**Gordon Pape** (right) is the best-selling author/co-author of many acclaimed investment books, including *6 Steps to $1 Million, Secrets of Successful Investing, Retiring Wealthy in the 21st Century, Head Start,* the annual *Buyer's Guide to Mutual Funds* and *Buyer's Guide to RRSPs,* and several more. He is editor and publisher of the *Mutual Funds Update* newsletter, a monthly publication on mutual fund investment strategies; the *Internet Wealth Builder* newsletter, a weekly e-mail advisory that focuses on stocks; and *Investing Today,* a monthly financial newsletter available free to visitors of his *Building Wealth on the Net* Web site at **www.gordonpape.com**. He is also senior editor of *The MoneyLetter,* one of Canada's most highly respected investment newsletters, and his financial columns appear regularly in *Fifty-Plus* magazine. His Smart Money commentaries appear weekly on *BTV (Business Television),* which is seen across Canada and the U.S.

**Eric Kirzner** (left) is a professor of finance at the Joseph L. Rotman School of Management, University of Toronto, and co-author of *Secrets of Successful Investing.* He serves on a number of advisory committees and is a director of the University of Toronto Asset Management Corporation and of Deutsche Bank, Canada. He served as technical expert on the development of the new Fundata FUNDGrade™ Mutual Fund Rating System.

# GORDON PAPE'S

# 2002 Buyer's Guide to Mutual Funds

**GORDON PAPE**

**ERIC KIRZNER**

Prentice
Hall
Canada

A Pearson Company
Toronto

**Canadian Cataloguing in Publication Data**

Pape, Gordon 1936-
        Gordon Pape's  buyer's guide to mutual funds

Annual.
1993-
ISSN 1193-9729
ISBN 0-13-062125-0 (2002 ed.)

       1. Mutual funds—Canada—Handbooks, manuals, etc. I. Title.

HG4530.P3          332.63'27         C93-030840-9

ISBN 0-13-062125-0

Editorial Director, Trade Division: Andrea Crozier
Acquisitions Editor: Andrea Crozier
Managing Editor: Tracy Bordian
Assisting Production Editor: Catherine Dorton
Copy Editor: Jodi Lewchuk
Proofreader: Karen Rolfe
Art Direction: Mary Opper
Cover Design: Sputnik
Cover Image: Chris McElcheran
Interior Design: Monica Kompter
Author Photograph: Lorella Zanetti
Production Manager: Kathrine Pummell
Page Layout: Beth Johnston/ArtPlus Ltd.

1 2 3 4 5  WEB  05 04 03 02 01

Printed and bound in Canada.

This publication contains the opinions and ideas of its author and is designed to provide useful advice in regard to the subject matter covered. The author and publisher are not engaged in rendering legal, accounting, or other professional services in this publication. This publication is not intended to provide a basis for action in particular circumstances without consideration by a competent professional. The author and publisher expressly disclaim any responsibility for any liability, loss, or risk, personal or otherwise, which is incurred as a consequence, directly or indirectly, of the use and application of any of the contents of this book.

Visit the Pearson PTR Canada Web site! Send us your comments, browse our catalogues, and more. **www.pearsonptr.ca**

A Pearson Company

# Get Winning
# Financial Advice
# FREE!

If you're interesting in getting the most for your money, you'll want to sign up to receive Gordon Pape's free monthly e-mail newsletter, *Investing Today*.

Every issue is packed with advice you can personally use, including stock recommendations from some of Canada's leading experts, information on the hottest mutual funds, money-making investing strategies, commentary on interest rate trends and how to profit from them, tax-saving advice, and more.

You'll be able to stay up to date on economic trends, market predictions, retirement strategies, and unusual profit opportunities. Plus you'll receive special offers for Gordon's books, newsletters, and other services at big discounts.

Best of all, *Investing Today* is absolutely free. There is no cost or obligation of any kind.

So don't wait. Sign up right now to start receiving up-to-the-minute information that will help you make informed financial decisions and increase your personal wealth.

Just log on to the Internet and go to: **www.gordonpape.com**. Click on the *Investing Today* banner, fill out the short form, and the next issue will be in your e-mail inbox soon.

# Contents

# Acknowledgments

As with any book this size, a lot of people have worked hard to make it all come together.

Special thanks to our long-time research assistant, Deborah Pape, for her hard work and persistence in gathering the vast amount of raw data that makes the ratings possible, and for tracking down answers to the many questions that arise every year. Thanks also to Diana Kirzner for her research and organizational help.

We would like to thank the mutual fund companies that co-operated by responding to our lengthy questionnaire, thereby contributing significantly to public knowledge and understanding of their products.

The statistical data in the pages that follow comes from a variety of sources, including the mutual fund companies themselves, *The Globe and Mail*, the *Globefund* Web site, the *National Post*, Southam's *Mutual Fund SourceBook*, and *The Fund Library*.

Finally, thanks to the editorial, production, and marketing team at Pearson PTR Canada for their assistance and support over the years. Special kudos to our hard-working editor, Jodi Lewchuk; to managing editor Tracy Bordian, who kept things flowing smoothly; and to editorial director Andrea Crozier, for her usual efficiency, good humour, and co-operation.

*Gordon Pape*
*Eric Kirzner*
Toronto, Ontario

# Introduction

This is the 12th annual edition of the *Buyer's Guide to Mutual Funds* and it represents a significant change in direction for us, one that we believe will make this book more practical and useful for fund investors.

In the past, we've taken an encyclopedic approach to our ratings and reviews. Any fund that was available to the general public and that had a track record of three years or longer received a write-up. Given the growth in the mutual funds world over the past decade, the entire book had to be devoted to reviews—there was no room for information on investing strategies, portfolio building, the process of fund selection, or anything else. When this *Guide* was originally launched, that kind of advice and information was our core content. But over the years, it got squeezed out as the total number of funds qualifying for entry moved past 500, then 1,000, and then 1,200.

Last winter, we sat down and did a complete review of what the *Guide* had become. We came to the conclusion that a great many of the funds we were reviewing were of only marginal interest to most people: some were very small, others were available only in limited areas of Canada, some were so consistently weak that no knowledgeable investor would want to touch them, and others still were out of sync with current market conditions.

As a result, we made a decision to return to our roots. We decided to cut back the total number of reviews and focus only on the funds we regard as being the best bets for your money in the current investment climate. We also decided to concentrate on the top fund companies, although we do include some smaller funds of special interest.

When you turn to the chapter on a specific company this year, you will find four categories of funds mentioned:

1. **Top Choices.** These are the funds we have selected as the best in the company's line-up at the time of writing. They should be highest on your priority list.

2. **Also Recommended.** The funds in this category may be useful for specific investment needs, such as income generation. The category may also include historically good funds that are going through temporary difficulties, and funds we feel are on the rise but have not yet reached the top rank.

3. **Promising Newcomers.** In the past, we did not include any funds that had not been in existence for at least three years. However, that meant we weren't able to alert readers to new funds showing exceptional promise. This new category now enables us to do that. Just remember that none of these funds has yet demonstrated long-term staying power.

4. **The Rest.** There are no individual write-ups and ratings for funds in this classification. We do not recommend any funds that appear in this category at the present time.

Additionally, every review of a recommended fund now contains a new feature called "Suitability." It tells you in a quick phrase what type of investor a particular fund will work best for. Within each fund company chapter you will find another new feature, "Investing Tips." Take a close look at this write-up. It offers little-known information about each company that may save you money when you buy funds.

Finally, we've added a wealth of new material at the front of the book that we hope you will find beneficial as you explore the mutual funds world. You'll find details about the new prospectuses and how to use them to your advantage, tax-saving tips and 2001 tax tables for every province and territory, guidance on risk assessment, advice on how to purchase specific types of funds, and much more. At the back of the book, you'll find our ever-popular FundLists and a new Question and Answer forum, which we invite you to participate in for future editions.

As you can see, there is a lot that's new, different, and, we hope, valuable.

The *2002 Buyer's Guide* is as up-to-the-minute as we can make it. But the mutual funds universe is a dynamic one, and things are constantly changing. So we suggest you consult with a financial advisor before making a final investment decision.

To keep on top of events, you may also wish to subscribe to the monthly *Mutual Funds Update* newsletter, which is produced in both electronic and print versions. If you have access to the Internet, we'd be pleased to offer you a free three-month trial subscription to the electronic edition. To take advantage of this offer, go to: **www.gordonpape.com/FreeMFU.html**. You'll also find current mutual fund information at the *Building Wealth on the 'Net* Web site: **www.gordonpape.com**.

We thank you for your past support and we hope this new and completely revised edition of the *Guide* will help you on the road to mutual fund prosperity.

*Gordon Pape*
*Eric Kirzner*
Toronto, Ontario

# A Time for Caution

*The terrible events of September 11, 2001, and their aftermath cast a pall over the investing world that is likely to linger for some time.*

As this book was preparing to go to press, everyone was still trying to cope with the shock of the destruction of the World Trade Center and the attack on the Pentagon, and trying to understand what it might mean for the future.

There is no way to predict how events will unfold over the next year or two, but clearly it is a time for mutual fund investors to exercise extreme caution. In times of turmoil, safety of capital should be of paramount importance. Risk needs to be minimized and profit expectations scaled way back.

The terrorist attacks exacerbated the already struggling economy and financial markets. The two years prior to September 11 had been extremely difficult. The high-tech crash that began in the late winter of 2000 and continued with only brief respites right through the first half of 2001 wiped out hundreds of millions of dollars in mutual fund valuations. Investors were left shocked, shaken, and unsure of what to do next.

Part of the problem was simply greed. During the late 1990s, many equity mutual funds soared in value as technology stocks headed to the moon. People began to take annual returns of 30 percent and more for granted. Those in more conservatively run funds became impatient with the underperformance of their managers and started switching into the high-flying growth and momentum funds—never bothering to consider the risk they were adding to their portfolios.

But the impact of the technology crash wasn't limited to that sector. Most other areas of the economy were affected, not only in North America but overseas. The result was a deceleration in the pace of economic growth that was already threatening to carry us into recession. The events of September 11 increased those gloomy prospects considerably.

The lesson for all fund investors is an old one, but it needs to be repeated again: Make sure your portfolio is well balanced and that the risk level is appropriate to your objectives and anxiety quotient.

There is absolutely no need to expose yourself to large losses in a mutual fund portfolio, even when the stock market is in deep distress and the economic outlook is weak. If you so choose, you don't even need to own a single equity fund, although that isn't a course we recommend. We suggest that, if you have not already done so, you take the time to apply some basic principles of portfolio building. Put together a selection of funds that will achieve the following goals:

1. Creates a proper balance between growth potential and capital preservation.

2. Minimizes equity risk by blending value and growth styles, with an emphasis on value in the current climate.

3. Contains a large percentage of fixed income securities.

4. Provides good geographic diversification.

5. Gives you some currency protection.

That may sound like a tough challenge. Surprisingly, it isn't. It's really fairly easy to accomplish as long as you have a clear-cut plan, use some self-discipline, and apply the fundamental principles contained in this book. The reward will be a fund portfolio that will enable you to weather any storm and enjoy a respectable average annual rate of growth.

Unfortunately, many Canadians have only a vague idea of how to invest in mutual funds. They're into funds because they've heard about them from friends, seen them discussed in the media, read an ad, or had a broker recommend them. In reality (though they'd be reluctant to admit it to anyone), they really don't understand what they've invested in. They aren't sure whether the funds they own are the right ones, if they've paid too much for them, how to go about judging them, when to sell them, or even what the fund portfolios hold in the way of securities.

This all-too-common scenario brings us to the cardinal rule of fund investing: Never buy a fund of any kind without a clear understanding of exactly what it is you're investing in and how it fits into your plan.

In the pages that follow, you'll find all the basics for that plan—everything you need for putting together a lifetime mutual fund portfolio. You'll get information about the many different types of mutual funds, guidance on how to decide which funds are right for you, details on the costs involved and how to keep them as low as possible, advice on how to pick winners and avoid losers, and a lot more. We've tried to keep the material here as practical and non-technical as possible, while at the same time covering all the key points you should know.

Before you become immersed in the details, however, a little background might help to put the tremendous growth of the Canadian mutual fund industry into some perspective.

## A History of Mutual Funds in Canada

At the start of the 1980s, most Canadians knew little to nothing about mutual funds. When it came to investing money, a bank savings account was the number-one choice by far. Canada Savings Bonds (CSBs) were also way up there on the popularity scale. The more adventurous Canadian might have committed some cash to guaranteed investment certificates (GICs), but would have done so with trepidation. A national survey commissioned by the Toronto Stock Exchange (TSE) in the autumn of 1983 found that only 1.5 percent of Canadians had money invested in equity (stock) mutual funds. By contrast, over 85 percent had savings accounts.

As the 1980s unfolded, we became a little more daring, swept along by a surging North American stock market that enjoyed a powerful five-year run from 1982 to 1987. Canadians unfamiliar with stocks began to search for other ways to participate in the bonanza. Mutual funds, which were already popular in the U.S., emerged as an obvious choice. When the TSE updated its survey in mid-1986, it found that savings accounts were as popular as ever. But the number of Canadians with money in equity mutual funds had risen to 6 percent.

Then came Black Monday—October 19, 1987. The financial world watched in shock as New York's Dow Jones Industrial Average plummeted more than 500 points. It was the biggest one-day loss in history, even worse than 1929. The TSE went on the same elevator plunge. Many investors panicked and dumped their shares and equity funds for whatever price they could salvage.

It took a long time for those wounds to heal. As the 1990s began, the Investment Funds Institute of Canada—the industry association of the mutual funds business, more commonly known as IFIC—reported that the total assets under management for all member companies was just under $23.5 billion. Of that, less than half—$11.2 billion—was invested in funds specializing in common stocks, either Canadian or foreign. The rest was in more conservative funds that focused on cash, bonds, mortgages, and preferred shares.

And then, suddenly, the explosion happened. Even with Canada mired in recession, money began flowing into mutual funds in the early 1990s. Assets of IFIC member companies tripled during the period from January 1, 1990 to the end of 1992. In part this was due to more mutual fund groups joining the umbrella organization. But much of the growth was directly attributable to rapidly declining interest rates, which pushed Canadians to start searching for other investment alternatives.

The stock market boom of 1993 started the Canadian mutual funds industry on the biggest growth spurt in its young history. In a single year, total assets under management surged from $67 billion to almost $115 billion, a one-year gain of $48 billion! The total invested in common stock funds alone rose to $50 billion, an almost fivefold gain in four years.

The pullback in stock and bond markets in 1994 slowed the frantic growth pace, but didn't stop it. At the end of October 1995, total mutual fund assets were almost $138 billion. Then came the huge bull market of the late 1990s, and there was no holding the fund industry back. By the turn of the century, assets under management by IFIC members had reached almost $390 billion. The stock market slump of 2000–01 slowed the growth rate, but at the end of July 2001, assets under management were almost $412 billion, a far cry from a decade earlier.

The explosion of the industry also brought with it a wide range of new options for fund investors. Sector funds (funds specializing in a specific industry or economic area) were pretty well limited to natural resource and precious metals funds a decade ago; today you can invest in funds that focus on everything from health care to consumer products. The range of fixed-income funds expanded as short-term bond funds and high-income bond funds made an appearance. High-income balanced funds began to offer portfolios of royalty income trusts (RITs) and real estate investment trusts (REITs), securities that were virtually unheard of at the start of the 1990s. Labour-sponsored venture capital funds were introduced, offering tax breaks to investors willing to take a higher-than-average risk. Geographic diversification became more complex with the appearance of Latin American funds, emerging markets funds, country-specific funds, and an expanded range of European, Pacific Rim, global, and international funds. Index funds added another, and somewhat controversial, dimension to the selection process. In addition, tax rules challenged the industry's innovative investing skills and the response was the birth of clone funds, to get around the foreign content limit in registered plans, and umbrella funds, to avoid capital gains tax liability when moving assets around.

While all of this was happening, the ways in which people bought and sold funds was evolving as well. Now you can choose from back-end loads, front-end loads, low-loads, and no-loads. You can get front-end loads with zero commission. Some dealers will give you rebates when you invest. You can also purchase funds online.

It is indeed a different world!

And yet, as rapid as the growth has been, there are those who predict the era of the mutual fund is over and suggest investors move on to building their own portfolio of carefully selected stocks and bonds.

We regard this projection as very unlikely.

The rush into mutual funds can indeed be seen as an investment fad, in the sense that a lot of money was directed into one business within a relatively short space of time. But to then predict the demise of the industry betrays a fundamental misunderstanding of what mutual fund investing is all about. People invest in mutual funds for three basic reasons:

1. They don't know how to build their own securities portfolio, or even if they do, they prefer to leave the decisions in the hands of professionals.
2. They don't want to devote the time needed to actively manage a securities portfolio.
3. They don't have the money to create a properly diversified stock and bond portfolio.

Mutual funds address all three problems. You can argue that the annual management fees make funds more expensive, but many people are quite content to pay for convenience and professional expertise, which is something that is not going to change. We don't expect the mutual fund industry to continue growing at anything close to the breathtaking pace it has in the past. But it *will* grow and continue to offer new choices for investors.

Your challenge is to make the industry work most effectively for you.

## SUMMARY

- Never invest in any fund without knowing exactly how it fits into your master plan.
- Proper diversification is the key to keeping risk at a minimum.
- The range of mutual funds available today allows investors to create any type of portfolio they wish.
- Mutual funds will continue to be the first choice of investors looking for convenience and professional management.

## FUND FACTS

TOP-PERFORMING CATEGORY. The best-performing mutual fund category over the decade ending May 31, 2001 was the U.S. Equity category. According to figures published in *The Globe and Mail*, the average fund of this type returned 13.3 percent annually over the 10-year period. Not a single fund lost money. The worst averaged 7.4 percent a year; the best averaged 18.5 percent.

WORST-PERFORMING CATEGORY. Over the same decade, real estate was the place to avoid. The average real estate fund gained only 0.2 percent a year over the period in question. Japanese equity funds were a close second for worst-of-the-decade honours, averaging just 1.3 percent annually.

BEST FUND. The best-performing fund in Canada over the 10 years to May 31, 2001 was the tiny Multiple Opportunities Fund, a high-risk micro-cap fund. It averaged 21.6 percent a year, but investors had to put up with some mind-bending volatility to get those returns.

# What Is a
# Mutual Fund?

*Most people who buy this book already know what a mutual fund is. But if you are*
*just starting out, you may not be exactly sure. There's nothing wrong with that. We all*
*have to start somewhere. And believe it or not, a lot of other people are in the same*
*situation, including some who actually own mutual fund investments.*

Here's how we explain the concept when we're giving beginners' seminars on
mutual fund investing. Pretend for a moment that you're sitting in a room with
1,000 other people listening to us discuss the subject.

Let's start by supposing each of you had to pay $10 to attend this seminar.
That's a total of $10,000 collected at the door. Now we surprise you by saying
we're not going to keep that money as our fee. Instead, we're going to invest it
on your behalf in Canadian stocks. In its simplest form, we're going to create a
Canadian equity mutual fund; we'll be the managers and all of you, the seminar attendees, will be the unitholders. Your $10 buys you one share in this new
venture and there are 1,000 shares in all, one for each person at the meeting. We
ask all of you to reconvene at this same place in exactly one year so we can tell
you how your investment has done. That will be our annual meeting.

The next day, we choose some stocks for the fund and purchase them on
behalf of the seminar attendees. Those picks become the fund's investment portfolio. Over the year, we buy and sell some stocks, hopefully producing some
profits along the way. For our services, we withdraw $25 from the fund's assets
each month, which is our management fee. You may think $25 seems like a
ridiculously small amount for the service we provide. But if the fund were to
grow in time to $1 million, the fee would increase 100 times to $2,500 a
month. When you consider that a number of mutual funds in this country have
assets in excess of $1 billion, you begin to appreciate the profit potential for

good money managers. The fund also incurs some other expenses, such as brokerage commissions for the shares purchased. These costs are paid out of the cash remaining in the fund.

At the end of the year, we reconvene and tell you what has happened over the past 12 months. If the news is good and your original $10 stake is now worth $15, we might ask for a performance bonus. Presumably, you'd all be feeling pretty happy about a 50 percent increase in your money, and you'd probably vote to grant the bonus.

But suppose the news is bad. It turns out that we are lousy money managers and your original $10 is now worth only $5. Chances are your immediate reaction would be to get out—to sell your unit, even if it means locking in the loss of half your stake and escaping while there is still something left. If this were a true open-end fund, the only way to do that would be to have us redeem the unit and pay you the cash from the fund's assets; you couldn't sell your share directly to another investor.

If you decide to hang in despite the rotten results, your alternative might be to demand that we quit as managers. Get someone else who can invest the money more effectively, the unitholders might say, or we'll all pull out our cash. This rarely happens in the real world, but it's a theoretical possibility if unitholders get angry enough. In any event, you wouldn't have to vote on a motion to grant a performance bonus—we'd be fighting just to keep our jobs.

There, in a microcosm, is the world of mutual funds. A fund is simply a pool of money put up by a number of individuals and handed over to a professional money manager to invest on their behalf. Certain criteria will govern the operation of the fund: what it can invest in, what fees it can charge, what kinds of risks it can take. These criteria will be detailed in a simplified prospectus, a document you must be provided with before any order can be finalized.

In this illustration, a Canadian stock fund has been used as an example. But a fund may invest in a wide range of other securities, from government bonds to gold bullion. One of the most common false assumptions made by beginning investors is that mutual funds and the stock market are the same thing. We've actually heard people say, "I won't invest any money in mutual funds because stocks are too risky." In fact, there are hundreds of mutual funds that don't own a single stock, and never will. Money market funds, for example, invest mainly in short-term notes issued by governments, banks, and large corporations. These funds would never hold a single share of stock.

Mutual funds come in a great variety of shapes and sizes. Some funds may have only a few hundred thousand dollars in assets, while some have grown to over $10 billion in size. There are over 3,000 mutual funds in Canada when all the variations and spinoffs (like clones and segregated versions) are taken into account. This is both a curse and a blessing.

The curse is the confusion created by such a dazzling choice of investment options. With so many funds to select from, some people become paralyzed with inertia, unable to decide which way to go. The blessing comes from the fact that this wide range of choice translates into greater profit potential and reduced risk. In the old days, there were few safe havens to turn to when the investment seas became rough. Today there are many funds that offer calm waters in which to ride out the storms that occasionally hit the real estate, stock, and bond markets.

Choosing the right funds from this expanding universe isn't easy and may be even less so in future, as more new entries appear. But it's well worth making the effort, because mutual funds offer the fastest and cheapest way to create a well-structured investment portfolio that is perfectly designed for your specific needs.

## SUMMARY

- A mutual fund is simply a pool of money from a number of individuals that is turned over to a professional manager to invest on their behalf.
- Mutual funds invest in a wide range of securities. Some funds focus exclusively on the stock market, but there are many funds that own no stocks at all.
- A mutual fund will earn profits or suffer losses based on how well the investments in the portfolio perform.

## FUND FACTS

MANAGEMENT FEES. Management fees and expenses normally range from a low of 0.5 percent of a fund's total assets to a high of about 4 percent. The lower the total management expense, the more profits that are left for distribution to investors.

OPEN- AND CLOSED-END FUNDS. An open-end mutual fund is one in which units are bought and sold directly by the fund's treasury, on the basis of the current market value of the portfolio. In most cases, the portfolio is revalued every day. A closed-end fund is one in which no new units are made available after the initial selling period. The only way to buy or sell shares is by dealing with another investor. Units in closed-end funds usually trade on a stock exchange.

THE PROSPECTUS. A simplified prospectus is a document summarizing all the terms and conditions governing a specific mutual fund or group of funds. Sales people are required by law to provide you with this document before finalizing an order. While no one ever reads these things from cover to cover, there are some key points you should routinely check out. See the section on this subject for details.

**BIG BERTHA.** The largest mutual fund sold in Canada is the Templeton Growth Fund. As of early 2001, it held assets totalling $10.3 billion.

**SOCIALISTIC CAPITALISM.** Richard Stone, president of the Stone & Co. Fund Group, describes mutual funds as "a socialistic way to participate in capitalism."

# The Advantages of
# Mutual Funds

*We've heard all kinds of excuses for not investing in mutual funds:*

*"They're too risky."*

*"I don't understand them."*

*"They're too expensive."*

*"I tried it once and lost money."*

*"The sales people use too much pressure."*

*"They're a fad."*

In specific cases, each of the above arguments could be valid; it's certainly true that some funds are high-risk, some cost too much, and some have a flavour-of-the-month quality. But to focus too closely on the flaws of mutual funds is a classic example of missing the forest for the trees. Mutual funds offer advantages that a small investor simply can't find anywhere else, which is why they've become so popular. The key benefits of mutual funds are as follows:

**PROFESSIONAL MANAGEMENT.** The people who run mutual funds are professional money managers, usually with impressive credentials and years of experience. This doesn't mean they are all good, however. As in any other business, you'll find some managers who are brilliant, some who are mediocre, and some who are downright inept.

The good news is that with mutual fund managers, it's somewhat easier than in most professions to sort the wheat from the chaff. The Canadian Medical Association isn't going to tell you which doctors are great and which are incompetent, and there are no published figures on a surgeon's percentage of successful operations in a given year. Similarly, the Canadian Bar Association doesn't publish a monthly won–lost record for trial lawyers. But mutual fund managers have the results of their labours on public display all the time. When the fund statistics come out each month, you can tell at a glance who has the hot hand and who is trailing the pack. Those statistics don't tell the entire story, of course. But they do provide public insight into a person's ability that few other professions outside of pro sports offer, or would even tolerate.

The investment world has become immensely complex over the past three decades. Very few people have the time, knowledge, or inclination to build and manage a diverse portfolio of stocks, bonds, cash, and real estate. As a result, money management has become a large and ever-expanding business. But hiring your own personal money manager can be very expensive. A professional usually won't even consider taking you on as a client unless you have at least $100,000 to invest—some won't consider less than $1 million. If you do have that kind of money, the fees can be expensive, usually 1 to 2 percent of your total assets under management.

Mutual funds provide an opportunity to obtain professional management even though you may have only a few hundred dollars available. In percentage terms, the price for fund management may be higher than you'd pay for individual attention. But the actual dollar amount will be low because most people don't have big bucks to invest. If you put $1,000 into a fund that has a management expense ratio (MER) of 2.5 percent, your actual annual charge for professional money management will be only $25.

If you think you can do better and save that fee, go for it. You don't need advice from us.

PORTFOLIO DIVERSIFICATION. One of the main problems faced by small investors is that they don't have enough money to properly diversify their holdings. To construct a solid stock portfolio, for example, you'd need to hold shares in about 16 companies. Properly chosen, these stocks would give you a position across about 80 percent of industry groups. If you were to buy a board lot (100 shares) of each company at an average price of $20 a share, it would require an outlay of $32,000. In the end, however, you would have only a basic stock portfolio. For proper balance, you'd need to add some fixed-income securities, such as bonds, and some money market funds to your mix. The total cost for a well-diversified plan? About $60,000.

But what, you may ask, is so important about diversification? Risk reduction, that's what. Professional money managers have two main goals. One is to achieve above-average returns. The other is to ensure that, in the event something goes wrong, their clients aren't hit any harder than is necessary.

Enter diversification. If you invest all your money in one stock and the company goes under, you've lost 100 percent of your assets. If you invest equally in two stocks and one collapses, you've lost 50 percent. If you spread the same amount among four stocks, you've lost 25 percent of your money. At 10 stocks, your loss drops to 10 percent. At 20 stocks, 5 percent. And that's the advantage of diversifying: by spreading your risk around, you limit the damage if one security goes south.

Mutual funds, of course, do the diversifying for you. When you buy units in a mutual fund, you're buying a share in that fund's investment portfolio. If you want to know exactly what the portfolio consists of, ask for a copy of the fund's latest financial statements. They'll tell you what assets the fund was holding as of the record date.

In some cases, there may be hundreds of individual securities within a portfolio. However, an extreme degree of diversification isn't necessarily a good sign; the more securities a fund owns, the more difficult it is for the manager and staff to keep on top of everything. Ideally, we prefer to see a portfolio of 25 to 50 securities. It gives us a higher level of confidence that the manager has the fund's investment policy under tight control and is able to carefully monitor everything in the portfolio on a day-to-day basis.

VARIETY. Only a few years ago, the mutual fund marketplace in Canada was very limited. Now there's a vast array of products on the shelf. At the start of 2001, there were more than 3,000 funds on offer, counting all the variations such as RRSP-eligible clone funds and segregated funds. And the total continues to grow. This growth has been good news for investors, on several counts.

To start, more funds mean greater choice. The chances of finding a fund that exactly matches your requirements improve as the number of funds available increase. Additionally, the range of investment options offered by funds has expanded. At the start of the 1990s, funds specializing in emerging markets, high-yield bonds, telecommunications, health sciences, Latin America, and technology were unknown in this country. Now all these choices, and more, are available. Furthermore, competition leads directly to better service and lower fees. When a few fund companies dominated the market, they could pretty well call the shots. That's no longer possible. One example of the benefits of a more competitive environment: the day of the mandatory 9 percent front-end load is long gone.

Finally, a larger industry means a lot more analysis and information. When we first started to write about mutual funds in the late 1980s—not all that long ago—there were very few books available on the subject, and the business media virtually ignored the topic. Now the press carries daily reports on the industry, mutual fund managers have become media stars, there are several newsletters devoted exclusively to fund investing strategies, and there are half a dozen annual consumer guides being published on mutual funds. There's no longer any reason to remain ignorant about mutual fund investing!

CONVENIENCE. Perhaps the biggest advantage mutual funds offer is convenience. They're quite literally available on almost every corner. Walk into any branch of a bank or trust company in this country and you can invest in mutual funds. You can pick up the phone and build a portfolio from your home. You can order funds by mail. You can buy them on the Internet. If you wish, some fund sales people will even come to your home and take your order in the privacy of your own living room. No other investment form has made itself so readily available to the ordinary investor.

PROFITABILITY. There's no guarantee that any given mutual fund will make money, of course. But if you hold a fund long enough, the odds favour that it will end up in the black. Over the decade ending May 31, 2001, not one Canadian equity fund out of the hundreds in existence at the time reported a negative average annual compound rate of return. Only one balanced fund lost ground during the decade.

In some cases, of course, the return was less than you could have earned by sticking your money into Canada Savings Bonds (CSBs), which earned 5.0 percent a year on average over the decade. But in most cases, the funds did much better. The average global stock fund returned 10.7 percent a year over that time, according to figures published in *The Globe and Mail.* The average U.S. equity fund spun annual profits of 13.3 percent. For more conservative investors, the average Canadian bond fund returned 8.0 percent a year. Ultra-conservative mortgage funds averaged 6.9 percent, almost two points better than CSBs.

So why invest in mutual funds? In a nutshell, to make money and reduce risk. Do you need any more reasons?

## SUMMARY

- Professional money management is one of the most important benefits offered to mutual fund investors. But if you think you can do it better yourself, go ahead!
- Portfolio diversification is difficult for stock investors to achieve without a substantial cash outlay. Mutual funds solve this problem.
- The variety of mutual funds available today is unmatched in our history. If it's legal, there's probably a fund that invests in it.
- There are no guarantees that your funds will be profitable. But over the long term, the odds are heavily in your favour.

## FUND FACTS

HIGH-FLYERS. Some of the new types of mutual funds have been among the hottest performers. In 2000, for example, the Talvest Global Health Care Fund, a sector fund that didn't even exist five years earlier, turned in the best result in the country with a gain of 120.9 percent.

**THE IMPORTANCE OF ONE PERCENTAGE POINT.** Just one percentage point can add up to a significant amount of money over time. If you were to invest $1,000 a year in a mutual fund each year for 30 years, earning an average of 8 percent annually, the fund's value would grow to just over $113,000. But if the fund returned an average of 9 percent, you'd have more than $136,000 in your portfolio, a gain of more than $20,000 from just a single percentage point!

# Types of Funds

*A few years ago, a woman approached Gordon Pape after a seminar and asked if it was too late for her to start investing in mutual funds. She was 70 years old (she didn't look it!) and wanted to know if funds were too risky a venture at her age.*

Her question alludes to one of the most common misconceptions about mutual funds: there is a strong tendency to assume that mutual funds and the stock market are the same thing. We can't tell you how many times we've heard people say that they won't invest in mutual funds because they're nervous about stocks. Well, if that false impression is what's holding you back, let us lay it to rest once and for all.

There *are* funds that invest in stocks, of course—lots of them. But there are also funds that invest in assets that have nothing whatsoever to do with the stock market, like mortgages, bonds, Treasury bills (T-bills), real estate, commodities, index futures, gold, and a whole variety of other securities. In fact, if it's a legitimate investment, you'll probably find a mutual fund that specializes in it. So even if you're scared to death of the stock market, there's no reason to pass up mutual funds. In fact, a fund may be an excellent option for you.

The catch is that you have to know which type of fund is right for you. The seminar attendee who asked if she was too old to buy funds is obviously not a candidate for high-risk ventures. But there are plenty of conservative, income-generating funds that are ideal for her needs, some of which have never had a losing year since they were launched. So let's take a look at the various groups and sub-groups of mutual funds currently being offered in Canada. You can then decide which ones are right for you.

## Cash-Type Funds

**MONEY MARKET FUNDS (CANADIAN).** These funds invest in a variety of short-term securities including federal and provincial T-bills, certificates of deposit, short-term corporate notes, bankers' acceptances, and term deposits. A few of these funds offer limited chequing privileges. The fund unit value is fixed, usually at $10.

MONEY MARKET FUNDS (U.S.). As the name indicates, these funds invest in short-term U.S. dollar securities like federal T-bills. The rate of return in recent years has been higher than that on Canadian money market funds because of the interest rate differential between the two countries. These funds are best suited for those seeking a safe hedge against a drop in the Canadian dollar, or those who require frequent access to U.S. cash.

T-BILL FUNDS. These funds are similar to money market funds, but hold only government T-bills. This gives them added safety, but the return is usually a bit less than from standard money market funds.

FOREIGN MONEY MARKET FUNDS. The weakness of the Canadian dollar in recent years has created a demand for money market funds that provide some currency protection, but offer potentially better returns than U.S. dollar funds. Foreign money market funds are the answer. These funds invest in short-term securities denominated in a range of currencies. Unlike other money funds, the unit value is not fixed, so these funds are subject to bigger gains and losses than other choices in this group.

PREMIUM MONEY MARKET FUNDS. Some fund companies, notably the big banks, offer special money market funds for those with a lot of cash to invest (the minimum entry fee is usually at least $100,000). The attraction here is a lower management fee, which translates into higher returns.

## Fixed-Income Funds

MORTGAGE FUNDS. These funds specialize in residential first mortgages, although they may hold other assets as well, such as short-term bonds or commercial mortgages. Mortgage funds are one of the lowest-risk types of fixed-income funds you can buy. The mortgages held in the portfolio will normally all mature within five years, making them less vulnerable to loss when interest rates rise (the longer the term of a fixed-income security, the more its price will be affected by interest rate movements). Mortgage funds are best suited for highly conservative investors looking for slightly better returns than are offered by guaranteed investment certificates (GICs). Your profits are usually in the form of interest income; capital gains potential is low.

**CANADIAN BOND FUNDS.** These funds invest in bonds issued by various levels of government, Crown corporations, municipalities, or major companies. They are somewhat higher risk than mortgage funds because the bonds in the portfolio will usually have longer maturity dates than mortgages. However, that higher risk is compensated by higher returns; bond funds can be expected to generate one to two percentage points more each year. For example, over the five-year period to May 31, 2001, the average Canadian mortgage fund had an annual return of 6.9 percent, according to figures published in *The Globe and Mail.* The average Canadian bond fund produced an 8.0 percent return. Bond funds generate interest income but also have the potential to produce capital gains if interest rates drop, as they did for much of the 1990s. But most people buy bond funds for the interest they produce, not for capital gains.

**SHORT-TERM BOND FUNDS.** These funds represent a cross between a regular bond fund and a money market fund. The managers invest in bonds with relatively short maturity dates. In some cases, three years is the maximum allowed; other funds will hold bonds with maturities up to five years. The goal is to create a defensive portfolio that will provide better returns than a money market fund but carry less risk than a standard bond fund. These funds will usually outperform regular bond funds when interest rates rise (as they did in 2000), but they won't experience the good gains normally associated with rates on the decline.

**HIGH-YIELD BOND FUNDS.** Relatively new on the scene, these funds invest mainly in corporate bonds issued by companies with a lower credit rating. They have been called "junk bond funds," but that's too harsh a description. When you invest in these funds, you're essentially accepting a higher degree of credit risk in exchange for potentially higher returns.

**FOREIGN BOND FUNDS.** These funds invest in international fixed-income securities, usually bonds. Some funds specialize in bonds issued by foreign governments and corporations. Others invest in Canadian bond issues denominated in foreign currencies (U.S. dollars, Japanese yen, sterling, euros), making them fully eligible for RRSPs. These funds are attractive during periods when the Canadian dollar is falling because of the profit potential from the fluctuations in currency exchange rates. For example, a bond denominated in U.S. dollars will be more valuable to a Canadian investor when our dollar is worth U.S.65¢ than it would be with the dollar worth U.S.70¢. For that reason, this category of fund performed well in 1998 when the loonie was weak, slipped badly in 1999 as our dollar recovered some ground, and then performed well again when the loonie came under pressure in early 2001. Foreign bond funds are somewhat higher risk than Canadian bond funds because of currency movements as well as interest rate exposure.

**DIVIDEND FUNDS.** True dividend funds (and many are not) invest in shares that pay a high dividend yield, allowing investors to benefit from the dividend tax credit if the units are held outside a registered plan. They're best suited for conservative investors in high tax brackets who want to improve their after-tax returns by making use of the dividend credit. In the past, the portfolios consisted mainly of preferred shares, but now many of these funds concentrate on high-yielding common stocks, such as the utilities and banks, making them nothing more than specialized blue-chip funds. True dividend funds are relatively safe, but their growth potential is limited, which is why they're included in this category.

**HIGH-INCOME BALANCED FUNDS.** Another newcomer to the scene, these funds invest in a variety of high-yield securities such as royalty income trusts (RITs) and real estate investment trusts (REITs). The goal here is to produce strong cash flow, much of which will be received on a tax-deferred basis. The trade-off is risk; royalty trusts have proven very volatile, and investors in these funds may see their unit values decline sharply in bad markets.

## Growth Funds

**CANADIAN EQUITY FUNDS.** These funds specialize in publicly traded shares of Canadian companies, although most contain some foreign stocks as well, within the foreign content limit. The degree of risk will depend on a fund's objectives; some emphasize security of capital by investing mainly in blue-chip stocks while others concentrate on more junior issues in a relentless pursuit of big capital gains. Your choice of which funds are most appropriate should be governed by your personal financial objectives.

**LABOUR-SPONSORED VENTURE CAPITAL FUNDS.** These funds were created to encourage new business development in Canada by investing in small- and medium-sized companies, most of which are not publicly traded. They're high-risk by nature, so governments have provided sweeteners in the form of tax credits to encourage people to take a chance.

**U.S. EQUITY FUNDS.** These funds invest mainly in American stocks. Some specialize in large blue-chip issues, some focus on small-cap stocks, but the majority are broadly diversified.

**INTERNATIONAL AND GLOBAL FUNDS.** These funds invest in stocks of several countries. Some limit themselves geographically to certain areas (e.g., Europe, the Pacific Rim, Latin America) while others roam the world. International funds do not invest in their home country, but global funds do. Hence, a true international fund will not invest in North America. But don't be guided by the fund name alone—it can be deceptive. There are many funds with the word "international" in their name that actually invest in all parts of the globe, including their home region.

COUNTRY-SPECIFIC FUNDS. These funds concentrate on stocks of a specific nation. After the U.S.–based funds, Japan funds are the most common type sold in Canada, but you can also buy funds that specialize in China, Germany, and India.

PRECIOUS METALS FUNDS. These funds invest mainly in gold, either directly by buying bullion or, more commonly, in shares of gold mining companies. Some funds also have holdings in other precious metals, such as platinum and silver. In recent years, shares in companies engaged in diamond exploration in the Northwest Territories have found their way into the portfolios of some of these funds. Precious metals funds are typically high risk by nature and will do well only during periods when bullion prices are strong.

NATURAL RESOURCE FUNDS. These funds invest in companies involved one way or another in the resources business. They will usually be heavily weighted toward the energy sector, but will also provide exposure to mining and forestry stocks. The stocks held by these funds are highly cyclical, so performance will vary significantly from year to year.

REAL ESTATE FUNDS. Here the managers specialize in commercial and industrial real estate. Profits are generated by capital gains and rental income, giving these funds a tax advantage. Real estate funds ran into serious problems when property values in many parts of the country tumbled during the recession of the early 1990s. As a result, only a handful of pure, open-end real estate funds are available today. However, there are a number of closed-end funds, or REITs, which trade on the Toronto Stock Exchange (TSE).

DERIVATIVE FUNDS. A new category, these funds have been developed for RRSP/RRIF investors who wish to go beyond the foreign content limit. Some hold most of their assets in Canadian T-bills, used as security for the purchase of index futures on international bond and stock exchanges, or on the portfolio of a parent fund. Others, the so-called "clone" funds, invest in futures that will rise and fall in value in accordance with a parent fund.

INDEX FUNDS. Growing in popularity, these funds are designed to track the performance of a benchmark stock index such as the TSE 300 or the S&P 500. They are known as "passive" investments because the manager does not make any buy-or-sell decisions.

**SECTOR FUNDS.** These funds specialize in a particular segment of the economy such as health services, science and technology, telecommunications, or infrastructure companies. Recently they have been growing in popularity, and some of these funds scored huge gains in the late 1990s before crashing to earth in the "tech wreck" of 2000–01.

## SUMMARY

- There are three main categories of mutual funds: cash, fixed income, and growth.
- Cash funds are lowest in risk, but provide the lowest return as well.
- Fixed-income funds specialize in investments that pay a fixed rate of return, such as bonds and mortgages. Funds like these are best suited for conservative investors wishing to minimize risk and for people who require regular income, such as retirees.
- Bond funds—a sub-group in the fixed-income category—aren't as safe as many people think, but they can produce above-average profits under the right conditions.
- Growth funds offer the biggest gains, but be prepared to take more chances. These funds are most appropriate for younger investors who have years to ride out any dips in the stock market.

## FUND FACTS

**CASH FUNDS.** When interest rates are low, as they were through most of the 1990s, yields on these funds are unattractive, except when they're used as an alternative to a savings account. When short-term rates are rising, as they were in 1999 and 2000, they're more attractive. Cash-type funds may also be useful as temporary parking places for money during turbulent economic times. They should not, however, be considered long-term investments.

**A ROSE MAY NOT BE A ROSE.** Don't rely on a fund's name to tell you what it invests in. Some T-bill funds hold assets outside of Treasury bills, while some supposedly more broadly based money market funds invest exclusively in Canadian Treasury bills. Ask to see a summary of the fund's portfolio before investing your money.

**FOR HIGH-ROLLERS ONLY.** The Bank of Montreal's regular Canadian Money Market Fund carries a management expense ratio (MER) of 1.25 percent. The fund's return for the year ending May 31, 2001 was 4.3 percent. Yet the bank's Premium Money Market Fund, which won't accept your money unless there's at least $100,000 on the table, had an MER of only 0.43 percent and a one-year return of 5.3 percent for the same period. The difference in return was almost entirely due to the management fee. It takes money to make money!

**WATCH THOSE RATES!** Fixed-income funds react strongly to movements in interest rates. When rates fall, they'll produce better-than-average returns, as they did for much of the period from 1995–98. But they'll lose value—sometimes very quickly—when rates rise, as in 1999–2000. Bond funds are particularly hard hit under those circumstances; some bond funds dropped in value by almost 10 percent in the last year of the century.

**TAX CREDIT LOSS.** As a general rule, don't hold dividend funds in registered plans like RRSPs, because the benefit of the dividend tax credit will be lost.

**BALANCED FUNDS.** As you explore the mutual fund world in more depth, you'll come across balanced and asset allocation funds. These can't be pigeon-holed into any specific class. As the name implies, funds of this type seek to build a balanced portfolio of cash-type investments, fixed-income securities, and stocks. Their objective is to achieve above-average growth while reducing risk exposure. Balanced fund managers will change the composition of their holdings depending on economic conditions. Consequently, a particular balanced fund may be heavily invested in bonds at one point in time, while at another time the emphasis may be on stocks.

# Coping with the Fine Print

*Before you buy units in any mutual fund, you should be given a copy of something called a "simplified prospectus." Most people ignored this prospectus in the past, as it was a boring-looking document filled with small print and legalese—a great cure for insomnia. But recently there have been significant improvements in the way fund prospectuses are being constructed, and they are now crammed full of useful information. Toss yours aside at your peril.*

The new prospectuses are especially valuable with regard to the specific information they provide about every fund being offered. Before you make any investment decision, you should read carefully the section on each fund you're considering. Here are some of the key points you'll find:

**REGISTERED PLAN ELIGIBILITY.** This is one of the first pieces of information you should come across. It will tell you if the fund is fully eligible for RRSPs, RRIFs, etc., or if it must be treated as foreign content within the prescribed limits.

**INVESTMENT OBJECTIVE.** This paragraph is a brief description of exactly what the fund is designed to do. It should tell you at a glance if the fund meets your broad objectives.

**INVESTMENT STRATEGIES.** This section provides a more detailed look at how the managers intend to achieve the fund's goals. It should tell you about the type of stocks the fund will buy (small, medium, or large companies); whether it will use derivatives and, if so, how; whether the manager will hold large amounts of cash under certain conditions; and more.

**TOP 10 HOLDINGS.** This listing will show you at a glance what kind of companies the fund invests in.

**RISKS.** This section should clearly define the risks associated with the fund.

**SUITABILITY.** Here you'll find a description of the type of investor for whom the fund is best suited. If you see a sentence like "You can accept high risk," believe it. You are being warned about potentially large swings in unit values. If you don't like taking on a lot of risk, this kind of statement is a red flag telling you to avoid the fund.

**PAST PERFORMANCE.** This section provides information about how the fund has done over time. Past results are useful to have, but don't assume you can project them into the future.

**DISTRIBUTION POLICY.** In this spot you'll find out how often the fund makes cash payments. If you're investing for income, you'll want at least quarterly distributions and perhaps even monthly ones.

**FINANCIAL HIGHLIGHTS.** This section holds useful statistical data. Note especially the management expense ratio (MER) figures because they represent the annual cost of the fund to you. Keep in mind that this equation has two parts. One is the actual fee that's paid to the management company. The other is the day-to-day operating expenses of the fund. It's not unusual for different funds within the same group to charge different management fees. In the case of any fund you're considering, see if the numbers are trending up or down; an increasing MER will have the effect of reducing net returns.

While you're perusing the numbers, look too at net assets. These figures will reveal the size of the fund. Anything over $500 million is considered large in Canada; under $10 million is small. You will also be able to see if the fund is growing or shrinking in size. The latter could be a danger sign, as it indicates either losses on investments or high redemptions that could force the sale of some of the fund's securities to raise cash.

Some of the other important points to look for in a prospectus are:

- *Fees and expenses.* There are a lot of numbers here, but check through them carefully. They outline exactly what costs you will have to pay, including sales commissions, annual fees, and expenses. If you're buying the fund using a deferred sales charge option, see how much you'll have to pay if you decide to sell. Also, check if the percentage is calculated on your original purchase price or on the market value of the units at the time of sale. If the fund increases in value, the latter method becomes much more expensive. In addition, many fund companies charge for early redemption, even on no-load or front-end load funds, so check for this catch. Sometimes you can find some angles for reducing your commissions here, such as low-load options or negotiable back-end loads.

- *Purchases, switches, and redemptions.* This segment provides all the key information you need about the actual procedure for buying fund units. Look especially at how much is required for the initial investment—you can't get into some funds unless you're prepared to invest several thousand dollars. In most cases, however, the minimum is $500 or $1,000.

- *Provincial limitations.* Some prospectuses will state that the funds are not sold in certain provinces. These restrictions exist when funds have not been registered with the provincial securities commissions in specific jurisdictions. In other cases, there may be no definitive statement of where the funds are available and you may have to contact the manager directly.

- *Income tax considerations.* If you're investing outside a registered plan, you'll want to take a close look at the tax implications. In doing so, remember that payments from mutual funds are taxed differently, depending on their source. The prospectus should outline which types of payments can be expected from the fund you're considering. There are several possibilities: capital gains dividends, Canadian stock dividends, foreign stock dividends, rental income, straight interest, and return of capital. You should understand which types of income you can expect to receive and determine if they make the best sense for you from a tax point of view. For example, if you want to shelter the maximum possible amount from taxes, you may look for funds that will generate capital gains, Canadian dividends, and return of capital instead of interest income. Once you've invested, the fund manager will issue an annual reporting slip for tax purposes, showing exactly how much of each type of income you received.

A mutual fund prospectus may seem daunting at first glance, but you don't have to read it cover-to-cover. Just go to the specific information on the funds you're considering and then look at the key points we have outlined here. By spending 15 or 20 minutes, you may avoid an investment mistake that could end up costing you hundreds or even thousands of dollars.

## SUMMARY

- A prospectus is a legal document that is approved by a securities commission before it is distributed to potential investors. It contains details of the terms and conditions of a securities offer, including all the costs involved, a summary of the risks, and the tax implications.
- Prospectuses have recently been given a major overhaul. The new form is much easier to follow and contains valuable information on each specific fund being offered, to which you should pay close attention.
- Look carefully at the section on sales commissions and expenses, so as to avoid unpleasant surprises down the road.
- A typical prospectus contains this vital information about the mutual fund:

  1. RRSP/RRIF Status
  2. Investment Objectives
  3. Investment Policies
  4. Top 10 Holdings
  5. Risk
  6. Suitability
  7. Part Performance
  8. Distribution Policy
  9. Financial Highlights

## FUND FACTS

**WHEN A PROSPECTUS IS NOT A PROSPECTUS.** Sometimes a prospectus is called an "Offering Memorandum." This document serves the same purpose as a prospectus, but the term indicates that shares in the security are being offered only to "sophisticated" investors on a private placement basis, and that a high minimum subscription will be required. The amount depends on the province where the issue is taking place and can range from a low of $25,000 to a high of $150,000. Clearly, any funds that are sold on an offering memorandum basis are intended only for the super-rich. There is currently a move under way to try to get the requirements for investing in such funds loosened a bit.

**EXPENSE SUMMARY.** You'll find a summary of all management fees as well as any expenses that will be charged directly to you somewhere in the prospectus. If you don't read anything else in the document, read this page.

**GETTING YOUR MONEY OUT FAST.** If you think you might need quick access to your invested money, check out the terms of redemption carefully before buying any units. Most funds make provisions for next-day redemption, but a few may only value their assets weekly or monthly, which means you would have to wait until the next valuation date. Also, some funds impose a penalty on assets withdrawn within 90 days of deposit.

# Know Yourself
# Before You Invest

*It was a week like none had ever seen before.*

In five trading sessions between April 10 and 14, 2000, the Nasdaq Composite Index recorded its two worst days ever, en route to a dizzying 25 percent free fall. Not to be outdone, the venerable Dow Jones Industrial Average, still the most-watched market indicator, recorded its biggest one-day loss in history, dropping more than 600 points. The TSE 300 didn't fare quite as badly, but the one-week drop of 10 percent was no picnic for investors either.

Mutual funds, especially those with heavy high-tech weighting, reacted accordingly. By the time the week was over, many were showing 30-day losses of greater than 20 percent. A few were down more than 30 percent. Never mind that many of these funds had just finished racking up eye-popping one-year returns; when you see your assets lose a quarter of their value in just a few days, the natural tendency is to get somewhat antsy. The nervousness was compounded by the fact that most investors in high-tech funds were relative newcomers. They weren't around for the big gains of 1999 and early 2000. They had just jumped on the bandwagon, many of them during RRSP season, and were stunned as their newly acquired units plummeted in value.

And that was just the beginning. After a brief respite during the summer, the stock market resumed its slide in the autumn of 2000, and the slide carried on through the winter of 2001. If you found yourself waking up in a sweat during that period, worrying about your money, take that as a sign that your fund portfolio wasn't properly designed for your investment personality.

Many investors became overly aggressive in the late 1990s, swept along by the excitement of Nasdaq and high tech. And it wasn't just the younger, inexperienced people who succumbed. At a seminar in February 2000, for example, a woman in her fifties asked how she could invest her RRSP money in a Nasdaq index fund. We suggested she might want to think twice about making such a move. Nasdaq had enjoyed a huge run, we told her. That run couldn't continue and the risks were high. Someone in her thirties could ride out any correction, but at her age . . . She was adamant, however. She was tired of the poor returns she was getting from her current mutual funds. She was going to invest a big chunk of her money in Nasdaq! We only hope she eventually decided that putting most of her RRSP assets into that one basket might not be such a good idea after all.

Market tremors are as inevitable as earthquakes along the San Andreas fault; everyone knows they are going to happen—we just can't predict exactly when. With that in mind, the moral of this story is simple: Before you decide which mutual funds to purchase, you must know exactly what your investment goals are. There are mutual funds to suit every need—the trick is matching up the right fund with your particular requirements.

To help you determine your personal priorities, we've developed a self-test to identify the type of investment personality you have. Take a moment to complete it now, before reading on.

| INVESTING STATEMENT | A (AGREE) | B (DISAGREE) | C (UNSURE) |
| --- | --- | --- | --- |
| I require regular investment income. | | | |
| The safety of my capital is essential. | | | |
| Growth is not an important factor. | | | |
| I am not prepared to accept more risk for a higher return. | | | |
| I don't want a manager with an aggressive style, even if he or she is good at it. | | | |
| I am within 10 years of my retirement. | | | |
| I cannot afford to lose any money. | | | |
| My spouse says mutual fund investing is too risky. | | | |
| I'm using RRSP/RRIF money for investment purposes. | | | |
| I'm more concerned with a comfortable lifestyle than with being rich. | | | |

Give yourself two points for every A answer and one point for every B response. Cs are worth zero points. The higher your point total, the more conservative you are, and the greater the degree of emphasis you should place on mutual funds that focus on steady income and protection of capital. If you scored 15 or more, you should concentrate on T-bill funds, money market funds, mortgage funds, and bond funds.

If your score is in the 7–14 range, you appear more willing and able to take greater risks in order to obtain better returns. In this case, you should be looking more seriously at equity funds (Canadian, U.S., and foreign) and specialized sector funds.

If your total score is less than seven, it's an indication you have done very little thinking about your investment objectives. You should take time to consider what you want to achieve before going any further.

Your personal investment goals will be influenced by several factors, including:

**AGE.** The younger you are, the more risk you can afford to take, although it's not a good idea to go overboard. If your first investments go sour, you may end up spooked for life. That's why it's a good idea to include a low-risk fund, such as a mortgage fund, in your initial purchases. This will allow you to gain some investing experience while keeping your money out of danger. As you develop a feel for what you're doing, you can experiment with other types of funds.

**INVESTING EXPERIENCE.** One of our cardinal rules for investors is to never put money in things you don't fully understand. Knowledge comes with experience, so until you feel comfortable with what you're doing, you'd be advised to set a goal of investing only in funds with policies and objectives you comprehend and agree with.

**INCOME NEEDS.** If you're relying on money from your fund investments to live on, you'll want to select one that provides a regular income stream.

**FAMILY SITUATION.** The greater your family responsibilities, the less money you can afford to risk. A single person with no dependants can usually absorb investment losses more readily than a married couple with three kids and a mortgage.

**RETIREMENT PLANS.** The closer you are to retirement, the more conservative you should be with your investment choices. You may no longer have the time to ride out a serious downturn in the stock market or a precipitous drop in the price of real estate or gold. This doesn't mean you should abandon growth funds entirely, but you do need some protection from inflation, which is unlikely to stay low forever. These growth funds should comprise a smaller portion of your portfolio, however.

**YOUR FINANCIAL AMBITIONS.** Some people feel they absolutely must be rich— whatever the risk involved. If you're one of these people, an aggressive growth fund is the way to go. Other people want only to enjoy a comfortable lifestyle, free from financial worries. They need to choose more conservative funds.

All of these factors must be taken into account when setting your mutual fund investment objectives. Only when you feel you know exactly what you want to achieve, and why, should you move on to the next stage.

## SUMMARY

- Set your investment goals before putting any money into funds.
- Know yourself. Your investing personality is one of the keys to intelligent fund selection.
- Start with lower-risk funds until you are comfortable with what you are doing.
- Younger investors should place emphasis on growth funds. As you approach retirement, income and safety should be your main priorities.

## FUND FACTS

**MONEY MARKET VS. MORTGAGE.** If you're looking for the ultimate in mutual fund safety, you can invest in a money market fund. However, returns are very low, especially during times when interest rates are down. A mortgage fund has slightly more risk, but your profits should be much better.

**BEWARE OF INFREQUENT INCOME.** Some so-called income funds make distributions only once or twice a year. If you're looking for regular income like a monthly cheque, ask how frequently money is paid out before you invest.

**SAFE SPECULATING.** Don't succumb to the "get rich quick" urge if you're investing inside an RRSP. If you take a hit, the money can't be replaced and you can't claim a capital loss for tax purposes. Keep your speculations outside your retirement plan.

# Picking Winning Funds

*With more than 3,000 mutual funds to choose from (including all the spinoffs), it shouldn't come as a big surprise that some are very good, some are very bad, and most float somewhere in between those two extremes. You obviously want only the very best funds for your portfolio—to heck with all the rest.*

You and everyone else.

There are just a couple of problems with that strategy. To begin with, trying to pick the best funds isn't easy, which is why people write books on the subject. Moreover, the best funds for you won't be the best funds for someone else—it all depends on what you're trying to achieve. There are some broad guidelines you can use to at least narrow down the field, however. Here they are:

**TRACK RECORD.** Mutual funds are like horses in the sense that they have a performance record that anyone can look up. They're also like horses in another way: the results of last year's races are no guarantee that they're going to win in the future. Past performance is simply an indication of form and nothing more. But at least the track record gives you some idea of how the fund has performed historically. And a fund that has consistently been in the first or second quartile of its category over several years (in other words, the top half) will likely continue to outperform.

Just remember when you're studying the numbers not to give too much credence to short-term results. Most equity funds will be negatively affected by downward moves in the market. Since performance numbers are recalculated monthly, this will be reflected in the results for all years being reported. The shorter the term you're looking at, the greater the impact of the most recent results. Keep in mind that the converse is also true, of course—upward moves in the equity markets will give a bigger boost to short-term (six month to three year) returns than to long-term (five and ten year) returns.

We're often asked what rate of return is necessary for a mutual fund to get back to a break-even point after a down year, taking commissions into account. Not surprisingly, there are a number of factors that come into play. For starters, the lower the sales commission, the faster you'll recoup any losses. That's why it's often (but not always) better to choose a back-end load sales option or a no-load fund. Next, remember that equity funds don't increase by a predictable amount each year; they follow the fortunes of the stock market. History shows that if you invest in good equity funds when the market is going through a tough period, you can expect to reap excellent returns when it rebounds.

You can find the performance history of every mutual fund in the country in a number of places. Most major newspapers publish monthly surveys of fund performance. Several organizations offer software to track fund results, allowing you to compare those you're interested in to the rest of the field. There are several annual mutual fund guides that assess comparative fund performance on a quantitative and qualitative basis. So there's no shortage of performance information. It's simply a matter of taking time to find it.

**TREND LINE.** Just because a fund has a great 10-year record, it doesn't mean it's still doing well. You have to look at the trend line, or how the fund is doing in comparison with other funds in the same category.

Consider the following examples. In each case, we're looking at a fund's ranking compared with all other funds in the same category over several years. See if you can spot the trend patterns:

| | 10 YEARS (73 FUNDS IN TOTAL) | 5 YEARS (136 FUNDS IN TOTAL) | 3 YEARS (151 FUNDS IN TOTAL) | 1 YEAR (202 FUNDS IN TOTAL) |
|---|---|---|---|---|
| Fund A rank | 3rd | 108th | 139th | 200th |
| Fund B rank | 1st | 2nd | 1st | 1st |
| Fund C rank | 48th | 91st | 11th | 19th |
| Fund D rank | 69th | 113th | 122nd | 147th |

The trends pop right out, don't they? Fund A is clearly in a long, steady decline. There's nothing in its trend line encouraging you to believe that next year the fund is going to finish near the top of the charts. Fund B proves itself a winner no matter what time frame you look at. Fund C is a case where something positive is happening. Over the past three years, it's been transformed from a weak performer to one that's in the top 10 percent in its class. And finally, Fund D is clearly a chronic also-ran—a fund that underperforms the competition no matter what time frame you look at.

VOLATILITY. Most Canadians are cautious by nature when it comes to their money. They don't like a lot of risk, and they don't like to own securities that bounce up and down like india rubber balls. None of us needs an ulcer brought on from worrying about the fluctuations in our investments. That's why most people would never put their money into a fund like Cambridge Growth, even though it has had years when it scored big gains—their nerves couldn't take it. Want proof? Look at the fund's year-by-year results during the past decade:

| YEAR | RANK |
| --- | --- |
| 1990 | −0.7% |
| 1991 | +13.6% |
| 1992 | +2.6% |
| 1993 | +61.7% |
| 1994 | −21.3% |
| 1995 | +2.7% |
| 1996 | +6.7% |
| 1997 | −31.5% |
| 1998 | −39.1% |
| 1999 | −19.4% |
| 2000 | −38.2% |

Be honest now. Sure, 1993 was a great year. But would you have stayed in the fund after that big 21-percent loss in 1994? Or after the back-to-back-to-back losses of 1997 through to 2000? Maybe you have nerves of steel, but most people don't.

We've used this example to illustrate why it's essential to look at volatility when you're trying to pick the best funds for your personal needs. Fortunately, the information is easy to find. Most of the business papers include volatility rankings in their monthly mutual fund reports, so you can tell at a glance how much grief you're letting yourself in for.

THE ECONOMY. Some types of funds will outperform others at certain stages in the business cycle. For example, you can make good money in a recession, especially in the early stages, by putting money into bond funds. That's because the Bank of Canada usually moves aggressively to lower interest rates when the economy turns sour, in hopes of encouraging investment and consumer spending. Bond prices rise in a falling interest rate environment, so bond funds will do well under tough circumstances.

Stock funds are normally the best performers when the economy is beginning to turn the corner into a recovery phase. The typical pattern is that stock prices get beaten down to bargain basement levels during a recession. When economic conditions start to look better, cheap shares attract investor attention and the markets take off.

The bottom line is that picking the winners isn't easy. But if you make the effort, there are a lot of valuable clues available to put you on the right track.

## SUMMARY

- Mutual funds are like horses—both have performance charts, but past results don't guarantee a future winner.
- Trend lines will help you identify which funds are on the way up and which are on a slippery slope.
- Some funds may produce fabulous results—but keep the Maalox handy!

## FUND FACTS

**SMALL CAN BE DECEIVING.** Be skeptical of spectacular performance results from small funds. Unusually high one-year returns should set off caution lights in your mind. There are a number of techniques managers can use to pump up the results of small funds, particularly on a short-term basis. So don't get too excited when a tiny new fund announces a big hit. Wait and see if the manager can keep up the pace for another year or two.

**VOLATILITY.** Volatility is a measure of a fund's tendency to fluctuate in value. A fund with a unit value that never changes has zero volatility. The greater the swings, the higher the volatility rating. There are several ways of measuring volatility, the most widely accepted being a mathematical calculation known as standard deviation. Many newspapers use a less complicated approach, however. For example, *The Globe and Mail* describes a fund's volatility as being low, average, or high. The higher the volatility rating, the greater a fund's inherent risk.

**MANAGER CHANGES.** Before you spend a lot of time studying history, find out some basic facts about a fund's consistency. For example, how long has the current manager been in place? How much of the record is his or her responsibility? If the manager has taken the helm only in the past year or two, then whatever happened before that time may not be particularly meaningful.

**MANDATE CHANGES.** Be sure the fund you're considering hasn't changed its mandate recently. You'd be surprised at the number of funds out there possessing objectives that are quite different today than they were when the fund started out. Just recently, one of the funds in the AIM group was suddenly transformed from a foreign bond fund into a Canadian bond fund. Obviously, any information about the fund before the switch became absolutely worthless from an investor's perspective. The fund's history as a foreign bond investment suddenly became irrelevant to its new Canadian bond fund status—it might as well have been a brand new fund.

**TIME HELPS.** Once a fund has been around for a while (three years minimum), it develops a certain standard compared to other funds in the same category. The longer the fund has been in existence, the more well defined that standard becomes. Some funds show themselves to be highly volatile, with big up and down swings in unit value. Some funds turn out to be consistent performers, with little variation month after month. Some funds regularly outperform their competition while some regularly underperform it. Once a clear pattern is established, there is a strong tendency for it to continue. Usually only a managerial change or a switch in the fund's investment mandate will break its long-term trend.

**WHAT'S IN A NAME?** Companies sometimes do strange things with their fund names, but here's one that looks especially odd, at least on the surface.

In July 2000, C.I. announced that it was closing the Signature Canadian Balanced Fund by merging it into the BPI Income & Growth Fund. This sort of thing happens a lot these days. But in the next breath, the company said that the name of the BPI fund was being changed to—get this—the Signature Canadian Balanced Fund. Wait a minute. Wasn't that the name of the fund they had just terminated? Yes, indeed. So what's going on? Why not just merge the BPI fund into the already existing Signature fund?

The BPI fund had a three-year track record, that's why. The Signature fund didn't. If the BPI fund had simply been merged into the Signature fund, its record would have been wiped out. By doing it the way C.I. did, the Signature Canadian Balanced Fund could display an above-average three-year annual compound rate of return.

This is just one example of how mutual fund statistics can sometimes be misleading.

# Cut Your Costs
# to the Bone

*Let's not kid ourselves. It's going to cost you some money to invest in mutual funds. The people who sell funds, manage the money, and publish your monthly statements don't work for nothing. They expect to be paid like everyone else. And the reality is, there's only one person who can pay them: you, the customer.*

So don't get hung up (as many people do) on the idea that no-load funds are somehow free. They're not. They don't have any sales commission attached, but you'll pay in other ways, as we'll explain below. In fact, there is a range of charges associated with mutual funds. Some are obvious and some are not, but all will have a direct impact on the return you receive on your investment.

Broadly, these charges break down into three categories: management fees, sales commissions (loads), and miscellaneous costs. A run-down on each group follows.

## Management Fees

Every fund has management fees of some kind. These fees comprise the charges levied against a fund to compensate the people who make the investment decisions. They're normally expressed as a percentage of a fund's total assets. Money market funds usually have the lowest fee; labour-sponsored venture capital funds have the highest.

Many critics of the industry feel that the management fees charged in this country are far too high in comparison with the U.S. Fund managers respond that they don't benefit from the same economies of scale so they must charge more. But competition is slowly forcing some changes that benefit investors, and companies now actively promoting their low charges include Sceptre, McLean Budden, and Phillips, Hager & North.

When you're considering a mutual fund, know what the average fee is for the category. You'll find this information in the monthly fund report in *The Globe and Mail*. For example, the average fee for a Canadian equity fund is 2.3 percent; the average bond fund fee comes in at about 1.7 percent. If the fee for the fund you're considering is higher, make sure it's worth the extra cost.

## Sales Commissions

Fund commissions can take several forms. Here's a summary of load charges:

FRONT-END LOADS. These commissions are charged at the time you make your investment and are deducted from the amount of money you initially put up. The amount of the commission is normally calculated as a percentage of your investment. So if a sales person charges a 5 percent front-end load, 95¢ out of every dollar you invest will go towards the purchase of fund units, while the other 5¢ is taken as commission.

The amount of commission charged will be determined by two factors:

1. *The maximum commission structure authorized by the mutual fund company.* The normal range for Canadian mutual funds has been between 2 and 9 percent, although many companies have reduced their maximum to the 5 to 6 percent range in recent years. Posted maximum rates often decline as the size of the investment increases.

2. *Your negotiating skills.* In most cases, the posted commission structure has the same effect as a manufacturer's suggested retail price. The commission rate is only a guideline; retailers may sell for less if they wish.

In the case of mutual funds, they usually do sell for less. Brokers, financial planners, and other fund sales representatives will generally charge a lower commission than the suggested rate—if you ask. You should never pay a front-end load of more than 4 percent, even if you're only investing $500. If you buy online or through a discount broker, you'll pay even less. Don't base your decision purely on monetary considerations, however; if you're receiving exceptional service from a sales rep, an extra point or two of commission may be good value for the advice you get.

The only situation in which you won't be able to negotiate a discounted rate is if the fund is sold exclusively by a so-called "captive" sales force, or representatives directly employed by the company. This kind of sales approach is found with insurance company funds and funds sold by organizations like Investors Group. In these cases, the posted rate is usually what you can expect to pay. Sometimes the commissions are unreasonably high; some companies are reducing the rates, however, to be more competitive. You may also find there is little room to manoeuvre if you buy your mutual funds through a discount broker.

These companies have already cut their rates substantially and can't drop the price any lower.

You should also be aware that if you purchase no-load funds through a broker or financial planner, you might be asked to pay a handling fee. Some sales reps will acquire the funds for you without charge as a goodwill gesture, but others will want to be compensated for their time (including discount brokers).

Front-end loads will cut into the return on your invested money, sometimes significantly. The table below shows how much a $1,000 investment will be worth after 5 years and 10 years with 3 funds, each of which posts a 12-percent average annual compound rate of return. Taxes aren't taken into account for purposes of this illustration.

| LOAD CHARGE | AMOUNT INVESTED | VALUE AFTER 5 YEARS | VALUE AFTER 10 YEARS |
| --- | --- | --- | --- |
| None | $1,000 | $1,762.34 | $3,105.85 |
| 5% | $ 950 | $1,674.22 | $2,950.56 |
| 9% | $ 910 | $1,603.73 | $2,826.32 |

As you can see, the longer the time frame, the more significant the impact of the front-end load on the fund's accumulated value.

The effect of front-end load charges is not taken into account in the performance records of mutual funds published in the business press. But you should be aware of them because they may affect your decision as to which fund to purchase.

Dr. David Fieldhouse, a mathematics professor at the University of Guelph, has provided a formula that you can use to determine the approximate real rate of return on any front-end load fund. A more precise calculation requires a more detailed formula, but in most cases this simplified version should do the trick:

$j = (1 + I) \times (1 - \{x/n\}) - 1$
$j$ = the adjusted annual rate of return
$I$ = the published rate of return
$x$ = the percentage of front-end load paid
$n$ = the number of years the units are held

(Note that percentages must always be expressed as decimals; for example, 8.5 percent becomes .085.)

To show you how this formula works, let's say you paid a front-end load of 4 percent for a fund three years ago. According to the monthly mutual fund performance report published in the financial press, its average annual compound rate of return since then has been 12 percent. At first glance, you'd be tempted to say this fund did better than a no-load fund with an 11 percent return over the same period. But did it? Let's use the formula and see:

$j = (1 + I) \times (1 - \{x/n\}) - 1$
$j = (1 + .12) \times (1 - \{.04/3\}) - 1$
$j = 1.12 \times (1 - .0133) - 1$
$j = (1.12 \times .9867) - 1$
$j = 1.105 - 1$
Actual return $= .105$ or 10.5%

Based on net performance, once the sales charge has been taken into account, the no-load fund has a better record in this case. Keep this formula in mind when you're assessing the relative merits of load and no-load funds.

> **SPECIAL TIP** Some brokers and planners will buy funds on a front-end load basis for good clients and charge zero commission. They do this to collect the annual "trailer fees" paid by the fund companies on the value of the accounts the advisor holds with them. The advantage to you is that you obtain units at no cost, without being tied in by deferred sales charges if you decide to sell later.

**BACK-END LOADS.** When you purchase a back-end load fund you pay no sales commission, so all your money goes to work for you immediately. But if you redeem your fund units before a certain number of years has passed (usually five to seven), you'll be assessed a redemption fee (also known as a deferred sales charge) at that time. This fee is usually structured on a sliding scale; the longer you hold your fund units, the less you'll pay.

The back-end load has proven itself extremely popular with investors. However, you shouldn't be too quick to automatically choose one. There's no question that, all things being equal, a back-end load fund will cost you less than a front-end load fund. The problem is that things are not always equal. In fact, deciding between a back- and front-end load option has become quite difficult in some cases. That's because, despite the attractiveness of paying nothing up-front, back-end load funds have certain disadvantages. These disadvantages are:

- *Inflexibility.* Because of the way back-end loads are structured, investors are often unwilling to switch their money elsewhere, even if it makes good sense to do so. A back-end load fund locks you in by setting a high premium on redemptions in the early years.
- *Inconsistency.* Back-end load charges are not always calculated in the same way. Sometimes you're charged on the basis of the market value of the fund at the time of redemption. However, some fund groups base the redemption fee on the original price you paid for the units. Find out which policy

is used by the fund you're considering; all else being equal, choose a fund that bases the redemption charge on your original investment.

- *Non-negotiability.* Unlike front-end load charges, back-end loads are usually non-negotiable.
- *Higher management fees.* Another drawback to watch for is a management fee step-up. Some back-end load funds are assessed a higher management fee than their front-end counterparts. What this means to you is that, if two funds produce exactly the same return, the back-end load units will end up with less in net yield.

Dr. Fieldhouse has also kindly provided a basic formula that can be used to determine the approximate real rate of return on back-end load funds:

$$j = (1 + I) \times (1 + q - \{p/n\}) - 1$$

All the factors are the same as before except:

p = the maximum penalty for early redemption
q = the amount by which the penalty declines annually

The formula is based on the assumption that the redemption fee will be assessed on the market value of the units when you cash them in (some funds base the charge on your original purchase cost, which is a better deal for you). A word of caution here, however: this formula only works if the redemption fee declines in equal stages over the years. If the pattern is asymmetric (e.g., there are annual declines of 0 percent, 0.5 percent, and 1 percent built in along the way), the formula can't be used.

## Miscellaneous Costs

There are a number of additional charges that may apply to the particular mutual fund you select. Inquire about them before making a purchase decision. The most common ones are as follows:

PENALTY FEES. A few funds have adopted the unpleasant policy of locking you in for a lengthy period by imposing a hefty penalty if you sell your units before a certain amount of time has passed. These penalties are over and above any normal redemption fees.

REDEMPTION FEES. You could find yourself having to pay a redemption charge even if you don't own any back-end load funds. Some discount brokers assess a fee to redeem units of any no-load fund except their own. Also, some funds (including some no-load funds) charge a redemption fee if you sell your units within a short time after purchase—90 days is common. The cost may be as much as two percent of the value of your assets. If you need to cash out early for some reason, check the prospectus before you place the sell order to avoid an unwelcome surprise.

**RRSP/RRIF FEES.** If the fund is held as a registered retirement savings plan or registered retirement income fund, a small annual trustee fee may be levied, although some companies have waived this fee. A fee may also be charged for RRSP cancellation.

**SET-UP FEES.** You may be assessed a charge for opening an account with a company. Altamira is one firm that operates this way.

**SWITCHING FEES.** You may be permitted to switch from one fund to another within the same company, but a charge will sometimes apply. Note that some companies, including Altamira, limit the number of free switches each year. If you're dealing with a discount brokerage, you may be assessed a fee even for switches within a no-load fund group.

**SYSTEMATIC WITHDRAWAL CHARGES.** Some investors wish to receive regular payments from their fund. These payments are called systematic withdrawals. Some companies charge an annual fee for this service; others charge a fee for each payment, and a few hit you for both.

**TERMINATION OR CLOSING FEES.** Some plans assess a nominal fee for closing an account. This practice is becoming more widespread.

**TRANSFER FEES.** This is a charge for transferring a registered account, such as an RRSP, to another financial institution or mutual fund group. This charge is also becoming increasingly common.

**WITHDRAWAL FEES.** A few funds charge a nominal fee for any withdrawals made from your account.

## SUMMARY

- Watch out for high management fees—they'll eat away at your returns.
- Never pay a front-end sales commission of more than 4 percent.
- Some advisors now sell front-end load units at zero commission. This is the best deal if you can get it.
- Don't automatically choose a back-end load over a front-end load. Deferred sales charges are sometimes a deterrent to investors who might want to move on to something else.

# FUND FACTS

**MANAGEMENT FEES EXPLAINED.** "Management fee" is a catch-all term that may cover a variety of charges against a fund's assets. Wages and bonuses for the fund managers are paid out of these fees. The fee may also be used to cover certain administration expenses, accounting and bookkeeping costs, brokerage charges, and marketing costs, depending on the policy of the individual fund.

**RATIO RATIONALE.** The management expense ratio (MER) of a mutual fund is calculated by adding together all management fees and other expenses (like brokerage commissions) charged to a fund and dividing that amount by the fund's total assets. Thus a fund with total expenses of $250,000 and assets of $10 million has a MER of 2.5 percent.

**WHERE TO FIND MERS.** You can find the latest MER of any mutual fund in the monthly fund reports published in *The Globe and Mail, National Post, The Toronto Star*, and other newspapers. They're also available on the Internet. You can use the Mutual Fund Directory on the Building Wealth Web site (**www.gordonpape.com**). Another excellent source is the GlobeFund Web site (**www.globefund.com**). Click on "Fund Selector" on the home page and choose the company in which you are interested. Then click on "Key Facts" and a page will appear that includes the MER for each fund.

**LOW-FEE COMPANIES.** Some fund companies have a policy of keeping their management fees as low as possible to enhance investor returns. Two such firms are Phillips, Hager & North of Vancouver and the McLean Budden Funds of Montreal/Toronto. It's no coincidence that their funds, on the whole, tend to generate above-average returns.

**TRAILER FEES.** These fees are annual commissions paid to the person who handles your mutual fund account, and they apply as long as you remain invested in the fund. The principle is similar to the one used in the life insurance industry, where an agent or broker continues to receive an annual commission as long as your policy remains in force. The mutual fund industry claims trailer fees ensure investors receive continuing service from a sales representative; it prevents the rep from losing interest in you once the sale has been made. Critics contend such fees discourage sales reps from advising clients to redeem their units, even though conditions may be right to do so—the lure of the fee prejudices the objectivity of the reps advice. Additionally, trailer fees represent a drain on a fund's assets, reducing the return to investors.

**GETTING A BETTER DEAL.** Some companies reduce or eliminate certain fees as a sales promotion tool. For instance, some fund groups have dropped trustee fees for RRSP accounts. Ask your sales representative if any special deals are available.

# Know Who Runs the Show

*A mutual fund may seem rather impersonal, but it's not. Somewhere behind the scenes people are making decisions every day on which securities to buy and which ones to sell, what companies look promising, how much cash the fund needs, and more. They're at a computer, on the telephone, meeting with business owners, or even travelling the world in search of bargains.*

These people are the fund managers, and they're the key to any fund's success. A good manager will consistently generate above-average returns for investors; a mediocre or poor manager will produce indifferent results, or worse.

The manager decides which securities the fund will buy and sell and what the portfolio composition should be at any given time. The manager is also responsible for ensuring that investment strategies are consistent with the stated objectives of the fund, maintaining adequate cash reserves to meet redemption requests, and complying with the regulations for mutual fund investing laid down by various securities commissions and other regulatory bodies. The manager's success or failure in making these decisions will determine how well a fund performs. The better the performance, the more investors the fund will attract and the more profitable it will be for the mutual fund company. So fund managers have an extremely heavy burden on their shoulders—and the best are paid very well for their services.

Conversely, a committee is effectively in charge of some funds; one person may be listed as the fund manager, but decisions are really made by a group. And while it doesn't matter if your fund is run committee-style as we've just described or by an individual manager, it is important that you know exactly how your fund is being controlled.

You may find a few companies that refuse, for reasons of their own, to disclose the name of a fund's manager, preferring to give only the name of the management company. In this case, you're operating in the dark about who actually runs the fund. If you encounter this situation, insist on more information about the credentials of the people to whom you're entrusting your money.

A few funds are directly associated with a manager's name, although in some cases that manager's responsibilities may have changed over the years. For example, Sir John Templeton remains the guiding genius behind the Templeton family of funds, but he doesn't actively run the funds any more. He lives in semi-retirement in Nassau, freely giving interviews to business journalists seeking the secrets of his success. But the actual decision making is in the hands of a new generation of fund managers who are well-steeped in Sir John's value investing approach.

At the beginning of the 1990s, most Canadian investors probably couldn't name a single mutual fund manager other than, perhaps, Sir John. But as mutual funds started to catch the public's attention in recent years, a new trend has begun to emerge. Many fund managers are now regularly quoted in the business press, have spots in television ads, and hold seminars that attract large audiences. Names like Kiki Delaney, Jerry Javasky, Veronika Hirsch, and Gerald Coleman are known to many fund investors.

That being said, the majority of fund managers in Canada toil in relative anonymity. But just because a manager isn't well known, it doesn't mean he or she isn't brilliant; the business press may simply not have discovered him or her yet. In fact, many managers have well-established credentials and solid track records. For instance, few investors know the name of Ian Mottershead, but he's been successfully overseeing the Canadian equity funds of Phillips, Hager & North for many years. He is just one example of the many little-known but extremely talented fund managers you can find out about with a bit of sleuthing.

Getting information about a fund's manager is becoming easier. Manager profiles now appear regularly in the business pages and in the monthly mutual fund supplements published by many major newspapers. In-depth analyses of individual funds and their management strategies have also become a fixture in the business press. There are several annual guides to mutual funds on the market, some of which contain profiles of leading fund managers. You can often dial in on the conference calls managers hold regularly with sales representatives, or get a free audio cassette and listen to them explain their current outlook and strategy. So there's no shortage of information, if you're prepared to look for it.

There are two essential points to consider when assessing how a fund's manager is likely to perform:

1. *Past record.* Check how the fund has done since the current manager took charge and how that performance compares with the fund's record prior to that time. If the performance has improved or remained stable at an above-

average level since the manager took over, it's a good sign (but no guarantee, of course) for the future.

2. *Stability.* A manager who has been in place for several years producing good results is reassuring to potential investors. A new manager brings an element of the unknown to your investment, unless he or she has established a track record with another fund.

Be extra cautious in the case of a fund run for several years by a manager who has recently departed. This is especially true if the manager was largely responsible for calling the shots (as opposed to working within a committee). In this situation, the fund's past record should be discounted in making a purchase decision. Keep in mind that you shouldn't react too quickly, however. Generally, the evidence suggests that you don't need to be in too much of a hurry to follow a departing manager. In many cases, the fund a departing manager has left behind performs better than the fund he or she takes over, at least for a while.

The bottom line: If the manager moves, stick with the old fund for at least six months and then reassess the situation.

## SUMMARY

- The manager is the key to a mutual fund's success.
- It's easy to find information about fund managers—if you take the time to look.
- Don't be too quick to follow a manager who leaves a fund; wait six months and review the situation.

## FUND FACTS

**COLOURFUL CUNDILL.** One of Canada's most successful value investors is Peter Cundill, founder of the Cundill Value Fund. He's known for his eye for value, but also for some of the off-the-wall things he sometimes does, like launching a lawsuit against Mississippi in an attempt to force the state to pay up on bonds it had defaulted on in the early 19th century. The Cundill funds are now part of the Mackenzie Financial organization.

**MANAGEMENT BY COMPUTER.** Believe it or not, there are a couple of mutual funds in Canada being run by a computer. The AGF American Tactical Asset Allocation Fund and the companion AGF Canadian Tactical Asset Allocation Fund both base their investment decisions on analyses prepared by a sophisticated computer program run by Barclays Global Investors. Both funds have generated above-average returns, so obviously the computer knows its business.

**MULTI-MANAGERS.** A few funds use what is known as a "multi-manager" approach where two or more managers are each given a portion of the assets to invest. The aim here is to achieve style diversification.

# Understanding Risk

*If you're going to invest money in mutual funds, you have to accept a degree of risk. If you can't cope with that, then keep your money in a savings account—although that's not entirely risk-free, either.*

Remember that the mutual fund risk scale is wide, ranging from minuscule to very high. You can pick any point on it that you like. If you want to keep risk to an absolute minimum, you can concentrate your mutual fund investments in money market funds and mortgage funds. No money market fund sold in Canada has ever lost money for investors (although it could theoretically happen under certain extreme circumstances). Some mortgage funds may occasionally decline in value, but there are some that have never lost a dime in any calendar year since they were created, and in some cases, that covers a span of more than two decades.

Another way to minimize risk is to invest in the segregated funds offered by insurance companies. All carry some degree of protection against loss, and in some instances the guarantee covers the full amount you invest. However, you'll usually pay higher fees for these funds, and the guarantee applies only if you die or hold the fund for at least 10 years.

As a general rule, the less risk you take, the lower your potential returns. If you want above-average profits from your funds, then you'll have to crank up the risk level a few notches. It goes with the territory.

If you'd quickly like to see just how much of a risk-taker you are, take this simple test:

| STATEMENT | AGREE | DISAGREE | UNSURE |
|---|---|---|---|
| I enjoy visiting a casino and regard any losses as simply the cost of an evening's entertainment. | | | |
| I enjoy playing games for money. | | | |
| I regularly buy lottery tickets. | | | |
| I'd rather take a one-in-ten chance to win $5,000 rather than a one-in-three chance to win $500. | | | |
| When renewing a mortgage, I prefer to take a shorter term with a lower rate rather than lock in at a higher rate for five years. | | | |
| When driving on the highway, I'll exceed the speed limit if no police are in sight. | | | |
| I delay planning holidays until the last minute in order to get discounts. | | | |
| I usually arrive late for appointments. | | | |
| I rarely worry about my investments. | | | |
| I want to be rich and I'll do whatever it takes to achieve that goal, within reason. | | | |

Score two points for every "Agree," one point for each "Unsure," and no points for all "Disagree" responses. Here's how to interpret the results:

15–20 points: You like to live on the edge. You have a high tolerance for risk and should plan your mutual fund investments accordingly.

8–14 points: You'll accept a degree of risk, but it may make you somewhat uncomfortable. A balanced fund portfolio looks like the appropriate approach for you.

0–7 points: You're very conservative by nature. Too much risk will give you bad dreams. Stick with funds at the lowest end of the risk scale.

Clearly, the risk/reward relationship must be a key consideration when you are deciding which mutual funds to buy. If preserving capital and avoiding loss is your prime concern, you'll select a conservative fund that shares these objectives. In this case, you'll give up some potential return for a higher measure of safety. On the other hand, if your objective is to maximize growth, and you're willing to incur greater risk to achieve this, you'll search out more aggressively managed funds—and there are plenty of those around.

Certain types of mutual funds are better suited for conservative investors than others. The following table gives a general guideline of the risk/return relationship of various types of funds. Keep in mind, however, that there may be exceptions within any particular group. Review the prospectus of any fund in which you're interested, and be sure its goals are consistent with your own.

| TYPE OF FUND | RISK POTENTIAL | RETURN POTENTIAL |
|---|---|---|
| Money Market | Low | Low |
| Mortgage | Low | Low |
| Bond | Low/Medium | Medium |
| Balanced | Medium | Medium |
| Dividend | Medium | Medium |
| Real Estate | Medium/High | Medium |
| International Equity (broad-based) | Medium | Medium/High |
| U.S. Equity (broad-based) | Medium/High | Medium/High |
| Canadian Equity (broad-based) | Medium/High | Medium/High |
| Regional | High | High |
| Emerging Markets | High | High |
| Small-Cap | High | High |
| Sector | High | High |

You can determine a specific fund's risk potential through the use of a more precise measure known as volatility (also called variability). Volatility is a mathematical calculation that measures the extent to which the actual monthly returns for a given fund swing up or down from its average return over a given period of time (usually three years).

Many people find this concept difficult to grasp, so look at it this way: suppose a fund has an average rate of return of 1 percent a month over five years. That average could have been achieved through a series of sharp ups and downs—a gain of 10 percent one month, a loss of 8 percent the next, a jump of 5 percent the next, and so on. In that situation, the fund would be said to have a high volatility rating and the risk factor would be significant.

However, if the actual returns throughout the whole period were exactly one percent each month—no movement up or down—the fund would have a volatility rating of one (or 0.1, or zero, depending on the scale being used). A low volatility rating implies a very conservative management strategy and a corresponding low risk rating.

The concept of volatility is useful, but it must be applied with a little common sense. For example, most money market funds have volatility ratings of one. That's because of the low-risk nature of their investments, which include T-bills, term deposits, and high-quality short-term corporate notes. An investment portfolio comprising this type of fund is as close to risk-free as you'll find, and will churn out consistent returns month after month. Since volatility scores put a premium on such virtues, money market funds are popular with conservative investors.

But if volatility were the only criterion applied, everyone would have all their cash in money market funds. In reality, there are other things to consider. The low volatility score achieved by money market funds correctly highlights their safety, but disguises the fact that their growth potential is nil and their income potential declines as interest rates fall. They will always perform well relative to risk because the risk is almost non-existent. The trade-off is that they cannot achieve the growth potential of an equity fund or even a bond fund. So don't get so carried away with studying volatility ratings that you lose sight of the underlying characteristics of the fund itself.

There are three other criteria to use in determining the risk/reward potential of a given fund. The first is to carefully study the section of the prospectus on management objectives. Words and phrases such as "will seek to maximize growth," "aggressive management approach," or "emphasis will be on above-average capital gains," are all tip offs that you're dealing with a higher-risk fund.

Second, make sure to review the annual performance record of the fund, going back 10 or 15 years. Look especially for losing years; funds that rarely suffer a loss over any 12-month period have shown excellent consistency regardless of their volatility rating.

Finally, in the case of equity funds, look for ones that have stood up especially well in hard times, like 1990, 1994, and 2000 through to 2001. If funds do well under harsh conditions, it indicates they are conservatively managed and priority is placed on capital preservation. That doesn't mean they will be top performers in bull markets, however. In fact, they probably won't outperform when markets are on the rise because of their cautious approach. Again, you have to decide where your priorities lie.

## SUMMARY

- All mutual funds contain a measure of risk. The question is how much risk you're prepared to accept.
- The more risk you take, the higher your potential returns should be, and vice versa.
- Volatility is a good measure of risk, but it can be misleading at times.

## FUND FACTS

STYLE MATTERS. A fund manager's investing style can also be a determining factor when weighing risk. Value managers usually look for stocks that are underpriced relative to the general market, so the downside risk should be less. Growth managers place less emphasis on current price and more emphasis on future potential; if the potential doesn't materialize, the stocks may fizzle.

**GO GLOBAL.** As a general rule, a global equity fund should be less risky than one that focuses on a specific country or region. The reason for this is that the manager has the whole world to make stock selections from and can avoid areas with high risk and low potential.

# Winning Fund Strategies

*Wouldn't it be great if all there was to mutual fund investing was to decide you want to do it and then go out and pick a few funds? Unfortunately, as with everything else in life, it's more complicated than that.*

In fact, there are five key components to making money in mutual funds:

1. Deciding to actually do it and committing your money.
2. Determining which types of funds are best for you.
3. Understanding the principles of picking winning funds.
4. Ascertaining a comfortable strategy. (That's the point we're at right now.)
5. Building a portfolio.

The strategy issue is critical. Investing in mutual funds is more than just buying a few funds and settling back to watch and hope. The right strategy provides a framework and a direction for your entire mutual fund programme.

There are a number of possible strategies available to you. The one you select at the outset will depend on your personality and objectives. But do decide on a course before you start—don't flounder around in uncertainty. You can always move in another direction later, or even mix strategies once you've attained a comfort level with what you're doing. In the beginning, though, decide on one basic strategic plan and stick to it for at least a year. Your options include:

BUY AND HOLD. This is the easiest strategy of all, so it's highly suitable for beginners. It simply involves buying and holding units in carefully selected mutual funds, and adding to your portfolio when you wish. The buy-and-hold approach is consistent with the attitude you should be taking toward mutual funds: they represent a long-term investment in your future. With the exception of money market funds and resource funds, people who use this strategy should rarely buy into a fund they are not prepared to hold for at least five years.

As with any other investment strategy, you should temper a buy-and-hold approach with common sense. As long as a fund is generating an above-average return for its type, you should continue to hold it. However, if performance slips below average for an extended period (18 months or more) you should review the situation. Ask questions about the fund management. Find out if key personnel have changed or if there has been a shift in investment philosophy. Ask for explanations as to why the fund has underperformed. If you're not satisfied with the answers, the time has come to shift your money elsewhere.

DOLLAR-COST AVERAGING. A more disciplined variation of the buy-and-hold approach is dollar-cost averaging. This technique involves investing a given amount of money in the funds of your choice at periodic intervals: monthly, quarterly, semi-annually, or annually.

The benefit of this strategy is twofold. First, it creates a system of forced savings, a discipline many investors need. Second, it reduces risk. If you stick to your plan, you'll avoid the classic investment trap of buying high and selling low; the peaks and valleys will be automatically smoothed out. This also means, of course, that your return won't be as high—but that's the price you pay for lower risk.

The psychology of this strategy is important. When the unit price of an equity fund is low, it probably means the stock market has fallen. This situation often scares off small investors who, in fact, should be taking advantage of the opportunity to add to their holdings at bargain prices. When unit prices are high, it probably means the market is going through a bullish phase, a time when many investors get carried away by enthusiasm and commit too much cash. Dollar-cost averaging acts as a control against these natural tendencies, which is why many investors swear by it.

To understand how dollar-cost averaging works, take a look at this simplified example. We've assumed an investor who has decided to put $500 every quarter into a hypothetical no-load equity fund.

| DATE OF PURCHASE | AMOUNT INVESTED | UNIT PRICE | NUMBER BOUGHT | TOTAL OWNED | MARKET VALUE |
|---|---|---|---|---|---|
| January 1 | $500 | $10 | 50.00 | 50.00 | $500.00 |
| April 1 | $500 | $9 | 55.56 | 105.56 | 950.04 |
| July 1 | $500 | $11 | 45.45 | 151.01 | 1,661.11 |
| October 1 | $500 | $12 | 41.67 | 192.68 | 2,312.16 |

Over the year, as you can see, the price our investor will pay for units in the fund ranges from a low of $9 to a high of $12. When the price is low, more units are acquired for $500; when it is high, fewer are purchased. The average cost of the 192.68 units bought during the year 2000 works out to $10.38 each; the per unit value at year-end is $12. So our investor has made an average profit of $1.62 per unit over the year.

Obviously, this investor would be better off buying all the units on April 1 when the price is lowest. But there is no way to predict that low in advance. Dollar-cost averaging enables you to take advantage of price dips when they occur while restraining you from over-investing when prices are high.

Now let's look at some strategies for more advanced investors:

SWITCHING. For some investors, buy-and-hold and dollar-cost averaging strategies are too tame. They want more action and faster growth, and they're willing to take the risks associated with those avenues. They also believe they can time market movements, at least to some extent. So they use a switching strategy, moving their money among different types of mutual funds depending on conditions.

This approach to fund investing first became popular in the U.S., where there are many large mutual fund companies that offer a wide variety of funds and charge very low fees (or no fees at all) to switch your money between them. Switching has become so widespread south of the border that many investment newsletters are devoted entirely to the subject.

In Canada, more fund companies are recognizing the growing importance of switching to many investors. As a result, they've aggressively added to the number of funds they offer, thus giving switchers more choice. In addition, they are removing some of the impediments to easy switching. For example, there was a time in the 1990s when the Mackenzie Financial Corporation operated three distinct groups of mutual funds: the Industrial Group, the Ivy Group, and the Universal Group. However, there was an impenetrable wall between them; if you held units in one group you absolutely could not switch into another group. You were forced to sell your holdings, perhaps paying a stiff back-end load in the process, and then had to make a new purchase into the group you wanted to access—paying a new commission, of course. This practice clearly discouraged switching, and probably cost Mackenzie business as a result.

But now the wall is down, and Mackenzie has become a switcher's paradise with over 100 funds and 4 distinct managerial styles from which to choose, not to mention the addition of the Cundill funds to the group. You can move among all four Mackenzie families without restriction, save for the nominal 2 percent switching fee your sales rep is allowed to charge (which you may be able to negotiate down to zero).

Several other companies have also moved to a multi-family approach, including C.I., Franklin Templeton, Guardian, and AIM (with the addition of the Trimark line). Of course, the no-load funds, such as those offered by financial institutions and fund companies like Altamira, Phillips, Hager & North, and McLean Budden, allow free switching among all their funds.

The dedicated switcher will want to search out companies that combine an attractive switching policy with high-performance funds. That's why it's especially important for switchers to carefully review the entire family and not base their investment decision on the performance of a single fund.

A basic switching strategy involves being heavily invested in equity funds at times when the stock market is strong and switching into money market and/or fixed-income funds at other times. The trick, obviously, is to get out of the equity funds before the stock market tumbles. If you're not confident in your ability to do that, a switching strategy probably isn't right for you.

More sophisticated switching strategies involve moving money around in different international funds, increasing holdings in countries that look like their markets are in a bull phase, and moving out of high-risk areas. Another approach is to switch on the basis of management style; a portfolio is weighted toward value funds when they are doing well and then holdings are switched to growth and momentum funds when they are strong. This is very tough thing to accomplish on a consistent basis, however. In fact, if you develop a knack for it, you should probably apply for a job as a fund manager yourself!

ASSET MIX. An alternative to switching for those who want to increase the growth potential of their funds is an asset mix approach. This involves structuring a fund portfolio in such a way as to give certain types of investments greater weight than others, in line with current economic conditions. The true asset mix investor will always hold some funds from each of the three key asset groups (cash, fixed-income, and growth) in his or her portfolio. The percentage of each will be shifted periodically, depending on a number of factors including age, risk tolerance, and general economic conditions. For example, a younger person who wishes to emphasize growth might use the following asset mix during good economic times:

| | |
|---|---|
| Cash-type funds: | 5%–15% |
| Fixed-income funds: | 15%–25% |
| Growth funds: | 60%–80% |

When the economy is heading for rougher times and the stock market looks vulnerable, this investor might vary the asset mix as follows:

| | |
|---|---|
| Cash-type funds: | 25%–40% |
| Fixed-income funds: | 25%–50% |
| Growth funds: | 30%–50% |

This combination produces a more balanced mix and reduces the fund's exposure to the stock market while encouraging a buildup of cash reserves in order to take advantage of future buying opportunities. The fixed-income section is also strengthened because deteriorating economic times frequently signal a drop in interest rates. This kind of situation will have a positive effect on the unit values of bond funds and, to a lesser extent, mortgage funds.

Rebalancing your asset mix can be achieved by using switching techniques, as long as that is possible at a minimal cost. It can also be done by directing new investment money to the asset categories you wish to strengthen.

There are several variations on the asset mix theme. You can incorporate geographic, currency, and style considerations into the equation if you wish. However, the starting point should always be asset class. If you do nothing more, at least take that initial step.

**LEVERAGING.** The idea behind leveraging is to increase your profit potential through the use of someone else's money. By using the leveraging strategy, you increase your bottom line return significantly. However, it's not as easy as it may seem at first glance. Always remember that there are two sides to the leveraging coin: it will increase your returns when investments perform well, but it can also leave you twisting in the wind if things turn sour. We'll explain with a few examples.

Suppose you want to build a mutual fund portfolio but you have only $10,000 to invest. If you decide to invest that money and nothing more, here's how you'd make out with a fund that grows at a rate of 10 percent annually, compounded (for simplicity, we've left taxes out of the calculation):

| | | VALUE AFTER | |
| INITIAL INVESTMENT | 1 YEAR | 3 YEARS | 5 YEARS |
| --- | --- | --- | --- |
| $10,000 | $11,000 | $13,310 | $16,105 |

Looks pretty good—after five years your asset base has increased more than 60 percent. If you sold your fund portfolio at the end of that time, you'd walk away with a profit of $6,105.

Now suppose you borrowed an additional $10,000 from the bank at 8 percent annual interest to add to your investment capital. Since the loan is for investment purposes, the interest is tax deductible. If you're in a 50 percent tax bracket, the true after-tax interest rate you pay is actually only 4 percent. By taking this loan, you increase your initial investment to $20,000. Here's how your results would look in that situation:

| | | VALUE AFTER | |
| INITIAL INVESTMENT | 1 YEAR | 3 YEARS | 5 YEARS |
| --- | --- | --- | --- |
| $20,000 | $22,000 | $26,620 | $32,210 |

Again, let's assume you liquidate your portfolio after five years. Here's what happens:

| | |
|---|---|
| Proceeds from the sale: | $32,210 |
| After-tax interest charges: | $ 2,000 |
| Repayment of loan principal: | $10,000 |
| Net proceeds: | $20,210 |
| Profit on $10,000 investment: | $10,210 |

Leveraging has paid off very handsomely in this case. By using other people's money, you've increased your overall return by more than $4,000, and the percentage return on your own money has jumped from about 60 percent to more than 100 percent. So if leveraging is so easy, why doesn't everyone do it?

Because there's a dark side to the moon. Everything is indeed rosy if your funds go up. But what happens if they drop in value? Suppose, for example, your fund loses five percent a year instead of showing a profit. Here's what happens if you put up only your own money:

| | | VALUE AFTER | |
|---|---|---|---|
| INITIAL INVESTMENT | 1 YEAR | 3 YEARS | 5 YEARS |
| $10,000 | $9,500 | $8,574 | $7,738 |

Your loss at the end of five years is $2,262.

Now here's what happens if you borrow an additional $10,000 and add it to your own stake:

| | | VALUE AFTER | |
|---|---|---|---|
| INITIAL INVESTMENT | 1 YEAR | 3 YEARS | 5 YEARS |
| $20,000 | $19,000 | $17,148 | $15,476 |

In this case, when you liquidate your holdings after five years your results will be as follows:

| | |
|---|---|
| Gross proceeds of sale: | $15,476 |
| After-tax interest charges: | $ 2,000 |
| Repayment of loan principal: | $10,000 |
| Net proceeds: | $ 3,476 |
| Loss on original $10,000: | $ 6,524 |

Your loss is almost three times as great as it would have been had you not leveraged your investment. So, as you can clearly see, a leveraging strategy can be risky business. Don't let spellbinding tales of huge potential profits lead you down a garden path to disaster!

## SUMMARY

- Choosing a strategy and sticking to it is a prerequisite for making money in funds.
- Buy and hold is a simple approach well suited to many investors.
- Dollar-cost averaging allows you to smooth out the ups and downs of the stock market, thus reducing your risk.
- Many fund investors are adopting an active switching strategy—but it is not without risk.
- An asset allocation approach is one of the most effective strategies available to you.
- Leveraging is a double-edged sword; don't undertake it without a thorough understanding of the risks involved.

## FUND FACTS

**OPPORTUNITY FUNDS.** Certain types of mutual funds are not suitable for a buy-and-hold strategy. These include highly volatile funds prone to experiencing large swings up and down that, over a long period, negate most of their gains. Natural resource funds are a good example here. There are times when these funds do well thanks to strength in particular sectors like oil and gas. However, over the long term, these funds have been duds. Average annual compound rate of return for the five years to May 31, 2001 in this category was -3.0%.

Resource funds are best treated like stocks; you should buy them when the prospects for strong growth are good. Then take your profits and move on. That's why we call them "opportunity funds."

**BULLS AND BEARS.** A bull market is a period when most securities of a certain type are rising in price. The term is usually associated with the stock market, but a bull market can occur in any investment area. There can be a bull market in bonds, real estate, gold, lumber futures, and so on. Bull markets in different investment areas may occur simultaneously or at completely different times. There can also be bull markets at different times in overseas markets; Japan's Nikkei Index might be in a bull phase while the Paris Bourse is falling. The opposite of a bull market is a bear market, a time when declining prices create opportunities for bargain hunters.

# Mutual Funds and Your RRSP

*If you're concerned about paying less tax, having enough money to live on when you retire, or both, you probably have an RRSP. And if you're like millions of other Canadians, you probably know very little about it.*

Don't believe that last statement? Try this self-test and see:

| STATEMENT | YES | NO |
|---|---|---|
| I know the total value of all my RRSPs within $500. | | |
| I know what return my RRSP earned last year. | | |
| I know what assets I have in all of my RRSPs. | | |
| I know how many RRSPs I have and where they're located, without having to look that information up. | | |
| I know the percentage of foreign content in my RRSPs. | | |
| I know where to invest this year's RRSP contribution to improve my returns. | | |
| I know how much I can contribute to my RRSP this year. | | |

Score one point for every "Yes" answer and zero for every "No." Here's how to interpret the results:

6–7: You're right on top of your retirement plan and have a clear idea of what you're doing.

4–5: You're making an effort, but more attention is needed.

2–3: A little knowledge is better than none—but it's not good enough.

0–1: You haven't a clue.

This isn't a book about RRSPs as such (see *Gordon Pape's 2002 Buyer's Guide to RRSPs* for more specific information on the subject), so we won't devote a lot of space to the topic. But we do think it's important to spend a few pages discussing the use of mutual funds in an RRSP because it's a mixture with the potential to either make your retirement years a lot more comfortable, or to blow all of your dreams out of the water and force you to keep working until age 80 (if anyone will have you).

## The Pros and Cons of Mutual Funds in Your RRSP

For starters, not every RRSP can be used to hold mutual funds. Only two types of plans enable you do to this, as described below:

- *Mutual fund plans.* These plans are RRSPs set up by mutual fund companies and financial institutions for the specific purpose of enabling you to buy their funds for your retirement plan. There is usually an annual trustee fee ($25–$50, plus GST) attached to these plans, but no other special fees. Usually (but not always) these plans are restricted to the funds offered by the sponsoring company.
- *Self-directed plans.* A self-directed plan enables you to hold any type of RRSP-eligible security, including mutual funds. In theory, then, you should be able to put any mutual fund you want into a self-directed plan. In reality, however, it doesn't work out that way. If you set up such a plan with a broker or financial planner, he or she may be reluctant to acquire certain no-load funds for you because he or she receives no sales commission. Discount brokers like TD Waterhouse will let you add such funds, but you usually have to pay a redemption charge—and that defeats one of the main attractions of no-load funds. So while a self-directed plan gives you more flexibility, you'll still find some restrictions. Fees typically run about $100–$125 a year.

There are several advantages to including mutual funds in an RRSP portfolio. First and foremost, it's the most effective way to diversify your retirement plan. Adding funds to your mix allows you to introduce some growth potential, which GICs and Canada Premium Bonds don't offer. Funds also enable you to move some of your RRSP assets outside Canada through the use of international funds. This gives you some protection against the ups and downs of the Canadian dollar and allows you to profit from faster economic growth in other parts of the world.

Mutual funds also substantially increase the profit potential of your RRSP. If you'd invested all your money into GICs over the five years ending May 31, 2001, your average annual return would have been 5.0 percent. The average bond mutual fund did slightly better (6.4 percent), but the top-performing bond funds like the Phillips, Hager & North Bond (which we've consistently recommended in this book) did much better at 7.7 percent.

The third major benefit of including mutual funds in an RRSP is flexibility. If you don't like the way things are going, you can simply switch your assets to another fund. You can't do that with a GIC—you're locked in until maturity. It's true that you're supposed to take a long-term view when making RRSP investment decisions. But tomorrow's vision of the future may be quite different from today's. Having the flexibility to adjust to changing conditions is a big advantage in any investment situation.

But there are also disadvantages to holding mutual funds in your retirement plan. It's important to understand them and to weigh all the pros and cons before plunging ahead.

One consideration is the expense. Mutual funds will cost your RRSP some money. It may be no more than an annual trustee charge plus the management fees that are deducted from the assets of the funds you hold. Or your costs may include some hefty sales commissions, depending on the type of funds you purchase. Unfortunately, these commissions have to be paid from within the RRSP.

The other potentially big disadvantage is loss. As we stated at the outset, adding mutual funds to your RRSP has the potential to blow your whole plan right out of the water. But that will happen only if you are careless or unwise with your investments.

## How to Make Mutual Funds Work in Your RRSP

Deciding how to invest your RRSP money is never easy. But for those who use mutual funds as the core of their retirement plans, it's especially difficult during times of market uncertainty, such as we've experienced recently.

One question frequently asked when markets are gyrating is if it's a good idea to hold the money in cash for a period of time and wait for the markets to settle down. A variation on that idea is to revert to plain-vanilla GICs. Even though they continue to pay unattractive rates of return, some investors prefer that alternative to taking risks with their RRSP money in volatile stocks or equity mutual funds.

We don't counsel either course. Holding cash in your RRSP earns very low returns. If you hold an excessive amount in money market funds, and the markets are turbulent over a lengthy period, you could end up with your money sitting relatively stagnant for a long time. As for GICs, they are just not a good investment these days, except for the most ultra-conservative investors who want safety at any price.

So what should you do? Go back to first principles. Take a long-term view. Build a balanced portfolio. And above all: simplify, simplify, simplify.

There are many ways to create and manage an RRSP. But one simple approach combines long-term growth potential, minimal risk, and ease of management. It's this: Choose a top-notch mutual fund company as your core manager and consolidate a large part (but not all) of your RRSP holdings there. It's easier than trying to build your plan by cherry-picking from a wide range of mutual funds and other securities (although that route does offer greater profit potential if it's done properly).

Want some evidence? Suppose you had moved all your RRSP money into the no-load firm Phillips, Hager & North at the beginning of March 1991. Let's say you had $50,000 at the time, and you had divided the money equally among five of their funds: Canadian Equity, Dividend Income, U.S. Equity (for foreign content), Bond, and Money Market. That's a well-balanced portfolio, with a relatively low risk factor.

Using average annual compound rates of return for each fund to February 28, 2001, your balance would have been $159,434. That works out to an annual gain of almost 12.5 percent and, in dollar terms, you've more than tripled your original investment. These figures are based on a one-time investment. The numbers would be even more impressive had regular contributions been made every year. Note also that we stuck with the low-performance money market fund throughout, which represented 20 percent of the portfolio, even though a real-world investor probably would have held less cash.

Despite the cash handicap, this simple one-family portfolio outperformed almost every balanced fund in Canada over the period in question. A handful of pure Canadian equity funds did better, but you'd have to have been very clever to pick them out back in 1991 when certain companies, including some of the fund sponsors described below, were almost unknown. Top-performing international funds aren't a factor here because of the RRSP limitations that would have held your foreign exposure to 20 percent for most of the time frame in our example.

So that's one possible approach if you're confused about what to do with your RRSP money this year: simply choose a good, solid company and go with it.

Not sure which company to go with? Here are some recommendations:

**PHILLIPS, HAGER & NORTH.** This is a conservatively run organization with an excellent long-term record. Best bets for your RRSP this year: Canadian Equity, Dividend, U.S. Equity, Bond, and Balanced. The company is based in Vancouver but you can order by phone from elsewhere; call 1-800-661-6141. No-load fees are payable when you buy direct from the company. You can also buy the funds through some discount brokers like TD Waterhouse, but in that case you'll pay a commission. The minimum initial investment when you open an account is $25,000.

**MCLEAN BUDDEN.** Hardly anyone has any money invested with this company, which is a shame since they have proven themselves to be dependable, no-nonsense managers year after year. There's nothing flashy here, just good, steady performance with a growth orientation on the equity side, although they now also have a value fund. They offer only seven funds, five of which are 100 percent eligible for an RRSP. These no-load funds can be purchased through the manager at 1-800-884-0436. The minimum initial investment is $10,000.

**INVESTORS GROUP.** There's a lot of chaff in the offerings of this Winnipeg-based giant, but enough good kernels of golden wheat to build a successful RRSP. The company has a huge repertoire of funds, 69 and expanding at last count. Best bets for your RRSP: Retirement Mutual, Dividend, Growth Portfolio, U.S. Large-Cap Value, Corporate Bond, and Government Bond. Investors Group funds are sold only by the company's representatives; check your phone book for the representative in your area. Sales commissions will apply.

**ETHICAL FUNDS.** If you're a credit union customer, this may be your group of choice. The family is distributed primarily through the credit union system in all provinces (Quebec registration was recently obtained) and offers several top-notch options for RRSP investors. The best of the bunch is the Ethical Growth Fund, which combines consistent above-average returns with a conservative, low-risk style. Also worth including in your plan: North American Equity, Balanced, and Income. Also noteworthy is the launch of four portfolios, each combining the company's funds in varying ratios with the goal of meeting different investment objectives. These funds are sold under the Credential name. The funds are no load, which adds to their attractiveness.

**MACKENZIE FINANCIAL CORPORATION.** As with Investors Group (they purchased Mackenzie in 2001), you have to be very selective, but the huge variety of funds available in the Industrial, Ivy, Universal, and now Cundill groups, virtually guarantees you'll find several decent holdings for your RRSP if you can filter through the deadwood that is bound to exist in any company of this size. The Universal Canadian Growth Fund and Ivy Canadian Fund make a good combination for the Canadian equity portion of your plan because of the very different styles these funds offer. To them, you can add a selection of other funds, including Cundill Security, Industrial Dividend Growth, Universal World Balanced RRSP, Industrial Pension, Ivy Growth and Income, and Industrial Bond. You can buy these funds through brokers and dealers anywhere in Canada. Sales commissions will apply.

**AGF FUNDS.** There's been a steady improvement in the AGF family in recent years and there are now several funds available that can be combined to make a strong core RRSP holding. The AGF Dividend Fund, which is not truly a dividend fund at all, provides a solid blue-chip Canadian stock position. To it, add the Canadian Bond Fund, Canadian Tactical Asset Allocation Fund, American Tactical Asset Allocation Fund, and, especially, the International Value Fund. There are clones of all the foreign content funds available if needed.

**FIDELITY FUNDS.** For many years, the lack of a decent Canadian equity fund kept them off this list, but Fidelity True North has been doing very well, as has Fidelity Disciplined Equity. Fidelity Canadian Bond Fund is a respectable performer and in 1998, the company added a Canadian Balanced Fund to its mix. Combine these funds with Fidelity's excellent international line-up, including the first-rate International Portfolio Fund (now offered in the form of an RRSP-eligible clone), and you've got a sound basis for a winning plan.

**FRANKLIN TEMPLETON FUNDS.** In the past, this company was not recommended for RRSPs because its domestic content was weak. However, in July 2000, Franklin Templeton announced it was acquiring the Calgary-based Bissett & Associates. This acquisition filled Franklin Templeton's greatest weakness by providing the organization with a strong family of RRSP-eligible Canadian equity and fixed-income funds. Combine Templeton's international expertise, the recent introduction of a new line of Franklin funds, and the deep value style Mutual Beacon Fund, and the overall result is a broadly diversified fund line-up with a number of attractive choices for RRSP investors.

**AIM FUNDS.** The acquisition of Trimark in 2000 earns this company a place on our list. AIM itself has several good funds, but the company's management style tends to be quite aggressive. With the Trimark funds in the fold, investors can put together a diversified portfolio that mixes value and growth styles very effectively. AIM funds are available through all financial advisors.

There are a number of mutual fund companies that are not appropriate to provide the foundation for your RRSPs, although some offer individual funds that are worth considering as add-ons. Remember, if you decide to limit your investments to a few fund families, the selected fund groups should offer the widest possible choice and the strongest possible performance in all areas. For the best results, you should pass on companies that are known for their expertise in one particular asset class but have notoriously weak offerings in others.

## SUMMARY

- Mutual funds can add profit potential to your RRSP—or blow your retirement plan out of the water.
- One big advantage of funds is flexibility; you can move your money at any time, although it may cost you something.
- You can hold up to 30 percent of your RRSP money in foreign funds. Some companies will keep a computer watch on your portfolio to make sure you don't stray over the line.

- If you want to exceed the foreign content limit, most companies offer clone funds that are fully eligible for registered plans.
- One simple way to create an RRSP portfolio is to choose one top-performing mutual fund company for your core holdings and build a long-term portfolio with it.

## FUND FACTS

**THE SHELL GAME.** RRSPs are not an investment in themselves, contrary to what many people believe. ("My RRSP is maturing next month," really means, "The GIC in my RRSP is maturing.") Think of an RRSP as a tax-sheltered empty shell, into which you can place almost any type of security you wish. Mutual funds licensed for sale in Canada are just one of the many securities that qualify.

**FOREIGN CONTENT PENALTIES.** If you exceed the 30 percent foreign content limit, the Canada Customs and Revenue Agency (CCRA) hits you with penalty interest of 1 percent a month on the excess.

**AUTOMATIC MONITORING.** You shouldn't have to worry about keeping your foreign content within the legal limit. Most RRSP administrators now automatically monitor your foreign holdings and advise you promptly if you stray over the boundary. Some will even automatically rebalance your plan if you get offside by selling enough foreign fund units to bring you back within the limit. As long as you correct before month-end, no penalty will apply.

**EXTRA CONTENT ROOM.** If you invest in a labour-sponsored venture capital fund, you get "bonus" foreign content room in your retirement plan. See the section on labour funds for full details.

**BOOK VALUE.** The foreign content limit is based on the book value of your plan, which is simply the original price you paid for any securities in your plan. The current value—what they could be sold for today—is known as the "market value." It's possible for your RRSP foreign content to exceed 30 percent of market value (for example, if your foreign funds have increased sharply in price), but that's not a worry as long as your book value stays onside.

**CHECK YOUR STATEMENT.** Some companies don't show the book value of your RRSP on the statements you receive—only the current market value. This makes it virtually impossible to stay on top of your foreign content percentage. If your plan isn't automatically monitored and you're not getting this information, you may have to take your business elsewhere.

# Building Fund Portfolios

*If you already own some mutual funds, take this simple test. Pull out your latest brokerage statement and review all the funds on the list. Do you know exactly how each fund fits into your investment plan? Are you satisfied that it represents the precise weighting you want?*

If you can answer yes to both questions, you probably don't need to read the rest of this chapter. But odds are that your response to one or both queries was "no." In that case, you need the information we're about to share with you. It may be worth thousands of dollars to your investments in the years to come.

Most mutual fund accounts grow like Topsy; they lack any coherent rationale. Your financial advisor says XYZ fund looks good, so you add it. You read that ABC fund is a hot performer, so you buy some units. Someone says bond funds should do well in the coming months, so you get one. The result is a mess of unrelated funds that underperforms for reasons you don't fully understand.

If the scenario above sound familiar, you need to make a fundamental change in the way you choose your funds. Your goal should be to create the perfect mutual fund portfolio for your own particular needs. It's not as hard as you might think; you just need to understand what you're trying to achieve and then have the discipline to do it.

The ideal fund portfolio should accomplish the following:

- Provide potential for steady growth at an average annual rate of at least 8 to 10 percent annually over the long term.
- Limit downside risk in falling equity markets.
- Offer some currency protection.
- Be well diversified by asset class, style, and geography.
- Be tax-efficient (for non-registered portfolios).

You should review these criteria every time you consider a new fund for inclusion in your plan. If the fund doesn't meet at least two of the objectives listed above, it should be bypassed.

Let's review each criterion in detail:

**GROWTH POTENTIAL.** The biggest mistake many fund investors make is succumbing to greed. It's the reason so many people got clobbered in the recent high-tech crash. They saw the huge returns that tech-weighted funds scored in 1998–99 and overloaded their portfolios in that direction. At the same time, they underweighted underperforming value funds and fixed-income funds.

A reasonable average annual return over the long haul (say 10 years or more) is 8 to 10 percent annually. With careful management, 10 to 12 percent is achievable. If you aim higher than that, you will have to accept a degree of risk that would make most people uncomfortable.

**DOWNSIDE RISK.** If you feel that your fund portfolio suffered higher losses than you would have liked in the recent market tumble, you may have built in too much risk. You need to rebalance your asset mix to put more emphasis on low-risk securities like money market funds, mortgage funds, bond funds, balanced funds, and value-oriented equity funds. However, don't go to the extreme of making your portfolio so safe that you reduce your return potential to less than 8 percent annually. While it's possible to make your portfolio bulletproof with ultra-secure funds, you will compromise your returns by doing so. The key is to find the right balance.

**CURRENCY PROTECTION.** There is no way of knowing where the loonie will go in the future. But we can say two things with certainty:

1. Our currency has been devalued by about one-third against the U.S. dollar in the past decade.
2. Every prediction that the loonie is about to rise to U.S.70¢ and higher has proven wrong to date.

Of course, these two things could change. But if past trends continue, the Canadian dollar will gradually lose more ground against the greenback in the coming years. That's why every fund portfolio should contain some currency protection. It's not a case of speculation; it's a matter of hedging against continued devaluation of the loonie.

Currency protection can be achieved by holding mutual funds that invest in U.S. dollar securities. These include U.S. equity funds, foreign bond funds, and U.S. dollar money market funds. Although many of the equity funds can be purchased in either Canadian or U.S. currency units, it really doesn't matter which you choose. As long as the securities in the portfolio are denominated in U.S. dollars, you will reap the benefit of any gain that currency makes against the loonie.

There is always the chance that our dollar may turn around and start to rise, so you wouldn't want to hold your entire portfolio in U.S. dollar funds (which you could, even in an RRSP). Decide on a U.S. dollar percentage that is appropriate for your plan (at least 25 percent is recommended) and be sure you choose funds able to provide that amount.

**DIVERSIFICATION.** There are several types of diversification that need to be considered when building your fund portfolio. Asset mix diversification is the most basic. It is, simply, the way in which you combine cash (money market funds), fixed-income, and equity funds in your portfolio. There is no "ideal" asset mix, but a 10–40–50 allocation is a reasonable target for a balanced portfolio.

Style diversification is becoming increasingly recognized as a key to superior fund performance. People with a good percentage of value funds in their equity mix withstood the recent market turmoil much better than those with equity mixes oriented heavily toward growth. However, growth funds will come back at some point in the future. The ideal portfolio has a mix of both, and requires some occasional fine-tuning to adjust the balance toward the style that is performing better at any given time.

Geographic diversification is essential. Canada is a small market with a weak currency. To tie up most or all of your fund assets in this country is therefore a mistake, unless you prefer to let patriotism rule over pragmatism. At least 40 percent of your fund portfolio should consist of U.S. and international funds.

**TAX EFFICIENCY.** Non-registered portfolios need to take tax efficiency into account during the fund selection process. The last thing you need is to be stuck with a big tax bill each year. For income-oriented portfolios, dividend funds and high-income balanced funds should be considered. They will generate income taxed at an advantageous rate in comparison with interest income from bond funds.

The distribution history of any equity fund should be carefully studied before you make a purchase. Distributions are taxed annually, and a fund with a record of high distributions may add a significant amount to your tax bill. Also consider "umbrella funds," which allow you to switch money among various fund classes without triggering capital gains tax liability. Several companies now offer these kinds of funds.

When you are buying funds for your "perfect" portfolio, think carefully about your purchase options. You want a selection of funds that provide the flexibility to make changes without triggering expensive penalty charges. Consequently, you should avoid back-end load funds if possible. No-load funds are the ideal choice, but there are other alternatives. Some companies, such as Franklin Templeton, have a no-load option for funds normally sold only by commission, however you can only get them if you have a fee-based arrangement with a financial advisor. Some companies offer "low-load" funds; they're mainly for institutional investors but if you're a good client, you may be able to get in on these. Keep in mind that some advisors will sell front-end load units at zero commission, just to get your business or because you have a large account.

If you must buy funds on a deferred sales charge (DSC) basis, choose families that offer plenty of switching options and make sure you will not be charged a switching fee when you want to move your money.

The above information may have seemed like a lot to digest in one sitting, but if you can master the basic rules found in this section, you can indeed build your own perfect mutual fund portfolio. For an example of how one such portfolio might look, check out the table below. Your own numbers may be somewhat different depending on your objectives, but if you use this as a model you won't go far wrong.

## A Sample Portfolio

Here is a sample fund portfolio that takes into account the criteria discussed above. This is a balanced portfolio that uses as a basic asset mix of 10 percent cash, 40 percent fixed income, and 50 percent growth. A more aggressive portfolio would increase the growth content while reducing the fixed-income segment accordingly. The "Model" column represents the basic allocation, which remains constant. The "Current" column represents the fine-tuning employed to reflect present market conditions, and should be reviewed quarterly. At the time of writing, conditions dictated that we favour value funds over growth funds.

| TYPE OF SECURITY | MODEL | CURRENT |
|---|---|---|
| Canadian Money Market Funds | 5.0% | 5.0% |
| U.S. Money Market Funds | 5.0% | 5.0% |
| Canadian $ Bond Funds | 20.0% | 20.0% |
| U.S. $ or Foreign Bond Funds | 20.0% | 20.0% |
| Canadian Equity Funds (value) | 12.5% | 15.0% |
| Canadian Equity Funds (growth) | 12.5% | 10.0% |
| U.S. Equity Funds (value) | 7.5% | 10.0% |
| U.S. Equity Funds (growth) | 7.5% | 5.0% |
| International Equity Funds (value) | 5.0% | 7.5% |
| International Equity Funds (growth) | 5.0% | 2.5% |
| Totals | 100.0% | 100.0% |

## SUMMARY

- Make sure every fund you select has a specific purpose.
- Be realistic when setting targets; an average annual return of 8 to 10 percent is very good.
- Don't become so cautious that you compromise your return potential.
- At least 40 percent of your portfolio should be in U.S. and international funds of various types.
- Ensure you have a blend of growth and value styles in your equity funds.
- Protect your portfolio against any further devaluation of the Canadian dollar.
- Make sure any non-registered portfolios are tax-efficient.

## FUND FACTS

DEALING WITH ONE COMPANY. If you restrict your fund investments to a single company, you may have a problem creating a properly balanced portfolio that resembles our model. For example, Phillips, Hager & North is an excellent fund management group, but they do not offer a foreign bond fund. AIC has some very successful funds, but they use a dedicated value approach. In cases such as these, you will have to add funds from other companies if you want to achieve full diversification.

CLONE FUNDS. Although the rules technically limit you to 30 percent foreign content in a registered plan, it is actually no problem to exceed that limit if you wish. Clone funds allow you to add U.S. and international holdings without encroaching on the foreign content limit. Many foreign bond funds are fully RRSP-eligible, but check before you buy.

# The 10 Biggest Fund Investing Mistakes

*It's sad, but true. Many investors—and not just the novices—put their money into mutual funds without having any clear idea of what they're doing, or why. Hopefully that won't happen to you after you finish reading this chapter.*

Here's a summary of the 10 worst mistakes investors make when buying mutual funds. Some of the points have been covered elsewhere in this book, but we felt it would be useful to pull them all together in one place. Novices can treat this chapter as a mutual fund investing checklist; experienced investors can regard it as a list of reminders.

**1. FAILING TO SET OBJECTIVES.** You should never invest in a mutual fund, or anything else for that matter, until you have established your personal financial goals. If you don't know what you want to achieve, you can't possibly select the right funds for your needs.

**2. FAILING TO UNDERSTAND RISK.** We've heard horror stories from conservative investors who plunged thousands of dollars into volatile funds like technology funds without comprehending the high risks involved. All mutual funds carry a degree of risk, but some are inherently more risky than others. Make sure you understand exactly what those risks are before you commit any money.

**3. FAILING TO UNDERSTAND THE RELATIONSHIP BETWEEN INTEREST RATES AND FIXED-INCOME FUNDS.** The rule is very simple: When interest rates rise, the unit values of bond and mortgage funds tend to decline; when rates fall, unit values rise. That's why fixed-income funds produced high returns during most of the 1990s and then lost ground when interest rates were pushed up in 1999 through to 2000 in an effort to slow down what was perceived as an overheated economy. But remember that even when unit values are declining, fixed-income funds still generate interest income for you. As long as you don't panic and sell at a loss, you'll do all right over the long term.

**4. GETTING HUNG UP ON PERFORMANCE RATINGS.** Past results are useful in assessing a mutual fund's consistency. But too many people base their investment decisions on history and nothing more. There are many other factors to consider, including managerial changes, current economic conditions, political events, trend patterns (how well has the fund done lately?), interest rate movements, and cost.

**5. FAILING TO GET ADVICE.** Many mutual fund investors dive right in without getting solid advice. The proliferation of no-load funds through banks, trust companies, credit unions, and telephone order firms like Altamira has contributed to this trend. That isn't to say no-load funds are bad—far from it. But if you buy no-load funds without any clear understanding of what you're doing, you may run into problems. If you're dealing with a financial institution, spend some time with a planning representative who knows what he or she is talking about (the level of expertise can be spotty, so be careful). Or you can consult a fee-for-service financial planner, one who charges by the hour but doesn't sell product. The key point here is that if you're not sure what you're doing, get help. Investment mistakes can be very expensive.

**6. PUTTING ALL YOUR MONEY IN ONE PLACE.** Diversification is one of the keys to investing success. In the case of mutual funds, diversification doesn't mean just distributing your assets among several funds; it also means using more than one fund group. Even though different managers may run the funds within a group, the managers usually talk to each other and often share similar investment philosophies. When they're wrong (it does happen) or out of sync with economic developments, the result can be below-average performance by many funds, not just one. This happened to Mackenzie Financial in the early 1990s and to Trimark later in the decade. The solution is to select three solid mutual fund companies and distribute your assets among them (you can use one as a core, if you wish). That way, if one falters, hopefully the other two will pick up the slack.

**7. HOLDING CYCLICAL FUNDS.** Most mutual funds should be purchased as long-term holds and a few should be actively traded. Cyclical funds—those that invest in sectors of the economy subject to boom and bust cycles—are classic examples of funds that should be sold when their upward move has about run its course. Natural resource funds, energy funds, technology funds, and financial services funds all fall into this category.

**8. FAILING TO USE ASSET ALLOCATION.** Many fund investors missed out on the big bond market profits of 1995–98 because they weren't using asset allocation techniques. If they had been, there would have been decent weighting of bond funds in their portfolios. In 2000, a large number of people suffered heavy losses because they did not have a good mix of value and growth equity funds. Proper asset mix is one of the most effective ways to reduce risk in a mutual fund portfolio while ensuring that at least a portion of your holdings will benefit from major upturns in the stock market, bond market, or interest rates.

**9. BEING UNREALISTIC.** Occasionally, a mutual fund will turn in an incredible one-year performance. When the high-tech craze was in full flight, some funds more than doubled in value in a single year. It's great when it happens. The problem is that those bonanzas can create unrealistic expectations in the minds of investors. Then, when things return to normal—as they inevitably do—disappointment sets in. So keep things in perspective; if an equity fund produces an average annual compound rate of return between 10 and 12 percent over a decade, it's doing very well. If the average annual return is over 12 percent, it's an outstanding performance.

**10. FAILING TO DIVERSIFY GEOGRAPHICALLY.** Canada is a small country economically, with limited industry and a volatile currency. Therefore, choosing only Canadian mutual funds limits your profit potential and increases your risk. We recommend you hold at least 40 percent of your mutual fund assets in non-Canadian funds.

## SUMMARY

- Investing mistakes aren't limited to novices by any means. Even experienced fund investors can trip up.
- Avoiding the most common mistakes can save you thousands of dollars over time.
- Some funds should be actively traded, just like stocks.
- An average annual return of 10 to 12 percent over a decade is very good for an equity fund.
- Don't confine your investments to Canada. At least 40 percent of your money should be in foreign mutual funds.

## FUND FACTS

**PANIC IN THE STREETS.** A classic example of how lack of advice can lead to big losses is the stock market free fall of October 1997. When the Asian crisis took hold and North American markets tumbled, some people panicked and sold, locking in losses and souring on mutual funds. Industry figures show that the great majority of sellers were investors in no-load bank funds. People with financial advisors were more likely to hold on, and they reaped the benefits of the big stock market rally from 1998 to early 2000; their funds recover all losses and much, much more.

**ELUSIVE GOAL.** Only four Canadian equity funds available to the general public managed an average annual return of better than 15 percent for the decade ending March 31, 2001. They were AIC Advantage (21.4 percent a year on average), ABC Fundamental Value (18.1 percent), Dynamic Power Canadian (17.1 percent), and Altamira Equity (15.8 percent).

# The Importance
# of Style

*The deeper you go into mutual fund investing, the more you'll hear about managers'
styles: this one is top-down, that one is bottom-up; this one is a value investor, that one
is a sector rotator.*

It can all get somewhat technical and confusing, the more so because some managers refuse to be pigeon-holed, claiming they use whatever approach works at
the time. But if you really want to understand what's happening inside the
mutual fund you're considering, you have to know the basic styles and what
they mean in real terms.

The styles we'll describe in this chapter all relate to equity funds. Fixed-
income managers also have their own styles, but they tend to be highly esoteric
and hardly understood outside the tight world of bond traders.

With that caveat in mind, here we go. We'll begin with the two basic management styles: top-down and bottom-up.

TOP-DOWN. This approach places emphasis on markets and sectors rather than
on individual stocks. The top-down manager for a Canadian stock fund will use
an analysis of the current economic situation as a starting point. From there, the
manager tries to identify sectors of the economy likely to outperform under a
projected scenario. The fund's portfolio will be most heavily weighted to those
sectors, and underweighted in areas the manager believes will do poorly. Once
all of that is accomplished, the actual stocks are selected, usually from industry
leaders in the most promising sectors.

Here's an example of top-down management in action. During the later
stages of an economic recovery, resource stocks and consumer issues often do
very well. Since interest rates are usually rising in that situation, utilities, which

are highly interest-sensitive, may do badly. So a top-down manager who normally would give oil and gas stocks a 10 percent weighting in the fund's portfolio might increase that allocation to 15 percent. Utilities stocks, which might normally get a 12 percent weighting, could be cut back to 8 percent.

Managers of top-down international funds take the same approach but do it on a country-by-country basis. A European fund manager, for example, might decide that Scandinavia, Britain, and Spain have above-average prospects for the coming year. Germany and France might be seen as having below-average potential. The manager would adjust the portfolio composition to reflect that particular view.

**BOTTOM-UP.** True bottom-up managers aren't indifferent to what's happening in the economy, but they don't view it as the number-one priority for stock selection. A bottom-up manager takes the position that what *really* matters is the quality of a company. If it's a well-managed firm with solid growth potential, that fact will eventually be reflected in the share value.

Bottom-up managers are essentially fundamentalists. They spend a lot of time analyzing company balance sheets, talking to managers, and visiting the plants or mining sites to see for themselves what's actually happening. In some ways, their style is more complex than that of a top-down manager because there's a higher degree of subjectivity involved. Is this company president really telling me the full story? Is this sales team capable of cranking up revenues by 30 percent next year? Is the new capital expenditure going to pay off as quickly as this chief financial officer calculated?

The economy is tough enough to predict, although the broad trends tend to be fairly evident at any given time. The bottom-up manager goes beyond that point, to make big bets on people and products—variables that are even more uncertain than the economic winds.

Top-down and bottom-up are basically different ways to select stocks. The next level of managerial styles gets more sophisticated, because it involves deciding what types of stocks will be chosen by the method being used. This is the level at which the character and the priorities of a mutual fund portfolio are established.

**VALUE.** The value manager's bible is Benjamin Graham's classic stock selection guide, *The Intelligent Investor*. In it, he sets out the basic principles of value investing, which are directed at seeking out stocks that represent a combination of low risk and excellent value. Many, many mutual fund portfolios have been built on these principles, some more successfully than others. Warren Buffett's fabled Berkshire Hathaway company in the U.S. (an investment firm) employs the Graham teachings in its stock selection approach: buy cheap and hold forever, if possible.

The main drawback to value investing is the emphasis it places on buying out-of-favour stocks that are trading at below the company's break-up value, and then waiting until the market recognizes the hidden gem and bids the price up to realistic levels. Sometimes this process can take a long time, so a fund built on value investing may not be the best choice for an investor seeking fast growth.

Some of the top value funds in Canada include those managed by the Trimark division of AIM Funds, the Cundill funds offered by Mackenzie Financial, the ABC Funds run by Irwin Michael, and the AIC Funds that have been faithfully constructed to replicate the Buffett style.

**GROWTH.** The growth manager doesn't really care if a stock is selling at a bargain price. This manager's main interest is in how fast the share price is likely to run up. So a growth portfolio will consist mainly of stocks of fast-growing companies with high earnings potential—hot stocks, if you like. You'll often find a lot of small- and mid-cap companies in a growth fund, because they offer the best opportunity for fast price movement.

Because of their style, growth portfolios are best suited for more aggressive investors seeking maximum capital appreciation. But be careful, because growth-oriented investments may be more risky than those based on a value approach. That's because many of the stocks in the portfolio may trade at high multiples—prices well in excess of where they should be based on traditional ratios like share price to profits (known as a price/earnings ratio). Investors often bid up the price of quality growth shares in anticipation of future earnings increases. If those increases fail to materialize, the stock can drop in a big hurry, as we saw with the dot.com stocks in 2000. So while growth-oriented funds may produce big gains when the manager gets it right, be prepared for losses if things turn sour.

**SECTOR ROTATION.** Sector rotation is the extension, or next level, of the top-down investing approach. A sector rotation manager focuses primarily on cyclical companies—those that tend to perform especially well at certain points in the business cycle. The idea is to overweight the portfolio with stocks that are likely to do better than the market in general and generate above-average returns for investors. Some of the favourite areas for this style of investing are automobile manufacturers, steel companies, forestry companies, mining firms, energy stocks, and airlines.

During periods when economic conditions are poor, the sector rotator overloads the portfolio with so-called "defensive" stocks—shares in companies that aren't as vulnerable to recessionary conditions. These might include utilities, pipelines, pharmaceutical companies, and banks.

A top sector rotator can produce outstanding returns for mutual fund investors. But there's a fair amount of guesswork involved in the process, and timing is a critical factor. If a manager takes a big position in a certain sector too early, the result can be a prolonged period of indifferent returns.

That's exactly what happened to the managers of Mackenzie Financial's Industrial Group of Funds through much of the 1990s. Funds like Industrial Growth and Industrial Horizon aren't technically sector rotation funds. However, the managers acted as if they were. They built up the resource sector of their portfolios, anticipating big moves in those stocks. The problem was that the great resource rally never happened, except in the energy sector. The result? Industrial Growth Fund, once the largest mutual fund in Canada, was among the worst performers in its category over the decade to the end of March 2001, with an average annual compound rate of return of just 2.2 percent.

MOMENTUM. The best way to describe this style of management is to say it's a cross between the growth and sector rotation styles; think of it as picking the hottest stocks in the hottest sectors. Momentum investing worked extremely well during the high-tech run-up in the 1990s, where some of the funds posted huge gains. But because most funds were still heavily invested in technology issues when the market collapsed, they were hard hit by the downturn. That's the risk of momentum funds: timing is everything, and it can be very difficult to anticipate and predict.

INDEXING. All of the styles we have described so far can be considered "active." Index investing is "passive" in the sense that the manager does not pick any stocks. Instead, the fund is structured to reflect the performance of a particular stock market index. Most index funds sold in Canada use either the TSE 300 or the S&P 500 as their benchmark.

In recent years, much more attention has been paid to the management style of mutual funds being selected for a portfolio. That's because each style will have periods when it does very well and other periods when it performs poorly. Funds using a growth approach (including momentum and sector rotation) generally did very well during the late 1990s, spurred by the dazzling performance of technology stocks. Value funds, by contrast, underperformed. When the high-tech bubble popped in 2000, however, most growth-oriented funds went into a nosedive while value funds enjoyed a resurgence.

For this reason, we recommend a style blend in your portfolio. You should include both value and growth funds in your mix; the proportions will depend on how you see the economy moving at any given time.

## SUMMARY

- A manager's investment style can tell you a lot about a fund's likelihood to produce above-average returns under certain economic conditions and the amount of risk you're taking on.
- Value managers try to buy $1 worth of assets for 40¢—and often succeed. These funds tend to be lower risk than most equity funds.
- The main interest of a growth manager is the potential of a stock to increase in value.
- Sector rotators can run into serious problems if the managers guess incorrectly about which areas of the economy will do best.
- Momentum investing is a cross between growth and sector rotation.
- Indexing involves tracking the performance of a specific stock market index, like the TSE 300.
- We recommend that investors have a mix of value and growth funds in their portfolios.

## FUND FACTS

**BUYING BERKSHIRE.** Berkshire Hathaway, Warren Buffett's great investment company, is the world's most expensive publicly traded stock. As of spring 2001, a single A share was going for almost U.S.$70,000, putting it well out of the range of most investors. But there's a much less expensive way to get in on the action. AIC Value Fund, based in Hamilton, Ontario, holds a large portion of its portfolio in Berkshire Hathaway shares or in companies that play a prominent role in the Berkshire portfolio. Predictably, AIC's record has been very good, with an average annual return of 15.2 percent for the decade ending March 31, 2001. And you can buy in for just $250.

**SIR JOHN'S LEGACY.** The godfather of value investing in Canadian mutual funds is the legendary Sir John Templeton, who build a financial empire by searching out bargains in all parts of the world. His original fund, Templeton Growth, has been churning out profits for almost 50 years (it started up in 1954 under the name Templeton Growth Fund of Canada). The Templeton organization delights in pointing out that if you'd invested $10,000 back then, you'd be a multi-millionaire today.

**SMALL-CAP FUNDS.** Small-cap companies are those that are just starting out or relatively modest in size. The definition of what constitutes a small-cap stock varies, but in Canada, companies with market capitalization (the collective value of all outstanding stock) under $150 million are usually considered to be in this class. In the U.S., a small-cap company may have a market capitalization up to U.S.$500 million.

**GOING FOR BIG GAINS.** Richard Driehaus, the Chicago-based manager of the AGF Aggressive Growth Fund, is regarded as one of North America's leading growth managers. He zeros in on small- and medium-sized companies he thinks have the potential to produce big returns. The fund stumbled badly when the tech market collapsed, but over the long-term investors have done very well. The five-year average annual compound rate of return to March 31, 2001 was 22.3 percent.

**VARIED STYLES.** One fund company has structured its lineup purely on the basis of style. It is Synergy Mutual Funds, run by Joe Canavan. At the time he launched the firm in late 1997, style diversification was not widely practised. Today, many investors and financial advisors recognize its importance.

# How to Buy Funds

*There's an old saying in the fund industry: "Mutual funds are sold, not bought."*

The implication of this phrase is obvious: you, the investor, would never purchase a mutual fund were it not for the persistent efforts of some sales person employing high-pressure tactics. Clearly this kind of thinking is a throwback to the days when mutual funds were in disrepute, thanks to the machinations of some unscrupulous promoters. Thankfully, that's no longer the case. Today's mutual fund industry is generally well run, reasonably well regulated, and offers a wide variety of legitimate investment options.

However, there are still several things to be careful about when buying fund units. Further along in this chapter, you'll find some tips for negotiating the sales jungle effectively. But first, let's take a look at the people with whom you'll be dealing when you make your purchase:

**STOCKBROKERS.** Mutual funds have become one of the main products for retail brokers, especially with their small investors who are nervous about the stock market but want to put their money in something more exciting than GICs. As a result, many brokers are very knowledgeable about the major fund companies. For the most part, however, it's been a self-education process because, surprisingly, many brokerage firms still do not employ mutual fund analysts to provide guidance and insight. As a result, the majority of brokers are familiar only with the funds of a half-dozen companies at most. Ask them about more obscure funds and they'll either try to bluff or will admit they don't know and say they'll get back to you. If recommendations and insights are important to you (and they should be if you're paying a broker's commission), using a stockbroker to buy funds is something of a hit or miss proposition. Protect yourself by doing some research on your own in advance and by probing the broker's knowledge about the funds in which you're interested. If the broker can't tell you anything you don't already know, consider taking your business to a discount broker who will charge less commission. One other disadvantage of buying through brokers is that they'll be reluctant to acquire no-load funds for you, unless you're a very good client.

**DISCOUNT BROKERS.** All the major banks now offer a discount brokerage service. As well, there are some independent discount brokerage companies, such as Charles Schwab Canada. The problem here is getting a handle on which discount broker offers the best combination of fees, service, and research (in the past, you didn't get any research from a discount broker, but intense competition has changed that). One of the best sources offering a comparison between the discounters can be found at the Quicken.ca Web site, and we recommend you refer to it before making a selection. You can often (but not always) acquire mutual funds through a discount broker at a lower commission than you'd pay a full-service broker. Be aware, however, that if you place an order for a no-load fund through a discount broker, there will usually be some kind of commission involved. In most cases, the commission is imposed when the units are sold.

**ONLINE BROKERS.** All the major discount brokers offer online trading, but some companies operate exclusively in this way. E*Trade Canada is the best known exclusive online brokerage firm in this country.

**FINANCIAL PLANNERS.** Many financial planners double as sales reps. You should be aware of this reality when you consult with one. A planner who operates strictly on a fee-for-service basis and is not interested in selling you anything can be relied on for unbiased advice. However, if the planner stands to benefit if you follow a particular recommendation—purchasing a specific mutual fund, for example—you should be aware of that fact; ask the planner up front about compensation.

The advantage of good financial planners is that they'll prepare a detailed mutual fund investment programme for you and construct a portfolio suited to your specific needs (brokers will rarely perform this time-consuming service). The disadvantage is that, as with brokers, a financial planner who is compensated through commissions may not be keen to add no-load funds to your mix, although some will do it as a service.

**MUTUAL FUND BROKERS.** These brokers are people who specialize in mutual fund sales only. Typically, they offer funds from a number of firms and will work with you to find the ones best suited for your needs. In most cases, however, they will not offer the traditional type of no-load fund. Their commissions will be similar to those charged by full-service brokers and financial planners, but they probably won't prepare a full-scale plan for you. Some mutual fund brokers now offer excellent deals on sales commissions to get your business. In some instances, they will acquire front-end load units for you at zero commission, giving you the freedom to cash out at any time at no cost (they make their money through the annual trailer fees paid by the fund company). Some brokers will even go so far as to pay you a rebate on the purchase of back-end load units. The landscape is constantly changing, so if you want to buy funds at a bargain rate, shop around.

**COMPANY SALES REPS.** Some fund companies employ their own sales people to promote and sell their products. Investors Group is a prime example of this type of sales approach. In the past, Investors Group reps offered only their own fund line, but competitive pressures have forced the company to expand their product range significantly.

**INSURANCE SALES PEOPLE.** The insurance industry offers its own type of mutual funds, known as segregated funds (see the section on seg funds for more details). These funds are often, but not always, tied in to some form of insurance contract and are sold by agents and brokers who represent specific companies. The major disadvantage of buying funds in this way is that commissions may be higher than for ordinary mutual funds and are normally not negotiable.

**FINANCIAL INSTITUTIONS.** Most banks and trust companies offer their own line of mutual funds on a no-load basis. A few large credit unions also have one or more funds, and the Ethical funds are sold through credit unions across the country. However, you may find that the mutual fund sales representative you deal with at a financial institution has limited knowledge of the field, and advice may be minimal. The banks have undertaken expensive staff training programmes to bring their reps up to speed, but staffing every branch with a quality person is expensive and the turnover is high.

Some financial institutions have become very innovative in their sales practices. For example, some TD funds are now available in "e-units." They can be purchased only over the Internet and carry a considerably reduced management fee compared to the standard units of the same fund. The management expense ratio (MER) on the regular A units of the TD Canadian Index Fund is 0.85 percent. But if you buy the e-units, your MER is just 0.31 percent. The effect of the reduced MER is an increase on your annual return by more than half a percentage point. TD is offering e-units only on their index funds so far, but if this style of investing is of interest to you, take advantage of the opportunity.

**FUND COMPANIES.** Some mutual fund companies sell units directly to investors over the phone or through their staff. Altamira was the pioneer of mutual fund telephone marketing in Canada and is still the only organization that has been able to make it work effectively. However, you can buy funds over the phone from other companies like the well-respected Vancouver firm of Phillips, Hager & North. Funds sold in this way are usually no load, although there may be some other fees involved. For instance, Altamira charges a one-time fee to set up a new account.

So much for the sales people you'll be dealing with along the way. Now here are those buying tips we promised at the beginning of the chapter:

- *Tip #1: Negotiate all commissions.* Treat the mutual fund marketplace as you would a street vendor—negotiate for the best possible price. Mutual fund companies authorize a range for commissions that may be charged for their products. In some cases, front-end loads can run as high as nine percent. Never pay that much. A discount broker will charge two to two-and-a-half percent (they'll go as low as one percent on large orders). Full-service brokers and financial planners will want three to four percent. Here again, if your order is large, you may be able to get rates that are even lower. A few back-end loads are also negotiable. Ask before you commit.
- *Tip #2: Negotiate sweeteners.* Mutual fund sales people want your business. Every purchase of a load fund means an immediate commission for them, plus an ongoing trailer fee to compensate them for continuing to service your account. As a result, they're often willing to toss in extras to attract you. Ask for no-fee switching and commission-free money market fund purchases for starters.
- *Tip #3: Find out what the management fees are.* Before making a decision on whether to buy a front-end, back-end, or no-load fund, ask what the management fees are in each case. You'll sometimes find that back-end and no-load units carry a higher management fee, which will eat into your returns over time.
- *Tip #4: Don't base your purchase decision on commission only.* Buying a no-load fund just as a means of saving the sales commission can be penny-wise and pound foolish. There are many good no-load funds available, but there are also a lot of mediocre and poor ones. Choose your funds on the basis of quality and their compatibility with your objectives.
- *Tip #5: Arm yourself with knowledge.* As with any other purchase, if you set out to buy mutual funds without doing any homework in advance, you'll be a sitting duck for any plausible sales pitch you encounter. Have some idea of what you want and why before you make contact with a sales person. If your sales person recommends something else instead, ask for an explanation as to why his or her suggestion is superior to your original choice.
- *Tip #6: Ask what kinds of units are available for the fund(s) in which you are interested.* The industry is rapidly moving to a multi-unit structure for funds. This means the same fund can be purchased in several different ways. For example, a single fund may be available in front-end load,

back-end load, no-load, and low-load units. Check the prospectus to see what options are available and decide on the one you prefer before placing an order. This is very important; the sales rep might not even mention a no-load or low-load option if you don't ask.

## SUMMARY

- Most questionable sales practices have been eliminated by the industry, but you still must be careful when making a purchase.
- Watch out for cursory "financial plans" that are in fact just disguised sales promotions.
- Discount brokers may save you money, but you could end up paying a fee to acquire supposedly no-load funds.
- Some companies, such as TD, offer savings if you buy their e-units online.
- Many fund companies are moving to multiple units. Check out all the purchase options before you place an order.

## FUND FACTS

**SAVE ON COMMISSIONS.** Some brokers and planners now use a fee-based system that involves paying an annual fee for their services based on your total assets, instead of a commission for every transaction you make. Ask if the sales person you deal with has this option available and see if you can benefit from it.

**NO-LOAD COMMISSIONS.** You can acquire traditional no-load funds without an up-front cost through TD Waterhouse. However, they'll hit you with a fee when you sell.

**FAKE PLANS.** Some sales people will offer a free "financial plan" as a come-on. It may be legitimate, or it may be designed primarily to persuade you to invest heavily in one or more of their funds. If you're suspicious about the plan you receive, ask some tough questions. It may just be a sales promotion gimmick; if so, don't let it influence your buying decision.

**DOES THE BAY SEND YOU TO SEARS?** Although banks sell third-party funds, they're not likely to praise the virtues of direct competitors. Scotiabank may offer a terrific line of funds, but don't expect a Royal Bank employee to let you in on that fact. If you're interested in acquiring a bank's no-load fund, do some research of your own.

**INFORMATION, PLEASE.** Don't be surprised when a sales person starts asking what seem to be very personal questions when you phone for the first time to place an order. All mutual fund sales organizations are required by securities regulators to "know the client." The idea is to ensure that any recommendations are consistent with the investor's objectives and financial position. Also, the brokerage industry is now required to obtain personal financial data as part of an agreement with the U.S. to combat money laundering. So don't be offended when you're asked about your goals, job, and income. It's part of the process. The only way to avoid it is not to invest.

**HOW TO PAY NOTHING AT ALL.** Some brokers will sell you a front-end load fund with no sales commission at all. The reason? Although they give up the immediate payment, they'll continue to collect trailer fees for as long as you own your units. If their sales volume is high enough, they can live very comfortably on just trailer fee income. A few small companies have sprung up that sell mutual funds this way exclusively.

**DON'T PAY MMF COMMISSIONS.** As a general rule, you should never pay a commission of any kind to purchase a money market fund. Some funds post maximum rates of two percent (a few are even higher). But if anyone actually tries to charge you that amount, resist. Returns on these funds usually aren't high enough to justify a commission fee of any kind. There are many excellent no-load money market funds around; choose one of them if the sales rep insists on a commission.

# Taxes and
# Your Funds

*Unfortunately, there's no escape. As soon as you start making money in mutual funds, the Canada Customs and Revenue Agency (CCRA) will be there with its hand out, wanting its share. The trick is to pay the folks at the CCRA (there's no way to avoid it), while keeping as much of your profits as you can. That's what this chapter is all about.*

There is only one way to avoid paying the government a share of your fund profits and that's to hold your units in some type of registered plan: a registered retirement savings plan (RRSP), registered retirement income fund (RRIF), life income fund (LIF), registered education savings plan (RESP), or a pension plan. You or the plan beneficiary will have to pay tax down the road at some point when money is withdrawn from the plan, but in the meantime the profits can compound tax-free.

Any funds held outside a registered plan will potentially be subject to tax each year, although in some cases you may have to pay little or nothing. The rules can be somewhat complex, so here's a summary of the various ways in which the CCRA may come at you:

## Distributions

Many mutual funds make periodic distributions to their unitholders. These distributions include net interest and dividend income earned by the fund during the year, as well as net capital gains realized by trading within the portfolio (such gains are independent of the purchase and sale of your personal units). In most cases, distributions are made once a year, but some funds make them quarterly or even monthly. These distributions are considered taxable income in your hands (unless they're inside a registered plan) and must be declared each year on your tax return. You'll receive a tax slip from the fund company before the end of February each year that provides all the details you need to complete your return. Distributions can take several forms, each of which may be taxed differently. They include:

**CAPITAL GAINS.** A capital gain is your share of the profits realized by the fund from the sale of securities inside the portfolio during the year. This form of distribution is taxed at the capital gains rate, which means the first 50 percent is tax-free. You pay at your marginal rate on the balance.

**DIVIDENDS.** A dividend is your share of the fund's earnings during the year. These payments are eligible for the dividend tax credit, so they'll be taxed at an advantageous rate. Dividends are one of the most effective ways to receive investment income in this country.

**FOREIGN INCOME.** If you own an international mutual fund, it may have received income from a number of foreign sources, including interest and dividends. This distribution is your share of that income. If the fund paid tax on that money to other governments, you can recover some of it through the foreign tax credit.

**OTHER INCOME.** This distribution usually comprises your share of any interest income earned by the fund. Interest doesn't receive any tax breaks, so you'll pay at your full rate.

**RENTAL INCOME.** This distribution comes from real estate mutual funds and real estate investment trusts (REITs). These investments receive special tax treatment because the fund managers normally use capital cost allowance (CCA) to shelter a large portion of the distribution from tax. You'll receive a special form for reporting this type of distribution on your return.

**RETURN OF CAPITAL.** This portion of a distribution is received on what is known as a "tax-deferred" basis because the income often has been partially tax-sheltered, perhaps as a result of exploration and development allowances. No tax is payable on this portion of a distribution in the year it is received. However, you must subtract the value of the tax-deferred distribution from the price you paid for your units for the purpose of calculating the taxable capital gain when you sell. This action produces what is known as an adjusted cost base (ACB). For example, if you pay $10 per unit and receive a $1 distribution that is tax-deferred, your new ACB is $9 ($10 − $1 = $9).

In order to assess the tax liability from fund distributions in non-registered accounts, you need to know the applicable rates for the various types of payments. The rates for the 2001 tax year follow in table form, below, and are listed by province. Gena Katz, principal, Ernst & Young Tax Practice, has graciously supplied the tables. The dollar amounts represent taxable income (not gross income). The tax rates are combined 2001 federal and provincial rates on employment income, incorporating all budget changes to July 2001. They include federal and provincial surtaxes and provincial tax reductions, where applicable. The basic personal tax credit has also been taken into account.

Quebec has taken over the dubious title of Canadian Tax King with the highest marginal rate in the country on regular income, at 48.72 percent. Alberta continues to be a tax haven for the wealthy, with a top marginal rate of 39 percent. Ontario's much-publicized cuts have taken the top rate in our most populous province to 46.41 percent, so high-income earners now get to keep slightly more than half of what they make once they hit the top bracket.

**BRITISH COLUMBIA**

| TAXABLE INCOME | INTEREST | DIVIDENDS | CAPITAL GAINS |
| --- | --- | --- | --- |
| $7,412 to $8,000 | 16.00% | 3.33% | 8.00% |
| $8,000 to $30,484 | 23.30% | 5.08% | 11.65% |
| $30,484 to $30,754 | 26.50% | 9.08% | 13.25% |
| $30,754 to $60,969 | 32.50% | 16.58% | 16.25% |
| $60,969 to $61,509 | 35.70% | 20.58% | 17.85% |
| $61,509 to $70,000 | 39.70% | 25.58% | 19.85% |
| $70,000 to $85,000 | 41.70% | 28.08% | 20.85% |
| $85,000 to $100,000 | 42.70% | 29.33% | 21.35% |
| $100,000 and up | 45.70% | 33.08% | 22.85% |

**ALBERTA**

| TAXABLE INCOME | INTEREST | DIVIDENDS | CAPITAL GAINS |
| --- | --- | --- | --- |
| $7,412 to $12,900 | 16.00% | 3.33% | 8.00% |
| $12,900 to $30,754 | 26.00% | 7.83% | 13.00% |
| $30,754 to $61,509 | 32.00% | 15.33% | 16.00% |
| $61,509 to $100,000 | 36.00% | 20.33% | 18.00% |
| $100,000 and up | 39.00% | 24.08% | 19.50% |

**SASKATCHEWAN**

| TAXABLE INCOME | INTEREST | DIVIDENDS | CAPITAL GAINS |
|---|---|---|---|
| $7,412 to $8,000 | 16.00% | 3.33% | 8.00% |
| $8,000 to $30,000 | 27.50% | 7.71% | 13.75% |
| $30,000 to $30,754 | 29.50% | 10.21% | 14.75% |
| $30,754 to $60,000 | 35.50% | 17.71% | 17.75% |
| $60,000 to $61,509 | 38.00% | 20.83% | 19.00% |
| $61,509 to $100,000 | 42.00% | 25.83% | 21.00% |
| $100,000 and up | 45.00% | 29.58% | 22.50% |

**MANITOBA**

| TAXABLE INCOME | INTEREST | DIVIDENDS | CAPITAL GAINS |
|---|---|---|---|
| $7,412 to $8,680 | 16.00% | 3.33% | 8.00% |
| $8,680 to $22,500 | 27.90% | 10.71% | 13.95% |
| $22,500 to $30,544 | 26.90% | 9.46% | 13.45% |
| $30,544 to $30,754 | 32.20% | 16.08% | 16.10% |
| $30,754 to $61,089 | 38.20% | 23.58% | 19.10% |
| $61,089 to $61,509 | 39.40% | 25.08% | 19.70% |
| $61,509 to $100,000 | 43.40% | 30.08% | 21.70% |
| $100,000 and up | 46.40% | 33.83% | 23.20% |

**ONTARIO**

| TAXABLE INCOME | INTEREST | DIVIDENDS | CAPITAL GAINS |
|---|---|---|---|
| $7,412 to $9,878 | 16.00% | 3.33% | 8.00% |
| $9,878 to $12,329 | 28.40% | 6.00% | 14.20% |
| $12,329 to $30,754 | 22.20% | 4.67% | 11.10% |
| $30,754 to $30,814 | 28.20% | 12.17% | 14.10% |
| $30,814 to $53,650 | 31.24% | 15.97% | 15.62% |
| $53,650 to $61,509 | 33.09% | 16.99% | 16.54% |
| $61,509 to $61,629 | 37.09% | 21.99% | 18.54% |
| $61,629 to $63,365 | 39.39% | 24.87% | 19.70% |
| $63,365 to $100,000 | 43.41% | 27.58% | 21.70% |
| $100,000 and up | 46.41% | 31.33% | 23.20% |

## QUEBEC

| TAXABLE INCOME | INTEREST | DIVIDENDS | CAPITAL GAINS |
|---|---|---|---|
| $7,201 to $7,412 | 17.00% | 7.71% | 8.50% |
| $7,412 to $26,000 | 30.36% | 10.50% | 15.18% |
| $26,000 to $30,754 | 34.61% | 15.81% | 17.31% |
| $30,754 to $52,000 | 39.62% | 22.07% | 19.81% |
| $52,000 to $61,509 | 42.87% | 26.13% | 21.44% |
| $61,509 to $100,000 | 46.21% | 30.31% | 23.11% |
| $100,000 and up | 48.72% | 33.44% | 24.36% |

## NEWFOUNDLAND

| TAXABLE INCOME | INTEREST | DIVIDENDS | CAPITAL GAINS |
|---|---|---|---|
| $7,412 to $29,590 | 26.57% | 5.30% | 13.29% |
| $29,590 to $30,754 | 32.16% | 12.28% | 16.08% |
| $30,754 to $58,598 | 38.16% | 19.78% | 19.08% |
| $58,598 to $59,180 | 39.61% | 20.59% | 19.81% |
| $59,180 to $61,509 | 41.64% | 23.12% | 20.82% |
| $61,509 to $100,000 | 45.64% | 28.12% | 22.82% |
| $100,000 and up | 48.64% | 31.87% | 24.32% |

## NEW BRUNSWICK

| TAXABLE INCOME | INTEREST | DIVIDENDS | CAPITAL GAINS |
|---|---|---|---|
| $7,412 to $30,754 | 25.68% | 12.36% | 12.84% |
| $30,754 to $60,509 | 36.82% | 19.86% | 18.41% |
| $60,509 to $100,000 | 42.52% | 26.98% | 21.26% |
| $100,000 and up | 46.84% | 32.38% | 23.42% |

## NOVA SCOTIA

| TAXABLE INCOME | INTEREST | DIVIDENDS | CAPITAL GAINS |
|---|---|---|---|
| $7,412 to $10,302 | 16.00% | 3.33% | 8.00% |
| $10,302 to $15,000 | 25.77% | 5.92% | 12.89% |
| $15,000 to $21,000 | 30.77% | 12.17% | 15.39% |
| $21,000 to $29,590 | 25.77% | 5.92% | 12.89% |
| $29,590 to $30,754 | 30.95% | 12.40% | 15.48% |
| $30,754 to $59,180 | 36.95% | 19.90% | 18.48% |
| $59,180 to $61,509 | 38.67% | 22.05% | 19.34% |
| $61,509 to $79,525 | 42.67% | 27.05% | 21.34% |
| $79,525 to $100,000 | 44.34% | 28.17% | 22.17% |
| $100,000 and up | 47.34% | 31.92% | 23.67% |

## PEI

| TAXABLE INCOME | INTEREST | DIVIDENDS | CAPITAL GAINS |
|---|---|---|---|
| $7,412 to $30,754 | 25.80% | 5.96% | 12.90% |
| $30,754 to $51,855 | 35.80% | 18.46% | 17.90% |
| $51,855 to $61,509 | 37.18% | 23.21% | 18.59% |
| $61,509 to $100,000 | 44.37% | 28.21% | 22.19% |
| $100,000 and up | 47.37% | 31.96% | 23.69% |

## NWT

| TAXABLE INCOME | INTEREST | DIVIDENDS | CAPITAL GAINS |
|---|---|---|---|
| $7,412 to $30,754 | 23.20% | 4.83% | 11.60% |
| $30,754 to $61,509 | 31.90% | 15.71% | 15.95% |
| $61,509 to $100,000 | 37.70% | 22.96% | 18.85% |
| $100,000 and up | 42.05% | 28.40% | 21.03% |

## NUNAVUT

| TAXABLE INCOME | INTEREST | DIVIDENDS | CAPITAL GAINS |
|---|---|---|---|
| $7,412 to $30,754 | 23.20% | 4.83% | 11.60% |
| $30,754 to $61,509 | 31.90% | 15.71% | 15.95% |
| $61,509 to $100,000 | 37.70% | 22.96% | 18.85% |
| $100,000 and up | 42.05% | 28.40% | 21.03% |

**YUKON**

| TAXABLE INCOME | INTEREST | DIVIDENDS | CAPITAL GAINS |
|---|---|---|---|
| $7,412 to $30,754 | 23.36% | 4.87% | 11.68% |
| $30,754 to $61,509 | 32.12% | 15.82% | 16.06% |
| $61,509 to $71,288 | 37.96% | 23.12% | 18.98% |
| $71,288 to $100,000 | 38.56% | 23.48% | 19.28% |
| $100,000 and up | 43.01% | 29.04% | 21.50% |

## Sales

Whenever you sell mutual fund units, a taxable event takes place. If you sell your units for more than you paid for them, you've earned a capital gain and will have to declare it for tax purposes. If you sell for less than you paid, you have a capital loss and you may be able to claim some tax relief.

The CCRA casts a very long shadow here. Transactions you may not consider to be a sale at all will be viewed as such by the tax department, and they'll want a piece of the action. Not sure of what constitutes a sale? Here are some examples:

SWITCHES. When you move money out of one fund and into another, CCRA regards the switch as two transactions: a sale and a purchase. If you've made a profit, the sale will trigger a tax liability.

RRSP CONTRIBUTIONS. If you have a self-directed RRSP, you're allowed to contribute securities directly into it, instead of converting them to cash first. But the government regards this "contribution in kind" as a sale, and you'll have to pay tax on any profits. The bad news is that if your fund units are on the losing end when you make this type of move, you cannot claim a capital loss.

GIFTS. If you give your fund units to someone else (your spouse, perhaps), it's considered a sale for tax purposes, and you must declare any profits.

DEATH. You won't have to worry about it personally, but if you die, your estate contends with the fact that the CCRA deems all your mutual fund assets (and everything else) to have been sold and any capital gains realized for tax purposes. The one exception is if your assets pass directly to your spouse, in which case no tax is assessed.

## Tax-Deflection Strategies

As you can see, the government is ready to pounce on your mutual fund profits in a number of ways. Your task is to deflect the blow and keep your taxes to a minimum. There are a number of strategies that will help you accomplish this. Here are the ones most commonly used:

**CLAIM ALL RELATED EXPENSES.** Taxable capital gains are calculated only after all legal expenses have been factored in. This is done in two stages: at the time of your initial purchase and when you sell.

When you buy your fund units, your cost for tax purposes will be adjusted to reflect any expenses you incurred in the process, such as sales charges and the transaction fee charged by securities commissions in some provinces. The result is the adjusted cost base, or ACB, the figure you use for determining capital gains or losses down the road.

When you sell, you deduct any related expenses from the gross proceeds of the sale. Expenses include such things as sales commissions, account closing fees, etc. The difference between the net proceeds you receive and the ACB is the amount subject to tax. If your proceeds are less than the ACB, you have a capital loss, which can be offset against any taxable capital gains you may have from other transactions.

**HAVE THE LOWER-INCOME SPOUSE DO THE FAMILY INVESTING.** If you're a two-income family, have the spouse with the lower income (who presumably is in a lower tax bracket) acquire the investments. That way, you'll pay less tax on any distributions or capital gains.

**DON'T BUY FUNDS AT THE YEAR'S END.** Many mutual funds make distributions only once a year, in December. This can create a tax trap, of which many people are unaware. The problem arises when you buy funds outside a registered plan just before the distribution date. Income earned over the previous 12 months is then paid out to investors—including you—and the fund's unit value is adjusted downward to reflect the payout. The effect is that you receive back some of the investment capital you've just put up, and you have to pay tax on it. This is definitely a situation to avoid.

**SET UP YOUR REGISTERED AND NON-REGISTERED PORTFOLIOS TO MINIMIZE TAXES.** A good rule of thumb is to use your RRSP to hold securities that attract the highest rate of tax. In the case of mutual funds, that would mean any fund designed to generate interest as the prime source of income, including money market funds, bond funds, and mortgage funds. Keep funds that enjoy a tax advantage outside the retirement plan, including stock funds (dividends and capital gains), dividend income funds (dividends), and real estate funds (rental income). It won't always be possible to set up your portfolios in such a perfect way, but apply this principle wherever it's feasible.

**INVEST IN FUNDS FOR YOUR CHILDREN.** You can reduce the family tax hit by putting some of your mutual fund investments into your children's names, but you must be careful. Any interest or dividends earned in this situation will be attributed back to you for tax purposes. But the capital gains won't be; they're considered the child's. So choose your funds here with care.

> **SPECIAL TIP** If the child has any independent income from an after-school job, that child can use that money to invest in funds (or anything else) without any tax being attributed back to you.

**TAKE ADVANTAGE OF LABOUR-SPONSORED FUNDS.** This category of mutual funds offers special tax breaks for investors. The federal government offers a tax credit of 15 percent of the total amount invested in qualifying funds, up to a total credit of $750 a year. Several provinces also offer similar credits against provincial taxes. As a result, in many parts of Canada, you can earn up to $1,500 in tax credits from a $5,000 investment. The credit is deducted directly from your tax payable, so you get the benefit of the full amount, not a percentage as in the case of personal tax credits. Units in these funds are eligible for RRSPs, so you can add to your tax break in that way. But a word of warning: these funds invest in small, start-up companies. Consequently, they're higher risk than the average mutual fund. And once you buy your units, you're locked in for eight years. (See the section on labour-sponsored funds for more details.)

**LOOK AT HIGH-INCOME BALANCED FUNDS.** Mention the term "high-income balanced funds" to most investors and you'll receive a blank stare. This relatively new fund category is not very well known or understood. But most of the funds in this group have turned in impressive numbers recently. And, more to the point as far as this chapter is concerned, they offer significant tax advantages for income-oriented investors. The reason for this is that most funds in this category invest primarily in royalty income trusts (RITs) and real estate investment trusts (REITs). Some of the income generated by these securities is eligible for tax breaks. As a result, the "return of capital" portion of the distributions from these funds tends to be fairly high. As we have just seen, income that falls into that classification is received on a tax-deferred basis.

The downside of these funds is that they can be quite volatile. RITs have had a checkered history since they appeared on the scene in the mid-1990s. They started off strong, but were then battered in the oil price slump of 1997–98; some have still not regained their issue price. As you might expect, the funds that invested heavily in these securities were beaten up as well. And make no mistake about it: the same thing could happen again. It's the nature of the beast. If oil prices tumble, the royalty trust market will start to resemble the recent tech wreck and these funds will look terrible again. That's the risk you run if you invest here. You have to decide if the tax advantages and the good flow of income are worth it.

USE UMBRELLA FUNDS. A major impediment to switching from one fund to another outside a registered plan is the government's view that any movement of assets constitutes a sale and a purchase for tax purposes. This means that if your units have increased in value since you bought them, a switch will trigger a taxable capital gain. No one likes that idea and, as a result, people tend to hold their investments when they should move on.

To combat this problem, some companies like AGF, C.I., AIM, Synergy, Mackenzie, and Clarington have set up "umbrella" funds composed of different "sectors" or "classes," each with its own area of investment specialization. Switching assets from one sector or class to another does not trigger a capital gain because the transaction takes place within the single umbrella fund. So you could move from AIM Global Health Care Class to AIM Global Telecommunications Class without incurring a tax liability, for example. But if you tried the same thing with funds not covered by this kind of umbrella, you'd be looking at a taxable gain.

As you can see, there are a number of strategies available for keeping your mutual fund tax bill as low as possible. But the plain fact remains that, as with anything else, if you make money from your mutual funds (which is, after all, the only reason to invest in them), you'll have to share at least some of it with the CCRA eventually. They wouldn't have it any other way.

## SUMMARY

- If you make money from your mutual funds, the CCRA will want a share—but there are ways to reduce its bite.
- Certain types of mutual fund distributions attract much less tax than others.
- Labour-sponsored funds offer huge tax savings, but you must be willing to accept the risks involved.
- High-income balanced funds offer tax advantages to income-oriented investors, but here, too, the risk factor is quite high.
- Umbrella funds enable you to move money around without incurring taxable capital gains in the process.

# FUND FACTS

**TAX-EFFECTIVE REBATES.** If you buy back-end load funds and get a rebate on the commission, the rebate is considered taxable income. But there's a way to avoid paying any tax right away: you can file a special election with your tax return to have the rebate applied to reduce the cost base of the fund units you purchased. There are two advantages to this action, says the Investment Funds Institute of Canada (IFIC). First, you defer paying any tax on the rebate until you dispose of your units. Second, making the election effectively transforms the rebate from ordinary income (fully taxed) to a capital gain (50 percent taxed).

To take advantage of this election, just include a written statement with your return saying you intend to apply the rebate to reduce the purchase price of the units. This statement should be filed with the tax return you prepare for the year the rebate is received.

**REINVESTMENTS TAXED TOO.** Most mutual funds offer an automatic reinvestment programme, where your distributions are used to buy more fund units. If you join, you won't actually receive any cash into your own hands. But beware: as far as the CCRA is concerned, that money is still taxable, even though you never see it.

**MARGINAL TAX RATE.** Your marginal tax rate is the rate payable on the last dollar you earn. Since we have a graduated tax system, your marginal rate increases as your income climbs. The highest Canadian marginal rate in 2001 belonged to Quebec where residents paid 48.72percent tax on every dollar earned after taxable income exceeded $100,000.

**DON'T OVERPAY!** In the past, some investors paid too much tax on rental income distributions because of poor reporting procedures by brokerage houses. There were cases where brokers holding units in REITs on the behalf of their clients classified the distributions as dividends rather than rental income. The result was an enormous difference in tax payable. The situation has been largely corrected, but if you do receive income from these securities, make sure your T3 slips are accurate.

**UNEXPECTED TAXES.** Here's an example of how a year-end mutual fund distribution can cost you money. As you can see, the net effect is that you end up paying tax on some of your own capital:

| | |
|---|---|
| Purchase of 100 units on December 1: | $1,000.00 |
| Yearly distribution on December 15 (taxable): | $75.00 |
| Value of units after distribution: | $925.00 |

Result: You end up paying tax on $75 of your original capital.

**CARELESS ADVISORS.** It may be difficult to believe, but some professional investment advisors fail to take taxes into account when constructing portfolios for their clients. We have seen cases where an investment counsellor has set up a registered and non-registered portfolio for an individual, each of which held exactly the same securities. By rearranging those portfolios for maximum tax benefit, significant tax savings could have been realized.

# Buying Money Market Funds

*Canadians have fallen in love with money market funds (MMFs). In the spring of 2001, we had almost $50 billion invested in this type of mutual fund. That's a lot of money!*

What's the attraction? Well, bank savings accounts used to be the most popular place to hold spare cash. But then the banks decided that they didn't want to encourage this practice any more. They slashed interest rates on savings accounts to the bone—some major banks now pay less than 1 percent on basic savings accounts. At the same time, they imposed fees on all kinds of services that used to be free. Bank profits soared, but customers gradually began to realize they should start seeking investment alternatives.

An excellent option was available just a teller's counter away and it involved money market funds. They offered a much better yield than savings accounts with no cost attached. The average Canadian MMF returned 4.5 percent for the 12 months to June 30, 2001. Few financial institutions offered a savings account that even came close to those numbers (the exceptions were some of the aggressive new banks or near banks, like ING Direct).

But the attractive yield (at least compared to savings accounts) wasn't the only reason for the rapid growth in these funds. Convenience was another big plus. Consequently, almost every bank and trust company now has at least one and perhaps as many as three or four MMFs available. CIBC, for example, currently offers eight different MMFs, including a regular CIBC Money Market Fund, a CIBC Canadian T-Bill Fund for those looking for an extra measure of security, a CIBC U.S. Dollar Money Market Fund, and several "premium" funds offering superior returns to investors with $100,000 or more to invest, including two that require $1 million just to get in the door.

Perhaps the biggest attraction of MMFs, however, is that they are seen as a safe haven for cash, even though they have no deposit insurance protection.

Some MMFs use Government of Canada Treasury bills as their core holding, giving them an image of soundness and stability. This image is reinforced by the fact that no Canadian MMF that we're aware of has ever lost money for its investors.

Unfortunately, many people who put their cash into MMFs don't fully understand what they're investing in, or they have unrealistic expectations for these funds. To start, it's important to realize that MMFs invest exclusively in short-term securities, usually with maturities of less than one year. A fund's holdings can range from high-grade T-bills to short-term commercial notes issued by corporations. The return paid by any given fund will therefore fluctuate on a daily basis. When interest rates are rising and new money can be invested in securities with an ever-higher yield, the total return from your MMF investment will steadily increase. But when short-term interest rates are falling, as they were through the first half of 2001, yields will decline as maturing securities have to be rolled over at a lower rate. The result is that the return on your investment will steadily decline. For anyone living on a fixed income, dependent on their investments to put bread on the table, this can be a serious problem.

And therein lies the danger of money market funds: by leaving your cash in them when interest rates are falling, you'll experience a lower return and miss opportunities to make bigger profits elsewhere.

That's not to say MMFs are bad or should not be used. As with all other forms of investing, it's a case of using them intelligently. MMFs have two valuable functions, after all. The first is that they provide a safe place for your money during periods of financial turmoil, especially when short-term interest rates are high. The second is that they are a substitute for deposit accounts.

In fact, there is no valid reason for holding large amounts of money in most bank savings accounts any more, as an increasing number of Canadians have concluded. You obviously need to retain a chequing account to handle current cash flow (although some MMFs do offer limited chequing privileges). But any cash you would otherwise keep in a savings account for easy access will work harder for you in an MMF and, in most cases, you can withdraw the funds just as quickly if required.

So which MMF should you choose? Since money market funds have taken off, the marketplace has been flooded with new products. There has also been some behind-the-scenes manoeuvering on the part of some mutual fund operators in an effort to gain a competitive edge. These industry movements have created confusion among investors looking for the best MMF deal. To help you make the right choice, here are some guidelines to follow when you're considering money market funds:

**DON'T PUT TOO MUCH EMPHASIS ON COMPARATIVE RATES OF RETURN.** The mutual fund industry has been going through a bitter internal conflict over the proper way to report MMF yields, and it's not over yet.

As things stand now, fund companies must use current yield in their advertising. However, there's no uniformity in the way this yield is reported. Some funds do the calculation daily, using a rolling seven-day average, while some tumble the numbers only once a week.

Funds are also allowed to promote their effective yield as long as it is not given greater prominence than the current yield in any ad. The effective yield brings the advantage of compounding into play. It is supposed to indicate what the fund will yield over the next 12 months, based on the current yield and assuming all interest is reinvested and compounded weekly. The Investment Funds Institute of Canada (IFIC) carries out and reports this calculation for its members. If you check the daily mutual fund reports in the business press, you'll find both yields shown for MMFs. However, both can be seriously flawed and should not be the sole factor considered when making a purchase.

Remember also that as interest rates drop, so will the effective yield of MMFs. You should not expect a fund that projects a 4.5-percent effective yield today to actually deliver that rate of return over the next 12 months if interest rates decline during that period. Of course, if rates rise, the yield will too. In short, there are no guarantees. In fact, the numbers quoted by the funds are not projected yields at all, but historical rates of return. They assume everything will remain the same for the next 12 months, which, of course, won't happen. So don't be misled into believing the quoted yields are what you'll actually receive.

**CONSIDER THE SAFETY FACTOR.** Although MMFs as a group have an excellent record, some are inherently less risky than others. You can expect to pay a price for increased safety, however.

Canadian MMFs are not as tightly regulated as those in the U.S. in terms of the quality of the securities they may hold. As a result, some funds have a greater degree of risk exposure than others. During good economic times this exposure may not seem particularly important, but when business is slow and bankruptcies are a problem, it's worth taking into account.

Funds that invest largely or exclusively in Government of Canada Treasury bills rank highest on the safety scale; they're usually called T-bill funds. Other MMFs may hold a higher percentage of commercial short-term paper in their portfolios. The yields on these securities will be higher than on government T-bills, but their safety rating will be lower.

You'll have to decide how much safety you're prepared to sacrifice for enhanced returns. Before you make that decision, ask for a copy of the fund's current portfolio and investment philosophy. Review both carefully to see how they fit with your needs.

**ASK ABOUT AVERAGE TERM TO MATURITY.** Yields on MMFs will rise or fall from current levels in the months ahead, depending on the course interest rates take. If rates are expected to drop, your objective should be to invest in a fund that will experience a slower-than-average yield decline, so you want one with a longer average term to maturity. The reverse holds true when rates are rising. In that case, the shorter the term to maturity the better, because the fund will be able to roll over its assets into higher-yielding securities at an earlier date.

**LOOK FOR NO-CHARGE SWITCHING.** An MMF should be regarded as a temporary parking place for cash. You should therefore select a fund that allows you to switch your assets easily, and without cost, to other types of funds like bond or equity funds. If you have to pay a fee to switch, it will cut into your yield significantly. And it may inhibit you from making a change that good investment sense would otherwise dictate.

**DON'T PAY ANY SALES OR REDEMPTION CHARGES.** The difference between the yields of competitive MMFs is usually so small that any load charge or redemption cost will almost always tip the balance in favour of a no-load fund. Most companies, even those that charge front- or back-end loads on all their other funds, will provide MMFs on a no-load basis. But you may have to negotiate with the sales person to get a no-load deal. If that doesn't work, contact the mutual fund company directly. If they still want to charge a fee, look elsewhere.

**TAKE A CLOSE LOOK AT THE MANAGEMENT FEES.** More than any other type of mutual fund, the returns on MMFs will be greatly affected by the management fee structure. That's because these funds usually generate relatively low returns in the first place. After management fees and expenses are deducted, the profit left for investors is small. A management expense ratio (MER) of about 1 percent is normal for an MMF. Anything over 1.5 percent is high. An MER under 0.75 percent is a bargain.

**CHECK THE SIZE OF THE FUND.** When it comes to MMFs, small is usually not beautiful. A bigger fund can spread its costs over a larger asset base, making it more efficient and reducing the drain on unitholder returns in percentage terms.

**ASK ABOUT REDEMPTION CHARGES.** Normally you can withdraw money from a no-load MMF without any charge. But some funds have instituted a 90-day waiting period for this privilege. If you pull your money out any sooner after opening an account, you could be hit with a fee of up to 2 percent.

**USE MMFS TO PROTECT YOUR CURRENCY BASE.** The Canadian dollar has been under attack for the better part of two decades and has lost a third of its value against the U.S. dollar in the past 10 years. This scenario has led many investors to look for ways to protect their assets from further currency debasement. U.S. dollar and international MMFs are one way to achieve this protection and many are now structured so that they can be held in a registered plan without any limitations.

**DON'T ASSUME YOU CAN'T LOSE MONEY.** The net asset value (NAV) of Canadian MMFs is supposedly fixed, usually at $10. For all other types of mutual funds, the NAV will fluctuate depending on the market value of the securities in the portfolio. This gives MMFs a unique advantage. You know (or think you know) that if you put in $100, you'll get that amount back plus interest when the time comes to cash out; it's sort of like a more flexible GIC.

Unfortunately, there's a potential trap for unwary investors here. The value of the securities in an MMF portfolio may indeed fluctuate, even if the fund invests exclusively in T-bills. For example, when interest rates took a dramatic leap in September 1992 in response to heavy pressure on the Canadian dollar from the referendum campaign on the Charlottetown Accord, the value of all fixed-income securities, including T-bills and short-term commercial notes, took a hit. As a result, some funds saw a sudden drop in the value of their portfolios. If MMFs were valued in the same way as all other mutual funds, this would have been reflected in a lower unit value. But since the value is fixed (albeit artificially), managers had to find some other way to make up the shortfall.

At least one company—Elliott & Page—did it by suspending interest payments for a month. Investors in their MMF received no return during that time. The units held their value, but the investors didn't earn any money.

The shorter the term to maturity an MMF portfolio has, the lower its risk. This is because the less time remaining to a security's redemption, the less vulnerable it is to interest rate fluctuations. But if wild movements in rates return, we could see a situation some time in the future when an MMF is forced to abandon the fixed-rate standard and pass on losses to investors in the form of a lower unit value. So while these funds are low risk, they are not entirely risk-free.

While we're on the subject of loss potential, remember that MMFs are *not* covered by deposit insurance, even if they're purchased at a financial institution that's a Canada Deposit Insurance Corporation (CDIC) member. The risk of serious loss is very low, but it cannot be dismissed entirely.

If you plan to invest in an MMF, don't make that decision in isolation. You probably won't leave your money in the fund forever, so you want to be sure you have good switching options available. Look at all the funds in the family of the MMF you're considering. See how they measure up compared to the competition and decide if you would consider investing in them on their own merits. If they don't look attractive, don't give the company your MMF business, especially if you're making the investment within a registered plan, such as an RRSP. You'll only create complications for yourself when the time comes to move on.

## SUMMARY

- MMFs are the safest type of mutual fund investment, but they aren't completely risk-free.
- Historical performance is of little importance in assessing the future potential of an MMF. The direction of short-term interest rates is much more significant.
- Big funds often offer lower expense ratios with higher returns.
- U.S. dollar MMFs offer protection against further devaluation of the loonie. Many of these funds are fully eligible for RRSPs.
- Don't buy an MMF in isolation. Check out the other funds in the family to see if you'd be happy switching into them later.

## FUND FACTS

CURRENT YIELD. The current yield is the actual return of an MMF over the past seven days, projected out over one year.

SMOKE AND MIRRORS. If you scan the monthly mutual fund reports in the business pages looking for low MERs, your eye may be drawn to the ICM Short-Term Investment Fund; it shows an MER of only 0.07 percent—just about the lowest in the industry. And the returns look terrific as well. But hold on: if something seems too good to be true, it probably is. That's certainly the case here. The MER on this fund looks so low because it doesn't reflect the negotiable annual management fee of up to 1 percent that you'll pay when you acquire units. In most funds, the management fee is deducted from the assets of the portfolio. But here, you're assessed the fee directly. Since ICM doesn't show this part of the equation when it publishes its results, it makes this fund look much better than it actually is.

A TALE OF TWO FUNDS. Take a look at the comparative annual rates of return of these two funds for the period ending March 31, 2001, as reported in *The Globe and Mail*. Note how much of the difference can be directly attributed to the management charges.

| FUND | MER | 1 YEAR | 3 YEARS | 5 YEARS |
|------|-----|--------|---------|---------|
| PH&N Canadian Money Market Fund | 0.48% | 5.3% | 4.8% | 4.3% |
| Elliot & Page T-Bill Fund | 1.86% | 4.1% | 3.4% | 2.9% |

**AN IMPORTANT DISTINCTION.** There are a few foreign MMFs that do not attempt to maintain a fixed-unit value. Their unit price will fluctuate up or down, depending on the market value of the securities in the portfolio. These funds carry a higher measure of risk than other MMFs, and can suffer losses as a result. The Altamira Short-Term Global Income Fund is an example of this type of fund.

# Choosing Fixed-Income Funds

*There's a tendency among younger people to think that fixed-income funds are for their parents; dull funds for old folks, if you like. There's no action in bond funds, no excitement in mortgage funds, and no drama in dividend funds. They may be okay some day when retirement income is needed, but not now. Please!*

Well, we have news for you. Yes, it's true that fixed-income funds are useful for generating retirement income. But there's a lot more to them than that. In fact, certain fixed-income funds offer significant capital gains potential (just remember that where there is potential for capital gain, there is also potential for risk).

Every mutual fund portfolio should contain some fixed-income funds. But exactly which type of funds and in what proportion will depend on your particular investment goals and on general economic conditions.

Before we get into the strategies of fixed-income investing, however, let's run through the different types of funds that are available:

REGULAR CANADIAN BOND FUNDS. These funds invest in a diversified portfolio of bonds and debentures issued mainly by Canadian government organizations and corporations. They may also contain mortgage-backed securities. The portfolio is usually a mix of short-, medium-, and long-term bonds, with the weighting adjusted by the manager depending on the prospects for interest rates and the bond market.

SHORT-TERM BOND FUNDS. These funds started appearing in the mid-1990s, mainly in response to the crash of the bond market in early 1994. Think of them as a cross between a regular bond fund and a money market fund. The managers invest only in debt securities with a term to maturity of less than five years. This makes the fund less risky than regular bond funds, which are vulnerable to loss during periods when interest rates are rising. The price you pay for this increased safety is a lower return and almost no capital gains potential. These are defensive funds, for people who want to keep risk to a minimum but obtain a better return than money market funds normally offer.

**HIGH-YIELD BOND FUNDS.** These funds specialize in high-yield bonds; you may be more familiar with their commonly used name, "junk bonds." Companies with a relatively low credit rating issue these bonds. As a result, the interest rate they pay to borrow is higher than would be charged to a blue-ribbon client like the federal government or a major bank. So you'll get a better return here, but with a higher risk—companies with weak credit ratings are more vulnerable to defaulting, especially in a recession. If you're risk-averse, you should steer clear of these funds.

**FOREIGN BOND FUNDS.** These funds invest in debt securities issued by foreign governments or companies, or in Canadian bonds denominated in foreign currencies. We have a lot of foreign currency issues in our country; all levels of government frequently issue U.S. dollar bonds, and you can also find issues in euros, Japanese yen, Swiss francs, sterling, and German marks. Funds that specialize in Canadian foreign currency issues are fully eligible for registered plans (the currency isn't what counts, it's the issuer). Those funds that invest offshore are considered foreign content for RRSP and RRIF purposes. Foreign bond funds perform best when global interest rates and the value of the Canadian dollar are falling in tandem.

**MORTGAGE FUNDS.** For the most part, these funds invest in residential first mortgages and mortgage-backed securities, which are guaranteed for both principal and interest by Canada Mortgage and Housing Corporation (CMHC or, in essence, the Government of Canada). However, a few also hold commercial mortgages. After money market funds, mortgage funds are considered the lowest-risk type of mutual fund you can buy. Defaults by mortgage holders in Canada are rare, and the relatively short term of these funds makes them less vulnerable to price changes due to interest rate fluctuations. A few fund companies even go so far as to guarantee that any defaulting mortgages will be repurchased from the fund with no penalty to unitholders (the Bank of Montreal does this for the BMO Mortgage Fund).

**DIVIDEND INCOME FUNDS.** We're including these funds in this chapter because there's no other logical place for them, but we do so reluctantly as there is no consistency in the offerings from different fund groups. A pure dividend income fund invests almost exclusively in preferred shares and high-yielding common stocks like banks and utilities. The objective is to maximize dividend income, which is taxed at a lower rate than interest due to the application of the dividend tax credit. However, several so-called dividend funds have portfolios that don't truly reflect this philosophy; they may hold bonds and common stocks that pay little or no dividend, or even hold foreign securities that don't qualify for the dividend tax credit at all. If tax-advantaged income is your main objective, be very selective with these funds.

**HIGH-INCOME BALANCED FUNDS.** Like dividend income funds, these funds do not fall perfectly into the fixed-income category, but there is no other logical place in which to slot them. These funds invest primarily in high-income securities like royalty income trusts (RITs) and real estate investment trusts (REITs). The goal here is to generate higher cash flow than you would receive from other types of fixed-income funds, often with some tax advantages. The trade-off is taking on more risk; like the securities in which they invest, these funds can be highly volatile.

**INCOME FUNDS.** These funds are something of a hybrid. Managers may choose to invest in just about anything on the fixed-income securities list, from long-term bonds to mortgage-backed securities to royalty trusts. Before putting any money into one of these funds, find out where the portfolio emphasis lies and decide if it's consistent with what you're trying to achieve.

That's the rather lengthy list of fixed-income options. As you can see, there's a lot to choose from, and not all the fund types will be right for everyone. The next step is to consider some of the most common fixed-income investing strategies and decide which of these funds best suits your specific goals.

Before we get into strategy, however, there's a basic principle of investing that *must* be taken into account whenever you're considering a fixed-income fund. It's this: **Interest rates and bond prices move in opposite directions**. Technically, this principle is an inverse relationship. When interest rates decline, bond prices rise, and vice versa. It seems very elementary, but many people aren't aware of it and don't understand how to use this principle to their advantage.

Although we've made reference to bond prices in stating this principle, it applies to all fixed-income securities, including mortgages and fixed-rate preferred shares. However, it's important to note that the degree of impact on the price of any given security will be directly affected by its term to maturity. The longer the time remaining until maturity, the more the price will move when rates rise or fall.

For example, suppose you have two bonds, each of which pays 7 percent annual interest. One matures next year while the other has 20 years to run. Interest rates drop and new issues are paying only 6 percent. That makes your bonds, with their higher coupon rate, more attractive to investors. But the bond with one year to maturity pays the premium rate only for a limited time; the other one continues to generate above-average income for two decades. It's not hard to figure out which one is worth more to other investors.

## Fixed-Income Fund Strategies

Keeping all of the above information in mind, let's now look at some fixed-income fund strategies:

THE COMPOUND INTEREST APPROACH. This approach is the one most commonly used for fixed-income funds. The idea here is to use the steady returns provided by these funds over time to maximize the effect of compound interest in your portfolio. You can achieve the same result with GICs, of course, but a well-selected group of fixed-income funds will usually provide a better return over time. Mortgage funds and conservatively managed bond funds work most effectively. This strategy works best inside a registered plan, such as an RRSP, where tax sheltering will maximize the return.

THE CAPITAL GAINS GAMBIT. Many new fund investors don't realize that bond funds are capable of producing some very healthy capital gains. This strategy seeks to take advantage of the interest rate/bond price relationship to generate a capital gains profit. The idea is to load up on bond funds during periods when interest rates are high and are expected to fall. As rates move down, bond prices will react and fund unit values will rise. Holdings are reduced when rates appear to be bottoming out in order to lock in the profits. Experienced investors employing this strategy seek out bond funds where the managers have overweighted their portfolios with long-term issues or find a pure long-term bond fund like Altamira Bond. These are the funds that will do best in a falling interest rate environment. Obviously, this is a higher-risk strategy—if you guess wrong and rates rise, you'll be looking at some heavy losses in your portfolio. If that happens, don't panic and sell. Rates will inevitably come back down. They always do.

THE STEADY INCOME PLAN. One of the strengths of fixed-income funds is their ability to generate a regular income stream for investors. This makes them especially useful for people who have reached retirement age and are planning to live on their investment income. If this is how you want to use your fixed-income portfolio, find out how often the funds you're considering make distributions. Some people prefer funds that offer monthly payments, to ensure a regular cash flow. Others are content with quarterly distributions. If a fund's distributions are less frequent (only once or twice a year), it won't be suitable for steady income.

THE TAX-ADVANTAGED INCOME TACTIC. Some fixed-income funds can be used to generate tax-advantaged income. This means your payments will be taxed at a lower-than-normal rate. Dividend income funds are a good choice here because a portion of the money they distribute to unitholders qualifies for the dividend tax credit. High-income balanced funds provide a degree of tax sheltering, as some of their distributions are treated as "return of capital," which means no tax is payable in the year the money is received. To take advantage of these opportunities, make sure you keep your fund units outside a registered plan and choose funds that invest mainly in securities that receive tax breaks.

THE CAPITAL PROTECTION STRATEGY. If safety is one of your prime concerns, fixed-income funds can be used effectively to protect your capital from loss. In this case, you'll want to focus on the lowest-risk types of fixed-income funds. Mortgage funds and short-term bond funds are the most suitable for this type of portfolio.

THE CURRENCY HEDGE. Finally, fixed-income funds can be used to give your mutual fund portfolio some protection against possible future declines in the value of the Canadian dollar. Unfortunately, our currency has a history of being highly volatile. In the past decade, the loonie has declined by more than 30 percent against the U.S. dollar—far too much for the comfort of any conservative investor. By adding foreign bond funds to your portfolio, you can reduce this risk to some extent by introducing securities denominated in some of the world's strongest currencies into your mix. But be careful: if the Canadian dollar should turn around and start to rise sharply in value against other currencies, especially the U.S. dollar, it will have a negative effect on the value of these funds. Currency volatility cuts both ways. We suggest using these funds as a long-term hedge against continued devaluation in our currency, especially if you require significant amounts of U.S. dollars now or in the future.

Every mutual fund portfolio should hold some fixed-income funds as part of its total asset mix. As a general rule, no less than 25 percent of your holdings should be in these funds, with a maximum of 75 percent for older people who are looking mainly for steady income and safety. We recommend that younger people who are just getting into fund investing begin with more conservative fixed-income funds. Psychology plays a big role in investing success; if you start with a high-risk fund and lose money, you could be put off fund investing for life. It's better to choose a low-risk fund at the outset. As it starts to show gains, your confidence level will increase and you can move into other areas.

## SUMMARY

- Fixed-income funds should be a part of every portfolio, but there are different types of funds for different needs.

- There are two types of foreign bond funds, one of which is fully eligible for RRSPs.
- Bond funds can generate some handsome capital gains, if used correctly.
- High-income balanced funds can be used to generate above-average cash flow, but the risk level is greater.
- Mortgage funds and short-term bond funds are the least risky types of fixed-income funds.
- Some fixed-income funds offer excellent tax advantages when held outside a registered plan.

## FUND FACTS

**THE NAME GAME.** The AGF Dividend Fund is not a true dividend fund at all. Its distributions are virtually non-existent and dividend income is not a priority for the managers. This is really a simple blue-chip equity fund with a misleading name.

**VITAL INFORMATION.** The *Mutual Funds Update* newsletter publishes an annual survey in March of each year on the yield and tax effectiveness of dividend income and high-income balanced funds. This information is not available anywhere else. To subscribe, go to **www.gordonpape.com**.

**THE DIVIDEND TAX CREDIT.** The dividend tax credit is intended to reduce the effect of double taxation by recognizing that corporate dividends are distributed to shareholders out of after-tax profits. This means a company has already paid tax once on the earnings. In theory, therefore, dividends should be received tax-free, but governments aren't that generous. The dividend tax credit is an exercise in compromise. To calculate the credit to which you're entitled, you must first "gross up" the actual dividend you receive by multiplying the amount by 125 percent. You then multiply that number by 13.33 percent. The amount of the credit is deducted directly from your federal tax payable. Note that the dividend tax credit will apply only to dividends your fund receives from taxable Canadian corporations. Dividends from foreign companies aren't eligible.

**SAFETY FIRST!** Here's how fixed-income funds rank on a safety scale, moving from the least amount of risk to the highest. Note that these ratings are generalizations. The style of individual portfolio managers will play a major role in the risk level of any fund.

| LOW-RISK | MEDIUM-RISK | HIGH-RISK |
|---|---|---|
| Mortgage Funds | Canadian Bond Funds | High-Yield Bond Funds |
| Short-Term Bond Funds | Foreign Bond Funds | High-Income Balanced Funds |
| | Dividend Income Funds | |

# Investing in Equity Funds

*Money market and fixed-income funds are valuable additions to any mutual fund portfolio, but the real action is in equity funds. This is where you can score the biggest gains—or suffer the worst losses if you choose poorly and the market moves against you. That's why you need to be extremely careful when you choose equity funds. You have to make sure you know exactly what you're buying and what risks are involved in the process. That's what this chapter is about.*

There is a broad range of equity funds to choose from. They fall into several categories, some of which may overlap. What follows is a rundown of the key ones. As you go through the list, keep in mind that a single fund may fit into more than one category; an international fund may specialize in small-cap stocks, for example.

**SINGLE-COUNTRY FUNDS.** These funds invest primarily, although not necessarily entirely, in shares from a single country. Canadian equity funds, by far the most common type of stock fund offered in this country, fall into this group. U.S. equity funds also fit in here. There are also about two dozen Japan funds, a Germany fund, two India funds, and some China funds, although most of these "China" entries can invest in Hong Kong and have the bulk of their assets in that market. No other single-country funds are offered directly here, although Canadian investors can buy a wide range of closed-end single country funds that trade on the New York Stock Exchange.

**REGIONAL FUNDS.** These funds invest in shares of companies located within a particular geographic region. Included in this group are European funds, Far

East funds, North American funds, and Latin American funds. The manager of a regional fund usually has the freedom to acquire stocks from any country in the designated area for the fund's portfolio. But sometimes there are restrictions. For example, several Far East funds specifically exclude Japanese stocks. The most obvious reason for this is that Japan is a developed country while the other Far East markets represent countries that are not. This distinction creates a conflict in the fund's investment approach. We believe the exclusion has more to do with marketing; many fund companies offer both a Far East fund and a Japan fund, and want to maintain a clear differentiation between the two.

**INTERNATIONAL AND GLOBAL FUNDS.** For the managers of these funds, the world (or most of it anyway) is their oyster. They have the freedom to invest wherever they want for the most part, and can stay completely away from countries they think are overpriced or are potential trouble spots. But these funds involve some subtle details you need to be aware of. For example, there is a technical distinction between the terms "international fund" and "global fund." An international fund will not invest in its home country or continent, whereas a global fund will. You may also find restrictions in the investment policies of different funds. The Templeton organization offers a good illustration here. The Templeton Growth Fund may invest anywhere in the world while the Templeton International Stock Fund excludes North American shares from its portfolio.

As a general rule, a well-managed global fund is the lowest-risk type of equity fund you can buy.

**LARGE-CAP FUNDS.** These funds invest mainly in the shares of large corporations. The theory is that these blue-chip stocks are more stable, so this type of fund represents less risk to an investor. This may be true to a degree, but the reality is that if the market goes into a dive, these stocks will too. There is a specific fund category devoted to domestic versions of these funds called Canadian Large-Cap Equity.

**SMALL-TO-MID-CAP FUNDS.** At the other end of the spectrum, these funds focus on shares in smaller companies deemed to have above-average growth potential. The definition of a small-cap stock differs from one country to another, so the portfolio makeup can differ between funds. Canadian investors can select from a wide range of small-cap stocks, some of which concentrate on this country, some of which invest mainly in U.S. companies, and some of which are international in scope. These funds are generally regarded as higher risk than those specializing in large-cap issues, but the rewards can be attractive. There are two official categories for such funds: Canadian Small-to-Mid-Cap Equity and U.S. Small-to-Mid-Cap Equity. International and global small-cap funds are lumped in with the broader Global Equity and International Equity categories.

**VENTURE CAPITAL FUNDS.** These funds invest primarily in young companies usually not listed on any stock exchange. The companies may be start-up operations or firms in need of capital to expand their business. This type of fund is considered extremely high risk, and investors potentially face heavy losses. As a result, most the venture capital activity is centred on labour-sponsored funds, which offer significant tax breaks as investment incentive (see the section on labour-sponsored funds).

**SECTOR FUNDS.** These funds invest in a specific area of the economy. For many years, the only sector funds available in Canada were in the natural resource and precious metals sectors. But that changed in the 1990s with the launch of a wide range of sector funds in such fields as health care, telecommunications, financial services, and technology. Some of these funds have experienced periods of tremendous growth, but they can be highly volatile as anyone who has invested in a technology fund can testify. Remember, when a particular sector is hot—as technology stocks were in 1998–99—the fund will do well; when the sector goes out of favour, unit values will fall, sometimes dramatically.

**INDEX FUNDS.** These are passive funds, designed to track the performance of a specific stock index, such as the TSE 300. They're designed for investors who want some exposure to the stock market, but don't want to incur a lot of risk. Their track record in Canada is mediocre at best.

**DIVIDEND INCOME FUNDS.** We've included these funds again here (a description also appears in the section on fixed-income funds, p. 107) because some dividend funds are really that in name only. Their portfolio composition actually makes them something else—balanced funds in some cases and large-cap funds in others. You'll have to look closely at the securities in the portfolio to determine where any one specific fund fits.

## Equity Fund Strategies

In mid-2000, there were more than 2,400 equity funds of various types available to Canadian investors. The selection process can be a difficult one, then, unless you have a sound strategy in place and stick to it. Here are some guidelines for helping you choose winning equity funds:

**CONTROL YOUR RISK.** Since equity funds represent the highest-risk element in any mutual fund portfolio, it's essential to manage that risk effectively. This can be done in several ways:

- *Decide on an acceptable percentage of equity fund holdings.* Conservative investors can reduce their risk in the equity area by limiting these funds to 25 to 30 percent of the total portfolio. (You can, of course, eliminate them entirely, but in doing so you lose all growth potential.) More aggressive investors may want to have their entire portfolio in equity funds, although that's not an approach we recommend. The general rule is that the greater the total percentage of equity funds you own, the higher the risk factor in your mutual fund portfolio.

- *Select fund types that best fit your philosophy.* You can limit your equity fund risk by concentrating on index funds and large-cap funds. Both will experience losses when markets drop, but those losses are likely to be less severe than with other types of funds. The highest-risk equity categories are small-cap, venture capital, emerging markets, and sector funds.
- *Diversify geographically.* If you choose only equity funds that focus on a single market (e.g., Canada), your portfolio will be more vulnerable (and therefore higher risk) than if it's well diversified internationally. Adding some broadly based global funds to your mix will enhance stability.
- *Diversify by style.* As a general rule, funds using a value approach to stock selection are less risky than those employing a growth style. A well-diversified portfolio will have room for both types of funds.

INVEST IN QUALITY. There are a lot of equity funds out there, but only a few have demonstrated the rare combination of top-quality management and first-rate long-term performance. These funds may not always hold their preeminent positions, of course, but history indicates that they'll stay at or near the top for at least a decade.

USE SPECIAL CAUTION WITH RRSPS. It's all right to include equity funds in your RRSP if that's the only investment portfolio you have. But if you have enough investment money to build a non-registered portfolio as well, keep the equity funds outside your retirement plan. This will reduce your RRSP's risk factor and allow you the full benefit of the tax advantages associated with equity funds: the dividend tax credit and the reduced tax rate on capital gains.

If you do buy equity funds for your RRSP, stick with the more conservative types; don't speculate with your retirement savings. Small-cap funds, for example, really aren't appropriate for RRSPs because of the risk involved.

SPREAD YOUR MONEY AROUND. Don't invest all the cash you've earmarked for equity funds into a single fund or even into a single company, no matter how stellar its reputation—overconcentration can lead to trouble. In the 1980s, for example, Mackenzie Financial's Industrial funds were the darlings of the industry. Investors were attracted by their good returns, and brokers loved to sell them because of the excellent commissions and special incentives (like exotic trips) they offered. But in the 1990s, they ran into trouble when the managers overcommitted all the equity portfolios to resource stocks. Those funds languished and investors complained bitterly. Mackenzie learned an important lesson from the situation; the company now offers four distinct fund groups, each with its own separate managerial team. We suggest you spread your equity fund investments among three good fund companies, although you may choose to use one company for your core holdings.

One last comment on equity funds: don't rush out and put a lot of money in them after an exceptionally good year. Chances are that after a big run, the markets will be due for a correction. Many people decided to get into equity funds for the first time after the spectacular success they enjoyed in 1998 through to 2000, when some funds more than doubled in value. Those same investors then watched in dismay as stock markets in most parts of the world hit rough waters in the early spring of 2000, starting a decline that continued well into 2001, causing most fund unit values to fall —in some cases dramatically.

The best approach to equity funds is to select carefully and take a long-range view. If the fund is well managed, it will enjoy some very good years along the way, and you'll profit accordingly. An average annual return of 10 to 12 percent over time is excellent; if you expect more, you are being unrealistic.

## SUMMARY

- Equity funds offer the greatest potential for large gains in the mutual funds world—but they can lose money too.
- Some sector funds have had spectacular gains, but they are vulnerable to big losses as well, as investors in tech funds have discovered.
- You can minimize your equity fund risk by diversifying globally and carefully monitoring the total percentage of stock funds in your portfolio.
- Value funds are inherently less risky than growth funds.
- An equity fund that produces an average annual return of 10 to 12 percent over the long term is doing very well.

## FUND FACTS

ADDING FOREIGN CONTENT. Many Canadian equity funds take advantage of the government's foreign content rules and hold up to 30 percent of their portfolio in U.S. and international equities. These holdings do not count against your personal foreign content limit if your fund units are in an RRSP or other registered plan. So if you want to increase the foreign holdings in a retirement plan, choose Canadian funds that make maximum use of this provision.

**EMERGING MARKETS FUNDS.** These funds are actually a sub-group of international funds. They focus on developing economies throughout the world, seeking to benefit from the higher growth potential. These funds have proven extremely volatile, with big swings in both directions. They're only for investors who are prepared to accept above-average risk.

**IUNITS.** The iUnits that trade on the Toronto Stock Exchange (TSE) provide a low-cost alternative to index funds. The original iUnits replicate shares in a basket of the stocks that make up the S&P/TSE 60 index, a blue-chip index. They trade under the symbol XIU. There are also several specialized iUnits, including technology index units (XIT), mid-cap stock units (XMD), energy units (XEG), and S&P/TSE Capped 60 Index units (XIC). All of these can be purchased through brokers, just like stocks. You'll pay a sales commission, but the annual management fee is lower than you'll find in a typical index fund, so your return will more closely mirror how the index itself performs.

# Index Funds

*There is no question that many actively managed funds fail to consistently beat their benchmark indexes. As a result, it's no surprise that a growing number of investors are using index-based securities in their portfolios. In some cases, they have chosen to go exclusively with indexing.*

There is a lot to be said in favour of indexing. You know (or you are at least fairly certain) that these securities will come close to matching the performance of their benchmark, whatever that may be. Additionally, index-based securities have a much lower annual cost than actively managed mutual funds (funds where the manager picks individual stocks or bonds).

The range of index-based products has expanded considerably in recent years.* Exchange-traded funds (ETFs) have become immensely popular in the U.S., and many new ones have been launched in Canada. The most popular of these funds are the i60 units, which track the S&P/TSE 60 Index. However, you can also buy Canadian ETFs that track specific market sectors, as well as bond indexes.

In the U.S., the range of ETFs is even broader. You can buy ETFs based on the performance of major markets like the S&P and the Dow. There are also ETFs that track specific sectors of the U.S. economy, ETFs based on various sub-indexes, and ETFs grounded in foreign stock markets (these funds are known as iShares).

The number of index mutual funds has also expanded, although they don't offer the range and diversity available through ETFs. Most index funds sold in Canada are based on one of the main TSE indexes and on the S&P 500, although there are some that track other U.S. indexes like the Wilshire 5000 and the Nasdaq Composite.

*We must disclose here that co-author Eric Kirzner is one of the creators of the FPX indexes published in the *National Post* and used by Talvest TVX as the base of their funds. Consequently, we will not discuss those specific funds in this chapter.

As a general rule, we recommend using ETFs instead of index funds in most situations. That's because they have a very low management expense ratio (MER) in comparison with index funds. For example, i60s have an MER of 0.17 percent as opposed to MERs of 0.75 percent to 1 percent for most Canadian index funds. Over several years, this difference will translate into a lot of extra money in your pocket. One caveat: you will have to buy ETFs through a broker and pay a commission for them; many index funds are no-load. So if you are planning to hold the units only for a short time, a no-load index fund may be the better choice. Alternately, some fund companies now offer special index units with very low MERs. For instance, you can buy "e" units of the TD Canadian Index Fund with an MER of only 0.31 percent. These units are sold only over the Internet.

Before you plunge into index funds and/or ETFs, however, there are some factors you should consider. One is that index funds tend to do relatively better in rising markets than in ones that are falling. Another is that, historically, Canadian index funds have not performed as well in relation to their U.S. counterparts.

Let's look at the bull/bear market issue first. When the stock markets were skyrocketing in the late 1990s, index funds looked very impressive. Not only were they were cheaper than other funds, but they were beating the pants off the majority of active managers. Why pay sales commissions and high MERs for inferior performance? Just buy the indexes—and many people did. But the bear market of 2000–01 revealed the other side of that coin. As the markets tumbled, index funds went right along for the ride. Meanwhile, many active managers—particularly those employing a value style—significantly outperformed both the indexes and the corresponding funds.

A detailed analysis of index funds shows that, over time, Canadian index funds have tended to be slightly below-average performers. Over the decade to April 30, 2001, for example, the TD Canadian Index Fund generated an average annual return of 10 percent, half a point below the average for the Canadian Equity category. The BMO Equity Index Fund did even worse, averaging 9.6 percent, while the Great-West Life Equity Index Fund, which has an extremely high MER, came in at just 8.4 percent.

Over the short term, the weaknesses of Canadian index funds in bear market situations have become glaringly apparent. The average Canadian equity fund lost 0.9 percent in the year to April 30, 2001. The TD Canadian Index Fund dropped 13.3 percent, the BMO fund lost 12.8 percent, the Royal Canadian Index Fund dropped 12.2 percent, and the CIBC Canadian Index Fund lost 14.8 percent. All were hit hard by the disproportionate weighting of Nortel Networks in the TSE indexes. These kinds of losses highlight one of the dangers in using indexing in a relatively small market like Canada's.

It's also important to recognize that there is a significant difference in the performance between funds, even when they are based on the same index. For example, the CIBC Canadian Index Fund dropped 14.8 percent over the year ending April 30, 2001. The Scotia Canadian Stock Index Fund fell 10.7 percent. That's a difference of more than four percentage points. CIBC claims the reason for this difference is that their fund had a full Nortel weighting throughout the year. "We didn't cheat going up, and we didn't cheat when Nortel went down," a spokesman said. So as you can see, each index fund may operate somewhat differently, thereby producing divergent results.

U.S. index funds have done much better by comparison over the long haul, and some even managed to outperform the averages during the bear market. The main reason for their superior results is that U.S. indexes do not become overweighted toward one or two stocks the way the TSE is prone to do. However, U.S. indexes can become overweighted toward a single sector, as Nasdaq is with technology.

Results also vary tremendously depending on which U.S. index is used. Any funds based on Nasdaq were obviously clobbered in the past year. But it may come as a surprise that there was a big difference between S&P 500–based funds and those that use the Dow 30 Industrials as a reference point. All the S&P funds were losers through the bear market, to varying degrees. But funds based on the Dow Jones Industrial Average made money in the year to April 30, 2001. The National Bank American Index RSP Fund rose 3.7 percent during the period in question while the TD Dow Jones Average Index Fund gained 4.9 percent (again, note the difference in return even though both funds track the same index).

There's another wrinkle to U.S. index funds that may catch many people by surprise: the RRSP versions from some companies are producing much different results from the non-registered funds. For example, the TD U.S. Index Fund, based on the S&P 500, recorded a loss of 10.4 percent for the year to April 30, 2001. The TD U.S. RSP Index Fund, also based on the S&P, lost 15.2 percent. That's a difference of almost five percentage points between two funds tracking the same index and run by the same company. How can this be possible? Currency exchange, says TD. The U.S. Index Fund has a portfolio of securities denominated in U.S. dollars. When the loonie tumbled against the greenback, the currency gain helped to offset the index losses. The RSP Index Fund is a clone that invests in future contracts tracking the parent U.S. Index Fund. Those contracts are all in Canadian dollars, so there are no currency exchange gains or losses. Thus the RSP Fund more accurately reflects the performance of the S&P 500—but that didn't help investors over the past year. The Royal U.S. Index Fund (–10.4 percent) and the Royal U.S. RSP Index Fund (–15.2 percent) also produced widely varying results, for similar reasons.

So what to make out of all of this? Here are some conclusions:

1. Canadian index funds have not proven they can outperform actively managed funds over the long haul. If you must use them, they should comprise only a small percentage of your portfolio.

2. U.S. index funds are better bets, but performance numbers vary considerably, even among funds based on the same index. Look for the funds with the best longer-term consistency or consider using exchange-traded funds like SPDRs (S&P 500) or DIAMONDS (Dow Industrials).

3. Diversify your U.S. index fund holdings. Include one Dow fund, one S&P fund and, if you're feeling adventurous, a Nasdaq fund.

4. Before you invest in a U.S. RRSP index fund, find out exactly how it differs from the non-registered fund in the same family (if there is one) and see which fund has done better over the longer haul. You don't have to buy the RRSP version for your registered plan if you have foreign content room available.

## SUMMARY

- Index funds and ETFs have become very popular in recent years.
- As a general rule, we recommend ETFs over index funds.
- Both index funds and ETFs will do relatively better under rising market conditions.
- Over time, Canadian index funds have been below-average performers. U.S. index funds have done better.

## FUND FACTS

AN ETF FUND. A new fund, Spectrum Tactonics, invests exclusively in ETFs. It was created in early 2001, and invests in ETFs traded in both Toronto and New York.

# Sector Funds

*A decade ago, sector funds were almost unknown in Canada. There were a few natural resource funds, even fewer precious metals funds, and that was pretty well it. Today, hundreds of sector funds are competing for your investment dollars. The question is, should you heed their siren call or ignore them altogether?*

Sector funds specialize in one area of the economy. All the stocks in the portfolio will be from companies operating within that sector, although sometimes the parameters can be rather loosely defined. You can now buy funds that specialize in technology, health sciences, financial services, real estate, consumer products, energy, and more. There are sub-sets of sector funds as well. For example, you will find technology funds that target specific industries like Internet companies, e-commerce, telecommunications, and biotechnology.

Sector funds have been big business in the U.S. for years, but it took the technology surge of the mid-to-late 1990s to bring the phenomenon to Canada in a major way. When Canadian investors saw the huge gains being scored by these stocks and the U.S. funds that specialized in them, they wanted to get in on the action. The fund companies were only too happy to oblige. Today, many of these funds have hundreds of millions of dollars in their coffers and one, Investors Global Science & Technology, actually topped the $1 billion mark despite getting off to a weak start after entering the field relatively late in October 1998.

As of the first half of 2001, Globefund listed 253 entries in the Global Science & Technology category and another 133 in the Specialty category, which is largely made up of sector funds. As well, there were 58 natural resource funds, 20 precious metals funds, and 17 real estate funds, bringing the total to 481. That's a lot of choice for Canadians.

As a result of this boom, many people now hold sector funds in their accounts. The question you need to ask yourself is: Should I be doing this? The answer in many, perhaps most, cases is: No!

In order to understand our concern about sector funds, you'll need a bit of background. History has shown us that while macro economies can experience ups and downs, the broad impact of such movements tends to be diluted. However, specific economic sectors may experience huge boom periods that are inevitably followed by a collapse.

Those marked highs and lows have been one of the problems with resource funds for years. Because the stocks they invest in (oil and gas, mining, and forestry) are cyclical in nature, resource funds as a group follow a similar pattern. Consequently, investors will experience times when their funds are doing extremely well and other periods when they record double-digit losses year after year. The long-term effect for the buy-and-hold investor is mediocre performance. Over the decade to April 30, 2001, the average Canadian natural resource fund returned 8.2 percent annually, according to figures published in *The Globe and Mail*. The average precious metals fund fared even worse, with an annual gain of just 4.3 percent. By comparison, the average broadly diversified Canadian equity fund, which from time to time may have held resource and precious metals stocks, gained 10.5 percent annually.

When the technology boom took flight, many people opined that tech stocks and funds would not be subject to these boom and bust cycles. Technology, the reasoning went, is the key to the future, and tech products would be in high demand for years. The collapse of 2000–01 gave lie to that myth. Science and technology funds that had enjoyed double- and even triple-digit annual gains in the late 1990s fell like rocks. None of these funds have been around long enough to have a 10-year track record, but our guess is that by the time they achieve the decade milestone, very few will outperform the average U.S. equity fund over the same period (we use the U.S. as the benchmark here because most technology funds are top-heavy in American stocks).

Our position on sector funds is that they are not useful buy-and-hold choices. They are extremely volatile, and we have yet to see evidence that any sector can outperform an average broadly based equity fund or even an index fund over the long haul.

These funds are better treated in the same way as stocks, which is why we have dubbed them "opportunity funds." They are best suited for active traders who will use a buy low and sell high approach, monitor the funds and the underlying sectors carefully, and take profits when appropriate. If you are comfortable running your fund portfolio (or a portion of it) in that way, then sector funds may be of some interest to you. But if you're like most Canadians, you do a thorough review of your holdings only once or twice a year, if that. In this case, we recommend leaving sector funds out of the equation. You're better off staying with funds that offer broad market diversification and let the professional managers make the calls on which sectors to move into and out of, and when.

## SUMMARY

- Sector funds specialize in a single area of the economy.
- Risk is much higher with sector funds than with more broadly based funds.
- Sector funds should be treated like stocks: buy when they are cheap and take profits after they run up.

## FUND FACTS

**POOR PERFORMER.** Precious metals funds are the worst-performing type of sector fund over the long haul. For the decade to June 30, 2001, the average fund in this category managed an annual gain of just 4.1 percent.

# Segregated Funds

*Life insurance companies have their own version of mutual funds, which are generically known as "egregated funds." It's not exactly an inspiring term—certainly no marketing guru thought it up. But just because the name is unattractive doesn't mean you should overlook these vehicles. They offer some unique features, albeit at a price.*

Segregated funds (so-called because the assets are held separately, or segregated, from those of the insurance company) differ from their mutual fund cousins in several ways. They offer advantages not available with other funds, but they have disadvantages as well. Let's focus on the advantages first. Here are three unique aspects to segregated funds, or seg funds, as they are commonly called:

GUARANTEES. With an ordinary mutual fund, your investment is totally at risk. Mutual funds are not protected by deposit insurance, and fund managers take pains to point out that a strong past performance record is no guarantee of future results. If a fund makes poor investments, the value of the assets it holds will decline and so will the value of your units. But with segregated funds, you are ensured a degree of protection. Some insurance companies guarantee that when the investment contract matures (normally at 10 years or at death), you or your estate will receive no less than 75 percent of the total amount you've invested in the fund over the years. Other companies looking for a competitive edge offer a guarantee equal to 100 percent of your invested cash. That's a no-loss guarantee, even if the stock market goes through the floor. Of course, if the investment climate ever got that bad, you'd have to wonder if the company would still be around to honour their guarantee. Bankruptcies in the insurance industry are not unknown.

CREDITOR PROTECTION. If a close family member is named as the beneficiary, segregated funds offer a degree of protection for your investments in the event you run into financial problems and have to declare bankruptcy. This protection is not absolute and may not apply in some cases, but recent court rulings have tended to uphold it. If creditor protection is important to you, get legal advice.

ESTATE PLANNING. Assets in a segregated fund pass directly to the beneficiary if you die. This means they avoid probate fees, which happen to be on the rise in some provinces. Also, assets in segregated funds may receive favourable tax treatment if the investment is being made as part of a life insurance contract. In this situation, no capital gains tax is payable on the profits when you die. Your beneficiary inherits the money tax-free, as part of the life insurance proceeds.

Those are pluses you'll enjoy if you choose seg funds. Before you get too excited, however, consider the disadvantages:

LACK OF FLEXIBILITY. Because these funds are usually used as a method of saving for an insurance or retirement annuity contract, investing in them can sometimes mean a lack of flexibility or some kind of penalty if you want to cash out early. It will depend entirely on the company; many will allow you to cash your units at any time, just as you would with a regular mutual fund. Policies vary from one firm to another, so make appropriate inquiries.

FORCED CONTRIBUTIONS. Some segregated funds can be purchased only through an investment contract with the insurance company that requires you put in a certain amount of money each month ("minimum premium" is the insurance terminology). A minimum monthly premium of $50 is typical unless you're prepared to invest at least $1,000 up front. In some cases, these premiums may be waived in the event you are disabled.

HIGH COMMISSIONS. Sales commissions for segregated funds can sometimes be high and, unlike commissions for ordinary funds, they are usually non-negotiable. Rates will vary from one company to another.

HIGH MANAGEMENT FEES. Some segregated funds are assessed unconscionably high management fees that end up reducing investor returns. In some cases, these fees are totally out of line with the industry in general. But note that this criticism doesn't apply to all insurance companies. Several have kept their fees at reasonable levels, but you'll have to search those firms out. It should also be noted that in some cases, the management expense ratio (MER) is high because the funds themselves are quite small. Since some expenses are fixed, a smaller fund will be charged a higher amount in percentage terms. For example, a $500,000 expenditure on a computer system will have a bigger proportionate impact on a $10 million fund than on one with $500 million in assets.

## A Changing Marketplace

Segregated funds went through an enormous growth spurt in the late 1990s, doubling their assets under management in about three years. This growth took place for two reasons:

1. *A new fund is born.* Manulife managed to put a seg fund wrapper on well-known mutual funds and sell them under the Guaranteed Investment Funds (GIF) label.

2. *Financial advisors and industry companies get aggressive.* As the 100 percent guarantee caught on in the industry, new seg funds were created that carried much more risk than these funds traditionally had in the past. Investors were told they could play the hot Nasdaq without risk to their money; if the bottom fell out (which it subsequently did), their original investment would be protected by the death and maturity guarantees. Furthermore, several companies introduced "reset" options, allowing investors to lock in gains and re-start the 10-year maturity clock.

Industry regulators watched the rapid growth of these funds with dismay. Clearly the insurance companies were taking on enormous risk and could find themselves in serious financial difficulty in the event of a prolonged stock market downturn. The regulators acted, imposing new capital reserve requirements on the insurers to provide extra coverage for their guarantees. This means that more capital has to be tied up and is therefore not available to the insurance companies for investment purposes.

The result has been turmoil in the industry. Some companies have closed their seg funds entirely. Others are raising fees to cover the new costs involved. Still others are reducing the guarantees to 75 percent. In all cases, the ultra-aggressive approach of the 1990s is gone. This means that if you invest in a seg fund today, you are entering a marketplace in a state of flux. You may find that your management fees escalate in the future, your fund is merged into another one for cost efficiency, the investment approach changes, or the company decides to withdraw from the seg fund business entirely.

In short, this is a time to be careful. If you do sign a seg fund contract, make sure that such key provisions as guarantees and reset features are locked in and not subject to unilateral change by the company. Here are a few other key points to keep in mind:

- *Know your funds.* Although the funds offered directly by life insurance companies are segregated funds, those available through subsidiary or affiliated companies may not be. In such cases, you will not receive the guarantees associated with segregated funds. Consequently, you may be offered a fund that, at first glance, appears to be a segregated fund because it bears the name of an insurance company. On closer examination, however, you may find it's just an ordinary mutual fund offered by a subsidiary of a life insurance firm.

An example here is Standard Life. The company's Ideal funds are all segregated and provide the benefits we have described above. However, the firm also offers Standard Life Mutual Funds. These funds are not segregated and carry none of the guarantees you might expect. If you invest with Standard Life, make sure you understand the distinction.

- *Clones and returns.* Some segregated funds, such as the Manulife GIFs, are clones of well-known mutual funds. However, this doesn't mean their returns will be the same. As a general rule, returns for the segregated version will be lower due to the cost of the insurance guarantee, which is added to the fund's MER. For example, over the year to April 30, 2001, the C.I. Harbour Fund posted a gain of 18 percent. The Manulife GIF version of the same fund gained 16.9 percent, more than one percentage point less. In essence, the difference is what the insurance premium for the guarantee is costing you.

## Tips for Investing in Segregated Funds

If you think you would like to take advantage of the options seg funds offer, here are some tips for making a sound investment:

DECIDE IF THE MATURITY GUARANTEE IS WORTH THE EXTRA MONEY. The chance of a well-diversified, conservatively managed equity fund losing money over a 10-year period is small. The chance of a bond or balanced fund losing money is even less. We don't believe maturity guarantees are needed at all, but we certainly cannot recommend paying high fees to insure a bond or balanced fund.

CONSIDER THE IMPORTANCE OF THE DEATH GUARANTEE. For older investors or those in uncertain health, the death guarantee could be the most attractive feature of a seg fund, especially if it offers 100 percent protection for your capital. This guarantee enables you to remain fully invested throughout your life, without having to retreat into low-paying, ultra-conservative securities for fear of jeopardizing the value of your estate.

REVIEW THE RESET FEATURE. As we have explained, this feature allows you to reset the maturity and death benefit guarantees. Not all companies offer it, so you may have to shop around.

The reset option kicks in if the fund increases in value. For example, suppose you invest $100,000 and six months later your fund is up 10 percent. Your investment is now worth $110,000, but your guarantee is for only $100,000. The reset privilege allows you to reset your maturity guarantee and death benefit to the new, higher value. You lock in your profit and, in the worst-case scenario, you—or your estate in the event of your death—will receive a minimum of $110,000 at maturity. Keep in mind that every time you use the reset option, you restart the clock. This means the maturity date is reset as well, to 10 years from the time of the reset. If you made your investment on January 1, 2002, your original maturity date would be January 1, 2012. But if you exercised your reset option on January 1, 2003, your new maturity date would be January 1, 2013.

We've commented that it is highly unlikely a maturity benefit would ever be exercised. However, the death benefit is something else again, and here the reset privilege has real value and represents a real potential cost to the insurance company—so much, in fact, that Manulife Financial had to rethink the reset privileges on its original line of GIFs. The new version of GIFs (called GIF Encore or GIF II) possess reset options that have been dramatically altered, making them automatic when tied to the death benefit. While this isn't a bad thing, it does show how important it is for you to read all of the fine print in your segregated fund contract before buying.

The bottom line: you must understand that if you buy into seg funds, you'll pay a premium price in the form of higher management fees. You may consider the cost worth the added benefits, but be sure you look at all the options carefully before you act. A traditional insurance company seg fund will often be less expensive and will offer performance potential that's every bit as good as the clones being offered by Manulife and others. For more information, check the section on the Top 10 Seg Fund Families later in the book.

## SUMMARY

- Segregated funds offer some unique advantages, such as a guarantee you won't lose any money. This guarantee comes with a price, however.
- High sales commissions and management fees are among the drawbacks to buying these funds in some cases.
- The seg fund industry is currently in a state of flux because of new regulations. Make sure you understand the full impact of the new rules before you invest.
- It is highly unlikely that a maturity guarantee will ever be needed. But death guarantees can be important in certain situations.
- Some companies offer a reset option for their funds, which can be useful in some circumstances.

# FUND FACTS

**NO PROFIT GUARANTEE.** A guarantee may look attractive at first glance, but remember that even with a 100 percent guarantee, you'll receive no return on your investment if it has to be invoked. You'll get back your original stake, but your money won't have earned anything during the years it was invested with the company. Still, many people like the idea of placing a limit on their potential losses, especially if they're investing in equity funds.

**TAX WARNING.** Not all segregated fund investments are made within life insurance contracts. You may be using segregated funds to build capital for an annuity when you retire, for example. In this case, any capital gains would be taxed in the normal way if you die before converting to an annuity.

**HIGH FEES.** Here are some examples of segregated funds charging management fees we consider excessive:

| FUND | MER* |
|---|---|
| Industrial-Alliance Mortgage Fund | 2.50% |
| Manulife AGF Canadian Bond GIF | 2.55% |
| Great-West Life Equity Index (NL) | 2.41% |
| Industrial-Alliance Money Market Fund | 2.50% |
| Zurich Scudder Global Fund | 3.63% |

*As reported in *The Globe and Mail*, May 17, 2001

# Closed-End Funds

*Just when you think you know everything about mutual funds, someone comes along and does it a little differently. That's the case with closed-end funds. Think of them as a hybrid, a cross between a mutual fund and a stock. These funds can sometimes offer unexpected profits, so it's important to understand how they work and when to take advantage of them.*

Most of the mutual funds you'll encounter are structured as open-end funds. This means there is no limit on the number of units they can distribute. Whenever an investor wants to buy in, the fund simply issues new units from its treasury at the current net asset value (NAV).

Under this structure, issuing new units does not reduce the value of those currently outstanding (the technical name for that process is "dilution"). For example, suppose a fund has 100,000 units outstanding at an NAV of $10 each. Total assets under management are therefore $1 million. If someone buys 1,000 new units at $10 each, the fund ends up with an additional $10,000 in assets from the cash acquired in the sale (assuming no sales commissions are involved). The fund now has $1,010,000 in assets and 101,000 units outstanding. The NAV per unit remains unchanged at $10.

An open-end fund will also redeem your units at the current NAV, usually with minimal notice. Again, there is no impact on the NAV of other unitholders when this happens; the purchase process is simply reversed. For instance, if you wanted to redeem 500 units of the fund we used in the above example, you would notify the company through your sales representative. It would issue you a cheque for $5,000 (500 units multiplied by the current $10 NAV). The fund would be left with assets of $995,000 and a total of 99,500 units outstanding. The NAV holds at $10.

The only way the NAV changes in an open-end fund is if the value of the underlying assets changes. Suppose, for example, that the fund receives dividends of $30,000 from stocks it holds. Total assets of the fund therefore increase to $1,030,000. The 100,000 units outstanding now have a NAV of $10.30 each, a 3 percent gain. If the fund distributes those dividends to its unitholders by issuing cheques, then the net assets of the fund will again be worth $1,000,000, and the NAV returns to $10. In the meantime, you'll have received a dividend of 30 cents per unit to compensate for the drop.

The overwhelming majority of mutual funds sold in Canada are the open-end type. But you may occasionally be offered an opportunity to buy into a closed-end fund. These funds issue a limited number of units. When the issue is fully subscribed, the offer is closed. No more units are made available at that time, although there may be additional offerings in the future. This means that if you want to buy units in a closed-end fund once the initial offering period is over, you have to find someone willing to sell them to you. To facilitate this process, units in most closed-end funds are listed on a stock exchange, where they can be bought and sold more easily. You'll find several closed-end funds traded on the Toronto Stock Exchange (TSE). Examples of these funds include the BPI Global Opportunities Fund, the Canadian General Investments Fund, the First Australia Prime Income Fund, the New Altamira Value Fund, and the Central Fund.

Unlike open-end funds, the NAV is not the determining factor in the selling price of a closed-end fund's units (or shares). The selling price is set by the market, and the market often decides a closed-end fund should sell for less than its underlying NAV. When this happens, a closed-end fund is said to be trading at a discount. Many Canadian closed-end funds trade at a substantial discount to their NAV, occasionally over 30 percent and sometimes as high as 40 percent. In this situation, you are essentially buying a dollar's worth of assets for 60 or 70 cents.

In early June 2001, for example, the United Corporations Fund was trading at a discount to its NAV of 40.4 percent. The Economic Investment Trust was 34.8 percent below its NAV, the Canadian General Investments Fund was at a 34.2 percent discount, and the Central Fund of Canada was trading at 28.2 percent below its NAV.

The reasons for the tendency of closed-end funds to trade at a discount are complex, but what it really comes down to is that the market penalizes these shares for their lack of flexibility and liquidity.

The situation is different in the U.S., where closed-end mutual funds are quite popular, especially with internationally minded people who want a stake in countries that are difficult to invest in directly. Hot funds traded on the New York Stock Exchange can sometimes carry very substantial premiums if investors expect their assets to rise rapidly in value. So closed-end funds don't always trade at a discount. But if they move to a high premium for any reason, you should probably sell. Sooner or later, investors will decide it's not worthwhile to pay $1.25 for a dollar's worth of assets.

One important implication in all of this for Canadian investors is to be wary of buying a closed-end fund when it's initially offered unless there is some overwhelming reason to do so—if the fund guarantees it will buy back your units at not less than issue price or close to it, for example. Without such a guarantee (which is rare because it defeats one of the main advantages of a closed-end fund from the manager's perspective), the market value of the fund will usually drop once the issue is completed and shares start trading on a stock exchange. If you like the concept of the fund, you'll probably be able to buy units more cheaply at that time. In recent years, some closed-end funds attempted to break this cycle by offering sweeteners designed to keep their share price near or above the NAV. These initiatives have been moderately successful, in most cases keeping the discount to around 5 percent.

## Closed-End Fund Strategies

The key to profiting from closed-end funds in Canada is to remember that they will normally trade at a discount, and it's the depth of this discount that will offer the greatest opportunities. So be on the watch for potential profits when a discount becomes unrealistically large. There are several possible strategies you can employ when you're keeping your eye peeled for closed-end funds:

BARGAIN HUNTING. Here an investor sees that shares in the fund are trading at a low price relative to the fund's assets. For example, suppose the NAV of shares in the High Flyers closed-end fund is $10, but they're trading for only $6 on the TSE, a 40 percent discount. Bargain hunters may bid the price up to $7, reducing the discount to 30 percent. If you bought in at $6, you'd make a quick profit of almost 17 percent in this situation.

RANGE WATCHING. Many closed-end funds trade within a predictable range, say a 25 to 35 percent discount to the NAV. Astute investors keep track of the price movements and buy when shares are trading in the low end of the range. When the price moves back to the high end, they sell and wait for the cycle to repeat.

FUND WINDUP. When a closed-end fund is wound up, all outstanding shares are redeemed at the final NAV. Anyone who bought in at a discount stands to make a profit in this situation. There are two kinds of windups:

- *Maturity.* When a fund is launched, a date is set for its windup. The process is an orderly one and the trading price of shares will gradually rise (or fall) toward the NAV as the windup date approaches.
- *Forced.* Here, shareowners force the windup of the fund by special resolution. This can happen when shares consistently trade at a deep discount to the NAV. By forcing liquidation, the shareowners are able to recover the full asset value of their holdings. Forced liquidations are unpredictable and, as a result, can produce windfall profits for investors who buy in at low prices.

CONVERSION. A fourth way to realize quick profits from a closed-end fund is in the conversion to open-end status. This scenario has occurred more frequently in recent years as shareowners, unhappy with low stock exchange prices, approve special resolutions converting what was originally a closed-end fund to open-end status. This enables shareholders to redeem their units at the NAV, rather than being forced to sell them on a stock exchange at a discount.

One recent example of a conversion from a closed- to an open-end fund involved the Templeton Emerging Markets Appreciation Fund, which was merged into the open-end Templeton Emerging Markets Fund in September 2001. The closed-end version had been trading at a significant discount to the NAV (13.7 percent as of June 2001) so the merger enabled unitholders to realize full value for their positions.

## REITs

A special category of closed-end fund is the real estate investment trust (REIT). Here the rules of the game are somewhat different in that the fund's profits come mainly from tax-advantaged cash flow.

REITs have been popular in the U.S. for years, but only emerged in Canada over the past decade. They began to appear when several open-end real estate funds were forced to convert to closed-end status when the property market crash of the early 1990s produced a flood of redemption requests that could be satisfied only by selling off assets at fire-sale prices. To protect unitholders who wanted to hold, the funds became closed-end. This enabled investors who wanted out to sell their units on the TSE without forcing fund managers to put their properties up for sale under impossible market conditions.

Since that time, a number of new REITs have appeared, some of which specialize in specific types of property like hotels and long-term care facilities. However, most REITs invest in commercial properties like shopping malls, office buildings, and medical centres. Their main source of income is the rent they generate. Profits are distributed to unitholders and are partially tax-sheltered through the use of capital cost allowance (CCA).

REITs were slow to gain investor favour because of the bad memories that lingered from the real estate crash. As a result, they tend to trade at bargain prices relative to the tax-advantaged income they generate. For example, Riocan, the largest Canadian REIT, paid a total distribution of just over $1.07 a unit in the calendar year 2000. Of that, 55 percent was received on a tax-deferred basis (you pay no tax when the income is received, but your liability for tax on capital gains is increased when you sell your units). When the markets opened for business on January 2, 2000, Riocan's price was $8.65. If you bought then, you received a 12.4-percent income return on your money through 2000, a large chunk of which was not taxed. In retrospect, Riocan was a bargain.

To determine if a REIT is a bargain at current prices, find out what it is expected to pay out in the year ahead and how much of that is likely to be tax-deferred (a broker should be able to provide that information). Compare that number to the market price of the units and see what the yield is. Of course, REITs can also appreciate (or depreciate) in value, so you need to take that into account when you're making a decision. By June 2001, Riocan was trading in a range of $10.25 to $10.50. Those who bought back when it was at $8.65 not only enjoyed great cash flow but also a capital gain.

## RITs

Another type of closed-end fund is the royalty income trust (RIT). These funds focus on a specific industry (e.g., a mattress factory or coal terminal) or sector (e.g., oil and gas). They are designed to generate above-average cash flow, but they can be quite risky as the market price may rise or fall dramatically. When oil prices slumped in 1998, for example, the energy-based RITs cut their distributions and the price of their shares crashed. When oil and natural gas prices recovered, the distributions hit record levels and so did the market price.

RITs are recommended only for knowledgeable investors who understand the risks they entail.

## Unit Trusts

A variation on the closed-end fund is the unit trust. This kind of investment is actually a hybrid, with attributes of both open- and closed-end funds. Here are the three main characteristics of a unit trust:

1. *They are on sale for a limited period only.* The units offered by First Trust, the largest seller of unit trusts in Canada, are open for only one year after their launch date. During that window, you can buy in at any time at the current NAV. At the one-year mark, the trust is closed.

**2.** *The stocks in the portfolio are not actively traded.* Once the shares are acquired, they are held for the duration of the trust in most cases. This practice keeps costs low.

**3.** *The trusts have a fixed termination date.* Typically the trust will be wound up after about five years, at which time investors will receive their pro rata share of the total assets. This means that if the trust is held outside an RRSP, you will face a capital gains tax liability when the trust is terminated (assuming it has earned a profit).

And here's how unit trusts are similar to ordinary open-end mutual funds:

- Units are valued daily.
- You can cash in your units at any time at the current NAV.
- Each trust has a clearly defined investment objective, which makes trusts similar to sector mutual funds.
- They do not trade on the stock exchange.

As you can see, there are numerous ways to invest in closed-end funds and their immediate cousins. However, this is a specialized area so you may wish to obtain professional advice before venturing in.

## SUMMARY

- Don't buy closed-end funds on the initial offering; you'll usually get a better price if you wait.
- REITs are a specialized form of closed-end fund and represent one of the best-kept tax-shelter secrets in Canada.
- RITs offer above-average cash flow, but their risk factor can be high.
- Unit trusts are a hybrid, a cross between open- and closed-end funds.

## FUND FACTS

NET ASSET VALUE. The NAV of a fund unit is calculated by dividing the net assets of the fund (the market value of all holdings less any liabilities) by the number of units outstanding at any given time. For example, if the fund had $100,000 in net assets and there were 1,000 units outstanding, the NAV of each unit would be $100. If it were an open-end fund, that's the price a new investor would pay to acquire units.

NAV CALCULATIONS. Most open-end mutual funds calculate their NAV on a daily basis. However, some closed-end funds do it less frequently—weekly or even monthly. You can find the current NAV of all Canadian mutual funds in the business pages of most major newspapers or in the financial press.

**MANAGERS LOVE THEM.** If closed-end funds usually trade at a discount, why does anyone bother with them? The simple answer seems to be that fund managers love them. They always know exactly how much money they have available; since investors can't sell units back to the treasury, there's no need to keep large cash reserves. And the managers will never be placed in the position of having to sell assets in a down market due to a rash of redemptions.

# How to Use the Mutual Fund Ratings

*The ratings on the pages that follow are designed to help you determine the suitability of specific investments you may be considering for your portfolio. The ratings should not be interpreted as buy or sell recommendations! Due to publishing deadlines, these ratings were compiled in summer 2001. Conditions may have changed significantly since then, so you should consult an investment advisor before making any final decisions. Obtain a copy of the simplified prospectus (the document that provides complete information about the fund and its management) and study it carefully before going ahead.*

For ongoing mutual funds information, please take advantage of the free three-month trial subscription to the electronic edition of our monthly newsletter, *Mutual Funds Update*. You can sign up by going to the following Internet address: **www.gordonpape.com/FreeMFU.html**.

Mutual fund information can also be obtained at the Building Wealth on the 'Net Web site: **www.gordonpape.com**.

## Key Ratings Considerations

The ratings that follow take into account a number of factors. These include:

RISK LEVEL. A higher-risk fund, even one that has a good performance record, will generally receive a lower rating than one that is less risk-prone, even though it may not promise as good a return. Risk levels are relative within each fund category. Equity funds, for example, are generally higher risk than fixed-income funds. So a medium-risk equity fund will have a higher degree of risk than a medium-risk fixed-income fund.

**PERFORMANCE RECORD.** Past results weigh heavily in the ratings, which requires some explanation. Previous performance is no guarantee of future success. A lot can happen over time: economic conditions may change, a mutual fund manager may depart, interest rates may move, two funds may merge and assume the best historical record—all these factors and more can have an impact on how relevant past returns may be. But to ignore history altogether is foolish. In the case of mutual funds, we can at least discern patterns in managerial style, risk levels, and consistency of performance that help us make an educated guess about the probability of where the fund is heading. Past performance is a far better indicator than throwing darts at a board, of course, despite what the newspapers may suggest. Because we regard performance records as being particularly important in judging the suitability of mutual funds, we give formal $ ratings only to funds that have been in existence for at least three years. When we review funds with a shorter track record, you will find an NR beside them, meaning "No Rating."

Performance ratings are based on results for the period ending June 30, 2001. Our information sources include data compiled by the *National Post, The Globe and Mail Report on Business, Globefund, The Fund Library,* Southam's *Mutual Fund SourceBook, PalTrak,* plus the mutual fund companies themselves.

We are also introducing a new rating system this year, one that has been developed by the Fundata organization with the technical assistance of one of our authors, Professor Eric Kirzner. It's called the FUNDGrade™ Mutual Fund Rating System, and it ranks mutual funds using historical data as follows:

| SCORE | DEFINITION |
|-------|------------|
| A | Superior past performance |
| B | Strong past performance |
| C | Average past performance |
| D | Sub-par past performance |
| E | Poor past performance |

The model rewards returns and consistency, but penalizes volatility. Recent results are weighed more heavily in the final calculations than distant results. Under this standard, weak performance in the latest years would swamp the performance in more distant years. Funds are ranked against both their peers in their asset class category, as well as against suitable benchmarks for the category. The benchmark for each fund group is that of the Investment Funds Standard Committee (IFSC). Currently, there are 33 categories in the IFSC universe.

Here are some of the key features of the FUNDGrade™ model:

- A *"highwater" hurdle.* To score an A grade, a fund must not only substantially outperform the category average but also beat the benchmark for the category. By ranking against both the asset class objectives group average and the benchmark, the fund categories that have overall relatively poor performance are appropriately downgraded. If none of the funds in a category beat the benchmark, the highest grade a fund can receive is a C.

- *Time-weighted adjustments for return, risk, and consistency.* The rate of return, risk, and consistency factors are time weighted. The use of time weighting means that recent fund performance is rated more heavily than distant performance. Recent results are likely to be more indicative of the current fund manager's policy, strategy, and success (or lack thereof) than older results.
- *Survivorship bias adjustment.* Most of the current mutual fund performance surveys suffer from survivorship bias. For example, if the survey starts with a current list of mutual funds and looks back at how they have done over the past 10 years, funds that disappeared over that time period would not be included on the list. Often it's the poorer-performing funds that disappear. The adjustment for survivorship bias means that the investor gets a clear picture of actual returns over the period examined.

Back testing was conducted on the historical record for all fund categories using 25 years of past data spanning the period 1975 through 2000. Overall, the Fundata FUNDGrade™ model discriminates by identifying top performers based on past results.

**ECONOMIC CONDITIONS.** The Fundata ratings are based on historic performance, but our own rankings take future considerations into account as well. For example, certain funds are more suitable under specific economic conditions. In late 2000 and early 2001, for instance, value funds performed much better as a rule than growth funds. Our ratings are adjusted for such factors, based on economic conditions as they were anticipated to develop in late summer 2001, in the wake of the events of September 11.

**STYLE.** The style used by a fund manager is increasingly recognized as an important element in judging risk and reward characteristics. For example, as we just mentioned, value funds came back into favour over the past year. We recommend that a well-balanced portfolio contain funds that employ both value and growth styles. Most recommended funds include a style description to help you with this selection.

**RRSP ELIGIBILITY.** We show which funds are fully eligible for registered plans by the RSP designation in the summary line. Funds that have a £ symbol are eligible for registered plans as foreign content only. Note that many companies offer RRSP-eligible clones of existing U.S. and international funds. These clones are not listed separately, but mention is made of them in the parent fund review where we believe the clone a worthy RRSP/RRIF alternative.

COSTS. High costs will impact negatively on a fund's rating. A low-cost fund (one with a low management expense ratio, or MER) earns brownie points. In cases where a front-end load (commission) is charged, assume the fee is negotiable unless the entry specifically states otherwise. Regardless of the posted commission scale, you should not pay more than 4 percent when purchasing a fund with a negotiable fee, even if the amount you're investing is small.

MANAGEMENT. Where management is a factor in performance, as it is in all actively managed mutual funds (as opposed to index funds), it has been taken into account in the ratings. We've included in each rating the name of the fund manager and the year he or she took over, if it could be obtained. Note that in some cases, companies refuse to give the name of a lead manager, claiming a team makes the decisions. You will also find some cases where a corporation is shown as manager, rather than an individual. We've complied with these designations in the reviews, since we didn't have much choice. But it has been our experience that in business, every team has a leader. Hopefully these firms will acknowledge this fact in future editions.

PERSONAL EXPERIENCE. Over the years, we've found that some funds have done better in our portfolios than others. These personal experiences are an important consideration in the mix because they tell a lot more than raw numbers.

This edition of the *Guide* focuses on the top mutual fund and segregated fund companies in Canada. Within each company's write-up, you will find four categories of funds listed, as follows:

1. **Top Choices.** The funds under this listing are the best choices in the company's line-up at the time of writing. We recommend you consider them first when making an investment decision.

2. **Also Recommended**. Funds in this category don't rank with the top group, but are worth a look. These funds may meet a particular need (e.g., tax-advantaged income), or may be funds that have done well in the past but are in temporary decline.

3. **Promising Newcomers.** Funds listed under this heading have been in existence less than three years and do not qualify for a formal rating. However, we feel they are worthy of attention for some reason, which will be explained in the review.

4. **The Rest.** This is a list of all the other funds offered by a company. We do not recommend them at this time.

Now for some other important points to note:

## Exclusions

We do not review funds that are open only to a specific group of people (e.g., doctors, teachers, public servants) or funds that are available only in limited areas of the country. We do not attempt to cover all the small funds and companies, but those worthy of special note are included in the section entitled "The Top Small Funds."

## Segregated Funds

You'll find a special section dedicated to segregated funds. These funds are identified by an "S" in the summary line. The whole segregated fund area is in a state of flux at the present time, and many companies have recently been forced to raise their MERs to comply with new government regulations. We therefore recommend that you consult with a financial advisor for the latest information.

## Rates of Return

Reference in the ratings to "compound average annual rates of return" describes the amount by which a fund would have grown each year over the period, assuming all dividends, interest, and capital gains were reinvested. Thus a fund said to have an average annual compound rate of return of 15 percent over 10 years is one in which $1,000 invested a decade ago would have grown at an average annual rate of 15 percent. All figures are based on results for the year ending June 30, 2001.

Rates of return of one year or less are simple rates of return, or how much your money would have increased in value since you made the investment.

## Load Charges and MERs

Load charges (sales commissions) are not taken into account in any of our calculations, as they will vary from one investor to another.

The reference to MER in the ratings describes the management expense ratio, which is the percentage of the fund's assets that is deducted each year to pay for management fees and other costs associated with the business. Investors don't pay this fee directly; in most cases it's deducted before the net asset value (NAV) of the fund is calculated. However, the net result acts to reduce your return. For example, if a fund earns a gross return of 10 percent and has an MER of 1.5 percent, the return you'll actually receive will be 8.5 percent. MERs are especially important in assessing the potential return from money market and fixed-income funds at a time of low interest rates. The lower the MER, the greater the likely return.

Wherever possible, we've used the MERs published in the fund company's latest annual report or in the prospectus.

## Average Quartile Rating

Some reviews refer to Average Quartile Rating (AQR). This is a measure of consistency. A perfect score is 1.00 (fund always in top quartile). The lowest score is 4.00 (fund always in last quartile).

## Availability

Not all mutual funds are sold in every province. Consult a sales representative in your area to determine whether any fund in which you're interested is available.

## Fund Categories

In 1999, the industry agreed on a reclassification of fund categories, in an attempt to get a better apples-to-apples comparison of funds of the same type. For example, Far East funds are now divided into three separate groups: Asia/Pacific Rim Equity (the fund can invest anywhere in Asia and Australia/New Zealand), Asia Ex-Japan Equity (the Japanese market is off-limits for the manager), and Japanese Equity.

The system is still being refined and we don't agree with all the fund designations, but we use the new categories in this book. You'll find a list of the symbols under the head "Mutual Fund Types," following.

Each entry is introduced with a series of symbols. Here's how to interpret them:

## OVERALL SUITABILITY

| | |
|---|---|
| $ | Below-average or higher-than-acceptable risk. There are better choices available. |
| $$ | Average. Returns will likely be about average for the category, or the fund may have a higher cost or risk level. |
| $$$ | Above average. Should be seriously considered. |
| $$$$ | Superior. Will usually perform in the top quartile of its category. |

## RISK LEVEL

| | |
|---|---|
| ↑ | High. Suitable only for investors willing to accept above-average risk for a fund of its type. |
| → | Medium. Some degree of risk involved. |
| ↓ | Low. Minimal risk for a fund of its type. |

## ASSET TYPE

| | |
|---|---|
| C | Cash or cash equivalent. |
| FI | Fixed-income. |
| G | Growth. |
| FI/G | Balanced. |
| G/FI | Balanced, with a growth bias. |

## CHARACTERISTICS

| | |
|---|---|
| # | Front-end load. |
| * | Back-end load. |
| #/* | Optional front- or back-end load. |
| #/*/No | Front-end, back-end, and no-load options. |
| #&* | Front- and back-end loads applicable. |
| No | No load. |
| S | Segregated fund |
| RSP | Fully eligible for RRSPs and RRIFs, without restriction. |
| £ | Foreign property in RRSPs and RRIFs. Limits apply. |
| MER | Management expense ratio. The costs charged against the assets of a fund before units are valued. The lower the MER, the better. |
| Fundata | The FUNDGrade™ rating as of June 30, 2001. |
| Style | The investing approach used by the fund's manager. |
| Suitability | A brief description of the type of investor who would find the fund most appropriate. |

## MUTUAL FUND TYPES

### Canadian Equity Funds

| | |
|---|---|
| CE | Canadian Equity. Invests in a broadly diversified portfolio of Canadian stocks. |
| CLC | Canadian Large-Cap Equity. Specializes in stocks of large Canadian firms. |
| CSC | Canadian Small-to-Mid-Cap Equity. Invests primarily in stocks of small- and mid-sized Canadian firms. |
| DIV | Dividend. Invests in high-yield common stocks, preferred shares, and other income securities with a goal of maximizing tax-advantaged cash flow. |
| LAB | Labour-Sponsored Venture Capital Fund. Invests in start-up companies. Offers special tax advantages. |

## U.S., International, and Global Equity Funds

USE        U.S. Equity. Specializes in stocks of larger American companies.

USSC       U.S. Small-to-Mid-Cap Equity. Specializes in small- to mid-sized American corporations.

NAE        North American Equity. Focus is on U.S. and Canadian stocks. May contain some Mexican content.

IE         International Equity. Invests in international stocks from countries outside North America.

GE         Global Equity. Invests in stocks from around the world, including North America.

PRE        Asia/Pacific Rim Equity. Invests in stocks through the Far East and the Pacific Rim.

JE         Japanese Equity. Specializes in Japanese stocks.

AXJ        Asia Ex-Japan Equity. Invests in stocks from all Asian countries except Japan.

LAE        Latin American Equity. Invests primarily in stocks from Mexico, Central America, and South America.

EE         European Equity. Invests in European stocks.

EME        Emerging Markets Equity. Invests in stocks from developing countries.

CSE        Country-Specific Equity. Focuses on stocks from a single country.

## Sector Funds

SPE        Specialty/Miscellaneous. Emphasis is on a specific sector or theme.

ST         Science & Technology. Invests in science and technology issues.

NR         Natural Resources. Specializes in natural resource stocks.

PM         Precious Metals. Invests in gold, precious metals, and shares in mining companies.

RE         Real Estate. Invests primarily in commercial real estate.

## Balanced Funds

CBAL       Canadian Balanced. Invests in a blend of Canadian equities and debt securities.

CTAA       Canadian Tactical Asset Allocation. Invests in a blend of Canadian equities, bonds, and cash using tactical asset allocation strategies.

CHIB       Canadian High-Income Balanced. Invests in a variety of income-generating securities including equities, royalty trusts, real estate investment trusts, and bonds.

GBAL       Global Balanced and Asset Allocation. Invests in a blend of foreign equities and debt securities. May use tactical asset allocation.

## Fixed-Income and Money Market Funds

CB       Canadian Bond. Invests primarily in Canadian dollar bonds and debentures with maturities of more than one year.

FB       Foreign Bond. Invests in bonds and debentures denominated in foreign currencies.

HYB    High-Yield Bond. Invests in bonds that pay higher yields (sometimes called "junk bonds").

STB    Canadian Short-Term Bond. Specializes in bonds with short maturities to reduce risk.

M        Canadian Mortgage. Invests mainly in residential first mortgages.

CMM   Canadian Money Market. Invests in Canadian short-term debt securities like Treasury bills.

FMM   Foreign Money Market. Invests in short-term securities denominated in foreign currencies, usually U.S. dollars.

# The Fund Awards

*Each year in this Guide, we single out funds, individuals, and corporations that we feel merit special mention for their accomplishments over the past 12 months. These Fund Awards carry no monetary prize and no plaque. They are intended only to recognize superior achievements in key areas of the industry.*

We also recognize that every year the fund business produces its share of disappointments and losers. Poor performances come with the territory and just because a fund has an off year, it doesn't necessarily mean it's a bad investment. But sometimes a negative result needs to be highlighted, as a warning to investors. You'll find some of these warnings at the end of this section.

All the performance figures quoted are based on results to June 30, 2001.

## FUND OF THE YEAR

AGF INTERNATIONAL VALUE FUND. The past 12 months witnessed the resurgence of value investing. The collapse of the high-tech sector, which had driven markets to record highs in the late 1990s and early 2000, signalled the end of the temporary reign of growth managers at the top of the mutual fund pyramid. Investors reverted to the tried-and-true methodology of Benjamin Graham, Sir John Templeton, and Warren Buffett. Old-fashioned measures like price/earnings ratios and book values came back into play as key determinants in deciding on a stock's value, while newfangled ideas like earnings momentum were pushed to the background. Many value funds thrived in this environment. But the one that impressed us most was the AGF International Value Fund, which is managed out of San Diego by the Charles Brandes organization. Brandes himself is a disciple of the late Dr. Benjamin Graham (Brandes once worked briefly with Graham) and has written his own book on the value discipline, so his credentials are legitimate. This fund gained 23.4% over the year to June 30/01 for the number-two position in the Global Equity category. But that result alone didn't win it Fund of the Year. What especially impressed us was the dependability this fund has shown over the years. Many value funds were eclipsed during the high-tech craze, but not this one. Even though its style was out of favour, it still managed to produce great returns. In fact, this fund produced double-digit profits for investors every single calendar year after the Brandes organization took it over in late 1994. That's a run of six straight, from 1995 to 2000. You can't beat that for consistency.

## COMPANY OF THE YEAR

**FRANKLIN TEMPLETON.** The problem with the Templeton organization in Canada for many years has been its tendency to be essentially a one-trick pony. The company offered some well-managed foreign equity funds, using the proven value techniques of the legendary Sir John Templeton. But once you got beyond Templeton Growth Fund and a couple of others, there was no depth. The Canadian stock funds were mediocre at best, the fixed-income funds were uninspiring, and there was no style differentiation. Now, in the space of a year, everything has changed. The major coup was the late 2000 acquisition of the Calgary-based Bissett funds. Bissett was one of the standout boutique firms in the country, with a strong line-up of Canadian equity funds and some very respectable fixed-income products. The acquisition of the Bissett line, which the company has wisely kept intact, solved the firm's biggest problem. Franklin Templeton (as the company is now called in recognition of its U.S. parent) now offers a credible range of Canadian options that are suitable for registered plans and complement Templeton's international strength. But the Bissett acquisition wasn't the company's only move.

Recognizing the importance of style diversification in today's market, the company imported several growth-oriented funds from the Franklin line-up in the U.S. These funds haven't performed well in the current value climate, but down the road they should provide an alternative that investors will welcome. Another important move, although one that was not recognized as such at the time, was the introduction of a deep value option called the Mutual Beacon Fund. This fund is another offspring of the U.S. parent firm, and could be regarded as the Franklin Templeton equivalent of Mackenzie's Cundill funds. Mutual Beacon, which invests in American stocks, has thrived in the recent market conditions and gained 24% in the year to June 30/01. So far investors don't appear to have noticed, as the fund has attracted only slightly more than $100 million in assets. But if those types of results continue, the dollars will come. All in all, Franklin Templeton has succeeded in pulling off a major overhaul in the past year, and has now positioned itself to be a much stronger force going forward. That accomplishment earns it the Fund Company of the Year title.

## MANAGER OF THE YEAR

PETER MARSHALL. Good mutual fund managers don't have to operate from Toronto's Bay Street, as Vancouver-based Phillips, Hager & North and Calgary-based Mawer and Bissett have proven over the years. This year, we salute a manager from Canada's East Coast. Peter Marshall works in relative obscurity from his Halifax base, but the results of his efforts have been making investors smile. He's the chairman and CEO of Seamark Asset Management and in that capacity he oversees accounts worth more than $6 billion. Although it's just a small part of that business, the outstanding results Marshall has achieved managing money for the Clarington funds is the reason we have chosen him as our Manager of the Year. He and his Seamark team have been the main force in imprinting the Clarington brand image into the minds of many investors. His conservatively run Clarington Canadian Equity Fund has been the top performer in the Canadian Large-Cap category in recent years, posting an average annual return of 12.7% over the three years to mid-2001. That gave it the number one ranking among its peers over that time frame. Marshall and Company even managed to deliver a profit in the 12 months to June 30/01, while the average fund of this type was losing 8.5%. And it doesn't stop there. His Clarington Canadian Balanced Fund ranked number five in its category over three years, out of a total of more than 350 funds. His Clarington Canadian Income Fund delivers a steady monthly income stream with some tax advantages as a bonus. It has never lost money over a calendar year since its launch in 1996. He also oversees the new Clarington Canadian Dividend Fund and the Clarington Global Income Fund. That's a heavy workload. Marshall is used to it, however; he has more than 30 years of experience in the business and worked with the near-legendary Bob Krembil at Bolton Tremblay before each went off to eventually start his own company (Krembil was a co-founder of Trimark). Marshall's a native Nova Scotian, so when the opportunity came to set up shop by the sea, he took it. National recognition has been long overdue. We hope to remedy that situation with this award.

## EXECUTIVE OF THE YEAR

DON REED. The Templeton organization in Canada was in trouble. The flagship Templeton Growth Fund, for so many years a magnet for investors' savings, had gone into eclipse. Other once-popular Templeton offerings like the Emerging Markets Fund saw assets draining away by the tens of millions. The company's domestic line-up was mediocre at best. It looked like the once-proud company was about to become an also-ran in an industry where to stand still is to die. So what did Canadian president Don Reed do? He made some phone calls. The Calgary-based Bissett organization had just experienced the retirement of its founder and driving force, David Bissett. Might the shareholders be interested in a buyout? Well, yes they were. The company had already come to the conclusion that it faced some serious obstacles to future growth, not the least of which would be the cost of providing international investment options to its clients. Bissett had a solid line-up of domestic and U.S. stock funds and some good income products, but customers wanted more diversification. The Templeton connection would be a perfect match: Bissett's domestic expertise aligned with Templeton's international experience. Reed got the ball rolling and then stepped back and let the financial suits from the parent Franklin organization negotiate the details. In fall 2001 the deal was closed and the Bissett line-up became part of the revamped Franklin Templeton, while still retaining its brand name and Calgary base. And that wasn't all. Reed also oversaw several other changes, which are described in our Fund Company of the Year write-up. Today, Franklin Templeton is the tenth-largest fund company in Canada in terms of assets under management and is once again a major player in the industry, thanks in large part to Don Reed.

## COMEBACK OF THE YEAR

**THE MACKENZIE INDUSTRIAL FUNDS.** Mackenzie Financial became the giant it is today on the strength of its Industrial Group of Funds. Back in the 1980s, when the fund industry first began to emerge as a viable option for Canadian investors, the Industrial Funds were the leaders of the pack. Industrial Growth became the biggest domestic fund in the country for a period of time. Industrial Horizon was the first major fund to offer a deferred sales charge option (back-end load), which made it an almost instant hit among both advisors and clients. But then came the 1990s, and the Industrial Funds fell on hard times. The management team placed big bets on the resource sector that never paid off. Returns drifted down and Mackenzie began to lose market share to go-go upstarts like Altamira. Only the fortuitous hiring of Jerry Javasky and Gerry Coleman and the subsequent launch of the Ivy Funds saved the company from becoming a distant also-ran. As the 1990s unfolded, the Industrial Group continued to underperform; Industrial Growth was especially weak. The fund lost more than three-quarters of its asset base as investors cashed in and moved on. Things weren't much better elsewhere in the family, as Mackenzie seemed more interested in its other brands: Ivy, Universal, and the newly acquired Cundill Funds. But now, after a decade-long hiatus, the Industrial Funds are back. A revamped management team headed by veteran Bill Procter has restored the line to respectability, and the funds turned in some very good results in the weak markets of 2000–01. Procter's Industrial Horizon Fund posted a 15.4% advance in the year to June 30/01, the third-best result in the Canadian Large-Cap category. Industrial Balanced, Industrial Income, and Industrial Pension all finished in the top 20 of the Canadian Balanced category—that's out of more than 350 funds. Even bedraggled Industrial Growth was revitalized. In the first eight months of 2001, the fund posted a big gain of 24%. Those investors who had hung on through thick and thin (mostly thin) rubbed their eyes in wonder when their statements arrived. Put it all together, and it's a remarkable turnaround. Now we have to hope that it can continue.

## SURPRISE FUND OF THE YEAR

**INVESTORS RETIREMENT MUTUAL FUND.** Mutual fund ads are always required to point out that past results are not indicative of future returns. The implication of the warning is not to expect a fund that gained 25% last year to pull off a repeat performance. But it works both ways. Occasionally a fund with a long history of mediocrity can rise up and post some eye-popping gains. This fund is an example. Except for a brief spurt in 1996, it has been an underachiever for most of the past decade. Its long-term record still ranks well down on the list in the Canadian Equity category. But the collapse of the technology markets and the return to value investing translated into a resurrection for this shop-worn entry. The fund gained more than 21% in the year to June 30/01, if you can believe it! New manager Dom Grestoni obviously gets a lot of the credit for this resurgence.

## BOND FUND OF THE YEAR

**TD REAL RETURN BOND FUND.** We don't often get repeat winners in a category, but it's impossible to overlook how well this fund continues to do in a tough bond market. It won this title last year when it posted a gain of 9.3%, one of the best results in the Canadian Bond category. Now it's pulled off the double. The fund earned 9.7% in the 12 months to June 30/01, making it the number one performer among its peers over that time frame. Its three-year average annual compound rate of return is also good for the number one spot. Real return bonds—this fund's specialty—are issued by the federal government and are indexed to inflation, both for principal and interest. So when inflation starts to edge up, so does the value of real return bonds. This is the only fund that invests in them and it profited accordingly. Last year we said it was probably a one-year wonder. It wasn't.

## CANADIAN SMALL-CAP FUND OF THE YEAR

**TRIMARK CANADIAN SMALL COMPANIES FUND.** This wasn't the number one performer over the past 12 months. That honour went to the tiny Resolute Growth Fund, which is also tops in the category over three and five years. But Resolute Growth is available only in some parts of the country and requires a large initial minimum. Trimark Canadian Small Companies is a small-cap fund anyone can buy into. It's a relative newcomer (launched in 1998), but it has shown steady improvement every year. Most of the Trimark funds struggled in the late 1990s, but this was a notable exception. The value investing style really showed its worth in the latest 12 months, as the fund added an impressive 28.7%, good for the number two spot in its category. Most of the Trimark entries are looking much better these days, but this one stands out from the crowd.

## SEGREGATED FUND OF THE YEAR

CANADA LIFE ENHANCED DIVIDEND FUND. This was a year when cautious and conservative won the race and this relatively new dividend fund from Canada Life proves it. Manager Philip Wootten of Laketon Investment used a deft mixture of common and preferred shares to fashion a portfolio that topped the list in its category over the latest 12-month period, with a gain of 26.4%. He also runs Canada Life's new Generations version of the same fund.

## GROWTH COMPANY OF THE YEAR

CLARINGTON FUNDS. In terms of asset growth, AIM Funds was the biggest year-over-year gainer, adding 232% to June 30/01. But it was growth by acquisition—the Trimark purchase was a huge plus. In terms of pure sales growth, the prize goes to the up-and-coming Clarington family, which gained 60% year over year. That's especially impressive in light of the weak stock markets that prevailed for much of that time. The secret to Clarington's success? A strong marketing campaign aimed directly at financial advisors and some great returns. See our Manager of the Year Award for more details.

## COLLAPSE OF THE YEAR

AGF AGGRESSIVE GROWTH FUND. In last year's edition, this entry won Fund of the Year honours on the strength of a 122% gain. Then the high-tech market went south and so did this fund. Loss for the 12 months to June 30/01 was a hair-raising 51.7%. That result was bad enough to rank this fund dead last in the U.S. Small-to-Mid-Cap category. Fame certainly is fleeting. Still, don't be surprised to see this one surge back with big gains again when the markets turn around, which they will. Manager Richard Driehaus is known as one of the best small-cap stock pickers in the U.S. He's out of sync right now, but that won't last forever.

## DISAPPOINTMENT OF THE YEAR

**SAGIT'S CAMBRIDGE FUNDS.** Investors who have money in the Cambridge line of this small Vancouver company must be feeling shell-shocked. Not only did every fund record double-digit losses, but most were down over 30% and some over 50% in the 12 months to June 30/01. The company declined to answer our questionnaire this year, saying they didn't want to participate in the 2002 edition. With numbers like that, we can't say that we blame them.

## LABYRINTH OF THE YEAR

**MACKENZIE FINANCIAL CORPORATION.** Let's see now. At the time of writing, Mackenzie was offering seven different fund lines: Cundill, Industrial, Ivy, Mackenzie, MAXXUM, Scudder, and Universal. Oh yes, then they had the STAR portfolios and the Keystone line, which has morphed into something different than it was before. It all adds up to more than 200 funds when you toss in the clones, seg funds, capital classes, U.S. dollar versions, and more. Too much, already! Fortunately, the higher-ups at Mackenzie think so too. They've assured us that by this time next year, a lot of the funds will be gone, through mergers and closures. Look for the MAXXUM line to be the first casualty.

# The Top 50 Mutual Fund Families

## Introduction to the Mutual Fund Reviews

The section that follows contains our selections for the top mutual fund companies in Canada, listed alphabetically. Within each corporate chapter, you will find the following headings:

THE COMPANY. This segment provides you with background information on the organization, including details of recent mergers, major managerial moves, significant fund changes, etc.

THE DETAILS. Statistical data about the company.

INVESTING TIPS. A new section this year, it contains practical investment guidance including advice on how to save money, capitalize on special deals, etc.

FUND SUMMARY. An at-a-glance look at our ratings for the company's funds.

FUND RATINGS. Detailed write-ups for the funds we are recommending this year.

# ABC FUNDS

## THE COMPANY

This small operation is directed by Irwin Michael, an MBA from the prestigious Wharton School of Finance who has established a reputation as one of Canada's top value managers. He is highly disciplined in his approach and doesn't stray from it, even when the financial tides are flowing strongly against him as they were in the late 1990s. During that period, which he describes as the most difficult one he has ever encountered with his fundamental value approach, his funds languished and investors became restless. But the collapse of the high-tech bubble brought value investing back into style and by mid-2001 both the ABC Fundamental-Value Fund and the ABC Fully Managed Fund were back among the top performers in their respective categories.

Michael and his colleagues spend most of their working hours poring over balance sheets and income statements, looking for hidden value within a company. They have shown themselves to be especially adept at identifying companies ripe for takeover bids—his funds were heavily into Gulf Canada Resources, which was taken out in the spring of 2001 for a fat premium. None of the funds in the group has ever used options, futures, or other derivatives.

The company maintains its own Web site at **www.abcfunds.com**, as well as a new one it recently launched called *The Value Investigator* (**www.valueinvestigator. com**). There you'll find detailed analyses of many of the stocks in the ABC portfolios. It's useful reading.

Irwin Michael is also a regular contributor to Gordon Pape's *Internet Wealth Builder* newsletter (**www.gordonpape.com/newsletter/iwbnl.cfm**).

## THE DETAILS

|  |  |
|---|---|
| Number of funds: | 3 |
| Assets under management: | $233.2 million |
| Load charge: | None |
| Switching charge: | None |
| Where sold: | Across Canada |
| How sold: | Directly through manager or through brokers and planners |
| Phone number: | 1-888-OPEN-ABC or (416) 365-9696 |
| Web site address: | www.abcfunds.com and www.valueinvestigator.com |
| E-mail address: | iamich@abcfunds.com |
| Minimum initial investment: | $150,000 |

# INVESTING TIPS

You need a lot of money to invest here. The minimum amount required to open an account is $150,000 (which can be split between spouses) and even then Irwin Michael may not accept your cash if he feels it represents too large a percentage of your total net worth (if things turn sour, he doesn't want to be responsible for wiping out an investor). But if you have the entry price and pass his admission test, this is a good place to stash some of your savings for long-term growth. And once you're in, you get first-class attention. The manager is accessible by phone and the firm offers monthly in-house briefings for its investors to keep them up to date on what's happening.

# FUND SUMMARY

|  |  |
|---|---|
| Top Choices: | Fundamental-Value, Fully Managed |
| Also Recommended: | American Value |
| Promising Newcomers: | None |
| The Rest: | None |

# FUND RATINGS

## Top Choices

### Canadian Equity Funds

### ABC FUNDAMENTAL-VALUE FUND    $$$$ → G No RSP CE

Manager: Irwin Michael, since inception (1989)

MER: 2.00%    Fundata: A    Style: Value

Suitability: Long-term value investors

Like most value funds, this one had a tough time in the late 1990s as investors ignored bargain basement shopping and focused on technology and other high-momentum stocks. The result was a weak showing in 1998 when the fund lost almost 14%. Michael returned it to profitability in 1999 and 2000, but it was in the first half of 2001, with the resurgence of value investing, that he regained the form he had shown in the mid-1990s. Investors enjoyed a big 22% gain in the first half of 2001, even as the TSE 300 was losing ground. That gain moved the fund back to near the top of its category and pulled up its longer-term averages considerably. This is the kind of fund you invest in and forget about; in fact, Michael is constantly urging his investors to show "patience, patience, patience." Historically the fund has an excellent safety record—years like 1998 are an aberration—and the long-term returns are first-rate. The price of admission is high, but if you have the money you won't find many better choices than this fund.

## Canadian Balanced Funds

### ABC FULLY-MANAGED FUND                    $$$$ ↓ G NO RSP CBAL

Manager: Irwin Michael, since inception (1988)

MER: 2.00%      Fundata: B       Style: Value

Suitability: Long-term conservative investors

Like the companion Fundamental-Value Fund, this fund struggled in 1998, losing just over 2%. But also like Fundamental-Value, it has been on the comeback
trail since then and scored a big 18% advance in the first six months of 2001.
Remarkably, manager Irwin Michael was able to achieve that gain despite very
large cash holdings during the period (at one point about 30% of the portfolio
was in cash). Fixed-income securities hardly played a part in this particular
advance; rather it was some good stock picks such as takeover target Gulf Canada
Resources that provided the impetus. Other solid gainers included Cominco,
Surrey Metro, and National Bank. The equity side of the portfolio is very com-
pact (only a dozen stocks as of March 31/01) so Michael takes relatively large
bets. That might suggest an undue amount of risk, but the fund has recorded
very few losing years and has a first-rate safety record. As for performance, it's
number one in the Canadian Balanced category over the past decade. That says
it all. The fund retains its $$$$ rating again this year. If value investing, low risk,
and steady returns are what you're looking for, this fund is for you.

## Also Recommended

## U.S. Equity Funds

### ABC AMERICAN VALUE FUND                    $$$ → G NO £ USE

Manager: Irwin Michael, since inception (1996)

MER: 2.00%      Fundata: B       Style: Value

Suitability: Long-term value investors

After honing his value investing technique in the Canadian markets, manager
Irwin Michael, the driving force behind the ABC Funds, decided to take his act
across the border in 1996 by launching this fund, the third in his stable. As with
his other funds, stocks are selected based on exceptional value, using a well-
developed set of screening techniques. The fund did very well for investors in
its first full calendar year, gaining just under 40% in 1997. But the fund went
into a tailspin from 1998 through to 2000. Although the U.S. market was
strong during that period, the value investing approach was definitely out of
sync with what investors wanted, which was high-tech stocks and fast growth.
As a result, this fund struggled to slightly better than break-even returns in 1998

and 1999 and then dropped 6.7% in 2000. Last year we commented that based on the track record of his other funds, we expected this one to eventually recover. Our prediction has now come to pass; the fund scored a big gain of 28.5% in the first half of 2001, at a time when the Dow, S&P 500, and Nasdaq were all tumbling. As with his other funds, this gain was achieved despite a large cash position. The portfolio is relatively small (16 stocks as of March 31/01), but Michael manages it well. We're moving the rating up to $$$ due to the good recent performance and the fact that value investing is once again working as it should.

## Promising Newcomers

None.

# ACUITY INVESTMENT MANAGEMENT

## THE COMPANY

This relatively small player in the Canadian mutual fund scene runs the Acuity family of funds in addition to several pooled funds. It's mainly known for its line of Clean Environment Mutual Funds. In the past, these funds were offered through Clean Environment Mutual Funds Ltd.; however, the name of the parent company has changed to Acuity Funds Ltd.

The funds marketed under the Clean Environment brand invest in environmentally friendly stocks, with a special emphasis on firms that are developing new technologies in the field. These include companies that have found new ways to reduce pollution, recycle materials, and use alternative energy sources. If you're a socially conscious investor, here's a way to put your money to work in a way that will allow you to sleep well at night and make some profits too. The funds are guided by a Scientific Advisory Council made up of key players from Canada's environmental sector.

Acuity has diversified its product line with the addition of four new funds marketed under the Acuity name. The new funds have investment themes that vary from capital preservation to growth. Two new funds debuted in the last year: the Acuity Global Environment Science & Technology Fund and the Acuity All-Cap 30 Canadian Equity Fund. The latter is a curious "all star fund," composed of up to 30 of what Acuity considers to be the most promising companies in the Acuity universe.

## THE DETAILS

| | |
|---|---|
| Number of funds: | 16 |
| Assets under management: | $600 million |
| Load charge: | Front: max.5%; Back: max. 5% |
| Switching charge: | 2% maximum |
| Where sold: | Across Canada |
| How sold: | Through brokers, dealers, and financial planners |
| Phone number: | 1-800-461-4570, ext. 4570 |
| Web site address: | www.acuityfunds.com |
| E-mail address: | mail@acuityfunds.com |
| Minimum initial investment: | $500 (generally) |

## INVESTING TIPS

Investors with ample resources may want to look at the company's pooled funds, which require a minimum investment of $150,000 but charge no commissions and offer low management fees. The pooled funds have generally had better comparative numbers than the regular Acuity mutual funds. Case in point: the Acuity Pooled Canadian Equity Fund has outperformed both the companion Canadian Equity Fund and the Clean Environment Equity Fund.

## FUND SUMMARY

| | |
|---|---|
| Top Choices: | None |
| Also Recommended: | Clean Environment Equity |
| Promising Newcomers: | Acuity All-Cap 30 Canadian Equity |
| The Rest: | Acuity Funds: Bond, Canadian Equity, G7 RSP Equity, Global Environment Science & Technology, Global Equity, High Income, Money Market, Social Values Canadian Equity, Social Values Global Equity; Clean Environment Funds: Balanced, Global Equity |

## FUND RATINGS

### Top Choices

None.

### Also Recommended

#### Canadian Equity Funds

#### CLEAN ENVIRONMENT EQUITY FUND                    $$ → G #/* RSP CE

Manager: Ian Ihnatowycz, since inception (1991)

MER: 3.21%        Fundata: E        Style: Bottom-up Value

Suitability: Socially conscious investors

This fund invests across all capitalization classes. The mandate directs the manager to look for companies that have shown a strong environmental commitment, avoiding industries such as tobacco and those that produce significant industrial waste. As of mid-2001, the fund had a diverse group of small- to large-cap stocks spread across a broad spectrum of industries, from financial services to consumer products to high technology. While longer-term returns have been consistently above average, the fund's 20.1% loss to June 30/01 was well below the peer group average and very disappointing. This poor showing accounts for its E rating in the Fundata model. We will treat the recent results as an aberration; the combination of our confidence in manager Ian Ihnatowycz, the longer-term good performance of this fund, and a reduction in the fund's high-technology concentration leads us to believe the recent weak performance is temporary. The fund's five-year return is 7.3% per annum.

**Promising Newcomers**

## ACUITY ALL-CAP 30 CANADIAN EQUITY                NR → G #/* RSP CE

Manager: David G. Stonehouse, since inception (September 2000)

MER: 2.50%      Fundata: N/A      Style: Bottom-up Value

Suitability: Growth-oriented investors willing to accept the risk of a fund with an extremely short track record

This fund is a recent debut and has an unusual portfolio strategy. Its objective is to provide long-term growth by investing in a diversified portfolio of up to 30 Canadian and foreign stocks selected as the best from the Acuity universe of eligible stocks. The portfolio at present is concentrated in industrial products (34%) and financial services (21%). In the six months to June 30/01 the fund had a 0.5% return compared with a 4.6% loss in its peer group. In the three-month period to June 30/01 the fund's 13.2% return far outstripped the 2.8% return of the peer group. It's still very early, but the fund has an intriguing portfolio strategy and a promising start. It's definitely worth a look.

# AGF GROUP

## THE COMPANY

It was a very busy year at AGF. In August 2000, the company surprised the mutual fund world with the announcement that it was acquiring Global Strategy in a deal valued at $483 million. Since then, the Global Strategy funds have been integrated into the AGF line-up and 2001 saw numerous managerial changes, name changes, mergers, and some windups (e.g., Global Strategy Europe Plus and Global Strategy U.S. Equity). As a result, the Global Strategy name has now disappeared from the AGF line-up.

The deal reinforced AGF's position as one of the leading players in the Canadian mutual fund industry. The company is now the seventh largest in the country with more than $29 billion in assets under management at the end of June 2001.

AGF is one of Canada's older fund companies; it's been in business since 1957 and for a period of time it seemed to be losing its zip. But several acquisitions and some new blood at the top have reinvigorated this warhorse and investors are finding a lot to like in the fund line-up.

The company has been making moves to ensure that pattern continues. AGF has created fully RRSP-eligible versions of some of its most popular international funds. Several new funds have been added to the line-up. But most important from an investor perspective, however, is the fact that many of the AGF funds are posting very impressive performance numbers. When a fund is making money, people will stick with it and add more cash as money becomes available to them.

## THE DETAILS

| | |
|---|---|
| Number of funds: | 73 |
| Assets under management: | $29.2 billion |
| Load charge: | Front: max 6%; Back: max 5.5% |
| Switching charge: | 2% maximum |
| Where sold: | Across Canada |
| How sold: | Through brokers, dealers, and financial planners |
| Phone number: | 1-888-243-4668 |
| Web site address: | www.agf.com |
| E-mail address: | tiger@agf.com |
| Minimum initial investment: | $1,000 (generally) |

## INVESTING TIPS

AGF offers an umbrella fund called AGF International Group Ltd. (It is also known as AGF All World Tax Advantage Group.) This Group is of special interest if you're investing outside a registered plan because it allows you to move your money among the different asset classes within the umbrella fund without triggering capital gains tax liability. Components of this master fund are designated by the word "class" in the name, such as AGF American Growth Class.

If you're considering using AGF "clone" funds for an RRSP or other registered plan, be aware that the performance numbers in some cases are not tracking the results of the underlying parent fund as closely as might be expected. For example, AGF International Value Fund recorded a one-year gain of 23.4% to June 30/01. But the RRSP-eligible clone gained only 19.3%. We've discussed this phenomenon with AGF on a number of occasions but have yet to receive an explanation that satisfies us. So we recommend that you avoid AGF clones and opt for the parent fund instead, at least until the returns come within half a point of one another.

## FUND SUMMARY

| | |
|---|---|
| Top Choices: | American Tactical Asset Allocation, Canada Class, Canadian Dividend, Canadian High Income, Canadian Stock, European Equity, International Stock, International Value, U.S.$ Money Market |
| Also Recommended: | Aggressive Growth, Asian Growth, Canadian Balanced, Canadian Bond, Canadian Growth Equity, Canadian Resources, Canadian Tactical Asset Allocation, China Focus, Emerging Markets Value, Global Government Bond, Global Real Estate Equity, RSP Global Bond, World Balanced |
| Promising Newcomers: | Global Financial Services |
| The Rest: | Aggressive Global Stock, Aggressive Japan, American Growth, Canadian Aggressive All-Cap, Canadian Aggressive Equity, Canadian Money Market, Canadian Opportunities, Canadian Small-Cap, Canadian Total Return Bond, Canadian Value, European Asset Allocation, Germany, Global Equity, Global Health Sciences, Global Resources, Global Technology, Global Total Return Bond, India, International Short-Term Income, Japan, Latin America, Managed Futures Value, Multi-Manager, Precious Metals, RSP International Equity Allocation, Special U.S., U.S. Value, World Companies, World Opportunities |

# FUND RATINGS

## Top Choices

### Canadian Equity Funds

#### AGF CANADA CLASS                                    $$$ → G #/* £ CE

Manager: Martin Hubbes, since September 1998

MER: 3.24%    Fundata: A    Style: Bottom-up Growth

Suitability: Long-term investors with non-registered accounts

Here's a rare bird: a Canadian equity fund that is foreign property for the purposes of RRSPs and RRIFs. It's considered foreign property because it's part of AGF's International Group. The term "Class" in the name indicates that investors may transfer units between any of the various "classes" (actually individual funds) within the Group without the worry of incurring capital gains. Manager Martin Hubbes uses a bottom-up investment style with a focus on large-cap growth stocks. The first two years following the 1997 launch saw the fund get beaten up pretty badly, but it has been doing much better lately. It gained 29.1% in 1999, 19.1% in 2000, and registered only a small loss of 3.1% in the first half of 2001, an excellent performance in turbulent markets. In the first half of 2001, the portfolio was heavily concentrated in energy, bank, and industrial stocks. We don't like the high MER here, which seems excessive. However, we do like the performance trend and are raising our rating to $$$.

#### AGF CANADIAN DIVIDEND FUND                          $$$ ↓ G #/* RSP CE

Managers: Gordon MacDougall, since inception (1985) and Martin Gerber (both of Connor, Clark & Lunn), since 1994

MER: 1.88%    Fundata: E    Style: Top-down Growth/Value

Suitability: Growth investors; not suitable for income investors

This entry is officially classified as a dividend income fund but any resemblance between this and a real dividend fund is purely coincidental. The fund throws off virtually no cash flow, which is supposed to be an integral feature of a true dividend fund. In fact, the annual study we do for the *Mutual Funds Update* newsletter consistently shows that this fund has a cash distribution so small you'd need a magnifying glass to find it. Keep that fact in mind if you're in income investor and maximizing the dividend tax credit is your main goal. AGF should consider renaming this fund to more accurately reflect its investment style because as things stand, investors are likely to be misled. Despite that criticism, this is not a fund to ignore. Viewed as purely an equity fund, it offers a well-structured portfolio of blue-chip stocks that includes a lot of banks and big industrial companies. The fund is conservatively managed by Gordon

MacDougall and Martin Gerber, who are with the investment house of Connor, Clark & Lunn. Returns have been consistently good. Especially impressive is the fact that this fund has never recorded a losing calendar year in the past decade. So approach this fund as a pure blue-chip entry for risk-averse investors and make your purchase judgment on that basis. Using that criterion, it's a winner. Formerly known as the 20/20 Dividend Fund and, in the distant past, the Sunset Convertible Preferred and Dividend Fund.

## AGF CANADIAN STOCK FUND                    $$$ → G #/* RSP CE

Manager: Martin Hubbes, since June 1996

MER: 2.43%      Fundata: B      Style: Bottom-up Growth

Suitability: Long-term growth investors

This fund is the product of a number of mergers. It was originally the AGF Canadian Growth Fund, and the Canadian Equity Fund merged into it in 1998. Then in 2001, the Global Strategy Growth & Income Fund and the Global Strategy Canadian Companies Fund were folded into it as well. Consequently, manager Martin Hubbes has had to juggle a variety of portfolios along the way. He's managed to do a good job of it, piloting the fund to gains of 32.6% and 20.2% in 1999 and 2000. The first half of 2001 saw a loss of 8.2%, but that was much better than the markets. Like most of the managers in the AGF stable, Hubbes is a bottom-up stock picker. The focus of this fund is on medium to large companies, with lots of banks but also some up-and-coming firms like Biovail Corp. Foreign content has been steadily increasing and now stands at almost 18%. This is a well-managed fund and a good choice for AGF investors. Formerly the DK Enterprise Fund in a long-ago life.

## Global and International Equity Funds

## AGF EUROPEAN EQUITY CLASS                    $$$ ↓ G #/* £ EE

Managers: John Arnold, since inception (April 1994) and Rory Flynn, since June 1996

MER: 3.13%      Fundata: A      Style: Bottom-up Value

Suitability: Long-term growth investors

This fund has a unique track record: it is among the few European equity funds never to record a losing calendar year since its inception. It even managed to come close to breaking even in the first half of 2001 when European stock markets were being clobbered. That's a remarkable record and one that should give investors confidence. Stock selection concentrates on companies that have shares down at least 30% from their 18-month highs, pay consistent dividends, and have clear value fundamentals. In the first half of 2001, the portfolio was heavily weighted to the U.K. (40.4% of assets), with France and Spain being the only other geographic holdings in double digits. That basic allocation is exactly the same as the previous three years, and it seems to be working well. Note that although the word "Growth" appears in the name of this fund, the management style is described as value. There is an RRSP-eligible clone of this fund, the AGF RSP European Growth Fund, which is tracking the performance of the parent fund reasonably well.

## AGF INTERNATIONAL STOCK CLASS    $$$ → G #/* £ IE

Managers: Charles Brandes and Jeff Busby, since inception (June 1997)

MER: 2.85%      Fundata: A      Style: Bottom-up Value

Suitability: Conservative investors

All the funds managed for AGF by the Charles Brandes organization of San Diego use a bottom-up value investment approach, examining the fundamentals of all prospective businesses with a view to acquiring shares at a cheap price. This has the effect of reducing risk, even in rough markets. That philosophy has been put to the test in the past year as overseas markets in both Europe and Asia have been in the dumps. However, the fund has fared reasonably well under these circumstances. It managed a small gain in 2000 and was down 6.5% in the first half of 2001. No one likes a loss at any time, but that result was good enough for a first-quartile result in its category. In fact, this fund has been an above-average performer every year since it was launched in 1997. Average annual return for the three years ending June 30/01 was a very good 13.2%. As of the first half of 2001, about a quarter of the assets were invested in the U.K., with Japan holding second spot with just under 20%. All of developed Europe combined was almost 58% of the fund's holdings. The portfolio normally contains between 35 and 75 stocks, and the top 10 list includes names like Unilever, Telefonos de Mexico, and British American Tobacco. This is a good choice if you're looking for a pure international fund (i.e., one with no North American content).

## AGF INTERNATIONAL VALUE FUND    $$$$ ↓ G #/* £ GE

Managers: Charles Brandes and Jeff Busby, since November 1994

MER: 2.80%      Fundata: A      Style: Bottom-up Value

Suitability: Conservative investors

This is one of the stars in the AGF firmament and is a must for anyone who has a portfolio with the company. Charles Brandes is one of America's great value investors, regarded by many as successor to the legendary Benjamin Graham. He has written his own book on the subject, *Value Investing Today*, and is frequently quoted in the U.S. media. The 20/20 Group, which has since been absorbed into AGF, scored a major coup in getting him to take over this fund in 1994, even though they had to change the fund's original mandate to do it. Brandes and his San Diego-based team scour the world for good values and the result is a well-diversified portfolio that has churned out returns that are well above the average since he took charge. The fund has never lost money over a calendar year since he and his team assumed responsibility. Their lowest one-year gain was 15% in 1995; the highest was 27.8% in 2000. The fund even managed to record a fractional gain in the first half of 2001, a remarkable achievement considering that stock markets around the world were sliding. The portfolio is well-diversified geographically, with just over half the assets in North America, a quarter in Europe, and the rest scattered around. This is a very good choice and is highly recommended. There's an RRSP-eligible clone available but it has not been tracking the parent fund as closely as we would like. Formerly known as the 20/20 U.S. Growth Fund and, subsequently, the 20/20 International Value Fund.

## Canadian Balanced Funds

### AGF CANADIAN HIGH INCOME FUND               $$$ ↓ FI #/* RSP CBAL

Managers: Clive Coombs, since inception (May 1989) and Tristan Sones, since June 2000

MER: 1.74%     Fundata: A     Style: Interest Rate Anticipation

Suitability: Conservative investors

In previous editions, we've commented that this fund was difficult to classify because of its unusual asset mix of mainly short-term bonds but with a large holding in preferred shares (19% in the first half of 2001). AGF describes it as a short-term bond fund, but it shows up in the media reports as a balanced fund. However you want to categorize it, this is a low-risk fund that offers decent cash flow (annualized yield of 5.75% in the first half of 2001), making it a useful holding for RRIF accounts. One-year return to June 30/01 was a very respectable 7%. Formerly known as the AGF Preferred Income Fund. Ignore returns prior to 1994, since the fund was operating under its old mandate before then.

## Global Balanced and Asset Allocation Funds

### AGF AMERICAN TACTICAL ASSET            $$$$ ↓ FI/G #/* £ GBAL
### ALLOCATION FUND

Manager: Barclays Global Investors, since inception (1988)

MER: 2.51%     Fundata: B     Style: Quantitative Value

Suitability: Conservative investors

The portfolio of this fund is adjusted between U.S. bonds, stocks, and short-term notes according to the dictates of a computerized asset allocation formula developed by the managers, a San Francisco-based company running hundreds of billions of dollars in assets worldwide. Results have been very good: the fund never had a losing calendar year through the turbulent 1990s, and even managed to earn a small profit for investors in 2000. However, it was down 4.8% in the first half of 2001, so it will be a test to maintain that unblemished record. Over the long haul, this is an excellent holding for conservative investors who want exposure to U.S. markets. The 10-year average annual compound rate of return of 13.3% to June 30/01 was the top performance in the category, so don't be discouraged by the recent short-term weakness—this is still a good place for your money. As of the first half of 2001, the portfolio was heavily weighted to S&P 500 Index stocks (75%) with 20% in bonds and 5% in cash. The RRSP-eligible clone of this fund, called the AGF RSP American Tactical Asset Allocation Fund, tracks the parent quite closely, though its returns are slightly lower. The parent fund is preferred if foreign content room in a registered plan is not a concern.

## Foreign Money Market Funds

### AGF U.S.$ MONEY MARKET ACCOUNT $$$ ↓ C #/* £ FMM

Manager: Tristan Sones, since June 2000

MER: 0.90%     Fundata: D

Suitability: Conservative investors seeking U.S. currency exposure

This fund invests mainly in U.S.-pay Canada T-bills. For the past three years, U.S. dollar money market funds have paid better returns than Canadian MMFs because of higher short-term interest rates in the U.S. As a result, this fund added 5.2% in the year to June 30/01 while its Canadian dollar counterpart gained just 4.1%. Of course, the lower MER on this fund also contributed to that differential. Keep an eye on Canadian dollar movements if you have money here. If our currency starts to rise, you may want to make a switch. Don't pay any commission to buy this fund, as the low return isn't worth it. If the sales rep won't provide it without charge, look for a no-load alternative. Also note that this fund is now eligible as foreign content for RRSPs or RRIFs.

## Also Recommended

## Canadian Equity Funds

### AGF CANADIAN GROWTH EQUITY FUND $$ → G #/* RSP CE

Manager: Bob Farquharson, since inception (April 1965)

MER: 2.95%     Fundata: D     Style: Bottom-up Growth

Suitability: Aggressive investors

This fund had been positioned as a small-to-mid-cap entry, but now it has been classified as an all-cap fund. Veteran manager Bob Farquharson, who has been running this fund for some 36 years, uses a bottom-up growth strategy and targets those areas of the economy expected to outperform the market as a whole. In the first half of 2001, his emphasis was heavily into industrial products (as it had been the previous two years), which included a lot of high-tech and leading-edge companies like Biovail and Celestica. A quick glance at the top 10 holdings list tells you why this is not a small-cap fund any more—giant names like Petro-Canada and Alberta Energy jump out at you. The mandate change comes after several years of spotty performance and it should help make the returns more consistent and reduce risk, although the fund did experience a 13.7% drop in the year to June 30/01. However, the switch in approach also makes the fund very similar to the companion Canadian Stock Fund, so we wonder how long the two will coexist. At this time, Canadian Stock would be our preferred choice between these two. The assets of the old Corporate Investors Stock Fund were merged into this fund in October 1994.

## Natural Resource Funds

### AGF CANADIAN RESOURCES FUND $$ ↑ G #/* RSP NR

Manager: Bob Farquharson, since January 1974

MER: 3.34%    Fundata: D    Style: Bottom-up Growth

Suitability: Aggressive investors with non-registered plans

If you've been in this fund over the long haul (it was originally the AGF Canadian Resources Fund), then you haven't done too badly. The average annual compound rate of return for the decade ending June 30/01 was 8.1%, which was better than average for the Natural Resources category. But 1997 and 1998 were trying times for investors here, with fund units losing almost half their value during that bleak two-year period. Things have looked better lately, however. The surge in energy prices propelled this fund to a gain of 11.3% in 1999 and 16% in 2000. The first half of 2001 was also strong, with an advance of 8.8%. Veteran manager Bob Farquharson continued to heavily weight the portfolio to oil and gas issues (51% of assets) in the first half of 2001, with Alberta Energy and Petro-Canada high on the top holdings list. But be warned: the risk element in this fund is very high. Treat it like a stock: buy low, sell high. And don't hold it in a registered plan!

## U.S. Small-to-Mid-Cap Equity Funds

### AGF AGGRESSIVE GROWTH FUND $$ ↑ G #/* £ USSC

Manager: Richard Driehaus (Driehaus Capital Management), since inception (June 1993)

MER: 2.45%      Fundata: E      Style: Bottom-up Growth

Suitability: Very aggressive investors willing to accept high risk for high return potential

Why, you may wonder, do we recommend a fund that lost more than 50% in the year ending June 30/01? Because when the markets turn, this fund has the potential to double in value over a single year. This is a classic example of a high-risk/high-reward fund. In 1999, it gained 195%. Recently, it's been on a steep downward slope. But one figure is intriguing. Despite the big recent loss, if you had been in this fund over the three years to June 30/01, you would have enjoyed an average annual compound rate of return of 24.6%. You would have also experienced some gut-wrenching ups and downs in the process, of course—this fund is not for the faint of heart. Manager Richard Driehaus is known as one of the top small-cap stock pickers in the U.S., but he takes big risks as the fund's performance indicates. So don't put your money here if you can't deal with that sort of thing. Even with the high-tech slump, Driehaus is still heavily into technology stocks (about a quarter the portfolio). He has also placed a size-able bet on the health care industry. As of August 2001, there were still no signs of a turnaround here so patience will be required. But this fund's time will come around again—we just can't predict exactly when.

## Global and International Equity Funds

### AGF ASIAN GROWTH CLASS $$ ↑ G #/* £ AXJ

Managers: David Chan, since September 1993 and Mary Tan, since January 1996

MER: 3.63%      Fundata: D      Style: Bottom-up Growth/Value

Suitability: Aggressive investors

We aren't big fans of Asian stocks these days, but if you must have a Far East fund in your portfolio, this has been one of the better performers. Singapore-based David Chan is the senior person on this management team. He is a bottom-up investor who concentrates on corporate fundamentals. He's wary of the fly-by-night operations that can crop up in Asia and prefers to focus on established companies with good long-term records. The fund invests in southeast Asia and there is no Japanese content. In the first half of 2001, Hong Kong was far and away the managers' favourite market, with 49.5% of the portfolio weighting, followed by Singapore and Korea. This is exactly the same pattern as last year. Recent results have been weak, with the fund dropping

23.3% in the year to June 30/01. But over three years, investors earned an annual return of 9.2%, comfortably above average for the Asia ex-Japan category. Remember, there's a lot of volatility here, so don't invest any money unless you can live with the risk.

## AGF CHINA FOCUS CLASS $$ ↑ G #/* £ CSE

Manager: Raymond Tse (Nomura Asset Management), since June 2000

MER: 3.95%    Fundata: A    Style: Bottom-up Growth/Value

Suitability: Aggressive investors

Most Far East funds have been hammered recently, but this is a notable exception. The fund produced an impressive return of just under 40% for the 12 months to June 30/01, which, interestingly, corresponds almost exactly with the tenure of manager Raymond Tse. Prior to his arrival on the scene, this had been a very undistinguished performer. Now the question is whether he can maintain the pace. Tse uses a combination of growth and value in his stock selection approach; AGF describes it as a "growth-at-the-right-price" style. Note that although the name is China Focus, the fund does not invest exclusively, or even primarily, in China. Rather, its mandate allows the manager to "invest in securities benefiting from growth in China." That's a lot of latitude, which the portfolio composition reflects with current holdings heavily based in Hong Kong (58%). Only 34% of the portfolio is invested in pure Chinese stocks. Don't put this one in an RRSP because it's too volatile. This is truly high-risk country, but the reward potential is clearly present. Rating moves up to $$.

## AGF EMERGING MARKETS VALUE FUND $$ → G #/* £ EME

Managers: Charles Brandes and Jeff Busby, since April 1994

MER: 3.18%    Fundata: A    Style: Bottom-up Value

Suitability: Aggressive investors

Let us state up front that we are not fans of emerging markets funds. They have a record of extreme volatility and the rewards have not been commensurate with the risk. Having said that, if you absolutely must have an emerging markets fund in your portfolio, this is one worth considering. The managers take a value approach to emerging markets investing, searching out what they regard as bargain stocks in developing countries. When these markets take off, stocks can shoot up in value overnight, but the opposite is also true as we saw in 1997 and 1998 when the fund struggled. Things picked up in 1999 as the fund posted a 58.4% advance. There was a loss of 17.3% in 2000, but the first six months of 2001 were surprisingly strong, with a gain of better than 5% under terrible market conditions. The portfolio is extremely well diversified, with the Pacific Rim and Latin America currently dominating. Brandes and Busby are seasoned pros and their style reduces volatility in what is normally a very high-risk category.

## Sector Funds

### AGF GLOBAL REAL ESTATE EQUITY CLASS $$ → G #/* £ RE

Manager: Steve Way, since inception (June 1998)

MER: 2.48%     Fundata: C     Style: Top-down Country/Bottom-up Value/Growth

Suitability: Aggressive investors with non-registered accounts

Manager Steve Way's primary focus here is country. He looks first for nations where the real estate market prospects are good and then uses a blend of value and growth to select individual stocks. North America was his favourite stamping ground in the first half of 2001, with about 55% of the portfolio in U.S. and Canadian real estate stocks. The fund started slowly, with small losses in its first two years. However, it scored a handsome gain of 16.5% in 2000 and added a 2.7% return in the first half of 2001. Just remember that real estate stocks are interest-rate sensitive: if rates start to rise, you may want to switch your money elsewhere.

## Canadian Balanced and Tactical Asset Allocation Funds

### AGF CANADIAN BALANCED FUND $$ → FI/G #/* RSP CTAA

Manager: Christine Hughes, since September 1999

MER: 2.57%     Fundata: E     Style: Top-down Growth/Interest Rate Anticipation

Suitability: Conservative investors

AGF announced in August 1999 that managerial responsibility for this poorly performing fund had been handed to Christine Hughes. She had previously been with Strategic Value, where she did a first-rate job with that company's Canadian Small Companies Fund. AGF also announced that the equities segment of the portfolio would be run more conservatively with the goal of managing risk more effectively (as balanced funds go, the risk associated with this fund tended to be higher than normal). The change is significant because the fund had been heavily tilted toward stocks. However, the asset mix in the first half of 2001 was very evenly balanced, with 51% in stocks, almost 39% in bonds, and the rest in cash. The fund scored a nice 11.4% gain in 2000, Hughes's first full year at the helm. It dropped 4.2% in the first half of 2001, but that wasn't bad considering the market conditions. This fund now looks like a much better choice. The Global Strategy Income Plus Fund, formerly managed by Tony Massie, was folded into this fund in May 2001. Formerly known as the AGF Growth & Income Fund and prior to that as Corporate Investors Ltd.

## AGF CANADIAN TACTICAL ASSET ALLOCATION FUND

$$$ → FI/G #/* RSP CTAA

Manager: Barclays Global Investors, since October 1993

MER: 2.41%     Fundata: D     Style: Quantitative Value

Suitability: Conservative investors

This fund is run by Barclays Global Investors, who use a computer programme to make the key asset allocation decisions. These are the same people who have done a bang-up job with the companion American Tactical Asset Allocation Fund. This fund actually did better than the U.S. version in the late 1990s, but has stumbled recently with a one-year loss of 13.8% to June 30/01. Longer-term results are still good, however, with a 9.2% average annual rate of return over the past decade. Portfolio mix in summer of 2001 was 61% Canadian stocks, 19% foreign stocks, 10% bonds, and 10% cash. This fund is a good choice if you want some stock market exposure with reduced risk, and it works well in an RRSP. However, we're pulling back the rating to $$$ until we see evidence that this fund is fully back on track.

## Global Balanced and Asset Allocation Funds

### AGF WORLD BALANCED FUND

$$ → G/FI #/* £ GBAL

Managers: John Arnold and Rory Flynn, since June 1996

MER: 2.50%     Fundata: A     Style: Top-down Country/Bottom-up Value

Suitability: Aggressive investors

The managers of this fund are based in Dublin, which has become something of a mini financial capital in recent years. The fund uses a three-way asset allocation approach taking asset class, currency mix, and geographic allocation into account. Individual stocks are selected using value criteria, with special emphasis on companies with a low p/e ratio and above-average yield and earnings growth. In the first half of 2001, the asset mix was heavily weighted toward stocks, which constituted almost 80% of the portfolio. Geographic exposure favoured Europe—too much, perhaps, with almost two-thirds of the holdings in European equities. Canadian stocks accounted for about 11% of the assets. Interestingly, U.S. stocks were almost non-existent. The fund's "neutral" position is 40% stocks, 40% bonds, and 20% cash, so the managers are taking a surprisingly aggressive stance at this juncture. We'll see if it pays off. Returns are usually above average for the Global Balanced category, with a five-year average annual gain of 7.8% to June 30/01, which corresponds with the tenure of the managerial team. Be especially wary of the RRSP-eligible clone here: it has performed much worse than the parent fund.

## Canadian Bond Funds

### AGF CANADIAN BOND FUND $$ → FI #/* RSP CB

Managers: Clive Coombs, since January 1990 and Scott Colbourne, since December 1997

MER: 1.88%    Fundata: D    Style: Interest Rate Anticipation

Suitability: Conservative investors

This fund has been a dependable performer for many years; never sensational but decent, with steady returns. This is a conservative fund from a portfolio safety perspective, investing almost exclusively in government or government-guaranteed issues. The fund gained 4% in the year to June 30/01, slightly below average in a weak bond market. However, long-term results are above average. The fund continues to be a sound choice in the AGF line-up and should do better as bond markets rally.

## Foreign Bond Funds

### AGF GLOBAL GOVERNMENT BOND FUND $$ → FI #/* £ FB

Managers: Clive Coombs, since inception (October 1986) and Scott Colbourne, since December 1997

MER: 1.91%    Fundata: D    Style: Currency and Interest Rate Anticipation

Suitability: Investors seeking currency diversification

AGF offers two foreign bond funds: this one, which invests directly in international bonds and can therefore only be held as foreign content in RRSPs, and the RSP Global Bond Fund, which is fully eligible for registered plans. The RRSP version has been the better performer recently. Over the long haul, there's not much difference between them. Foreign bond funds have not been very profitable for investors over time, but some people find them useful for currency diversification. They do especially well when the Canadian dollar is sliding; in 1998 this fund enjoyed its best year in a decade with a gain of almost 18%, thanks to a heavy weighting toward the U.S. dollar at a time when the loonie was in a tailspin. But since then it, along with other foreign bond funds, has struggled. Loss for the 12 months to June 30/01 was 1.3%. As a general rule, an increase in the value of the loonie against major international currencies will not be good news for this kind of fund. Also remember that if you hold these units in a registered plan, they will chew into your foreign content allocation. If you decide to put units into your RRSP despite this warning, be careful: this fund pays interest monthly. If you have opted for automatic reinvestment and hold the fund in an RRSP, the additional units you receive could push you over the foreign content limit. The Global Strategy World Bond Fund was merged into this one in May 2001.

## AGF RSP GLOBAL BOND FUND $$ → FI #/* RSP FB

Managers: Clive Coombs, since inception (August 1993) and Scott Colbourne, since December 1997

MER: 2.00%     Fundata: D     Style: Currency and Interest Rate Anticipation

Suitability: Investors seeking currency diversification in a registered plan

This fund has the same management team as the Global Government Bond Fund, so it shouldn't come as a great surprise that the broad strategies are similar. The difference is that this fund invests only in RRSP-eligible bonds to minimize risk and make the fund fully eligible for registered plans. Over the years, this fund has gone through several incarnations. At various times it has been known as the 20/20 Foreign RSP Bond Fund, the Strategic Income Fund, and the Convertible Income Fund. Because of the changes, any results prior to late 1993 are not relevant when measuring historical returns. Since then, results have been about average for the Foreign Bond category (average annual compound rate of return of 2.5% for the five years to June 30/01). Until recently, the companion Global Government Bond Fund was the better choice, but this one has looked better lately.

## Promising Newcomers

## Sector Funds

## AGF GLOBAL FINANCIAL SERVICES CLASS NR → G #/* £ SPE

Manager: Rory Flynn, since inception (May 2000)

MER: 2.92%     Fundata: N/A     Style: Bottom-up Value

Suitability: Investors seeking greater exposure to the financial sector

As the name suggests, this fund specializes in companies that are involved in the financial sector in some way, including banks, insurance companies, mutual fund companies, brokerage houses, etc. As with any sector fund, this specialization means performance will tend to be more volatile than with broadly diversified funds. However, the ups and downs here should not be as great as you'd experience in a high-tech or natural resource fund. The time of greatest risk in a fund of this type is when interest rates are rising, so keep an eye out for that situation. Initial returns have been good: the one-year gain to June 30/01 was a respectable 15.7%.

# AIC GROUP

## THE COMPANY

The Burlington, Ontario–based AIC was, at one time, one of the fastest growing mutual fund companies in Canada. Growth rates have slowed lately, as the performance numbers of this high flier waned during the late 1990s. As of mid-2001, the company had just under $13 billion in assets under management. AIC has continued to introduce new funds, adding two in late 1999 and two more in May 2000, in addition to the launch of ten new foreign funds early in 1999. The latest additions are sector funds: AIC Global Developing Technologies Fund, AIC Global Science & Technology Fund, AIC Global Medical Science Fund, and RRSP-eligible versions of each were introduced in October 2000.

In previous editions, we told you that Jonathan Wellum left the AIC employment ranks, as did former CIBC financial services analyst Mark Maxwell. The two started their own money management firm, Georgian Capital Partners, in which AIC became a significant investor. Georgian Capital Partners continues to manage a number of AIC funds, including Advantage Fund II, American Advantage Fund, and Diversified Fund. With Wellum's departure, AIC's founder, Michael Lee-Chin, assumed the reins of both the Advantage Fund and the Income Equity Fund.

AIC also recruited star manager Larry Sarbit, formerly of Investors Group, to launch a new family of funds called the Focus Series. The series has one initial offering in three guises, the American Focused Fund, which is available in a Canadian or U.S. dollar version, plus an RRSP-eligible clone. The new series preserves AIC's investment principles, but with an important difference: with the Focus Series, the goal is to buy excellent companies at prices well below the intrinsic value of the business. The objective is to provide protection of principal on one hand while giving the investor potential upside capital appreciation on the other. By buying "great businesses" at discounted prices, these funds, in theory, should provide risk minimization and above-average rates of return on a long-term basis.

AIC continues to offer its three original fund types:

- *The Advantage Series.* The focus of these funds is financial services companies, although the degree of concentration on that sector has fallen to about 55% in recent years. This is partly the result of the sector's poor performance, and partly because new money has flowed into other sectors. Nonetheless, the performance of these funds will be tied very closely to financial markets. When they're strong, as they were in much of 2000–01, these funds do well. When the financial markets are weak, the Advantage funds will likely underperform a more diversified portfolio.

- *The Diversified Series.* The portfolios of these funds are more broadly based then those of the Advantage Series, reducing their potential for explosive returns to some extent, but also cutting the risk in bad markets.
- *The Income Series.* The goal of these funds (Income Equity Fund and American Income Equity Fund) is to focus on tax-efficient, stable monthly cash flow.

Finally, a bit of trivia some people have asked about: AIC stands for Advantage Investment Counsel, the original name of the company.

## THE DETAILS

| | |
|---|---|
| Number of funds: | 43 |
| Assets under management: | $13 billion |
| Load Charge: | Front: max. 6%; Back: max. 6% |
| Switching charge: | 2% maximum |
| Where sold: | Across Canada |
| How sold: | Through licensed financial advisors |
| Phone number: | 1-800-263-2144 |
| Web site address: | www.aicfunds.com |
| E-mail address: | info@aicfunds.com |
| Minimum initial investment: | $250 |

## INVESTING TIPS

AIC's Diversified Canada Fund, launched in 1999, is the first mutual fund that can be purchased on a split-share basis. Both AIC Capital Shares (symbol ADC) and the AIC Preferred Shares (symbol ADC.PR.A) trade on the Toronto Stock Exchange (TSE), and both are eligible investments inside an RRSP, RRIF, and DPSP. Split shares divide a security into two separate investment components: the part generally known as capital shares is eligible for capital gains while the other half, known as preferred shares, receives dividends flowing to the units. Investors seeking dividend income would purchase the preferred shares, while those seeking capital gains would buy the capital shares. The split shares will have a life of 10 years, after which the capital and preferred shares will be redeemed. Split shares are an innovation for the mutual fund industry. We believe this option offers a viable alternative for investors, depending on their needs.

In April 2001, AIC launched 19 new funds under the AIC Corporate Fund Inc. banner. This new family of funds is structured as a corporation, not as traditional mutual fund trusts. There are 19 new share classes available and most have a U.S. dollar clone, thus the total number of new funds is 35. Each of the 19 funds has its own distinct investment objective, and AIC provides investors with plenty of options. Part of AIC's investment philosophy has always been to help investors maximize their after-tax returns. This new Corporate Funds family provides investors with two distinct benefits, both of which address the detrimental effects of taxation. First, investors will enjoy AIC's commitment to a buy-and-hold philosophy. Second, they can shift their assets among any of the 19 share classes without realizing taxable capital gains, increasing the potential for portfolio growth.

## FUND SUMMARY

|  |  |
|---|---|
| Top Choices: | Advantage, Diversified Canada, Value |
| Also Recommended: | Advantage II, American Advantaged, Money Market |
| Promising Newcomers: | American Focused Fund |
| The Rest: | American Income Equity, Bond, Canadian Focused, Global Advantage, Global Bond, Global Developing Technologies, Global Diversified, Global Health Care, Global Medical Science, Global Science and Technology, Global Technology, Global Telecommunications, Income Equity, World Advantage, World Equity |

## FUND RATINGS

### Top Choices

### Canadian Equity Funds

### AIC ADVANTAGE FUND                                $$$ ↑ G #/* RSP CE

Manager: Michael Lee-Chin, since inception (1985)

MER: 2.45%      Fundata: C      Style: Bottom-up Value

Suitability: Aggressive value investors

The stock-picking duties here are now solely in the hands of Michael Lee-Chin, who was the architect of this fund and has been involved with it since inception. Chin took over when Jonathan Wellum left to start his own management firm. Needless to say, this change had little impact on the fund since it has long promoted a buy-and-hold philosophy. The fund invests mainly in wealth management companies of various types (including mutual funds, insurance firms, and brokerages), accounting for about 53% of Canadian stock holdings at mid-2001. For added diversification, the fund invests in other sectors such as communications, precious metals, consumer goods, and merchandising. Its top holdings include Warren Buffett's Berkshire Hathaway, not surprising considering the buy-and-hold strategy. But when you think about it, you are buying a value fund that has a major position in another value fund, and both funds charge an MER. This fund has been a steady top-quartile performer since inception. Its value orientation and strength of management showed through royally last year. Over the year to June 30/01, the fund gained 4.5% compared with the 5.8% loss for its peer group and the whopping 23.1% decline on the TSE. What this result demonstrates is how dramatic swings can be when a fund's portfolio is tilted toward one sector of the economy. Looking ahead, we see a continued rebound in financial services. We also want to point out that a buy-and-hold strategy means that this fund has been very tax efficient. Sounds good, but should the manager have to sell any securities, it will trigger huge capital gains exposure for investors. We are raising this fund to a $$$ rating.

## AIC DIVERSIFIED CANADA FUND $$$ → G #/* RSP CE

Manager: Jonathan Wellum (Georgian Capital Partners), since inception (1994)

MER: 2.26%      Fundata: A        Style: Bottom-up Value

Suitability: Long-term value investors

For several years, everybody loved the AIC funds because of the great returns they generated. Their performance was tied mainly to two strategies: a strong emphasis on financial service companies and a commitment to the value investing approach of Warren Buffett. When value investing took on a Dark Ages look in the go-go Nasdaq boom, and bank stocks were pounded by rising interest rates and merger disappointments, AIC's funds took heavy losses and investors fled. But it's a new day and AIC's approach suddenly looks pretty sound again as we look ahead to slowing growth, sober markets, and the likelihood of declining interest rates. Financial services make up the largest sector in this portfolio at 36%, while industrial products make up 27%. The top 10 holdings include Bombardier, Celestica, and TD Bank. The fund has a sizeable position in Buffett's Berkshire Hathaway Inc. Returns have steadily improved as the focus of the market has shifted. Over the year to June 30/01 this fund added 12.9%, an excellent performance during a difficult period. We expect more of the same going into 2002. Therefore, we have raised the rating to $$$.

## U.S. Equity Funds

## AIC VALUE FUND $$$ → G #/* £ USE

Manager: Neal Murdoch, since 1994 and Michael Lee-Chin, since 1987

MER: 2.41%      Fundata: A        Style: Top-down Value

Suitability: Long-term value investing

This fund was selected as the U.S. Equity Fund of the Year in 1996 and 1997 by the mutual fund industry, which may be the worst thing that can happen to any fund. Investors chasing last year's returns were hit hard with this fund, despite the fact that it has been in the top quartile in its category more years than not since inception. Its long-term strategy will focus on the financial services sector and global multinationals—not surprisingly given AIC's interests. The fund invests predominately in large-cap, blue-chip U.S. stocks, while staying clear of technology issues, a sector that AIC believed was overvalued. This belief proved correct, but it took some time as the tech sector lead the economy through the late 1990s. The value orientation here is obvious and is concentrated on a core group of about 50 stocks, which is small enough for the managers to adequately supervise, but large enough for diversification purposes. At mid-2001, the fund was nearly fully invested, representative of its long-term view. As for performance, the last three years have been disappointing. In the year ending June 30/01, the fund lost 5.1%, although the average U.S. equity fund lost 13.8%. Five-year numbers are now right at average for U.S. equity funds. Like other AIC funds, this one has a heavy financial services weighting at 52.4%. Nevertheless, we are keeping this fund at a $$$ rating. An RRSP-eligible clone of this fund is available, as well as two segregated fund versions.

## Also Recommended

### Canadian Equity Funds

### AIC ADVANTAGE II FUND $$ ↑ G #/* RSP CE

Manager: Michael Lee-Chin, since inception (1996)

MER: 2.72%    Fundata: B    Style: Bottom-up Value

Suitability: Aggressive value investors

When their wildly successful Advantage Fund was capped, AIC needed somewhere to put the trainloads of cash coming into the company. Enter the Advantage II Fund, which initially was a virtual clone of Advantage I except for a higher MER. It got off to a strong start, but two weak years have dropped the three-year average annual compound rate of return to June 30/01 to –3% compared with the Canadian Equity category at 4.8%. For the year to June 30/01, this fund gained 2.9% compared with a loss of 5.8% for the average Canadian equity fund. That kind of result is characteristic of AIC funds with relatively high volatility due to several factors: AIC is very focused in one area (the Canadian wealth management sector); the portfolio contains a relatively small number of names; and the fund follows a buy-and-hold discipline (that is, it buys a few good companies and holds for the tax efficiency). Unfortunately, this strategy doesn't allow the manager to soften the impact of large swings in the value of issues held. Traditional positions include pension and mutual fund management companies, insurance companies, and brokerages. But the Advantage II

Fund also holds a number of issues that are outside of that core focus, including MDS Inc., Thomson Corp., and Loblaws Companies. These companies were selected for their perceived ability to add shareholder value, which AIC defines as a compounding cash flow stream. They should also help to soften the volatility going forward. This fund is a decent choice as long as you maintain a long-term perspective and are comfortable with the wealth management focus. It will also have less capital gains exposure than the Advantage Fund. We'll maintain our $$ rating for the fund. Note that the MER for this fund is considerably higher than for Advantage I, which may be a factor in your choice.

## U.S. Equity Funds

### AIC AMERICAN ADVANTAGE FUND                $$$ ↑ G #/* RSP USE

Manager: Jonathan Wellum, since inception (1997)

MER: 2.72%      Fundata: C      Style: Bottom-up Value

Suitability: Long-term value investors

The value-based AIC funds are looking good again after a couple of poor years. There are two reasons for this: the return to favour of value investing and the improved showing of financial services stocks. The Advantage series is heavily weighted toward the financial sector (94% of portfolio as of mid-2001), which tells you why recent results here have been strong. One-year gain to June 30/01 was 5.9% compared with a 13.8% average loss for the peer group. Three-year average annual compound rate of return is 11.3%. Be aware of the fact that, as this portfolio is currently constituted, you are buying a U.S. financial services sector fund, even though it's not apparent from the name. You are putting all your eggs in one basket here, so don't use this as a core fund.

## Canadian Money Market Funds

### AIC MONEY MARKET FUND                $$ → C #/* RSP CMM

MER: 1.07%      Fundata: B

Suitability: Conservative investors

This fund invests primarily in commercial paper. Performance over every time frame is right around the average. But because it has front- or back-load fees, we recommend looking at no-load money market funds or, alternatively, negotiate to pay no load.

## Promising Newcomers

### AIC AMERICAN FOCUSED FUND                    NR → G /* RSP USE

Manager: Larry Sarbit, since inception (November 1999)

MER: 2.68% Fundata: N/A          Style: Bottom-up Value

Suitability: Aggressive value investors

AIC's value approach to investing went out of favour during the go-go markets of the late 1990s. But now the "buy-good-companies-and-hold-them-forever" approach, which the company's borrowed from U.S. multi-billionaire Warren Buffett, is back in the money management saddle and all their funds are performing well. This fund is one of the firm's latest additions. Launched in the fall of 1999, it is under the direction of Larry Sarbit, who ran the Investors U.S. Growth Fund with great success for many years. In true AIC fashion, he employs Buffett's classic approach to stock selection. In fact, one of its top 10 holdings is Buffett's own Berkshire Hathaway Company. The portfolio is very conservative in nature, making this a good choice for low-risk investors. Performance has been excellent so far, with a one-year gain of 28.3% to June 30/01. The only problem is that money has been pouring in faster than the manager can deploy it. As a result, AIC reported with some dismay that 75% of the portfolio was in cash as of the end of June 2001. However, given the lousy performance of the markets, that large cash position wasn't such a bad thing for unitholders. There is an RRSP-eligible clone available if foreign content room is a problem in your registered plan.

# AIM FUNDS MANAGEMENT

## THE COMPANY

AIM has moved from being a virtually unknown company in Canada to the status of industry giant in just a few short years. It now has more than $33 billion under management, placing it third behind Investors Group and Royal Funds among Canada's biggest mutual fund companies.

The company, which is controlled from London by AMVESCAP PLC, started in this country by acquiring the small Admax group. It then gobbled up the GT Global Funds in 1998, a transaction that put it on the investment map. Its biggest coup, however, was the megadeal in mid-2000 that saw Trimark sell its company and its funds to AMVESCAP, who merged them into the AIM Canada family. That one deal was enough to vault the AIM/Trimark combo into the top three in the nation in terms of assets under management.

The deal that brought the two companies together closed on August 1, 2000. Unlike many other fund company mergers, AIM has kept the Trimark name largely intact, although a few of that company's more aggressive funds have been rebranded under the AIM logo. The consolidation provides the company with a degree of style diversification it never had in the past, as the Trimark funds are more conservatively managed. Investors can switch freely between the two groups.

## THE DETAILS

| | |
|---|---|
| Number of funds: | 57 |
| Assets under management: | $33.5 billion |
| Load charge: | Front: max 5%; Back: max 6%; Low-load option also available |
| Switching charge: | 2% maximum |
| Where sold: | Across Canada |
| How sold: | Through registered brokers, dealers, and financial planners |
| Phone number: | 1-800-874-6275 |
| Web site address: | www.aimfunds.ca |
| E-mail address: | inquiries@aimfunds.ca |
| Minimum initial investment: | $500 |

## INVESTING TIPS

AIM offers two "umbrella" funds for investors with non-registered portfolios who want the option of moving money around without incurring capital gains tax liability. They are the AIM Canada Fund Inc. and the AIM Global Fund

Inc. Tax-free switches may be made among the individual "classes" (mini-funds, really) within each umbrella fund. However, you may not move assets between the two master funds without the risk of incurring a tax bill.

Because of stricter rules relating to segregated funds, AIM announced increases to the annual fees and expenses charged to the Trimark line of seg funds. These increases took effect on January 1, 2001, and will reduce the net returns to investors. The company also cut back the number of segregated funds it offers to a core of five.

We recommend you look very carefully at the high cost of the segregated fund option before making an investment decision. For example, the regular Trimark Select Canadian Growth Fund has a management expense ratio (MER) of 2.52%. But the segregated version carries an MER of 4.35%—almost two percentage points higher. This is a hefty annual premium to pay for the guarantees offered by the seg funds.

## FUND SUMMARY

### AIM Funds

|  |  |
|---|---|
| Top Choices: | Canadian First Class |
| Also Recommended: | Canada Income, Canadian Balanced, Canadian Bond, Canadian Premier Fund, Global Bond, Global Blue Chip, Global Health Sciences (Fund and Class) |
| Promising Newcomers: | Canadian Leaders |
| The Rest: | American Aggressive Growth, American Blue Chip Growth, American Mid-Cap Growth, Canada Money Market, Canadian Leaders, Canadian Premier Class, Dent Demographic Trends, European Growth, Global Aggressive Growth, Global Financial Services, Global Growth & Income, Global Energy, Global Sector Managers, Global Technology, Global Telecommunications, Global Theme, Indo-Pacific (Fund and Class), International Growth, Latin America Growth, Short-Term Income |

### Trimark Funds

|  |  |
|---|---|
| Top Choices: | Canadian, Canadian Bond, Canadian Endeavour, Canadian Resources, Canadian Small Companies, Government Income, Income Growth, Interest, Select Canadian Growth, Select Growth Fund (Class), Trimark Fund |

Also Recommended: Advantage Bond, Americas Fund, Europlus, Select Balanced

Promising Newcomers: Enterprise, Global Balanced, Global High-Yield Bond, U.S. Companies, U.S. Money Market

The Rest: Discovery, Enterprise Small-Cap, International Companies

# FUND RATINGS

## Top Choices/AIM Funds

### Canadian Equity Funds

### AIM CANADIAN FIRST CLASS $$$ → G #/* RSP CE

Managers: Robert Mortimer and Ronald Sloan

MER: 2.80%     Fundata: A     Style: Event-Driven Value

Suitability: Conservative investors

The AIM fund line-up doesn't contain many funds that are well suited to risk-averse investors (see Trimark for those); however, this fund is an exception. The managers look for stocks that are attractively priced in relation to historic earnings, cash flow, and valuations. They especially like companies offering a potential catalyst that could unlock hidden values. The top portfolio holdings in mid-2001 included several banks, Canadian Pacific (which was going through a corporate breakup), Molson, E-L Financial, and Onex. The portfolio has a strong foreign content position, with more than 20% of assets in U.S. securities. Results have been good, and the fund has been a consistent first- or second-quartile performer since it was launched in 1997. After a small loss in calendar 1998, it produced a gain of more than 40% in 1999 and followed that with a 23% advance in 2000. In the first half of 2001, it was just slightly below break-even, a good result in very weak market conditions. This fund is making its debut appearance here and we're starting it off with a well-merited $$$ rating. Formerly called AIM Canada Value Class.

## Also Recommended/AIM Funds

### AIM CANADIAN PREMIER FUND $$ ↑ G #/* RSP CE

Managers: Clas Olsson, since October 1997 and Jason Holzer, since 2000

MER: 2.70%     Fundata: C     Style: Earnings Momentum

Suitability: Aggressive investors

This is a classic momentum fund that invests across the full spectrum of Canadian businesses, as well as offering a significant foreign content component.

This is high-risk territory, as momentum funds chase the hot stocks of the day, which could come crashing down. Funds like this tend to perform much more impressively when markets are strong, and this particular one is no exception. It had a one-year gain of 44.3% to June 30/00 and showed a three-year average annual compound rate of return of 21.9% to that date. But what a difference a year makes. In the 12 months to June 30/01, it gave back 23% and the three-year average annual compound rate of return fell to 11.3%. If you are going to put any money here, you have to be aware of these risks. As of mid-2001, the portfolio had a strong blue-chip feel to it, with companies like Canadian Pacific, Bombardier, Loblaws, George Weston, and Molson in the top 10 holdings. We were also seeing the first indications that the fund was bouncing back from the big losses sustained earlier in the year. The same team runs the companion AIM Canadian Premier Class. Its recent record is much weaker, but it offers a tax advantage to non-registered portfolios because it comes in under an umbrella fund (AIM Canada Fund Inc.), allowing you to move assets around without triggering capital gains. The Class version was formerly known as AIM Canada Growth Class.

## Sector Funds

### AIM GLOBAL HEALTH SCIENCES FUND (CLASS)          $$ → G #/* £ ST

Manager: Thomas R. Wald, since 2000

MER: 2.93%     Fundata: A     Style: Growth

Suitability: Aggressive investors

This was one of the first industry sector funds to appear in Canada. The mandate is to invest in the health care industry throughout the world, including everything from pharmaceutical manufacturers to nursing homes. This should continue to be a huge growth area as the North American population ages. The fund got off to a quick start, then sagged somewhat following a managerial change in 1996 and has yet to return to its early glory days. There was another managerial change in 2000, with Thomas Wald assuming portfolio responsibility, and the fund showed signs of regaining some steam in the second quarter of 2001. This is not our top pick among health sciences funds by any means, but it is a respectable entry in the field. This fund has a stablemate, AIM Global Health Care Class. It has the same manager and a very similar portfolio. Safety record to date is quite good for a single industry fund. The main difference is that the Class units fall within an umbrella fund, which means you can switch assets around without attracting capital gains tax liability.

## AIM GLOBAL BLUE CHIP FUND $$ → G #/* £ GE

Managers: Lindsay Davidson, since July 1996 and Michele Garren, since 2000

MER: 3.01%    Fundata: A    Style: Value

Suitability: Middle-of-the-road investors

Here's a rarity: a value fund in the AIM group that is much more focused on growth and momentum. The fund's mandate allows it to invest anywhere in the world, with a focus (as the name tells you) on large company stocks. As of mid-2001, the largest geographic holding in the portfolio was in the U.S. (about 40% of the assets). Because of value investing's return to favour, we expected to see much better recent results from this fund, but they have been somewhat disappointing. The portfolio lost 6.3% over the year to June 30/01. Compared with world stock market performances that wasn't awful, but many value managers came up with handsome gains over the same time frame (take a look at AGF International Value Fund). We're keeping this fund on our Recommended List because it is one of the better bets in the AIM line-up at the present time, but we're not wildly enthusiastic about it. Be guided accordingly. On December 18/98, the AIM Tiger Fund, AIM Korea Fund, and AIM Nippon Fund were merged into this fund. Name changed from AIM International Value Fund in 2001.

## Dividend Income Funds

## AIM CANADA INCOME CLASS $$ → G/FI #/* RSP DIV

Managers: Rob Leslie, Roger Mortimer, and Ronald Sloan, since 2000

MER: 2.12%    Fundata: E    Style: Value/Growth

Suitability: Income investors

The goal of this fund is to generate steady income through an annual yield of about 8% while providing growth potential for investors. To achieve this, it invests in a mix of dividend-paying Canadian stocks, foreign stocks, and real estate investment trusts (REITs). To supplement cash flow, the managers also write covered call options. The fund has done a good job of living up to the income part of its mandate. In calendar 2000, the units paid out distributions of 45¢ each, bang on the 8% target yield. As a bonus, all the payments came in the form of tax-advantaged dividends and capital gains, which means this fund works much better outside a registered plan. The growth side of the equation has not been as impressive, however. Three-year performance numbers show an average annual loss of 0.3% to June 30/01, meaning capital losses within the portfolio have exceeded the distributions over that time. Note that the volatility here will be greater than for a more traditional dividend fund because of the high percentage of common stocks and REITs in the mix. This fund would be most appropriate for retirees looking for good cash flow. It might also work in a RRIF for the same reason, although any tax advantages would be lost. We give it a $$ rating on the strength of its income stream.

## Canadian Balanced and Asset Allocation Funds

### AIM CANADIAN BALANCED FUND                    $$ ↑ G #/* RSP CBAL

Manager: Clas Olsson, since October 1997; Robert Alley, Jan Friedli, and Jason Holzer, since 2000

MER: 2.46%      Fundata: C       Style: Earnings Momentum/Credit Analysis

Suitability: Balanced investors

This fund is somewhat more aggressively managed than the usual Canadian balanced entry and the results show it: the fund recorded a handsome gain of 32% in 1999 when markets were strong and added another 9% and change in 2000. But it was weak in the first half of 2001, losing almost 6%. The objective is to maintain a blend of approximately 60% stocks and 40% bonds, with little variation. The fund has been sticking closely to that goal. The portfolio at mid-2001 was weighted toward stocks, but bonds were a healthy part of the mix at around 40% of total assets. Equities are selected from the entire universe (no large- or small-cap bias), using an earnings momentum approach to stock selection, which AIM claims is unique among Canadian balanced funds. The bond segment is a middle-of-the-road mix of government and corporate issues, although the managers favoured the corporate side in the first half of 2001, as they had in the year previous. This is a decent fund and worthy of consideration for an RRSP if you don't mind the higher risk. Formerly known as the Admax Asset Allocation Fund.

## Canadian Bond Funds

### AIM CANADIAN BOND FUND                        $$ ↑ FI #/* RSP CB

Managers: Carolyn Gibbs, since October 1997; Robert Alley and Jan Friedli, since 2000

MER: 2.15%      Fundata: E       Style: Credit Analysis

Suitability: More aggressive bond investors

This new fund is really an old fund. In its previous guise it was known as the AIM Global RSP Income Fund and invested in a portfolio of international securities. But now it has been given a tighter Canadian mandate and a new name to reflect that directive. The portfolio focuses heavily on corporate bonds, both Canadian and U.S., which gives it a higher risk profile than bond funds that hold more government issues. Part of the Canadian holdings is in the form of U.S. pay bonds. So what you're getting here is a Canada/U.S. currency mix. This fund is a good choice for people who need regular income and who are willing to accept the higher risk that comes with this portfolio mix. One-year return (to June 30/01) was 7.5%, a significant improvement from the year previous and good enough to propel the fund to a first-quartile ranking. As a result, we are raising our rating a notch. Formerly known as the Admax World Income Fund.

## Foreign Bond Funds

### AIM GLOBAL BOND FUND                    $$ ↑ FI #/* £ FB

Managers: Carolyn Gibbs, Robert Alley, and Jan Friedli, since 2000

MER: 2.62%      Fundata: A      Style: Credit Analysis

Suitability: Investors seeking U.S. currency exposure

This fund is run by the same team that manages the companion Canadian Bond Fund and the approach is very similar: a strong emphasis on corporate issues. The major difference is that most of the cash flow generated here is in U.S. dollars. About two-thirds of the portfolio was in U.S. bonds (most of them corporate) in mid-2001, with about 20% of the assets in Canadian issues. There was a sprinkling of bonds from other countries (Mexico, Italy, Australia, Germany, and Brazil), but to describe this as a "global" bond fund based on its composition is stretching matters. It's really a North American fund, with U.S. dollars as the driving force. If that's what you want, take a look at it. Returns have been decent as far as foreign bond funds go, with a gain of 6.4% over the year to June 30/01. However, cash flow is not particularly strong and income is paid only quarterly as opposed to monthly in the Canadian Bond Fund. This is a true international bond fund with a well-diversified portfolio, including some developing countries issues. Not recommended for RRSPs—although it is eligible—because it will eat into your precious foreign content room.

## Promising Newcomers/AIM Funds

## Canadian Equity Funds

### AIM CANADIAN LEADERS FUND                    NR → G #/* RSP CE

Managers: Robert Mortimer and Ronald Sloan, since inception (January 2001)

MER: N/A      Fundata: N/A      Style: GARP

Suitability: Conservative investors

This brand-new fund is run by the same team that manages the strong AIM Canadian First Class. Their growth-at-a-reasonable-price (GARP) approach is in tune with current market conditions, which is why we are including this fund on our Promising Newcomers list, even though it has no track record to date. This is a large-cap fund that will hold a small portfolio of about 30 stocks. The managers make good use of foreign content (about 19% of assets in mid-2001). Recent top holdings included Royal Bank, Vincor International, Seamark Asset Management, Molson, and Magna International. We like the approach here, and the fact it offers another value option for the AIM brand name.

# Top Choices/Trimark Funds

## Canadian Equity Funds

### TRIMARK CANADIAN FUND                    $$$ → G #/* RSP CE

Managers: Ian Hardacre and Carmen Veloso, since 1999

MER: 1.63%/2.52%      Fundata: A      Style: Value

Suitability: Conservative investors

The late 1990s were rough on this one-time favourite, as value investing went out of style and returns foundered. But what goes around comes around, and this entry is looking very good again. Over the latest 12 months, to June 30/01, the return was 11.5% (10.8% for the back-end load, or DSC version), well above average for the category. It's the first time since 1996 that this fund has been in above-average territory in the Canadian Equity category—a long wait for faithful investors. Many didn't hang around; an investor exodus led Trimark to replace lead manager Vito Maida in February 1999 with the team of Ian Hardacre, who joined the company in 1997 after coming over from the Ontario Teachers' Pension Plan, and Carmen Veloso. The fund showed a quick rebound after the change but then slipped back into mediocrity for a time. Part of the problem was the investing style. When Trimark was an independent company, it used to say that its approach was "to buy good companies at attractive prices." That statement really meant that the fund employed a value/growth style blend, with a tilt toward value, and value was out of favour until this past year. But now it's back, and so is this fund. A look at the top 10 holdings in mid-2001 shows several banks and blue chips like Telus. But, interestingly, we also find some high-tech companies that were notably absent in years past, such as CAE Inc. In fact, almost 10% of the portfolio was in tech stocks at that point, showing that the managers were bargain hunting in the beaten-up sector. Last year we commented that this looked like an Old Economy fund, but that seems to be changing. Note the two purchase options carefully. The back-end load (DSC) version carries a much higher MER that will cut deeply into your net returns. We recommend the front-end units. Try to persuade your advisor to sell them to you at zero commission. If you're a good client, it may work.

### TRIMARK CANADIAN ENDEAVOUR FUND          $$$ ↓ G */# RSP CE

Manager: Geoff MacDonald, since 1998

MER: 2.14%      Fundata: A      Style: Value

Suitability: Conservative investors

The distinctions between the various Trimark Canadian equity funds are somewhat difficult for the average investor (and even the professional advisor) to discern. This fund takes a somewhat more value-oriented approach than Trimark Canadian and as a result, its recent returns have been significantly higher. One-year gain to June 30/01 was a sparkling 18.8%. However, we can't be sure if this is only a temporary advantage due to market conditions or an indication that manager Geoff MacDonald is a superior stock picker. Due to this uncertainty, we're giving this fund a $$$ rating, the same as the other Trimark Canadian entries. But we note that at the time of writing, this fund is the strongest of the bunch. The thrust of the portfolio is toward mid- to large-cap stocks, but the manager has extensive small-cap knowledge so some smaller companies may also show up here. Major holdings in mid-2001 included several banks, Power Corp., Telus, and U.S. firms Newell Rubbermaid and McDonald's. This is a very sound choice in the current environment and is recommended for RRSPs. Formerly the Trimark RSP Equity Fund.

## TRIMARK SELECT CANADIAN GROWTH FUND $$$ → G #/* RSP CLC

Manager: Heather Hunter, since 1999

MER: 2.52%     Fundata: A     Style: Value

Suitability: Conservative investors

This is another Trimark entry that struggled through the late 1990s but is experiencing a renaissance with the re-emergence of value investing. It's run by Heather Hunter, who moved over to Trimark from the Ontario Teachers' Pension Plan. She favours large-cap stocks that offer long-term growth potential. The portfolio is well diversified, but was more defensive than its stablemates in mid-2001 with a cash position of almost 15%. Hunter prefers a buy-and-hold approach, typically retaining a stock for three to five years. Returns have been improving; the fund gained 11.5% in the year to June 30/01. Many of the top holdings also show up in other Trimark portfolios, but there is obviously enough differentiation to have an impact on returns. We're increasing the rating to $$$.

## Canadian Small-to-Mid-Cap Funds

## TRIMARK CANADIAN SMALL COMPANIES FUND $$$ → G #/* RSP CSC

Managers: G. Keith Graham, since inception (May 1998) and Rob Mikalachki, since 2000

MER: 2.57%     Fundata: A     Style: Value

Suitability: Aggressive investors

Many Canadian small-cap funds performed well in the first half of 2001, despite the weakness of the stock markets. This fund was one of the best, gaining 22.1% in the first six months of the year, which was remarkable in light of what else was going on in the markets. In fact, this fund has been steadily improving since its launch, gaining 12.5% in 1999 and 16.5% in 2000. That's a tribute to the investing acumen of lead manager Keith Graham and his associate, Robert Mikalachki. The portfolio is well diversified, with industrial products and consumer products being the largest categories. The managers were also holding a relatively large amount of cash (13%), which makes the recent performance even more impressive. Foreign content represents slightly more than 20% of the holdings. This is one of the best-looking Canadian small cap funds around right now. We'll see if they can keep up the pace. Debuts with a $$$ rating.

## Global and International Equity Funds

### TRIMARK FUND $$$$ → G #/* £ GE

Manager: Bill Kanko, since 1999

MER: 1.62%/2.50%    Fundata: A    Style: Value

Suitability: Conservative investors

We're delighted to report that this long-time favourite is back on track after running into a rough patch in the late 1990s. Lead manager Bill Kanko took over in May 1999 from Robert Krembil, who had run this fund since it was created back in 1981. Kanko restored the fund to first-quartile status in 2000 and kept that top ranking in the first half of 2001. His value approach worked especially well in the rough market conditions that prevailed in late 2000 and early 2001, and the fund produced a gain of 11.5% (load version) over the 12 months to June 30/01. The fund continues to be heavily weighted toward U.S. stocks (63% as of mid-2001). Japan represented about 12% of the assets and there was a fairly large cash position at 12%. European stocks were almost non-existent. Sector emphasis was on consumer products stocks, which accounted for about a quarter of the assets, followed by financial services at 14%. We are returning this fund to the $$$$ status it enjoyed in this *Guide* for many years. Note that we recommend the purchase of front-end load units (try to get them at zero commission) for long-term investors because of the high MER attached to the DSC units.

### TRIMARK SELECT GROWTH FUND (CLASS) $$$ → G #/* £ GE

Manager: Bill Kanko, since 1999

MER: 2.50% Fundata: A Style: Value

Suitability: Conservative investors

This started out as an optional front- or back-end load companion to the front-end Trimark Fund. However, now that the Trimark Fund also offers two purchase options (albeit with different MERs), we wonder how long the two funds will remain separate. This fund features the same manager (Bill Kanko), the same style, and a similar—but not identical—portfolio. In theory, nominal returns should generally be slightly below those of the original Trimark Fund front-end (SC) units because of the higher MER, and that was indeed the case over the past year with this fund generating a 10.4% return to June 30/01. This fund originally grew more rapidly because of the public preference for back-end load funds, but that distinction no longer holds. If you're going to buy one of these funds on a back-end load basis, it really doesn't matter which one you pick, but our preference is for the SC units of the Trimark Fund. Yet another version of this fund, Trimark Select Growth Class, was launched in June 2001 as part of the umbrella AIM Global Fund Inc. Investors with non-registered portfolios who make frequent switches may want to look at that option, as it permits you to move money around without exposing yourself to capital gains tax. Also comes in the form of an RRSP-eligible clone fund.

## Sector Equity Funds

### TRIMARK CANADIAN RESOURCES FUND          $$$ → G */# RSP NR

Manager: Geoff MacDonald, since inception (May 1998)

MER: 2.57%     Fundata: A       Style: Value

Suitability: Aggressive investors

This fund has emerged as one of the top-performing Canadian resource entries in recent years under the guidance of Geoff MacDonald. Although the resource sector is inherently high-risk, he minimizes this concern to some extent by using a value approach to stock selection. Companies must be attractively priced in relation to historic profits and valuations. As well, he looks for firms with sustainable cash flow and improving balance sheets. In other words, you won't find a lot of speculative issues in this portfolio. MacDonald also makes good use of the foreign content allowance to diversify geographically, with positions in countries like the U.S., Australia, Mexico, and Finland. As of mid-2001, he wasn't overloaded in any one sector, the kind of balance we like in this type of portfolio. As for returns, they have been just fine so far. One-year gain to June 30/01 was a sparkling 26.9%. Three-year average annual compound rate of return was 13.4%. We are impressed so far and are starting this fund off with a $$$ rating.

## Canadian Balanced and Asset Allocation Funds

### TRIMARK INCOME GROWTH FUND          $$$ → FI/G #/* RSP CBAL

Managers: Patrick Farmer, since 1997; G. Keith Graham, since 1999; Rex Chong, since 2000; and Vince Hunt, since 2001

MER: 1.67%/2.44%     Fundata: A       Style: Value/Credit Analysis

Suitability: Conservative investors

The revival of value investing has revived the fortunes of this fund after it spent several years wandering in the wilderness. The portfolio is broadly diversified, although the bond holdings were on the low side in mid-2001, representing about a quarter of the assets. Stock selection tends more toward value than growth, with emphasis placed on issues that are attractively priced in relation to historical earnings and valuations. Results have been steadily improving, and the one-year gain to June 30/01 was a terrific 18.4% (SC units), one of the best in the category. That result pulled up the three-year average annual compound rate of return to 8.5%. This fund comes with two purchase options and we strongly recommend the SC units, which have a much lower MER. That makes a big difference to your net return; the one-year gain for the DSC units to June 30/01 was more than a percentage point less, at 17.2%. Rating moves up to $$$.

## Canadian Bond Funds

### TRIMARK CANADIAN BOND FUND                    $$$ ↓ FI #/* RSP CB

Managers: Patrick Farmer, since inception (1994); Rex Chong, since 2000; and Vince Hunt, since 2001

MER: 1.31%      Fundata: B       Style: Credit Analysis

Suitability: Conservative investors

This is a very respectable fixed-income entry from the Trimark family. The managers also run the companion Advantage Bond Fund, but this fund's mandate doesn't include the high-yield component that drives its stablemate. Like Advantage Bond, the safety record here is very good and the portfolio mix suggests it should stay that way. Over the five years to June 30/01 this fund gained an average of 6.7% annually, the same as Advantage Bond, which is above average for the Canadian Bond category. The portfolio is a mixed bag of federal and provincial bonds, corporate issues, mortgage-backed securities, asset-backed securities, and even a few preferred shares. A good choice for conservative investors.

### TRIMARK GOVERNMENT INCOME FUND              $$$ ↓ FI #/* RSP STB

Managers: Patrick Farmer, since inception (1993); Rex Chong, since 2000; and Vince Hunt, since 2001

MER: 1.31%      Fundata: C       Style: Credit Analysis

Suitability: Conservative investors

This is a defensive bond fund. The securities are all government or government-guaranteed issues, and all have relatively short maturities, none of which exceed five years. Some mortgage-backed securities are included in the mix. A portfolio like this one will produce below-average returns in strong markets, but will preserve capital when bond markets weaken. In the past, this fund suffered by being compared to the total bond fund universe. Now it has been placed in the new Short-Term Bond category where it fits more comfortably and shows rates of return that are average to slightly above. Five-year average annual gain to June 30/01 was 4.8%. This one is for investors who don't want to take on a lot of risk.

## Canadian Money Market Funds

### TRIMARK INTEREST FUND $$$ → C #/* RSP CMM

Manager: Patrick Farmer, since 1993; Rex Chong, since 2000; and Vince Hunt, since 2001

MER: 0.89%/1.87%     Fundata: B     Style: Credit Analysis

Suitability: Conservative investors

This fund invests almost entirely in commercial paper, which boosts returns but adds a slightly higher degree of risk. Average annual return over the five years to June 30/01 was 4% (SC units). The average fund in the Canadian Money Market category returned a shade less, at 3.8%. But a word of warning: the DSC units, which were launched in October 2000, carry a much higher MER, resulting in returns that are consistently below average. As a result, these DSC units are not recommended. Opt for the SC units only and insist on paying a zero front-end load. If your advisor won't concede, choose a no-load money market fund from another organization.

## Also Recommended/Trimark Fund

## Global and International Equity Funds

### TRIMARK EUROPLUS FUND $$ → G #/* £ EE

Managers: Richard Jenkins, since 1997, and Dana Love, since 2000

MER: 2.79%     Fundata: A     Style: Value

Suitability: Aggressive investors

European funds as a group have struggled recently, but this one has struggled just a bit less. It posted a decent 9% gain in 2000. In the first half of 2001, it gave back 5.5%, but that wasn't bad considering the weak state of European markets. The mandate allows the managers to invest throughout Europe, including the countries of the former Iron Curtain bloc and Russia. However, most of the portfolio in mid-2001 was in Western Europe, with an emphasis on Germany, Denmark, the U.K., and Ireland. This is a decent European entry and worth a look if you'd like that type of regional fund for your portfolio. An RRSP-eligible clone is available.

## Canadian Balanced and Asset Allocation Funds

### TRIMARK SELECT BALANCED FUND                $$ → FI/G #/* RSP CBAL

Managers: Patrick Farmer, since 1997; Ian Hardacre and Carmen Veloso, since 1999; Rex Chong, since 2000; and Vince Hunt, since 2001

MER: 2.44%    Fundata: A    Style: Value/Credit Analysis

Suitability: Conservative investors

The equity side of this portfolio has a different management team than the companion Income Growth Fund, and the bond holdings here were even more meagre in mid-2001 at 20%. Those are the main differences between the two funds, apart from the purchase options. In terms of results, this one has done respectably but it has not been as strong lately as Income Growth. Our recommendation is that you choose the Income Growth SC units if you are in for the long haul.

## Specialty Equity Funds

### TRIMARK AMERICAS FUND                $$ ↑ G #/* £ SPE

Managers: Jim Young and Bruce Harrop, since 2000

MER: 2.89%    Fundata: C    Style: Value

Suitability: Aggressive investors

The aim of this fund is to offer investors some exposure to Latin America, but with a healthy dose of U.S. stocks added (82% of the portfolio in mid-2001). The U.S. additions are mainly small- to mid-cap companies, so the composition of this fund is more aggressive than the typical Trimark entry. Returns haven't been bad: gain for the year to June 30/01 was 7%, and the three-year average was 7.4%. The main problem, as we have noted in the past, is that it's hard to get a reading on this fund. The Latin exposure is very small (less than 14%) so what this really comes down to is a small- to mid-cap U.S. fund with some Brazilian and Mexican stocks tossed in. If that somehow fits your portfolio mix, fine. Most people find it's difficult to locate a proper niche for this fund and move on to something more clearly defined. There's an RRSP-eligible clone available, but we don't recommend this fund for registered plans.

## Canadian Bond Funds

### TRIMARK ADVANTAGE BOND FUND                    $$ → FI #/* RSP HYB

Manager: Patrick Farmer, since inception (1994); Rex Chong, since 2000; and Vince Hunt, since 2001

MER: 1.30%     Fundata: A        Style: Credit Analysis

Suitability: Aggressive bond investors

This is a somewhat unusual bond fund in terms of its portfolio structure. The managers hold a core of federal government bonds for stability and then blend in some high-yield issues to boost returns. Results have been reasonably good, especially given the recent weakness of the high-yield bond market. Average annual compound rate of return for the five years to June 30/01 was 6.7%, tops in the High-Yield Bond category. However, the fund's position relative to its competitors has slipped recently, which gives us enough concern to reduce the rating to $$. Given the fact that corporate bonds make up about 70% of the portfolio, you'd expect this fund to have a higher-than-normal risk level, but in fact it has never suffered a loss over any given calendar year. Still, the portfolio mix is such that the potential for an above-average loss at some point is always present.

## Promising Newcomers/Trimark Funds

## Canadian Equity Funds

### TRIMARK ENTERPRISE FUND                        NR → G #/* RSP CE

Manager: Catherine (Kiki) Delaney, since inception (June 1999)

MER: 2.51%     Fundata: B        Style: Value

Suitability: Middle-of-the-road investors

Kiki Delaney made headlines in the financial pages when she resigned as portfolio manager of the Spectrum Canadian Equity Fund in 1999 to move over to Trimark and start this new entry. She hasn't shot out the lights with it so far, but performance has been respectable. The fund gained 12.8% in 2000, its first full calendar year, and recorded only a small loss of about 2% in the first half of 2001. The focus is on mid- to large-cap stocks with strong growth potential. Recent top holdings included CAE, CIBC, CNR, Petro-Canada, and Sun Life. We expect this will be a decent performer over the long haul, but it's up against some tough competition from within its own organization now that Trimark's other Canadian equity funds have pulled up their socks.

## U.S. Equity Funds

### TRIMARK U.S. COMPANIES FUND (CLASS)  NR → G #/* £ USE

Managers: Bruce Harrop, since 2000, and Jim Young, since 1999

MER: 2.70%    Fundata: N/A    Style: GARP

Suitability: Middle-of-the-road investors

This is the same team that runs the Trimark Americas Fund. Here they search out high-quality companies that are attractively priced and offer investors some kind of edge: a technological advantage, a strong competitive position, exceptional management, etc. The top portfolio holdings in mid-2001 included many familiar corporate names: Pepsico, Kimberly-Clark, Target, Wells Fargo, etc. Initial results have been good, with a 10.7% gain in the year to June 30/01. This fund is one to watch. There's an RRSP-eligible clone if needed. Also comes in a "Class" version that is suitable for non-registered portfolios.

## Global Balanced and Asset Allocation Funds

### TRIMARK GLOBAL BALANCED FUND  NR → FI/G #/* £ GBAL

Managers: Rex Chong, since 1999; Patrick Farmer, since 1999; Vince Hunt, since 2001; Richard Jenkins, since 1999; and Dana Love, since 2000

MER: 2.70%    Fundata: N/A    Style: Value/Credit Analysis

Suitability: Conservative investors

This new global balanced entry offers a well-diversified portfolio in geographic terms, with about a third of the assets in the U.S. as of mid-2001 and the rest nicely scattered around the globe. In terms of asset mix, the emphasis was on stocks, with bonds accounting for only about a quarter of the portfolio. Performance has been good. The fund gained just over 20% in 2000, its first full calendar year, and more than held its own with a 4.4% advance in the first half of 2001. This looks like a welcome new addition to the Trimark fold. Also comes in an RRSP-eligible clone.

## Foreign Bond Funds

### TRIMARK GLOBAL HIGH-YIELD BOND FUND  NR ↑ FI #/* £ FB

Managers: Rex Chong and Patrick Farmer, since 1999, and Vince Hunt, since 2001

MER: 2.17%    Fundata: N/A    Style: Credit Analysis

Suitability: Aggressive investors

The Trimark fixed-income team has proven their skill in the Canadian high-yield bond market with the Advantage Bond Fund. Now they've taken their act to the global stage and so far it's playing well. U.S. junk bonds make up the largest single segment of the portfolio, but there are some Canadian high-yield issues as well, along with some more conservative government bonds and mortgage-backed securities. Initial results have been good: the fund returned 8.7% in the year to June 30/01. Just remember that the risk here is much higher than in a regular bond fund. There's an RRSP-eligible clone available if you don't want to eat up foreign content room.

## Foreign Money Market Funds

### TRIMARK U.S. MONEY MARKET FUND      NR → C #/* £ FMM

Managers: Rex Chong and Patrick Farmer, since 2000, and Vince Hunt, since 2001

MER: 1.07%/1.88%      Fundata: N/A      Style: Credit Analysis

Suitability: Investors seeking U.S. currency exposure

This is another entry from the very fine Trimark fixed-income team. The portfolio is mainly in short-term U.S. corporate notes with some T-bills. The fund generated an above-average return of 4.9% in the year to June 30/01 (SC units). We do not recommend the DSC units, as they have a much higher MER.

# ALTAMIRA INVESTMENT SERVICES

## THE COMPANY

Altamira went through a difficult period in the mid-1990s but is now on the road to recovery under the leadership of its president, Gordon Cheesbrough. A high-profile media campaign has helped refurbish the company's image but, more importantly, several of its key funds produced impressive results during the bull market of the late 1990s. However, Altamira has a lot of funds that are performing poorly and some of its recent launches (such as the e-Business Fund) have been disasters.

There are some good funds in the family, but you have to choose carefully. Altamira tends to place big bets in specific sectors. Its heavy concentration in growth-based technology stocks has hurt returns badly over the past year.

Like others in the business, Altamira has launched its own line of index funds in an obvious attempt to capitalize on the financial media's preoccupation with high MERs. The Precision family is now quite extensive, including the Altamira Precision Canadian Index Fund based on the S&P/TSE 60 Index—Canada's major index composed of large-capitalization, broadly based stocks. The Precision U.S. RSP Index Fund is based on the S&P 500, while the Precision International RSP Index Fund derives its performance from the Morgan Stanley Capital International Europe, Australasia, and Far East Index (MSCI EAFE Index). There are also two Precision European Index funds. One is a derivative-based, fully RRSP-eligible fund. The other is not derivative based, and is considered foreign content within an RRSP. Both of the Precision European Index funds track the Euro Top 100 Index, which is an index of the 100 largest companies in Europe. There is also a Precision Dow 30 Fund based on the Dow Jones Industrial Average (considered foreign content), a Precision Pacific Index Fund (based on the performance of the MSCI Pacific Index and considered foreign content), and, finally, a Precision U.S. Mid-Cap Fund (foreign content) designed to track the S&P 400 Mid-Cap Index.

## THE DETAILS

|                            |                                                                   |
| -------------------------: | ----------------------------------------------------------------- |
| Number of funds:           | 51                                                                |
| Assets under management:   | $5.8 billion                                                      |
| Load charge:               | None                                                              |
| Switching charge:          | 2% on sector funds switched within 90 days of purchase            |
| Where sold:                | Across Canada                                                     |
| How sold:                  | Directly through the manager or through brokers, dealers, and financial planners |

Phone number:  1-888-NO-LOADS (1-888-665-6237)
Web site address:  www.altamira.com
E-mail address:  advice@altamira.com
Minimum initial investment:  $5,000 for Precision family; $1,000 for all others

## INVESTING TIPS

Altamira is one of the few non-bank fund lines that offer no-load sales by telephone to investors right across Canada. You can open up an account by phone and, by completing a form, make switches in the same way. There is a one-time account-opening fee.

## FUND SUMMARY

Top Choices:  Asia Pacific, Bond, Global Diversified, Japanese Opportunity, North American Recovery, Short-Term Canadian Income, T-Bill

Also Recommended:  Balanced, Equity, European, Global Small Company

Promising Newcomers:  Biotechnology

The Rest:  Altafund Investment Corporation, Capital Growth, Dividend, e-Business, Global 20, Global Bond, Global Discovery, Global Financial Services, Global Telecommunications, Global Value, Growth & Income, Health Sciences, High-Yield Bond, Income, Leisure & Recreation, Precious & Strategic Metals, Precision Canadian Index, Precision Dow 30 Index, Precision Euro RSP Index, Precision European Index, Precision International RSP Index, Precision Pacific Index, Precision U.S. RSP Index, Precision U.S. Mid-Cap Index, Resource, RSP Balanced Portfolio, RSP Biotechnology, RSP e-Business, RSP Global Telecommunications, RSP Global 20, RSP Global Diversified, RSP Growth & Income Portfolio, RSP Growth Portfolio, RSP Health Sciences, RSP Income & Growth, RSP Income, RSP Japanese Opportunity, RSP Maximum Growth, RSP Stable Income Portfolio, Science & Technology, Select American, U.S. Larger Company

# FUND RATINGS

## Top Choices

### Canadian Equity Funds

**ALTAMIRA NORTH AMERICAN RECOVERY FUND**                $$$ → G NO RSP CSC

Manager: David Taylor, since 1995

MER: 2.39%     Fundata: N/A     Style: Bottom-up/Sector Growth

Suitability: Aggressive growth-oriented investors

While investors were fleeing to the safety of large-cap stocks, it was difficult for smaller turnaround stocks to record any sustained gains. When markets go south, it's generally these struggling firms that are the first to be sold. As a result, this relatively diversified fund investing in distressed North American stocks deemed to be undervalued has found it a challenge to mount any offensive. A loss of 4.1% over the year ending June 30/00, coming on top of a loss of 10.1% the previous year, created considerable investor concern. However, in the latest year ending June 30/01, the fund recorded an impressive 12.8% return compared with an average loss for the category. We'll maintain a cautious $$$ rating for this fund given its recent healthy rebound. Note that although this is called a North American fund, most of the assets are in Canada in order to give it full RRSP eligibility.

### Global and International Equity Funds

**ALTAMIRA ASIA PACIFIC FUND**                $$$ ↑ G NO £ PRE

Manager: Mark Grammer, since 1997

MER: 2.55%     Fundata: A     Style: Bottom-up Value

Suitability: Aggressive investors

This fund has a solid record in a volatile category. In the year ending June 30/01, its 21.4% loss was painful, but not as bad as the 30.1% average loss for the category. The three-year return at 16.1% per annum is well above the 6.1% gain for the category. The five-year return is also above average. The real question is whether Asia can recover any time soon. The key to this region remains Japan, and based on recent economic data there are many uncertainties that have yet to be fully addressed, including slow domestic demand, rising unemployment, and a fragile banking system. However, if you want Asia/Pacific in your portfolio, this is one of the better choices. Rating maintained at $$$.

## ALTAMIRA JAPANESE OPPORTUNITY FUND $$$ ↑ G NO £ JE

Manager: Mark Grammer, since 1997

MER: 2.52%    Fundata: A    Style: Bottom-up Value

Suitability: Aggressive investors

The Altamira Japanese Opportunity Fund was one of only three Japan funds to earn an A rating from Fundata in its June 30/01 reporting period. Although the fund suffered a huge loss during the year, its three-year average annual compound rate of return was a very good 15.3%. The category as a whole had average gains of less than 5%. Mark Grammer, an Asian specialist, has been doing a wonderful job in spite of the hurdles in his path. The fund invests primarily in small- to mid-sized companies, so there is added growth potential as well as risk to this fund. The recent signs are encouraging, and while it is still very early in the Japanese recovery, we like the prospects in the longer term. This fund is a good choice—albeit an aggressive one—for when this region turns around. We are keeping our rating at $$$, bearing in mind the aggressive nature of this sector. An RRSP-eligible clone of this fund was launched in 2000, but this fund may be too aggressive for most registered plans.

## Global Balanced and Asset Allocation Funds

## ALTAMIRA GLOBAL DIVERSIFIED FUND $$$ ↑ G/FI NO £ GBAL

Manager: Chuck Bastyr, since 1998

MER: 2.14%    Fundata: C    Style: Top-down/Interest Rate Anticipation

Suitability: Aggressive investors

This is a very flexible balanced fund that has no restrictions on asset investment, whether equities or fixed-income. As a result, the fund could be fully invested in stocks if the manager so decides. This strategy leaves the onus on the manager to make the right calls. As of mid-2001, the fund had 79% of its assets in equities, with a focus on financial services, communications, and technology. Only 20% of the assets were in fixed-income securities, with the remaining 1% in cash. For investors who bought this fund expecting a more balanced approach, a surprise awaited them. At the end of June 2001, this fund had a strong U.S. flavour, with over 50% of its holdings there, followed by investments in Europe. Since taking over in 1998, Chuck Bastyr seems to be turning this fund around. However, after two years of strong performance, the fund faltered in the latest year, suffering an 18.7% loss in the 12 months ending June 30/01. Be warned that this fund, in its present state, is a bit aggressive and not recommended for those looking for a conservative balanced fund. But we are giving the manager the benefit of the doubt and are maintaining our rating at $$$.

## Canadian Bond Funds

### ALTAMIRA BOND FUND $$$ ↑ FI NO RSP CB

Manager: Robert Marcus, since 1991

MER: 1.42%    Fundata: E    Style: Interest Rate Anticipation

Suitability: Aggressive investors

After a couple of years of remarkable performance where it was one of the top three bond funds in Canada, this fund has slipped badly over the last 30 months. One- and three-year numbers for the period ending June 30/01 are now below average, although five-year numbers are still in the top 25% of the peer group. Mind you, long-term holders of this fund should be used to this type of performance: the fund manager makes big bets on the bond market, so when he is right, the fund is a top-quartile performer. But when he is wrong, he becomes a fourth-quartile performer. If you can stand the roller-coaster ride, this fund has a 10-year average annual compound rate of return of 10.4%, making it number one in the Canadian Bond category over the past decade. To achieve these numbers, the fund's mandate emphasizes long bonds, which made up about 83% of the portfolio in the early part of 2001, with most being in federal bonds. The fund normally has a long average duration. (Duration is a technical measure of the number of years it will take to receive today's present value of a bond in future payments. The longer the duration, the more sensitive a bond portfolio will be to interest rate movements. A bond fund with a long duration will increase proportionately more in value when interest rates fall, and lose more when rates rise.) At mid-2001, the fund had an average duration of 12.3 years, with an average maturity of 19.8 years. Overall, this is a good risk/reward bond fund designed with the long-term investor in mind. If you recognize the risks and want to have some of your assets in bonds, this fund is a good choice.

### ALTAMIRA SHORT-TERM CANADIAN INCOME FUND $$$$ ↓ C NO RSP CMM

Manager: Edward Jong, since 1997

MER: 0.60%    Fundata: N/A    Style: Index

Suitability: Conservative income investors

This is what investors like to find: a number one performer in its first three years, with rock-bottom volatility, low MER, and no fees. If there's a tiny downside, it's the minimum deposit to get into this fund, which is $5,000. The fund invests primarily in Treasury bills and other short-term debt instruments issued or guaranteed by the Canadian federal or provincial governments, the U.S. government, Canadian chartered banks, or Canadian corporations. "Short-term" is just what it means: the portfolio will maintain an average term to maturity of less than one year. Edward

Jong manages the fund actively, trying (and apparently succeeding) to anticipate changes in short-term interest rates. Recently the fund held no U.S. securities, though it can go up to 30% of assets while maintaining full RRSP eligibility. The average annual return for the three years ending June 30/01 was 5.4%—well above average for the category. This is a first-rate money fund and deserves a $$$$ rating.

## ALTAMIRA T-BILL FUND $$$ ↓ C NO RSP CMM

Manager: Edward Jong, since 1998

MER: 0.39%     Fundata: C     Style: Index

Suitability: Conservative income investors

Manager Edward Jong seems to have a touch for anticipating short-term interest rate movements. This T-bill fund, which invests in Canadian Treasury bills and other short-term federal and provincial debt instruments, has been a consistent top performer. It produced a return of 5.2% for the year ending June 30/01, well above average for the category, but below the number posted by the companion Short-Term Canadian Income Fund, hence the difference in the rating. This is Altamira's most conservative fund. The portfolio generally has an average term to maturity of between 90 and 180 days. The attractive results are matched by low volatility, no fees, and a very nice MER. We'll keep this fund at a $$$ rating.

## Also Recommended

### Canadian Equity Funds

## ALTAMIRA EQUITY FUND $$$ ↑ G NO RSP CE

Manager: Ian Ainsworth, since 1998

MER: 2.48%     Fundata: D     Style: Top-down/Sector Growth

Suitability: Aggressive investors

This fund had shown signs of a major turnaround since a new management team under the direction of Ian Ainsworth was appointed in mid-1998, after the sudden departure of Frank Mersch following problems with securities regulators. Mersch's active trading style and stock-picking acumen were responsible for the huge gains this fund enjoyed in the early 1990s, but in the years prior to his leaving he seemed to have lost his touch. Ian Ainsworth and Co. shifted gears and took the fund in a different direction, with a heavy emphasis on the technology sector. This strategy worked at first (the fund gained 56% in the year ending June 30/00, following a top-quartile performance for the year ending June 30/99), but resulted in severe losses in the latest year (to June 30/01), when the fund dropped 25.3%. The fund is in a higher-risk category and performance is volatile. For now, the rating is maintained at $$$.

## Global and International Equity Funds

### ALTAMIRA EUROPEAN EQUITY FUND                    $$ → G NO £ EE

Manager: Chuck Bastyr, since 1999

MER: 2.53%      Fundata: B      Style: Top-down/Sector Growth

Suitability: Aggressive investors

In late 1999, Altamira brought the management of this fund in-house, terminating the services of Banque Pictet of London and replacing them with the company's own global team, with Chuck Bastyr as the fund's lead manager. The new team has had to contend with very rough European markets, and the fund posted a loss of 18.2% for the year to June 30/01. But that was better than the average result for the category, and the three-year returns are also above average. We will wait to see how Bastyr and his team do when the markets turn back up before considering a rating change.

### ALTAMIRA GLOBAL SMALL COMPANY FUND               $$ → G NO £ GE

Manager: Chuck Bastyr, since inception (1996)

MER: 2.54%      Fundata: B      Style:   Top-down/Sector Growth

Suitability: Aggressive investors

This global fund will shop anywhere. While it may invest in the emerging markets of Africa, Asia, and Latin America, it tends to focus on small-cap stocks in developed countries, including the U.S., U.K., Netherlands, Japan, and Norway. Manager Chuck Bastyr looks for companies with market caps of less than $2 billion, and may also invest in government and corporate debt instruments. There are two points of caution with respect to global small-cap investing. The first is variable economic and political factors, and sometimes questionable foreign stock market conditions. Second, the stocks held may be from companies with short operating histories and limited products, markets, and financial resources. In short, they're more vulnerable and are therefore likely to be more volatile (although so far this fund has a good record in that regard). The average annual three-year return to June/01 of 14.8% was well above average for global equity funds as a group, and substantially above the Morgan Stanley Capital International Index. We'll maintain the rating at $$.

## Canadian Balanced and Asset Allocation Funds

### ALTAMIRA BALANCED FUND $$ → FI/G NO RSP CBAL

Manager: Shauna Sexsmith, since 1997

MER: 2.20%     Fundata: E     Style: Top-down/Interest Rate Anticipation

Suitability: Long-term balanced investors

Taking over this moribund fund in 1997, Shauna Sexsmith began turning things around and performance numbers were improving. The fund gained 23.7% in the year to June 30/00, which made three straight years of above-average results. However, the year ending June 31/01 was disappointing, as this balanced fund recorded a 10.2% loss compared with a 2.6% loss for its peer group. That result also meant that three- and five-year returns came down to average/below average for the Canadian Balanced category. The fund increased its exposure to equities to 59% at mid-2001, up from 48% at mid-2000. The equity side is quite diversified across a range of industries and includes some large-cap, blue-chip dividend stocks. Added diversification is derived through the 13% of assets invested in stocks from around the world. This component is accomplished through investing in other Altamira funds, with Europe, Japan, and the U.S. as the favourite areas as of mid-2001. The fixed-income portion is conservatively managed and includes a mix of government and high-grade corporate bonds and T-bills. Over 40% of Canadian bond holdings are short-term in nature, resulting in minimal interest rate risk. We are down-grading the fund to a $$ rating pending a return to the form of the previous three years.

## Promising Newcomers

### ALTAMIRA BIOTECHNOLOGY FUND NR ↑ G NO £ ST

Manager: Wendy Chua, since inception (September 2000)

MER: 2.83%     Fundata: N/A     Style: Bottom-up Sector

Suitability: Aggressive investors

This sector fund debuted in September 2000 and invests primarily in biotech companies. In its short life it is showing some promising signs. Although it had a loss in its first six months (reflecting a severe decline in U.S. biotech stocks), for the three months ending June 30/01, the fund recorded a 14.3% return compared with 6% for its peer group. If you are thinking about biotech investing, this fund is worth a look. Just be sure you can handle the risk.

# ASSANTE ASSET MANAGEMENT

## THE COMPANY

Founded in 1987, Assante Asset Management (formerly Loring Ward Investment Counsel) is a Winnipeg-based firm that provides investment management, personal wealth management, and offshore services. The company specializes in servicing high net worth individuals and prides itself on its innovative approaches to money management.

There are two mutual fund lines under the Assante banner: Optima Strategy and Artisan. The Optima Strategy funds are pools intended for individuals and families with $25,000 or more to invest, so they are aimed at the high-end market. The Artisan funds are actually portfolios of other companies' funds. You'll find funds from such organizations as AGF, AIM, C.I., Dynamic, and Fidelity represented in the various portfolios. We have adopted a policy of not reviewing funds of funds, so the individual Artisan portfolios are not reviewed here. However, most of the underlying funds in which they invest are rating elsewhere in this book, so you can assess the individual components of each Artisan portfolio in that way.

## THE DETAILS

|  |  |
|---|---|
| Number of funds: | Optima Strategy: 18; Artisan: 14 |
| Assets under management: | $3.5 billion |
| Load charge: | Front: max. 4%; Back: max. 6% |
| Switching charge: | 2% maximum |
| Where sold: | Across Canada |
| How sold: | Through Assante and other select financial planning groups |
| Phone number: | 1-877-943-7215 |
| Web site address: | www.assante.com/canada/financialservices |
| E-mail address: | access@assante.com |
| Minimum initial investment: | Optima Strategy Funds: $25,000; Artisan Funds: $2,000 |

## INVESTING TIPS

In the past, the Optima Strategy funds showed very low MERs (management expense ratios). That's because management fees of up to 2.5% were charged directly to investors. However, new rules on how MERs are calculated and presented went into effect in 2000, so the figures shown in this edition (as of Dec. 31/00) are an accurate reflection of the total non-optional fees and expenses you will be assessed. You will see that they are quite high, well above average by industry standards in most cases. Keep this fact in mind when you are considering an investment. In some cases, the manager absorbs certain expenses, which are included in the MER nonetheless. However, the company is under no obligation to continue this practice.

Regardless of how the numbers are expressed, each investor is charged an annual management fee for the funds held. This fee varies depending on the type of fund. The base rate for equity funds is 2.5% a year, for fixed-income funds it is 1.5% to 2% annually, and for the money market fund it is 0.75% a year. Investors who use the company's asset management service receive a discount of 0.25% a year on most of the funds, but you must have a total of $100,000 with Optima Strategy funds to qualify. Those who invest more than $250,000 can qualify for additional reductions. This is an unusual pricing mechanism, so be sure that you understand exactly what you'll be paying and what services you will receive for your money.

Optima operates "umbrella" funds that allow for switches without triggering capital gains tax liability in non-registered portfolios. This programme is similar to the ones offered by AIM, AGF, C.I., Clarington, and a few other firms.

Although we don't rate the Artisan Portfolios, we can report that none of the Canadian equity entries with a three-year track record came close to matching the return of the average Canadian balanced fund over that time frame (to June 30/01). The only two global portfolios with a three-year record, High Growth and Moderate, did outperform the category average, however.

## FUND SUMMARY

### Optima Strategy Pools

| | |
|---|---|
| Top Choices: | Canadian Equity Value, Canadian Fixed-Income, Real Estate Investment, Short-Term Income, U.S. Equity Value |
| Also Recommended: | Global Fixed-Income |
| Promising Newcomers: | Canadian Equity Diversified |
| The Rest: | Canadian Equity Growth, Canadian Equity Small-Cap, Cash Management, International Equity Diversified, International Equity Growth, International Equity Value, U.S. Equity Diversified, U.S. Equity Growth |

### Artisan Portfolios

(Note: We do not review or rate funds of funds.)

| | |
|---|---|
| Top Choices: | N/A |
| Also Recommended: | N/A |
| Promising Newcomers: | N/A |

The Rest: Canadian T-Bill, Conservative, Global Advantage, Growth, High Growth, Maximum Growth, Moderate, Most Conservative, New Economy, RSP Global Advantage, RSP Growth, RSP High Growth, RSP Maximum Growth, RSP Moderate

# FUND RATINGS

## Top Choices/Optima Strategy Pools

### Canadian Equity Funds

### OPTIMA STRATEGY CANADIAN EQUITY VALUE POOL

$$$ → G #/* RSP CE

Manager: Daniel Bubis, since 1994

MER: 3.13%    Fundata: A    Style: Value

Suitability: Conservative investors

This fund uses a disciplined value investing approach to its stock selection, looking for undervalued companies trading at a low price/earnings multiple. This kind of approach normally signals a fund with low volatility, but this one has experienced some unusually high performance swings in recent years as value investing went out of favour and then came roaring back with the high-tech collapse. So we've gone from a small gain of 4.2% in the year to June 30/00, when markets were generally strong, to an impressive advance of 27.7% in the 12 months to June 30/01, at a time when stock markets were generally weak. In fact, that result made this fund the number two performer in the country over that period. What a comeback! The portfolio makes good use of foreign content with a selection of U.S. stocks and is well diversified by sector, with energy stocks in the dominant position (22%) entering 2001. The value approach of manager Daniel Bubis is back in vogue and this fund is looking much better as a result. Rating rises to $$$.

### U.S. Equity Funds

### OPTIMA STRATEGY U.S. EQUITY VALUE POOL

$$$ → G #/* £ USE

Manager: Thomas F. Sassi (Scudder Kemper Investments), since 1994

MER: 3.13%    Fundata: A    Style: Contrarian Value

Suitability: Conservative investors

Like the Canadian Equity Value Pool, this portfolio is value-driven. The advisor is New York-based Scudder Kemper Investments, which was formed from a complex corporate arrangement that absorbed Dreman Value Advisors, who had been handling the management previously. The manager uses a contrarian approach to stock selection, focusing on stocks with very low price/earnings ratios. The goal is not only to produce good returns but also to provide good downside protection in bad markets. Unfortunately, something went badly amiss in 1999–2000. Results had been very good, with a three-year average annual compound rate of return to June 30/99 of 31.8%—terrific for a value fund. To that point, there had not been a single 12-month period when this fund has shown a loss, so the risk rating was excellent. That combination prompted us to boost this fund's rating all the way to $$$$ in the year 2000 edition of this *Guide*. So what happened? This supposedly low-risk value fund proceeded to lose 22.7% in the year to June 30/00. Granted, it wasn't a great time for value funds, but that result was totally out of sync with its previous history and was one of the worst results in the U.S. Equity category. In the 2001 edition, we cut back the rating but commented that we expected the fund would recover, as Scudder Kemper has a long and successful history of value investing. Well, that's just what happened. The fund staged a huge turnaround and chalked up a big 31.1% gain in the 12 months to June 30/01, good enough to rank it among the top three in the U.S. Equity category. As a result, we are somewhat gingerly moving the rating back up to $$$. We would just like to see a little more consistency here—and so, we expect, would unitholders.

## Sector Funds

### OPTIMA STRATEGY REAL ESTATE INVESTMENT POOL

$$$ → G #/* £ RE

Manager: Robert H. Steers (Cohen & Steers), since 1996

MER: 3.16%     Fundata: D     Style: Value

Suitability: Conservative investors

This fund does not invest directly in property but rather in a portfolio of real estate stocks and investment trusts, mainly in the U.S. and Canada. The mix is well diversified and includes holdings in hotel groups (e.g., Starwood), health care facilities, office managers and developers, retail malls, etc. It has been the top performer in the small Real Estate category over the past three years. One-year return to June 30/01 showed a very fine gain of 24.9%, with a three-year average annual return of 7.9%. The goal of the managers is a combination of income and long-term capital gain. You won't make a big killing with this one, but it should provide steady—if modest—returns.

## Canadian Bond Funds

### OPTIMA STRATEGY CANADIAN FIXED-INCOME POOL

$$$ → FI #/* RSP CB

Manager: Nestor Theodorou, since 1994

MER: 2.62%   Fundata: A

Suitability: Conservative investors

This fund invests mainly in Government of Canada bonds with varying maturities, as well as some provincial issues and a few corporates. Returns have been consistently above average over the past five years. Even a modest gain of 5.4% in the year to June 30/01 was better than what most funds in the Canadian Bond category could do, and earned it a ranking among the top performers over that time. Longer-term results are above the norm as well, even with the high management fee. A good choice from this company, especially for a registered plan.

### OPTIMA STRATEGY SHORT-TERM INCOME POOL

$$$ ↓ FI #/* RSP STB

Manager: Nestor Theodorou, since 1994

MER: 1.97%   Fundata: A   Style: Yield Curve Analysis

Suitability: Conservative investors

This fund is designed for investors who want less risk in their bond holdings. The portfolio holds government and corporate issues with maturity dates of no more than five years. In fact, the average duration of the portfolio (a measure of risk) has been much less than that for some time. This type of fund will typically underperform when bond markets are strong, but will protect your asset base when bonds hit the skids. The relatively high MER cuts into returns here, but the 5.5% average annual compound rate of return for the three years to June 30/01 was still above average. This is a good choice if capital preservation with modest returns is your goal.

## Also Recommended/Optima Strategy Pools

## Foreign Bond Funds

### OPTIMA STRATEGY GLOBAL FIXED-INCOME POOL

$$ → FI #/* £ FB

Manager: Gary Cooper, since 2001

MER: 2.64%   Fundata: D   Style: Top-down Value

Suitability: Investors seeking currency diversification

There has been a change at the top for this fund, which had been run for several years by MFS Investment Management, a top U.S. company. Assante has brought the management in-house, giving the assignment to Gary Cooper. This move causes us some concern, because MFS had done a good job with this fund over time, making it one of the best in the foreign bond category. We hope that Cooper is able to fill MFS's shoes but we are cutting the rating a notch until we see the evidence. This fund invests in government and government-guaranteed issues from around the globe, with broad currency diversification. Results are better than average for the Foreign Bond category, even with the high management fee. However, that's not saying much because foreign bond funds haven't been very profitable lately. The five-year average annual compound rate of return to June 30/01 was just 4.3%. Still, if you want a fund of this type in your portfolio for the currency diversification, this is a pretty good one. There's an RRSP-eligible clone if required.

## Promising Newcomers/Optima Strategy Pools

### OPTIMA STRATEGY CANADIAN EQUITY DIVERSIFIED POOL

NR → G #/* RSP CE

Managers: Catherine (Kiki) Delaney, Ian Hardacre, and Heather Hunter (all of AIM), since inception (May 2000)

MER: 3.08%     Fundata: N/A     Style: Value

Suitability: Conservative investors

Now here's an interesting fund. You can't get the combined talents of these three good managers in one fund within the AIM organization as they all manage different portfolios under the Trimark banner. But this new fund combines the best of their ideas and all that talent should spell good things for Optima investors, at least in theory. We haven't had much time to see how it will work out, but the initial signs are good. The fund gained 8.3% over the year to June 30/01, a very positive result in a tough market. Of course, that should come as no surprise since the Trimark funds have also done well in this environment. We would have liked to see some style diversification here by adding a growth manager from AIM to the mix but that's a quibble, at least at this stage. This fund is one worth your attention if you have investments with the company.

## Top Choices/Artisan Portfolios

N/A

## Also Recommended/Artisan Portfolios

N/A

## Promising Newcomers/Artisan Portfolios

N/A

# BANK OF MONTREAL (BMO INVESTMENTS INC.)

## THE COMPANY

The Bank of Montreal is the fourth-largest marketer of mutual funds among Canada's five major banks. While getting off to a slow start initially, the bank has come on strong in the past several years and now offers an extensive line of 47 funds across many categories. In late April 2000, the bank renamed its funds BMO Mutual Funds to better integrate the bank's investment products and lines of business. The fund company name is now BMO Investments Inc.

BMO debuted a number of new global funds in non-registered and registered form in November 2000; most are off to a slow start. Another significant push recently has been into U.S.-oriented mutual funds. Responsibility for the U.S. funds is under Harris Investment Management Inc. The other key manager is Jones Heward Investment Counsel Inc., a subsidiary of the bank, which handles the Canadian funds. Global funds are managed by an assortment of outside advisors, including Edinburgh Fund Managers PLC, J.P. Morgan, Quadravest Capital Management Inc., Rothschild Asset Management Limited, Sanford C. Berstein & Co., State Street Global Advisors and Grupo Financiero Bancomer.

The bank has reduced the management expense ratio (MER) on many of its funds. In terms of performance, the majority of the funds are average compared to their peer group.

## THE DETAILS

|  |  |
|---|---|
| Number of funds: | 47 |
| Assets under management: | $11.4 billion |
| Load charge: | None |
| Switching charge: | None |
| Where sold: | Across Canada |
| How sold: | Through any Bank of Montreal branch, Nesbitt Burns, BMO Funds Call Centre, and through InvestorLine |
| Phone number: | 1-800-665-7700 or 1-888-636-6376 (Quebec) |
| Fax number: | 1-888-840-2817 or (416)867-6203 |
| Web site address: | www.bmo.com/mutualfunds and www.bmo.com/fonds |
| E-mail address: | English: mutualfunds@bmo.com; French: fonds@bmo.com |
| Minimum initial investment: | BMO funds: $1,000; MatchMaker: $1,000; Custom Select: $10,000 |

## INVESTING TIPS

For those investors who like BMO funds but who also want some professional advice in determining the right mix to suit their needs, the bank offers the MatchMaker product line. Based on your investment objectives, a MatchMaker portfolio will be recommended to you. These portfolios simply buy and switch between different BMO Funds depending on the investment climate.

The most confusing aspect of the packaged portfolios offered by various fund groups are the names. They may make sense to the promoters, but to anyone else they're cryptograms. The MatchMaker series is, unfortunately, no exception. You'll need a detailed explanation to figure out what each portfolio invests in and the type of person for whom it is best suited.

Overall these portfolios have turned in only a fair performance so far. The best performers have been the Strategic Balanced Portfolios 1 and 2. However, returns are below that of the BMO Asset Allocation Fund over three years, so you might as well choose the fund itself instead.

If you have a lot of spare cash, BMO has a premium money market fund that performs very well due to its low 0.43% expense ratio. The fund has an above-average record with a one-year return of 5.2% compared with 4.5% for the average in the category. The three-year return at 4.9% is about 65 basis points above the average. The catch is that the fund has an initial minimum investment of $150,000.

## FUND SUMMARY

| | |
|---|---|
| Top Choices: | Asset Allocation, Dividend, Equity, NAFTA Advantage, Precious Metals, U.S. Special Equity |
| Also Recommended: | Bond, Mortgage, Special Equity, U.S. Value |
| Promising Newcomers: | U.S.$ Bond |
| The Rest: | Air Miles Money Market, Emerging Markets, Equity Index, European, Far East, Global Balanced, Global Bond, Global Financial Services, Global Health Sciences, Global Opportunities, Global Science & Technology, Global Technology, International Bond, International Equity, Japanese, Latin American, Money Market, Monthly Income, Premium Money Market, RSP European, RSP Global Balanced, RSP Global Financial Services, RSP Global Opportunities, RSP Global Science & Technology, RSP Global Technology, RSP International Index, RSP Japanese, RSP Nasdaq Index, RSP U.S. Equity Index, Resource, Short-Term Income, T-Bill, U.S. Dollar Bond, U.S. Dollar Equity Index, U.S.$ Money Market, U.S. Growth, U.S. Value |

# FUND RATINGS

## Top Choices

### Canadian Equity Funds

### BMO EQUITY FUND                                              $$$ → G NO RSP CE

Manager: Michael Stanley (Jones Heward), since 1994

MER: 2.34%     Fundata: B     Style: Value

Suitability: Long-term value investors

This is a large-cap, value-oriented fund that you could buy for your RRSP and forget about until retirement. It was formerly known as the BMO Growth Fund, but the name change better reflects its value bias. The fund is composed of a diversified group of well-capitalized Canadian blue-chip companies representing areas like industrial products, metals and minerals, and utilities. Consequently, the fund is quite defensive in nature. The mandate is to invest in a core portfolio of between 40 and 50 good stocks. Results continue to be above average. The loss for the year to June 30/01 was 6.6%, slightly better than the 8.5% average loss of the peer group. Three- and five-year average annual returns of 7.2% and 13.6% are also well above average. So far in its short history, the fund appears to be better than average in both up and down markets. This is a good choice for your portfolio.

### Dividend Income Funds

### BMO DIVIDEND FUND                                         $$$ → G/FI NO RSP DIV

Manager: Michael Stanley (Jones Heward), since inception (1994)

MER: 1.77%     Fundata: C     Style: Value

Suitability: Income investors with an equity bias

If you want a top-performing Canadian dividend fund that looks for capital growth over regular income, this may be your choice. At mid-2001, this $1.3 billion fund (down from $1.9 billion a year ago) held a core portfolio of value-oriented, large-cap, high-yielding companies like banks, utilities, and pipelines. But since the fund pays only quarterly distributions, it is not recommended for investors seeking steady monthly income. Compared with the average Canadian dividend fund, this one has a strong focus toward common shares, which account for about 84% of its assets. Comparable funds offer more of a mix of common shares, preferred shares, trust units, and bonds. Returns have been generally high across the board. Three-year average annual return to June 30/01 was way above average at 10.4%. The 23.0% return in the latest year was highly impressive, given the 11.7% average for the peer group. The fund is recommended as a relatively low-volatility equity holding in an RRSP. The name change from BMO Dividend Income Fund reflects the capital appreciation bias.

## U.S. Small-to-Mid-Cap Funds

### BMO U.S. SPECIAL EQUITY FUND                    $$$ → G NO £ USE

Manager: Paul Kleinaitis (Harris Investment Management Inc.), since 1999

MER: 2.17% Fundata: B  Style: Small- and Mid-Cap Value

Suitability: Aggressive value investors

The fund manager here concentrates on small- and mid-cap companies with market capitalization of $500 million or less. The fund is off to a solid start in its short history. The three-year return to June 30/01 is 12.4% per annum, compared with 8.3% for the peer group and 6.4% for the Russell 2000 (Canadian $) Index. Although it posted a 1.5% loss in the year ending June 30/01, the average fund in the category lost a whopping 11.3%. So far we are impressed with what we see, thereby giving it a $$$ rating.

## Global and International Equity Funds

### BMO NAFTA ADVANTAGE FUND                    $$$ → G NO £ NAE

Managers: Jones Heward Investment Counsel Inc., Harris Investment Management Inc., and Grupo Financiero Bancomer, since inception (1994)

MER: 2.15%     Fundata: B     Style: Value

Suitability: Long-term equity investors

The mandate of this fund is to search for quality issues within the NAFTA countries: the U.S., Canada, and Mexico. At least 20% of the assets must be invested in each of the three countries. At mid-2001, this large-cap value fund had about 45% of its stocks in the U.S. market. The fund's exposure to Mexico (23% at mid-2001) was constructive, as Mexico was one of the world's few winning markets at that point in time. The fund recorded a 4.1% loss in the year ending June 30/01, compared with the average 10.1% loss for the North American Equity category. Longer-term returns are above average as well. This is a fully invested fund, with virtually all of the assets in stocks at mid-2001. The risk factor here will be higher than a comparative pure U.S. or Canadian fund, due to its exposure to the more volatile Mexican market. Keep that detail in mind when making your investment decision. All in all this is solid, well-managed fund, and we are maintaining our $$$ rating.

## Sector Funds

### BMO PRECIOUS METAL                     $$$ ↑ G NO RSP PM

Manager: Bill Belovay (Jones Heward), since 1999

MER: 2.33%     Fundata: A     Style: Growth

Suitability: Sector investors willing to accept high volatility

This precious metal fund is off to a great start. The fund concentrates primarily on Canadian gold exploration and production companies, although it also holds some foreign companies. Its return in the year ending June 30/01 was a remarkable 27.1%, compared with the 8.1% return of the precious metal group. The three-year return is just as impressive, given that the average for the group was a loss of 3.4%. Since taking the reins in 1999, Belovay, with his 15-plus years of experience in the mining and resource sector, has done a nice job picking stocks with this sector fund. The Fundata score of A supports our assessment. The fund is well worthy of a $$$ ranking.

## Canadian Balanced and Asset Allocation Funds

### BMO ASSET ALLOCATION FUND          $$$ ↓ FI/G NO RSP CTAA

Manager: Jones Heward Investment Counsel, since 1996

MER: 2.07%     Fundata: A     Style: Tactical Asset Allocation

Suitability: Long-term balanced investors

This is a conservatively managed fund on both its equity and fixed-income sides. The equity component is well diversified, with a large-cap value orientation. It held a relatively large portfolio of over 160 stocks at mid-2001, representing about 51% of its assets. Its fixed-income side is concentrated mainly in government bonds and in relatively short-duration fixed-income securities including a 12% allocation to money market securities, resulting in below-average interest rate risk. The fund's performance has been steadily improving. The three-year return for the year to June 30/01 was 5.2% per annum, over twice that of its peer group. In the latest year to June 30/01 the fund lost 2.9% compared with the 5.3% loss of its peer group. The safety record is quite good for a fund of this type. This performance merits a boost in its rating to $$$. A good RRSP choice.

## Also Recommended

### Canadian Small-to-Mid-Cap Funds

#### BMO SPECIAL EQUITY FUND $$ → G NO RSP CSC

Manager: Lesley Marks (Jones Heward), since 1998

MER: 2.35%      Fundata: N/A      Style: Growth

Suitability: Long-term growth investors

In 1998, Lesley Marks replaced ex-manager James Lawson, who had generated some decent returns during his tenure. This fund searches primarily for stocks with a market capitalization of under $500 million at the time of purchase. As a result, the fund consists mainly of growth-oriented stocks, which produces added risk. To alleviate some of this risk, the portfolio at mid-2001 was well diversified across industries with a focus on industrial products and oil and gas. The growth emphasis also means the fund was underweighted in commodities. In her short tenure, Marks has had to deal with plenty of turbulence in the small-cap sector. Results so far are not overly impressive. The fund lost 9.1% for the year to June 30/01, which was below the 6.7% average loss for the peer group. This had been a pretty good aggressive long-term fund, but given its recent showing, we are feeling cautious and are downgrading to a $$ rating.

### U.S. Equity Funds

#### BMO U.S. VALUE FUND $$ → G NO £ USE

Manager: Don Coxe (Harris Investment Management Inc.), since inception (1997)

MER: 2.20%      Fundata: B      Style: Value

Suitability: Long-term value investors

Value is the approach here, and that has been a rough road to follow in the U.S. over the last few years. Management seeks out high-quality U.S. firms that have strong competitive positions, are financially sound, and are currently undervalued. This is a widely diversified portfolio, with entries from computer manufacturers, automakers, banks, insurance, telecommunications, and retail—mostly household names. 1997 was a super year for this fund: it returned some 32%. But the next three years were weak. The average annual return for the three years ending June 30/01 is only 3.1%, though that is slightly above average for the category. Big, profitable companies will shine again, and this fund should do well in a value-based rally. We are upgrading to a $$ ranking.

## Canadian Bond Funds

### BMO BOND FUND                    $$ ↓ FI NO RSP CB

Manager: Mary Jane Yule (Jones Heward), since 1996

MER: 1.59%      Fundata: B       Style: Term Structure Analysis

Suitability: Conservative income investors

This fund is managed more conservatively than the average Canadian bond fund. At mid-2001, a large percentage of the bonds were in Government of Canada issues, with a secondary focus on high-quality corporate issues. But while conservative, this fund has been able to outperform its peer group in most years. In the year to June 30/01, it returned an above-average 6.1%, and over the past three years its 4.1% return compares favourably with the 3.9% average for the group. If you want a conservative, no-nonsense, low-risk bond fund, you may want to look here.

## Canadian Mortgage Funds

### BMO MORTGAGE FUND                 $$ → FI NO RSP M

Manager: Mary Jane Yule (Jones Heward), since 1996

MER: 1.50%      Fundata: C       Style: Interest rate anticipation

Suitability: Conservative income investors

For pure mortgage investment, this fund has long been a top performer within its group. Since inception in 1974, this fund has had only one losing calendar year (1994) when it was down 0.5%. A major plus is its MER, which is about 25 basis points lower than the average for its group. The safety profile of this fund over the long term is somewhat erratic. Historically, there was only a 1% chance of losing money in any one-year period, with the worst loss over any 12-month period coming in at just 2.1%. As an added guarantee, the Bank of Montreal has committed to the repurchase of any defaulting mortgages from the fund, at no penalty to unitholders. However, short-term volatility is high by the Canadian Mortgage category standard. Returns going out to three years have slipped to average compared with other mortgage funds of this type. In the latest year to June 30/01, the fund returned 6.6%, slightly above the average. Conservative investors may like this fund. It used to be our top-rated mortgage fund, but no more. Rating maintained at $$.

## Promising Newcomers

### Foreign Bond Funds

**BMO U.S.$ BOND FUND**                            NR ↓ FI NO £ FB

Manager: Maureen Syagera (Harris Investment Management Inc.), since inception (1998)

MER: 1.59%     Fundata: N/A     Style: Term Structure Analysis

Suitability: Conservative income investors

This fund's objective is to provide current income in U.S. dollars while preserving capital. The portfolio as of mid-2001 was allocated to U.S. federal government bonds and had a relatively high duration for a fund of this type. It makes monthly distributions. It is off to an impressive start with an 8.8% return in the year ending June 30/01, well above the group average.

# BEUTEL GOODMAN MANAGED FUNDS

## THE COMPANY

This 34-year-old company has its roots in managing money for pension funds, pooled accounts, and individuals with high net worth. It was not until March 1991 that it began to offer its line of mutual funds to the general public. Since then, several of the funds have achieved top-quartile returns over both the short and long term, which has not only added to Beutel Goodman's own sales of mutual funds but also attracted the attention of other mutual fund companies looking for outside managers. Moreover, if you like stability among fund managers then you'll like Beutel, since all of its funds, with the exception of two, have retained the same managers for over five years.

This is a small but very strong fund family. Most of the funds have good recent and longer-term performance records. Management expense ratios (MERs) are not only relatively low but, contrary to general industry trends, have been falling. The family is not for everyone, however, as the minimum investment is $10,000 for each of its funds.

## THE DETAILS

| | |
|---|---|
| Number of funds: | 7 |
| Assets under management: | $452 million |
| Load charge: | Front: max. 4% |
| Switching charge: | 2% maximum |
| Where sold: | Across Canada (but directly in Ontario only) |
| How sold: | Directly through the manager or through brokers, dealers, and financial planners |
| Phone number: | 1-800-461-4551 or (416) 932-6400 |
| Web site address: | www.beutel-can.com |
| E-mail address: | marketing@beutel-can.com |
| Minimum initial investment: | $10,000 |

## INVESTING TIPS

If you live in Ontario, you can purchase Beutel Goodman funds on a no-load basis by ordering directly from the company. See the phone number above. Elsewhere in Canada, you must purchase through an investment dealer and pay a sales commission of up to 4%.

In addition to its regular mutual funds, Beutel also markets a line of pooled funds under the "Private" brand name. On the surface, these appear to be clones of the underlying mutual funds but, in reality, different fund managers direct them. These funds tend to produce better returns, in part because of the lower fees associated with them. Also, they offer a no-load feature, whereas the regular funds are front-end load. However, you can't buy into the Private fund line unless you have $500,000 to invest.

## FUND SUMMARY

|  |  |
|---:|:---|
| Top Choices: | Income, Money Market, Small-Cap |
| Also Recommended: | Balanced, Canadian Equity |
| Promising Newcomers: | None |
| The Rest: | American Equity, International Equity |

## FUND RATINGS

### Top Choices

#### Canadian Small-to-Mid-Cap Funds

**BEUTEL GOODMAN SMALL-CAP FUND**          $$$$ → G #/NO RSP CSC

Manager: Team

MER: 1.46%     Fundata: A     Style: Value

Suitability: Long-term value-based equity investors

This is a premier small-cap fund if you want a good risk/reward trade-off. The fund holds only 41 stocks, with an average market cap of about $655 million. It has managed to beat the average fund in its category the majority of the time, making this a top selection among small-cap funds. In the latest year to June 30/01, it had a 13.9% return, compared with a loss of 6.7% for the group average. Over the past three years, the fund's 14.1% average annual return has dramatically outstripped the 2.7% average for the group. For a small-cap fund, this one is rather conservative, with a sprinkling of real estate investment trusts (REITs). Overall, you'll find a good blend of growth and value here, along with below-average risk and good returns. A high Fundata rating shows the strong positive contribution by the managers. Recommended with the long-term investor in mind. A solid fund, and we are upgrading its rating to a well-deserved $$$$.

#### Canadian Bond Funds

**BEUTEL GOODMAN INCOME FUND**          $$$ → FI #/NO RSP CB

Manager: David Gregoris, since 1992

MER: 0.67%     Fundata: D     Style: Term Structure Analysis

Suitability: Long-term income investors

As far as bond funds go, this is one of the steadier performers in the peer group, with returns consistently in the top 25% of its class. This kind of performance has attracted plenty of new capital into this actively managed fund. Default risk—always a concern in a bond fund—is low, as evidenced by the portfolio's composition of mainly Government of Canada bonds and high-quality corporate debt, with the latter rated at least A by a recognized bond credit agency. In terms of interest rate risk, the fund is relatively defensive with only 20% in long bonds as of late spring 2001, and a low average duration (a measure of average bond maturity). Add a low MER and you have a decent fund for fixed-income investors.

## Canadian Money Market Funds

### BEUTEL GOODMAN MONEY MARKET FUND $$$ ↓ #/NO RSP CMM

Manager: Team

MER: 0.61%     Fundata: C

Suitability: Conservative investors

Since inception, this fine money market fund has been batting a thousand. It's beaten the average in every year since 1991. This top-quartile performer is conservatively managed, mixing government T-bills with higher-yielding short-term corporate debt, all with a maturity of under one year. The volatility is below average as well. A recommended fund for your temporary cash as well as your RRSP. One of our favourite money market funds.

## Also Recommended

## Canadian Equity Funds

### BEUTEL GOODMAN CANADIAN EQUITY FUND $$ → G #/NO RSP CE

Manager: James Lampard, since 1991

MER: 1.32%     Fundata: A     Style: Value

Suitability: Value-based equity investors looking for relatively low volatility

The fund selects its stocks mainly from the TSE 300, which gives it a bias toward large-cap issues. However, the fund can hold small-cap stocks for added growth potential. This fund has underperformed the TSE 300 during most of its history, and has fared better than the average Canadian equity fund only 50% of the time. However, its recent performance has been stellar, reflecting its value bias. The fund holds a concentrated group of about 40 stocks, with an overweighting in industrial products, oil and gas, and financial services. In the year ending June 30/01, the fund returned a healthy 15.1% compared with the 5.8% loss for the average Canadian equity fund. Over the past three years, its 5.8% per annum return beat the average by close to a full percentage point. The fund has relatively low volatility as measured by both its low standard deviation and very low beta (a measure of risk). A high cash balance of 7.4% in mid-2001 highlights this defensiveness. The fund has a strong short-term record, but in a bull market this conservative approach to equities has limited its upside. We'll maintain its $$ rating for now although we'll consider an upgrade if the fund maintains its current pace.

## Canadian Balanced and Asset Allocation Funds

### BEUTEL GOODMAN BALANCED FUND $$ ↓ FI/G #/NO RSP CBAL

Manager: Denis Marsh, since 1991

MER: 1.11%     Fundata: B     Style: Value

Suitability: Conservative long-term balanced investors

If a conservative balanced fund is your heart's desire, this one may be for you. Its performance has been slightly above average throughout its history, as you might expect from a fund of its conservative nature. However, its return in the year ending June 30/01 was a solid 6.5% compared with a 2.6% loss for the peer group. The portfolio mix as of mid-2001 was about 60/40 stocks to bonds. The equities side has a value orientation that favours large-cap stocks with fairly good yields, but small caps are added for some growth potential. The fixed-income side is conservatively managed, as federal and provincial bonds compose the bulk of the bond portfolio. The overall portfolio risk is low versus the market, which accounts for its generally lower-than-average returns compared with its peer group. In all, this is a lower-risk/average return fund that would suit conservative investors.

## Promising Newcomers

None.

# C.I. FUND MANAGEMENT

## THE COMPANY

This is one of the more active and most complex fund companies in Canada, with over $30 billion in assets under management, including the purchase of BPI Financial Corp. in 1999.

Over the past year, the somewhat opaque C.I. structure has become more transparent. There are now four distinct lines in addition to the C.I. family of funds: the Harbour line, managed by Gerald Coleman, an ex-Mackenzie star; the Signature line, which includes several funds managed by Wally Kusters, formerly of Trimark, and Eric Bushell, who came over from BPI; a line that still bears the BPI name; and the Landmark line, operating under momentum-based Webb Capital Management. Additionally, there is a group of "sector" funds, explained in more detail below. Moreover, many of the funds offer a U.S. dollar option. Talk about a buffet of funds!

A recent trend at C.I. has been an increase in the in-house portfolio management staff. Other fund companies have had a large in-house staff but, prior to 1997, C.I. had all of its assets managed by external firms. Over the past few years, C.I. has aggressively recruited top managers, like Gerald Coleman for the Harbour Funds and more recently, Wally Kusters, an equity specialist who was previously with O'Donnell and, prior to that, with Trimark. The firm can now boast a strong internal team, with both domestic and international expertise.

We should note that there is some inconsistency in the names used by this firm. The company itself is officially known as C.I. Fund Management. Note the periods between initials. But the fund names drop those periods, and are shown as simply CI.

## THE DETAILS

| | |
|---|---|
| Number of funds: | 123 |
| Assets under management: | Over $30 billion |
| Load charge: | Front: max. 5%; Back: max. 5.5% |
| Switching charge: | 2% maximum |
| Where sold: | Across Canada |
| How sold: | Directly through the manager or through brokers, dealers, and financial planners |
| Phone number: | 1-800-563-5181 |
| Web site address: | www.cifunds.com |
| E-mail address: | service@cifunds.com |
| Minimum initial investment: | $500 (generally) |

# INVESTING TIPS

As mentioned, C.I. Fund Management has several funds that include the word "sector" in their names. Even more confusing is fact that there are actually two different types of funds involved here. One group is essentially identical to a parent fund with the same name (e.g., CI Global Sector Shares are the same as the CI Global Fund). However, the sector shares are grouped together under a single umbrella fund (CI Sector Fund Limited) so that assets can be transferred between the sectors without triggering capital gains liability. This tax-deferred choice allows active investors to trade frequently in non-registered accounts without worrying about any capital gains impact. Returns tend to be lower than those of the parent funds, mainly due to the fact that sectors hold more cash to provide liquidity for the frequent switching. Since these sector funds are essentially the same as the parent funds, they are not reviewed separately.

The other funds with "sector" in the name invest in specific areas of the economy (this is the classic definition of a sector fund). So you'll find CI Global Technology Sector Shares, CI Global Health Sciences Sector Shares, and so on. They are also part of the umbrella CI Sector Fund Limited, but they have no corresponding stand-alone fund, so you can buy them only as part of the overall Sector Fund.

We noted a long time ago that C.I. Fund Management would do itself a favour if it could somehow manage to simplify its structure. Well, things are starting to move in that direction. Over the past year C.I. merged a number of its funds into similar, existing funds. Overall, the C.I. family has a number of top-performing funds, but its propensity for name changes and mergers makes overall measurement difficult due to the inherent survivorship bias.

If you've selected a generic CI fund you are interested in, remember that for many of the funds in the C.I. family there are RSP clones, U.S. dollar versions, sector versions, and segregated versions available.

C.I. has three funds that fit into the "absolute return" or "hedge fund" category. The BPI American and Global Opportunities Fund and the Trident Global Opportunities Fund are structured as hedge funds. The manager uses derivatives, long–short positions, and other techniques to isolate fund performance from the market. Minimum initial investments reflect the provincial exempt market conditions, which are $97,000 in P.E.I, New Brunswick, Manitoba, Alberta, B.C. ($25,000 for purchasers qualifying as sophisticated investors), and the Yukon, and $150,000 in the other provinces and territories. Definitely worth a look if you are interested in hedge funds.

# FUND SUMMARY

## CI Funds

|  |  |
|---|---|
| Top Choices: | Canadian Bond, Global Consumer Products, Global, Global Energy, Global Financial Services, International Balanced, Money Market, U.S.$ Money Market |
| Also Recommended: | Emerging Markets, Global Boomernomics, Global Bond RSP, World Bond |
| Promising Newcomers: | None |
| The Rest: | American Managers, Canadian Balanced, Canadian Growth, Canadian Income, European, Global Biotechnology, Global Business to Business, Global Focus Value, Global Health Sciences, Global Manager, Global Technology, Global Telecommunications, Global Value, International, International Value, Japanese, Latin America, Pacific, Short-Term, Trident Global Opportunities, Trilogy Global Opportunities |

## Harbour Funds

|  |  |
|---|---|
| Top Choices: | Harbour |
| Also Recommended: | Growth & Income |
| Promising Newcomers: | None |
| The Rest: | None |

## Signature Funds

|  |  |
|---|---|
| Top Choices: | Canadian Resource, Dividend, Dividend Income, High Income, Select Canadian |
| Also Recommended: | Canadian Balanced, Global Small Companies |
| Promising Newcomers: | None |
| The Rest: | American Small Companies, Canadian, Explorer |

## BPI Funds

|  |  |
|---|---|
| Top Choices: | American Equity |
| Also Recommended: | None |
| Promising Newcomers: | None |
| The Rest: | American Opportunities, Global Equity, Global Opportunities, International Equity |

**Landmark Funds**

| | |
|---|---|
| Top Choices: | None |
| Also Recommended: | None |
| Promising Newcomers: | None |
| The Rest: | American, Canadian, Global |

## FUND RATINGS

### Top Choices/CI Funds

**Global and International Equity Funds**

**CI GLOBAL FUND**                                    $$$ → G #/* £ GE

Manager: William Sterling, since 1995

MER: 2.53%     Fundata: C     Style: Growth

Suitability: Investors seeking global exposure with a U.S. emphasis

This fund is officially designated as a global equity fund, but it had about 57% of its holdings invested in U.S. stocks as of mid-2001, followed by Japan and Europe, along with stocks from the Americas, the Middle East, the Pacific Rim, and Africa. The large portfolio has been a steady outperformer since inception, especially under the helm of Bill Sterling, a Harvard-educated economist. The heavy exposure to U.S. stocks has clearly helped returns in the past. In the year to June 30/00 the fund returned 36.3%, way above average for its peer group. However, in the year ending June 30/01, the fund lost 22.5%, bringing its three-year average annual compound rate of return down to 4.9%. Over five and ten years, this fund has outperformed the group average. Overall, this fund is a good and steady performer for long-term investors. However, its massive U.S. exposure raises questions about how well the fund reflects global investing. The CI Global Equity RSP Fund is a clone that is fully eligible for registered plans.

**Sector Equity Funds**

**CI GLOBAL CONSUMER PRODUCTS**                       $$$ → G #/* £ SPE
**SECTOR SHARES**

Manager: John Hock, since 2000

MER: 2.40%     Fundata: A     Style: Value

Suitability: Aggressive investors

There are a lot of trends at work for this fund. Some of the largest countries in the world, (in terms of population) are only now beginning to exercise the type of consumer demand that we have known in the West for two generations—China alone represents a quarter of the world's population. Over half of

Indonesia's population, the globe's fifth largest, is under 24 years of age. Vast numbers of the citizens of these and numerous other countries are just reaching the age of household formation, with all of its attendant purchases. As the economies of these countries strengthen, wages—and thus disposable income—are on the rise. This fund has been able to capitalize mightily on these trends during its first three years. The fund turned in an average annual return of 23.6% for the three years ending June 30/01. It did this with a very reasonable risk rating as well, one comparable to the middle third of Canadian equity funds over the same time period. In the latest year to June 30/01, the fund's 1.2% return was realized in a tough market. This fund keeps a well-merited $$$ rating.

## CI GLOBAL ENERGY SECTOR SHARES $$$ → G #/* £ NR

Manager: Robert Lyon, since 2000

MER: 2.54%     Fundata: C     Style: GARP

Suitability: Aggressive investors

This energy-specific fund has recorded a 14.5% per annum return to June 30/01 since its launch just over three years ago. The latest year showed a solid 22.7% return. Both numbers are well above group and benchmark averages. The fund invests strictly in energy companies; top holdings as of mid-2001 included Exxon Mobil, BP Amoco, and Total Fina. Fund manager Robert Lyon has taken a defensive posture; the fund's cash position was 16.7% as of mid-2001.

## CI GLOBAL FINANCIAL SERVICES SECTOR SHARES $$$ → G #/* £ SPE

Manager: John Hock, since 2000

MER: 2.58%     Fundata: B     Style: Value

Suitability: Specialty equity investors

John Hock, who runs his own company in partnership with C.I., is doing a good job so far with this fund, which focuses on financial services companies from around the world. The three-year average annual compound rate of return here was 11.5% to June 30/01, and the one-year gain was 11.6%. Both numbers are well above the group average. About 45% of the portfolio is in U.S. stocks, with Japan (14.1%) and Germany (11.6%) the other major geographic players. This is one of the better specialty funds in this area, worthy of a $$$ rating.

## Global Balanced and Asset Allocation Funds

### CI INTERNATIONAL BALANCED FUND                    $$$ ↓ G/FI #/* £ GBAL

Manager: William Sterling, since inception (1994)

MER: 2.35%    Fundata: B    Style: Generally Growth

Suitability: Conservative investors

If you want a conservative, low-risk/high-return global balanced fund with a growth bias, then this may be the one for you. This fund held 57.1% of its assets in stocks as of mid-2001, with the rest in bonds, preferred shares, and income trusts, including 21.4% in cash. Regional diversification is strong, with holdings from all around the world and a bias toward the U.S. market. There is no restriction as to where or in what percentage the fund can invest. Its mandate includes both developed and emerging markets for maximum diversification. The stock side is growth oriented, while the bond side is conservatively managed. In terms of performance, this fund has been reasonably strong in its six years of existence. Its five-year average annual compound rate of return to June 30/01 of 9.1% is well ahead of its peer group. Recent numbers have been weaker, however, and the fund suffered a 16.1% loss in the latest year. Nevertheless, this is a decent choice among international balanced funds. The CI International Balanced RSP Fund has been transformed into an RRSP-eligible clone of this fund.

## Canadian Bond Funds

### CI CANADIAN BOND FUND                    $$$ → FI #/* RSP CB

Manager: Jeffrey Herold, since inception (1993)

MER: 1.68%    Fundata: D    Style: Term Structure Analysis

Suitability: Conservative investors

Jeffrey Herold has made this into one of the better-performing bond funds. It has easily beaten the average for its category the majority of the time and has been a top-quartile performer over its life. The five-year average annual return of 7% is nicely ahead of the peer group's 6.2% per annum return. Holdings consist mainly of Government of Canada bonds, with the remainder in high-quality corporate issues and provincial debt. As such, the fund's default risk is low. This fund is recommended as a core holding for the fixed-income section of your portfolio and would fit well in an RRSP or RRIF.

## Canadian Money Market Funds

### CI MONEY MARKET FUND $$$ → C #/* RSP CMM

Manager: Wally Kusters, since September 1999

MER: 0.85%     Fundata: D     Style: Value

Suitability: Conservative investors

This is a strong performer in the Money Market category. With a significant bias toward short-term corporate debt, this fund has continued to shine among its peers by beating the average in each of the past nine years. The main risk is derived from the fact that this fund has an unusually high percentage of its assets in corporate debt compared with other Canadian money market funds. We recommend this fund as a temporary haven for your excess cash. Tip: Don't buy this or any other money market fund on a back-end-load basis. Try to get the front-end load waived as well.

## Foreign Money Market Funds

### CI U.S.$ MONEY MARKET FUND $$$ ↓ C #/* RSP FMM

Manager: Wally Kusters, since September 1999

MER: 0.85%     Fundata: E     Style: Value

Suitability: Conservative investors

This fund has outperformed the average of its group in each of the past five years by investing in any U.S.-dollar-denominated debt of less than 365 days, whether marketed by the U.S. or Canada. A relatively low management expense ratio (MER) helps with the returns here. The fund's risk is low and tracks that of the 30-day T-bill. Currency risk is derived from holding U.S.-denominated investments. The main holdings of this fund at mid-2001 included short-term debt issued by the Export Development Corp. denominated in U.S. dollars and U.S. T-bills. Note: If you can get this fund on a no-charge basis (front-end load option with zero commission), it's worth considering if it meets your needs. This fund is fully eligible for registered plans.

## Also Recommended/CI Funds

### Global and International Equity Funds

### CI EMERGING MARKETS FUND $$$ ↑ G #/* £ EME

Manager: Nandu Narayana (Trident Asset Management), since 1997

MER: 2.85%     Fundata: A     Style: GARP

Suitability: Aggressive investors

Fund manager Nandu Narayana has a good sense of timing. This fund's cash balance was reduced from 30% to as low as 5.2% in mid-1999 (just in time, as the fund returned 24% in the year to June 30/00). In the latest year, the cash balance was increased again and stood at 20.9% in mid-2001. This cash play helped the fund withstand a terrible downturn in the emerging market sector. Although the fund lost 15.9% in the year ending June 30/01, the average for both the peer group and the MSCI Emerging Markets benchmark was a 24.1% loss. The three-year return at 6.9% per annum is well above average. The fund has good geographical diversification with Mexico, Brazil, the Pacific Rim, and South Africa as its top countries and regions in mid-2001. Other regions include Europe, Africa, and the Middle East. This is a decent fund of its type, consistently in the top half of its group. Narayana did a great job with the BPI Emerging Markets Fund, which was merged into this one in 2000. Emerging markets funds are high risk by nature, but this impresses us as one of the best of the bunch at this time. The fund's rating goes to $$$, despite the loss this year. This fund is available in a fully RRSP-eligible equivalent, although we can't get excited about holding volatile emerging markets funds in registered plans.

## Global Balanced and Asset Allocation Funds

### CI GLOBAL BOOMERNOMICS SECTOR SHARES          $$ ↑ G #/* £ GBAL

Managers: Stephen Waite and William Sterling (C.I. Mutual Funds), since 1998

MER: 2.65%     Fundata: E       Style: Growth

Suitability: Aggressive investors

This fund scored a bottom-of-the-list "E" on the Fundata model due to its 22.5% loss in the year ending June 30/01. However, we are still putting it on our Recommended List given its otherwise strong track record. In calendar years 1999 and 2000, the fund recorded gains of 42.8% and 5.8% respectively. Put it all together and the fund's 13.4% three-year return to June 30/01 is healthy indeed compared with the return on the blended benchmark (60% MSCI World and 40% Lehman Brothers Fixed Income). The fund invests in both equity and fixed-income securities, targeting the rapidly growing segments of the population. As of mid-2001, the portfolio was allocated as 70% stocks, 27% cash, and 3% bonds. The fund debuts with a $$ rating.

## Foreign Bond Funds

### CI GLOBAL BOND RSP FUND                    $$ ↓ FI #/* RSP FB

Managers: Kent Osband and William Sterling, since July 2000

MER: 2.47%     Fundata: N/A     Style: Term Structure Analysis

Suitability: Conservative RRSP/RRIF investors seeking currency diversification

This is a foreign bond fund that is 100% RRSP/RRIF-eligible. The eligibility is achieved by using bond futures contracts from different countries. The portfolio focuses primarily on developed countries but may hold some emerging market securities for added growth. The fund holds its primary assets in Canadian dollars, avoiding any significant currency risk. Returns have been consistently above average compared with the peer group. The fund's five-year average annual compound rate of return to June 30/01 was 3.9%, better than the average for its class. The overall portfolio risk here is minimal. Take a look at this fund if you want the extra foreign bond exposure. A decent long-term holding for an RRSP.

### CI WORLD BOND FUND                               $$ → FI #/* £ FB

Managers: Kent Osband and William Sterling, since July 2000

MER: 2.15%     Fundata: B     Style: Term Structure Analysis

Suitability: Conservative investors seeking currency diversification for non-registered accounts

The composition of this bond fund's portfolio includes government debt from Latin America, Western and Eastern Europe, Canada, and the U.S. The fund has a strong track record and has outperformed the average fund over both the short and long term. Its five-year annual return of 4.4% places it near the top of foreign bond funds. This fund should not be purchased inside a registered plan since it will use up valuable foreign allowances. Another benefit of this fund is its lower volatility. For RRSPs/RRIFs, we recommend buying the companion Global RSP Bond Fund, which offers 100% eligibility.

## Promising Newcomers/CI Funds

None.

## Top Choices/Harbour Funds

### Canadian Equity Funds

### HARBOUR FUND                                  $$$ ↓ G #/* RSP CE

Manager: Gerald Coleman, since inception (1997)

MER: 2.46%     Fundata: A     Style: Value

Suitability: Conservative investors

The introduction of the Harbour family of funds was based on the arrival of highly regarded money manager Gerald Coleman at C.I. The name and logo of the fund family (a square-rigged sailing ship with all sails set) could not be more appropriate for the fund's objectives and Coleman's investment style. Harbour funds are intended for long-term, conservative investors who want superior returns and low risk. So far it's been a case of mission accomplished. The "harbour" in question is well inside the territory we like best, the one referred to as low-risk/high-return. The fund's average annual return for the three years ending June 30/01 was 7.8%, compared with 4.8% for the category. Risk is low. The trick for Coleman is to select a portfolio of only 30 to 40 holdings on which he can keep close watch. Canadian enterprises in the fund are well diversified, with banks, retail, metals, oil, and manufacturing represented. Selected companies must exhibit sound fundamentals as well as staying power and the potential for growth. Yes, more stratospheric returns have been available elsewhere, but for the conservative investor, this fund has offered a comfortable and profitable voyage. We'll maintain a $$$ rating.

## Also Recommended/Harbour Funds

### Canadian Balanced and Asset Allocation Funds

### HARBOUR GROWTH & INCOME FUND　　　　$$ ↑ G/FI #/* £ CBAL

Manager: Gerald Coleman, since inception (1997)

MER: 2.30%　　　Fundata: B　　　Style: Asset Allocation

Suitability: Balanced investors with an equity bias

This fund's name should be taken literally. Its first aim is growth, with income secondary, and recently it held some 62% of assets in equities. Not surprisingly, the stocks in the portfolio were similar to those in the companion Harbour Fund, which Gerald Coleman also manages. The average annual return for the three years ending June 30/01 was an above-average 5.2%. This is an asset allocation-driven fund, although it officially falls into the Canadian Balanced category. Coleman will switch between equity and fixed-income asset classes as required in an attempt to achieve high total returns and minimize volatility. The return for the year ending June 30/01 was a solid 9.6%. We'll give it an increase to a $$ rating.

## Promising Newcomers/Harbour Funds

None.

## Top Choices/Signature Funds

### Canadian Equity Funds

### SIGNATURE SELECT CANADIAN FUND                 $$$ → G #/* RSP CE

Manager: Eric Bushell, since 1998

MER: 2.57%      Fundata: A       Style: Value

Suitability: Conservative investors

Eric Bushell, who also manages the two Signature dividend funds, runs this fund. As of mid-2001, the fund's heaviest sector allocations were to communications and media (22.2%), financial services (14.4%), and oil and gas (13.3%). Bushell concentrates on large-cap companies and so far he is doing a great job selecting stocks. The fund had a 21.6% return in the year ending June 30/01 and a 21% annual compounded return over the three years ending June 30/01. Throw in a below-average volatility rating and you can see why this fund scores an "A" from Fundata. It debuts here with a $$$ rating.

### Dividend Income Funds

### SIGNATURE DIVIDEND FUND                         $$$ ↓ FI/G #/* RSP DIV

Manager: Eric Bushell, since 1999

MER: 2.00%      Fundata: A       Style: Value

Suitability: Conservative income investors

After languishing in the bottom half of the category in its first three years, this fund has come to life under Eric Bushell, who took over in 1999. The fund ranked near the top of the Dividend Income category for the year ending June 30/01, with a return of 17.2%. Bushell's focus on preferred shares and high-yield common shares has certainly paid off so far. The fund also generates good cash flow, although not as good as the companion Dividend Income Fund. We'll move the fund up to a $$$ rating.

### SIGNATURE DIVIDEND INCOME FUND                  $$$$ ↓ FI/G #/* RSP DIV

Manager: Eric Bushell, since 1995

MER: 1.50%      Fundata: A       Style: Value

Suitability: Income-oriented investors

In April 2000, the name of this fund was changed (it used to be the BPI Dividend Income Fund), but its other details remained the same. This is not only a genuine income fund but also a very effective one—just look at the Fundata score. The fund offers a portfolio of preferred shares and dividend-paying common stocks that generate excellent cash flow for investors seeking steady income. Total return has generally been above average for the Canadian Dividend category since Eric Bushell took over as manager. In the year ending June 30/01, the fund recorded a well-above-average 17.3% return. In mid-2001, the fund had 47% allocated to preferred shares and 35% to common shares. The safety record of this fund is very good. It's a solid choice if you're looking for a combination of dividends and modest capital gains. The fund keeps its $$$$ rating. Note: C.I. said in early 2001 that it plans to cap this fund, but it was still open for business at the time of writing. If it is still available, we recommend this one over the companion Dividend Fund.

## Sector Equity Funds

### SIGNATURE CANADIAN RESOURCE FUND $$$$ → G #/* RSP NR

Manager: Robert Lyon, since 1999

MER: 2.60%     Fundata: A     Style: Value

Suitability: Aggressive investors

This fund, previously known as the CI Canadian Resource Fund, has enjoyed a great run recently. Thanks to a 31% return in the year ending June 30/01, the fund's average annual gain for the three years ending June 30/01 was 13.5%, compared with 4.3% for the peer group. And its volatility was among the lowest in the group, albeit in relative terms—this is a high-risk category by definition. The fund is populated with many high-profile Canadian enterprises, including Rio Alto Exploration, Abitibi-Consolidated, and Alcan Aluminium. Given its high return, low volatility, Fundata A rating, and management expertise, we are going to raise it to a  $$$$ rating. This rating means it's a top choice among resource funds generally, but only when that sector is doing well.

## Canadian Balanced and Asset Allocation Funds

### SIGNATURE HIGH INCOME FUND $$$ ↑ FI/G #/* RSP CHIB

Manager: Benedict Cheng, since 1997

MER: 1.75%     Fundata: C     Style: Credit Analysis

Suitability: Aggressive income investors

The name of this fund was changed from BPI High Income in April 2000. This is one of the new high-income balanced funds aimed at investors seeking above-average, tax-advantaged cash flow. Real estate investment trusts (REITs), royalty income trusts (RITs), and high-yield corporate bonds are the focus, generating high, consistent monthly income. The fund paid 85.2¢ per unit in the year to June 30/01. Its 18.7% return placed it well above average. Over the past three years, the fund scored an 8.8% average annual gain. However, risk was also higher than average for the category. We'll maintain the fund's $$$ rating based on the good tax-advantaged cash flow, but be aware of the high volatility here.

# Also Recommended/Signature Funds

## Global and International Equity Funds

### SIGNATURE GLOBAL SMALL COMPANIES FUND $$ ↑ G #/* £ GE

Manager: Andrew Waight, since 1999

MER: 2.57%    Fundata: B    Style: GARP

Suitability: Aggressive investors

C.I. announced a managerial change for this fund at the end of 1999, with Andrew Waight taking over at the helm. It's a move that gave investors some pause because this fund had been on a real hot streak, with a gain of 76% for the year ending June 30/00. Any time a fund is doing that well, no investor wants to see any tinkering, much less the departure of the manager who had been making it all happen. Unfortunately, concern heightened as the fund lost 17.3% in the year to June 30/01. However, the terrible market conditions that prevailed don't allow a true test of Waight's ability here. The fund invests in small-cap companies internationally, but small-cap in this case is defined as anything up to U.S.$750 million in market capitalization! Some "big" Canadian companies are smaller by comparison. This fund's longer-term record merits a strong rating but we are downgrading to a $$ score given Waight's uncertain debut performance thus far.

## Canadian Balanced and Asset Allocation Funds

### SIGNATURE CANADIAN BALANCED FUND $$ → FI/G #/* RSP CBAL

Manager: Wally Kusters, since 1999

MER: 2.55%    Fundata: B    Style: Value

Suitability: Balanced investors with an equity orientation

This fund began life as BPI Income & Growth but moved into the C.I. empire when that company bought out BPI. The manager's job was handed to Wally Kusters, a veteran of the industry (one of the many ex-Trimark types around) and highly respected among his peers. Kusters runs a tight ship, with a portfolio of no more than 40 to 50 positions. The current weighting of this balanced fund is in favour of equities, which compose 57% of the portfolio. The fund gained 4.8% for the three years to June 30/01, above average for the Canadian Balanced category. The risk rating is just slightly worse than average. Not a first choice, but worthy of consideration.

## Promising Newcomers/Signature Funds

None.

# Top Choices/BPI Funds

## U.S. Equity Funds

### BPI AMERICAN EQUITY FUND                    $$$ → G #/* £ USE

Manager: Paul Holland, since 1997

MER: 2.59%     Fundata: E        Style: GARP

Suitability: Aggressive investors

This fund changed its name from the BPI American Equity Value Fund to the current version in 2000. Dropping the word "value" better reflects the management style of this fund, which tends to have a growth bias. The fund's mandate is to invest in undervalued blue-chip stocks, such as Citigroup, Motorola, and General Electric. You'll also find a lot of up-and-coming tech stocks here. Holland and his team have a knack for picking stocks just before they hit a growth spurt. It had been one of the hottest performers in the U.S. Equity category in the late 1990s. The one-year return to June 30/99 was 41.1% and the one-year return to June 30/00 was 34%. However, the fund stumbled badly in the latest period with a loss of 34.6% in the year ending June 30/01. Here's what kind of effect a bad run can have: the three-year average annual return has dropped from 39.7% at this time last year to 7.4% as of June 30/01. However, that's still well above the U.S. equity fund average. We are dropping the rating down to $$$ for now but we are assuming that Holland can regain his touch once stock markets start to firm up. There is an RRSP clone of this fund available, the BPI American Equity RSP Fund. It should be used in registered plans to save foreign content room.

## Also Recommended/BPI Funds

None.

## Promising Newcomers/BPI Funds

None.

## Top Choices/Landmark Funds

None.

## Also Recommended/Landmark Funds

None.

## Promising Newcomers/Landmark Funds

None.

# CIBC MUTUAL FUNDS

## THE COMPANY

All the banks have taken steps to strengthen their no-load fund line-ups in recent years. CIBC is no exception and has become a leader in the promotion of index funds with a wide range of offerings that cover markets worldwide.

As with the other banks, CIBC has been adding new fund options. They introduced a number of new funds this year, but given the weak market environment most are off to a slow start.

One of the bank's most intriguing initiatives was the move a few years ago to offer so-called "Protected Funds" as an alternative to segregated funds. Five of these funds were launched with a mandate to provide growth potential through participation in various equity and bond indices. On top of this, the funds offered a 100% guarantee against loss that applied after a five-year holding period. This was a very aggressive offering, providing a guarantee period that was half the standard for segregated funds and was probably too much of a strain on CIBC's balance sheet. As a result, the funds were quickly withdrawn from sale—despite their popularity—and are no longer available.

The majority of the bank's funds are managed by TAL Investment Counsel, in which the bank owns a 65% interest. In the interest of full disclosure, note that co-author Eric Kirzner is an advisor to the CIBC Securities Investment Committee.

## THE DETAILS

|  |  |
|---|---|
| Number of funds: | 51 |
| Assets under management: | $19.2 billion |
| Load charge: | None |
| Switching charge: | None |
| Where sold: | Across Canada |
| How sold: | Directly through any CIBC branch, CIBC Investor's Edge (discount brokerage), CIBC Wood Gundy (full-service brokerage), as well as other dealers and discount brokerage services. You can also buy direct by signing up for CIBC's Direct Trading service. |
| Phone number: | 1-800-465-3863 or (416) 980-3863 |
| Web site address: | www.cibc.com/MutualFunds |
| E-mail address: | angela.andrisani@cibc.com |
| Minimum initial investment: | $500 |

## INVESTING TIPS

CIBC is a leader in the marketing of index funds so if you're an index investor, this is a good place to start your shopping.

CIBC now offers five 100% RRSP-eligible index funds that also include a CIBC International RRSP offering and a U.S. RRSP Equity Index fund. The former tracks Morgan Stanley's Europe Australia and Far East Index (MSCI EAFE) while the latter mirrors the S&P 500 Composite Index. In terms of equity index funds, CIBC is the only company to offer a U.S. Equity Index fund that tracks the Wilshire 5000 Index. The Wilshire is a capitalization-weighted index that captures the performance of more than 95% of all U.S.-traded stocks.

CIBC also offers a family of bond index funds, including the CIBC Bond Index Fund that tracks the ScotiaMcLeod Bond Universe, and the CIBC Short-Term Bond Index Fund that tracks the ScotiaMcLeod Short-Term Bond Index.

Unfortunately, the bank has not yet produced an answer to TD's "e" units, which allow investors who buy online to obtain much lower management expense ratios (MERs) on their index funds.

## FUND SUMMARY

|  |  |
|---|---|
| Top Choices: | Canadian Short-Term Bond Index, Canadian Emerging Companies, Financial Companies, U.S. Small Companies |
| Also Recommended: | Capital Appreciation, Canadian Bond Index, Canadian Small Companies Energy, Global Technology, Money Market, Mortgage, U.S.$ Money Market, U.S. Equity Index |
| Promising Newcomers: | None |
| The Rest: | Asia Pacific, Balanced, Canadian Imperial Equity, Canadian Index, Core Canadian Equity, Canadian Real Estate, Dividend, Emerging Economies, Emerging Markets Index, European Equity, European Index, European Index RRSP, Far East Prosperity, Global Bond, Global Bond Index, Global Equity, High-Yield Cash, International Index RRSP, International Index, Japanese Equity, Japanese Index RRSP, Latin America, Monthly Income, N.A. Demographics, Nasdaq Index; Nasdaq Index RRSP, Precious Metals, Premium T-Bill, U.S. Equity Index RRSP |

# FUND RATINGS

## Top Choices

### Canadian Small-to-Mid-Cap Funds

### CIBC CANADIAN EMERGING COMPANIES FUND    $$$ → G NO RSP CSC

Manager: Robert Tattersall, since October 1998

MER: 2.14%    Fundata: A    Style:    Bottom-up Growth

Suitability: Aggressive investors

This fund's primary objective is capital appreciation through investing in small and emerging companies in the bottom third of the TSE 300 Index as well as non-Index stocks. So this fund goes after the really little guys. It's headed up by Robert Tattersall, an extraordinary manager who has more than proven his worth with the stellar performance of the Saxon Small-Cap Fund over the years. So far he has this fund humming. Its return in the year ending June 30/01 was a solid 10.4% compared with a 6.7% loss for the peer group and a 2.4% loss on the Nesbitt Burns Canadian Small-Cap benchmark. The risk level is slightly below the average as well. This fund debuts with a well-deserved $$$ rating.

### U.S. Small-to-Mid-Cap Funds

### CIBC U.S. SMALL COMPANIES FUND    $$$ ↑ G NO £ USSC

Manager: James A. Rullo (Wellington Management), since 1997

MER: 2.60%    Fundata: B    Style: Bottom-up Momentum

Suitability: Aggressive investors

This is a small-cap U.S. equity fund that searches for companies that are under-valued or have solid growth potential, and have a market cap of under $1 billion at the time of investment. After a slow start, this fund is really starting to deliver under James Rullo. The fund has outperformed its peer group through almost all time periods. Over the last year, ending June 30/01, the fund returned 8.2%, compared with an 11.3% loss for its peer group. Over the last three years, the fund's 12.6% per annum beat the peer group by 4.2 percentage points per year. We'll upgrade to a $$$ rating.

## Sector Equity Funds

### CIBC FINANCIAL COMPANIES FUND $$$ → G NO RSP SPE

Manager: Sharon Ranson, since September 1999

MER: 2.60%     Fundata: B     Style:    Bottom-up Growth

Suitability: Aggressive investors

Here's another new offering from CIBC. This speciality fund invests, for the most part, in the Canadian financial services industry, focusing primarily on banks, investment companies, and financial services. It's unique in the world of Canadian mutual funds, as it is currently the only RRSP-eligible fund specializing in financial services. This fact, coupled with a good performance record, might make it a fund worthy of your attention. In the latest year to June 30/01, the fund returned 13.5%; in the last three years it earned 9.5% per annum. Holdings include household names like Royal Bank, Bank of Nova Scotia, and Sun Life Financial Services. The risk level is average. This fund debuts with a $$$ rating.

## Canadian Bond Funds

### CIBC CANADIAN SHORT-TERM BOND INDEX FUND $$$ ↓ FI NO RSP STB

Manager: Jacques Prevost, since July 1999

MER: 0.90%     Fundata: C     Style: Index

Suitability: Conservative investors

If you are very risk conscious but want higher returns than money market funds or T-bills, this fund may be the solution. The fund tries to emulate the return of the Scotia Capital Markets Short-Term Bond Index by investing in the various securities that make up the Index. As of mid-2001, the portfolio was invested primarily in federal bonds, followed by high-quality corporate debt. Moreover, with the majority of investments in short-term bonds, this fund has minimal interest rate risk. Returns have been consistently above the average for the peer group. That's enough for us to maintain the rating on this fund at $$$. You can buy this fund if you are seeking a little more than you will get from a comparative money market fund.

# Also Recommended

## Canadian Small-to-Mid-Cap Equity Funds

### CIBC CAPITAL APPRECIATION FUND $$ → G NO RSP CSC

Manager: Jean Michaud, since April 2001

MER: 2.56%    Fundata: D    Style:    Bottom-up Value

Suitability: Aggressive investors

After a number of years of outperformance, this fund slipped considerably in the latest year to a 14% loss. But longer term, three- and five-year numbers have been stellar, outdistancing both the benchmark—the Nesbitt Burns Small-Cap Index—and the peer group. The fund is well diversified, but with more than $500 million in assets, its size may start to become a liability. Liquidity is a problem when trying to build a small-cap portfolio with a large fund. The fund tries to find diamonds in the rough in emerging technologies and knowledge industries. Given the recent weak performance and the change in management this year, we are downgrading the rating on this fund to $$.

### CIBC CANADIAN SMALL COMPANIES FUND $$ ↑ G NO RSP CSC

Manager: Jean Michaud, since April 2001

MER: 2.48%    Fundata: B    Style:    Bottom-up Value

Suitability: Aggressive investors

After two strong years, this fund tanked in the latest year to June 30/01, taking an 11.7% loss. But the three-year return was solid indeed, as the fund concentrates on the smaller companies in the TSE 200 Index (the bottom two-thirds of the TSE 300). The fund's performance relative to both the peer group and the Nesbitt Burns Small-Cap Index was highly impressive. In the three-year period ending June 30/01 the fund realized a 19.5% return compared with a 2.7% average for the category and 4.9% for the benchmark. We'll start this fund out with a $$ rating.

## U.S. Equity Funds

### CIBC U.S. EQUITY INDEX FUND $$ → G NO £ USE

Manager: Susan M. Ellison, since 1998

MER: 0.97%    Fundata: D    Style: Index

Suitability: Index investors

Since rejigging its investment strategy from that of a large-cap U.S. equity fund to one that tracks the Wilshire 5000 Index, this fund has had some decent returns. The Wilshire 5000 Index covers a group of more than 7,000 securities that represent 95% of the U.S. stock market. Its portfolio is well diversified and investors are effectively buying the entire U.S. stock market. As you would expect, the fund is large, with about 2,000 stocks at mid-2001, including some technology heavyweights and other blue chips. Volatility should be close to that of the broader market. With a passive management style reflective of an index fund and low fees, this fund has beaten the average large-cap U.S. fund over the past several years. For example, the five-year return to June 30/01 was 12.8% compared with 11.8% for the peer group. In the shorter term, however, the fund has fallen behind some actively managed U.S. equity funds, mainly due to the divergence in the market between Old Economy and New Economy stocks. With a broadly based index fund like this one, you have exposure to both sectors of the economy, whereas active managers can play one segment of the economy off against the other.

## Sector Equity Funds

### CIBC ENERGY FUND                                          $$ ↑ G NO RSP NR

Manager: Normand Lamarche, since May 2001

MER: 2.50%      Fundata: D      Style:   Bottom-up Momentum

Suitability: Aggressive investors

This fund has posted some impressive returns since its inception. Recent numbers are particularly good, thanks to a resurgence in the energy sector. The three-year return to June 30/01 was 9.5%, more than double that of the peer group and well ahead of the 6.9% return for the benchmark index (TSE 100 Resources Index). In the latest year to June 30/01 the fund returned 7.2%, well below the peer group. We like this fund but are downgrading it a notch to a $$ rating because of a managerial change (even though Lamarche is a veteran and knows his field) and the possibility that energy stocks have seen their peaks for this cycle. Don't lose sight of the high risk involved here.

### CIBC GLOBAL TECHNOLOGY FUND                              $$ ↑ G NO £ ST

Manager: Stephen Kahn, since inception (November 1995)

MER: 2.77%      Fundata D       Style: Bottom-up Growth

Suitability: Very aggressive investors

This is your typical high-risk/high-return technology-oriented fund. When the market is strong this fund may soar, but when the market declines, it is extremely vulnerable because it is tied to a specific sector, which happens to be very volatile. Here's some evidence: Stephen Kahn's one-year return to June 30/00 was 152.1%, or more than twice the average for his peer group and almost four times the average for the benchmark index (the Nasdaq Composite). But in the year ending June 30/01, the fund lost 62.7% compared with a 37.8% loss for the peer group. Not surprisingly, this fund is heavily weighted in U.S. tech stocks, although some of the biggest holdings in the fund are not household names. Companies such as Flextronics, Amdocs, and Agere Systems head the list. When buying these types of funds, you should think long and hard about dollar-cost averaging your way into them by purchasing a little now and a little more when the fund dips. This kind of approach is especially important with CIBC Global Technology, as Kahn tends to be more aggressive than his peer group. If you are looking for some sizzle in your portfolio, this fund may suit your needs, but keep in mind that this year's loss more than wiped out last year's gains, although the three-year return is an above-average 15.7%. Given it's the fund's latest performance, we are lowering to the rating to a $$. However, when the tech market recovers, watch for this fund to shoot up again.

## Canadian Bond Funds

### CIBC CANADIAN BOND INDEX FUND $$ ↓ FI NO RSP STB

Manager: Jacques Prevost, since July 1999

MER: 0.96%     Fundata: C     Style: Index

Suitability: Conservative investors

The fund is very similar to the Canadian Short-Term Bond Index Fund. It tries to emulate the return of the Scotia Capital Markets Universe Bond Index by investing in the various securities that make up the Index. As of mid-2001, the portfolio was invested primarily in federal bonds, followed by high-quality corporate debt. Returns thus far are encouraging. In the three years ending June 30/01 the fund returned 3.8% per annum compared with 3.2% for the peer group. We'll start this fund at $$.

## Mortgage Funds

### CIBC MORTGAGE FUND $$ → FI NO RSP M

Manager: John W. Braive, since December 1999

MER: 1.81%     Fundata: C     Style: Credit Analysis

Suitability: Conservative investors

John Braive took over the management of this fund in December 1999. The fund has a respectable record despite the fact that it has the highest MER of any fund of its type offered by the five major banks. The portfolio is made up almost entirely of high-quality NHA-insured mortgages. The fund will suit ultraconservative investors who want a higher return than they'd get from money market funds. However, this fund will be somewhat more vulnerable to rising interest rates. Its performance in the year to June 30/01 was 7.4%, nearly 100 basis points above the group average.

## Canadian Money Market Funds

### CIBC MONEY MARKET FUND                    $$ ↓ C NO RSP CMM

Manager: Steven Dubrovsky, since 1994

MER: 1.17%      Fundata: B      Style: Index

Suitability: Conservative investors

Since inception, this fund has had mixed results compared to its peer group. Returns have hovered around the average, but have failed to beat the average the majority of the time. On the positive side, this fund has been a steady performer and is geared toward CIBC clients who demand a higher return than comparative savings deposit accounts. Due to the additional risk it takes on by holding the majority of its assets in short-term corporate debt, this fund will tend to have slightly better returns than the companion Canadian T-Bill Fund. If you have the minimum $100,000 required, the Premium Canadian T-Bill Fund would be a better choice due to its lower fees and higher returns.

## Foreign Money Market Funds

### CIBC U.S.$ MONEY MARKET FUND              $$ → C NO RSP FMM

Manager: Steven Dubrovsky, since 1994

MER: 1.17%      Fundata: C      Style: Index

Suitability: Conservative investors

The distinguishing feature about this U.S. dollar fund is that it's fully RRSP-eligible. The fund invests mainly in short-term Canadian securities, such as federal government T-bills, corporate notes, and provincial T-bills, all of which are denominated in U.S. dollars. Performance wise, this fund has returned above-average profits compared to the Foreign Money Market category. Buy this fund if you want more U.S. dollar exposure or want to increase your U.S. dollar assets within a registered plan. Be warned that a rise in the Canadian dollar will impact returns here, especially if you have to convert to Canadian dollars.

## Promising Newcomers

None.

# CLARICA MUTUAL FUNDS

## THE COMPANY

Clarica used to be the Mutual Fund Group, owned by Mutual Life. In mid-1999, the company went through a demutualization process and changed its name to Clarica Life. The names of the mutual funds were changed as well, but they are not segregated funds and are not tied to any kind of insurance contract. However, Clarica does offer a line of segregated funds that invest directly in the underlying mutual funds from this group and carries a 75% return on capital guarantee (which means you will get no less than 75% of your money back at maturity) and a 100% death benefit.

In total, Clarica offers 33 segregated funds sold under two brand lines. Those bearing the SF designation are replicas of the mutual funds listed below. There is also a line known as the MVP Funds, several of which are just seg fund wrappers for an underlying mutual fund, like Fidelity Small-Cap America or AGF Dividend. We will not review the segregated funds separately; use our comments on the recommended mutual funds to make your decisions.

Most of the Clarica mutual funds are available on an optional no-load or DSC (back-end load) basis, with the exception of those in their Leader series: Clarica Bond Fund, Clarica Diversifund 40, Clarica Equifund, and Clarica Amerifund. These funds are sold with a front-end load of up to 3.75%.

In January 2001 the company launched several index funds designed especially for RRSPs, which track a number of U.S. and international stock markets.

The Clarica funds are managed by seven outside advisors, including Perigee Investment Counsel; Mackenzie Financial (Summit Series), AGF (Alpine Series); State Street Research; AMI Partners; Knight, Bain, Seath & Holbrook Capital Management; and TD Asset Management. The company does not supply the names of the lead portfolio managers for their funds, only a management company. We think this is unfortunate and strongly believe that investors have a right to know who is responsible for looking after their money and when a key person joins or moves on.

## THE DETAILS

|  |  |
|---|---|
| Number of funds: | 36 |
| Assets under management: | $4.2 billion |
| Load Charge: | Front: max. 3.75% (for Bond, Diversifund 40, Equifund, and Amerifund); Back: max. 6% (remaining funds in the group) |
| Switching charge: | None, but special rules apply |
| Where sold: | Across Canada |

| How sold: | Exclusively through Clarica Investco agents |
| Phone number: | 1-888-864-5463 (English) |
| | or 1-888-456-2843 (French) |
| Web site address: | www.clarica.com |
| E-mail address: | clarica@clarica.com |
| Minimum initial investment: | $500 |

## INVESTING TIPS

Most of the Clarica funds (except for the Leader series) now offer both a no-load and a DSC purchase option. If you choose the DSC units, you will have to pay a sales charge of up to 6% if you cash in prior to the seventh year after purchase. The no-load units are exactly that. What's the catch? The DSC units carry a higher management expense ratio (MER)—the annual expense deducted from the fund's assets. It's not a big difference, however—in most cases 10 basis points (0.1%) or less.

Your sales representative may press you to choose the DSC units because he or she won't get any commission if you opt for the no-load version. The rep will receive annual trailer fees in both cases, however. Which should you select? Our preference is for the no-load units. The MER difference isn't significant and it's a small price to pay for the freedom to be able to move your money out quickly and cost-free if you don't like the results you're getting.

We should also comment here that the MERs on these funds are quite high—above the industry norm in many cases. You may wish to take this cost into consideration when making an investment decision. The MERs shown below are for no-load units.

## FUND SUMMARY

| Top Choices: | Summit Canadian Equity, Summit Dividend Growth, Summit Foreign Equity, Summit Growth & Income |
| Also Recommended: | Alpine Growth Equity, Alpine Canadian Resources, Diversifund 40, Premier Bond |
| Promising Newcomers: | Canadian Growth Equity, Growth, Short-Term Bond |
| The Rest: | Alpine Asian, Amerifund, Asia and Pacific Rim Equity, Bond, Bond Index, Canadian Equity Index, Equifund, European Equity, Global Bond, Income, Money Market, Premier American, Premier Blue Chip, Premier Diversified, Premier Emerging Markets, Premier Growth, Premier International, Premier Mortgage, RSP European Index, RSP |

International Index, RSP Japanese Index, RSP
U.S. Equity Index, RSP U.S. Technology Index,
U.S. Growth Equity, U.S. Small-Cap

# FUND RATINGS

## Top Choices

### Canadian Equity Funds

### CLARICA SUMMIT CANADIAN EQUITY FUND $$$ ↓ G */NO RSP CLC

Manager: Mackenzie Investment Corp.

MER: 3.01%     Fundata: A     Style: Bottom-up Value

Suitability: Conservative investors

This fund invests primarily in large-cap Canadian equities, with a goal of providing long-term capital growth. The portfolio will generally hold no more than 75 companies at a time, making it easier for the managers to follow the investments. Its largest sector is the financial services industry. The portfolio is well diversified, with industrial products the top sector in the first half of 2001 (28%) followed by financial services (20%). It also holds about a quarter of its assets outside Canada, primarily in the U.S. Management is defensive: the fund held about 12% in cash entering 2001. These numbers lead us to believe that the fund is run by Mackenzie's crack Ivy team. It would be nice if Clarica would confirm our management hunch, as it would certainly be useful knowledge for investors. Initial returns following the fund's launch in mid-1997 were weak because value investing was out of style. But this fund is now looking much better. Gain for the year to June 30/01 was 6.6% (no-load units), a good result in a falling stock market. That return was good enough to pull up the three-year figure to above average. This fund shows less volatility than most Canadian equity funds (this may be partially due to its tendency to hold large amounts of cash), which means that conservative investors should feel more comfortable with it.

### Dividend Income Funds

### CLARICA SUMMIT DIVIDEND GROWTH FUND $$$ → G/FI */NO RSP DIV

Manager: Mackenzie Investment Corp.

MER: 2.98%     Fundata: A     Style: Bottom-up Value

Suitability: Conservative investors

The objective of this fund is to provide reasonable returns using high-yielding common stocks and preferred shares. However, the portfolio may also hold royalty income trusts or RITs (e.g., Westshore Terminals) and real estate investment trusts or REITs (e.g., Riocan). But blue-chip common stocks make up the bulk of the assets here. As we're seeing with an increasing number of dividend funds, U.S. stocks have appeared in the portfolio, representing close to 15% of the assets in the early part of 2001. Recent returns have been quite good (first quartile), with a one-year gain of 17.5% to June 30/01 (no-load units). Distributions are paid monthly and have been running at about 60¢ a year. All in all, not a bad fund with a good and steady income stream.

## Global and International Equity Funds

### CLARICA SUMMIT FOREIGN EQUITY FUND          $$$ → G */NO £ GE

Manager: Mackenzie Investment Corp.

MER: 3.14%      Fundata: A      Style: Bottom-up Value

Suitability: Conservative investors

This is another Summit fund that we believe is managed by Mackenzie's conservative Ivy team. The style is certainly in the same mode as the Ivy Foreign Equity Fund. This fund invests primarily in U.S. companies (58% entering 2001) but holds overseas positions as well. Names like American Express, Unilever PLC, and Pepsico appear in the 10 largest holdings list. The value approach helps to shield investors from excessive risk, and the fund posted a very respectable gain of 10.6% in the year to June 30/01. That return was a little less than Mackenzie's Ivy version, but the MER here is higher. This is the type of fund that will probably lag behind in surging markets, but will give you a high comfort level when times are tough. Recommended.

## Canadian Balanced and Asset Allocation Funds

### CLARICA SUMMIT GROWTH          $$$ ↓ G/FI */NO RSP CBAL
### & INCOME FUND

Manager: Mackenzie Investment Corp.

MER: 2.99%      Fundata: A      Style: Value

Suitability: Conservative investors

This balanced fund leaves asset allocation decisions to the full discretion of the managers (whom we again believe to be Mackenzie's Ivy group). Entering 2001, it held about 35% in bonds, 3% in cash, and the rest in stocks, of which U.S. and foreign equities made up 23%. The value approach hurt returns in the initial years after launch but saved the fund from disaster when markets plunged in 2000–01. The one-year return to June 30/01 was 8.5% for the no-load units, well above average. Three-year returns have also improved to above average. This fund has a lower risk level than the average fund in its class, so if you invest here you are making a trade-off: reduced risk for lower returns when markets are on the rise. Recently, that was a trade-off many people were happy to accept.

## Also Recommended

### Canadian Small-to-Mid-Cap Funds

### CLARICA ALPINE GROWTH EQUITY FUND           $$ → G */NO RSP CSC

Manager: AGF Funds Inc.

MER: 3.17%      Fundata: D      Style: Bottom-up

Suitability: Aggressive investors

This fund invests in shares of small-to-mid-cap companies, although there is no upside limit on the size of the firms. Consequently, the fund may also hold large-cap stocks as the manager sees fit, and had significant positions in Nortel, Petro-Canada, MDS, and Talisman Energy entering 2001. So this is not a pure small-cap fund by any means. That's too bad, as many small-cap funds have done well recently. This fund was held back by some of its larger holdings like Nortel. After a big gain of 33.7% over the year to June 30/00, the return dropped sharply with a loss of 13.7% (no-load units) in the 12 months to June 30/01. We're keeping this one on the Recommended List for now because of previous good results, but it is hanging on by a thread. Rating drops to $$.

### Sector Funds

### CLARICA ALPINE CANADIAN           $$ → G */NO RSP NR
### RESOURCES FUND

Manager: AGF Funds Inc.

MER: 3.21%      Fundata: D      Style: Bottom-up

Suitability: Aggressive investors

This fund can invest in companies engaged in the discovery, development, and extraction of natural resources. The mandate is to focus on small- and mid-cap equities, but the managers haven't been sticking very closely to that mandate. Entering 2001, the list of top 10 positions included such resource giants as Petro-Canada, Talisman Energy, Alberta Energy, and Canadian Natural Resources Ltd. As you might gather from that list, the fund has been heavily weighted toward the energy sector, helping to produce a return of 7.3% for the year to June 30/01. Still, we would have expected better given the strength of the oil and gas sector for much of that period. This is not our first choice among resource funds by any means, but it's okay if you have assets with the company and you like the sector.

## Canadian Balanced and Asset Allocation Funds

### CLARICA DIVERSIFUND 40 $$ → FI/G # RSP CTAA

Manager: Perigee Investment Counsel

MER: 1.94%     Fundata: D     Style: Blend

Suitability: Conservative investors

Until 1996, this group offered three "Diversifunds," with the only difference between them being the percentage of stocks held in each portfolio. The three funds are now one with this, the most balanced of the options, as the sole survivor. Stocks may make up between 25% and 55% of the portfolio, depending on conditions, while bonds and other fixed-income securities will account for at least 45% of the holdings at any time. This allocation means the fund is managed more conservatively than the companion Premier Diversified Fund, which may hold a much higher percentage of stocks. The performance had been consistently better than average, but the fund slipped to below par in the year to June 30/00—the first time in six years—and is coming off another weak performance, with a 6.5% drop in the 12 months to June 30/01. If matters don't improve, it will be gone from our Recommended List in the next edition.

## Canadian Bond Funds

### CLARICA PREMIER BOND FUND $$ → FI */NO RSP CB

Manager: Perigee Investment Counsel

MER: 2.14%     Fundata: D     Style: Interest Rate Anticipation

Suitability: Conservative investors

This is the no-load/DSC companion to Clarica's older Bond Fund, which is available only on a front-end load basis. In this case, the manager places more emphasis on capital growth. Income is not a primary goal, so keep that fact in mind if good cash flow is important to you. Results have been somewhat better than those of the Bond Fund, with a 4.5% return for the year to June 30/01, compared with 3.6% for the Bond Fund. Of the two, this is the better choice. However, it's just an average performer in relation to the total Canadian Bond category. If you need income, look to the new Clarica Income Fund, which makes monthly payments.

## Promising Newcomers

### CLARICA CANADIAN GROWTH EQUITY FUND   NR → G */NO RSP CLC

Manager: AGF

MER: 3.11%   Fundata: N/A   Style: Bottom-up Growth

Suitability: Middle-of-the-road investors

This new Clarica entry, run by the folks at AGF, is growth oriented, in contrast with the value approach of the companion Summit Canadian Equity Fund. Growth funds on the whole did not fare well during 2000–01, but this one, which draws its portfolio mainly from TSE 300 companies, didn't do badly. It showed a small loss of 0.4% for the year to June 30/01, a much better performance than the TSE Index. And this result was achieved despite the fact that plunging Nortel Networks represented a whopping 13.3% of the portfolio entering 2001! Obviously the managers had some other good things going for them. There is no foreign content here, so it's an all-Canada entry.

### CLARICA GROWTH FUND   NR → G */NO RSP CE

Manager: AMI Partners Inc.

MER: 3.83%   Fundata: N/A   Style: Bottom-up Growth

Suitability: Middle-of-the-road investors

This is another new growth fund from Clarica, managed by AMI Partners. The investment approach is long term, buy and hold, so this should be a tax-efficient fund for non-registered portfolios. Unlike the Canadian Growth Equity Fund, this one includes foreign content. Initial results have been respectable, with the fund coming in a little below break-even in the first part of 2001, a better performance than the TSE.

## Canadian Bond Funds

### CLARICA SHORT-TERM BOND FUND   NR → FI */NO RSP STB

Manager: Perigee Investment Counsel

MER: 2.26%   Fundata: N/A   Style: Interest Rate Anticipation

Suitability: Conservative investors

As the name tells you, this is a short-term bond fund. In this case, very short term—investments will not be for terms longer than three years. This approach makes the fund useful for investors who want to keep risk to an absolute minimum. Initial performance has been about average for the category; the no-load units gained 5.1% over the year to June 30/01. The major drawback is the MER, which is very high for a fund of this type.

# CLARINGTON FUNDS

## THE COMPANY

Since introducing its first fund in September 1996, Clarington, under the direction of Terry Stone, the former head of Bolton Tremblay Funds, has grown its fund family to 26 core funds and almost $1.9 billion in assets under management. Its ability to attract new capital has resulted from a combination of some good performance numbers and a broad selection of funds to satisfy most investors' needs.

Clarington uses the services of several third-party portfolio management teams, including respected firms such as New York–based Oppenheimer Funds Inc., Boston-based Keystone Investment Management, and San Francisco–based Montgomery Asset Management.

One note: Despite repeated attempts, we were not able to persuade the folks at Clarington to respond to our requests for updated information this year, which we found rather surprising considering the company's aggressive marketing programme. Therefore, some of the data that follows may be out of date. Check with your financial advisor for the most up-to-date information.

## THE DETAILS

|  |  |
|---|---|
| Number of funds: | 26 |
| Assets under management: | $1.9 billion |
| Load charge: | Front: max. 5%; Back: max. 5% |
| Switching charge: | 2% maximum |
| Where sold: | Across Canada |
| How sold: | Through independent brokers, dealers, and financial planners |
| Phone number: | 1-888-860-9888 or (416) 860-9880 |
| Web site address: | www.claringtonfunds.com |
| E-mail address: | funds@clarington.ca |
| Minimum initial investment: | $500 |

## INVESTING TIPS

The company offers an "umbrella" fund that is useful for investors wishing to reduce tax exposure in non-registered accounts. It's called the Clarington Sector Fund Inc. and it contains eight "classes," each of which is the equivalent of a fund within a fund. The advantage is that you can move assets among the various classes without triggering liability for capital gains tax. One word of warning: All investments in this umbrella fund are considered foreign content in an RRSP, including the Canadian Equity Class and the Short-Term

Income Class. However, we see no reason why anyone would want to hold these units within a registered plan, since the tax advantages of the umbrella fund would be lost.

## FUND SUMMARY

|  |  |
|---|---|
| Top Choices: | Canadian Balanced, Canadian Equity, Canadian Income, Canadian Microcap, Canadian Small-Cap |
| Also Recommended: | Money Market |
| Promising Newcomers: | Canadian Dividend |
| The Rest: | Asia Pacific, Canadian Bond, Canadian Equity Class, Digital Economy Class, Global Communications, Global Communications Class, Global Equity, Global Equity Class, Global Health Sciences Class, Global Income, Global Small-Cap, Global Small-Cap Class, International Equity, Navellier U.S. All-Cap, Short-Term Income Class, U.S. Equity, U.S. Smaller Company Growth, Technology |

## FUND RATINGS

## Top Choices

### Canadian Equity Funds

### CLARINGTON CANADIAN EQUITY FUND $$$$ ↓ G #/* RSP CLC

Manager: Peter Marshall (Seamark), since inception (1996)

MER: 2.90%     Fundata: A     Style: Value

Suitability: Conservative investors

This Canadian equity fund has been a steady above-average performer most of the time since its inception in late 1996. Its first year was a little weak, but since then returns have been solid and the fund was a first-quartile performer in 2000 and the first half of 2001. On a three-year basis (to June 30/01) this fund returned 12.7% annually, far better than the 4% return for the average fund in the Canadian Large-Cap category. As a bonus, the risk profile is tops in its class—the fund has not recorded a losing calendar year since it was started. The Canadian equity portion of the portfolio is populated with well-known names: Thomson, Nortel, several of the big five banks, and Alcan. The fund also takes advantage of its eligible foreign content by having 26% in U.S. and international stocks. We like the look of this one and are rewarding it with a top $$$$ rating in recognition of continued good performance.

## Canadian Small-to-Mid-Cap Funds

### CLARINGTON CANADIAN MICROCAP FUND $$$ ↑ G #/* RSP CSC

Manager: Leigh Pullen (QVGD Investors), since inception (1997)

MER: 3.12%     Fundata: A        Style: Value/Growth

Suitability: Aggressive investors

This fund got off to a rocky start, losing 15.7% in its first full calendar year (1998). But it has since righted itself and has been turning in impressive results with gains of 28.5% in 1999, 18.8% in 2000, and 9.1% in the first half of 2001. The mandate is to invest in companies with a market capitalization of less than $100 million, so we're talking small stuff here. You've probably never heard of any of the top 10 holdings, with the possible exception of Danier Leather, which does a lot of newspaper advertising. No matter. The managers have shown they know how to find winners in this area and that's what counts. The fund has been very volatile since its launch, but it has produced superior returns compared with its peers. The average annual return for the three years ending June 30/01 was 10.6%, putting it in the top 20% of group. The main drawback is the MER, which is high for the category. All things considered, this is a good choice for a micro-cap investment, but we recommend that it represent no more than 5% of your investable assets because of the risk involved. We'll launch this fund with a $$$ rating.

### CLARINGTON CANADIAN SMALL-CAP FUND $$$ → G #/* RSP CSC

Manager: Leigh Pullen (QVGD Investors), since inception (1997)

MER: 3.01%     Fundata: A        Style: Value/Growth

Suitability: Aggressive investors

Leigh Pullen and his team at QVDG Investors are doing the same good job for this fund as they are for the companion Microcap Fund. The difference is that this fund can invest in much larger companies—up to $800 million in market cap—making it potentially less volatile than Micro-Cap, although there is still quite a bit of risk here. Like Microcap, which was launched at the same time, this fund also got off to a slow start, losing 13.6% in its first year. It took longer to pick up steam but has looked strong recently with a gain of 18.3% in the first half of 2001. That result was good enough for a first-quartile ranking. We'll give this one a $$$ rating in its debut appearance here.

## Canadian Balanced and Asset Allocation Funds

### CLARINGTON CANADIAN BALANCED FUND $$$ ↓ FI/G #/* RSP CBAL

Manager: Peter Marshall (Seamark), since inception (1996)

MER: 2.90%    Fundata: A    Style: Value

Suitability: Conservative investors

This is one of those sound little funds that too few people know about. It has produced consistent low-risk/high-return results ever since its launch back in 1996, with an average annual compound rate of return of 8.9% for the three years to June 30/01—way above average for its category. The fund was slightly tilted toward equities (55%) in mid-2001. However, there was a 13% cash holding and a good mix of government and corporate bonds as well. Manager Peter Marshall uses the foreign content allowance liberally, with about a quarter of the assets held outside Canada. The top stock holdings included several banks, Thomson, Lafarge, and Shaw Communications. The MER is a bit above average but with results like these, we don't think we'll be hearing any complaints.

### CLARINGTON CANADIAN INCOME FUND $$$$ ↓ FI #/* RSP CBAL

Manager: Peter Marshall (Seamark), since inception (1996)

MER: 2.51%    Fundata: A    Style: Value

Suitability: Income-oriented conservative investors

This fund is officially classified as balanced, but it operates more like a dividend income fund. The objective is to provide a reliable monthly income stream of 8¢ per unit with tax advantages. Results have been very good. The average annual return for the three years ending June 30/01 was 8.1%, and risk has been very low—the fund has never lost money over a calendar year since it was launched. But income is where the fund really shines. It has spun off 96¢ a unit for each of the past four years, as advertised, with a significant portion being received on a tax-deferred basis. The asset mix in mid-2001 was 47% equities, all blue-chip companies. Fixed-income composed 32% of the total, mostly in short- to medium-term issues, with the rest in cash. Anyone looking for tax-advantaged income should include this one on their short list. It fulfills its mandate very well and as a result, we're moving it up to a $$$$ rating.

## Also Recommended

### Canadian Money Market Funds

### CLARINGTON MONEY MARKET FUND $$ ↓ C #/* RSP CMM

Manager: Peter Marshall (Seamark), since inception (1996)

MER: 0.80%　　Fundata: A

Suitability: Conservative investors

This fund appears to be pretty simple, and that may contribute to its success. It is invested exclusively in Canada T-bills, which means the assets are about as safe as it gets. Three-year returns are a tick above average for the category.

## Promising Newcomers

### CLARINGTON CANADIAN DIVIDEND FUND NR → FI #/* RSP CBAL

Manager: Peter Marshall (Seamark), since inception (1999)

MER: 2.91%　　Fundata: N/A　　Style: Value

Suitability: Income-oriented conservative investors

Peter Marshall's Seamark Asset Management is running a string of winners for Clarington and this relative newcomer is no exception. Like the companion Canadian Income Fund, income is the key to the mandate, and the fund aims at distributing 8¢ per unit each month. The portfolio composition is much different here, however—there are no bonds in the mix. This is a pure equity fund but only shares in dividend-paying companies are held. Surprisingly for a dividend fund, there is a large amount of foreign content (25%), but that doesn't appear to have been a problem to date. Results so far have been good, with the fund generating a return of 12.3% over the year to June 30/01. A promising new addition to the Clarington line-up.

# CREDENTIAL FUNDS (ETHICAL GROUP)

## THE COMPANY

In major centres, where the banks and their brokerages are so dominant, it's easy to forget that there are other financial services providers available to meet Canadians' investment needs. One of these alternatives is the credit union system. Canada's credit unions have a well-deserved reputation for service and product innovation and a laudable focus on the community. Their umbrella organization is the Credit Union Central of Canada. As the needs of members turned more to wealth management, the Credit Union Central saw an important niche that needed to be filled. Enter the Credential Group, a wholly owned subsidiary of Credit Union Central of Canada, providing wealth management services for member credit unions and their clients.

Credential Group pursues its wealth management mandate through two subsidiaries, Ethical Funds and Credential Asset Management. You may already be familiar with the former.

Ethical was the first group of "socially responsible" mutual funds in Canada, and it is currently the largest. The initiative was undertaken in 1986 by the Vancouver City Savings Credit Union, who perceived a nascent demand for this type of investment vehicle. In the years since, the family has grown to 10 core funds. The philosophy that drives this group is a belief that one doesn't have to sacrifice basic moral principles to get superior returns. While investment decisions are based on financial considerations, close attention is paid to social and environmental concerns as well. Once considered fringe players in the market, the respectable showing of Ethical Growth and other funds in the group has propelled this company into the mainstream.

The folks at Ethical have developed a very effective Web site. It discusses the specifics of their funds, of course, but that's far from all you'll find there. The site provides a lot of detail about the topic of socially responsible investing (SRI). If this subject interests you, the Web site is well worth a look.

The Credential Portfolio Funds are a product of the October 1999 alliance between Quebec's Mouvement Desjardins and Credit Union Central of Canada. This union brought together Canada's two largest financial services co-operatives, collectively boasting more than nine million members nationally. In January 2000, Credential Asset Management launched its first four funds under the Credential Portfolio Funds brand name. These are actually "funds of funds," based on 10 funds from the Desjardins line-up. Each portfolio provides a specific strategic asset allocation by combining mutual funds from various asset classes. Each Portfolio uses a model designed to maximize returns for a given level of risk. All are 100% RRSP eligible.

In December 2000, Credential launched a second line of portfolio funds, under the "Select" banner. These portfolios are made up of funds from the Ethical group as well as from three outside organizations including AGF, Fidelity, and AIM (Trimark funds).

We're pleased to note that the management expense ratio (MER) for all of the Ethical funds has dropped from last year.

## THE DETAILS

|  |  |
|---|---|
| Number of funds: | 16 |
| Assets under management: | $2.2 billion |
| Load charge: | None |
| Switching charge: | 2% maximum |
| Where sold: | All provinces except Quebec |
| How sold: | Directly and through brokers, dealers, and financial planners |
| Phone number: | 1-877-384-4225 |
| Web site address: | www.credential.com |
| E-mail address: | clientrelations@credential.com |
| Minimum initial investment: | $500 (generally) |

## INVESTING TIPS

Eventually, it is expected that units in both fund groups will be available in A, B, C, and D shares. A units are those most familiar to retail investors. However, there is a bit of a wrinkle here. If you invest over $250,000 in A units, you can apply for a 0.25% reduction in the annual management fee, which will have the effect of boosting your returns by a like amount (Ethical Money Market Fund excepted). B units will offer an as yet unspecified guarantee of principal. C units will be available on some form of self-serve basis, and will attract a lower management fee. Finally, D units are offered to institutional purchasers making a minimum initial purchase of $150,000, and have a negotiable management fee.

At the present time, only A units of the Credential portfolios are available. Ethical Funds are sold in A and D units.

## FUND SUMMARY

### Ethical Funds

|  |  |
|---|---|
| Top Choices: | Special Equity |
| Also Recommended: | Growth, Income, North American Equity |
| Promising Newcomers: | Canadian Equity |
| The Rest: | Balanced, Global Bond, Global Equity Money Market, Pacific Rim |

## Credential Portfolio Funds

(Note: Our policy is not to review or rate funds of funds. Therefore, only the Ethical Funds are rated below.)

|  |  |
|---|---|
| Top Choices: | N/A |
| Also Recommended: | N/A |
| Promising Newcomers: | N/A |
| The Rest: | N/A |

## FUND RATINGS

### Top Choices/Ethical Funds

#### Canadian Small-to-Mid-Cap Equity Funds

**ETHICAL SPECIAL EQUITY FUND**                $$$ → G NO RSP CSC

Manager: Leigh Pullen (QVDG Investors Inc.), since 1997

MER: 2.76%      Fundata: A      Style: Value

Suitability: Aggressive investors

This is one of Ethical's more recent additions, a small-cap entry that offers higher return potential with enhanced risk. It got off to a weak start, in part because its value approach didn't work well in the go-go markets of the late 1990s. But it came into its own in 2001, posting a six-month gain of 17.5% to June 30. Longer-term numbers have moved to above average as a result. The fund invests in companies with a market capitalization of less than $500 million who pass, of course, the company's ethical screens, designed to weed out companies that don't meet the standards that have been established. Some of the top holdings in the portfolio in mid-2001 were GTC Transcontinental, Cryptologic, Cascades, Aur Resources, and E-L Financial. We are impressed by the turnaround and are raising the rating to $$$ as a result.

### Also Recommended/Ethical Funds

#### Canadian Equity Funds

**ETHICAL GROWTH FUND**                $$ → G NO RSP CE

Manager: Martin Gerber, since 1992 and Larry Lunn (Connor, Clark & Lunn), since 1986

MER: 2.31%      Fundata: C      Style: Value

Suitability: Conservative, socially conscious investors

This is the flagship fund of the Ethical group, and it has the honour of being the first socially responsible fund ever created in this country (in 1986). It was the first mutual fund in Canada to combine profits with conscience by investing in companies that meet specific standards of practice. It was taken over by the Credit Union Central of Canada in late 1992 to form the cornerstone of a new Ethical Funds family. The managers are with the firm of Connor, Clark & Lunn. They bring a conservative style to the fund, at times moving heavily into cash to protect capital, an approach that has worked especially well in bear market situations. For example, with the markets slumping in mid-2001, the fund held a large 26% cash position. Ethical screens to exclude firms involved in military contracts, the tobacco industry, nuclear power, and unfriendly environmental activities. The performance numbers used to be very good, but the fund has been in a prolonged slump in recent years, which even the resurgence of a value investing style has not helped. Despite the large cash position, the fund lost 10.5% over the year to June 30/01, a time when many value funds were posting nice gains. That result pulled the three-year average annual compound rate of return into negative territory, at –2.6%. Over the past decade, the fund showed an average annual return of 8.1%, but even that is well below par for the peer group. We have a great deal of admiration for this family and we would like to see this fund performing up to previous standards, but as things stand right now we have no option but to drop the rating to $$—and even that designation is on the generous side. Under the present circumstances, we can recommend this fund only to dedicated socially responsible investors.

## Global and International Equity Funds

### ETHICAL NORTH AMERICAN EQUITY FUND $$ ↑ G NO £ USE

Manager: Cynthia Frick (Alliance Capital Management), since 1992

MER: 2.42%    Fundata: E    Style: Growth

Suitability: Aggressive investors

This is another former high-flyer in the Ethical family that has fallen on hard times. From 1995–99, this fund ran off a string of double-digit gains, topped by a 62.6% advance in 1998. But since then it has been a tough go for investors here. The fund lost more than 19% in 2000 and dropped another 11% in the first half of 2001. Those recent bad numbers help account for the low Fundata rating. Part of the problem is that, unlike most of the other funds in this group, this fund's manager has a growth orientation. Even with the collapse of the high-tech sector, there were still several technology/telecommunications stocks among the top 10 holdings in mid-2001, including Vodaphone, AT&T Wireless, and AOL Time Warner. The strong position in financial services stocks wasn't enough to offset that drag. Although this is billed as a North American Fund, the portfolio is invested mainly in large-cap U.S. stocks. There hasn't been a single Mexican equity in the fund for several years and Nortel

Networks was the only Canadian representative entering 2001. This mix could change of course, but if you're considering an investment this should be viewed as a U.S. fund rather than a North American one. Manager Cynthia Frick is with Alliance Capital Management, a company based in Minneapolis. Unlike the companion Ethical Growth Fund, this one is fully invested, which means there is little or no cash in the mix. That helps to boost returns when stock markets are strong, but has the opposite effect when they are falling. Volatility is on the high side—there is more risk here than in most Ethical funds. We are reducing the rating to $$, and the fund earns that designation only because of past glories. There is an RRSP-eligible clone if you prefer to use that in your registered plan. Started out as the Co-operative Trust Growth Fund.

## Canadian Bond Funds

### ETHICAL INCOME FUND $$ → FI NO RSP CB

Manager: Jim Lorimer (Co-operators Investment Counselling), since 1992

MER: 1.71%     Fundata E     Style: Term Structure Analysis

Suitability: Conservative investors

This is a respectable bond offering from the Ethical group, although it has slipped relative to its peers in recent years. The one-year and three-year returns have fallen to just slightly below average for the category, with the twelve-month advance to June 30/01 coming in at 4.4%. Risk is about average for the Canadian Bond category. The portfolio is heavily weighted to provincial and federal government bonds, with a 31% weighting in corporate issues. An okay bond fund, but not great.

## Promising Newcomers/Ethical Funds

### ETHICAL CANADIAN EQUITY FUND NR → G NO RSP CE

Manager: Joel Raby (Magna Vista Capital Management), since inception (January 2000)

MER: 2.40%     Fundata: N/A     Style: GARP

Suitability: Middle-of-the-road investors

The recent weak performance of the flagship Growth Fund appears to have prompted the Ethical folks to offer another alternative for Canadian equity investors. This fund, run by Joel Raby of Magna Vista, uses a slightly more aggressive growth-at-a-reasonable price (GARP) approach to stock picking. The focus is on blue-chip companies, with several banks, BCE, Power Corp., and Thomson Corp. among the top 10 holdings in mid-2001. The fund hasn't been around long enough for us to get a handle on how well it will do over time, but early results are encouraging. It was a first quartile-performer in the first half of 2001. It suffered a small loss of 2.3% over that period, but that was much better than the result posted by the TSE 300. Check into this one if you like the Ethical approach but aren't happy with the recent returns of Ethical Growth.

## Top Choices/Credential Portfolio Funds

N/A

## Also Recommended/Credential Portfolio Funds

N/A

## Promising Newcomers/Credential Portfolio Funds

N/A

# DESJARDINS FUNDS

## THE COMPANY

Desjardins is a household name in Quebec, where the company is one of the dominant players in the financial services field through its omnipresent credit union and trust company network. Its mutual fund family has expanded greatly in the past few years, and the funds are now available outside Quebec as well. Some of them are very good performers and worthy of your attention. All the funds are managed by Elantis. Three new funds in their Ethical line debuted in January 2000. All, unfortunately, are off to weak starts.

Desjardins funds are now marketed under the name Fiducie Desjardins and some are also available through the Credential network.

In October 2000, 10 new funds called Maestral Funds were launched under the Desjardins Trust banner. Thus far, all, with the exception of the money market fund, are off to disappointing starts.

## THE DETAILS

|  |  |
|---|---|
| Number of funds: | 29 |
| Assets under management: | $4.4 billion |
| Load charge: | None |
| Switching charge: | None |
| Where sold: | All provinces, except Desjardins Select Cartier Fund (Quebec residents only) |
| How sold: | Through Desjardins Trust and Credit Union branches |
| Phone number: | 1-800-361-2680 or (514) 286-3225 |
| Web site address: | www.desjardins.com |
| E-mail address: | info@fiducie-desjardins.com |
| Minimum initial investment: | $1,000 (generally) |

## INVESTING TIPS

The new Desjardins Ethical funds are actually "funds of funds" portfolios based on the Vancouver-based Ethical family of funds. For example, the Ethical Income Fund is 34% weighted to the Ethical Income Fund, 23% to the Ethical Growth Fund, 15% to the Ethical International Bond Fund, 15% to the Ethical North America Fund, 5% to the Ethical Money Market Fund, 5% to the Ethical Special Equity Fund, and 3% to the Ethical Pacific Rim Fund. If you are looking to build an all-Ethical portfolio, have a look at these Desjardins offerings.

# FUND SUMMARY

## Desjardins Funds

|  |  |
|---|---|
| Top Choices: | American Market, Quebec |
| Also Recommended: | Bond, Dividend, Growth, Mortgage |
| Promising Newcomers: | None |
| The Rest: | Balanced, Asia/Pacific, Diversified Ambitious, Diversified Audacious, Diversified Moderate, Diversified Secure, Equity, Environment Ethical Balanced, Ethical Income, Ethical North American, Europe, Global Science & Technology, High-Potential Sectors, International, International RSP, Money Market, Select American, Select Balanced, Select Canadian, Select Cartier, Select Global, Worldwide Balanced |

## Maestral Funds

|  |  |
|---|---|
| Top Choices: | None |
| Also Recommended: | None |
| Promising Newcomers: | None |
| The Rest: | American Equity, Asset Mix, Canadian Bond, Canadian Equity, Global Equity, Global Equity RSP, Growth, Health & Biotechnology, Market, Technology & Telecommunications |

# FUND RATINGS

## Top Choices/Desjardins Funds

### U.S. Equity Funds

### DESJARDINS AMERICAN MARKET FUND          $$$ → G NO RSP USE

Manager: Elantis Management Team

MER: 2.16%      Fundata: C      Style: Value/Growth

Suitability: Long-term aggressive RRSP investors

This fund makes use of derivatives to provide investors with exposure to the U.S. stock market while retaining 100% RRSP eligibility. After a strong start, results have been slipping lately. One-year loss to June 30/01 was 15.5%, compared with a 13.8% loss for the average fund. Five-year average annual return was 11%, slightly below the 11.8% average for the category. The safety record to date is excellent. A decent choice for RRSP investors looking for more U.S. equity for their plans. Rating stays at $$$, but we are looking for improvement if the fund is to maintain its high rating with us next year.

## QUEBEC GROWTH FUND $$$ ↑ G #/* RSP SPE

Manager: André Marcotte, since 1999

MER: 2.00%     Fundata: B     Style: Value/Growth

Suitability: Quebec investors

The portfolio here is allocated primarily to Quebec stocks, although it will hold some other Canadian issues. It seeks out companies that the manager believes offer good earnings and significant growth potential. The Quebec focus exposes the fund to some obvious political risk, but for investors who have been prepared to accept that fact the rewards have generally been good. The fund stubbed its toe over the year to June 30/01, losing 9.1%. That loss came after several excellent years of performance, however, which shows in the 20.4% five-year average annual compound rate of return. André Marcotte (who took over the fund in February 1999) is off to a decent start. This fund was recently purchased from Montrusco Bolton.

## Canadian Balanced and Asset Allocation Funds

## DESJARDINS QUEBEC FUND $$$ ↓ FI/G NO RSP CBAL

Manager: Elantis Management Team

MER: 2.08%     Fundata: N/A     Style: Tactical Asset Allocation

Suitability: Aggressive balanced investors

Here's an example of a fund that isn't categorized for accurate comparison with its peers. While it is classed as a specialty equity fund, its recent portfolio makeup was 32% bonds and 60% equities, with a smattering of cash. The fund's stated objectives even read like those of a balanced fund: to provide investors with a reasonable income and long-term capital appreciation. It is fortunate that the fund managers have the likes of Bombardier, BCE, CNR, and Alcan to choose from; as a group, they compose roughly half the equity holdings. On the fixed-income side, Hydro Quebec and Quebec provincials dominate, and are pretty evenly split with regard to maturity. Compared with its specialty peers, this fund has done extremely well, with an average annual return of 7.4% for the three years ending June 30/01 (the group's average was 4.3%). If we were to compare it with Canadian balanced funds, its results would look even more favourable, as the average annual return in the balanced category was 3.5% over the past three years. The one-year return was a respectable 4.1% when compared with the 2.9% average loss in the category. The risk rating for the last three years gives this fund a very desirable high-return/low-risk profile. For that reason, we'll upgrade the fund to a $$$ rating.

## Also Recommended/Desjardins Funds

### Canadian Small-to-Mid-Cap Funds

**DESJARDINS GROWTH FUND**                          $$$ ↑ G NO RSP CSC

Manager: Elantis Management Team

MER: 2.15%      Fundata: NA      Style: Growth

Suitability: Long-term growth investors

Desjardins Growth is the mid-cap offering in this group, investing in medium-sized companies with good growth potential. Sometimes the manager stretches that mandate a bit, but generally the portfolio is quite faithful to the overall objective. Results have been very good by the standards of the new Canadian Small-to-Mid-Cap category. Returns for all time periods are well above average, with a five-year average annual gain of 10.5% to June 30/01. There's greater risk here because of the nature of the mandate. This is a very good fund for its type, although its 11.2% loss in the year ending June 30/01 was disappointing (the average in the category was a 6.1% loss).

### Dividend Income Funds

**DESJARDINS DIVIDEND FUND**                         $$$ → G NO RSP DIV

Manager: Elantis Management Team

MER: 2.12%      Fundata: C      Style: Value

Suitability: High-bracket income investors

The objective of this fund is to generate above-average dividend income that is eligible for the dividend tax credit. The portfolio is structured for that purpose, with a mixture of preferred shares and high-yielding common stocks. The fund had consistently produced above-average total returns until recently, when its performance slipped a bit. In the latest year to June 30/01, the fund realized an 11.3% gain, which is average for the category. Longer-term results are slightly above average for the Dividend category. If you're looking for a fund that will generate consistently high tax-advantaged income, there are better choices. But as a conservatively managed stock fund for an RRSP, this is a decent selection. This fund barely maintains its $$$ rating.

## Canadian Bond Funds

### DESJARDINS BOND FUND                          $$ ↓ FI NO RSP CB

Manager: Elantis Management Team

MER: 1.83%       Fundata: C        Style: Credit Analysis

Suitability: Conservative fixed-income investors

Desjardins Bond is an average performer, with returns generally around the median mark. The portfolio was about 64% in federal, provincial, and municipal government bonds in mid-2001, with 34% in corporate bonds and the remainder in cash. Returns for the year ending June 30/01 were 4.7% compared with 4.5% for the average bond fund. Okay if you're a Desjardins client, but not a fund you'd cross the street for.

## Canadian Mortgage Funds

### DESJARDINS MORTGAGE FUND                      $$ ↓ FI NO RSP M

Manager: Elantis Management Team

MER: 1.83%       Fundata: A        Style: Term Structure Analysis

Suitability: Conservative income investors

Returns for this usually steady mortgage fund have recovered nicely in the past three years and are now running slightly above average. The gain for the year to June 30/01 was a solid 7%, compared with 6.4% for the peer group. The three-year annual return at 4.8% also exceeded the average by about 25 basis points per annum. Although residential mortgages make up the bulk of the portfolio, a portion of the fund (23%) was invested in bonds in mid-2001. The big attraction here is a great safety record: this fund has never recorded a losing 12-month period in its history, and that goes all the way back to 1965. It's a decent core holding for a conservatively managed RRSP.

### Promising Newcomers/Desjardins Funds

None.

### Top Choices/Maestral Funds

None.

### Also Recommended/Maestral Funds

None.

### Promising Newcomers/Maestral Funds

None.

# DUNDEE MUTUAL FUNDS

## THE COMPANY

Over the past several years, Dundee has pursued an extremely active strategy of acquiring mutual funds and expanding into the area of wealth management.

The Dundee funds are currently divided into three lines: the original Dynamic Funds, which generally—but not always—adopt a bottom-up value approach; the Dynamic Power Funds, which emphasize growth; and the Dynamic Focus Plus Funds, which were previously part of the Infinity family of Fortune Financial management (Dundee acquired Fortune in 1999.)

The company's offerings have expanded greatly over the past year. A number of new funds in the global area debuted in October 2000 and February 2001, including several global sector funds and RRSP versions of the Global Technology and Health Sciences funds. These add to the company's clone fund group, which includes the Americas, Europe, Far East, International, and Power Americas funds.

In February 2001, the company launched its Dynamic Global Fund Corporation, which allows investors to switch from one investment style to another without triggering a disposition and hence a capital gain. There are 16 fund classes included in the programme.

Then, in March 2001, Ned Goodman announced he was returning to active management as lead manager of the Focus Plus family. The funds continue to emphasize a team approach with regard to management; Goodman & Company Investment Counsel still oversees the portfolios. The team includes over 20 analysts and senior managers. However, unlike past years, some of the funds are now highlighting the lead manager.

You have to wade carefully through the Dynamic offerings. There are a few good funds but a lot of underperformers as well. Dynamic's propensity to merge or change the names and focus of weak performers means you should take extra care when evaluating this line.

## THE DETAILS

| | |
|---|---|
| Number of funds: | 67 |
| Assets under management: | $6.5 billion |
| Load charge: | Front: max. 5%; Back: max. 6% |
| Switching charge: | 2% maximum |
| Where sold: | Across Canada |
| How sold: | Through brokers, dealers, and financial planners |
| Phone number: | 1-800-268-8186 or (416) 365-5100 |
| Web site address: | www.dynamic.ca |
| E-mail address: | invest@dynamic.ca |
| Minimum initial investment: | $1,000 |

## INVESTING TIPS

Dundee has launched a group of five protected funds under the "Dynamic" brand name. They are similar to segregated funds in several ways, but are not tied to any kind of insurance or annuity contract. Each protected fund is a replica of a regular Dynamic fund and must be held for at least 10 years to be eligible for a 100% guarantee (meaning that if you suffer a loss over that time, you'll receive an amount equal to your original investment). The funds are also redeemable at the original investment amount or current market value—whichever is greater—should the investor die prior to the end of the 10-year holding period. These funds offer capital preservation and the opportunity for appreciation and will allow the investor to lock in market gains twice a year for added security. Unlike pure segregated funds, the insurance cost on these funds will remain constant for the life of the fund. All of Dynamic's protected funds are eligible for RRSPs, RRIFs, and RESPs. For further information about the specifics, talk to a financial advisor.

One point to be aware of when buying and selling Dynamic Funds is the short redemption schedule available on a deferred sales charge basis. If you redeem in the first three years, it may be possible to pay as little as 3% in redemption charges. That's not bad when compared with the industry norm.

## FUND SUMMARY

|  |  |
|---|---|
| Top Choices: | Focus Plus Wealth Management |
| Also Recommended: | Americas, Dynamic Fund of Canada, Far East, Global Precious Metals, International, Power Canadian Growth, Precious Metals, Quebec |
| Promising Newcomers: | Canadian Resources |
| The Rest: | Canadian Real Estate, Canadian Value Class, Diversified Income Trust, Dividend, Dividend Growth, Dollar Cost Averaging, Equity Hedge, Europe, Europe Value Class, Far East Value Class, Focus Plus American, Focus Plus Balanced, Focus Plus Canadian, Focus Plus Canadian Class, Focus Plus U.S. Class, Fund of Funds Global Bond, Global Financial Services, Global Health Science, Global Income & Growth, Global Partners, Global Real Estate Class, Global Resource, Global Technology, Health Sciences, Income, International Value Class, Money Market, Partners, Power American, Power Balanced, Power Bond, Power Canadian Growth Class, Power European Growth Class, Power International Growth Class, Power U.S. Growth Class, QSSP, Real Estate Equity, Small-Cap, U.S. Value Class |

# FUND RATINGS

## Top Choices

### Sector Equity Funds

### DYNAMIC FOCUS PLUS WEALTH MANAGEMENT FUND                    $$$ ↑ G #/* RSP SPE

Manager: Goodman and Company Team

MER: 2.67%     Fundata: A     Style: Bottom-up Momentum

Suitability: Aggressive investors

This fund was renamed this year (it was previously the Dynamic Infinity Wealth Management Fund) and is now under the leadership of well-known manager Ned Goodman. The investments in this fund are restricted to the financial services industry. Its portfolio holdings are generally limited to 35 to 40 names and include banks, mutual fund companies, and insurance companies. The fund takes full advantage of its eligible foreign content, as it provides the only diversification. The three-year return is relatively equal to the TSE Financial Services Sub-Index and well above the TSE 300 Composite Index. The one-year return to mid-2001 was an impressive 11.8% given the weakness in Canadian equity markets over that period. This fund's risk is higher than that of a more diversified Canadian equity fund. What it provides is an opportunity to play exclusively in a sector we like over the next year. We'll maintain its $$$ rating.

## Also Recommended

### Canadian Equity Funds

### DYNAMIC FUND OF CANADA                    $$ → G #/* RSP CE

Manager: David Goodman, since 1997

MER: 2.54%     Fundata: B     Style: Bottom-up Value

Suitability: Middle-of-the-road investors

In spite of this fund's long track record (it's been around since 1957), its returns over the past decade have been only average. It is a conservatively managed value fund that invests primarily in established large-cap companies, which has been its mandate since inception. In 1998, the fund was hampered by an underexposure to financial services. It changed direction in 1999 and re-allocated its assets to emphasize financial services and oil and gas—at just about the time both of those sectors were soft. Since then, both sectors have gained momentum and returns this year have improved somewhat. In the 12 months to June 30/01 the fund gained 4.8%, almost a full 15 percentage points above the category average. Three- and five-year returns are now in the second and third quartile among peer group entries. Given the value-based style and the lower-than-average risk, we are upgrading the rating to $$.

## DYNAMIC POWER CANADIAN GROWTH FUND          $$ ↑ G #/* RSP CE

Manager: Rohit Sehgal, since 1999

MER: 2.61%      Fundata: D      Style: Top-down Sector Growth

Suitability: Aggressive investors

The Dynamic Power Canadian Fund was merged into this fund in October 2000. Rohit Sehgal, who joined Dundee a few years ago, is now running this fund. Sehgal's appointment was not surprising given the fund's poor past performance and the fact that Sehgal is an equity specialist, having managed the London Life Canadian Equity Fund for 17 years. Furthermore, this fund has been brought into the Power line of funds, which are Sehgal's responsibility. The fund invests across all capitalization classes but will always have 50% in large caps. Its approach is top-down growth, focusing on earnings momentum—market timing, in other words—which makes this a very active fund. Very little is held in cash. As of mid-2001, this well-diversified fund was overweighted in financial services and under-weighted in industrial products. This mix exhibits the fund's top-down approach, focusing on the best potential growth sectors. Since the management change, returns have been much stronger. Although the fund suffered a 15.7% loss in the year ending June 30/01, the fund returned 56.4% a year ago. The three-year average returns are now above the norm for Canadian equity funds as a group. We are maintaining our rating at $$.

## Specialty Equity Funds

## DYNAMIC QUEBEC FUND          $$ ↓ G #/* RSP SPE

Managers: Ned Goodman, since inception and Ed Ho, since 1998

MER: 2.84%      Fundata: D      Style: Bottom-up Value

Suitability: Quebec-oriented investors

The fund invests in Quebec companies, or any business that is expected to benefit from Quebec's economic activity. Despite the fact that the Quebec economy was slow to enjoy its share of the general upturn in Canada in the 1990s, Ned Goodman and his team have managed to make some beneficial investments. Many of the names in the portfolio will come as no surprise: Molson, Bank of Montreal, Quebecor, and Cogeco Cable. The fund was an average performer over the last three years, with an average annual return of 1.9% to mid-2001. When set head-to-head against the only other exclusively Quebec-based fund— Montrusco Bolton's Quebec Growth—this one comes in second. Quebec Growth produced an average annual gain of 7.7% over the same period.

However, Quebec Growth is available only to investors in that province, so people in other parts of the country who would like to get in on the action are limited to this fund. Risk level has been very good. If you can buy Quebec Growth, however, it is our preferred choice.

## U.S. Equity Funds

### DYNAMIC AMERICAS FUND                                    $$ → G #/* £ USE

Manager: Todd Beallor, since 2000

MER: 2.48%     Fundata: D      Style: Bottom-up Value

Suitability: Value-oriented investors

This fund has had a spotty record since its inception. It employs a bottom-up approach, looking for undervalued situations or companies with strong expected earnings growth. All capitalization classes are considered. In the year to June 30/01, the fund held up well, suffering a small loss of 1.3% versus an average loss of 13.4% for U.S. equity funds. Three-year numbers are below average, but five-year numbers are still slightly above. The fund holds only a small core group of stocks, usually between 30 and 35 names in the portfolio. As a result, correct stock selection becomes more critical. An obvious absence of more growth-oriented companies hurt returns in the past, but the fund's value orientation should be constructive in the future. Due to the conservative nature of this fund, it will tend to err on the defensive side compared with its peer group. For now we will we keep the $$ rating.

## Global and International Equity Funds

### DYNAMIC FAR EAST FUND                                    $$$ ↑ G #/* £ PRE

Manager: Joe Evershed, since 1995

MER: 3.22%     Fundata: C      Style: Bottom-up Value

Suitability: Aggressive Far East investors

Simply stated, this is a good fund in an otherwise precarious region. That said, after a number of years of solid performance this fund bombed badly in the year ending June 30/01, when it suffered a 37.2% loss. At mid-2001, the portfolio had a bias toward Hong Kong and Japan. Despite its dismal performance this past year, its three- and five-year numbers remain above the returns for its peer group or its benchmark index. In fact, the fund made money over those time frames, which was not the case for most Pacific Rim funds. For example, in the year to June 30/00, the fund made an impressive, above-average 35% gain (compared with 26.1% for the peer group) as the Far East staged a major rebound. In terms of risk, the fund is below the average of its group, due to its value orientation (but it's still high risk in absolute terms). This fund is a good choice for investors who want to be in this region, but we have lowered our rating to $$$. An RSP version of this fund is available if you want full RRSP eligibility; however, we do not generally recommend funds with this much volatility for registered plans.

## DYNAMIC INTERNATIONAL FUND $$ → G #/* £ IE

Managers: Joe Evershed, since 1995; Chuk Wong, since 1996; and Todd Beallor, since 2000

MER: 2.68%     Fundata: C     Style: Bottom-up Value

Suitability: Value-oriented investors

It appears that when funds do poorly, they are often merged into another fund. Case in point: the Global Millennia Fund was merged into this entry two years ago. Then the Dynamic Israel Growth Fund and the Dynamic Latin American Fund were also folded into this one. As of mid-2001, this global fund had an American flavour to it, with the U.S. representing about one-third of its stock holdings, followed next by allocations to Western Europe and other European countries. It is interesting to note the lack of holdings in Latin America, given the merging of Dynamic Latin America into this one just two years ago. Stocks are selected for their value and long-term potential through a bottom-up approach, and there is a definite large-cap feeling to the portfolio. Returns have been inconsistent throughout the fund's history. In the latest year, the fund suffered a 21.7% loss although the three-year, five-year, and ten-year numbers have placed the fund in the top half of its category, and reasonably comfortably within that range. This result is predominantly due to the strong returns over the year ending June 30/00 when this fund doubled the return of the median fund. Looking ahead, the instability of these numbers is a concern, and we are downgrading to a $$ rating.

## Sector Equity Funds

## DYNAMIC GLOBAL PRECIOUS METALS FUND $$ ↑ G #/* £ PM

Manager: Goodman and Company Team

MER: 2.97%     Fundata: A     Style: Bottom-up Value

Suitability: Aggressive investors

Despite stagnant gold prices, the metal sector showed some life recently as major gold mining companies started to generate positive cash flows. This fund can seek out the best gold resource companies around the globe. At present, however, most of the best companies are in Canada; as of mid-2001, the fund had over 60% of its assets in Canadian resource stocks. The rest of the fund is primarily invested in the Pacific Rim, Africa, and the U.S. The fund had its best period since inception in the 12 months to June 30/01, returning an impressive 16.6%. With lower-than-average volatility and high recent returns, it scored the second-highest Fundata score of the 19 funds in the precious metals category. If you want exposure to this sector, this is certainly one of the better funds to work with. We are increasing the rating to $$.

## DYNAMIC PRECIOUS METALS FUND $$ ↑ G #/* RSP PM

Manager: Jonathan Goodman

MER: 2.59%     Fundata: C     Style Bottom-up Value

Suitability: Aggressive investors

This fund has a long-term, buy-and-hold approach, purchasing established medium and large companies, including East Africa Gold and Agnico Eagle. The marketing material says it all: "for long-term investors who await the anticipated recovery of the bullion sector." Unfortunately, the long term hasn't been good at all. If you bought in a decade ago, you would have earned a paltry 2.2% per annum and that number is positive only because of the most recent year's (to mid-2001) 22% return. And it's not the manager's fault that the sector has not co-operated—Jonathan Goodman is certainly a knowledgeable person to have at the helm If you are going to hold a precious metal fund, this one isn't bad. Upgraded to a $$ rating.

### Promising Newcomers

## DYNAMIC CANADIAN RESOURCES FUND NR → G #/* RSP NR

Managers: Goodman and Company Team, since May 2000

MER: 2.46%     Fundata: C     Style: Bottom-up Value

Suitability: Aggressive investors

This fund specializes in resource-based companies, primarily Canadian ones. At mid-2001, its major holdings included Aber Diamond, Gabriel Resources, Talisman Energy, and Nexen. The fund has had a couple of good years since inception and recorded a 27.7% return in the year ending June 30/01, compared with the 17% return for its TSE 100-Resources Index benchmark. With increased investor attention to this sector and a decent track record to date, this is a fund worth considering. Just beware of the historic volatility associated with resource funds.

# ELLIOTT & PAGE FUNDS

## THE COMPANY

Elliott & Page (E&P)—a member of the Manulife Financial group of companies—has been around since 1949. E&P provides investment management to Canadian companies, pension funds, institutions, individuals, and mutual funds. The company entered the mutual fund business in 1988.

The company has taken over the former Manulife Cabot Funds, which are now being sold as the E&P Cabot Funds.

In summer of 2001, Elliott & Page introduced three new Multi-Advisor portfolios. Two of them are asset allocation portfolios: the E&P Manulife Balanced Growth Fund and the E&P Manulife Maximum Growth Fund. The third is the E&P Tax-Managed Growth portfolio.

## THE DETAILS

| | |
|---|---|
| Number of funds: | 23 |
| Assets under management: | $1.8 billion |
| Load charge: | Front: max. 5%; Back: max. 5% (except Cabot funds acquired through Manulife Securities) |
| Switching charge: | 2% maximum, depending on initial sales charge |
| Where sold: | Across Canada |
| How sold: | Through brokers, dealers, and discount brokerage firms. Cabot funds available through Manulife Securities. |
| Phone number: | 1-888-588-7999 |
| Web site address: | www.elliottandpage.com |
| E-mail address: | info@elliotandpage.com |
| Minimum initial investment: | $500 |

## INVESTING TIPS

The firm's load structure, previously one of the most confusing in the industry, has been simplified and now aligns more closely with industry norms. Here's an overview. Salespersons can charge between 0% and 5% on a front-end load basis. The DSC (back-end load) option, which is what most investors use, is based on a 5% fee to the mutual fund dealer. The new DSC programme took effect in July 2000 and is based on the following redemption schedule:

| Year 1: | 6.0% |
| --- | --- |
| Year 2: | 5.5% |
| Year 3: | 5.0% |
| Year 4: | 4.5% |
| Year 5: | 4.0% |
| Year 6: | 3.5% |
| After Year 6: | 0% |

In short, investors who hold the funds for at least six years can redeem at zero cost. The exception to this charge is the money market fund, which continues to be sold as a no-load alternative.

## FUND SUMMARY

### Elliott & Page Funds

| | |
| --- | --- |
| Top Choices: | Monthly High Income |
| Also Recommended: | American Growth, Asian Growth |
| Promising Newcomers: | Growth Opportunities |
| The Rest: | Active Bond, Balanced, Equity (capped), European Equity, Generation Wave, Global Equity, Global Momentum, Growth & Income, Money, RSP American Growth, RSP Global Equity, RSP U.S. Mid-Cap, Sector Rotation, T-Bill, U.S. Mid-Cap, Value Equity |

### E&P Cabot Funds

| | |
| --- | --- |
| Top Choices: | None |
| Also Recommended: | None |
| Promising Newcomers: | None |
| The Rest: | Blue Chip, Canadian Equity, Global Multi-Style |

# FUND RATINGS

## Top Choices/Elliott & Page Funds

### Canadian Balanced and Asset Allocation Funds

### ELLIOTT & PAGE MONTHLY HIGH INCOME FUND
$$$ → FI/G #/* RSP CHIB

Manager: Alan Wicks, since 2000

MER: 2.43%     Fundata: A     Style: Top-down

Suitability: Balanced investors

This balanced fund is off to a great start. Against its peer group (high-income balanced funds), the fund's one-year return to June 30/01 was remarkable (26% versus 14.3% for the category average). It also outperformed the fund's benchmark index (the Globe Canadian High Income Balanced Peer Index). As of mid-2001, the portfolio was concentrated in royalty trusts (38%), high-yield Canadian stocks (27%), and REITs (15%). The rest was allocated to government and corporate bonds and cash. It was the only one of four funds in the high-yield category to score a Fundata "A." We are starting it off with a $$$ rating. The risk level is about average for a fund of this type, but keep in mind that high-income balanced funds, as a group, will be more volatile than regular balanced funds because of their large holdings in royalty trusts.

## Also Recommended/Elliott & Page Funds

### U.S. Equity Funds

### ELLIOTT & PAGE AMERICAN GROWTH FUND
$$$ ↓ G #/* £ USE

Manager: Robert Jones (Goldman Sachs), since 1995

MER: 2.52%     Fundata: D     Style: Bottom-up Growth

Suitability: Diversified U.S. equity investors

Given the performance of growth funds in general, it is not surprising that Robert Jones continues to outperform the average U.S. large-cap fund. This fund uses a quantitative multi-factor model developed by Goldman Sachs in the quest for undervalued stocks. The S&P 500 Index is used as a comparative benchmark when allocating the fund's assets in terms of its industry weighting. By overweighting and/or underweighting specific companies within this framework, the manager attempts to beat the S&P 500. Although the longer-term record is good, the fund has recently underperformed its peers. That's likely the result of the fund's reliance on growth stocks like Microsoft and Cisco. In the year ending June 30/01, the fund lost 14.3% compared with an average loss of 13.8% for the peer group. The three-year record is below average as well. However, given strong management and a well-below-average risk profile, the fund hangs on to its $$$ rating.

## Global and International Equity Funds

### ELLIOTT & PAGE ASIAN GROWTH FUND$$ ↑ G #/* £ PRE

Manager: Edmond Leung, since 2000

MER: 4.10%     Fundata: B     Style: Top-down Growth

Suitability: Aggressive investors

In June 2000, Edmond Leung of ABN AMRO Asset Management took over at the helm of this fund. His goal is to model the Asian Growth Fund after the ABN AMRO Far East Fund, which has outperformed the MSCI Pacific benchmark by as much as 670 basis points on an annual compound basis over a five-year period. Unfortunately, Leung assumed management responsibility at the wrong time. Like other Asian investors, this fund suffered a large loss in the latest year. In the year ending June 30/01 it fell by 30.9%, about equal to its peer group and a little worse than the MSCI Far East Index. Why are we retaining a $$$ rating? Well, we see a fundamentally sound model plus a stellar longer-term record. In the three years to June 30/01 the fund returned 16.7% compared with 6.1% for the average fund and 6.8% for the index. At mid-2001, its major allocations were to Japan (26.9%), Australia (18.9%), Hong Kong (18.5%) and Korea (10.1%). If you are looking for an Asian investment, this fund is worthy of your consideration.

## Promising Newcomers/Elliott & Page Funds

## Canadian Small-to-Mid-Cap Equity Funds

### ELLIOTT & PAGE GROWTH OPPORTUNITIES FUND   NR ↑ G #/* RSP CSC

Manager: Ted Whitehead, since 1998

MER: 2.93%     Fundata: B     Style: Top-down Growth

Suitability: Aggressive investors

This small-cap specialty fund is off to a solid start. Fund manager Ted Whitehead focuses on small- and medium-sized companies with high growth potential. At mid-2001, the fund's heaviest sector allocations were to industrial products, consumer products, and merchandising. These areas composed over 46% of the portfolio. The fund's two-year annual compounded return to June 30/01 was 28.7%. In the latest year it realized an 11.5% gain against a 6.1% average loss for its peer group. Let's call this a "highly promising" newcomer!

## Top Choices/E&P Cabot Funds

None.

## Also Recommended/E&P Cabot Funds

None.

## Promising Newcomers/E&P Cabot Funds

None.

# FIDELITY INVESTMENTS

## THE COMPANY

Fidelity Canada is a subsidiary of the Boston-based Fidelity Investments, a behemoth in the mutual fund industry with 16 million customers and more than U.S.$900 billion under management worldwide. On any given day, Fidelity trading accounts for 5% to 8% of the total business on the New York Stock Exchange.

The company claims that it researches more stocks than any other money manager in the world, which involves investigating more than 5,000 companies. To carry out this Herculean task, it employs more than 500 portfolio managers, analysts, and traders in its Boston, London, Hong Kong, Tokyo, and Toronto offices. Overall, Fidelity employs more than 33,000 people.

Since Fidelity's initial foray into the Canadian mutual fund business in the late 1980s, the company has accumulated more than $33 billion in fund assets and now stands as the number four company in the nation in terms of size. The majority of the funds are managed via Fidelity's traditional bottom-up approach to stock picking, which considers individual stocks on their own merit rather than focusing on economic sectors or geographic locations.

Fidelity has decided to label all their funds as having a GARP style: growth at a reasonable price. The bias is slightly toward the growth side in most cases but a few of the managers, like Alan Radlo, have a slight value bias.

## THE DETAILS

|  |  |
|---|---|
| Number of core funds: | 29 |
| Assets under management: | $33.1 billion |
| Load charge: | Front: max. 5%; Back: max. 6% |
| Switching charge: | 2% maximum |
| Where sold: | Across Canada |
| How sold: | Through registered brokers, financial advisors, or insurance agents |
| Phone number: | 1-800-263-4077 (English, French, and Cantonese) |
| Web site address: | www.fidelity.ca |
| E-mail address: | cs.english@fmr.com (English); sc.francais@fmr.com (French) |
| Minimum initial investment: | $500 |

## INVESTING TIPS

The company restructured its deferred sales charge option (DSC) for units purchased after April 2, 1999. Prior to that date, the DSC was calculated on the market value; however, under the revised format, the DSC will be determined on the entry price of the units. This change makes DSC fees more predictable for investors and, for funds that have moved up in value, the DSC will be lower if you decide to bail out. On the other hand, for funds that have declined in value, a higher DSC will apply since it will be calculated on the higher original cost. Further, the "10% free amount" in reference to redemptions will also be based on the original price instead of the market value.

All the commissions cited above apply to the company's A units, which are the ones most often purchased by investors. However, Fidelity also offers F units, which carry no sales commissions and no switching fees. These units are usually sold by advisors for fee-based accounts—those where you pay an annual percentage of total assets to the advisor for his or her services. If you have that type of account, be sure to ask for F units so you don't end up being charged twice.

## FUND SUMMARY

| | |
|---|---|
| Top Choices: | Canadian Asset Allocation, Canadian Growth Company, Canadian Short-Term Bond, Small-Cap America, True North, U.S. Money Market |
| Also Recommended: | Canadian Bond, Canadian Large-Cap, Canadian Money Market, European Growth, Far East, Focus Consumer Industries, Focus Financial Services, Focus Health Care, Focus Natural Resources, Global Asset Allocation, International Portfolio, Japanese Growth |
| Promising Newcomers: | American Opportunities, Disciplined Equity |
| The Rest: | American High-Yield, Canadian Aggressive Growth, Canadian Balanced, Emerging Markets Portfolio, Focus Technology, Growth America, Latin American Growth, Overseas |

# FUND RATINGS

## Top Choices

### Canadian Equity Funds

### FIDELITY TRUE NORTH FUND                           $$$ ↓ G #/* RSP CE

Manager: Alan Radlo, since inception (September 1996)

MER: 2.51%      Fundata: B      Style: GARP

Suitability: Conservative long-term investors.

This fund got off to a very rocky start. It was launched amid much fanfare and anticipation as Fidelity's vehicle for its new star manager, Veronika Hirsch. Then Ms. Hirsch ran into a spot of trouble with regulatory authorities and she and Fidelity parted company. The firm scrambled desperately to find a replacement and came up with Boston-based Alan Radlo. Talk about making a silk purse out of a sow's ear! Radlo, who uses a fundamental value approach to stock picking, quickly put his mark on the fund and gave Fidelity a highly respectable entry in the Canadian Equity category. The fund generated an average annual compound rate of return of 11.2% for the three years to June 30/01, although it had a small one-year loss. Those numbers put the fund firmly in the high-return/low-risk category. The portfolio is widely diversified, with no sector predominating. Industrials, financials, and energy are the top three holdings, totalling about 48% of assets. The management expense ratio (MER) is spot on the average for its peer group. Pretty good work from a fellow who's based in the States! We continue to be impressed by this fund. Definitely recommended.

### Canadian Small-to-Mid-Cap Funds

### FIDELITY CANADIAN GROWTH COMPANY FUND     $$$ ↓ G #/* RSP CSC

Manager: Alan Radlo, since inception (July 1994)

MER: 2.52%      Fundata: B      Style: GARP

Suitability: Long-term investors seeking above-average growth potential

The fine job Alan Radlo has done with this fund is reflected in an above-average long-term performance and the amazing fact that this small-cap fund has never recorded a losing calendar year since its inception, despite the volatility of the sector. That said, there's some cheating here on Radlo's part. Although the focus of the fund is on small-to-mid-cap stocks, there are lots of biggies in the portfolio as well, and these add stability and reduce risk. In the first half of 2001, for example, the top 10 holdings including such well-known (and hardly small-cap) names as Sun Life, Bombardier, and Onex. At that time, industrial products, oil and gas, and financial services accounted for more than half of the total assets, so the fund will take heavy weightings in specific sectors. The fund also had a 17% cash position, which made it quite defensive in nature (large cash holdings reduce risk). Radlo's philosophy is to search for companies with the capacity to become market leaders. He especially looks for stocks that are undervalued compared with their potential. So far, returns have been solid. The fund had a fractional gain in the year to June 30/01, but over five years the average annual return of 15.9% left most of the competition in the dust. These solid returns were accomplished with below-average volatility; the fund has a very low beta of 0.81 (1.00 would mean the fund was matching the market). Average quartile ranking (AQR) is an excellent 1.86 over seven years. This is a first-rate small-cap addition for long-term investors.

## U.S. Small-to-Mid-Cap Funds

### FIDELITY SMALL-CAP AMERICA FUND $$$$ → #/* £ USSC

Manager: James Harmon, since July 2000

MER: 2.56%    Fundata: A    Style: GARP

Suitability: Aggressive investors

After three managerial changes in as many years, this fund has taken off under the direction of the new man at the helm, James Harmon. He took over in July 2000 and look what's happened since: in the year to June 30/01, this fund gained 43.3%! No other fund in the category was within shouting distance. Despite this great run, Harmon feels there is a lot more profit potential in the U.S. small-cap market. He particularly likes the prospects for health care and education stocks, which he believes are still undervalued. The portfolio is well balanced: the top 10 names account for only about 23% of the total assets. Risk is on par with the fund's benchmark index, the Russell 2000. This is not a core holding, but it would be a valuable addition for more aggressive investors who want some exposure to the strong American small-cap market. A U.S. dollar-denominated version of this fund is also available, but there is no RRSP-eligible clone. Rating moves up to a top $$$$.

## Canadian Balanced and Asset Allocation Funds

### FIDELITY CANADIAN ASSET ALLOCATION FUND $$$$ ↓ FI/G #/* RSP CTAA

Manager: Dick Habermann, since inception (December 1994)

MER: 2.49%    Fundata: B    Style: GARP

Suitability: Core fund for conservative investors

This big $6.3 billion fund operates using a team approach with Dick Habermann as lead manager, along with input from Alan Radlo on the equities side and Jeff Moore on the bond side. The fund was relatively defensive in the first half of 2001, with the fixed-income, and cash positions accounting for 44% of total assets. "Neutral" weightings would be 65% stocks, 30% fixed-income and 5% money market, so the managers were clearly concerned about the direction of the equity markets. However, the weightings are constantly monitored and changed to reflect market conditions, so check the current weightings if you're considering an investment. The fund's diversified group of stocks is conservatively managed, with many large-cap, dividend-paying issues. The bond portion has average risk. The strategy here is working: the five-year average annual return of 13.1% to June 30/01 is tops in the Canadian Tactical Asset Allocation category. The fund has never lost money in any calendar year, and has a fine AQR of 1.43 over seven years (1.00 would be perfect, meaning it was always in the top quartile). This is a good Canadian balanced fund for your RRSP or RRIF and we are moving the rating up to $$$$ in recognition of the long-term consistency and low risk.

## Canadian Bond Funds

### FIDELITY CANADIAN SHORT-TERM BOND FUND    $$$ ↓ FI #/* RSP STB

Manager: Jeff Moore, since October 2000

MER: 1.34%     Fundata: C       Style: Credit Analysis

Suitability: Risk-averse investors and RRIF portfolios

Canadian Jeff Moore took over the direction of this fund in the fall of 2000, but the conservative, low-risk style remains the same. Unlike the companion Canadian Bond Fund, this fund avoids all exposure to higher-risk long bonds in order to preserve capital. This fund is geared toward those who need regular monthly income and it has a good record for payouts. In the calendar year 2000, distributions totalled $0.58 per unit for a yield of 5.7%, making this fund an especially good choice for a RRIF (the combination of steady returns and low risk is perfect in that situation). Moore's strategy focuses more on fundamental research than the state of interest rates. As with the Bond Fund, bonds of cyclical companies are avoided to minimize risk. Corporate and federal bonds comprise the majority of the portfolio. The risk here, however, is far less than with the Bond Fund. Returns are generally above the peer group, which is the Canadian Short-Term Bond category. In the year to June 30/01, the fund realized a 6.3% return, more than a percentage point above the average for the category. This fund used to be known as the Fidelity Canadian Income Fund.

## Money Market Funds

### FIDELITY U.S.$ MONEY MARKET FUND    $$$ → C #/* £ FMM

Manager: Robert Duby, since inception (November 1994)

MER: 1.02%    Fundata: D

Suitability: Non-registered accounts requiring U.S. dollar cash flow

This fund invests primarily in short-term commercial notes and is geared toward those who want monthly income in U.S. dollars. The cash flow has been very good; in calendar 2000, the fund distributed U.S.53¢ per unit for a yield of 5.3%. The only problem here is that this fund is considered foreign content, so you'll eat up your 30% allocation if you buy this one for an RRSP or RRIF. For a non-registered account where U.S. dollars are required, it will work just fine, however. Gain to June 30/01 was 5%, nicely above the average for the Foreign Money Market category. Longer-term numbers are also well above the average for the peer group. The risk inherent in this fund is from holding U.S. dollars when the Canadian dollar rises. If you do decide to buy outside your RRSP, try to avoid paying any load.

## Also Recommended

## Canadian Equity Funds

### FIDELITY CANADIAN LARGE-CAP FUND    $$ → G #/* RSP CLC

Manager: Robert Haber, since June 1998

MER: 2.39%    Fundata: C    Style: GARP

Suitability: Conservative investors

This fund struggled for years under its original name of Capital Builder, but it staged an impressive reversal after Robert Haber took control in mid-1998 and the mandate was changed to make it a large-cap fund. Last year we reported the fund had a great 50.3% return in the 12 months ending June 30/00. The latest numbers are nowhere near as exciting; the fund lost 6.2% in the year to June 30/01, and dropped to a third-quartile ranking in the first half of 2001. Still, it was a top-quartile performer in calendar years 1999 and 2000. Last year the fund had substantial exposure to the interest-sensitive utilities and financial services sectors, with these two sectors accounting for 44% of the stock holdings as of mid-2000. Haber has been steadily reducing this weighting, however, and in the first half of 2001 it was down to about 22%. In the meantime, industrial products and oil and gas were way up. This fund has now become a respectable addition to Fidelity's Canadian equity line-up.

## Global and International Equity Funds

### FIDELITY EUROPEAN GROWTH FUND $$ \rightarrow$ G #/* £ EE

Manager: Thierry Serero, since July 1998

MER: 2.54%    Fundata: D    Style: GARP

Suitability: Balanced investors seeking to add European exposure

This was a consistently good fund under the leadership of Sally Walden, but a managerial change in mid-1998 saw her promoted within the Fidelity organization and responsibility passed to Thierry Serero. He's had his problems here and the fund squeaks into our Also Recommended category by the skin of its teeth. We'll grant that European markets have been in a funk recently, but this fund has been even funkier. The three-year average annual compound rate of return to June 30/01—which pretty well covers the period since Serero took over—is an unimpressive –4.6%. The average fund in the category also lost money, but slightly less than this fund. And there were some European funds that managed to eke out a profit over that time. As of mid-2001, the fund's top positions were in the U.K. and France. Surprisingly, there was also a 7% U.S. allocation—strange for a European fund. This is not one of our top European picks, but there are certainly worse choices around. A U.S. dollar-denominated version of this fund is also available, as is an RRSP-eligible clone.

### FIDELITY FAR EAST FUND $$ ↑ G #/* £ AXJ

Manager: K.C. Lee, since inception (September 1991)

MER: 2.68%    Fundata: C    Style: GARP

Suitability: Aggressive investors seeking more Asian exposure

Asian markets were weak for most of 2000 and the first part of 2001, so manager K.C. Lee can't be blamed too much for this fund's 13.6% loss for the 12 months to June 30/01. Despite that loss, he managed to post a three-year average annual compound rate of return of 15.6%, almost triple the category average. Another key point in Lee's favour is that this is a low-risk fund, at least as far as other Asian funds are concerned (we classify it high-risk because all Far East funds are more volatile than broadly based global funds). This fund shows a beta of 0.94, which means it is less volatile than its benchmark index. The fund is heavily weighted to Hong Kong and has been for several years. Lee focuses on Old Economy stocks and places great emphasis on quality of management. There is a heavy concentration on just a few companies here: Hutchison Whampoa, Cheung Kong Holdings, and HSBC Holdings account for 46% of all the assets in the fund. If any of them should run into serious trouble, watch out! This type of weighting is great when you are on the right side of the trade, but it can be disastrous if you bet wrong. The fund is recommended only for those who are comfortable with

Lee's Hong Kong focus. The fund is worthy of a $$$ rating based on its performance record relative to the competition, but we want to see clear evidence of an Asian recovery before we move it to that level. A U.S. dollar-denominated version of this fund is also available, as is an RRSP-eligible clone.

## FIDELITY INTERNATIONAL PORTFOLIO FUND $$ → G #/* £ GE

Manager: Dick Habermann, since March 1993

MER: 2.50%     Fundata: D     Style: GARP

Suitability: Conservative long-term investors

This is a good fund that has gone into what we hope is just a temporary slump. Nonetheless, the drop of 16.7% in the year to June 30/01 makes us nervous, since it is below the average for the category. In fact, the fund has been a third-quartile performer over the past two-and-a-half years and no one should be sanguine about that, least of all manager Dick Habermann. This is one of Fidelity's largest funds, with over $7 billion in assets (including the RRSP-eligible clone). But that asset base is slowly starting to erode, something that Fidelity can't afford to tolerate for long. Long-term results still look good, but fund investors are an impatient lot these days. The fund invests across a broad spectrum of countries and sectors and follows a bottom-up growth-oriented strategy, looking at the strengths and weaknesses of each individual company. As was the case in the previous year, the fund remained overexposed to the U.S. market in the first half of 2001 (54.6%), followed by Japan (10.8%), and the U.K. (9.9%). We are continuing to show this fund on our Also Recommended list, but we don't have the same degree of confidence we did in the past and we suggest shopping around. We're dropping the rating from $$$$ to $$ while awaiting a turnaround. A U.S.$ denominated version of this fund is also available.

## FIDELITY JAPANESE GROWTH FUND $$ ↑ G #/* £ JE

Manager: Jay Talbot, since July 1998

MER: 2.71%     Fundata: D     Style: GARP

Suitability: Aggressive investors

Sooner or later Japan will come roaring back and when it does, this fund will look great. In the meantime, however, it's hard times. The fund lost 33.9% in the year to June 30/01. That's bad, but the average Japan fund actually did a bit worse. Over three and five years, this fund is number one in the Japanese Equity category, so manager Jay Talbot is doing well with the tough mandate he's been given. That said, Japanese funds are volatile and only investors who can handle the risk should consider them. A U.S.$ denominated version of this fund is also available, as well as an RRSP-eligible clone.

## Sector Funds

### FIDELITY FOCUS CONSUMER INDUSTRIES FUND     $$ → G #/* £ SPE

Manager: John Porter III, since September 1999

MER: 2.67%     Fundata: B     Style: GARP

Suitability: Active investors who do a lot of switching

This fund got off to a roaring start, with a gain of more than 35% in its first calendar year. Since then, it hasn't done much of anything. Still, its 1.5% gain in the 12 months to June 30/01 looks pretty good when compared with the horrendous losses incurred by other sector funds, especially in the high-tech category. Frankly, we aren't big fans of sector funds of any type. We feel they should be treated more like stocks, bought and sold at appropriate times. Because of the boom and bust cycles they experience, sector funds are not good buy-and-hold candidates. However, if you must have a sector fund, this would appear to be more stable in nature than most. The portfolio contains such blue-ribbon names as Wal Mart, Procter & Gamble, Coke, and Gillette. It also holds Disney, Kimberly Clark, Phillip Morris, and Avon—nothing wrong with any of these other than their being temporarily out of fashion. The fund can invest anywhere, but clearly the focus is in the U.S. The fund's only serious competitor in the specialty consumer funds sector comes from the C.I. stable. The C.I. fund made a much heavier bet on the technology side and exploded during the late 1990s. As a result, it has a better-looking three-year record. Fidelity's bottom-up investment approach, however, is tried and true. They crunch the numbers and they interview management in their target firms. That doesn't mean they can't be offside occasionally, but this is a pretty basic fund. We're not excited but if this one turns your crank, go ahead and invest.

### FIDELITY FOCUS FINANCIAL SERVICES FUND     $$ → G #* £ SPE

Manager: James Catudal, since February 2000

MER: 2.67%     Fundata: C     Style: GARP

Suitability: Active investors

The term "financial services" does not just refer to banks. Also included under the definition's umbrella are brokerage firms; investment management firms; life, property, and casualty insurers; loan companies; investment bankers; and S&Ls. While this fund can invest globally, the focus is definitely in the U.S. Fidelity uses a well-established bottom-up approach to find companies with unique product or marketplace position that are believed to represent good sources for consistent returns and growth. The falling interest rate environment in 2000–01 helped this fund out a lot; it produced a return of just under 25% for the 12 months to June 30/01. Despite that good result, this fund finished down the track over three years compared to other funds operating in the same sector. It's an okay choice if you want to stick with Fidelity but if you're shopping around for this type of fund, look at the C.I. entry first.

## FIDELITY FOCUS HEALTH CARE FUND $$ → G #/* £ ST

Manager: Yolanda Strock, since June 2000

MER: 2.68%      Fundata: A      Style: GARP

Suitability: Active investors

Fidelity offers several sector funds that while fine, are not the leaders in their particular area of specialization. This is one of those funds. The one-year loss of 8.3% to June 30/01 looks absolutely sensational when compared to the average loss for the whole category, and that's what earns the fund an A rating from Fundata. But the category is Science & Technology, which was pummelled something awful during the period. When you compare this fund to others with a strict health care focus, it comes off as much less impressive. The fund invests primarily in the U.S., although it may invest anywhere in the world. Its recent top holdings strongly emphasized pharmaceuticals: Merck, Eli Lilly, Abbott Labs, Pfizer, and Bristol Myers Squibb. The fund's goal is to achieve long-term capital growth by investing in companies with products or services related to medicine and health care. It has produced respectable returns so far for investors, but there are other funds of this type that have done much better.

## FIDELITY FOCUS NATURAL RESOURCES FUND $$ ↑ G #/*£ NR

Manager: Scott Offen, since September 1999

MER: 2.67%      Fundata: C      Style: GARP

Suitability: Aggressive investors

The natural resource sector has been a good place to be in the past couple of years. Most of the funds in this category have been chalking up double-digit gains, and this one is no exception. Manager Scott Offen invests worldwide and the fund was top-heavy in oil and gas stocks in the first part of 2001. Lots of energy big berthas here: Chevron, Exxon Mobil, Texaco, and Royal Dutch (Shell) are all in the top 10 holdings. Alcan also squeezes in as the only big metals and mining entry. The fund's aim is long-term capital growth by investing in companies that own or develop natural resources anywhere in the world using Fidelity's traditional bottom-up investment approach. This mandate could include anything from agriculture, paper and forest products, and precious metals, to oil and natural gas. This is a decent fund of its type, but there are better ones in the resource sector. Also, be very aware of the volatility traditionally associated with this type of fund. Don't hang around if resources go into a nosedive.

## Global Balanced and Asset Allocation Funds

### FIDELITY GLOBAL ASSET ALLOCATION FUND     $$ → G/FI #/* £ GBAL

Manager: Dick Habermann, since inception (January 1993)

MER: 2.50%     Fundata: C     Style: GARP

Suitability: Investors seeking a core global balanced fund

Dick Habermann is the lead manager on this fund; John Chow provides advice on U.S. equities and Charles Morrison does the same with fixed-income securities. Chow is a newcomer to this mix as of last year, but Habermann has been overseeing this show since the fund was launched back in 1993. This scenario makes it tempting to suggest that Chow may be responsible for this fund's sudden fall from grace—it had recorded double-digit profits every year from 1995–99, but lost 7% in 2000 and was down almost 8% in the first half of 2001. Pointing the finger at Chow would be unfair, however, considering that both the U.S. and most international markets were in the red during this period. Also, the heavy equity rating (73% in the first half of 2001) didn't help returns. We'll have to wait for a rebound to get a better fix on how he'll perform on the U.S. equities side over the long haul. In the meantime, however, we are downgrading our rating to $$ because of the below-average performance over the past 18 months. This is still a fund worth considering when you look at the Fidelity line-up, but it is in a bit of a slump at present. A fully RRSP-eligible clone of this fund is also available.

## Canadian Bond Funds

### FIDELITY CANADIAN BOND FUND     $$ → FI #/* RSP CB

Manager: Jeff Moore, since October 2000

MER: 1.54%     Fundata: D     Style: Credit Analysis/Yield Curve Strategies

Suitability: Investors looking for a core bond fund

We've seen a change at the helm here, with Canadian Jeff Moore taking control from Ford O'Neil in October 2000. Moore's a graduate of the University of Waterloo and the University of Western Ontario, so he brings a home-grown touch to this portfolio. The fund offers a mix of federal, provincial, municipal, corporate, and agency bonds and is slightly higher in risk than its benchmark index (RBC Dominion Canadian Bond Market Index). During the first half of 2001, the fund's duration (a measure of risk) was 5.42 years, about twice that of the companion Canadian Short-Term Bond Fund, which Moore also manages. That fund has actually outperformed this one over the past three years and would be the preferred choice for risk-averse investors. Still, a duration of 5.42 years is not high for a bond fund so there is not a lot of interest rate risk here. The three-year average annual return to June 30/01 was a slightly above average

3.6%. The one-year return was also above average. Not the top Canadian bond fund around, but respectable.

## Money Market Funds

### FIDELITY CANADIAN MONEY MARKET FUND       $$ → C #/* RSP CMM

Manager: Robert Duby, since inception (January 1991)

MER: 1.02%     Fundata: B

The name of this fund was changed from the Canadian Short-Term Asset Fund in September 1999, but it's essentially the same fund. The MER is down a bit from last year, which has helped to improve returns to slightly above average. If you decide to buy, try to avoid paying any load. The fund invests mainly in high-quality commercial paper. Not the best money fund around, but okay.

## Promising Newcomers

## Canadian Equity Funds

### FIDELITY DISCIPLINED EQUITY FUND       NR ↓ G #/* RSP CE

Manager: Robert Haber, since inception (September 1998)

MER: 2.51%     Fundata: C       Style: GARP

Suitability: Conservative long-term investors

An equity fund manager has to deal with many variables. It's not simply a matter of picking good stocks. They have to be the right stocks, in the right sectors, at the right time, at the right price—that's not an easy task to pull off consistently. One of the ways to improve the odds is to reduce the number of variables. Index funds are the prime example of this: with these funds, all variables are taken out of the equation except the movement of the underlying index (in foreign index funds, exchange rates create an additional variable). This particular fund removes the variable of sector weighting. This means that veteran manager Robert Haber does not need to concern himself about which sectors of the TSE 300 Composite Index are likely to outperform and which are likely to be laggards. He doesn't need to place a bet on energy versus media or on financial services instead of forest products. The fund's portfolio is structured so as to reflect the actual sector weightings of the Index, so all Haber has to concern himself with is stock selection. This enables him to concentrate on choosing the companies within each sector that are deemed to have the best growth potential. So the success or failure of this fund will come down to the stock-picking acumen of Haber and the large Fidelity research team that backs him up. So far, the results have been very good. The fund gained almost 50% in 1999, its first full calendar year, and managed a decent 15.8% gain in the tough markets of 2000. It slumped somewhat in the first half of 2001, but so did the overall market. Recent top 10 holdings included several banks, Canadian Pacific, Alcan, Bombardier, and Manulife. We like the concept and expect this fund to do well in the future.

## U.S. Equity Funds

### FIDELITY AMERICAN OPPORTUNITIES FUND                    NR ↓ #/* £ USE

Manager: John Muresianu, since inception (July 2000)

MER: 2.00%     Fundata: N/A     Style: GARP

Suitability: Conservative investors

This Fidelity entry has been around for only about a year but we like the feel of it. It's certainly performed better so far in its young life than its older sibling, Fidelity Growth America, which we are not recommending at this time. Manager John Muresianu uses the S&P 500 Index as his benchmark. So far, he's slightly below the S&P performance, but his conservative style of stock selection holds promise. In the first half of 2001, for example, he avoided the New Economy stocks that he felt were still overpriced and concentrated instead on old-line stocks in the energy and materials sectors. We don't suggest rushing out and loading up on this one just yet, but keep your eye on it. It may emerge as Fidelity's top core U.S. offering.

# FRANKLIN TEMPLETON INVESTMENTS

## THE COMPANY

The Templeton funds have been well known to Canadian investors since the 1950s. The company has officially adopted the name of its parent firm—the Franklin Templeton Group of San Mateo, California—which is one of the world's largest investment companies. In terms of assets under management, Franklin Templeton ranks tenth in Canada, in part due to a key acquisition it made in 2000 when it purchased the Calgary-based Bissett fund group.

The company's ability to attract capital has a lot to do with some strong performers in its fund group. The rigorous investment philosophy of the Templeton fund line was put in place by the company's founding owner, Sir John Templeton, and remains the guiding force for the investment team. However, there have been some significant changes among its Templeton funds in the past three years with a number of acquisitions, new launches, and managerial shifts.

The most significant move was the Bissett acquisition. It brought an entirely new dimension to the organization, giving it domestic strength and a depth it never had previously. In fact, we regard the Bissett family among the strongest mutual fund line-ups in Canada.

But the change didn't stop there. Just a little over four years since the Canadian launch of the very successful Franklin U.S. Small-Cap Growth Fund, Templeton bolstered that family with the addition of a number of Franklin funds. These funds take a more aggressive investing approach, providing investors with a growth-oriented option. The timing for the launches wasn't great—growth funds did not do well in 2000–01—but over the long term these funds will bring an important new dimension to the organization.

As a result of the overhaul, the company now offers four distinct fund groups to investors: the Templeton line of traditional value funds, the more aggressive Franklin funds, the deep value Mutual Beacon Fund, and the GARP-style Bissett funds.

Franklin Templeton's most significant managerial change in the past year was the appointment of George Morgan to head the venerable Templeton Growth Fund; he took over at the beginning of 2001. It was an important moment for investors, considering it's the third managerial switch in two years for the once proud fund that has been having its troubles lately. But it was also a nationalistic milestone: Morgan is a Canadian, the first ever named to run the fund, which was launched in this country back in the 1950s and marked the birth of what became the worldwide Templeton empire. Morgan is an MBA graduate of the University of Western Ontario. He runs the fund from Templeton's Nassau office.

## THE DETAILS

Number of funds: 36

Assets under management: $20.1 billion

Load charge: Front: max. 6%; Back: max. 6%

Switching charge: 2% maximum

Where sold: Across Canada

How sold: Through brokers, dealers, financial planners, TD Bank, Sunetco, CT Securities, and London Life

Phone number: (416) 364-4672, 1-800-387-0830 (English), 1-800-897-7281 (French), or 1-800-661-3339 (Chinese)

Web site address: www.templeton.ca

E-mail address: tor-webmaster@templeton.ca

Minimum initial investment: $500 (generally)

## INVESTING TIPS

If you owned units in any of the Bissett funds prior to the takeover, you should retain them. They are known as F units and carry a lower management expense ratio (MER) than the new A units, which are sold on an optional front- or back-end load basis (as are the other funds in the Franklin Templeton group). As a result, the return on the F units should be slightly higher.

Note that the historic rates of return for the Bissett funds are based on the no-load, low MER units sold by the company prior to the takeover. Most investors buying in now will have to purchase the new A units, which have a higher MER (in some cases, substantially higher). Returns from these funds will be reduced, so take that fact into account if you are considering a purchase. We show the MERs for the A units in the reviews, since they will be the ones that apply to most new sales.

Among the Bissett funds, the Retirement Fund is a good choice for balanced investors. However, we do not formally review or rate it, as it is a "fund of funds," investing entirely in other Bissett funds.

In June 2001, the company announced the creation of a new series of tax-efficient funds designed for Canadians investing outside a registered plan. They're called Tax Class Funds and they allow investors to switch between different Franklin Templeton Investment funds without triggering a tax event like a capital gain. The concept is similar to the umbrella fund approach already used by several other companies, such as AGF, C.I., and Mackenzie. The Tax Class Funds are actually individual pools within an overall corporate structure. An investor can move money among the various pools without tax consequences, unlike a switch between two stand-alone funds, which is considered a sale and purchase by the Canada Customs and Revenue Agency (CCRA). There are 19 core funds available in Tax Class options.

Investors holding units in the Templeton International Balanced Fund should note that it was scheduled to be merged into the Templeton Global Balanced Fund in fall 2001. Likewise, the Templeton Canadian Bond Fund was to be merged into the Bissett Bond Fund.

## FUND SUMMARY
### Templeton Funds

| | |
|---|---|
| Top Choices: | Balanced, Canadian Asset Allocation, Growth |
| Also Recommended: | Canadian Stock, Global Smaller Companies, International |
| Promising Newcomers: | None |
| The Rest: | Canadian Bond, Emerging Markets, European Tax Class, Global Balanced, Global Bond, International Balanced, Treasury Bill |

### Franklin Funds

| | |
|---|---|
| Top Choices: | None |
| Also Recommended: | None |
| Promising Newcomers: | None |
| The Rest: | Japan Tax Class, Technology, U.S. Aggressive Growth, U.S. Large-Cap Growth, U.S. Money Market, U.S. Small-Cap Growth, World Health Sciences & Biotech, World Growth, World Telecom |

### Mutual Beacon Funds

| | |
|---|---|
| Top Choices: | Mutual Beacon |
| Also Recommended: | None |
| Promising Newcomers: | None |
| The Rest: | None |

### Bissett Funds

| | |
|---|---|
| Top Choices: | Bond, Canadian Equity, Income, Microcap, Money Market, Multinational Growth, Small-Cap |
| Also Recommended: | Dividend Income |
| Promising Newcomers: | None |
| The Rest: | American Equity, International Equity, Large-Cap |

# FUND RATINGS

## Top Choices/Templeton Funds

### Global and International Equity Funds

### TEMPLETON GROWTH FUND                    $$$ → G #/* £ GE

Managers: George Morgan, since January 2001

MER: 2.04%      Fundata: A      Style: Value

Suitability: Patient, long-term investors

Launched back in 1954, this entry has become the largest mutual fund in Canada, with assets of more than $10 billion (including all spinoff funds) in mid-2001. Investors have been attracted by Templeton's reputation and the fund's excellent history. For years this fund was a first- or second-quartile performer, and those results came to be taken for granted. There was tremendous pressure on the manager to consistently outperform, and the failure of the fund to live up to those high expectations in the late 1990s created a lot of distress among faithful followers. The fund holds more than 200 stocks, which may seem like a lot, but given its asset base, it is not unreasonable. Areas of investment are indicative of Templeton's global reach and include Canada, the U.S., Asia, Europe, Mexico, South/Central America, and Africa. The main problems recently have been the fact that value stocks were out of favour, plus a premature decision to reduce U.S. stock holdings. However, the fund held its own when markets went into a dive. In the year to June 30/01, the fund gained 1.5% versus a 15% average loss for the peer group. The three-year average annual return was only 4.1%, but that was slightly above the average for its category. Looking back a decade, however, we find the fund produced an average annual gain of 13.5%, which is quite respectable. This fund is best suited to patient, long-term investors who want to know their money is in the hands of a large, conservative organization and don't expect to see shoot-out-the-lights results. If that's what you're looking for, don't hesitate. But if you want a big score right away, try another company. We are maintaining the rating at $$$ on what is probably the most famous mutual fund in the world. Note that George Morgan has taken over the day-to-day management of this fund, the first Canadian ever to hold that position. He's the fund's third manager in the past two years, a clear indication that the organization has not been satisfied with the recent performance. There's an RRSP-eligible clone of this fund if you'd prefer.

## Canadian Balanced and Asset Allocation Funds

### TEMPLETON BALANCED FUND $$ → FI/G #/* RSP CBAL

Managers: Jeffrey Sutcliffe, since 1998 and Peter Moeschter, since 1999

MER: 2.13%    Fundata: A    Style: Value

Suitability: Aggressive balanced investors

This is another Templeton fund that experienced deteriorating performance in recent years, but it seems to be on the upswing again. It has also gone through a managerial change. The team of Neil Devlin and George Morgan has been replaced by Jeffrey Sutcliffe in fixed income and Peter Moeschter in equities. With 64% of the portfolio in common stocks, including a significant foreign holding at mid-2001, this fund should provide some good capital appreciation potential. The fund gained 7.5% in the year to June 30/01, well above average for the Canadian Balanced category. That result helped to pull the annual gain over the past five years to 10.4%, well above average for the category. Foreign content is maximized and includes holdings from all around the world. On the fixed-income side, default risk is low, with the majority of the assets in government bonds, while interest rate risk is average.

### TEMPLETON CANADIAN ASSET $$$ ↓ G/FI #/* RSP CBAL
### ALLOCATION FUND

Manager: Jeffrey Sutcliffe, since 1998

MER: 2.30%    Fundata: B    Style: Value

Suitability: Balanced investors

You'd expect this fund to be somewhat more aggressive than the companion Templeton Balanced Fund, and it is. The managers employ an asset allocation approach to investing, with a target of 65% equities and 35% fixed-income. However, at mid-2001, there wasn't much difference between the two funds. This one's asset mix was 64% in common stocks, which was virtually identical to the Balanced Fund. The fixed-income portion here is also weighted heavily in government bonds, with marginally higher-than-average interest rate risk. One-year gain to June 30/01 was a very good 8.9%. Three-year average annual compound rate of return was 5.8%, almost identical to the Balanced Fund and much better than the 2.4% average for the category. Surprisingly, the safety profile of this fund is somewhat better than that of the Balanced Fund. So the choice of which fund to go with depends on your needs. For higher returns, the Balanced Fund has the better long-term record (although this one has beaten it recently). If you want a lower level of risk, history tells us this one works better.

## Also Recommended/Templeton Funds

### Canadian Equity Funds

### TEMPLETON CANADIAN STOCK FUND $$ → G #/* RSP CE

Manager: Peter Moeschter, since 2001

MER: 2.61%       Fundata: B       Style: Value

Suitability: Diversified Canadian equity investors

There's been a recent change at the top here, with new manager Peter Moeschter replacing George Morgan, who took on Templeton Growth. Besides holding established large companies such as Bank of Montreal, National Bank, and Alcan, the fund will also buy smaller issues. The portfolio is well diversified across all sectors. Moreover, the fund's foreign component does not have the typical U.S. exposure, but rather includes holdings from a diversified mix of regions such as Asia, Europe, South/Central America, Mexico, and the Middle East. This strategy aims to leverage Templeton's global investing expertise. Returns have been generally inconsistent, but recent performance has been encouraging. In the 12 months to June 30/01, the fund gained 12% compared with a 5.8% average loss for the other funds in the category. Its three-year average annual return of 5.7% was also above average. The direction here is right, and this fund is in line for an upgrade if we see another good year under the new manager.

### Global and International Equity Funds

### TEMPLETON INTERNATIONAL STOCK FUND $$ → G #/* £ IE

Manager: Donald Reed, since 1989

MER: 2.64%       Fundata: A       Style: Value

Suitability: Middle-of-the-road investors seeking to diversify outside North America

The difference between this and the companion Growth Fund is that this fund is restricted from holding North American stocks. At first glance, being shut out of the strong U.S. market would appear to be a detriment. However, this fund actually outperformed the Growth Fund for much of the past decade, although not in the past year. As of mid-2001, the fund remained significantly overweighted in Europe. The fund lost 10.1% in the year ending June 30/01, which, while disappointing, was better than the 20.1% loss for the category. Longer-term numbers continue to be well above the average for the peer group. Overall, this fund is a decent choice for investors looking to diversify outside the North American market. However, it is worthy only of a $$ rating at this stage. There's an RRSP-eligible clone of this fund if you'd prefer.

## TEMPLETON SMALLER COMPANIES FUND $$ → G #/* £ GE

Manager: Brad Radin, since 1999

MER: 2.76%     Fundata: A        Style: Value

Suitability: Aggressive investors

This fund invests in small companies from both developed and emerging markets worldwide. Companies generally have a market cap of under U.S.$1 billion and may include those with strong earnings growth or in a turnaround situation. At mid-2001, this diversified fund of over 150 names had holdings from Asia, Europe, Mexico, South/Central America, Africa, the U.S., and the Middle East. Brad Radin, who joined the company in 1995 and is a vice-president in the Global Equity Management Group, took over the fund in 1999 and results are encouraging. For the year to June 30/01, returns were 6.9% compared with a 15% loss for the category. We are upgrading to a $$ rating.

### Promising Newcomers/Templeton Funds

None.

### Top Choices/Franklin Funds

None.

### Also Recommended/Franklin Funds

None.

### Promising Newcomers/Franklin Funds

None.

### Top Choices/Mutual Beacon Funds

### U.S. Equity Funds

## MUTUAL BEACON FUND $$$ → G #/* £ USE

Manager: Lawrence Sondike (Franklin Capital Advisors), since 1998

MER: 2.67%     Fundata: A        Style: Value

Suitability: Conservative investors

This is the only fund in the "Mutual" series offered by the Franklin Templeton organization in Canada. The name Templeton says "value investing," but this offering goes beyond that mandate. Manager Lawrence Sondike is known as a "deep value" investor, which means his criteria for stock selection are even more demanding than those normally associated with the Templeton funds. He is a disciple of legendary value manager Michael Price and seeks his stocks from among out-of-favour companies, particularly those in financial distress. Prudence dictates that all selections and the fund itself focus on capital preservation in good times and bad. Long-term growth is the aim, with income a secondary goal. The value approach was out of favour in the period that followed the launch of this fund in 1997, so it did not fare well immediately. But it has looked much better recently, with a one-year return to June 30/01 of 24.1% compared with an average loss for its peer group of more than 14%. That's a huge outperformance! This fund is unlikely to soar to the heights of some of the go-go growth funds in hot markets, but it's a good safe haven in troubled times. A companion fund, the Mutual Beacon RSP Fund, is available for RRSP/RRIF investing.

## Also Recommended/Mutual Beacon Funds

None.

## Promising Newcomers/Mutual Beacon Funds

None.

## Top Choices/Bissett Funds

### Canadian Equity Funds

### BISSETT CANADIAN EQUITY FUND                    $$$$ ↓ G NO RSP CE

Manager: Fred Pynn, since 1994

MER: 2.34%       Fundata: A        Style: GARP

Suitability: Conservative investors

This fund went into a slump in 1999, falling all the way to a fourth-quartile performance (bottom 25% of its class), its worst showing ever. But everything is relative. The net result was a one-year gain of 19.5% to June 30/00. Most people would be more than happy with that kind of return, but with the Canadian stock markets churning out great numbers, it was a sub-par result. In the year ending June 30/01, the fund gained 5.0%, which was a lot lower in absolute terms. But in relative terms, it was a top performer considering the category average was a 5.8% loss. The five-year annual return of 15.4% per annum is way above the peer group average. Longer-term results are also comfortably above average and the risk level of this fund is relatively low. The manager uses a bottom-up approach to stock selection, with emphasis on a company's fundamentals. He wants growth, but at reasonable stock valuations. Expenses are very low—way below average for the Canadian Equity category, in fact. This is a first-rate entry, and we will retain its $$$$ rating.

## Canadian Small-to-Mid-Cap Equity Funds

### BISSETT MICROCAP FUND                    $$$ → G NO RSP CSC

Manager: Garey Aitken, since 2000

MER: 3.54%      Fundata: B        Style: Bottom-up Growth

Suitability: Aggressive investors

This fund concentrates on companies with a market capitalization of under $75 million at the time of purchase. It has a very strong record thus far. The three-year return to June 30/01 was 18.4% compared with 2.7% for the peer group. The latest one-year return of 2.8% compares favourably with the 6.1% loss suffered by the peer group. With a slightly below-average risk rating for its category, this fund is well worthy of a $$$ debut rating. The difference between this and the companion Small-Cap Fund is that the companies held in this portfolio will typically be smaller and may be start-ups. The risk here is therefore potentially higher, although this fund has actually done better in that regard than Small-Cap in the past few years.

### BISSETT SMALL-CAP FUND                   $$$ → G NO RSP CSC

Manager: Garey Aitken, since 2000

MER: 3.11%      Fundata: A        Style: Bottom-up Growth

Suitability: Aggressive investors

There has been a change at the top here and it's paying off. Gene Vollendorf, who had been associated with the fund since 1996, left in the spring of 2000 to, as the corporate jargon goes, "pursue other opportunities." The fund had not been performing well under his direction; average annual compound rate of return for the three years to June 30/00 was –3.2%. However, new manager Garey Aitken has the fund back on the right foot. One of his first moves was to increase the fund's exposure to the energy sector, and he added more exposure to financial services as well. In the year ending June 30/01 the fund recorded a 16.6% return compared with a 6.1% loss for the category. A solid turnaround, indeed.

## Global and International Equity Funds

### BISSETT MULTINATIONAL GROWTH FUND $$$ → G NO £ GE

Manager: Jeffrey Morrison, since 1999

MER: 2.48%    Fundata: A    Style: Bottom-up Growth

Suitability: Conservative investors

The mandate of this fund is somewhat unusual. The manager seeks out European and North American companies that operate on a multinational level and offer a growing dividend stream. These aren't your traditional blue-chip stocks in most cases, but the next level down, or major firms on the rise. Return for the year to June 30/01 was 3.2%, which is hardly inspiring until you realize that the average fund in the peer group had a 15% loss! Five-year performance was well above average, at 15.5% annually. The risk level is below average for the category as well. Decent returns and below-average risk justify the $$$ rating.

## Canadian Balanced and Asset Allocation Funds

### BISSETT INCOME FUND $$$ ↑ FI NO RSP CHIB

Manager: Leslie Lundquist, since 1998

MER: 2.44%    Fundata: C    Style: Bottom-up Income

Suitability: Aggressive income investors

This fund generates a high level of income, paid quarterly, from a variety of real estate investment trusts (REITs), royalty income trusts (RITs), and similar types of securities. Payout in the 12 months to June 30/01 was $1.15 a unit, so cash flow is very good. Moreover, over half the distribution was received on a tax-deferred basis if the fund was held outside a registered plan. But you need to understand where those payments are coming from and the volatility involved here. The trust units held in this fund are subject to big swings in market value. As a result, while the cash distributions may be large, total return may be negligible. In fact, over the three years to June 30/00, this fund produced an annual loss of 0.2%—not a lot, but still a loss. However, the royalty trust market snapped back in the first half of 2000 and results have been much better since. In the year ending June 30/01, the fund returned 29.8%. This fund is worth considering in two situations: first, for investors looking for tax-advantaged income in a non-registered portfolio; second, for an RRIF if strong cash flow is required, although the risk is on the high side for that purpose. However, a small loss in NAV over time is not necessarily a bad thing in an RRIF. Remember that the minimum annual withdrawal is based on the market value of the RRIF each January 1. If you own stocks or funds that shoot up in value, you'll have to take out more money and, of course, pay the taxes accordingly.

## Canadian Bond Funds

### BISSETT BOND FUND $$$ → FI NO RSP CB

Manager: Michael Quinn, since inception (1986)

MER: 1.40%     Fundata: D     Style: Laddered Spread

Suitability: Aggressive income investors

This fund has been a first- or second-quartile performer since 1994, except for a lapse in 1999 that saw it slip to the third quartile. Nonetheless, it remains a very sound entry and the low management fee helps to bolster investor profits. The portfolio is a mix of federal, provincial, and corporate issues, and it was the latter position that was a drag on returns in early 2000. One-year gain to June 30/01 was 6.3% and that was well above average for the peer group. From a risk perspective, this fund shows worse-than-average month-to-month volatility, with about a one-third chance of being down in any given month. But over a year, the unit value changes tend to even out, and overall risk is moderate. The Templeton Canadian Bond Fund was scheduled to be merged into this fund in the fall of 2001.

## Canadian Money Market Funds

### BISSETT MONEY MARKET FUND $$$$ ↓ C NO RSP CMM

Manager: Michael Quinn, since 1993

MER: 1.09%     Fundata: D     Style: Income

Suitability: Conservative investors

For a fund it doesn't get much better than this: First- or second-quartile performance in its category over all time periods, plus low management fees that contribute significantly to the good result. The fund's main holding is federal T-bills, but the fund also holds short-term corporate notes. A good, safe place for parking money temporarily.

## Also Recommended/Bissett Funds

## Dividend Income Funds

### BISSETT DIVIDEND INCOME FUND $$ → G/FI NO RSP DIV

Manager: Juliette John, since 1998

MER: 2.64%     Fundata: B     Style: Balanced

Suitability: Conservative income investors

From 1994 to 1998, this fund was consistently an above-average performer in its category. But then it went into a two-year slump, performing well below the average for its peer group. However, it is now back on the right track. In the year to June 30/01 the fund realized a total profit of 17.9%, compared with an average for the category of 11.7%. The portfolio is a mix of Canadian, U.S., and international common stocks, preferred shares and bonds, with a bit of cash. The distributions from this fund are generally quite good, so it is a fine choice for investors who require regular income.

## Promising Newcomers/Bissett Funds

None.

# GBC ASSET MANAGEMENT

## THE COMPANY

GBC Asset Management is the marketing and distribution division of Pembroke Management Ltd., which was set up in 1968. Not that there is much marketing to be done. This is one of those rare companies that really, truly, doesn't want a lot of new business. They have a good thing going for them, they do well by their clients, and they don't want a flood of new money that would be difficult to place.

The company's focus is on high net worth individuals and special institutional situations, which explains why the company requires a minimum of $100,000 to open an account with them. The firm has special expertise in North American small-to-mid-cap equities, and the three funds they manage inhouse are overseen by a team, and genuinely so, as no one person is given the ultimate decision power. Mutual funds requiring detailed knowledge of other markets (e.g., international equities, bonds) are run by outside firms.

This is a company for which we have a great deal of respect, as was shown when we named their Canadian Growth Fund the Small Cap Fund of the 1990s.

## THE DETAILS

|  |  |
|---|---|
| Number of funds: | 5 |
| Assets under management: | $607 million |
| Load charge: | None if purchased directly through GBC, otherwise front: max. 3% |
| Switching charge: | None |
| Where sold: | All provinces |
| How sold: | Through GBC in Ontario and Quebec; through brokers and dealers elsewhere. |
| Phone number: | 1-800-668-7383 (Toronto) or 1-800-667-0716 (Montreal) |
| Web site address: | www.gbc.ca |
| E-mail address: | info@gbc.ca |
| Minimum initial investment: | $100,000 |

## INVESTING TIPS

If you'd like to put some money with GBC, you can pool your family resources to meet their $100,000 minimum. You may not have that much in a single account, but by adding in your spouse's investments and RRSPs, you may be able to qualify.

# FUND SUMMARY

|  |  |
|---|---|
| Top Choices: | Canadian Growth |
| Also Recommended: | Canadian Bond, North American Growth |
| Promising Newcomers: | None |
| The Rest: | International Growth, Money Market |

# FUND RATINGS

## Top Choices

### Canadian Equity Funds

### GBC CANADIAN GROWTH FUND $$$$ ↓ G #/NO RSP CSC

Manager: Pembroke Management Ltd., since inception (1988)

MER: 1.95%     Fundata: D     Style: Growth

Suitability: Long-term growth investors

The mandate of this fund is to invest primarily "in common shares of small and medium-sized Canadian corporations" and shares of companies "the fund initially invested in when they were small- and medium-sized and has continued to hold as the corporations maintain above-average growth." That helps explain why you'll find names like MDS Inc. and Fairfax Financial in the portfolio, companies that have grown quite large in recent years. However, the main focus is still on smaller firms and the managers generally do very well in their selection process. This fund usually turns in above-average returns, although it slipped to below average for the category in 2000 and the first half of 2001. The fund gained just 2% in 2000 and the advance in the first half of 2001, when many small-cap funds were strong, was a disappointing 2.5%. But over the long term, this fund's performance is excellent and given the proven record of the management team, we expect to see a return to form before long. As a bonus, the safety record is very good for a fund of this type—small-cap funds are traditionally quite volatile. Bottom line: When it comes to Canadian small-cap funds, they don't come much better than this one. If you have the price of admission, take a look.

# Also Recommended

## U.S. Small-to-Mid-Cap Funds

### GBC NORTH AMERICAN GROWTH FUND $$$ → G #/NO £ USSC

Manager: Pembroke Management Ltd., since inception (1988)

MER: 1.88%     Fundata: C     Style: Growth

Suitability: Long-term growth investors

This fund emphasizes smaller North American companies and uses the Russell 2000 Index as its benchmark. Although the majority of the holdings are in U.S. equities, this fund also holds some Canadian stocks, like Fairfax Financial. The focus is on high-growth companies in which management has a large ownership position. This fund has been a good performer for a long time. However, it has to be compared to the correct peer group to highlight that fact. The recent creation of a new U.S. Small-to-Mid-Cap fund category made that possible. Within the category, this fund is among the better long-term performers even though it has stumbled recently, dropping 4.6% in the first six months of 2001. The risk profile of this fund is about average for the category. This is a respectable choice for anyone looking for exposure to the U.S. small-to-mid-cap market, if you have the price of admission.

## Canadian Bond Funds

### GBC CANADIAN BOND FUND $$$ → FI #/NO RSP CB

Managers: TD Quantitative Capital, since 2000

MER: 1.20%     Fundata: D     Style: Optimization

Suitability: Conservative investors

This has been a first-rate bond fund for years. However, it slipped to third-quartile position in the first half of 2001. Greydanus Boeckh and Associates, who had run this fund since its launch in 1984, was acquired in 1999 by TD Quantitative Capital, a division of TD Asset Management, and that company now shows as the manager of record. The bulk of the portfolio is in federal and provincial government bonds, with about a quarter of the assets invested in corporate issues to provide higher returns. This is a change from the previous policy, where the managers had avoided corporate issues because of the additional risk they carry. This is normally an above-average performer, in part due to a relatively low management expense ratio (MER). The safety profile of this fund is quite good as well.

## Promising Newcomers

None.

# GUARDIAN GROUP OF FUNDS (GGOF)

## THE COMPANY

Merger mania caught up with the Guardian organization in May 2001 when it was announced that ownership of the firm had been purchased by Bank of Montreal. For investors, however, it's simply business as usual. BMO is maintaining Guardian as a stand-alone unit, just as it has with Jones Heward, which it also owns. There has not been any merger of the BMO and Guardian fund lines and none is anticipated.

This is just the latest of many changes at GGOF. The previous year, the company announced it was creating three distinct fund groups to provide clients with style diversification. The fund groups are as follows:

- *GGOF Alexandria Growth Funds*. These are equity funds that use a growth-style approach to portfolio selection. The domestic funds are run by Greystone Capital Management of Regina, while the international funds are managed by Dresdner RCM Global Investors.
- *GGOF Centurion Value Funds*. The Centurion Funds employ a value style. The domestic funds are managed in-house by Kevin Klassen, who moved over to Guardian from the BPI organization after it was absorbed by C.I. The international funds are in the hands of Lazard Asset Management and Matthews International Capital Management of San Francisco, a firm that specializes in Asian investing.
- *GGOF Guardian Funds*. This group includes most of the traditional Guardian funds and employs the company's traditional growth-at-a-reasonable price (GARP) style.

## THE DETAILS

|  |  |
|---|---|
| Number of funds: | 32 |
| Assets under management: | $2 billion |
| Load charge: | Front: max. 9%; Back: max. 6% |
| Switching charge: | 2% maximum |
| Where sold: | Across Canada |
| How sold: | Through registered brokers, dealers, and financial planners |
| Phone number: | 1-800-668-7327 or (416) 947-4099 |
| Web site address: | www.guardianfunds.com |
| E-mail address: | clientservices@guardianfunds.com |
| Minimum initial investment: | $500 |

## INVESTING TIPS

GGOF funds are sold in two types of units. Classic units are offered on a front-end load basis only. They have a lower management expense ratio, or MER (about 0.6% less on average), making them the better choice for long-term investors in most cases. Some brokers and planners now offer front-end load funds at zero commission to good clients; this would be your best option if you can get it. The other type of units, Mutual Fund units, can be purchased on either a front- or back-end load basis. Minimum initial investment for either unit type is $500.

Although in most cases the Classic units are the better choice, you have to give some careful thought regarding which to choose if you are buying one of the GGOF income funds, such as Guardian Monthly High Income. The management expense ratio for this fund is 2.5% on the Mutual Fund units, but only 1.85% on the Classic units. Since the payout is the same for both types, the difference in the MER shows up in the net asset value (NAV), which will be lower for the Mutual Fund units. Essentially, this means the yield on the Mutual Fund units will be higher. For example, in the spring of 2001, the NAV of these units was $8.79. With an annual distribution of 72¢, that produced a cash yield of 8.2%. At the same time, the current yield on the Classic units, priced at $9.02, came in at just under 8%. On the other hand, the Classic units offered slightly higher capital gains potential because the 0.65% difference in the MER eventually shows up in the NAV.

Which type of unit you choose will therefore depend on your priorities. The same amount of dollars will buy more Mutual Fund units because of their lower price. At the NAV we've quoted, a $10,000 investment gives you 1,137.656 Mutual Fund units generating a distribution of $819.11 over 12 months. The same amount invested in Classic units buys 1,108.647 units, with a one-year cash flow of $798.23. So if more immediate cash is your priority, buy Mutual Fund units. If you're more interested in longer-term gains, the Classic units are your choice.

Note that in the ratings, "C" stands for Classic units and "MF" for Mutual Fund units.


## FUND SUMMARY

|  |  |
|---|---|
| Top Choices: | Centurion American Value, Guardian Monthly Dividend, Guardian Monthly High Income |
| Also Recommended: | Alexandria Canadian Balanced, Guardian Canadian Equity, Guardian Canadian Money Market, Guardian Enterprise |
| Promising Newcomers: | Alexandria Canadian Growth, Centurion Global Value, Guardian Canadian High-Yield Bond |

# FUND RATINGS

## Top Choices

### Canadian Equity Funds

**GGOF GUARDIAN ENTERPRISE FUND**        **$$$ → G #/* RSP CSC**

Manager: Gary Chapman, since 1994

MER: 2.98%%    Fundata: B      Style: GARP

Suitability: Growth-oriented investors willing to accept higher risk

The mandate of this fund is to concentrate on small- and medium-sized companies with a strong entrepreneurial bent. Chapman's style is to look for companies with strong growth prospects and then hold them while they expand. As you might expect from a small-cap fund, this approach has resulted in a relatively high degree of volatility over the years. Right now, however, the fund is working very well for investors and was one of the better performers in its category in the year to June 30/01 with a gain of 7.6% (C units). The portfolio is broadly diversified, with 149 separate companies represented in the first half of 2001. Of these, 84 were foreign holdings although they accounted for only 8.5% of total assets. There is good sector diversification, with no one segment of the market dominating. Risk is better than average for a fund of this type, but is obviously greater than you would find in a large-cap fund. We expect small-cap stocks to perform well over the next year, so we are moving the rating up to $$$.

## Dividend and Income Funds

### GGOF GUARDIAN MONTHLY DIVIDEND FUND          $$$ → FI #/* RSP DIV

Manager: John Priestman, since 1988

MER: 1.94%     Fundata: B (C), C (MF)     Style: Income

Suitability: High-bracket income investors

After being closed for more than five years, this fund was reopened to investors on January 15/01. That's good news because this is one of the best dividend funds around in terms of cash flow (though not total return). It is also a true dividend fund, with the bulk of the portfolio in preferred shares. There are also some royalty trusts in the mix to boost yields. Monthly payout is still 3.5¢ a unit. Recent returns have been slightly above average for the Dividend Income category. However, keep in mind that capital gains potential is limited because of the large percentage of preferred shares in the portfolio. Because of the tax-advantaged cash flow, units are best held outside a registered plan.

### GGOF GUARDIAN MONTHLY HIGH          $$$ → FI #/* RSP CHIB
### INCOME FUND

Manager: John Priestman, since inception (1996)

MER: 2.13%     Fundata: N/A     Style: Income

Suitability: High-bracket income investors willing to accept greater risk

This fund invests in resource and real estate trusts, including familiar names like Pengrowth, Superior Propane, Athabasca Oil Sands, and Summit Real Estate. The primary goal here is above-average cash flow, with some tax advantages. In terms of total return, this wasn't an exciting place to be in the late 1990s when royalty trust prices were hard hit. But the resurgence of energy-based trusts in 2000–01 propelled this fund to a total return of 24.7% (C units) over the 12 months to June 30/01, one of the best in its category. That result pulled the three-year numbers to above the average as well. From the point of view of income generation, this fund has always been attractive. The units pay 6¢ a month (72¢ a year), so the cash flow is first-rate. At this time you can enjoy a combination of good income plus capital gains potential. This fund is worth considering for non-registered accounts where tax-advantaged income is desired because some of the income is not taxable in the year received. It could also be considered for an RRIF with its above-average cash flow. In that case the tax breaks will be lost, but the high yield may offset that downside for many people. There is above-average risk here as far as income funds go. However, as long as the distributions continue at the current level—and there is no reason to think they won't in the foreseeable future—this fund is worth a close look.

## U.S. Equity Funds

### GGOF CENTURION AMERICAN VALUE FUND    $$$ → G #/* £ USE

Manager: Andrew Lacey (Lazard Asset Management), since 2000

MER: 2.65%    Fundata: B    Style: Value

Suitability: Conservative long-term investors

The highly respected New York house of Lazard Asset Management took control of the portfolio in January 1998, and immediately set out to reposition it. The fund targets three types of stocks: takeover candidates, companies that are out of favour with investors for various reasons, and what Lazard calls "undercovered" opportunities—mid-cap stocks that have been inadequately covered by Wall Street analysts. The style here is bottom-up value and the portfolio is well diversified, with about 50 positions. Results are above average for the U.S. Equity category, even though the fund was in the red for the year to June 30/01 with a loss of 5.4% (C units). Three-year results, which cover the period since Lazard took over, show solid gains, however, with an average annual return of better than 10%. The portfolio is well balanced, with no one sector having a weighting of more than 16.3% in the first half of 2001. A decent choice. There's an RRSP-eligible clone available if you wish to make use of it. Formerly known as the Guardian American Equity Fund.

**Also Recommended**

## Canadian Equity Funds

### GGOF GUARDIAN CANADIAN EQUITY FUND    $$ → G #/* RSP CE

Manager: Mike Weir, since 2000

MER: 2.88%    Fundata: C    Style: GARP

Suitability: Long-term growth investors

There's a new face at the top here: Mike Weir (not the golfer!) has taken the reins from veteran John Priestman. But the style remains unchanged (growth at a reasonable price) and the fund continues to have an Old Economy feel to it. As of the first half of 2001, Nortel was the only high-tech holding among the fund's top 25 positions. Instead of high-tech holdings, investors in this primarily mid- to large-cap fund were given a bunch of banks, several energy-related companies, and classic industrial stocks like Bombardier. Weir has made one key change, however, by reducing the foreign content of this fund significantly, to just under 10% of assets, although the fund has 71 foreign stocks in its portfolio. If you are considering investing in this fund, make sure this type of portfolio mix is what you're looking for. The absence of tech stocks helped the fund in the past year, though it posted a loss of 6.2% in the 12 months to June 30/01. We are keeping the rating at $$ for now while we see how Weir fares in his new role, but this fund has been looking better lately. Previously known as the Guardian Growth Equity Fund and prior to that as the Guardian Vantage Fund.

## Canadian Balanced Funds

### GGOF ALEXANDRIA CANADIAN BALANCED FUND

$$ → FI/G #/* RSP CBAL

Manager: Rob Vanderhooft (Greystone Capital Management), since 1994

MER: 2.45%      Fundata: B      Style: Growth

Suitability: Long-term balanced investors with a growth bias

This balanced fund provides a combination of interest and dividend income from Canadian and global sources, plus some growth potential. The fund is managed by Rob Vanderhooft of Regina-based Greystone Capital. In the first half of 2001, the fund held about 60% of its assets in equities, about 36% in bonds, and the rest in cash. The top stock holdings include a bunch of banks and energy companies with some industrials like Bombardier sprinkled in for good measure. Foreign equities represented about 18% of the asset base. Volatility has been moderately low, and the fund has generally been a decent performer, although it has slipped a bit recently. The five-year average annual compound rate of return remains above average, however, at 9.1%. We're giving this fund a $$ rating for now, but there are signs it is strengthening again. The Guardian Growth and Income Fund was merged into this one in mid-2000.

## Canadian Money Market Funds

### GGOF GUARDIAN CANADIAN MONEY MARKET FUND

$$$ → C #/* RSP CMM

Manager: Stephen D. Kearns, since 1998

MER: 0.86% (C) Fundata: B

Suitability: Low-risk investors

This fund invests entirely in short-term, high-grade corporate notes. That approach should produce above-average returns for this category, and indeed that's been the case for the C units, which show above-average returns for all time periods. But that's because they have a much lower MER (0.86%) than the MF units (1.55%), which are optional front- or back-end load. The latter produce sub-par results because of their high management fee. So consider the $$$ rating as applicable to the C units only. They are front-end loaded, so we don't recommend this purchase unless you can get them with zero commission. Don't buy this fund on a back-end load basis, whatever you do! Previously called the Guardian Short-Term Money Fund.

## Promising Newcomers

### Canadian Equity Funds

#### GGOF ALEXANDRIA CANADIAN GROWTH FUND          NR → G #/* RSP CE

Manager: Robert Vanderhooft, since inception (1999)

MER: 2.68%      Fundata: N/A      Style: Growth

Suitability: Conservative investors looking for growth potential

Here's a surprise: a growth fund that actually managed to almost break even over the year to June 30/01. While most growth funds were taking a beating as the high-tech bubble burst, this one was down less than 2%. That may not seem all that great but when you stack it up against the double-digit losses of most growth funds, it's very impressive. There are twin secrets to this success. The first is that manager Robert Vanderhooft overweighted the portfolio toward the energy sector in 2000 and this move benefited from the surge in oil and gas stocks. The second is that he saw the Nortel meltdown coming and sold off a large part of the fund's position in that company in May 2000, before the collapse in the share price. That kind of good anticipation is impressive and we like the prospects for this fund in the future.

### Global and International Equity Funds

#### GGOF CENTURION GLOBAL VALUE FUND          NR → G #/* £ GE

Manager: Ronald Saba (Lazard Asset Management), since inception (September 2000)

MER: 2.25%      Fundata: N/A      Style: Value

Suitability: Long-term value investors

This fund appeared on the scene at a propitious moment, just as value investing was coming back into vogue. Manager Ron Saba is a veteran with a quarter-century of investment experience. Geographic diversification is first-rate; unlike so many so-called "global" funds, this one avoids the trap of heavily overweighting the portfolio with U.S. issues. There will usually be 35 to 50 companies held.

## Fixed-Income Funds

### GGOF GUARDIAN CANADIAN HIGH-YIELD BOND FUND

NR ↑ FI #/* RSP HYB

Manager: Stephen D. Kearns, since inception (January 1999)

MER: 2.21%     Fundata: A     Style: Credit Analysis

Suitability: Income investors willing to accept higher risk

This is a junk bond fund, to put it crudely. But so far in its young life, it has been a very impressive junk bond fund, with a one-year gain of more than 12% for the period to June 30/01. That return is somewhat misleading, however, because this is not a pure bond fund. More than 15% of the assets are invested in royalty trusts like PrimeWest and Superior Propane, and real estate investment trusts, such as Royal Host. There are also some preferred shares in the mix. So although this is technically classified as a high-yield bond fund, it is more akin to a high-yield balanced fund in its composition. The risk is therefore somewhat higher than you would expect in a pure bond fund, so keep that fact in mind if you are considering this one for your portfolio.

# HSBC INVESTMENT FUNDS

## THE COMPANY

HSBC Investment Funds (HSBC stands for Hongkong and Shanghai Banking Corporation) is the successor of the Hong Kong Bank family of funds. HSBC Asset Management Ltd., a HSBC Bank Canada subsidiary, manages all the funds in this group. The domestic funds are under the direction of HSBC Asset Management (Canada) Ltd., which was formerly M.K. Wong & Associates Ltd. The firm has been a part of the HSBC group since 1996, but the name wasn't changed until mid-1998. This company offers a large number of high-quality funds, including eight that earned $$$ ratings this year. It's an organization that deserves careful consideration from any fund investor. Its latest offering, launched in December 2000, is the Global Technology Fund.

## THE DETAILS

|  |  |
|---|---|
| Number of funds: | 17 |
| Assets under management: | $2.34 billion |
| Load charge: | None |
| Switching charge: | 2% maximum |
| Where sold: | Alberta, B.C., Manitoba, Ontario, Quebec, New Brunswick, Newfoundland, Nova Scotia, Saskatchewan |
| How sold: | Directly through branches of HSBC Bank Canada and through registered brokers and investment dealers. Lotus Funds are sold directly through HSBC Investment Funds (Canada) Inc. by phone (1-800-665-9360), mail, or in person by visiting their Vancouver or Toronto offices. |
| Phone number: | 1-800-830-8888 |
| Web site address: | www.hsbc.ca/funds |
| E-mail address: | info@hsbc.com; assetmanagement@hsbc.ca |
| Minimum initial investment: | $500 (generally) |

## INVESTING TIPS

The Lotus Group of Funds, previously distributed through M.K. Wong, was incorporated into the HSBC family, and these four funds retain their identity. They are generally top performers and always worthy of a careful look.

# FUND SUMMARY

Top Choices: Canadian Bond, Canadian Money Market, Dividend Income, European, U.S.$ Money Market, U.S. Equity, Lotus Bond, Lotus Income

Also Recommended: Canadian Balanced, Equity, Lotus Balanced, Mortgage

Promising Newcomers: None

The Rest: Asia Pacific, Emerging Markets, Global Equity, Global Equity RSP, Global Technology, Small-Cap Growth, RSP World Bond RSP, Lotus Canadian Equity

# FUND RATINGS

## Top Choices

### Dividend Income Funds

#### HSBC DIVIDEND INCOME FUND                    $$$ → G/FI NO RSP DIV

Managers: HSBC Asset Management (Canada) Ltd., since 1994

MER: 1.96%      Fundata: C      Style: Value

Suitability: Conservative income investors

This fund is designed to produce a combination of long-term capital gains plus dividend income, using a mix of preferred shares and high-yielding common stocks. It's doing well on both counts. Its distribution record is above average, at 34¢ per unit in the year ending June 30/01. Total return for the three years to that same date averaged 7.2% annually, compared with a 5.3% an average for its peers. That's an excellent record, good enough to maintain a $$$ rating this year. The fund's good safety record is a bonus. The fund uses covered call writing from time to time to lock in profits and enhance income.

### U.S. Equity Funds

#### HSBC U.S. EQUITY FUND                    $$$ → G NO £ USE

Managers: HSBC Asset Management (Americas) Inc., since 1994

MER: 2.25%      Fundata: D      Style: Growth

Suitability: Growth-oriented investors

Technically, this fund invests in U.S. equities and can hold up to 10% in Latin American stocks. So far, however, the Latins haven't made the cut and the fund has focused almost exclusively on the States. The fund lost 20% in the year ending June 30/01 following its 13.6% gain in the previous 12 months. But despite that one-year drop, this fund remains a very good choice in its category. Five-year average annual compound rate of return is an impressive 14.9% compared with the peer average of 11.8%. The portfolio is composed mainly of large-cap stocks including Microsoft, Exxon, AOL Time Warner, and Pfizer, with some retailers mixed in; if it's on the Dow, it's probably here. Very good safety record to go along with the solid returns. There's an RRSP-eligible clone available if you're bumping up against the foreign content limit in your registered plan.

## Global and International Equity Funds

### HSBC EUROPEAN FUND $$$ → G NO £ EE

Managers: HSBC Asset Management (Europe) Ltd., since 1994

MER: 2.40%    Fundata: C    Style: Top-down Value/Growth

Suitability: Aggressive investors

Managed in London, this is a traditional European fund that focuses on E.U. member states. So you'll find lots of stocks from the U.K., Germany, France, and Switzerland, but nothing at all from Eastern Europe. This fund has been one of the best performers in the European Equity category. For example, it ranked first in its group for the year ending June 30/99 with a 4.1% return. That may seem low, but it was a stellar result in the face of a slump in European markets. Despite a 21.5% loss in the latest year ending June 30/01 (about equal to the average loss in its peer group), the fund's record remains strong. In the five-year period ending June 30/01, its 15.1% return was well above the category average. This is one of our favourite European funds.

## Canadian Bond Funds

### HSBC CANADIAN BOND FUND $$$ ↓ FI NO RSP CB

Managers: HSBC Asset Management (Canada) Ltd., since 1994

MER: 1.18%    Fundata: D    Style: Credit and Term Structure Analysis

Suitability: Conservative investors

This portfolio favours government bonds, mainly federal, along with some Ontario and New Brunswick issues. The fund also had 34% of its assets in high-quality corporate securities in the first half of 2001. Performance has been better than average over two, three, and five years, and well above average for the past year. Average annual compound rate of return for the five years to June 30/01 worked out to 6.8% annually, with a very attractive risk rating. A good choice for conservative investors. It would be a very comfortable fit for an RRSP.

### LOTUS BOND FUND $$$ ↓ FI NO RSP CB

Managers: HSBC Asset Management (Canada) Ltd., since 1994

MER: 0.96%      Fundata: D      Style: Credit and Term Structure Analysis

Suitability: Long-term income investors

This is a good-looking bond fund with a nice mix of government and corporate issues. It gained 5.2% in the year to June 30/01, well above average in a tough year, and sports a solid three-year average annual compound rate of return of 4%. There really isn't much to distinguish this fund from the HSBC Canadian Bond Fund, except for the fact that this one is extremely small. We expect it to be absorbed into the larger fund before long. With less than $1 million in assets, it's uneconomical.

## Canadian Money Market Funds

### HSBC CANADIAN MONEY MARKET FUND $$$ → C NO RSP CMM

Managers: HSBC Asset Management (Canada) Ltd., since 1988

MER: 0.96%      Fundata: B

Suitability: Conservative income investors

This is a relatively aggressive money market fund. In early 2001, it held 56% of its assets in corporate notes, which is an above-average allocation for money market funds. Returns out to five years have been slightly elevated for the money market category.

### HSBC U.S.$ MONEY MARKET FUND $$$ → C NO £ FMM

Managers: HSBC Asset Management (Canada) Ltd., since 1997

MER: 1.12%      Fundata: N/A

Suitability: Conservative income investors

This money market fund is denominated in U.S. dollars and holds very high-quality U.S. and Canadian issuer money market securities. In the three years to June 30/01, the fund's 4.7% average annual gain outperformed the peer group's by a healthy 64 basis points (0.64%) per annum. In the latest year to June 30/01, the fund earned 5%. A solid choice for a U.S. money market investment.

### LOTUS INCOME FUND $$$ ↓ C NO RSP CMM

Managers: HSBC Asset Management (Canada) Ltd., since 1988

MER: 0.90%      Fundata: C Style: Credit Analysis

Suitability: Conservative income investors

It's hard to know where to put this fund. Its mandate suggests that it's a short-term bond fund; the portfolio may have an average term to maturity of not more than five years and may hold securities with maturities up to seven years out. In practice, however, the managers have been running it as a money market fund, investing primarily in Canada T-bills, with some corporate notes thrown into the mix. Recently, T-bills and short-term corporate bonds represented virtually the entire portfolio. Before you invest any money, you may wish to obtain clarification from the management team regarding their future plans. The fund has had good results: its compound annual 10-year rate of return is above average at 4.8%. Subsequent periods have seen it perform slightly above average, making it a low-risk/high-return choice in the Canadian Money Market category. However, it may not be long for this world because of its small size (less than $1 million). It's an obvious candidate for a merger into the HSBC Money Market Fund.

## Also Recommended

### Canadian Equity Funds

### HSBC EQUITY FUND                                    $$ → G NO RSP CLC

Managers: HSBC Asset Management (Canada) Ltd., since 1988

MER: 1.93%      Fundata: D        Style: Value/Growth

Suitability: Long-term Canadian equity investors

This entry was an index fund until the fall of 1992. At that time, the mandate was changed to make it a fully managed equity fund. Recently, performance has been slipping; the fund lost 18.7% (the category average was an 8.5% loss) for the year ending June 30/01. But the three-year results are still above average, at 4.8% annually. It's one of only 34 large-cap Canadian equity funds with a 10-year history and it ranks fifth over that time frame with an average annual compound rate of return of 11.2%. The portfolio favours large-cap issues, with some smaller-growth stocks mixed in for extra oomph. There is also a 10% U.S. equity position. Given the recent performance, we are downgrading to a $$.

### Canadian Balanced and Asset Allocation Funds

### HSBC CANADIAN BALANCED FUND             $$ → FI/G NO RSP CBAL

Managers: HSBC Asset Management (Canada) Ltd., since 1992

MER: 1.88%     Fundata: D        Style: Tactical Asset Allocation

Suitability: Long-term balanced investors

This is one of only three funds in the HSBC family with a 10-year history, and it's a respectable one. This fund has been turning in consistently good results since effecting a strategy change on the equity side a couple of years back that placed greater emphasis on larger, more stable companies to reduce volatility. Banks and utilities are still a large part of the equity portion of the portfolio.

Three-year annual return to June 30/01 at 5.7% was better than average for the balanced fund category. Its five-year record of 9.5% per annum beat the average Canadian balanced fund by 1.6 points per annum. However, performance slipped in the latest year to an 8% loss. The portfolio continues to be weighted toward equities (57% in the first half of 2001), with a 40% bond component. This fund is a good choice for a conservative investor.

### LOTUS BALANCED FUND $$ → FI/G NO RSP CBAL

Managers: HSBC Asset Management (Canada) Ltd., since 1984

MER: 2.14%    Fundata: D    Style: Tactical Asset Allocation

Suitability: Long-term balanced investors

This entry has been around for a decade, with generally strong results. The past few years have produced substantially better-than-average profits, although the fund's performance slipped badly to a 9.3% loss in the 12 months to June 30/01. It had an above-average compound annual rate of return of 5.5% for the three years to that date. The bond section of the portfolio, recently 46% of assets, is conservatively managed, with a mix of Government of Canada, provincial, and high-grade corporate bonds, along with some mortgage-backed securities. The stock section, about 51% of assets, is more aggressive, with many of the same holdings as the companion HSBC Canadian Equity Fund, although in this case a few more blue chips like the banks, BCE, Cognos, Nortel, and Bombardier are tossed in. We are downgrading to a $$ rating due to the recent underperformance.

## Canadian Mortgage Funds

### HSBC MORTGAGE FUND $$ → FI NO RSP M

Managers: HSBC Asset Management (Canada) Ltd., since 1992

MER: 1.56%    Fundata: C    Style: Credit Analysis

Suitability: Conservative income investors

This fund offers relatively low risk and decent returns in a low-paying fund category. Average annual compound rate of return for the five years to June 30/01 was 5.7%, above par for the peer group. Three-year returns were also above average. The one-year gain here was 6.9%. This is a useful fund to hold in the fixed-income section of an RRSP or RRIF, as long as you don't expect big profits from it.

## Promising Newcomers

None.

# INTEGRA MUTUAL FUNDS

## THE COMPANY

Integra is an investment management firm that was one of the first in Canada to employ a multi-manager, multi-style approach. Its primary business is in institutional money management and high net worth clients. However, it does maintain a relatively small (in terms of its total assets under management) mutual funds operation.

The firm is the Canadian subsidiary of Old Mutual PLC, one of the largest and most diverse financial services companies in the world. Old Mutual, headquartered in London, England, owns more than 50 international specialist investment firms and provides multi-style, multi-national asset management services globally.

The Integra philosophy is that no one style of investment management is rewarded consistently through all phases of a market cycle and plan sponsors can significantly reduce the risk of short-term underperformance by employing a multi-team/multi-style investment management strategy. The company says that its multi-style approach results in reduced volatility and more consistent rates of return.

Management of funds is handled by a core group of teams, divided into value managers (Lincluden Management) and top-down/growth mangers (Gryphon Investment Counsel).

## THE DETAILS

|  |  |
|---|---|
| Number of funds: | 10 |
| Fund assets under management: | $781.8 million |
| Load charge: | None |
| Switching charge: | None |
| Where sold: | Across Canada |
| How sold: | Directly through Integra Capital Corporation |
| Phone number: | 1-877-799-1942 |
| Web site address: | www.integra.com |
| E-mail address: | info@integra.com |
| Minimum initial investment: | $5,000 |

## INVESTING TIPS

Beginning in April 1996, investors were charged management fees directly, so the management expense ratios (MERs) on these funds published in the media will appear unusually low. As a result, the returns you see in the monthly mutual fund reports are somewhat inflated, since most other funds deduct expenses before performance numbers are calculated. However, the company has supplied us with the maximum fees that apply for each fund, and these appear in the individual ratings. Keep in mind that the fees are applied on a sliding scale, so numbers in our reviews represent the highest amount you might pay. Actual expenses incurred by the fund are added to determine the true MER, so even these numbers are on the low side.

There is a $5,000 minimum purchase, but the company can waive this criterion in certain circumstances.

## FUND SUMMARY

|  |  |
|---|---|
| Top Choices: | Balanced, Bond |
| Also Recommended: | Equity, International Equity, Short-Term Investment |
| Promising Newcomers: | U.S. Small-Cap Equity, U.S. Value Growth |
| The Rest: | Canadian Value Growth |

## FUND RATINGS

### Top Choices

#### Canadian Balanced and Asset Allocation Funds

**ICM BALANCED FUND**                    **$$$ ↓ FI/G #/NO RSP CBAL**

Managers: Gryphon Investment Counsel and Lincluden Management, since inception (1987)

MER: 1.75%      Fundata: A      Style: Value/Growth

Suitability: Conservative investors

There are two teams running this fund and several other ICM portfolios. Each employs a different style for their half of the assets. Gryphon uses a top-down investing approach, which involves identifying key sectors of the economy expected to do well and selecting large-cap stocks that will profit as a result. Lincluden takes a value-oriented, bottom-up approach, selecting stocks on the basis of their intrinsic value without reference to overall trends. The managers can shift freely between asset classes to maximize returns. Results have been showing steady improvement in recent years, although the figures shown in the media do not reflect the full impact of the expense charges levied against individual unitholders. This is unfortunate because it makes comparisons difficult for ordinary investors, who may be left with an inaccurate impression. The good news here is that the risk level is very low. If safety is your primary concern, this fund is worth considering; the last time it recorded a loss over a calendar year was back in 1994, and even then it was only a fraction of a percentage point.

## Canadian Bond Funds

### ICM BOND FUND                                    $$$ ↓ FI NO RSP CB

Managers: Gryphon Investment Counsel and Lincluden Management, since 1990

MER: 1.30%      Fundata: B        Style: Interest Rate Anticipation/Credit Analysis and Yield

Suitability: Conservative investors

This fund has been a consistent above-average performer, even after discounting the returns to take the full management fee into account. It invests mainly in Government of Canada issues, with a few provincial corporate bonds tossed in. Corporate bonds comprise about 16% of the portfolio. The management style is conservative. Here again we see a very good safety profile, as is the case with almost all ICM funds. The fund has not shown a calendar year loss since it started.

## Also Recommended

## Canadian Equity Funds

### ICM EQUITY FUND                                    $$ ↓ G NO RSP CE

Managers: Gryphon Investment Counsel and Lincluden Management, since 1987

MER: 1.75%      Fundata: B        Style: Value/Growth

Suitability: Conservative investors

This fund can invest in a wide variety of Canadian equities and bonds convertible into equities. It's an interesting combination but it has produced below-average returns over the long term, even with the artificial boost provided by the unusual way of charging fees. However, the most recent results have shown improvement; in fact, the fund was a first-quartile performer in the first half of 2001. As with the companion Balanced Fund, the risk level of this fund is quite low compared to the peer group. From 1996–2000, the fund showed only one losing calendar year in 1998. So what we have here is a low-risk, low-return entry that appears to be on an upswing. We are raising the rating to $$ as a result.

## International Equity Funds

### ICM INTERNATIONAL EQUITY FUND                       $$ → G NO £ IE

Managers: Phillips & Drew and Murray Johnstone International, since 1993

MER: 1.95%      Fundata: A        Style: Value/GARP

Suitability: Conservative investors

The mandate of this fund is to invest in non-North American companies, with a focus on Europe, the Far East, and Australia. The managers use a combination of country allocation and value stock selection to make their picks. Phillips & Drew takes a value approach for their portion of the portfolio, while Murray Johnstone International is a growth-at-a-reasonable-price (GARP) manager. The portfolio is well diversified and is concentrated in more developed countries, holding the likes of Hitachi, Canon, Nestle, and Bayer. Numbers over the past 18 months look shaky, but both the Asian and European markets have been weak. In reality, this fund was above average for its type during the period, despite recording losses. Managers have to do the best they can with the mandate they're given, and this team has done a respectable (although not sensational) job. This is not a fund we would recommend you go out of your way to buy, but if you have money with the company you may want to include some units to provide overseas diversification.

## Canadian Money Market Funds

### ICM SHORT-TERM INVESTMENT FUND   $$ ↓ C NO RSP CMM

Managers: Gryphon Investment Counsel and Lincluden Management, since inception (1992)

MER: 0.75%     Fundata: D     Style: Multi-Style

Suitability: Conservative investors

Pick up the newspaper and check the monthly mutual fund performance numbers: this fund will stand out in the Money Market category. Its average annual return is either right at the top of the list or close to it. But like its sister funds, it quotes returns before deducting management fees. For the three years ending June 30/01, for example, the paper says you earned an average of 5.2% annually with this fund—one of the better results in the category. But knock three-quarters of a percentage point off that result if you're a retail investor (institutions and group RRSPs get a reduction), and you're down to around 4.5%, about average for money market funds. Keep this scenario in mind before you invest. That doesn't mean this is a bad fund—it's not. It just means you have to know how to interpret all the numbers.

# Promising Newcomers

## U.S. Equity Funds

### ICM U.S. VALUE GROWTH FUND  NR ↓ G NO £ USE

Managers: Pell, Rudman Trust Co. and Barrow, Hanley, McWhinny & Strauss, since inception (1998)

MER: 1.95%   Fundata: A   Style: Value/Growth

Suitability: Conservative investors

In this managerial tandem, the Pell, Rudman group handles the U.S. mid-cap growth side of the portfolio while Barrow, Hanley *et al.* are large-cap value specialists. The fund only invests in companies with a market cap of more than U.S.$1 billion and is structured to minimize risk. The portfolio is stuffed with household names, from RadioShack to Bristol-Myers Squibb. Results have been good so far with the fund recording an 8.6% gain (before deducting managerial fees) over the year to June 30/01, a time when many rival funds were losing ground. This looks like a promising choice for conservative investors within this group.

## U.S. Small-to-Mid-Cap Funds

### ICM U.S. SMALL-CAP EQUITY FUND  NR → G NO £ USSC

Managers: Rice, Hall, James & Associates and Sterling Capital Management, since inception (1998)

MER: 2.25%   Fundata: A   Style: Value/GARP

Suitability: Aggressive investors

The mandate of this fund allows the managers to invest in companies with a market capitalization of up to U.S.$2.5 billion. In Canada, a company of that size would be at least mid-cap, so it gives you an idea of the difference in scale between the two countries. As a result, the portfolio contains many names you may be startled to learn classify as "small-caps," including Bell & Howell, Barnes & Noble, Rayonier, and Crane. Nonetheless, the majority of names will be totally unfamiliar to the average investor. The managers certainly seem to know how to make the mix of value and GARP work effectively. The fund showed a one-year gain of 28.5% to June 30/01. It got off to an initial slow start, but has been a top-quartile performer in the past 18 months. It looks promising, but remember that small-cap funds are somewhat riskier by nature.

# INVESTORS GROUP

## THE COMPANY

This Winnipeg-based giant is Canada's largest mutual fund company in terms of assets under management. In addition to its extensive line of 82 active funds, the company markets a broad range of mortgage and insurance products through its vast network of over 3,600 sales reps, 66 mortgage planning specialists, and 100 Financial Planning Centres nationwide. It is a publicly traded company and a member of the Power Financial Corporation group. In recent years, Investors has been very active in expanding its leadership in the fund business through key alliances and new funds.

In a much-publicized takeover in 2001, Investors Group acquired control of another Canadian fund giant, Mackenzie Financial Corporation. However, unlike most other recent acquisitions of this kind, Mackenzie is continuing to operate as a stand-alone company and its funds have not been integrated with those of Investors Group. Therefore, we will continue to treat it as a separate entity for purposes of this *Guide*. See the section on Mackenzie Financial for a review of their funds.

Many of the Investors Group funds are run by outside portfolio managers to allow for more diversity in style. The list includes AGF, Beutel Goodman, Sceptre, and funds marketed under the AGF, Beutel Goodman, Fidelity, Janus MAXXUM, Scudder Sceptre, and Templeton names.

Investors Group has raised its profile in the Quebec market with the establishment of a Montreal-based investment management operation. Christine Décarie, the equity specialist who ran Montrusco's successful Quebec Growth Fund for several years, was hired as a partner and portfolio manager responsible for the Quebec operation. Décarie is involved in the creation of new funds for the Investors Master Series (this name is now applied to Investors Group's original proprietary line of funds). The newest fund added to this series is the Investors Quebec Enterprise Fund, which invests in small-to-mid-cap companies located in or doing business in Quebec.

As a result of all the changes, the company now boasts a total of 82 funds, including both the Masters Series and the partnerships with other organizations.

Investors interested in having their asset allocation decisions made for them may want to take a look at Investors Portfolio Funds, which offer eight different investment objectives and invest in a broad mix of Investors Funds. These portfolio funds generally rank among the better of this type of product—performance is superior to the bank-based structured portfolios. They are not reviewed separately, however.

Investors Group funds are sold only by their own representatives and are not available through any outside third party. The ratings section that follows is divided into three distinct groups: the Investors Masters Funds, the GS Funds advised by Rothschild Asset Management, and the IG funds managed by various outside managers.

## THE DETAILS

| | |
|---|---|
| Number of funds: | 82 |
| Assets under management: | $46.2 billion |
| Load charge: | Front: max. 2.5%; Back: max. 3% |
| Switching charge: | None |
| Where sold: | Across Canada |
| How sold: | Exclusively through Investors Group representatives |
| Phone number: | 1-888-PHONE IG or 1-888-746-6344 |
| Web site address: | www.investorsgroup.com |
| E-mail address: | Through Web site |
| Minimum initial investment: | Non-registered: $1,000 (generally); RRSP: $500 (generally) |

## INVESTING TIPS

Investors Group has an unusual commissions structure. There is no front-end load for equity or balanced funds if your total investment in all funds exceeds $10,000 (it's 2.5% if your holdings are less than that amount). A redemption charge will apply if you sell before seven years (maximum 3%), meaning that if you invest less than $10,000, you'll potentially face both a front- and back-end load. Equity funds are also assessed an annual "service fee" of 0.5% on the market value of your investments (this is over and above the normal management fee). If your total assets are between $35,000 and $150,000, you'll receive a partial rebate of this service fee. With assets over $150,000, you get it all back. The rules are somewhat different for fixed-income and money market funds. Investors Group representatives can give you more details regarding this rather complex payment structure.

## FUND SUMMARY

### Investors Masters Funds

| | |
|---|---|
| Top Choices: | Mutual of Canada, Natural Resources, Real Property, North American Growth, Summa, U.S. Large-Cap Value |
| Also Recommended: | European Growth, Global, Retirement Mutual, U.S. Opportunities, U.S.$ Money Market |
| Promising Newcomers: | Euro Mid-Cap Growth, Mergers & Acquisitions |

The Rest:  Asset Allocation, Canadian Balanced, Canadian
Enterprise, Canadian Equity, Canadian Money
Market, Canadian High-Yield Income, Canadian
Small-Cap, Canadian Small-Cap II, Corporate
Bond, Dividend, Global Bond, Global
e-Commerce, Global Financial, Global Science
& Technology, Government Bond, Growth Plus
Portfolio, Growth Portfolio, Income Plus
Portfolio, Income Portfolio, Japanese Growth,
Latin American Growth, Mortgage, Pacific
International, Pan Asian Growth, Quebec
Enterprise, Retirement Growth Portfolio,
Retirement High Growth, Retirement Plus
Portfolio, U.S. Large-Cap Growth, World
Growth Portfolio

## GS Funds

Top Choices:  None
Also Recommended:  None
Promising Newcomers:  None
The Rest:  GS American Equity, GS Canadian Balanced,
GS Canadian Equity, GS International Bond, GS
International Equity

## IG Funds

Top Choices:  IG Beutel Goodman Canadian Small-Cap
Also Recommended:  IG Beutel Goodman Canadian Equity, IG
Scudder U.S. Allocation
Promising Newcomers:  IG MAXXUM Dividend
The Rest:  IG AGF Asian Growth, IG AGF Canadian
Growth, IG AGF Canadian Diversified Growth,
IG AGF U.S. RSP, IG AGF U.S. Growth, IG
Beutel Goodman Canadian Balanced, IG FI
Canadian Allocation, IG FI Canadian Equity, IG
FI Global Equity, IG FI U.S. Equity, IG Janus
American Equity, IG Janus Global Equity, IG
MAXXUM Income, IG Sceptre Canadian
Balanced, IG Sceptre Canadian Bond, IG
Sceptre Canadian Equity, IG Scudder Canadian
All-Cap, IG Scudder Emerging Markets Growth,
IG Scudder Europe Growth, IG Templeton
International Equity, IG Templeton World
Allocation, IG Templeton World Bond

# FUND RATINGS

## Top Choices/Investors Masters Funds

### Canadian Equity Funds

### INVESTORS SUMMA FUND $$$$ → G * RSP CE

Manager: Scott Morrison, since December 2000

MER: 2.93%      Fundata: D      Style: Growth

Suitability: Socially responsible investors

This fund is designed for those investors who want socially responsible companies as part of their portfolios. Investment screens preclude companies involved in tobacco, alcohol, munitions, pornography, and gambling. Stocks are chosen from across all capitalization classes, but the manager favours value-oriented, large-cap issues. Diversification is achieved across a broad range of industries and by maximizing foreign exposure. At mid-2001, a high cash balance of 14% gave the fund some flexibility and a defensive stance in the prevailing market weakness. Recent results have been disappointing in light of this fund's strong record in years past. The fund lost 12.4% for the year to June 30/01, compared with the 5.8% average loss for the category. However, the fund was showing clear signs of getting back on track in the second quarter of 2001 under new manager Scott Morrison. The three-year average annual return of 9.5% was more than double that of its peer group and the longer-term record remains stellar as well. Despite a disappointing year we'll maintain the $$$$ rating on the assumption that Morrison has this one going the right way again.

### U.S. Equity Funds

### INVESTORS U.S. LARGE-CAP VALUE FUND $$$ → G * £ USE

Manager: Terry Wong, since 1997

MER: 2.97%      Fundata: A      Style: Value

Suitability: Conservative investors

Investors Group has recently made several changes in its U.S. fund line-up. This fund was previously called the Investors U.S. Growth Fund, which was a misnomer because it has always had a value bias in its management style. The new name reflects this bias. This is a classic buy-and-hold fund, with $2.4 billion in assets and a core group of 30 value stocks. Terry Wong, who took over this fund in June 1998, had big shoes to fill when long-time manager Larry Sarbit left for Berkshire Investment Group. When Sarbit was running the fund, it achieved a 10-year average annual return of close to 20%. Under his regime, the portfolio emphasized stocks with good growth potential and was managed on a highly disciplined basis, never holding more than about 20 to 25 companies. Sarbit didn't do a lot of trading, preferring to find good companies and hold them for the long term. Wong was the portfolio assistant under Sarbit for over a decade, so his style with the fund should be similar. Unfortunately, in his first full year at the helm, the fund gained a below-average 10.5% for a third-quartile placement. Return in the year ending June 30/00 (–9.1%) was even worse compared with its peers. This was a disappointing start, but the fund has since gone on a tear. With value investing back in vogue, the fund scored a gain of 23% in the year to June 30/01 at a time when most U.S. stock funds were being hammered. That performance merits an upgrade to $$$.

## Global and International Equity Funds

### INVESTORS NORTH AMERICAN GROWTH FUND  $$$ → G * £ NAE

Manager: William D. Chornous, since 1995

MER: 2.96%     Fundata: A     Style: Value

Suitability: Conservative investors

This fund scored the highest Fundata grade in the North American category. As the name implies, the fund invests primarily in U.S. and Canadian stocks. Its top holdings consist of some very large U.S. and Canadian corporations, making it a good buy-and-hold investment. The fund recorded an average annual compound rate of return of 8.9% over the five years to June 30/01, compared with 6.2% for the category. In the latest year, the fund gained a remarkable 16.3% versus a 10.1% loss for the average North American equity fund. The long-term record is very strong. We are upgrading the fund to a $$$ rating.

## Sector Equity Funds

### INVESTORS CANADIAN NATURAL RESOURCES FUND $$$ → G * RSP NR

Manager: Kevin Nysol, since 1996

MER: 2.99%     Fundata: B     Style: Value

Suitability: Aggressive investors

This fund, despite a so-so performance in the latest year, has been impressive so far as a consistent top-quartile performer. The fund recorded an annual compounded return of 8.4% in the three years ending June 30/01, almost double that of the average resource fund over the same period. Over the most recent 12 months the fund slipped a bit, gaining 4.8%, which was well below the category average. Risk is relatively low for a fund of this type, but remember that all resource funds will be more volatile than a broadly diversified equity fund. Resource funds are cyclical, but right now the tide is running in their favour. We'll maintain the fund at its $$$ rating.

## INVESTORS REAL PROPERTY FUND                    $$$ ↓ G #/* RSP RE

Manager: Murray Mitchell, since 1989

MER: 2.73%      Fundata: A      Style: Sector

Suitability: Real estate sector investors

If you always wanted to be a landlord, this fund might suit your fancy. Unlike some other real estate-oriented funds, this one actually accumulates income-producing real property instead of stocks. It resembles a real estate investment trust (REIT) in the sense that it collects rents, deducts expenses, and passes on the remainder to unitholders. As of mid-2001, most of the assets were in real property with the remainder in cash-equivalent securities. As a result, the fund is not impacted by the stock market (it holds no stocks). As long as buildings are rented and rents come in, the fund should maintain a regular income stream. Gain for the year to June 30/01 of 8% was below average for the small Real Estate category. However, the fund's three-year and five-year records are above average. Over the past 10 years the fund has achieved an annual compound rate of return of 4% per annum, compared with a mere 0.2% for the category. The fund is well deserving of its A rating from Fundata. Its beta of zero (meaning it is independent of the market) makes it a useful alternate investment. Furthermore, the standard deviation is well below that of stocks and bonds. This fund is 100% eligible for RRSPs and RRIFs, but you'll give up the tax breaks if you hold units in registered plans. A good choice for income-oriented investors looking for some tax-sheltered cash flow. We are moving it up to a $$$ rating given its consistency and low volatility.

## Canadian Balanced and Asset Allocation Funds

## INVESTORS MUTUAL OF CANADA                    $$$ ↑ FI/G * RSP CBAL

Manager: Christine Décarie, since January 2000

MER: 2.94%      Fundata: D      Style: Primarily Value

Suitability: Aggressive balanced investors

For most of its history this fund has been inconsistent. Returns have bounced around compared with the average of the peer group. In the latest year, to June 30/01, the fund recorded a 4.1% loss compared with the 2.6% loss in the category. But over the past five years, the fund's 9.9% annual compound return beat the Canadian Balanced category average by two percentage points per year, placing the fund in the top quartile. As of mid-2001, the portfolio had about 42% in bonds, preferred shares, and cash, and 58% in Canadian and foreign stocks (mainly U.S. stocks). The equities side has a blue-chip bias, with some growth stocks mixed in to boost returns. The fixed-income side is the most aggressive of the Canadian balanced funds, with the highest average duration (a measure of bond risk). Rating remains at $$$.

# Also Recommended/Investors Masters Funds

## Canadian Equity Funds

### INVESTORS RETIREMENT MUTUAL FUND $$ → G * RSP CE

Manager: Dom Grestoni, since 2000

MER: 2.93%     Fundata: A     Style: Value

Suitability: Conservative investors

Here's an example of how a fund can sometimes turn on a dime. This one has been a laggard for years. But the collapse of the technology markets and the resurgence of value investing translated into a resurrection for this grand old lady. The fund gained more than 21% in the year to June 30/01, if you can believe it! New manager Dom Grestoni obviously gets some of the credit for this turnaround. Let's hope it continues. Rating moves up one notch.

## U.S. Equity Funds

### INVESTORS U.S. OPPORTUNITIES FUND $$ → G * £ USSC

Manager: Terry Wong, since 1997

MER: 2.97%     Fundata: A     Style: Value

Suitability: Aggressive investors

Investors Group states the objective of this fund as simply as anyone could want: to provide long-term capital growth. We only wish the fund's history were as simple to decipher. In the peer group of 23 small-and-mid-cap U.S. equity funds with three-year results, this fund had the second-poorest showing for the period ending June 30/00, with an average annual return of only 2.1%. So it came as a real shock when the fund recorded a 39.1% return in the year ending June 30/01, compared with an 11.3% loss for the peer group! The fund's concentration on small companies meant manager Terry Wong did some stellar stock picking in the latest year to achieve that kind of result. One year doesn't erase weak past results, but this is a fund definitely worth watching.

## Global and International Equity Funds

### INVESTORS EUROPEAN GROWTH FUND $$ ↓ G * £ EE

Manager: Martin Fahey, since 2000

MER: 3.02%     Fundata: B     Style: Growth

Suitability: Growth-oriented investors

This is the second-largest fund in the European Equity category, trailing only the Fidelity European Growth Fund in terms of assets. The fund is diversified across Western Europe. As of mid-2001, the largest allocations were to France, the U.K., and Germany; these three holdings compose over 40% of the portfolio. A minor portion of the fund is also allocated to emerging Eastern European markets for added growth and diversification. The fund lost 9.4% in the year to June 30/01, compared with an average loss of 20.6% for the category. Longer-term results to five years are well above average for the European category. The conservative nature of this fund makes it a good long-term holding if you're an Investors client. The safety record is among the best for this type of fund.

## INVESTORS GLOBAL FUND                          $$ → G * £ GE

Manager: Peter O'Reilly, since 2001

MER: 3.00%      Fundata: B         Style: Generally Value

Suitability: Diversified investors

Investors Group offers a broad selection of global and international funds to its clients. The mandate of this fund allows the manager to invest anywhere he sees good opportunities, with a focus on large and well-managed companies. In recent years, the fund has been heavily focused in U.S. stocks (38.1% as of June 30/01). The fund held quite steady in the vicious global market downturn this year; its focus on strong fundamentals paid off in solid stock picking. The 1.5% loss for the year to June 30/01 compared favourably with the 15% average loss recorded by the peer group. Longer-term results are above average as well. The safety record of this fund is very strong in comparison with the group, but that is due in part to a very large cash position (12.8% as of mid-2001). We are maintaining the $$ rating.

## Foreign Money Market Funds

## INVESTORS U.S.$ MONEY MARKET FUND          $$$ ↓ C NO RSP FMM

Manager: Patsy Rogers, since January 1999

MER: 1.21%      Fundata: C

Suitability: Conservative U.S. income investors

If you are looking to park U.S. cash somewhere, this is a good choice. The average annual return for the three years ending June 30/01 was 4.5%, about 50 points per year above average. The management expense ratio (MER) is high, but performance has been there. We'll give it a $$ rating.

## Promising Newcomers/Investors Master Funds

### Global and International Equity Funds

#### INVESTORS EURO MID-CAP GROWTH $\quad$ NR → G * £ EE

Manager: Martin Fahey, since June 2000

MER: 3.11%     Fundata: N/A     Style: Growth

Suitability: Aggressive investors

The fund has a short history but a very promising future. The fund manager invests primarily in mid-sized European companies (between U.S.$1 billion and $5 billion in capitalization). At mid-2001, the heaviest allocations were to the United Kingdom (31.1%), the Netherlands (11.4%), and Ireland (6.0%). Obviously manager Martin Fahey was in no hurry to commit—the fund's cash position was 38.9% at mid-year. Results have been impressive. In the year ending June 30/01, the fund recorded a 9.4% return compared with the 20.6% loss for the Europe category. That's enough to earn it special recognition here.

### Specialty Funds

#### INVESTORS MERGERS & ACQUISITIONS FUNDS $\quad$ NR → G * £ SPE

Manager: John Campbell, since June 2000

MER: 3.61%     Fundata: N/A     Style: Value

Suitability: Aggressive investors

This unusual fund is structured to invest in small-to-medium-cap companies in sectors that are posed for a consolidation through mergers, acquisitions, and takeovers. The portfolio as of June 30/01 had a 53.4% allocation to financial services, 12.3% to consumer products, and 9.5% to industrial products. Fund manager John Campbell racked up a remarkable 32.3% return in the latest year. The record is very short but the outlook is very promising.

### Top Choices/GS Funds

None.

### Also Recommended/GS Funds

None.

### Promising Newcomers/GS Funds

None.

## Top Choices/IG Funds

### Canadian Small-to-Mid-Cap Equity Funds

### IG BEUTEL GOODMAN CANADIAN SMALL-CAP FUND $$$ ↓ G * RSP CSC

Manager: Stephen Arpin, since September 2000

MER: 3.24%     Fundata: A     Style: Value

Suitability: Middle-of-the-road investors

If you're picking one of the Beutel Goodman-managed funds from Investors Group, here's your best choice. The focus is small-cap stocks, and the fund had a 13.5% three-year average annual compound rate of return to June 30/01. That result was way above average for Canadian small-cap entries over that period. Shorter-term results have been significantly above average as well. The one-year gain of 13% was 19 percentage points above the category average! The mandate is to invest in Canadian issues that, at time of purchase, have a market cap of no more than 0.1% of the TSE 300 market cap. There are recognizable names in the fund's top holdings, such as Open Text, Riocan REIT, and Moore Corp. A major plus is a good safety score in what can be a high-risk category. The fund easily keeps its $$$ rating and could be worthy of an upgrade next year.

## Also Recommended/IG Funds

### Canadian Equity Funds

### IG BEUTEL GOODMAN CANADIAN EQUITY FUND     $$ → G * RSP CLC

Manager: Mark Thomson (Beutel Goodman), since September 2000

MER: 3.27%     Fundata: A     Style: Value

Suitability: Middle-of-the-road investors

This blue-chip-oriented fund has made a nice recovery from a terrible start. Its 12.3% return in the year ending June 30/01 (compared with the 8.5% average loss in the Canadian Large-Cap category) indicates that the vaunted Beutel Goodman value approach is starting to pay off. The fund is well diversified across all sectors. At mid-2001 its heaviest allocations were to industrial products (20.8%), financial services (18.8%), and oil and gas (8.2%). We are raising the rating to $$.

## Global Balanced and Asset Allocation Funds

### IG SCUDDER U.S. ALLOCATION FUND $$ → G/FI * £ GBAL

Manager: Gary Langbaum (Scudder), since 1999

MER: 3.26%    Fundata: B    Style: Value/Growth

Suitability: Balanced investors

This fund's goal is to generate capital growth and income through holding U.S. securities. It may invest up to 25% of its assets in non-U.S. issues, but so far it has stayed primarily in the States. With 61.1% of the portfolio in stocks at mid-2001, this fund is more growth-oriented than the average global balanced fund. Stocks tend to be large-cap value, with some growth issues added in. The fixed-income side is conservatively managed, with below-average bond risk. Returns have been good to date, with a five-year average annual compound rate of return of 8.2%, well above the norm for its peer group.

## Promising Newcomers/IG Funds

### IG MAXXUM DIVIDEND FUND NR → G #/* RSP DIV

Manager: Bill Procter, since October 2001

MER: 3.31%    Fundata: B    Style: Value/Growth

Suitability: Income-oriented equity investors

This income-oriented fund invests in Canadian common and preferred shares with the objective of generating above-average dividend returns. As of mid-2001 the portfolio was allocated 87.6% to stocks and 12.4% to bonds and cash. In the year ending June 30/01, the fund generated a 16.3% return compared with 11.7% for the dividend category. A promising start indeed. The only problem is that the manager who achieved these results has been replaced. The fund is passing into the hands of Bill Procter of Mackenzie Financial and will likely be merged into one of that company's funds before long.

# iPERFORMANCE FUND CORP. (FORMERLY HIRSCH ASSET MANAGEMENT CORP.)

## THE COMPANY

If you've been following mutual funds at all, you know the name of Veronika Hirsch. She was the high-profile manager who made very large waves in 1996 when she left AGF, who had promoted her heavily on television, to join Fidelity as manager of its then new True North Fund. Shortly thereafter, she ran into some problems with securities regulators and she and Fidelity parted ways. She later reached a settlement with the Ontario and B.C. Securities Commissions and returned to doing what she does best: running mutual funds. She then started her own fund group under the name Hirsch Asset Management. At the end of 2000, the assets of the company were acquired by iPerformance Fund Inc., which took over management responsibilities. Hirsch was retained as manager of the Canadian Growth and Natural Resource Fund and handles the equities portion of the Balanced Fund; all still bear her name.

The new ownership group launched four hedge funds in January 2001 under the iPerform trade name, and signed several top managers to run them. Marc Gabelli of New York's well-known Gabelli & Partners handles the iPerform Gabelli Global Fund. Kevin Landis of Silicon Capital Management runs the iPerform Silicon Valley Fund. Hirsch and Chris Guthrie of Hillsdale Investment Management share responsibility for the iPerform Canadian Opportunities Fund. The fourth fund, iPerform Select Leaders, is a fund of funds that combines the styles and strategies of all these managers. Although these funds are still very new, the Canadian Opportunities Fund was very impressive out of the gate, gaining more than 15% in the first half of 2001 at a time when the stock market as a whole was slumping.

## THE DETAILS

| | |
|---|---|
| Number of funds: | 8 |
| Assets under management: | $45.6 million |
| Load charge: | Hirsch Funds: Front: max. 5%; Back: max. 5.75% |
| | iPerform Funds: Front: max. 5% |
| Switching charge: | 2% maximum |
| Where sold: | Hirsch Funds: Across Canada, except Nunavut |
| | iPerform Funds: Across Canada, except Quebec |
| How sold: | Hirsch Funds: Through registered dealers |
| | iPerform Funds: By offering memorandum only |

Phone number: 1-866-473-7376 or (416) 216-3566
Web site address: www.hirschfunds.com and www.iperform.com
E-mail address: mailbox@iperform.com
Minimum initial investment: Hirsch Funds: $1,000
iPerform Funds: $150,000

## INVESTING TIPS

The two fund groups operated by this company are completely different in their nature and sales approach. The Hirsch funds are conventional, with optional front- or back-end loads, a reasonable minimum investment, and distribution through the usual sources. The iPerform hedge funds, by contrast, are for "sophisticated" investors only, and require a minimum investment of $150,000. This puts them out of the buying range for most people.

## FUND SUMMARY

Top Choices: None
Also Recommended: Hirsch Canadian Growth
Promising Newcomers: Hirsch Natural Resource
The Rest: Hirsch Funds: Balanced, Fixed-Income
iPerform Funds: Canadian Opportunities,
Gabelli Global, Select Leaders, Silicon Valley

## FUND RATINGS

### Top Choices

None.

### Also Recommended

### HIRSCH CANADIAN GROWTH FUND                    $$ ↑ G #/* RSP CE

Manager: Veronika Hirsch, since inception (1997)

MER: 2.89%      Fundata: E      Style: Bottom-up/Growth Bias

Suitability: Aggressive investors

This fund had a big year in 1999 with a gain of more than 40%, but it hasn't been very impressive since. In the first half of 2001, it dropped about 13% and was a fourth-quartile performer. Risk is on the high side. However, manager Veronika Hirsch has done very well in the past, so we're not about to write off this fund entirely. The style is growth, after all, and value has been the place to be in the past year. When growth stocks come back into favour, this fund should do well again. Top holdings in the first half of 2001 included several of the big banks, Manitoba Tel, and Nortel. The fund also had a significant position in Gulf Canada Resources, which turned out to be very profitable when a takeover bid was made for the company. There's more risk associated with this fund than we're comfortable with, but some people may be prepared to accept that in exchange for greater return potential.

## Promising Newcomers

### HIRSCH NATURAL RESOURCE FUND        NR ↑ G #/* RSP NR

Manager: Veronika Hirsch, since inception (1998)

MER: 3.05%      Fundata: D      Style: Bottom-up/Growth Bias

Suitability: Aggressive investors

Veronika Hirsch's main strength has always been natural resource stocks, and that expertise shows in this fund. It hasn't had a losing calendar year since its launch, with gains of 15.8% in 1999, 4.7% in 2000, and 3% in the first half of 2001. To keep things in perspective, however, those returns were below average for the Natural Resources category. Top holdings in the first half of 2001 included many big name companies like Alcan, Enbridge, and Canadian Natural Resources. This is a credible resource fund for those who want to specialize in that sector, even though it would not be our number one selection.

# JONES HEWARD GROUP

## THE COMPANY

This is an investment counselling firm now owned by Bank of Montreal, but it continues to operate its own independent fund group in addition to handling the management duties for several of the bank's First Canadian Funds. The small family of five basic funds plus one spinoff clone possesses a long history, but has undergone many changes in recent years. Under the new management team, these funds look much more attractive.

## THE DETAILS

|  |  |
|---|---|
| Number of funds: | 6 |
| Assets under management: | $180 million |
| Load charge: | Front: max. 5% (except Money Market: max. 2%); Back: max. 5% |
| Switching charge: | None |
| Where sold: | Across Canada |
| How sold: | Through brokers, dealers, and financial planners |
| Phone number: | 1-800-361-1392 or (416) 359-5000 |
| Web site address: | www.jonesheward.com |
| E-mail address: | Through Web site |
| Minimum initial investment: | $1,000 |

## INVESTING TIPS

The funds are sold with the usual front- or back-end load option, although the back-end load is somewhat less onerous than the norm, with a maximum charge of 5% if you cash out before the end of two years. If possible, try to obtain the units on a front-end load basis paying zero commission. This will give you maximum flexibility to move out, which is important in a small family without many switching options.

## FUND SUMMARY

|  |  |
|---|---|
| Top Choices: | Bond, Money Market |
| Also Recommended: | Jones Heward, American |
| Promising Newcomers: | None |

# FUND RATINGS

## Top Choices

### Canadian Bond Funds

#### JONES HEWARD BOND FUND                      $$$ → FI #/* RSP CB

Manager: Jones Heward Investment Team

MER: 1.75%      Fundata: C

Suitability: Conservative investors

This is a pretty good bond fund, with above-average returns in recent years. Performance has been in either the first or second quartile since 1999. Corporate bonds represent over 40% of the assets, helping to bolster returns. The portfolio is conservative and the strategy is defensive to protect capital. That approach pulled down the long-term results to slightly below average. This fund is best suited for investors seeking a conservatively managed bond fund for the fixed-income side of their portfolio, and who don't mind sacrificing a bit of return for greater safety—the fund scores well on that count.

### Canadian Money Market Funds

#### JONES HEWARD MONEY MARKET FUND              $$$ → C # RSP CMM

Manager: Dorothy Biggs, since 1994

MER: 0.54%      Fundata: C

Suitability: Conservative investors

The 1998 cut in the management expense ratio (MER) of this fund from 1% to 0.5% provided a nice boost to returns. Since then, the fund has been returning almost half a percentage point more on an annualized basis than the average Canadian money market fund. Only a few funds of this type offer as low an MER and most of them require very high minimum investments. You can get into this fund for as little as $1,000. The fund is sold only on a front-end load basis, with a maximum commission of 2%. If you can get that fee waived, you've got a real bargain here. The portfolio is a mix of government and corporate notes.

## Also Recommended

### Canadian Equity Funds

### JONES HEWARD FUND                                    $$$ ↓ G #/* RSP CE

Manager: Jones Heward Investment Team

MER: 2.68%       Fundata: B       Style: GARP

Suitability: Long-term growth investors

Last year we were advised that this was a value fund. This year the style description provided by the company is growth at a reasonable price (GARP). That's a value-oriented style, but somewhat more aggressive than a traditional value fund. Despite this change in nuance, the fund continues to perform well with above-average scores over all time periods. The stocks are chosen using a fundamental, bottom-up approach and the portfolio is diversified across all capitalization groups (small, mid, and large). The main holdings in the first half of 2001 were of the blue-chip variety—a lot of banks, BCE, Nortel, Bombardier, Suncor, CP, and the like. Risk rating is very good. This is not one of the first-tier Canadian stock funds, but it is quite respectable. The fund was founded in 1939 as Group Investment Ltd., making it one of the oldest continuous funds in Canada.

### U.S. Equity Funds

### JONES HEWARD AMERICAN FUND                          $$ ↑ G #/* £ USE

Manager: Harris Bretall Sullivan & Smith LLC, since May 1995

MER: 2.68%       Fundata: E       Style: Growth

Suitability: Growth investors who can tolerate volatility

This is one of those feast or famine funds so if you invest here, be prepared. The San Francisco–based managers got off to a slow start after taking over in 1995, but they really hit their stride during the period from 1997 through to 1999 when technology was in the ascendancy, posting gains of 30%-plus each year. But the bubble burst in 2000 and after three straight top-quartile years the fund sank to the bottom of the pack, losing 37.5% over the 12 months to June 30/01. It was starting to show signs of recovery by the second quarter of 2001, however, and the next 12 months shouldn't be anywhere near as bleak. The managers use top-down economic analysis to identify those areas of the economy where they expect to outperform, and then use a bottom-up approach to choose the best large-cap stocks in the sectors they have picked. In the first half of 2001, the portfolio continued to be weighted toward technology stocks (31%) in anticipation of a recovery in that sector, but it also had good diversification in other areas. If a recovery does happen, all will be well, but that approach makes this fund more risky than many of its counterparts.

## Promising Newcomers

None.

# LAURENTIAN BANK OF CANADA

## THE COMPANY

In August 1998, the Laurentian Bank of Canada unveiled the IRIS Group of Funds, created from the amalgamation of the Cornerstone (North American Trust) and Savings and Investment Trust families of funds. Nine funds resulted. With the addition of 4 new funds the following month, the family grew to 13, and it has now expanded to 15.

The bank didn't stop there, however, in its move into the mutual funds business. In 1999, Laurentian teamed up with the Edmond de Rothschild Group to establish a joint venture mutual fund management company, BLC-Edmond de Rothschild. The fit was a good one, giving each partner access to new, sought-after territory. Rothschild gained a foothold in North America without having to establish a presence in the U.S., and Laurentian Bank gained much-needed expertise in European and Asian fund management. The fact that both institutions were francophone was icing on the cake.

The product of this marriage is a second group of funds, known as the R Funds. BLC-Edmond de Rothschild employs a top-down approach to investment, determining the regions of the globe they believe will outperform. Then they apply quantitative analysis to identify a pool of investment candidates. Finally, they narrow the field to final choices using a more qualitative approach: reviewing financials, interviewing management, etc.

There are now 10 core funds in this group, plus eight clones that are fully RRSP eligible. All focus on the large-cap end of the spectrum and there are no fewer than three separate European funds, reflecting Edmond de Rothschild's roots. Unfortunately, most of the R Funds have had a rough ride so far, with some recording huge losses in the year to June 30/01. As a result, we were not able to find any we could recommend at the present time. Note also that BLC-Edmond de Rothschild assumed the managerial role of manager of the IRIS funds.

Although we list a Web site for these funds, the information available there has been extremely sketchy. The company has taken note of the criticism we made in this regard in the last two editions, however. Rock Dumais, president of LBC Financial Services, a Laurentian Bank subsidiary, wrote us in mid-2001 to advise that improvements are on the way and should be in place by the time you read this edition. The updated site will include performance numbers, fact sheets, and daily asset values for all the funds sold through the bank. We welcome this initiative as it will make it much easier for investors to get the latest information about all the funds.

We would also like to see Laurentian provide names of the individual fund managers, rather than supplying only a corporate name. We believe that investors have a right to know who is looking after their money and to be informed if there are key managerial changes.

## THE DETAILS

| | |
|---|---|
| Number of funds: | IRIS: 15 |
| R Funds: | 10 |
| Assets under management: | $687.5 million |
| Load charge: | IRIS: None |
| | R Funds: Front max. 5%; Back max. 6% |
| Switching charge: | IRIS: None |
| | R Funds: 2% maximum |
| Where sold: | Across Canada except R Funds, which are not available in P.E.I. |
| How sold: | Through branches of Laurentian Bank, LBC Financial Services representatives, or independent dealers |
| Phone number: | IRIS: 1-800-565-6513 |
| | R Funds: 1-877-876-6989 |
| Web site address: | www.laurentianbank.ca |
| E-mail address: | N/A |
| Minimum initial investment: | $500 |

## INVESTING TIPS

Although both fund families are sold through Laurentian Bank branches, they are very different in their commission structure. The IRIS family is a no-load group, so in that respect it is similar to other bank fund families. The R Funds carry an optional front- or back-end load. Minimum initial investment is the same for both fund families. A mutual fund decision should not be made on the basis of commissions alone. However, if you are planning to invest through Laurentian Bank, you may wish to take their structure into account before making your final selection.

## FUND SUMMARY

### IRIS Funds

| | |
|---|---|
| Top Choices: | None |
| Also Recommended: | Balanced, Bond, Dividend, Global Equity, Mortgage, North American High-Yield Bond, U.S. Equity |
| Promising Newcomers: | Small-Cap Canadian Equity |

|  |  |
|---|---|
| The Rest: | Canadian Equity, Canadian Equity Index Plus, Money Market, Nasdaq 100 RSP Index, Strategic Income Option Balanced, Strategic Growth Option Balanced, Tactical Option Balanced |

## R Funds

|  |  |
|---|---|
| Top Choices: | None |
| Also Recommended: | None |
| Promising Newcomers: | None |
| The Rest: | American, Asian, Canadian Leaders, European, Europe Techno-Media, Life & Health, Money Market, Small- & Mid-Cap European, Techno-Media, World Leaders |

## FUND RATINGS

### Top Choices/IRIS Funds

None.

### Also Recommended/IRIS Funds

**Dividend Income Funds**

### IRIS DIVIDEND FUND                           $$ ↑ G NO RSP DIV

Manager: BLC-Edmond de Rothschild, since 2000

MER: 1.97%     Fundata: A     Style: Value

Suitability: Income investors prepared to accept higher risk

The objective of this fund is to generate tax-advantaged income (eligible for the dividend tax credit) and moderate capital accumulation. The managers may invest in common stocks, preferred shares, income trusts, or fixed-income securities. This was previously the Savings and Investment Trust Dividend Fund. Returns were above average for 1996 and 1997 under that name, but the fund then lost steam. It is on the road to recovery, however, and posted a good 21.1% gain over the year to June 30/01. This is not a pure dividend fund; only a small portion of the portfolio is in preferred shares. Most of the assets are invested in high-yielding common stocks, like banks and royalty trusts. Distributions are good, but the risk profile here is somewhat higher than with a typical dividend fund. In fact, this one actually recorded losses in calendar years 1998 and 1999. Give that history some thought when you're making your decision.

## U.S. Equity Funds

### IRIS U.S. EQUITY FUND $$ → G NO £ USE

Manager: BLC-Edmond de Rothschild, since 2000

MER: 2.26%      Fundata: C      Style: Top-down Growth

Suitability: Long-term growth investors

This fund invests mainly in S&P 500 companies, although the managers are not limited to that list. This is the old Savings and Investment Trust American Fund, merged with the Cornerstone U.S. Fund. It slipped to a third-quartile position in 1999, but moved back to above average in 2000 and the first half of 2001. A contributing factor to the relatively weak performance in 2000 was the heavy portfolio weighting in information technology (a third of the assets at the start of the year). However, the loss was only 6.1%, which was not bad considering the state of the markets. The fund slipped a further 4.7% in the first half of 2001. The portfolio is well diversified with familiar names like Citibank, Wal-Mart, and General Electric in the top 10 list in the first half of 2001. This fund is currently in a slump but should recover well when growth stocks come back into favour.

## Global and International Equity Funds

### IRIS GLOBAL EQUITY FUND $$ → G NO £ GE

Manager: BLC-Edmond de Rothschild, since 2000

MER: 2.41%      Fundata: C      Style: Top-down Growth

Suitability: Long-term growth investors

This fund is the amalgamation of the Savings and Investment Trust International Fund and the Cornerstone Global Fund. Its mandate allows it to invest around the world, including the U.S. Portions of the portfolio may also be placed in emerging markets. In the first half of 2001, this fund had toned down its previous leaning toward high-tech and presented a top 10 list that included several major oil companies and old standbys like Nestle. The fund recorded consistently strong gains through the mid-to-late 1990s, but lost 10% in 2000 and was down another 14% in the first half of 2001. As a result, we are reducing its rating to $$.

## Canadian Balanced and Asset Allocation Funds

### IRIS BALANCED FUND $$ → FI/G NO RSP CBAL

Manager: BLC-Edmond de Rothschild, since 2000

MER: 2.32%     Fundata: C     Style: Top-down Growth

Suitability: Long-term balanced investors

This portfolio holds a well-diversified mix of Canadian and international stocks, government and corporate bonds, and short-term notes. But it's a so-so performer and the portfolio actually declined by 6.6% over the year to June 30/01. Still, that wasn't terrible considering the general state of the markets. There's a lot of indexing going on in this portfolio, however, with S&P 500 deposit receipts, TSE i60 units, and MSCI Japan and U.K. iShares all in the top 10 holdings. An emphasis on indexing can work to an investor's advantage when markets are rising, but not so much when they're falling. This was the Cornerstone Balanced Fund, which merged with the Savings and Investment Trust Retirement Fund.

## Canadian Bond Funds

### IRIS BOND FUND $$ → FI NO RSP CB

Manager: BLC-Edmond de Rothschild

MER: 1.68%     Fundata: D

Suitability: Conservative investors

The mandate here is to invest in high-quality bonds, both government and corporate. Returns for the fund are below average over the long term, with a three-year average annual compound rate of return of just 3.3%. But the fund looked somewhat better in the first half of 2001, posting a small gain in a tough bond market. Not a great bond fund, but acceptable.

## Foreign Bond Funds

### IRIS NORTH AMERICAN HIGH-YIELD BOND FUND $$ ↑ FI NO RSP HYB

Manager: Elliott & Page, since 1998

MER: 2.31%     Fundata: B

Suitability: Aggressive investors

The mandate here permits this fund to invest in Canadian and U.S. corporate bonds, which may include unrated securities or even those that are in default at the time of purchase. Obviously there is more risk here than in an ordinary bond fund, but the potential returns are higher as well. The fund, under its revised mandate, got off to a good start under the direction of Elliott & Page, then ran into some problems. It appears to be back on track, however, and is coming off a good year with a gain of 7.9% for the 12 months to June 30/01. A decent choice in the high-yield category, but don't lose sight of the risk. Formerly the Savings and Investment Trust Global Bond Fund.

## Canadian Mortgage Funds

### IRIS MORTGAGE FUND                                    $$ → FI NO RSP M

Managers: BLC-Edmond de Rothschild

MER: 1.94%       Fundata: E

Suitability: Very conservative investors

Mortgage funds haven't been an exciting place to be in recent years, but they have looked better lately as short-term interest rates started falling. This fund recorded a nice 7.6% gain over the year to June 30/01 and it has become a respectable choice in its category. Formerly the Savings and Investment Trust Mortgage Fund.

## Promising Newcomers/IRIS Funds

### IRIS SMALL-CAP CANADIAN EQUITY FUND          NR ↑ G NO RSP CSC

Manager: Elliott & Page

MER: 3.32%       Fundata: A          Style: Growth

Suitability: Aggressive investors

So far this new small-cap entry from the IRIS group looks very good. With Elliott & Page as the portfolio advisors, the fund broke strong from the gate, posting a 32.8% gain in 1999, its first full calendar year. The managerial team followed that performance up with a 20.8% advance in 2000 and kept up the pace with an 11% gain in the first half of 2001. And remember that much of this was achieved in a period when the markets were very weak. The portfolio includes both small- and mid-cap companies, with names like Investors Group, Canadian Utilities, and parent company Laurentian Bank in the portfolio in the first half of 2001. We're impressed by the quick start of this fund. Let's hope E&P can keep it up.

## Top Choices/R Funds

None.

## Also Recommended/R Funds

None.

## Promising Newcomers/R Funds

None.

# LEITH WHEELER INVESTMENT COUNSEL

## THE COMPANY

This is a Vancouver-based, employee-owned company, founded in 1982 by Murray Leith and Bill Wheeler. It has been working hard to establish a foothold in the crowded mutual funds market place; most Canadians, however, are still not familiar with it. The firm currently manages more than $3.2 billion worth of assets for individuals, foundations, charitable organizations, and pension funds. The mutual fund line is just a small part of its total business, with $287 million in assets under management. Its managerial style is a conservative, value-oriented approach. Initially available in only B.C. and Alberta, the funds may now also be purchased by residents of Ontario, Manitoba, and Saskatchewan.

## THE DETAILS

|  |  |
|---|---|
| Number of funds: | 6 |
| Assets under management: | $287 million |
| Load charge: | None |
| Where sold: | Alberta, B.C., Manitoba, Ontario, and Saskatchewan |
| How sold: | Directly through Leith Wheeler or through brokers |
| Phone number: | 1-888-292-1122 |
| Web site address: | www.leithwheeler.com |
| E-mail address: | info@leithwheeler.com |
| Minimum initial investment: | $50,000 (The International Fund is open only to clients with a portfolio of $500,000 or more) |

## INVESTING TIPS

If you're considering investing in these funds, we recommend you buy your units directly from the company on a no-load basis. Although units are technically available through brokers and planners, they may be reluctant to acquire them for you because Leith Wheeler pays no trailer fees—they are one of the last holdouts in the industry. There is a toll-free number you can call to place an order (see The Details section).

Note that the minimum initial investment here is $50,000. It can be divided among several funds if you wish.

# FUND SUMMARY

Top Choices: Balanced, Canadian Equity, Fixed-Income, Money Market

Also Recommended: None

Promising Newcomers: N/A

The Rest: None

# FUND RATINGS

## Top Choices

### Canadian Equity Funds

### LEITH WHEELER CANADIAN EQUITY FUND $$$ ↓ G NO RSP CE

Manager: Leith Wheeler Investment Committee, since inception (1994)

MER: 1.40%    Fundata: C    Style: Bottom-up Value

Suitability: Low-risk investors, especially with non-registered portfolios

Like most value funds, this buy-and-hold entry experienced hard times in the late 1990s. As a result, its three-year average annual compound rate of return is a sickly looking 2.9% (to June 30/01). Like most other value funds, however, it staged a comeback starting in the second half of 2000 and is looking much stronger these days. If you are looking for a fund for a non-registered portfolio, this one may be of interest to you. All securities are purchased with the intention of retaining them for two to four years, so there isn't a lot of active trading going on. This makes for a tax-efficient portfolio with little in the way of annual distributions to attract the attention of the Canada Customs and Revenue Agency. The portfolio mainly consists of large-cap stocks, but a few small- and mid-cap companies are mixed in. Interest-sensitive stocks (financial services and utilities) were by far the largest holding in the first part of 2001, with a weighting of more than 40%. Technology positions were non-existent. Historically, this fund has always been defensive by nature. That means it will tend to underperform in bull markets, but protect your assets in bear markets. As a recent example, the fund actually made a profit in the first half of 2001 when the overall TSE was falling.

## Canadian Balanced Funds

### LEITH WHEELER BALANCED FUND $$$ ↓ FI/G NO RSP CBAL

Manager: Leith Wheeler Investment Committee, since inception (1987)

MER: 1.10%     Fundata: D     Style: Bottom-up Value

Suitability: Conservative investors

The story here is similar to that of the companion Canadian Equity Fund: the fund spent years wandering in the value wilderness and is now being rewarded with above-average gains. The portfolio of this fund is constructed well and it makes good use of U.S. stocks to add foreign content and boost returns. The investment parameters of this fund have narrowed somewhat in recent years. In the past, the managers enjoyed a fairly wide latitude in determining their asset allocation: the fund could hold between 25% and 75% in equities. Now, however, the equity range is usually limited to between 45% and 65% of the total portfolio. In the first half of 2001, the balance was 60% stocks (39% of which were Canadian) with the rest in bonds and cash. As you might expect, three-year returns are below average. But longer-term results are comfortably above par, as are the most recent results. Like the Canadian Equity Fund, this one is defensive in nature, making it a sound choice in turbulent markets. The fund name changed from Leith Wheeler All-Value Balanced Fund in 1994.

## Canadian Bond Funds

### LEITH WHEELER FIXED-INCOME FUND $$$ ↓ FI NO RSP CB

Manager: Leith Wheeler Investment Committee, since inception (1994)

MER: 0.75%     Fundata: B     Style: Value

Suitability: Conservative investors

This portfolio invests mainly in government issues, but the portion of corporate bonds in the portfolio has been steadily increasing in an effort to boost returns and is now up to almost 40%. The fund is an above-average performer over all time periods, due in part to its low management expense ratio (MER). Until 1999, this fund had a great safety record; it was one of the few bond funds we'd encountered that had never been in the red over any calendar year since its inception. But that changed in the down market as the fund slipped about 2%. It has bounced back nicely since then, however, and was one of the top performers in its category over the year to June 30/01 with a gain of 5.9%.

## LEITH WHEELER MONEY MARKET FUND          $$$ ↓ C NO RSP CMM

Manager: Leith Wheeler Investment Committee, since inception (1994)

MER: 0.60%          Fundata: E          Style: Value

Suitability: Conservative investors

This fund is consistently among the better performers in the Canadian Money Market category, helped by its low MER of 0.6%. It invests primarily in high-grade corporate notes, with slightly less than a third of the portfolio in T-bills.

## Also Recommended

None.

## Promising Newcomers

N/A

# MACKENZIE FINANCIAL CORPORATION

## THE COMPANY

The big story of the year in the mutual fund business was the purchase in early 2001 of giant Mackenzie Financial by the even bigger giant, Investors Group, which in turn is majority-owned by Power Corporation. However, this is a takeover with a difference: in all previous acquisitions of this kind, the company being purchased has effectively disappeared. In many cases, so has its line of mutual funds (e.g., Global Strategy into AGF). However, some fund lines have retained their own brand names while forming part of the new group (Bissett [Franklin Templeton] and Trimark [AIM] are notable examples).

In this case, Mackenzie is continuing to operate as a stand-alone company; no attempt has been made to integrate its funds with those of Investors Group. One of the reasons for this independence is that they are sold through different distribution channels—Investors has its own captive sales force, while Mackenzie funds are sold through all brokers, planners, and fund dealers.

This current practice doesn't mean there won't be some rationalization in the future. In fact, it has already begun. It was announced in July 2001 that the Scudder and MAXXUM funds, also owned by Investors Group, are being brought under the Mackenzie banner. This move is clearly designed to reduce costs and may well lead to fund mergers down the road.

At the time of the announcement, Mackenzie also revealed that it was dismissing all the MAXXUM fund managers except the U.S.-based Janus organization and replacing them with people from its existing team. Therefore, all historical MAXXUM results have to be treated with extreme caution. Also, because of the wholesale managerial changes, we are recommending very few MAXXUM funds at this time. We expect that most—if not all—of the MAXXUM funds will be folded into existing Mackenzie funds and the trade name will vanish.

No announcement had been made by our writing deadline about the future management of the Scudder funds, but Mackenzie senior officials did say they were reviewing these funds closely as part of a total corporate overhaul. So there may well be changes by the time you read this book.

As a result of these changes, we are showing MAXXUM and Scudder as families within the Mackenzie line-up for the purposes of this edition.

The changes outlined above are not likely to be the only ones. A senior Mackenzie official told us that the company's entire line-up is under review. There is no question that it has become unwieldy; counting MAXXUM and Scudder, the company currently has more than 200 stand-alone funds and portfolios on offer. To that, add another 40-plus segregated funds, launched in combination with Great-West Life (which is also part of the Power Corp. empire), and you have a range of choices so broad that even the most experienced investor will need a road map.

So expect more changes going forward. Some may even have been announced by the time you read this edition of the *Guide*, so check with a financial advisor before investing.

## THE DETAILS

| | |
|---|---|
| Number of funds: | 141 funds plus 17 STAR and 19 Keystone funds and portfolios |
| Assets under management: | $32.8 billion |
| Load charge: | Varies. Front: max. 5% (generally); Back: max. 5.5% (generally) |
| Switching charge: | 2% maximum |
| Where sold: | Across Canada |
| How sold: | Through brokers, dealers, and financial planners |
| Phone number: | 1-888-653-7070 or (416) 922-5322 |
| Web site address: | www.mackenziefinancial.com |
| E-mail address: | invest@mackenziefinancial.com |
| Minimum initial investment: | $500 |

## INVESTING TIPS

There are now seven fund families under the Mackenzie roof: Cundill, Industrial, Ivy, Universal, MAXXUM, Scudder, and a pure Mackenzie line with no other brand designation. It's important to differentiate among them when making your investment decisions. Here's a capsule summary of each group's approach:

- *Cundill.* Deep value bias. Stocks at 50¢ on the dollar is the goal. Contrarian in approach; Peter Cundill typically buys stocks in markets that no one else will touch. These funds tend to lag in strong markets but are very good performers when stocks in general are falling.
- *Industrial.* Mackenzie's roots. Funds here still place a big emphasis on the resource sector, although Bill Procter is trying to steer them into different directions. Traditional approach.
- *Ivy.* Growth with reasonable risk. No big chances here. A conservative, straightforward style that most investors will feel comfortable with.
- *Universal.* The go-go family. Higher risk and higher reward potential. Best suited to more aggressive investors.
- *MAXXUM.* The new managers of the funds are mainly from the Industrial group. Look for this line to be merged into that brand.

- *Scudder.* Traditionally value investors, akin to Ivy in their approach. It would not surprise us to see a matchup of those two lines.
- *Mackenzie.* Mainly fixed-income and money market funds.

Mackenzie also offers 17 STAR portfolios, managed by Garmaise Investment Technologies. These are portfolios of Mackenzie funds that provide an asset allocation approach to investing suitable for a range of needs and objectives. There are four different classes of portfolios, as follows:

- *Registered.* Eligible for registered plans and contains foreign content up to the allowable limit.
- *Canadian.* Eligible for registered plans, contains no foreign content funds, but does provide foreign exposure through derivatives.
- *Investment.* Blend of Canadian and foreign funds, not intended for registered plans.
- *Foreign.* Complete foreign content, no Canadian exposure.

In line with our policy of not reviewing "funds of funds," the STAR portfolios are not rated. Check the details of the underlying funds.

Mackenzie had been promoting a second portfolio-based product line called Keystone. It offered a blend of Mackenzie funds along with those from other companies. However, it underwent a complete overhaul in late 2000. The revamped Keystone line offers stand-alone versions of funds actually managed by several outside firms, such as AGF, Altamira, Beutel Goodman, C.I., Saxon, Sceptre, Spectrum, and U.K.-based Premier, which is 25% owned by Mackenzie. These funds can be purchased separately or in combination through what is called the Keystone Strategic Asset Allocation Program. Frankly, we have some difficulty seeing the usefulness of this plan for most investors. Except for the Premier line, all the Keystone funds can be purchased independently in their original versions, often on a no-load basis and with lower MERs. The Keystone approach does allow a financial advisor to mix funds in one portfolio that are both load and no-load in their basic versions, something an individual investor might find difficult—but not impossible—to achieve. However, we have to wonder just how viable this new approach really is, and we suggest you approach it with caution. We will not review these funds separately, as they are basically other funds with a Keystone branding. See the write-ups on the underlying funds for information and ratings.

In another recent initiative, Mackenzie announced the creation of a series of "Capital Class" funds. The concept is similar to the umbrella funds already offered by companies like C.I. (who started it all), AGF, AIM, Clarington, and others. The "classes" are pools of money within a master fund. Investors can switch among the various pools without attracting capital gains tax liability. If you're investing in a non-registered portfolio and you move your money around a lot, take a look at them. They are essentially versions of existing Mackenzie funds, so they will not be reviewed separately.

At the same time, Mackenzie unveiled two innovative tax-efficient funds: Mackenzie Canadian Managed Yield Capital Class and Mackenzie U.S. Managed Yield Capital Class. Essentially, both are money market funds that have been structured in such a way so as to yield capital gains rather than interest income. They're suitable only for non-registered plans, and then only if you keep a lot of cash in money market funds and want to reduce the tax bite.

Mackenzie's new line of segregated funds offers two levels of guarantees. One group provides only 75% protection against loss, while the other guarantees 100% of your principal. The company says the new line-up has been structured in accordance with the recent regulatory changes, which have resulted in many seg funds closing shop and others raising their management fees. The Mackenzie/Great-West product is "built to last" and is competitively priced, the company claims. Check with a financial advisor for full details before you buy. These funds are simply existing Mackenzie mutual funds with a segregated wrapper (guarantees, etc.), so they will not be reviewed or rated separately.

Also in the past year, Mackenzie launched its own version of a hedge fund for high net worth investors. It's called Mackenzie Alternative Strategies Fund, and the entry fee is a cool $150,000. It's too early to tell if it's worth the price of a ticket.

For MAXXUM and Scudder investors, note that Scudder discontinued the sale of its no-load Classic units early in 2001, so the only versions now offered are the Advisor series, which carry an optional front- or back-end load. However, investors in the Classic units may retain them and we recommend doing so because they carry a much lower management expense ratio (MER). Special units of the MAXXUM and Scudder funds are also sold by the Quadrus Group of Funds.

## FUND SUMMARY

### Cundill Funds

| | |
|---:|:---|
| Top Choices: | Canadian Security, Value |
| Also Recommended: | None |
| Promising Newcomers: | Canadian Balanced, Global Balanced, Recovery |
| The Rest: | None |

### Industrial Group of Funds

| | |
|---:|:---|
| Top Choices: | Balanced, Dividend Growth, Horizon, Income, Pension |
| Also Recommended: | None |

Promising Newcomers: None
The Rest: Bond, Equity, Growth, Short-Term Segregated

## Ivy Funds

Top Choices: Canadian, Enterprise, Foreign Equity,
Growth & Income
Also Recommended: None
Promising Newcomers: None
The Rest: Global Balanced

## Universal Funds

Top Choices: Canadian Growth, Canadian Resource
Also Recommended: Canadian Balanced, Future, Precious Metals,
World Income RRSP, World Real Estate, World
Tactical Bond
Promising Newcomers: Financial Services, World Resource
The Rest: Americas, Communications, European
Opportunities, Far East, Global Ethics, Health
Sciences, International Stock, Internet
Technologies, Japan, Select Managers, Select
Managers Canada, U.S. Blue Chip, U.S.
Emerging Growth, World Balanced RRSP, World
Emerging Growth, World Growth RRSP, World
High-Yield, World Precious Metals Capital
Class, World Science & Technology, World Value

## MAXXUM Funds

Top Choices: Dividend
Also Recommended: Money Market, Natural Resource
Promising Newcomers: None
The Rest: Canadian Balanced, Canadian Equity Growth,
Income, Janus American Equity, Janus Global
Equity, Precious Metals,

## Scudder Funds

Top Choices: Canadian Bond
Also Recommended: Canadian Short-Term Bond,
Canadian Small Company
Promising Newcomers: None

The Rest: Canadian Equity, Canadian Money Market,
Emerging Markets, Global, Greater Europe,
Pacific, U.S. Growth & Income

## Mackenzie Funds

Top Choices: Cash Management
Also Recommended: Mortgage, U.S. Money Market
Promising Newcomers: Yield Advantage
The Rest: Money Market

## FUND RATINGS

## Top Choices/Cundill Funds

### Canadian Equity Funds

**MACKENZIE CUNDILL CANADIAN**      **$$$$ ↓ G #/* RSP CE**
**SECURITY FUND**

Managers: Alan Pasnik and Peter Cundill, since September 1998

MER: C Units 2.47% Fundata: A    Style: Core Value

Suitability: Conservative investors

This fund used to be classed as a small-cap, but now the mandate has been expanded and it invests in all types of stocks. Top 10 holdings in mid-2001 included well-known names like National Bank, Royal Bank, and Noranda Inc. Like all the funds in the Cundill line, the managers take a deep-value approach to investing, meaning they buy only stocks that are trading at significant discounts to their underlying value. It's an approach that can produce indifferent results when stock markets are raging, but it works wonders in bear markets. No surprise, then, that this fund has been shining lately. The one-year gain to June 30/01 was a terrific 20.5% (C units), one of the best in the category. The three-year average annual return for the A units (no longer sold) is a very good 12.8%. The C units will produce a slightly lower return because of a higher management expense ration (MER), but it's not a big deal when the fund is doing well. We are upgrading this fund to a $$$$ rating, and it is a good choice in the current investment climate. A segregated version is also available.

### MACKENZIE CUNDILL VALUE FUND                    $$$$ → G #/* £ GE

Managers: Peter Cundill, since 1974 and David Briggs and Tim McElvaine, since 1998

MER: C Units 2.65%      Fundata: A      Style: Core Value

Suitability: Conservative investors

This fund is looking much better these days after a prolonged slump. That's largely because manager Peter Cundill went shopping in Japan while it was cheap. He was then able to sit back and watch as his prescience paid off big time in 1999, propelling the fund to a one-year gain of 16.6% as of June 30/00. During a period when most value funds were taking it on the chin, that was a pretty good result. What is somewhat surprising is that in mid-2001, the portfolio was still heavily concentrated in Japan (42%), at a time when that country was struggling economically and the Nikkei Index was sagging. Again, it's an example of the Cundill approach at work: look for bargains where most managers fear to tread. Interestingly, Canadian stocks led by Fairfax Financial occupied the number two rank, at 15% of assets. No one has ever accused Peter Cundill of running with the herd! The result was a one-year gain of 22.6% in the year to June 30/01, at a time when most global funds were recording losses. That performance was good enough to put the fund in the top five of the category. Three-year average annual return for the A units (no longer sold, but the only ones with a three-year record) was 18.4%. This fund has an historic pattern of performing very well in down markets and very poorly in strong ones. So while we are raising the rating to $$$$ in the current investment climate, we caution that the fund is not likely to retain its lofty level once a market recovery takes hold in earnest. Right now, however, it's one to own. An RRSP-eligible clone of this fund is also available, as well as a segregated version and a Capital Class version.

### Also Recommended/Cundill Funds

None.

## Promising Newcomers/Cundill Funds

### Global and International Equity Funds

### MACKENZIE CUNDILL RECOVERY FUND NR → G #/* £ GE

Managers: Peter Cundill and James Morton, since inception (September 1998)

MER: C Units 2.95%     Fundata: A     Style: Core Value

Suitability: Conservative investors

Here's a fund that is perfectly in tune with the Cundill philosophy of looking to buy a dollar for fifty cents. Its mandate is to invest in companies that are underperforming, in turnaround situations, or have low credit ratings—or any combination thereof. You've heard of junk bond funds? This might be described as a junk stock fund. As such, it may have a higher degree of risk than you would normally expect to find in a global equity fund. However, it has not been in existence long enough for statistical data to bear that theory out, so we are classifying it as medium risk for now. It is certainly off to a fine start. One-year gain to June 30/01 was an excellent 19.5%. Where were the managers finding the "junk" that was doing so well? Mainly in the U.K., surprisingly, which accounted for 27% of the assets in mid-2001. Canada was the next best choice for junk stocks, with 17% of the portfolio. Japan and China were other happy hunting grounds. If you like this concept, Cundill and his team are probably the best in the business at pulling it off. But beware of the risk.

### Canadian Balanced and Asset Allocation Funds

### MACKENZIE CUNDILL CANADIAN BALANCED FUND NR → G #/* RSP CBAL

Managers: Alan Pasnik and Peter Cundill, since inception (September 1998)

MER: C Units 2.53%     Fundata: A     Style: Core Value

Suitability: Conservative investors

With the Cundill equity funds doing so well, it is hardly a surprise that this relatively new balanced fund is also turning in some impressive numbers. The one-year gain to June 30/01 was a fine 17% for the C units. The segregated version actually did even better, with a 21.8% gain—good enough for number one in the Canadian Balanced category. However, that result was really a matter of investment timing, and the discrepancy between the versions is unlikely to continue. The equity portfolio is similar to that of the Canadian Security Fund (same management team). Bonds formed 30% of the mix in mid-2001 and there was a 7% cash position. This fund is likely to show the same pattern as the other Cundill entries, with the best results in down markets. Risk should be medium to low.

## Global Balanced and Asset Allocation Funds

### MACKENZIE CUNDILL GLOBAL BALANCED FUND    NR → G #/* £ GBAL

Managers: Alan Pasnik, David Briggs, and Peter Cundill, since inception (October 1999)

MER: C Units 2.53%    Fundata: N/A    Style: Core Value

Suitability: Conservative investors

This is the Cundill line's global balanced entry. It's the most recent fund to be added to this group and, like the others, it performed very well as markets tumbled in 2000–01. One-year gain to June 30/01 was 11.3%, good for a number two ranking in the category. The equities side of the portfolio (54.2% in mid-2001) contains many of the names from the Cundill Value Fund. The bond side (30%) consists mainly of Government of Canada issues. This fund is a good conservative choice in the current climate.

## Top Choices/Industrial Group of Funds

### Canadian Equity Funds

### MACKENZIE INDUSTRIAL HORIZON FUND    $$$$ → G #/* RSP CLC

Manager: Bill Procter, since November 1996

MER: 2.48%    Fundata: A    Style: Value/Growth

Suitability: Middle-of-the-road investors

Bill Procter assumed portfolio responsibility for this long-time laggard in November 1996 and immediately started to implement changes. The natural resource component of this fund was pared down while the financial services and industrial products sectors were boosted. The number of stocks held was cut in half, from 80 to about 40. The mandate was clearly defined to focus on large-cap companies in established industries. Procter is a bottom-up manager who chooses stocks on the basis of fundamentals. The fund did well in the first full year under his mandate, gaining 14.7% in 1997. But it slumped in 1998 and 1999 before recovering in 2000–01. In other words, its performance has been all over the place since Procter took charge. Right now, it's doing well. The one-year gain to June 30/01 was 15.4%, very good in light of the rough stock market conditions. The style is officially listed as a value/growth blend, but the performance and the portfolio suggest that value is really in the ascendancy here. The fund focus is on banks, conglomerates, and a few energy companies like Talisman. So what you're really getting here is a middle-of-the-road large-cap fund. We moving this one up to a $$$$ rating because a value-investing, Old Economy approach seems to be back in favour among investors and this fund fits the bill. A segregated version is offered, and there's a Capital Class version as well.

## Dividend Income Funds

### MACKENZIE INDUSTRIAL DIVIDEND GROWTH FUND

$$$ ↑ G #/* RSP DIV

Manager: Bill Procter, since December 1994

MER: 2.47%     Fundata: A     Style: Value/Growth

Suitability: Investors seeking a combination of income and growth

This is not a classic dividend fund. The portfolio is heavily weighted toward dividend-paying common stocks rather than preferreds, with names like Bank of Montreal, BCE, and Brascan among the largest holdings. And there is a relatively large U.S. stock component (20% in the first half of 2001) that does not fit into a genuine dividend fund. So this continues to be a fund for those who want a combination of income and growth, rather than pure income. The fund pays a monthly distribution of 5¢ per share, and some of that is tax-sheltered if received outside a registered plan. For example, in calendar 2000, almost half of the distributions from this fund were treated as "return of capital," accordingly received on a tax-deferred basis. The fund's total returns slumped in the late 1990s, but have picked up over the past two years. The fund recorded a gain of 11.6% for the 12 months to June 30/00 and followed that with an advance of 18.7% in the latest year. Longer-term results out to five years are above average for the Dividend Income category. This is a decent choice for a conservative portfolio held outside an RRSP/RRIF, although risk is somewhat higher than you'd expect from a true dividend fund. A segregated version of this fund is also available.

## Canadian Balanced and Asset Allocation Funds

### MACKENZIE INDUSTRIAL BALANCED FUND     $$$ ↑ G/FI #/* RSP CBAL

Managers: Tim Gleeson and Chris Kresic, since December 1997

MER: 2.48%     Fundata: B     Style: Value/Interest Rate Anticipation

Suitability: Balanced investors willing to accept higher risk

Although officially described as a balanced fund, this entry's managers have been steadily moving away from anything resembling true balance in the past couple of years. They have been increasingly weighting the fund toward equities, and stocks made up more than 80% of the portfolio in mid-2001. As a result, you should expect a higher degree of risk from this fund than from a typical balanced entry. Despite this weighting and plunging stock markets, the fund managed to produce a very respectable gain of 11.5% in the year to June 30/01. Some of the stocks in the portfolio did very well, including Talisman Energy, Manulife Financial, and Oxford Properties. We don't like this fund for a conservatively managed portfolio such as an RRIF, but it could work well in a younger person's RRSP. Rating moves up to $$$. A segregated version is available.

## MACKENZIE INDUSTRIAL INCOME FUND $$$ ↓ FI/G #/* RSP CBAL

Managers: Tim Gleeson, since 1992 and Bill Procter, since 1998

MER: 1.93%    Fundata: A    Style: Relative Value

Suitability: Conservative investors

This is not a true fixed-income fund (despite the name), hence its inclusion in the balanced section. Federal government bonds are the core holding, but the manager may invest a portion of the fund's assets in stocks and the fund also holds some real estate investment trusts (REITs). In the first half of 2001, equities represented 40% of the portfolio. The A units are the original ones, and pay an annual distribution of $1 each, a portion of which is a non-taxable return of capital (which means the portfolio is not generating enough cash to make up the whole amount, so it gives you some of your money back). The B units pay an annual distribution of about 40¢ each. Both the A and B units are otherwise the same. Mackenzie warns that A unitholders who receive distributions in cash will deplete their investment in the fund over time, which will lead to "administrative complexities." The company encourages Class A unitholders to make a non-taxable switch to Class B shares to avoid this problem, and no longer offers A units for sale. If you own A units and stay with them, the fund is better held outside a registered plan so you can take advantage of the tax-deferred income you will receive. If you choose the B units, more money will be left in the fund and the value of your units will be worth more over time. As far as total returns are concerned, the fund gained 9.4% in the year to June 30/01. This fund comes in a segregated version as well.

## MACKENZIE INDUSTRIAL PENSION FUND $$$ → G/FI #/* RSP CBAL

Manager: Bill Procter, since March 1995

MER: 2.48%    Fundata: A    Style: Value/Growth

Suitability: Middle-of-the-road investors

This fund invests mainly in stocks, with a small bond component tossed in (23% in the first half of 2001 plus an 8% cash position). So this is a fund to choose if you're looking for a Mackenzie entry that emphasizes stocks (although to a lesser extent than the companion Industrial Balanced Fund) while offering some fixed-income exposure as well. In the past year it was the best performer among the Industrial group's three-horse balanced entry, with a nice gain of 15.9%. There is no monthly cash flow here, however, so if that's your need, look to Industrial Income. There's a segregated version if you'd prefer.

## Also Recommended/Industrial Group of Funds

None.

## Promising Newcomers/Industrial Group of Funds

None.

## Top Choices/Ivy Funds

### Canadian Equity Funds

**MACKENZIE IVY CANADIAN FUND**               $$$ ↓ G #/* RSP CE

Managers: Jerry Javasky and Chuck Roth, since June 1997

MER: 2.47%      Fundata: A      Style: Value/Growth

Suitability: Conservative investors

Mackenzie officially says the style of this fund is a value/growth blend, and that's a good description. Co-manager Jerry Javasky is known in the financial community as an ultraconservative value manager, but Chuck Roth brings a growth orientation to the portfolio. It's a mix that's working, although not as spectacularly as the Cundill entries at the present time. Gain for the 12 months to June 30/01 was 6.7%, well above average for the Canadian Equity category. The managers aim for a core of about 25 positions, each representing about 4% of the total assets. The objective is to provide above-average returns with below-average risk. The fund generally does that job quite well—returns for all time periods are above the group average, while the risk level is low. That combination tells you why it earns an A rating from Fundata. If you're a conservative investor, you should take a close look at this fund. It's one of the better entries in the Mackenzie stable. Segregated and Capital Class versions are also available.

### Canadian Small-to-Mid-Cap Equity Funds

**MACKENZIE IVY ENTERPRISE FUND**               $$$ ↓ G #/* RSP CSC

Managers: Joe Mastrolonardo and Stephanie Griffiths, since November 1999

MER: 2.50%      Fundata: A      Style: Value/Growth

Suitability: More aggressive investors

This fund struggled in 1998 and 1999 but it has looked much better since being taken over by a new team late in 1999. Performance has been much stronger and the fund gained a solid 7.7% in the year to June 30/01. The three-year results are still below average for the category, but the trend is right. Another factor in the fund's favour is that risk is quite low for a small-cap entry. As of mid-2001, the managers had a large cash position (19.3%) to help cushion the asset base in a falling market. Rating moves up to $$$. Segregated and Capital Class versions are also available. Formerly called Mackenzie Equity Fund.

## Global and International Equity Funds

### MACKENZIE IVY FOREIGN EQUITY FUND $$$ ↓ G #/* £ GE

Manager: Jerry Javasky, since April 1999 (previously 1992–97)

MER: 2.49%    Fundata: A    Style: Value/Growth

Suitability: Conservative investors

It's déjà vu: Jerry Javasky ran this fund from 1992 to 1997 before handing over portfolio responsibility to Bill Kanko; now Kanko is running the Trimark Fund for AIM and Javasky is back in charge. This fund's main emphasis is on U.S. stocks (57% of the portfolio in the first half of 2001), but there are several other countries represented as well, with Europe quite prominent. The fund was also sitting on a big chunk of cash (16%) in mid-2001. Returns had been above average for the Global Equity category, but they slipped in 1999–2000 with a loss of 0.3% for the year to June 30/00. However, Javasky has made a good recovery and the fund scored a gain of 11.4% in the latest 12-month period, bringing its average returns over all time periods (to five years) to well above par for funds of this type. Historically, the fund has a better-than-average safety rating. In early 1999, Mackenzie launched an RRSP-eligible clone of this fund, the Ivy RSP Foreign Equity Fund. It should be your choice if you want to hold this fund in a registered plan. There is also a segregated version and a Capital Class version. The Universal Growth Fund was merged into this one in mid-1998.

## Canadian Balanced and Asset Allocation Funds

### MACKENZIE IVY GROWTH & INCOME FUND $$$ ↓ FI/G #/* RSP CBAL

Manager: Jerry Javasky, since June 1997

MER: 2.20%    Fundata: A    Style: Value/Growth

Suitability: Conservative investors

This entry has evolved into a true balanced fund since Jerry Javasky assumed portfolio responsibility in 1997. However, this fund has no set asset allocation parameters, so the ratios can swing dramatically in any direction at any time. For example, in the first half of 2001, bonds represented only 34% of the mix, down from 42% the previous year. Cash was another 5%, and the rest was in Canadian and foreign (mainly U.S.) stocks. Returns have recovered somewhat after a brief slump; the fund gained 10.3% over the 12 months to June 30/00 and followed that performance up with a 6.6% advance to June 30/01. Long-term results are well above average for the Canadian Balanced category. Good safety record. If you're looking for a sound balanced fund with growth potential for your RRSP, this is a good choice. Also available in a segregated version.

## Also Recommended/Ivy Funds

None.

## Promising Newcomers/Ivy Funds

None.

## Top Choices/Universal Funds

### Canadian Equity Funds

#### MACKENZIE UNIVERSAL CANADIAN GROWTH FUND $$$ ↓ G #/* RSP CE

Managers: Dina DeGeer, since August 1995 and Dennis Starritt, since November 1996

MER: 2.48%      Fundata: B        Style: Value/Growth

Suitability: Middle-of-the-road investors

Two former Trimark managers oversee this fund. They maintain a relatively small portfolio of about 25 to 30 Canadian companies, plus a few U.S. and international stocks selected (without overpaying) on the basis of growth potential. The fund went through a rough patch in 1999, gaining just 4.9% and dropping to the bottom 25% of its peer group. However, things perked up in the first half of 2000, with a 14.4% advance, spurred by good results from companies like BCE, Cognos, and Westaim. In the latest 12 months to June 30/01, the fund finished just above break-even, although that was much better than average for the category. Longer-term results are also above average. The fund invests across all capitalization classes, so you are likely to find some names you don't recognize in the portfolio. It's somewhat more volatile than Ivy Canadian, for example, although overall risk is still well below average for the category. As of the first half of 2000, the managers were sitting on a lot of cash (25% of the assets), which gave the portfolio a defensive cast. We like the prospects for this fund, although the Ivy or Cundill entries look better in the current environment. The rating is maintained at $$$. A segregated version is also offered.

## Sector Equity Funds

### MACKENZIE UNIVERSAL CANADIAN RESOURCE FUND

$$$ → G #/* RSP NR

Manager: Fred Sturm, since 1991

MER: 2.52%     Fundata: A     Style: Value/Growth

Suitability: Aggressive investors

Resource investors finally caught a break! Most funds in the category did very well in the past year, but this one did better than most, posting an advance of 25.7% for the 12 months to June 30/01. That result was enough to pull the returns over all time periods to well above average. The portfolio is well diversified, with a slight tilt toward energy. But the risks are high in the resource category, and this fund is about average in that regard. If you're considering putting money here because you expect the boom in resource stocks to continue, don't lose sight of that fact. Make sure you understand what you're getting into and be prepared to take profits when they occur and exit. The $$$ rating is reflective of this fund's relatively good results within its own category.

## Also Recommended/Universal Funds

## Canadian Equity Funds

### MACKENZIE UNIVERSAL FUTURE FUND

$$ ↑ G #/* RSP CE

Manager: John Rohr, since October 1993

MER: 2.48%     Fundata: D     Style: Value/Growth

Suitability: Aggressive investors

The mandate of this fund is to focus on technology companies, and we all know what has happened to them in the past year. The balance is supposed to be invested in other growth-oriented stocks, although 17.4% of the portfolio was in cash in the first half of 2001. Although this entry is perceived as a small-cap fund by some people, the portfolio actually contains many large companies such as BCE, Bombardier, Nortel, Thomson, and Celestica—so don't be misled. Foreign content is kept near the maximum limit to allow significant investment in the U.S. technology market. Recent results have been poor (as you might expect), but not as poor as those chalked up by pure science and technology funds. The fund lost 21.9% over the year to June 30/01. However, its longer-term results are above average, which is why it remains on our Recommended List. There is a segregated version available. Note that the name was changed from Industrial Future Fund in January 1998.

## Sector Equity Funds

### MACKENZIE UNIVERSAL PRECIOUS METALS FUND   $$$ ↑ G #/* RSP PM

Manager: Fred Sturm, since inception (February 1994)

MER: 2.56%     Fundata: A     Style: Value/Growth

Suitability: Aggressive investors

This fund has a widely diversified portfolio across the precious metals sector that includes both senior and junior companies. Like most precious metals funds, it was a laggard through most of the 1990s. But recently the whole sector has come to life and this entry turned in a terrific gain of 38.1% over the year to June 30/01. That pulled up longer-term results to above average, but let's keep matters in perspective: even with that great one-year performance, this fund still shows an average annual compound rate of return over five years of –6.3%. This isn't a buy-and-hold type of fund, but if you think the gold rush is going to last a while, be our guest. Just remember that a high level of risk is involved.

## Canadian Balanced and Asset Allocation Funds

### MACKENZIE UNIVERSAL $$ → FI/G #/* RSP CBAL
### CANADIAN BALANCED FUND

Managers: Dina DeGeer and Dennis Starritt, since inception (November 1996)

MER: 2.29%     Fundata: B     Style: Value/Growth

Suitability: Middle-of-the-road investors

This is the same managerial team that runs the companion Universal Canadian Growth Fund, so the equities side of the portfolio is very similar. As of mid-2001, just over half the assets were in the stock market. There was a 38.7% bond position and 9.7% in cash, so this is a true balanced fund. Foreign content is used well, composing 15% of the portfolio. The latest one-year return of 4% (to June 30/01) was above average. Three-year results are about on a par for the Canadian Balanced category. Risk is slightly better than average.

## MACKENZIE UNIVERSAL WORLD INCOME RRSP FUND

$$ → FI #/* RSP FB

Manager: Richard Gluck, since October 1998

MER: 2.24%     Fundata: C     Style: Top-down

Suitability: RRSP investors seeking foreign currency exposure

Formerly the Universal Canadian Bond Fund, this entry has been converted into an RRSP-eligible international bond fund, investing in mainly foreign bonds and bond index futures, although there are some Canadian issues in the mix. Recent results have been slightly above average, with a small gain of 2% for the year to June 30/01. Not great, but okay if you really want some currency diversification in your registered plan. A segregated version is also offered.

## MACKENZIE UNIVERSAL WORLD TACTICAL BOND FUND

$$ ↑ FI #/* £ FB

Manager: John Ricciardi (Cursitor-Eaton Asset Management), since inception (November 1994)

MER: 2.32%     Fundata: E     Style: Top-down

Suitability: Income investors seeking currency diversification

The goal of this fund is to invest in the world's largest bond markets, but that doesn't mean minimal risk because there's a lot of trading going on. In fact, Mackenzie warns about the volatility that may be associated with this fund, something you don't normally expect in a bond entry. It would be nice to report all this action has produced some good gains, but lately there's been a whole lot of nothing going on. Return for the year to June 30/01 was a loss of 1.7% and over three years the fund was virtually at break-even. Still, it did slightly better than the average for the category. The bonds are all government issues so there's no doubt that from a credit perspective, you won't get much better quality, but the returns leave a lot to be desired. A segregated version is also offered.

## Promising Newcomers/Universal Funds

### Sector Equity Funds

### MACKENZIE UNIVERSAL FINANCIAL SERVICES FUND NR → G #/* £ SPE

Managers: Frank Lin and Grace Yeo (United Overseas Bank); Gregory Anderson and Daniel Johnson (UBS Brinson); and DWS Financial Services Team (Deutsche Bank), since inception (April 2000)

MER: 2.86%     Fundata: N/A     Style: Value/Growth

Suitability: Middle-of-the-road investors

This fund invests in financial companies of all types (banks, insurance companies, brokers, etc.) from around the globe. It's a sector fund, which means the risks are higher than in an entry that is more diversified. But as sectors go, this one is less volatile than most. Initial results have been positive, with a one-year gain of 6.6% to June 30/01. There are lots of blue-chip stocks in the top holdings, from Bank of New York to the National Australia Bank. A good choice if you want to add a sector fund to your mix.

### MACKENZIE UNIVERSAL WORLD REAL ESTATE FUND   NR → G #/* £ RE

Manager: John Partridge (Henderson Real Estate Strategy Group), since inception (October 1997)

MER: 2.68%     Fundata: E     Style: Value/Growth

Suitability: Aggressive investors

This fund invests in shares of companies associated with the real estate business, not in actual buildings and land. So this is a sector fund that operates in what can be a volatile area. The companies represented are truly diversified internationally, with the U.S. being the largest block at about a quarter of the assets. Returns have been above average for the small Real Estate category: one-year gain to June 30/01 was 10.2%.

### MACKENZIE UNIVERSAL WORLD RESOURCE FUND     NR ↑ G #/* £ NR

Manager: Fred Sturm, since inception (February 1999)

MER: 2.73%     Fundata: B     Style: Value/Growth

Suitability: Aggressive investors

Manager Fred Sturm has done so well with the companion Canadian Resource Fund lately that Mackenzie has allowed him to take his act on to a broader stage. This fund takes a similar approach but Sturm can now roam the world for stocks. He does exactly that: you'll find everything here from oil fields in central Asia to forestry companies in China to mining operations in South America. So far he's done well with this mix. The one-year gain to June 30/01 was a rousing 30.4%. This fund isn't for everyone but if you like resources and you can handle the risk, take a look.

## Top Choices/MAXXUM Funds

### Dividend Income Funds

### MAXXUM DIVIDEND FUND                    $$$ ↑ G #/* RSP DIV

Manager: Bill Procter, since October 2001

MER: 2.40%      Fundata: B      Style: Value/Growth

Suitability: Investors seeking a mix of income and growth

Under the direction of the now-departed Jackee Pratt, this fund invested mainly in blue-chip stocks, including some U.S. issues that we wouldn't normally expect to find in a true Canadian dividend fund. Distributions tended to be on the low side, which meant it really wasn't well suited for income investors. Now responsibility for the portfolio has been assumed by Bill Procter, one of Mackenzie's more successful managers. He already runs the Industrial Dividend Growth Fund, and we would not be surprised if this fund were merged into that one before long. We like what Procter has done with Industrial Dividend Growth, although the risk level is a bit higher than you would normally expect in a dividend fund. We expect he'll use exactly the same approach here, which is why we are classifying it as a Top Choice fund. Formerly known as the Prudential Dividend Fund.

## Also Recommended/MAXXUM Funds

### Sector Funds

### MAXXUM NATURAL RESOURCE FUND              $$ ↑ G #/* RSP NR

Manager: Fred Sturm, since October 2001

MER: 2.70%      Fundata: B      Style: Growth

Suitability: Aggressive investors

This fund was doing very well under the direction of Jackee Pratt, who was relieved of her duties when the MAXXUM funds were moved to Mackenzie. One-year gain to June 30/01 was 21.7%. Replacing Pratt is Fred Sturm, who manages the Universal Canadian Resources Fund. That fund did even better over the same period, gaining 25.7%, and has a three-year average annual compound rate of return of 11.4%. Therefore, we see no reason why this fund shouldn't continue to perform in much the same way it has been—until it is merged into the Universal fund, which we suspect will eventually happen.

## Canadian Money Market Funds

### MAXXUM MONEY MARKET FUND $$$ → C NO RSP CMM

Manager: Tim Gleeson and Chris Kresic, since October 2001

MER: 0.85%     Fundata: B

Suitability: Conservative investors

This has been a consistent second-quartile performer and we see no reason why that should change, even with the managerial shake-up. Composition of the portfolio heavily favours short-term corporate notes, with some Canadian T-bills as well. Formerly the Prudential Money Market Fund.

## Promising Newcomers/MAXXUM Funds

None.

## Top Choices/Scudder Funds

### Canadian Bond Funds

### SCUDDER CANADIAN BOND FUND $$$ ↓ FI NO RSP CB

Manager: Cameron Laird, since 2000

MER: 2.08%     Fundata: N/A

Suitability: Conservative investors

This fund has been a decent performer despite the high MER of its Advisor units, which are the only ones you can buy. The portfolio focuses on government issues, with provincial bonds being the largest block. However, about 25% of the assets are in corporate bonds. Returns are above average, with a one-year gain of 4.5% to June 30/01. However, if you hold the Classic units, you did much better (5.6%) because of their much lower MER.

## Also Recommended/Scudder Funds

### Canadian Small-to-Mid-Cap Equity Funds

### SCUDDER CANADIAN SMALL COMPANY FUND $$ → G NO RSP CSC

Manager: Shahram Tajbakhsh, since 2000

MER: 2.83%     Fundata: N/A     Style: Blend

Suitability: Aggressive investors

This fund had a managerial change in 2000 and has been looking much better since. It was a first-quartile performer in 2001, with a gain of almost 10% in the six months to the end of June (Advisor units). The portfolio is well diversified and includes a few names that would be recognizable to most investors, such as Laurentian Bank, Cara Operations, and Cott. Not the top small-cap fund, but certainly a respectable one. Our main reservation is we don't know what will happen to it now that it is part of Mackenzie.

## Canadian Bond Funds

### SCUDDER CANADIAN SHORT-TERM BOND FUND    $$ ↓ FI NO RSP STB

Manager: Cameron Laird, since 2000

MER: 1.64%    Fundata: N/A

Suitability: Conservative investors

The original Classic units of this fund were among the top performers in the category. However, the Advisor units, the only ones you can buy now, don't look as good because their higher MER (1.64% versus 0.91%) cuts deeply into returns, especially when interest rates are low. However, this fund is still a decent choice for conservative investors who want a higher monthly income than is available from GICs, but with less risk than medium- and long-term bond funds. Holdings are mainly government and corporate bonds.

## Promising Newcomers/Scudder Funds

None.

## Top Choices/Mackenzie Funds

## Canadian Money Market Funds

### MACKENZIE CASH MANAGEMENT FUND       $$$$ ↓ C # RSP CMM

Manager: Mackenzie Team, since 1986

MER: 0.54%    Fundata: A

Suitability: Conservative investors

This is one of the better money market funds in the country. It combines above-average returns with a high degree of safety (the entire portfolio is normally invested in Government of Canada T-bills). Returns are well above average, thanks in part to a very low MER. Try to get it without paying any load fee (maximum is 2%). The name has been changed from Industrial Cash Management Fund, and some of the terms are different so check the details before buying.

## Also Recommended/Mackenzie Funds

### Canadian Mortgage Funds

### MACKENZIE MORTGAGE FUND                    $$ ↓ FI #/* RSP M

Manager: MRS Trust, since February 1994

MER: 1.95%    Fundata: E

Suitability: Conservative investors

This fund invests mainly in NHA-insured residential first mortgages of varying maturities. This means that, from a safety perspective, you won't do much better from the asset quality point of view. But if you want profits, that's something else entirely. With interest rates so low, mortgage funds haven't been very exciting lately and the relatively high MER of this fund doesn't help. However, it did manage to return a slightly above-average 6.9% for the year to June 30/01. Longer-term results are a tad below par for the category, however. The fund pays distributions on a monthly basis, which makes it useful for cash-flow purposes. Average payment is about 8/10 of a cent a month per unit. Based on a unit price of about $2, that works out to an annual cash-on-cash yield of about 4.7%, which is not bad for a fund of this type. The combination of income and safety makes this fund a decent choice for a RRIF, but not for much else. If Mackenzie would lower the MER to a more reasonable level, this fund would be a lot more attractive. A segregated version is available. Formerly the Ivy Mortgage Fund.

### Foreign Money Market Funds

### MACKENZIE U.S. MONEY MARKET FUND          $$ ↓ FI #/* £ FMM

Manager: Mackenzie Team, since 1994

MER: 1.32%    Fundata: E

Suitability: Conservative investors seeking currency diversification

This fund generates returns that are usually around the average for the category. It's not one we're excited about—the MER is on the high side—but it isn't bad. However, it should not be held in a registered plan, as it will eat up valuable foreign content room. Formerly the Universal U.S. Money Market Fund.

## Promising Newcomers/Mackenzie Funds

### Canadian Bond Funds

## MACKENZIE YIELD ADVANTAGE FUND NR ↑ FI #/* RSP HYB

Manager: Chris Kresic, since inception (October 1999)

MER: 2.13%     Fundata: N/A     Style: Relative Value

Suitability: Aggressive fixed-income investors

This new addition is a high-yield bond fund. It invests in companies with below-average credit ratings, although the overall weighted average rating for the portfolio must be BB or higher to limit risk. The manager is also permitted to hold some stocks, and 6.6% of the assets were in equities in mid-2001. Initial results have been good, with a one-year gain of 9% to June 30/01. Distributions are paid quarterly. There's also a seg fund version. The Industrial Mortgage Securities Fund was merged into this one in October 2000.

# MAWER INVESTMENT MANAGEMENT

## THE COMPANY

This Alberta company has been in business since 1974. The firm originally restricted itself to investment management for individuals, pension plans, and foundations, but in 1987 the company launched a family of no-load mutual funds, which has since grown to 10 in total.

Their investment style is a modified GARP. Normally, this acronym stands for "growth at a reasonable price"; however, the Mawer people prefer the phrase "growth at the right price." The distinction, as they see it, is that their version employs a somewhat more conservative approach. The "right" price to a Mawer manager means a stock is trading at a discount to its intrinsic value.

With the acquisition of the Bissett organization by Franklin Templeton in 2000, Mawer is the only remaining independent Calgary-based fund manager of any significance. This situation gives rise to speculation that Mawer is a logical takeover candidate and company officials acknowledge that their phones have been ringing. However, they have stated a merger isn't in their current plans.

In early 2000, Mawer launched a new product for high net worth investors called TEAM (tax effective asset management). The programme uses a number of tax-sensitive portfolio management techniques to maximize returns while minimizing tax liability in non-registered accounts.

## THE DETAILS

|  |  |
|---|---|
| Number of funds: | 10 |
| Assets under management: | $410.8 million |
| Load charge: | None |
| Switching charge: | None |
| Where sold: | Across Canada |
| How sold: | Through investment dealers or directly through the manager (see "Investing Tips" for more details) |
| Phone number: | 1-888-549-6248 |
| Web site address: | www.mawer.com |
| E-mail address: | webmaster@mawer.com |
| Minimum initial investment: | See "Investing Tips" |

## INVESTING TIPS

Mawer funds are registered for sale in all provinces. However, the minimum investment required will vary depending on where you live and from whom you buy your funds. Residents of Alberta and Saskatchewan can buy units directly from the company. In that case, there's an initial minimum of $25,000 per account, although the company has the discretion to waive that requirement. Residents of other provinces can also buy direct from Mawer, but in their case, the minimum initial investment rises to $100,000. Alternatively, funds may be purchased through a licensed dealer, in which case the initial minimum is $5,000 per fund (note the distinction between "per fund" and "per account"). Although the funds are no-load, a dealer or broker may levy some kind of fee for his or her service.

## FUND SUMMARY

|  |  |
|---|---|
| Top Choices: | Canadian Bond, Canadian Balanced Retirement Savings, Canadian Diversified Investment, Canadian Equity, Canadian Income, Canadian Money Market, New Canada |
| Also Recommended: | High-Yield Bond, World Investment, U.S. Equity |
| Promising Newcomers: | N/A |
| The Rest: | None |

## FUND RATINGS

### Top Choices

**Canadian Equity Funds**

### MAWER CANADIAN EQUITY FUND $$$ → G NO RSP CLC

Managers: Jim Hall, since January 2000

MER: 1.55%     Fundata: A     Style: Value

Suitability: Conservative investors

This fund specializes in shares of medium to large Canadian corporations. The investment style is shown as value, but it's actually GARP (meaning "growth at the right price" in this case), which is a variation on the value approach. Stocks are selected using a fundamental, bottom-up technique. The fund had been languishing, but has looked much better in the past 18 months. Part of the recovery may be due to the resurgence of value investing, but it's interesting to note that the fund picked up around the time Jim Hall took over responsibility, first as co-manager and then as manager in his own right. The fund recorded a solid gain of 10.7% over the year ending June 30/01, at a time when many Canadian stock funds lost money. The portfolio in the first half of 2001 had a distinct Old Economy look to it, just as it had the previous year, with lots of banks, utilities, and oil companies, and only a smattering of tech issues. Surprisingly, however, Nortel Networks was in the mix; the Mawer managers started buying stock at around $30, feeling at that price, it was trading below its intrinsic value. Unfortunately, Nortel continued to drop, contributing significantly to the small loss the fund suffered in the first half of the year. The fund's long-term record is comfortably above average and it was a first-quartile performer in 2000 and the first half of 2001. Safety record is solid so the fund gets points for its good risk/reward profile. A good choice.

## Canadian Small-to-Mid-Cap Funds

### MAWER NEW CANADA FUND                    $$$ ↓ G NO RSP CSC

Manager: Martin Ferguson, since December 1998

MER: 1.59%      Fundata: A      Style: Value

Suitability: Aggressive investors

This fund zeros in on small-cap stocks with good growth potential, including start-up operations. The strategy here is to buy and hold for the long term to maximize growth potential. The fund had a rough year in 1998, losing almost 18%, but looked much steadier in 1999 (+9.4%) and 2000 (+8.1%) under the direction of Martin Ferguson, who took over in late 1998. The fund exploded in the first half of 2001, gaining 23% in the first six months of the year, making it one of Canada's top small-cap funds during that time. Stocks are chosen from companies with a market cap of less than $500 million. Safety record is good for a fund of this type (small-cap funds are notoriously volatile), despite the setback in 1998. The fund name changed from Mawer North American Shares Fund in January 1994.

## Canadian Balanced and Asset Allocation Funds

### MAWER CANADIAN BALANCED          $$$$ ↓ FI/G NO RSP CBAL
### RETIREMENT SAVINGS FUND

Manager: Donald Ferris, since inception (January 1988)

MER: 1.10%      Fundata: A      Style: Strategic Asset Allocation

Suitability: Conservative investors

This fund is fully RRSP-eligible while the companion Canadian Diversified Investment Fund is not. It's a high-quality balanced fund, investing in short-term notes, bonds, and Canadian and foreign equities, within the foreign content limit. It also holds positions in other Mawer funds, including the New Canada Fund, World Investment Fund, and U.S. Equity Fund. Performance has been good, with above-average returns over all time frames. The safety record is very good as well: this fund has not had a calendar-year loss since 1994. The portfolio in mid-2001 was well diversified, with 38% in fixed-income securities, 34% in Canadian stocks, 13% in international equities, and 12% in U.S. stocks.

Manager Don Ferris has been around for more than 10 years, so there's real stability at the top. Management expense ratio (MER) is low (although it's up from last year). You can't ask for much more than this from a fund. An excellent candidate for your RRSP.

## Global Balanced and Asset Allocation Funds

### MAWER CANADIAN DIVERSIFIED INVESTMENT FUND
$$$ ↓ FI/G NO £ GBAL

Manager: Donald Ferris, since inception (January 1988)

MER: 1.31%     Fundata: A     Style: Strategic Asset Allocation

Suitability: Conservative investors

The higher foreign content helps to distinguish this fund from the companion Balanced Retirement Savings Fund, which is designed for registered plans. This fund is better suited for non-registered accounts, and manager Donald Ferris pays close attention to tax efficiency as a result. Foreign content in the first half of 2001 was 31%, so most of the assets are Canadian. Historically, this fund has tended to produce slightly lower returns than the Retirement Savings Fund, which is something of a surprise given the greater scope for diversification. It's still a decent performer, although Retirement Savings is our preferred choice. The fund showed a 8.7% advance in 2000, but lost a little ground (less than a percentage point) in the first half of 2001. The safety record is very good. We're repeating yet again a suggestion we've offered in the past: given the increased foreign content, change the name of this fund to the Global Diversified Investment Fund, which better describes its mandate.

## Canadian Bond Funds

### MAWER CANADIAN BOND FUND
$$$ ↓ FI NO RSP CB

Manager: Gary Feltham, since February 1993

MER: 1.13%     Fundata: C     Style: Enhanced Core

Suitability: Conservative investors

This is one of those steady performers that never get much attention despite turning in above-average results year after year. In fact, it's been a second-quartile performer every single year since 1994. You can't ask for greater reliability than that. Government of Canada bonds make up about half the portfolio, with corporate issues accounting for about a third. The rest comprises provincials and municipals. The manager closely tracks the Scotia Capital Markets Universe Bond Index in duration terms, within a 0.5% range on either side. Safety rating is very good.

## MAWER CANADIAN INCOME FUND $$$ ↓ FI NO RSP STB

Manager: Gary Feltham, since February 1993

MER: 1.37%     Fundata: E     Style: Bottom-up Value

Suitability: Very conservative investors and RRIF investors

This fund was included in the balanced category until 1999, but it is now offi-cially classified as a Canadian short-term bond fund. This category switch explains the low Fundata rating; the fund has actually been an above-average performer in its new category since the change. It's now a pure bond fund that focuses on the short-to-medium term. No securities are held with maturities beyond 10 years, greatly reducing the risk inherent in the portfolio, which had been quite high in its previous incarnation due to the inclusion of royalty trusts. The portfolio tilts toward government bonds, but there is a large percentage in corporate issues to increase overall yield. You can arrange for regular distribu-tions from this fund on a monthly or quarterly basis, which is useful for retirees. The low risk and good cash flow makes this a fine holding for an RRIF. The only thing we find troubling is the fact that this fund has a significantly higher MER than the companion Canadian Bond Fund.

## Canadian Money Market Funds

## MAWER CANADIAN MONEY MARKET FUND $$$ → C NO RSP CMM

Manager: Bill MacLachlan, since September 1993

MER: 0.87%     Fundata: B

Suitability: Very conservative investors

This fund invests mainly in corporate notes, with a few government T-bills tossed in. Returns are consistently above average, thanks in part to the low management fee.

## Also Recommended

## U.S. Equity Funds

## MAWER U.S. EQUITY FUND $$ → G NO £ USE

Manager: Darrell Anderson, since November 1994

MER: 1.39%     Fundata: D     Style: Value

Suitability: Conservative investors

This U.S. stock fund seeks to generate a combination of capital gains and dividends for investors. There are lots of big names (e.g., Tyco, Wendy's) in the portfolio, which consists of 40 to 50 positions, but there's a smattering of smaller growth stocks and medium-size companies as well. As with all Mawer equity funds, the investment style is bottom-up GARP (growth at the right price), which is a variation on the value theme. This fund was a good performer in the past, but hit a rough patch in the late 1990s when value was out of favour. It actually lost a bit in the first half of 2001, but its performance was good enough for a first-quartile ranking nonetheless. Longer-term performance numbers have slipped to below average. On the plus side, the safety record is good, but we would like to see a return to the strong results of the mid-1990s.

## International Equity Funds

### MAWER WORLD INVESTMENT FUND                    $$ → G NO £ IE

Manager: Gerald Cooper-Key, since inception (November 1987)

MER: 1.56%      Fundata: A      Style: Value

Suitability: Conservative investors

This fund invests in equities outside North America, specifically Europe, the Pacific Basin, and Latin America. Overseas stocks have been weak recently, and the fund recorded a loss of 6% in 2000 and was down more than 10% more in the first half of 2001. Nonetheless, it was a second-quartile performer in 2000 and first-quartile performer in the first six months of 2001. This result tells you the manager is doing a good job in rough market conditions. European stocks continue to dominate the portfolio, but the manager has built the emerging markets holdings, which accounted for 15% of the assets in mid-2001. Long-term results are consistently above average. However, the short-term results aren't going to pick up until international markets emerge from the malaise that gripped them in the first part of 2001.

## Canadian Bond Funds

### MAWER HIGH-YIELD BOND FUND                    $$ ↑ FI NO RSP HYB

Manager: Gary Feltham, since April 1996

MER: 2.18%      Fundata: B      Style: Bottom-up Value

Suitability: Aggressive investors

The goal of this fund is to achieve a combination of high income and capital gains by investing in fixed-income securities of lower-rated and non-rated Canadian companies. Technically it's a "junk bond" fund, although that term is misused in the Canadian context since we don't really have a lot of junk issues in this country. High-yield bonds payable in U.S. dollars, Treasury bills, and investment-grade securities may be used occasionally. This is a fund that would be of interest to investors who can live with higher risk and who want above-average cash flow. For example, in the first half of 2001, the gross yield on this fund was 7.7%. In absolute terms, however, the numbers here are quite low. The fund gained just 4.1% in the year to June 30/01, and the three-year average annual compound rate of return was less than 2%. Given the additional risk that you have to accept by investing here, we don't regard that kind of return anywhere near sufficient. The companion Canadian Bond or Canadian Income funds are better choices. However, if you want a high-yield bond fund for your portfolio for diversification, you could do worse than this one.

## Promising Newcomers

None

# MCLEAN BUDDEN FUNDS

## THE COMPANY

This company is mainly a pension fund manager that offers some small mutual funds almost as a sideline. It also manages funds for some other companies, including Spectrum Investments (to which it's related as part of the Sun Life organization) and Stone & Co. Its investment style in the past was strictly growth-oriented and it has been among the best at that type of money management. Recently it added a value management group and launched a new Canadian Equity Value Fund in the fall of 1999.

Apart from offering funds that perform well, the company has some of the lowest management fees in the industry, which enhances the return to investors.

This is an often-overlooked company that deserves more attention. Fortunately, its funds are now becoming available through more distributors. Our only complaint with McLean Budden is that they do not provide the name of the lead manager on each fund; we regard this information as very important to investors.

## THE DETAILS

|  |  |
|---|---|
| Number of funds: | 8 |
| Assets under management: | $433.3 million |
| Load charge: | None (if purchased through a dealer, however, certain charges may apply) |
| Switching charge: | None |
| Where sold: | Across Canada |
| How sold: | Through registered dealers or directly from the company in Ontario, Quebec, Alberta, and B.C. |
| Phone number: | 1-800-884-0436 |
| Web site address: | www.mcleanbudden.com |
| E-mail address: | Through Web site |
| Minimum initial investment: | $10,000 |

# INVESTING TIPS

If you live in any of the provinces where the company sells direct to clients, buy your units from them rather than going through a financial advisor or a discount broker to ensure you won't have to pay any commissions or other charges.

# FUND SUMMARY

|  |  |
|---|---|
| Top Choices: | American Equity, Balanced Growth, Canadian Equity, Growth, Fixed-Income, Money Market |
| Also Recommended: | None |
| Promising Newcomers: | Canadian Equity Value |
| The Rest: | International Equity Growth |

# FUND RATINGS

## Canadian Equity Funds

### MCLEAN BUDDEN CANADIAN EQUITY GROWTH FUND                    $$$$ → G NO RSP CLC

21.29

Manager: Team

MER: 1.30%     Fundata: A        Style: Large-Cap Growth

Suitability: Long-term conservative investors

This fund invests primarily in shares from the largest 100 companies on the TSE 300 Index. The managerial team has gradually been increasing the foreign content component of this fund, which was up to almost 20% in the first half of 2001. The foreign assets are held in units of the companion American Equity Fund and International Equity Fund. This fund has a fine consistency record. It has been a first- or second-quartile performer every year since 1995 and shows an eight-year average quartile ranking (AQR) of 1.75, which is very good. Despite being growth in style, the fund weathered the market storms of 2000–01 quite well, gaining 18.4% in 2000 while giving back a modest 5%-plus in the first half of 2001. The portfolio consists of 30 to 40 securities, and included Magna, Torstar, Royal Bank, BCE, and Alcan in the first half of 2001. This continues to be one of the best choices around for investors looking for a well-balanced, conservatively run growth fund. We're moving the rating up to $$$$ in recognition of this fund's steady performance and above-average returns over many years.

31.29

## U.S. Equity Funds

### MCLEAN BUDDEN AMERICAN EQUITY FUND        $$$$ → G NO £ USE

Manager: Team

MER: 1.30%      Fundata: B        Style: Large-Cap Growth

Suitability: Long-term conservative investors

Here's another McLean Budden fund with a fine consistency record. Since 1994, it has been below the second quartile in only one calendar year (1999) when it dipped to third quartile despite a respectable gain of 11.9%. Its AQR over eight years is an impressive 1.50 (1.00 is perfect, 4.00 is the worst). The goal of this fund is long-term growth by investing in a diversified portfolio of 40 to 50 U.S. stocks selected from the S&P 500. Emphasis is on large companies like PepsiCo, Colgate Palmolive, Microsoft, and General Motors, although you will find a few unfamiliar names in the mix. In the first half of 2001, the portfolio was weighted toward consumer goods and services, with about 33% of the assets, although the emphasis on this sector was down significantly from the previous year. Technology stocks accounted for 28% of the mix. Over the long haul, very few U.S. equity funds have done better than this one. The fund did not record a losing calendar year from 1994–2000. It did slip about 4% in the first half of 2001, but that was a much better performance than the S&P and good enough for a first-quartile ranking. A very good selection, the rating moves up to $$$$.

## Canadian Balanced Funds

### MCLEAN BUDDEN BALANCED GROWTH FUND $$$ → FI/G NO RSP CBAL

Manager: Team

MER: 1.00%      Fundata: B        Style: Large-Cap Growth          15.54

Suitability: Long-term balanced investors

This fund employs a conservative investment strategy, combining stocks of large companies (e.g., CN Rail, Bombardier, banks) with bonds and debentures, and securing at least an "A" safety rating. On the equities side, McLean Budden's trademark large-cap growth approach is used. On the fixed-income side, the company employs a number of active bond strategies to maximize returns, including interest rate anticipation, yield enhancement (overweighting provincial and corporate issues), special feature bonds, and U.S.-pay bonds. The managers maintain a truly balanced portfolio with the equity component between 40% and 60%. Results have been good in recent years and the fund consistently shows above-average returns. It gave up a little ground in the first half of 2001, but the loss was minimal compared with the general decline in the markets. Worthy of your attention. A good choice for an RRSP.

## Canadian Bond Funds

### MCLEAN BUDDEN FIXED-INCOME FUND          $$$ → FI NO RSP CB

Manager: Team

MER: 0.70%      Fundata: D       Style: Multiple

Suitability: Conservative investors

This small fund specializes in high-quality government and corporate bonds. It generally produces very good results and has never been below second quartile since 1994. It managed to turn a small profit in the first half of 2001 when many bond funds lost ground, mainly because the managers increased their short-term positions and these bonds performed well during the period. Returns over all time periods are well above average for the Canadian Bond category. The low management expense ratio (MER) is a big help here. Another good choice in this sound family.

## Canadian Money Market Funds

### MCLEAN BUDDEN MONEY MARKET FUND        $$$$ → C NO RSP CMM

Manager: Team

MER: 0.60%      Fundata: E       Style: Maximizing Risk-Adjusted Returns

Suitability: Conservative investors

This fund invests in a mix of Canadian T-bills, bankers' acceptances, and corporate short-term notes. The team seeks to add value in several ways, including credit quality management aimed at generating the best possible return on a risk-adjusted basis. The results speak for themselves: the fund has been a first-quartile performer every year since 1995. The low MER is a big plus. Rating moves to $$$$. This is one of the best money funds you'll find.

## Also Recommended

None.

# Promising Newcomers

10.90

## Canadian Equity Funds

### MCLEAN BUDDEN CANADIAN EQUITY VALUE FUND   NR → G NO RSP CE

Manager: Team

MER: 1.30%     Fundata: N/A     Style: Large-Cap Value

Suitability: Long-term conservative investors

McLean Budden made its reputation as a growth manager. The addition of a value team marks a departure for the company but a welcome one, because it gives the investor the option of style diversification. There are four members in this group: Brian Dawson, Alan Daxner, Susan Shuter, and Ted Thompson. This new fund is their collective baby. So far in its young life it has been impressive, with a second-quartile performance in 1999 and first-quartile showing in 2000 and the first half of 2001. The emphasis is on large-cap value stocks, although some mid-cap stocks may also be held (market valuation between $500 million and $1 billion). The major holdings in the first part of 2001 included several banks, TransCanada PipeLines, Alcan, Cominco, Canadian Pacific, and Westcoast Energy. The fund lost a little ground during the first six months of 2001 but its performance was better than the TSE 300. A good complement to the companion Canadian Equity Growth Fund.

# MERRILL LYNCH INVESTMENT

## THE COMPANY

Merrill Lynch is Canada's largest independent full-service securities firm, with more than 100 offices nationwide. In 1999, the company launched its own line of mutual funds, which has been steadily growing since.

The company is part of the worldwide Merrill Lynch organization, which operates in 22 countries and employs more than 900 investment professionals globally. It makes use of this talent pool in the fund management process, as well as employing top outside management houses in specialized fields.

The Atlas funds (originally created by Midland Walwyn, which was purchased by Merrill Lynch) have been renamed and incorporated into the Merrill fund line-up. Original managers have been retained in funds that bear the word "Select" in their name.

## THE DETAILS

| | |
|---|---|
| Number of funds: | 29 |
| Assets under management: | $4.2 billion |
| Load Charge: | Front: max. 5%; Back: max. 5.5% |
| Switching Charge: | 2% maximum |
| Where Sold: | Across Canada |
| How Sold: | Merrill Lynch financial consultants and other distribution channels |
| Phone Number: | 1-888-888-3863 |
| Web Site address: | www.mlfunds.ca |
| E-mail address: | Through Web site |
| Minimum initial investment: | $500 |

## INVESTING TIPS

Merrill Lynch funds offer a purchase option that not many people are aware of. It's called "low-load" and is distinct from the Class F units now being offered by many companies for use by fee-based financial advisors.

The low-load option is exactly what it sounds like: it's an alternative with a commission structure less than the one applied if you buy units on a normal front-end load basis. This option is usually offered only to very good customers and/or those investing a lot of money. But if you're planning to buy units in any of these funds, ask about it.

# FUND SUMMARY

| | |
|---|---|
| Top Choices: | Canadian Core Value, Canadian Income Trust, Canadian Small-Cap, Select Canadian Balanced, Select Global Value, U.S. Basic Value |
| Also Recommended: | Canadian Growth Fund, International RSP Index, U.S. Fundamental Growth, U.S. Money Market |
| Promising Newcomers: | Canadian Balanced Value |
| The Rest: | Canadian Bond, Canadian High-Yield Bond, Canadian Money Market, Canadian T-Bill, Developing Capital Markets, Euro, Global Growth, Global Sectors, Internet Strategies, Select International Growth, Triple A, U.S. RSP Index |

# FUND RATINGS

## Top Choices

### Canadian Equity Funds

### MERRILL LYNCH CANADIAN CORE VALUE FUND $$$ ↓ G #/* RSP CE

Managers: Kim Shannon and Gaelen Morphet, since 1999

MER: 2.61%    Fundata: A    Style: Value

Suitability: Conservative investors

Kim Shannon, the chief investment officer at Merrill Lynch, first came to our attention when she took over the moribund Spectrum Canadian Investment Fund and made it a winner. She and management partner Gaelen Morphet still run that fund for Spectrum, and bring the same talent for value investing to this Merrill Lynch entry, into which the Atlas Canadian Large-Cap Value Fund was merged last year. The portfolio emphasis is on medium- to large-sized companies with a market capitalization of $1 billion-plus. Recent large holdings included Bank of Montreal, Magna International, Atco Ltd., and Westcoast Energy. Financial services was the largest single group, with about a quarter of the assets. This fund is a very good choice for more conservative investors and would fit well in an RRSP.

## Canadian Small-to-Mid Cap Funds

### MERRILL LYNCH CANADIAN SMALL-CAP FUND  $$$ → G #/* RSP CSC

Managers: Kim Shannon and Gaelen Morphet, since 2000

MER: 2.91%     Fundata: A     Style: GARP

Suitability: Aggressive investors

This fund grew out of an amalgamation of three former Atlas funds: Emerging Growth, Small-Cap Value, and Small-Cap Growth. The new management team of Shannon and Morphet took over the revamped entity in 2000 and they have been doing good things with it ever since. The fund gained 13.6% in 2000, and kept up the pace with an 11.8% advance in the first six months of 2001. This management team is known for their value approach to investing, although the fund's style is officially described as growth at a reasonable price (GARP). As a result, we expect the risk level here to be somewhat lower than you might expect with a small-cap fund. We're impressed with the results to date and we know about Shannon and Morphet's competence from past experience, so we have no hesitation in giving this fund a $$$ rating.

## U.S. Equity Funds

### MERRILL LYNCH U.S. BASIC VALUE FUND  $$$ ↓ G #/* £ USE

Managers: Kevin Rendino and Carrie King, since inception (December 1998)

MER: 2.84%     Fundata: A     Style: Value

Suitability: Conservative investors

As the name suggests, this fund searches out undervalued stocks with low price/earnings and price/book ratios. This approach keeps the risk level relatively low, which has worked well for investors recently. While many equity funds suffered, this one returned a handsome 13.7% over the year to June 30/01. The portfolio tends to favour large-cap stocks like AT&T, IBM, Allstate, and Du Pont. There are a few non-U.S. stocks in the mix, including positions in the Cayman Islands, the Netherlands, and South Africa. But at its core, this is a blue-chip, low-risk U.S. equity offering. Recommended. The Atlas American Advantage Value Fund was folded into this one in 2000.

## International and Global Equity Funds

### MERRILL LYNCH SELECT GLOBAL VALUE FUND      $$$ → G #/* £ GE

Manager: Anthony Rawlinson (Global Value Investment Portfolio Management), since 1998

MER: 2.65%      Fundata: B      Style: Value

Suitability: Conservative investors

This was one of the few former Atlas funds to retain its existing manager after the Merrill Lynch takeover. Anthony Rawlinson brings a value approach to stock selection and has built a well-diversified portfolio that invests in companies of all sizes. He adopted a defensive position in the first half of 2001 with 18% of his assets in cash, and that helped the fund to a small gain in the first six months of the year. Over the three years to June 30/01, this fund produced an average annual compound rate of return of 16.4%, very good for its category. Unlike many global funds, U.S. stocks play a relatively minor role here, comprising less than a quarter of the assets in the first half of 2001. The value approach helps to reduce risk, an important consideration in current markets. Previously known as the Atlas Global Equity Fund.

## Canadian Balanced and Asset Allocation Funds

### MERRILL LYNCH SELECT CANADIAN      $$$ ↓ FI/G #/* RSP CBAL
### BALANCED FUND

Manager: Len Racioppo (Jarislowsky Fraser Ltd.), since inception (1984)

MER: 2.32%      Fundata: A      Style: Blend

Suitability: Conservative investors

When you have good fund managers, you should do everything possible to retain them. This fund is a case in point. When Merrill Lynch assumed control of the old Atlas Canadian Balanced Fund and renamed it, they asked Len Racioppo, president of the renowned Montreal-based investment firm Jarislowsky Fraser, to stay at the helm. He did, and it's been a good thing for investors. This fund has easily outperformed the average fund in the Canadian Balanced category over the last several years by investing in a relatively conservative and diversified portfolio of blue-chip stocks along with a blend of government and high-quality corporate bonds. With a 20% position in foreign stocks, this fund also offers good geographic diversification. Moreover, with a strong bias toward short- and mid-term bonds, this fund is also less sensitive to interest-rate risk. The fund has been an above-average performer in its class over almost all time frames. Its one-year gain was 5.7% in the year to June 30/01; three-year average annual gain was 5.8%. Overall, a good low-risk choice and well-suited for a registered plan.

## Canadian High Income Balanced Funds

### MERRILL LYNCH CANADIAN INCOME TRUST FUND          $$$ → G/FI #/* RSP CHIB

Managers: Kim Shannon and Gaelen Morphet, since 2000

MER: 2.03%     Fundata: B     Style: Bottom-up

Suitability: Aggressive investors

This fund is designed for investors seeking above-average, tax-advantaged income and who are prepared to accept a higher degree of risk. The portfolio is made up primarily of real estate investment trusts (REITs) and royalty income trusts (RITs). These securities can generate very attractive cash flows, but their market prices have proven volatile, especially in the case of energy trusts. If you can't live with ups and downs, you should not be investing here. The fund has been very good at fulfilling its mandate. In calendar 2000, it paid out 75¢ per unit, which amounted to a yield of 11.6% based on the unit price at the start of the year according to a survey done by the *Mutual Funds Update* newsletter. More than half of that income was received on a tax-deferred basis if units were held outside a registered plan. Total return for the year to June 30/01 was 28.3%. This is a good choice if you're looking for strong cash flow, but don't lose sight of the market risk.

### Also Recommended

## Canadian Equity Funds

### MERRILL LYNCH CANADIAN GROWTH FUND          $$ → G #/* RSP CE

Managers: James Ellman and Andrea Mitroff, since 2000

MER: 2.57%     Fundata: C     Style: Momentum

Suitability: Aggressive investors

The new style of prospectus being issued by mutual fund companies contains a lot more useful information than in the past. But it is still lacking one important detail: the provenance of a specific fund. In this case, the most recent Merrill Lynch prospectus makes it appear as if this fund has been around since 1985, producing very good results over that time. But that's a misleading impression to give. This was previously the Atlas Canadian Large-Cap Growth Fund. It had been managed since 1995 by Fred Pynn of Bissett and Associates, whose style was quite different from the momentum approach currently being used by the new managers. Earnings momentum is an aggressive method of stock selection, which may produce big gains or big losses depending on market conditions. That's what we've been seeing here: a gain of 17% in 2000 and a loss of 10% in the first half of 2001. None of this is to say this is a bad fund; we want to point out only that to rely on past history to promote the fund is misleading. The portfolio emphasis is on mid-to-large-cap companies, and recent top holdings included Alberta Energy, Canadian Pacific, and Royal Bank. There's a strong foreign component in the mix, accounting for almost a quarter of the fund's assets in the first part of 2001. We'll give this fund a $$ rating for now until we see more performance numbers under the new team.

## U.S. Equity Funds

### MERRILL LYNCH U.S. FUNDAMENTAL GROWTH FUND
$$ → G #/* £ USE

Managers: Lawrence Fuller and Thomas Burke, since 2000

MER: 2.69%    Fundata: B    Style: Growth

Suitability: Middle-of-the-road investors

This fund is a companion to the U.S. Basic Value Fund. Here, the emphasis is on large-cap growth stocks, specifically companies with above-average sales growth rates, improving profit margins, and leading market share. Since growth stocks have been in a decline recently, it will come as no surprise that this fund has not fared as well as its value-driven counterpart. However, it hasn't done badly: loss for the year to June 30/01 was just 2.3%. Large holdings in the first half of 2001 included Exxon Mobil, Phillip Morris, and Kimberley Clark. This fund should be a decent performer when the market for growth stocks recovers.

## International and Global Equity Funds

### MERRILL LYNCH INTERNATIONAL RSP INDEX FUND
$$ → G #/* RSP IE

Manager: MLIM Quantitative Advisors

MER: 2.21%    Fundata: B    Style: Index

Suitability: Middle-of-the-road investors

This fund uses futures contracts to track the performance of various international stock exchanges (non-North American), making it fully eligible for registered plans. International markets did not perform well in the first half of 2001, so it's not surprising that this fund lost 7% during that period. What may be surprising is that those results were above average for the category. This is a useful fund to consider if you want international exposure in your RRSP without using up foreign content room.

## Foreign Money Market Funds

### MERRILL LYNCH U.S. MONEY MARKET FUND      $$$ → C #/* £ FMM

Managers: Michael Walsh and Cindy Macaulay, since 1998

MER: 1.20%      Fundata: D      Style: Duration

Suitability: Conservative investors

Merrill's two Canadian money funds don't impress us, but this U.S. entry is a consistent second-quartile performer and is worth your attention if you're looking for some U.S. dollar exposure. Returns have been good, with a one-year gain of 5% to June 30/01 and a three-year average annual compound rate of return of 4.6%. Main portfolio emphasis is on corporate bonds.

## Promising Newcomers

## Canadian Balanced and Asset Allocation Funds

### MERRILL LYNCH CANADIAN BALANCED VALUE FUND      NR ↓ FI/G #/* RSP CBAL

Managers: Kim Shannon, Gaelen Morphet, and Greg Maunz, since inception (March 1999)

MER: 2.54%      Fundata: A      Style: Value

Suitability: Conservative investors

Here's another entry from the fine team of Shannon and Morphet. This conservative balanced fund is just the ticket if you're looking for a core holding in a registered plan. Stocks are of the blue-chip, low-risk variety while the fixed-income side contains a mix of government bonds and high-quality corporate issues. Performance has been very good so far, with a gain of 15.3% in 2000 and an advance of 2.1% in the first half of 2001.

# MONTRUSCO BOLTON INVESTMENTS

## THE COMPANY

Montrusco Bolton, Inc., with over $10.1 billion total assets, is the entity that resulted from the merger between Montrusco Associates and Bolton Tremblay in February 1999. It is a prominent Montreal-based investment firm that manages assets for pension plans, high net worth clients, and mutual fund companies such as Scotia Funds, C.I. Mutual Funds, Altum Funds, and Excel Fund Management.

The firm offered one fund that was available to all investors, the Quebec Growth Fund. However, it was announced in October 2001 that the fund was being sold to Desjardins. See the listing there.

The company also announced several fund mergers and closures, and that it is dropping the "Select" name from its line-up. This is part of a major refocusing that effectively removes the firm from the retail market with the exception of high net worth investors.

## THE DETAILS

| | |
|---|---|
| Number of funds: | 18 |
| Assets under management: | $2.3 billion |
| Load charge: | Front: max. 6%; Back: max. 5% |
| Switching charge: | None |
| Where sold: | Across Canada |
| How sold: | Through sales representatives |
| Phone number: | (514) 842-6464 (Nicole Charland) |
| Web site address: | www.montruscobolton.com |
| E-mail address: | invfms@montruscobolton.com |
| Minimum initial investment: | Generally $150,000 |

## INVESTING TIPS

This company really only wants your business if you have a lot of money to invest. The minimum requirement is $150,000.

Note that the management fee is charged directly to the investor rather than to the fund itself.

## FUND SUMMARY

| | |
|---|---|
| Top Choices: | Bond Index Plus, T-Max |
| Also Recommended: | TSE 100 Momentum, U.S. Index |
| Promising Newcomers: | None |
| The Rest: | Balanced, Balanced Plus, Canadian Companies, Canadian Small Cap, Continental Europe Equity, Fixed Income, Global Equity, Growth, International Equity, Taxable US Equity |

## FUND REVIEWS

### Top Choices

**Canadian Bond Funds**

#### MONTRUSCO BOLTON BOND INDEX PLUS FUND                    $$ → FI #/* RSP CB

Manager: Yves Paquette, since 1996

MER: 0.13%     Fundata: C     Style: Index

Suitability: Moderate risk income investors

The goal of this portfolio is to track the Scotia McLeod Universe Bond Index. Tracking error has been low; the fund misses the index by about 40 points per year on average. The fund's five-year return is 7.4% per annum, some 1.2 percentage points per annum above the average in the Canadian Bond category.

## Canadian Money Market Funds

### MONTRUSCO BOLTON T-MAX FUND $$$ ↓ C #/* RSP CMM

Manager: Yves Paquette, since 1995

MER: 0.05%     Fundata: C

Suitability: Conservative investors

This is a good money market entry with above-average returns and a fine safety record. The 4.8% per annum five-year return to June 30/01 is 1.1 percentage points above the average in the money market fund category.

## Also Recommended

## Canadian Equity Funds

### MONTRUSCO BOLTON TSE 100 MOMENTUM FUND $$$ ↑ G #/* RSP CE

Manager: Tom Valks, since 2000

MER: Charged direct to investor     Fundata: B     Style: Momentum

Suitability: Very aggressive investors.

This fund uses momentum-based strategies to filter out stocks and to select the top 10 stocks at any time in the TSE 100 Index. This is a classic high risk/high potential reward fund. It lost 27.3% in the year ended June 30/01. However, it the average annual return over the three years to that date was 22%. The volatility is about as high as you can find. Only suitable for the very aggressive.

## U.S. Equity Funds

### MONTRUSCO BOLTON U.S. INDEX FUND $$$ → G #/* £ USE

Manager: Tom Valks, since 1999

MER: 0.10%      Fundata: D      Style: Value

Suitability: Tax-motivated investors

This U.S. equity fund is designed for use in registered plans as foreign content, or by tax-exempt investors. Otherwise it is a fairly standard U.S. index fund. Returns until recently have been extremely good. The fund lost 15.1% in the year to June 30/01 but returns over longer time periods are above average. Safety record is average.

# NATIONAL BANK MUTUAL FUNDS

## THE COMPANY

National Bank doesn't register that high on the radar scopes of investors outside Quebec, but it is the sixth-largest bank in the country after the Big Five. The National Bank funds are its in-house line. As of January 1, 1999, all of the former General Trust funds were absorbed by their respective National Bank funds.

There are a few good funds in the National Bank family, but the funds are available for sale only to residents of Quebec, Ontario, and New Brunswick.

Note that all these funds were formerly known as "Invesnat." The name has been changed to identify them more closely with the parent bank. Most of the funds are run by an in-house firm, Natcan Investment Management.

National Bank teamed up with well-known Fidelity Investments (who acts as manager) to create five NBC/Fidelity Funds, which debuted in October 2000. At this stage all are off to mediocre starts, reflecting the market conditions that have prevailed over the time period.

## THE DETAILS

|  |  |
|---|---|
| Number of funds: | 47 |
| Assets under management: | $4.3 billion |
| Load charge: | None |
| Switching charge: | None |
| Where sold: | Quebec, Ontario, and New Brunswick |
| How sold: | Through branches of National Bank or by phone |
| Phone number: | 1-888-270-3941 |
| Web site address: | www.invesnet.com |
| E-mail address: | webtrade@invesnet.com |
| Minimum initial investment: | $500 (generally) |

## INVESTMENT TIPS

If you have large sums to allocate to money market funds from time to time and you live in an eligible province for NBC, the family has some big ticket, low management expense ratio (MER) money market funds. The top of the line is the NBC Treasury Management Fund. The MER is 0.27%, about as low as you will see in this field. Last year, the fund scored a return of 5.6%, beating the average fund by over a full percent (that's the MER effect). To enter, however, you will need a cool million. NBC has some other good performers in the money market field with minimum investments of $50,000 and $100,000. These funds are especially worth consideration from businesses looking for a short-term place to park cash reserves.

# FUND SUMMARY

## National Bank Funds

|  |  |
|---|---|
| Top Choices: | Corporate Cash Management, Dividend, Mortgage, Small Capitalization, Treasury Bill Plus, U.S. Money Market |
| Also Recommended: | Bond |
| Promising Newcomers: | Canadian Opportunities |
| The Rest: | Aggressive Diversified, American Index Plus, American RSP Index, Asia Pacific, Canadian Equity, Canadian Index, Canadian Index Plus, Conservative Diversified, Emerging Markets, European Equity, European Small-Cap, Future Economy, Future Economy RSP, Global Equity, Global Equity RSP, Global RSP Bond, Global Technology, Global Technologies RSP, International RSP Index, Intrepid Diversified, Moderate Diversified, Money Market, Natural Resources, Protected Canadian Bond, Protected Canadian Equity, Protected Global RSP, Protected Growth Balanced, Protected Retirement Balanced, Presumed Sound Investments, Retirement Balanced, Secure Diversified, Short-Term Government Bond |

## NBC/Fidelity Investments Funds

|  |  |
|---|---|
| Top Choices: | None |
| Also Recommended: | None |
| Promising Newcomers: | None |
| The Rest: | Canadian Asset Allocation, Focus Financial Services, Global Asset Allocation, Growth America, International Portfolio Growth Balanced, Protected International, Protected Retirement Balanced, Secure Diversified, Treasury Management |

# FUND RATINGS

## Top Choices/National Bank Funds

### Canadian Small-to-Mid-Cap Equity Funds

### NATIONAL BANK SMALL CAPITALIZATION FUND $$$$ → G NO RSP CSC

Manager: Robert Bearuregard, since January 1999

MER: 2.35%      Fundata: A      Style: Value

Suitability: Growth-oriented investors

As one of the old General Trust funds that were brought into the National Bank line-up in August 1998, the mandate of this fund is to invest in growth-oriented stocks with an emphasis on small-to-mid-cap companies. Despite a management change in 1999, the results for this fund have been consistently above par for the small-cap category, with an average annual compound rate of return of 15.3% for the decade to June 30/01. The one-year return to June 30/01 was 18.7%, so dramatically higher than the 6.1% loss for the category that it is hard to believe they are in the same universe. The fund's volatility is well below the category average. With successful long- and short-term track records, this fund is worthy of a $$$$ rating.

### Dividend Income Funds

### NATIONAL BANK DIVIDEND FUND                    $$$ ↓ FI NO RSP DIV

Manager: Jacques Chartrand, since 1992

MER: 1.73%      Fundata: A      Style: Value

Suitability: Conservative income-oriented investors

This relatively small fund has a portfolio that is in keeping with a true dividend fund, with the majority of the investments in preferred shares (about 65% of the total in mid-2001). Longer-term performance has lagged behind other dividend funds over five years because of the high percentage of preferreds in the fund. However, it scored near the top in the year ending June 30/01 with a 13.2% return, bringing the three-year annual compounded return to 8.9% compared with an average 7.2% for the dividend fund category. The fund's volatility has been much lower than the average, making this a low-risk vehicle. Reason: the blue-chip common stocks held by many other "dividend" funds actually make them large-cap stock funds in disguise. This is a good choice for National Bank customers looking for tax-advantaged income at minimal risk.

## Mortgage Funds

### NATIONAL BANK MORTGAGE FUND $$$ ↓ FI NO RSP M

Manager: Gilles Tremblay, since inception (1991)

MER: 1.68%    Fundata: D    Style: Term Structure Analysis

Suitability: Conservative investors

This fund is a decent choice in the Mortgage category. Recent returns have shown improvement and longer-term results are above average with a five-year average annual gain of 5.4% to June 30/01. Plus, the safety record is unblemished. This fund has never gone through a 12-month period with a loss, although shorter-term volatility is higher than normal for a mortgage fund. This fund even managed to stay in the black in 1994 when many mortgage funds recorded small losses. A worthwhile option if you're looking for a mortgage fund, but don't expect it to make you rich in these times of low interest rates. The General Trust Mortgage Fund was merged into this one on January 1, 1999.

## Canadian Money Market Funds

### NATIONAL BANK CANADIAN CORPORATE CASH MANAGEMENT FUND $$$ → C NO RSP CMM

Manager: Richard Lévesque, since 1995

MER: 0.46%    Fundata: C    Style: Value

Suitability: Conservative investors

The emphasis here, as you might guess by the name, is on corporate short-term notes. However, about a third of the portfolio is invested in federal T-bills, so this is not a pure corporate play. This is the best performer among the bevy of money market entries on offer from National Bank, but you'll need $100,000 to get into it. If you have the cash, this is a consistent leader among its peers; its three-year return to June 30/01 is 5% (thanks to its low MER), against an average of 4.3% for the category.

### NATIONAL BANK TREASURY BILL PLUS FUND $$$ ↓ C NO RSP CMM

Manager: Richard Lévesque, since 1995

MER: 0.85%    Fundata: B    Style: Money Market

Suitability: Conservative investors

You need $50,000 to get into this fund. For that price, you get a fund that invests about 67% of assets in Ontario and Quebec T-bills in addition to having a lower management fee than the companion Money Market Fund. The returns here are consistently above average. You can expect to receive an annual yield that's about 30 basis points (0.3 percentage points) higher than the Money

Market Fund's, which—not coincidentally—is about the difference in the two management fees. Formerly the Natcan Treasury Bill Fund.

## Foreign Money Market Funds

### NATIONAL BANK U.S. MONEY MARKET FUND       $$$ ↓ C NO RSP FMM

Manager: Richard Lévesque, since 1995

MER: 1.11%     Fundata: E

Suitability: Conservative investors

This is a fully RRSP-eligible fund that invests in Canadian debt securities denominated in U.S. dollars. Last year, the portfolio was mainly in Government of Canada T-bills. In the latest year to June 30/01, the fund returned a solid 4.9%, well above average. It has a good-quality portfolio with above-average returns and the second-lowest risk rating in its category. A good hedge against future declines in the Canadian dollar.

## Also Recommended/National Bank Funds

## Canadian Bond Funds

### NATIONAL BANK BOND FUND                     $$ → FI NO RSP CB

Manager: Gilles Chouinard, since 1994

MER: 1.48%     Fundata: D      Style: Value

Suitability: Moderate-risk income investors

Once the old General Trust Bond Fund, this fund was renamed in August 1998 but the manager and the mandate remained the same. The portfolio is a blend of Government of Canada bonds, Quebec and Ontario government issues, and some corporate and municipal bonds. This fund has been consistently in the middle of the pack among its peers, moving just above or just below average on annual returns. Over the five years to June 30/01, the fund generated an average annual gain of 6.4%, slightly above the norm for the Canadian Bond category. The risk rating is also average, so we'll give it an average $$ rating.

## Promising Newcomers/National Bank Funds

**Canadian Equity Funds**

### NATIONAL BANK CANADIAN OPPORTUNITIES FUND  NR → G NO RSP CE

Manager: Natcan Investment Management, since inception (December 1999)

MER: 2.21%      Fundata: N/A      Style: Sector Rotation/Growth

Suitability: Aggressive investors

This fund is a Canadian equity sector rotator, which means the managers alter their sector allocations with the changing economic outlook. As of mid-2001, the fund had a clear positioning, as its top allocations were 43.1% to industrial products, 10.4% to utilities, and 9.5% to metals and minerals. In the year ending June 30/01, the fund realized a 16.6% return compared with a 5.8% loss for the category. Definitely worth a look if you're a more aggressive investor and it is available in your province.

## Top Choices/NBC/Fidelity Investments Funds

None.

## Also Recommended/NBC/Fidelity Investments Funds

None.

## Promising Newcomers/NBC/Fidelity Investments Funds

None.

# NORTHWEST MUTUAL FUNDS

## THE COMPANY

The Northwest Funds organization was established in 1997 when a group headed by mutual fund marketing expert Michael Butler purchased the Concorde fund family and transformed it. Butler, who had previous industry experience with Mackenzie, Spectrum, and Talvest, remains the driving force behind the company.

Under the Concorde name, the funds had been managed by a Quebec-based firm, TPR Investment Management, with indifferent results. However, TPR is now gone and Northwest currently uses the services of several outside managers.

In 2000, the company added the Marathon funds to its line-up, and now runs them under the "Specialty" trade name; they're more aggressively managed than the original Northwest funds. Also during 2000, the Northwest Dividend Fund was merged into the Northwest Balanced Fund, and the Northwest Income Fund changed its name to Northwest Specialty High-Yield Bond Fund and adopted a different investment mandate.

Don't confuse these Northwest funds with the segregated funds offered by North West Life. This is a completely different group with no corporate affiliation to the insurance firm. So why did they choose the name at all, you may ask, especially since they are based in Toronto? Well, the name refers to what is known as the northwest quadrant on a risk–return chart. The funds that appear in the northwest quadrant are those that combine the best returns with the lowest degree of risk.

Northwest has done a lot of work to improve its Web site, which we noted in the past was quite weak. It's much better now, with some useful information about the funds in this group. However, we could do without the annoying pop-up graphics and sound.

## THE DETAILS

|  |  |
|---|---|
| Number of funds: | 9 |
| Assets under management: | $357 million |
| Load charge: | Front: max. 6%; Back: max. 6% |
| Switching charge: | 2% maximum |
| Where sold: | Across Canada |
| How sold: | Through brokers and dealers |
| Phone number: | 1-888-809-3333 and (416)594-6633 |
| Web site address: | www.northwestfunds.com |
| E-mail address: | marketing@northwestfunds.com |
| Minimum initial investment: | $500 (except for the Specialty Equity and Specialty Resource funds, which require a $1,000 minimum) |

## INVESTING TIPS

Be wary of the funds in the Northwest Specialty series. These funds can be extremely volatile and are prone to huge valuation swings. For example, the Northwest Specialty Aggressive Growth Fund lost a breathtaking 72.4% in the year ending June 30/01. It may be hard to believe, but the Northwest Specialty Momentum Fund did even worse, dropping 74.4%. Not all the Specialty funds are losers, however. In fact, the Specialty Equity Fund gained 20.1% over the same period. Perhaps not surprisingly, the company is taking steps to merge the Specialty Aggressive Growth and Specialty Momentum funds into Specialty Equity, which will have the effect of expunging their records from the history books.

## FUND SUMMARY

| | |
|---|---|
| Top Choices: | Balanced, Growth |
| Also Recommended: | International, Specialty Equity |
| Promising Newcomers: | None |
| The Rest: | Money Market, Specialty Aggressive Growth, Specialty High-Yield Bond, Specialty Innovations, Specialty Momentum, Specialty Resource |

## FUND RATINGS

### Top Choices

**Canadian Equity Funds**

### NORTHWEST GROWTH FUND                    $$$ → G #/* RSP CE

Manager: Richard Fogler (Kingwest and Company), since 1997

MER: 2.89%     Fundata: A     Style: Value

Suitability: Conservative investors

Richard Fogler took over this fund in 1997 and it has been an above-average performer ever since. He is a veteran money manager with more than 25 years of experience, but he's not well-known to investors. He uses a disciplined stock selection style called economic value added (EVA), which was developed in the 1970s by Joel Stern of the New York investment house, Stern Stewart. The objective of the complicated analytical process is to identify companies that consistently add shareholder value, thereby improving the price of their stock. Essentially, Fogler uses this approach to analyze what a company will be worth in the future, and buys stocks in the firms with the best potential. If he doesn't see the potential for 40% to 50% growth within two years, the stock doesn't make the buy list. In the first half of 2001, some of the stocks that met his tough criteria were Sears Canada, Bombardier, Shaw Communications, Alberta Energy, and Bank of Montreal. The portfolio is kept small (about 35 stocks) and turnover is minimal, which is good from a tax-efficiency perspective if the fund is held outside a registered plan. The fund was a first-quartile performer in 2000 and again in the first half of 2001, during a very difficult time for the stock markets. One-year gain to June 30/01 was a scintillating 12.5%. Three-year average annual compound rate of return was a very good 11.6%. This fund is one of those hidden gems that deserve more attention.

## Canadian Balanced Funds

### NORTHWEST BALANCED FUND                    $$$ → G/FI #/* RSP CBAL

Manager: Richard Fogler (Kingwest and Company), since 1997

MER: 2.78%      Fundata: A       Style: Value

Suitability: Conservative investors

This is a conservatively managed balanced fund that uses a "sleep at night" approach to investing, in the words of Northwest president Michael Butler. Domestic stocks are selected using the same EVA analysis employed in the companion Growth Fund. There is also a very good foreign component to this fund, with both U.S. and global stocks (these stocks are selected by OpCap, which runs the companion International Fund). The fixed-income side consists mainly of short-term bonds, which provide some income while reducing overall volatility. There may also be large cash holdings: in the first half of 2001, some 20% of the assets was in T-bills. Results using this blend of styles since Fogler took charge at the end of 1997 are good. In fact, this fund has been a first-quartile performer in its category since 1999. Three-year average annual compound rate of return to June 30/01 was 7.2%. Weighting in the first half of 2001 was tilted toward equities, but the large cash reserve served as a cushion. A decent performer all around. Good for an RRSP.

## Also Recommended

## Canadian Small-Cap Funds

### NORTHWEST SPECIALTY EQUITY FUND           $$$ ↑ G #/* RSP CSC

Manager: Wayne Deans (Deans Knight Capital Management), since 1994

MER: 2.68%      Fundata: A       Style: Value

Suitability: Aggressive investors

Take caution here: The word "Specialty" in this fund's name signals a more aggressive investing approach. And that's just what Wayne Deans brings to this volatile small-cap fund. It can, and has, experienced huge swings both up and down. In 1998, for example, it lost a whopping 33.3%. But recently it has been on a roll, with a gain of more than 23% in the first half of 2001, a remarkable performance in a down market. Deans seeks out fast-growing companies with good balance sheets and a clear competitive edge. His mandate allows him to choose stocks with a market cap of up to $1 billion—that's a lot for a small-cap fund. In the first half of 2001, the fund was heavily weighted toward the resource sector, which did well, explaining the strong returns. There's a lot of profit potential here, but you must be willing to accept the risk that goes with it.

## Global Equity Funds

### NORTHWEST INTERNATIONAL FUND                 $$$ → G #/* £ GE

Manager: Eliza Mazen (OpCap Advisors), since 1998

MER: 3.10%      Fundata: A       Style: Value

Suitability: Conservative investors

The goal of this fund is to invest in the "best 100 companies in the world." That's obviously a challenge, but OpCap Advisors (a subsidiary of Oppenheimer Capital of New York) has been doing a decent job with this fund since assuming management responsibility at the start of 1998. During that year, the fund gained 26.3%, good enough to place it in the top 10% of performers in its category according to Globefund. Results in 1999 weren't quite as impressive; the fund gained 18.9%, good for a high third-quartile ranking. In 2000, the advance was a modest 4.5%, but that was good enough for a first-quartile ranking in a weak market. You'll probably be familiar with some of the top names in the portfolio, such as McDonald's (U.S.) and Canon (Japan). But other companies may be new to you, like Nordea AB (Denmark) and Telekomunikacja Polska SA (Poland). Note that although the fund is called "International," it is actually a global fund since it invests in North America as well as overseas. One negative to consider is the high MER. An RRSP-eligible clone of this fund is also available, but it has a very high MER of 3.80%.

## Promising Newcomers

None.

# PERIGEE INVESTMENT COUNSEL

## THE COMPANY

The Perigee organization has been in business for almost 30 years, but its mutual funds are still unfamiliar to most people. That's because they were previously available only as pooled funds to pension plans and Perigee's own high net worth clients. When the company decided to provide its expertise to average investors by offering their line of pooled funds in a slightly more expensive retail mutual fund version, all the historic returns were recalculated to factor in the appropriate management fees, making the performance numbers consistent with those in the rest of the industry.

But make no mistake: the Perigee line of mutual funds is a low-cost entry when compared to other fund companies. There are no load charges and the average MER of the Perigee line of funds is well below the industry average.

The 13 Perigee mutual funds provide broad diversification with money market, fixed-income, U.S. equity, international equity, and four Canadian equity offerings. We also like the balanced structure of this fund family. Perigee created three balanced funds to follow different benchmark asset mixes; there's the very conservative Accufund, the moderate-risk Symmetry Balanced Fund, and the slightly more aggressive Diversifund.

Of special note is the company's Web site, which posts quarterly reports for each fund. The reports proffer some candid comments about performance, including what's worked well recently and what hasn't.

Note that Perigee also manages many of the Clarica funds, so you can also acquire their expertise through that source.

The firm is owned by Legg Mason, a U.S. money management house.

## THE DETAILS

|  |  |
|---|---|
| Number of funds: | 13 |
| Assets under management: | $5.3 million |
| Load charge: | None |
| Switching charge: | None |
| Where sold: | In all provinces, but not in the territories |
| How sold: | Through brokers, dealers, and financial planners |
| Phone number: | 1-888-437-3333 |
| Web site address: | www.perigeemutualfunds.com |
| E-mail address: | funds@perigeemutualfunds.com |
| Minimum initial investment: | $2,500 per fund |

## INVESTING TIPS

Although Perigee's funds are no-load, they can no longer be acquired directly through the company, which is a departure from past practice. This means you must buy online or through a dealer and you may be assessed some type of charge. Be sure to clarify this point before you place an order. Sales people receive a trailer fee of 0.5% annually from Perigee, so you may be able to negotiate a no-charge arrangement. Note that the B units are the ones sold to the general public.

## FUND SUMMARY

| | |
|---|---|
| Top Choices: | Accufund, Active Bond, Index Plus Bond, T-Plus |
| Also Recommended: | Global Bond, International Equity |
| Promising Newcomers: | Legg Mason U.S. Value |
| The Rest: | Batterymarch U.S. Equity, Canadian Sector Equity, Canadian Select 35 Equity, Canadian Aggressive Growth Equity, Diversified, North American Equity, Symmetry Balanced. |

## FUND RATINGS

### Top Choices

### Canadian Balanced Funds

**PERIGEE ACCUFUND**                             **$$$ ↓ FI/G NO RSP CTAA**

Manager: Gia Steffensen, since 1992

MER: 1.02%     Fundata: B     Style: Top-down Growth

Suitability: Conservative investors

This is Perigee's lowest-risk balanced fund offering. Like all Perigee funds, this fund is managed using a team approach. In this case, the managers follow a conservative asset mix, split about 70%/30% between debt instruments and equity. In the first half of 2001, the fund had 45% of its assets in government bonds, mortgages, and mortgage-backed securities, with 16% invested in cash. U.S. equity exposure was being increased. Returns are slightly above average for the fund's peer group over the one- and three-year time frames. This fund is an excellent low-cost choice for conservative investors and would fit well into an RRSP or RRIF, but lacks the sizzle more aggressive investors would want. Aggressive investors can opt for one of the other two Perigee balanced offerings, but we are recommending neither at this time because of recent poor performance.

## Canadian Bond Funds

### PERIGEE ACTIVE BOND FUND $$$ ↑ FI NO RSP CB

Manager: David L.H. Yu, since 1996

MER: 0.75%     Fundata: A     Style: Interest Rate Anticipation

Suitability: Investors seeking above-average returns, willing to accept more risk

For this fund to perform well, the managers have to guess correctly about the future course of interest rates. The emphasis of the portfolio is therefore constantly shifting, depending on whether they expect rates to rise or fall. During the first half of 2001, the focus was on short-term bonds, which were seen as benefiting most from interest rate cuts in the U.S. and Canada. One advantage of this fund is its attractive MER, which becomes especially important during times of low interest rates. That situation helped the fund gain 5.9% for the year ending June 30/01, well above average for the category. Three-year figures are also superior and this fund has outperformed the companion Perigee Index Plus Bond Fund on both a one- and three-year basis. It moves up to a $$$ rating, but the risk here will be somewhat higher than with the Index Plus Bond Fund.

### PERIGEE INDEX PLUS BOND FUND $$$ → FI NO RSP CB

Manager: David L.H. Yu, since 1996

MER: 0.75%     Fundata: C     Style: Index

Suitability: Long-term conservative investors

The goal of this fund is to track the Scotia Capital Markets Universe Bond Index, with slight variations to provide added value. Most of the bonds in the portfolio are government issues, with some corporate issues added for extra return potential. Performance has been very good over all time periods, with a fine average annual compound rate of return of 8.9% for the 10 years to June 30/01. The low MER is a big help in producing those good numbers. Risk is slightly better than average and somewhat lower than with the companion Active Bond Fund. Overall, this fund is an excellent low-cost alternative in this category. We'll maintain our $$$ rating.

## Canadian Money Market Funds

### PERIGEE T-PLUS FUND $$$$ ↓ C NO RSP CMM

Manager: Owen D. Phillips, since 1986

MER: 0.48%     Fundata: D     Style: Index

Suitability: Short-term conservative investors

This is a first-rate money market fund with good returns. In fact, it was one of the top-performing funds in the category over the decade to June 30/01 with an average annual return of 5.4%. The good numbers are encouraged by the low MER, although the fees and costs have been inching up in recent years. The portfolio is mainly invested in T-bills, with a few bankers' acceptances in the mix to provide higher yields. Safety profile is excellent. Rating moves up to $$$$.

## Also Recommended

### Global and International Equity Funds

### PERIGEE INTERNATIONAL EQUITY FUND $$ → G NO £ IE

Managers: Greg Jones and Susan Kenneally (Clay Finlay Inc.), since 1995 and 1999

MER: 1.70%    Fundata: A    Style: Top-down Growth

Suitability: Long-term investors seeking non-North American exposure

This is a true "international" fund as the term is used in the industry; that is, it invests only outside North America. With funds of this type, the major decision comes down to how to play the Europe–Asia mix, as everything else is incidental. In the first half of 2001, just over 20% of the portfolio was in Japan, but that was about it as far as Asia was concerned. The heaviest deployment of assets was in Europe, with Great Britain and France each holding 16% positions. Past results from this fund have been exceptional, but it stumbled badly over the past year, losing 26% over the 12 months to June 30/01. Even with that setback, longer-term results are much better than average so we assume that this fund will get back on track. Until we see evidence of that happening, however, we will downgrade the rating to $$.

### Foreign Bond Funds

### PERIGEE GLOBAL BOND FUND $$ → C NO RSP FB

Manager: David L.H. Yu, since 1996

MER: 1.41%    Fundata: B    Style: Index

Suitability: Investors seeking foreign currency diversification

On the whole, foreign bond funds have been weak performers over the years. The average annual rate of return for the category over the decade to June 30/01 was an unimpressive 5.7%. The main attraction of these funds is to provide fixed-income currency diversification in a portfolio. This fund does well on that score and also has produced better-than-average gains over all time frames covering five years. As a bonus, it is RRSP-eligible, meaning you will not impinge on foreign content restrictions when purchasing units. Foreign bond funds generate the best results when the Canadian dollar is falling and interest rates are declining. We don't expect to see this tandem at work in the coming year, so it is likely that returns here will be unexciting. However, if you like the idea of having some exposure to foreign currencies, this fund offers a reasonable cost approach when playing that game.

## Promising Newcomers

### PERIGEE LEGG MASON U.S. VALUE FUND NR → G NO £ USE

Managers: Bill Miller and Mary Chris Gay (Legg Mason), since inception (December 2000)

MER: 2.17%    Fundata: N/A    Style: Value

Suitability: Long-term investors seeking a tax-efficient fund

This is the first fund to emerge from Perigee's new relationship with U.S.-based Legg Mason. It's run by Legg Mason president Bill Miller, who was named Fund Manager of the Decade in a 1999 poll run by Morningstar.com. The Canadian version is modelled on the Legg Mason Value Trust Fund, also run by Miller, which beat the S&P 500 every year through the 1990s. This result indicates a disciplined approach to value investing and a very low turnover; the average holding period for a stock is five to seven years, which means this will be a very tax-efficient fund for non-registered portfolios. With value investing back in vogue these days, and given the track record of the manager, this fund looks like an almost sure-fire winner.

# PHILLIPS, HAGER & NORTH INVESTMENT MANAGEMENT

## THE COMPANY

This is a highly respected Vancouver-based investment house with some outstanding performers in its stable. The firm has been in business since 1964 and manages money for pension plans, individuals, foundations, and the like, as well as operating its family of mutual funds. Management fees are among the lowest in the industry. The funds in this group are best suited for conservative, long-term investors. Minimum initial investment is a hefty $25,000 per account, with subsequent minimum purchases of $1,000.

PH&N has always used a team approach with regard to its fund management. However, they have provided us with the names of all their key investment decision personnel. Here they are:

- *Overall investment strategy.* Company partners Tony Gage and David Heal.
- *North American equity.* The Canadian team is headed by Ian Mottershead and also includes Chris Cumming, Dale Harrison, and Dan Lewin.
- *Fixed-income.* Scott Lamont is the key person here. Others include Michael Borden, Richard Durrans, Tony Gage, David Heal, Christine Hu, Lili Leung, Hanif Mamdani, Dan Russell, Rob Menning, and Chris Suzuki.
- *Global equities, including the U.S.* Geoffrey Randalls is the senior manager. Other team members include Jeff Black, Jeff Clay, Bernard Gauthier, Trevor Graham, Pat Naccarato, Jeff Tiefenbach, and Lorne Yawney.
- *Macroeconomics.* David Heal, Gene Hochachka, and Cameron Kerr.

The company uses a growth-at-a-reasonable-price (GARP) investment strategy, which means the managers will not buy overpriced issues for their portfolios.

One significant development during the past year was the decision to fold the Euro-Pacific Fund into the new Overseas Equity Fund. This move was approved by unitholders in February 2001.

## THE DETAILS

|  |  |
|---|---|
| Number of funds: | 16 |
| Assets under management: | $8.8 billion |
| Load charge: | None |
| Switching charge: | None |
| Where sold: | Across Canada |

How sold: Directly through PH&N or through brokers, dealers, and financial planners
Phone number: 1-800-661-6141
Web site address: www.phn.com
E-mail address: info@phn.com
Minimum initial investment: $25,000

## INVESTING TIPS

Some investors have been purchasing PH&N fund units through discount brokerage firms. In some cases, large amounts of money are involved. We were informed about one case in which a gentleman said he paid several hundred dollars in commissions by going this route.

Although we generally support the idea of discount brokers, we advise against buying PH&N funds through them if you are going to be charged any sort of commission, either when you make the purchase or when you sell. Set up an account directly with the company and save all sales charges.

Note that the company's Vintage Fund, which has been an excellent performer, is closed to new investors. However, existing unitholders can add to their positions. Because it is effectively closed, we do not show it on our Recommended List.

## FUND SUMMARY

Top Choices: Balanced, Bond, Canadian Equity, Canadian Growth, Canadian Money Market, Dividend Income, Short-Term Bond and Mortgage, U.S.$ Money Market
Also Recommended: None
Promising Newcomers: None
The Rest: Global Equity RSP, High-Yield Bond, Overseas Equity, Total Return Bond, U.S. Equity, U.S. Growth, Vintage

# FUND RATINGS

## Top Choices

### Canadian Equity Funds

### PHILLIPS, HAGER & NORTH CANADIAN EQUITY FUND
$$$ → G NO RSP CE

Manager: Team, headed by Ian Mottershead

MER: 1.14%     Fundata: B     Style: GARP

Suitability: Conservative investors

This is a pure Canadian stock fund with no foreign content (the companion Canadian Growth Fund holds foreign stocks). It is a growth-oriented fund but as with all funds in this group, the managers will not overpay for stocks. The main holdings are in medium- to large-sized companies. In their 2001 second-quarter report, the managers said they were looking carefully at the battered technology sector for bargains, but were not yet prepared to make a major commitment. Financial services stocks continued to dominate the portfolio at that point, representing over a third of the total assets. The fund chalked up very good gains in both 1999 and 2000, with advances of 21.2% and 20.8% respectively. It gave back 6.3% in the first half of 2001, but that was a much better performance than the TSE 300. Over time, the fund has been a consistent above-average performer, with a brief dip into the third quartile in 1998—the only blemish in recent years. Average annual compound rate of return over the decade to June 30/01 was 11.4%. Bottom line: steady above-average returns with an acceptable degree of risk. The low management expense ratio (MER) and no load charges add to the fund's attractiveness.

### PHILLIPS, HAGER & NORTH CANADIAN GROWTH FUND
$$$ → G NO RSP CE

Manager: Team, headed by Ian Mottershead

MER: 1.19%     Fundata: C     Style: GARP

Suitability: Conservative investors

The performance pattern here is similar to the company's Canadian Equity Fund, so the same broad comments apply. The portfolios are also similar; the main difference is that a chunk of this fund's holdings (about 24%) is in U.S. and international securities, thus providing global diversification. Like its Canadian Equity Fund stablemate, this fund is also a consistent above-average performer. However, recent results have lagged behind those of the Canadian Equity Fund because the Canadian market generally held up better than global markets in late 2000 and in the first half of 2001. As a result, the fund lost 9.9%

in the year to June 30/01. However, the 10-year average annual return remains strong at 11.3%. If you prefer your Canadian fund to have some foreign content in it, this is the one to choose. Formerly known as the Canadian Equity Plus Fund and prior to that as the RSP/RIF Equity Fund.

## Dividend Income Funds

### PHILLIPS, HAGER & NORTH DIVIDEND INCOME FUND          $$$$ ↓ G/FI NO RSP DIV

Manager: Team, headed by Ian Mottershead

MER: 1.21%     Fundata: C      Style: GARP

Suitability: Conservative investors

This portfolio concentrates on high-yielding common stocks rather than preferreds (in fact, you'd be hard-pressed to find a preferred share here). However, the stock selection process puts a high degree of emphasis on safety (there are no cyclicals in the portfolio). As well, only new stocks that have a dividend yield exceeding the average of the TSE are added. The fund has a great performance record, but cash flow is not its strongest suit so keep that in mind if you're an income-oriented investor. However, on a total return basis, this fund is one of the consistent leaders in the dividend fund category and is usually a first-quartile performer, meaning it is in the top 25% of all funds in the group. Calendar year 1999 was an exception, with the fund producing a mediocre 2.6% return. It rallied smartly, however, in 2000 to gain an amazing 51.6%! During the first half of 2001 it came in just below break-even, with a 1.2% decline. Over a decade, it's the top-performing dividend fund in Canada with an average annual return of 17.1%. Just remember that this is not a conventional dividend fund. It's more like a blue-chip stock fund and, as such, it will be especially vulnerable to developments like a big pullback in bank share prices. Still, for a long-term investor, you won't do much better if you're seeking a conservative, well-managed Canadian stock fund. It's a good choice for RRSPs and RRIFs for that reason.

## Canadian Balanced Funds

### PHILLIPS, HAGER & NORTH BALANCED FUND  $$$ ↓ FI/G NO RSP CBAL

Manager: Team

MER: 0.92%     Fundata: C      Style: GARP

Suitability: Conservative investors

This is a well-diversified fund, with a portfolio made up of a carefully chosen mix of Canadian stocks; U.S. stocks; federal, provincial, and corporate bonds; plus a 25% foreign content holding. That last position is responsible in large part for the 5.5% loss the fund experienced in the first half of 2001. Until now, it has never recorded a losing calendar year going all the way back to its launch in 1991. Historically, this fund tends to be a second-quartile performer, which means it does slightly better than the average for the Canadian Balanced category. This one won't shoot the lights out, but at least you won't toss and turn at night worrying about your money. Good choice for an RRSP.

## Canadian Bond Funds

### PHILLIPS, HAGER & NORTH BOND FUND          $$$$ ↓ FI NO RSP CB

Manager: Team, headed by Scott Lamont

MER: 0.58%      Fundata: D       Style: Interest Rate Anticipation plus
                                          Active Trading

Suitability: Conservative investors

This is one of the better bond funds around. Both short- and long-term results are well above average. The fund gained 5.6% in the year to June 30/01, a good result in a tough bond market. Over the past decade, the average annual compound rate of return is 9.4%, which ranks this entry in the top 10% of bond funds in Canada. The portfolio is weighted to government securities, with some corporate issues, foreign bonds, and mortgages thrown into the mix. An extra benefit is the very low MER, which makes this one of the best values you'll find in bond funds from that point of view. The fund tracks the Scotia Capital Markets Universe Bond Index with some leeway in terms of the managers' duration call, meaning they may increase or decrease the risk level slightly from that of the Index, depending on their views of where the bond market is going. They also do some active trading. The risk rating is excellent. If you're looking for a long-term buy-and-hold bond fund, they don't come much better than this one.

### PHILLIPS, HAGER & NORTH SHORT-TERM          $$$$ ↓ FI NO RSP CB
### BOND AND MORTGAGE FUND

Manager: Team, headed by Scott Lamont

MER: 0.62%      Fundata: D

Suitability: Conservative investors

This is a halfway house between the company's successful Bond Fund and their money market funds. The idea is to generate a better return than you'll get from money funds, but with less risk than a conventional bond fund would carry. To achieve that, the fund invests in bonds that mature within five years, in addition to conventional mortgages. Consequently, the safety record is very good, as you would expect. What is somewhat surprising is that over the year to June 30/01, this fund actually outperformed the Bond Fund, gaining 6.8%. It also has a better three-year record and usually ranks as a top-quartile performer in its category. If you're looking for a defensive fund with decent returns, this one will work well. A useful holding for a conservatively managed RRSP or RRIF. Rating is raised to $$$$.

## Canadian Money Market Funds

### PHILLIPS, HAGER & NORTH CANADIAN MONEY MARKET FUND                    $$$$ → C NO RSP CMM

Manager: Team, headed by Scott Lamont

MER: 0.48%     Fundata: E

Suitability: Conservative investors

This portfolio invests mainly in high-grade corporate notes, which enhances the return with slightly more risk. Major advantage: one of the lowest management fees in the business, which contributes significantly to the above-average performance numbers. In fact, it is a first-quartile performer in its category almost every year. Consistently good returns, timeliness, and no-load status earn it a top rating.

## Foreign Money Market Funds

### PHILLIPS, HAGER & NORTH U.S.$ MONEY MARKET FUND                    $$$$ → C NO RSP FMM

Manager: Team, headed by Scott Lamont

MER: 0.55%     Fundata: E

Suitability: Conservative investors

This is a solid U.S. money fund that offers the bonus of full RRSP eligibility. The managers invest in short-term notes issued by Canadian governments and corporations that are denominated in U.S. currency. The fund offers one of the lowest management fees in this category, in addition to being no-load. It's been a first-quartile performer every year since it was launched in 1990. You don't get better consistency than that. A good choice, especially for those who want to hold U.S. dollars in their RRSPs or RRIFs.

## Also Recommended

None.

## Promising Newcomers

None.

# ROYAL MUTUAL FUNDS

## THE COMPANY

The Royal Bank is the premier company in Canada in terms of no-load funds. Based on assets under management, it is number one among the banks and second overall, behind the giant Investors Group.

Royal's extensive product line of 54 funds brings together many different investment management styles, objectives, sectors, and geographic regions. Several of Royal's mutual funds have undergone name changes. Its Strategic line of funds—managed by James P. O'Shaughnessy, a highly regarded U.S. quantitative analyst—are now known as the O'Shaughnessy Funds. All three have strong performance records. The three balanced funds formerly marketed under the Royal Trust Advantage name are now known as the Royal Select funds. In all cases, however, the money management strategies stay the same.

Nine global funds focusing primarily on the new economy were launched in December 2000 and January 2001. The most promising of these at present is the Royal Health Sciences Sector Fund.

The primary manager for the majority of the funds is Royal Bank Investment Management (RBIM); however; some of the index and foreign funds use outside managers.

## THE DETAILS

|  |  |
|---|---|
| Number of funds: | 54 |
| Assets under management: | $34.4 billion |
| Load charge: | None |
| Switching charge: | None |
| Where sold: | Across Canada |
| How sold: | Directly through any Royal Bank or Royal Trust branch or through brokers, dealers, and financial planners |
| Phone number: | English: 1-800-463-FUND (3863); French: 1-800-668-FOND (3663) |
| Web site address: | www.royalbank.com/rmf/index.html |
| E-mail address: | funds@royalbank.com |
| Minimum initial investment: | Non-registered: $1,000 (generally); Registered: $500 (generally) |

## INVESTING TIPS

Royal has a line of six index funds, which were launched in response to the increasing popularity of this type of fund. These index funds offer exposure to

Canadian, international, and U.S. indices, with the foreign funds having a fully eligible RRSP/RRIF option, designated by "RSP" in the fund name. Four of the index funds have a low management expense ratio (MER) of 0.58%, while two premium index funds have had their MERs capped at 0.30%. However, you need an initial $250,000 minimum purchase to get in on these funds.

## FUND SUMMARY

| | |
|---|---|
| Top Choices: | Canadian Growth, Canadian Money Market, Canadian Value, Dividend, Energy, Monthly Income, O'Shaughnessy Canadian Equity, O'Shaughnessy U.S. Growth, O'Shaughnessy U.S. Value, U.S.$ Money Market |
| Also Recommended: | Select Income, U.S. Equity |
| Promising Newcomers: | Global Health Sciences Sector |
| The Rest: | Asian Growth, Balanced, Balanced Growth, Bond, Bond Index, Canadian Equity, Canadian Index, Canadian Small-Cap, Canadian T-Bill, DS Premier Canadian Bond Portfolio, e-Commerce, European Growth, Global Balanced, Global Bond, Global Communications & Media, Global Consumer Trends Sector, Global Education, Global Financial Services Sector, Global Infrastructure Sector, Global Resources Sector, Global Technology Sector, Global Titans, International Equity, International RSP Index, Japanese Stock, Latin American, Life Science & Technology, Mortgage, Precious Metals, Select Balanced Portfolio, Select Choices Aggressive Growth, Select Choices Balanced, Select Choices Growth, Select Choices Income, Select Growth, U.S. Index, U.S. Mid-Cap Equity, U.S. RSP Index, Zweig Strategic Growth |

# FUND RATINGS

## Top Choices

### Canadian Equity Funds

### ROYAL CANADIAN VALUE FUND       $$$ → G NO RSP CLC

Manager: Christina Poole and Ina Van Berkel, since March 1998

MER: 2.15%     Fundata: A     Style: Bottom-up Value

Suitability: Conservative investors

This fund is holding nice and steady in a truly tough environment. The fund managers use classic value-based fundamental analysis to select companies, and they are doing a good job. In the year ending June 30/01, the fund recorded a 2.1% return. That seems a very modest result until you recognize that the average fund in the large-cap category had an 8.5% loss. In the three years to the same date, the rate of return was 5.5% per annum, which was 1.5 points above the category average. As of mid-2001, the fund had a large cash position (22%) as a defensive measure. The fund debuts with a $$$ rating.

### O'SHAUGHNESSY CANADIAN EQUITY FUND     $$$ → G NO RSP CLC

Manager: James P. O'Shaughnessy, since November 1997

MER: 1.60%     Fundata: A     Style: Value

Suitability: Conservative investors

This fund has everything you want in a large-cap Canadian equity fund: a skilled and experienced manager, a relatively low MER for the category, transparent investment strategy, and a great record. This fund holds about 50 Canadian stocks, which are chosen by combining both value and growth measurements. As of mid-2001, the portfolio was fully invested (virtually no cash) in a cross-section of Canadian sectors with the largest allocations to financial services (27.2%) and utilities (14.4%). All the O'Shaughnessy funds use what might be called an active/passive approach: many of the same principles used by index funds are employed, but his system modifies this method by actively selecting key stocks using specialized criteria he has developed. In the year ending June 30/01, the fund had a sterling 12.8% return. The fund debuts with a $$$ rating. It looks quite attractive in the current climate.

## Canadian Small-to-Mid-Cap Equity Funds

### ROYAL CANADIAN GROWTH FUND $$$ → G NO RSP CSC

Manager: Eden Rahim, since 1994

MER: 2.31%     Fundata: C     Style: Growth

Suitability: Aggressive investors

Over the past two years, Eden Rahim moved this small-to-mid-cap fund away from a resource bias and into growth sectors such as technology and biotechnology in hopes of revitalizing it. Part of the strategy included reducing the number of stock positions to concentrate on fewer names. The fund's focus on commodity stocks was reduced and there was a significant overweight position in the growth-oriented industrial products group, as well as consumer products. Rahim's stewardship is bearing fruit. The fund broke even in the 12 months to June 30/01 (the peer group lost 6.1%), after gaining 39.2% in the 12 months to June 30/00. The three-year numbers are now well above average at 8.4% annually. The fund was also holding substantial cash (nearly 18%) in mid-2001 as a defensive measure. We are upgrading the rating to $$$.

## Dividend Income Funds

### ROYAL DIVIDEND FUND $$$$ ↑ G/FI NO RSP DIV

Manager: John Kellett, since 1993

MER: 1.88%     Fundata: C     Style: Value

Suitability: Balanced investors

The stated goal here is to maximize tax-advantaged income through the use of the dividend tax credit, as well as to generate capital gains. In both cases, it has excelled. Like many dividend funds, this one is heavily invested in interest-sensitive bank and utility stocks—which accounted for 49% of assets at mid-2001—making the fund vulnerable to rising interest rates, a fact that should always be in the back of your mind when you are considering a purchase. Otherwise, the portfolio is generally defensive in downturns. In terms of its holdings, this fund has 85% of the portfolio in high-yielding common stock, making it more aggressive than dividend funds that lean more toward preferred shares. The result of this asset mix was reflected in recent returns, when the market was focusing on interest rates. During the 12 months to June 30/01, the fund gained 17.4%, which was a first-quartile result. Returns over longer time frames remain well above average. As long as you're aware of the sensitivity of this fund to interest rates (which results in above-average risk compared with dividend funds as a group) it remains one of the best choices in the Canadian dividend category and is highly recommended whether you need regular cash flow or capital gains. This fund is an especially good choice for an RRSP or RRIF.

## U.S. Equity Funds

### O'SHAUGHNESSY U.S. GROWTH FUND  $$$ ↑ G NO £ USE

Manager: James P. O'Shaughnessy, since November 1997

MER: 1.60%     Fundata: C     Style: Growth

Suitability: Aggressive investors

This is a specialty fund that includes a lot of small-cap stocks. The fund manager uses the O'Shaughnessy U.S. Growth Strategy Index, which is a fundamental momentum-based filter model that identifies firms with low price to sales ratios, rising earnings, and a rising share price. So far the fund is off to solid start. In the three years ending June 30/01, the fund recorded an annual compound rate of return of 7.6% per annum compared with a 2.6% average for the peer group. One caution: the fund is more volatile than the U.S. equity fund average as it has a high standard deviation and beta, meaning the risk is above normal. The fund debuts with a $$$ rating.

### O'SHAUGHNESSY U.S. VALUE FUND  $$$$ → G NO £ USE

Manager: James P. O'Shaughnessy, since November 1997

MER: 1.60%     Fundata: B     Style: Value

Suitability: Middle-of-the-road investors

This fund is a mirror of the companion Growth Fund. The manager uses the O'Shaughnessy U.S. Value Strategy Index, which identifies firms with high dividend yields and higher-than-average sales and capitalizations. After a slow start, the fund has rebounded and the three-year annual compound rate of return of 8.2% per annum compares very favourably with a 2.6% average for the peer group. The one-year gain was an amazing 29.3%. The fund has average volatility and appears to be well positioned to take maximum advantage of the current market climate. We don't often give a fund a debut rating of $$$$, but we believe it is justified here in the present conditions.

## Sector Equity Funds

### ROYAL ENERGY FUND  $$$ ↑ G NO RSP NR

Manager: Gordon Zive, since 1994

MER: 2.37%     Fundata: C     Style: Growth

Suitability: Aggressive investors

This is an example of a well-managed fund doing quite well in a tough sector that is often unforgiving and very cyclical. Manager Gordon Zive reduces portfolio risk by holding large-cap, well-established Canadian producers and integrated oil companies, with the latter being more defensive in downturns.

With oil prices surging, the fund reported a return of 16.6% in the year ending June 30/01, which followed nicely on the heels of 8.5% and 24.2% returns in the two previous years. These numbers are all well above the average for the Natural Resources category. Over longer time frames (five to ten years) this fund has a solid record as well. This is one of the best energy-oriented funds available in Canada. Be aware that the risk here is high and this is not a fund for your RRSP. Recommended only for aggressive investors.

## Canadian Balanced and Asset Allocation Funds

### ROYAL MONTHLY INCOME FUND $$$ ↓ FI/G NO RSP CHIB

Manager: John Varao, since 1997

MER: 1.26%    Fundata: A    Style: Tactical Asset Allocation

Suitability: Conservative balanced investors

This fund invests in high-yield, fixed-income securities, including corporate bonds, preferred shares, and income trusts, as well as holding some common shares. As at mid-2001, the fund's allocation was 50% to bonds, 45% to stocks, and the remainder to cash. After a weak start the track record is strong. Return in the year ending June 30/01 was 19.1% compared with 14.3% for the category. Volatility is well below the norm. This is a very good choice if above-average cash flow is a priority. Debuts with a $$$ rating.

## Canadian Money Market Funds

### ROYAL CANADIAN MONEY MARKET FUND $$$ → C NO RSP CMM

Manager: Walter Posiewko, since 1999

MER: 1.00%    Fundata: B

Suitability: Conservative investors

Walter Posiewko has replaced Barry Edwards as the manager of this fund, in addition to the companion U.S. Money Market, Premium Money Market, and Canadian T-Bill funds. It's amazing what a lower MER can do for a fund's return, especially in this category where a slight variation in the MER can lead to quite different results. Case in point: prior to reducing its MER by 33 basis points, this fund was an underachiever. With the lower fees, the fund is returning slightly above-average numbers, with less-than-average volatility. The $$$ rating reflects this change.

## Foreign Money Market Funds

### ROYAL U.S.$ MONEY MARKET FUND
$$$ ↓ C NO RSP FMM

MER: 1.16%    Fundata: D

Suitability: Conservative investors

This fund invests primarily in high-quality, short-term debt that is denominated in U.S. dollars. The securities may be issued or guaranteed by Canadian or foreign governments, banks, or corporations. Holdings favour commercial paper and bankers' acceptances. Returns have generally been average. Risk is low for a fund of this type, but don't lose sight of the currency risk that comes with holding U.S.-dollar denominated securities. Full RRSP eligibility.

## Also Recommended

## U.S. Equity Funds

### ROYAL U.S. EQUITY FUND
$$ ↓ G NO £ USE

Manager: Raymond Mawhinney, since 1999

MER: 2.23%    Fundata: C    Style: Value/Growth

Suitability: Middle-of-the-road investors

This is the largest of the extensive line of Royal U.S. equity offerings. The mandate is to invest in major U.S. companies, with a blend of blue chips and medium-sized firms. Current emphasis is on industrial products, consumer goods, and financial services. Returns have been inconsistent in recent years. Three- and five-year numbers are almost exactly at the averages. However, the fund lost 15.5% in the year ending June 30/01, compared with a 13.8% average loss for the category. The bonus with this fund is its safety record. However, we need strong proof of consistent outperformance to justify a high rating. We are downgrading to a $$.

## Canadian Balanced and Asset Allocation Funds

### ROYAL SELECT INCOME FUND
$$ ↓ FI/G NO RSP CBAL

Manager: John Varao and Mark L. Arthur, since 1999

MER: 1.93%    Fundata: A    Style: Tactical Asset Allocation

Suitability: Conservative investors

There are three Select funds, each of which fulfills a specific investing goal. This is the Select Fund for conservative investors seeking income versus capital growth. In terms of volatility, it has the lowest risk of any of Royal's balanced funds, due to its large weighting toward fixed-income securities. The neutral weighting for this fund is about 67% in income funds and 33% in equity funds.

As of mid-2001, the equities side accounted for 40% of assets, with the remainder in a mix of fixed-income securities. Gain for the three years to June 30/01 averaged 4.4% annually, which was above the norm for the peer group. If safety and a decent return is a useful combo for you, try this one.

## Promising Newcomers

### ROYAL GLOBAL HEALTH SCIENCES SECTOR FUND    NR ↑ G NO £ SPE

Manager: Heather Pierce, since December 2000

MER: 2.75%     Fundata: N/A     Style: Bottom-up Growth

Suitability: Aggressive investors

This recent debut invests in companies engaged in the health services industry. In its first six months of operation it earned 7.9%—a promising start. It's much too early to predict how it will perform in comparison with some of the well-established health care funds like the Talvest entry, but it's one worth watching.

# SAXON FUNDS

## THE COMPANY

Established in 1985, Saxon Mutual Funds are owned and managed by Toronto-based Howson Tattersall Investment Counsel. The firm stresses a disciplined value approach to its stock selection and is widely known for its expertise in the small-cap sector. Besides mutual funds, the company's investment team also manages in excess of $250 million of portfolios or portions of portfolios for institutional and individual clients. Management of the company's line of five mutual funds is under the direction of the company's principals, Richard Howson and Robert Tattersall.

This small fund company has found it difficult to attract money to its funds despite several advantages, including no-load charges, very low management expense ratios (MERs), and some very good performance numbers. In terms of availability, the company began marketing its no-load funds across Canada about two year ago, and all are now available nationwide. Despite this increase in availability, however, assets under management have not grown significantly.

The family is a model of consistency and transparency: nothing fancy, no special features, no confusing name changes, and no shifting objectives. What we see instead is good old-fashioned performance—high returns and relatively low volatility.

## THE DETAILS

|  |  |
|---|---|
| Number of funds: | 5 |
| Assets under management: | $103 million |
| Load charge: | None if purchased directly through the manager, otherwise 2% max |
| Switching charge: | None |
| Where sold: | Across Canada |
| How sold: | Directly through the manager in Ontario or through brokers, dealers, and financial planners |
| Phone number: | 1-888-287-2966 |
| Web site address: | www.saxonfunds.com/~saxon |
| E-mail address: | saxon@saxonfunds.com |
| Minimum initial investment: | $5,000 |

## INVESTING TIPS

Investors have advised us that they have had difficulty acquiring the Saxon funds through a discount broker. We aren't sure why this would be a problem, but it may explain why the company's fund assets under management are not growing more quickly despite their excellent results. If you live in Ontario, you can acquire the funds directly through Saxon (see the phone number above). We recommend that you obtain funds in this way, as no sales commission of any kind will be involved. Residents of other provinces may be told initially that the funds are not available. If this happen to you, ask why. Request a supervisor's assistance to determine if the firm does not offer them, or if the original sales person simply made an error. If you are told you cannot acquire the funds through your company of choice, call Saxon's toll-free number. Tell them about the problem, and ask which companies in your area offer their funds.

## FUND SUMMARY

|  |  |
|---|---|
| Top Choices: | High Income, Small-Cap, Stock |
| Also Recommended: | Balanced, World Growth |
| Promising Newcomers: | None |
| The Rest: | None |

## FUND RATINGS

### Top Choices

### Canadian Equity Funds

#### SAXON STOCK FUND $$$$ ↓ G NO RSP CLC

Manager: Richard Howson, since 1989

MER: 1.75%    Fundata: A    Style: Bottom-up Value

Suitability: Conservative investors

This is a winning Saxon fund but unlike the companion Small-Cap Fund, the stock selection criteria here encompasses not only bottom-up research but also top-down analysis in the never-ending search for Canadian stocks of all capitalization classes. In addition to small companies, this fund also holds some blue-chip Canadian stocks for steady long-term appreciation. Normally there is no crossover between this fund and the Small-Cap Fund in terms of the top 10 holdings, so each has a unique portfolio. Stocks are held for the long term— between three and five years—but the manager may sell if the stock reaches its price target. Composition is more diversified in terms of industry allocation than the Small-Cap Fund, which in theory makes this fund more defensive and therefore less risky. In the year to June 30/01, this fund gained 24.4%, a huge score over the average Canadian equity fund, which lost 5.8%. The three-year, five-year, and ten-year numbers are way above average. Over the past five years, the fund's 13.6% annual compound rate of return beat the average fund by 380 basis points and the benchmark index by close to 300 basis point per annum.

Those results were achieved with a significantly below-average standard deviation and, surprisingly, a low beta (both are measures of risk). This fund is well worthy of a $$$$ rating.

## Canadian Small-to-Mid-Cap Equity Funds

### SAXON SMALL-CAP FUND                    $$$$ ↓ G NO RSP CSC

Manager: Robert Tattersall, since 1985

MER: 1.75%      Fundata: A        Style: Bottom-up Value

Suitability: Middle-of-the-road investors seeking small-cap exposure

The expertise of manager Robert Tattersall is clearly reflected in the performance of this fund, which specializes in Canadian companies that trade on either the TSE or ME, with a market capitalization of less than $150 million at the time of purchase. For added diversification, the fund may also invest in stocks outside Canada, within the foreign content limit. The fund generally adopts a buy-and-hold format, holding stocks for between three and five years, but an option allows it to divest the position if the stock either reaches its price target or if the market cap surpasses $300 million. In reality, many of the companies are well below the capitalization limit and the manager shows some fondness for microcaps—stocks with market caps normally under $100 million. Commodity stocks are underweighted, while industrial products, including growth sectors, are overweighted. The average stock in this portfolio is quite attractive on a valuation basis. Risk is minimized by employing a value approach and by holding over 95 stocks for good diversification. In the latest year to June 30/01, Tattersall recorded a 14.1% return compared with the 6.1% peer group average. Furthermore, over the long term, this diversified fund has managed to be a top-tier performer on a three-year, five-year, and ten-year basis. With a three-year average annual gain of 10.1% and a five-year average gain of 17%, most other small-cap funds are left in the dust, with the average funds returning only 2.7% and 5.3% respectively over the same periods. As of mid-2001, its weighting of only 8% cash was more aggressive than the average small-cap fund. Despite this aggressiveness, the fund continues to show lower volatility than the average fund in its segment. This fund is one of the clear choices if you want exposure to the small-cap market. The fund keeps its $$$$ rating.

## Canadian Balanced and Asset Allocation Funds

### SAXON HIGH INCOME FUND $$$ → FI/G NO RSP CHIB

Manager: Richard Howson, since 1997

MER: 1.25%    Fundata: A    Style: Bottom-up Value

Suitability: Aggressive income investors

This fund is designed to earn high income through a portfolio of Canadian dividend-paying stocks, income trusts, and fixed-income securities. After three mediocre performance years, manager Richard Howson finally struck gold. In the year ending June 30/01, the fund recorded a 26.3% return compared with an average of 14.3% for the High Income Balanced category. Howson's concentration on income, royalty, and real estate trusts is the major factor underlying his success this year. In fact, as of mid-2001, all of the fund's top holdings were allocated to these investment products. The beta of this fund is a very low 0.21, reflecting the relatively low correlation between income trusts and stock market indexes. The fund debuts with a $$$ rating.

## Also Recommended

## Global and International Equity Funds

### SAXON WORLD GROWTH FUND $$ ↓ G NO RSP GE

Manager: Robert Tattersall, since inception (1985)

MER: 1.75%    Fundata: A    Style: Bottom-up Value

Suitability: Conservative investors

Manager Robert Tattersall brings the same value-oriented stock selection criteria used for the Small-Cap Fund to this multi-country entry. The mandate here directs the manager to look for small-to-mid-cap companies trading outside of Canada, while at the same time seeking a balance between the various capitalization classes. Geographic and sector allocation is secondary to the main focus of identifying value stocks. In the first half of 2001, the portfolio was weighted heavily to the U.S., which represented nearly 50% of assets, followed by Japan and Europe. Tattersall's stock-picking ability is shining through. Despite an 18.1% decline in the MSCI World Composite Index benchmark, the fund eked out a 4% gain in the year ending June 30/01. The three- and five-year numbers are average to slightly above. The risk profile, like that of the other Tattersall funds, is impressive. We'll maintain a $$ rating for now, but another good year will see it move up.

## Canadian Balanced and Asset Allocation Funds

### SAXON BALANCED FUND                      $$ → FI/G NO RSP CBAL

Manager: Richard Howson, since 1989

MER: 1.75%      Fundata: A        Style: Bottom-up Value

Suitability: Balanced investors with an equity orientation

In terms of Canadian balanced funds, this one is somewhat spotty. After turning in several years of sub-par results, manager Richard Howson rebounded with a vengeance in the year ending June 30/01, when the fund recorded a 19.3% gain compared with a 2.6% loss for the average balanced fund. This propelled both the three- and five-year numbers way above the average. In terms of its allocation, as of June 30/01 the fund had 68% in stocks and 32% in bonds, income trusts, and cash. The stock side is diversified across a range of industries and doesn't discriminate based on capitalization, so company sizes are represented. As of mid-2001, the fixed-income component was split about equally between government and corporate issues. We'll keep the rating at $$ for now because of indifferent past results, but this fund is in line for an upgrade if the positive trend continues.

### Promising Newcomers

None.

# SCEPTRE INVESTMENT COUNSEL

## THE COMPANY

Sceptre is one of the country's larger investment counselling firms, with almost $14 billion in assets under management. The company has been in business since 1955 and its clients include pension funds, institutions, other fund companies, and individuals.

These are tough times for Sceptre, however. The firm's asset base diminished by over $4 billion in 2000 as a result of weak stock markets and lost client business. This led to a shakeup in top management, with William J. Malouin taking over as president and CEO and a move to create a strategic alliance with the giant U.S. Putnam organization.

For many years the Sceptre funds were excellent performers, producing above-average returns. But the performance of the family as a whole was very weak in the late 1990s as the company's value approach to stock selection was out of tune with the high-tech frenzy. We expected the funds would fare better as value returned to favour, but they have disappointed. The story is summed up by one simple fact: in the first six months of 2001, the Money Market Fund was the company's second-best performer. You're not going to build much business that way.

A word of explanation is in order about the MERs of these funds. The figures shown in the Fund Ratings are different from those included in the annual report. The reason is that Sceptre has been absorbing some expenses to keep the actual MERs low. However, there is no guarantee they will continue to do this in future. The figures below show the actual MERs in 2000. If the company should reduce or end the cost absorption, the numbers we've would be significantly higher.

## THE DETAILS

|  |  |
|---|---|
| Number of funds: | 7 |
| Assets under management: | $424 million |
| Load charge: | None if purchased directly from manager; otherwise, Front: max. 2% |
| Switching charge: | None (up to six transfers a year) |
| Where sold: | Across Canada |
| How sold: | Through brokers, dealers, and financial planners, or directly through the manager in Ontario, Manitoba, New Brunswick, Saskatchewan, and B.C. |
| Phone number: | 1-800-265-1888, (416) 360-4826, and (604) 899-6002 |

Web site address: www.sceptre.ca
E-mail address: mail@sceptre.ca
Minimum initial investment: $5,000

## INVESTING TIPS

If you live in any of the five provinces where the funds are sold directly by the manager, you should definitely acquire them that way. Otherwise, you may have to pay a small sales commission.

## FUND SUMMARY

Top Choices: Bond, Money Market
Also Recommended: Balanced Growth, Equity Growth
Promising Newcomers: None
The Rest: Canadian Equity, Global Equity, U.S. Equity

## FUND RATINGS

### Canadian Bond Funds

### SCEPTRE BOND FUND                              $$$ → FI NO RSP CB

Manager: Richard L. Knowles, since March 2000

MER: 1.03%      Fundata: C        Style: Value/Modest Timing

Suitability: Conservative investors

The portfolio of this fund is divided into three distinct components. Federal and provincial government securities account for slightly more than half the assets, providing security and liquidity. Corporate bonds make up about 40% of the total, generating higher yields. Finally, foreign currency bonds may be used when appropriate. The net result is a fund that consistently turns in above-average results. In fact, it has been a first- or second-quartile performer every year except one since 1994. That's called consistency. At a time when Sceptre has very few funds to feel good about, this one stands out as a notable exception. It's especially useful for the fixed-income section of registered plans.

## Money Market Funds

### SCEPTRE MONEY MARKET FUND $$$$ ↓ C NO RSP CMM

Manager: Richard L. Knowles, since March 2000

MER: 0.80%     Fundata: C

Suitability: Conservative investors

This fund has a wonderful consistency record. It has been an above-average performer for as far long as we can remember, never sinking below second quartile since at least 1994. The portfolio is about equally divided between government and corporate notes, which provides a good combination of security and decent returns. The low MER helps as well. The safety rating is among the best in the category.

## Also Recommended

### Canadian Small-to-Mid-Cap Funds

### SCEPTRE EQUITY GROWTH FUND $$ → G NO RSP CSC

Manager: Alan Jacobs, since May 1993

MER: 1.70%     Fundata: D     Style: Bottom-up Growth with Value

Suitability: Aggressive investors

This formerly top-performing fund has been going through a difficult period, but there are signs it may be coming out of its long funk. After below-average results from 1997–2000, the fund recorded a modest gain of about 3% in the first half of 2001, good for a second-quartile performance. That's a long way from the heady days of the mid-1990s when this fund was chalking up big profits, but manager Alan Jacobs has shown before that his bottom-up value approach is capable of outstanding results. We aren't yet ready to upgrade the rating on this fund but if you own units in it, you should continue to hold them. The worst may be over.

### Canadian Balanced Funds

### SCEPTRE BALANCED GROWTH FUND $$ → FI/G NO RSP CBAL

Manager: Lyle A. Stein, since March 1993

MER: 1.74%     Fundata: C     Style: Bottom-up Growth with Value

Suitability: Conservative investors

Historically, this is a good balanced fund. However, like other Sceptre entries, it went through some difficult times in the late 1990s, generating below-average returns for unitholders. During 1998–99 it was a fourth-quartile performer— the bottom of the mutual fund barrel. However, it enjoyed a modest turnaround in 2000 and in the first half of 2001, moving back up to second quartile, or slightly above average. Gain in 2000 was 8.2%, while in the first half of 2001 it slipped slightly, by 3.2%. In the first half of 2001 the portfolio was fairly evenly divided between stocks and bonds. This fund still has a long way to go to regain the form it showed in the mid-1990s when it was a top performer, but manager Lyle Stein appears to have started on the long road back.

## Promising Newcomers

None.

# SCOTIA FUNDS

## THE COMPANY

The Bank of Nova Scotia is the smallest of Canada's five major banks in terms of fund assets under management. Its line of 45 active funds has grown through both internal expansion and by the key acquisitions of the Montreal Trust and National Trust families of funds. The fund lines have been reorganized under the Scotia brand, with the end result being an extensive line-up that offers some strong entries.

The management of the funds is primarily under the wing of Scotia Cassels Investment Counsel, formed from the merger of Cassels Blaikie, which ran the National Trust funds, and Scotia Investment Management. Several other funds are managed by Montreal-based Montrusco Bolton, which was created by the merger of Montrusco & Associates and Bolton Tremblay.

One of the fund family's major strengths is consistency—something we applaud. Fund names and portfolio objectives remain relatively consistent from year to year, which means that investors have a clear performance picture. It also means low survivorship bias when measuring performance. Survivorship refers to the fact that funds that have disappeared (typically the weaker ones) and are excluded from typical backward-looking performance surveys. Survivorship bias means that performance results are upwardly biased as a result, which may give investors misleading impression.

## THE DETAILS

| | |
|---|---|
| Number of funds: | 45 |
| Assets under management: | $11 billion |
| Load charge: | None |
| Switching charge: | None |
| Where sold: | Across Canada |
| How sold: | Through branches of the Bank of Nova Scotia, Scotiabank and Trust, Scotia Discount Brokerage, and Scotia McLeod |
| Phone number: | (416) 750-3863, 1-800-268-9269 (English), or 1-800-387-5004 (French) |
| Web site address: | www.scotiabank.ca |
| E-mail address: | mail@scotiabank.com |
| Minimum initial investment: | Money market funds: $2,500; Other mutual funds: $500 (generally) |

## INVESTING TIPS

Scotia has one of the strongest stables of short-term income funds and money market funds of any mutual fund family in Canada. If you are looking for conservative, short-term investing opportunities or a place to park money temporarily, whether in Canadian or U.S. dollars, take a close look at Scotia's offerings.

## FUND SUMMARY

|  |  |
|---|---|
| Top Choices: | Canadian Balanced, Canadian Dividend, Canadian Income, Canadian Mid-Large Cap, Canadian Small-Cap, CanAm U.S.$ Money Market Fund, CanAm U.S.$ Income, Mortgage Income |
| Also Recommended: | Canadian Short-Term Income, Money Market |
| Promising Newcomers: | None |
| The Rest: | American Growth, American Stock Index, Canadian Blue Chip, Canadian Bond Index, Canadian Growth, Canadian Stock Index, CanAm Stock Index, CanGlobal Income, Capital Global Discovery, Capital Global Small Companies, Capital International Large Companies, Capital U.S. Large Companies, Capital U.S. Small Companies, Emerging Markets, European Growth, Global Income, International Growth, International Stock Index, Latin American Growth, Mortgage Income, Nasdaq Index, Pacific Rim Growth, Precious Metals, T-Bill, Total Return, Young Investors |

## FUND RATINGS

### Top Choices

### Canadian Equity Funds

### SCOTIA CANADIAN MID-LARGE CAP FUND          $$$ → G NO RSP CE

Manager: Britton Doherty

MER: 1.51%     Fundata: B     Style: Growth

Suitability: Middle-of-the-road investors

As the name implies, the fund searches for mid-to-large-cap stocks, but with a definite large-cap bias. Its top holdings are similar to those of the companion Blue Chip and Canadian Growth funds. With about 7% in cash at mid-2001, this is one of the more defensive funds in Scotia's Canadian equity line-up. The portfolio hasn't changed much over the year as it still has a heavy allocation to financial services, utilities, and industrial products. The overall portfolio risk is average. The fund recorded a 6.3% loss in the year ending June 30/01, about on par with its peer group. However, in the previous 12 months it had an above-average 35.5% return. Its five-year average annual return of 12.5% is 2.7 percentage points above the average for the category. The fund's relatively low management expense ratio (MER) helps. This is a solid performer within the Mid-to-Large-Cap category.

## Canadian Small-to-Mid-Cap Equity Funds

### SCOTIA CANADIAN SMALL-CAP FUND $$$ ↑ G NO RSP CSC

Manager: Allaster MacLean

MER: 2.39%     Fundata: D     Style: Growth

Suitability: Aggressive investors

This fund's mandate is to invest in small- to medium-sized growth companies. However, a look at the portfolio's average capitalization indicates a small-cap bias. The portfolio includes an assortment of interesting small companies that specialize in emerging technologies, including some biotech companies. Since the end of 1998, the fund has decreased its exposure to consumer products while increasing its exposure to the industrial products (23.6% at mid-2001) and oil and gas sectors (19%). The shift into the rebounding oil and gas sector plus some good old-fashioned stock picking paid off with a dramatic gain of 46.2% for the year to June 30/00. In the latest 12 months the fund lost 5.2%, about one percentage point less than the average for the category. Three- and five-year numbers are well above the average for the Small-Cap category as well as the Nesbitt Burns Canadian Small-Cap Index. One caution: the fund is quite volatile with standard deviation well above average. Nevertheless, this is one of the top small-cap funds, well worthy of at least a $$$ rating.

## Dividend Income Funds

### SCOTIA CANADIAN DIVIDEND FUND $$$ → G/FI NO RSP DIV

Manager: Paget Warner

MER: 1.14%     Fundata: C     Style: Yield/Moderate Growth

Suitability: Conservative investors

Despite being classified as an income fund, this has been one of the best-performing Canadian equity funds in Scotia's stable. The focus is to provide favourable tax-advantaged income to unitholders, along with capital appreciation. It is the most conservative of Scotia's Canadian equity line and has the lowest volatility in the Scotia equity family. Low volatility is achieved by holding the majority of its assets in common stocks (90% at mid-2001), with the remainder in preferred shares and income trust units. At mid-2001, over 50% of its assets were in bank and utility stocks, making this fund very sensitive to rising interest rates. Over the past five years the fund has been a first-quartile performer. The three- and five-year average annual returns of 6.5% and 17.1% are well above the averages in its category. For investors seeking regular quarterly income or looking for a conservative blue-chip equity fund, Canadian Dividend should be on the shortlist. Holding it outside a registered plan allows the benefit of tax-advantaged cash flow.

## Canadian Balanced and Asset Allocation Funds

### SCOTIA CANADIAN BALANCED FUND $$$ → FI/G NO RSP CBAL

Manager: Britton Doherty

MER: 1.63%     Fundata: C     Style: Growth Bias

Suitability: Conservative investors

This is a conservatively managed fund on both the equity and fixed-income sides. Stocks have a blue-chip orientation, with strong valuation and dividends. Risk is minimized through both industry and foreign stock diversification, including a heavy weighting of U.S. stocks. The bond side is conservative, with lots of federal and corporate issues and below-average interest rate risk. At mid-2001, the fund was allocated at roughly 54% stocks and 46% fixed-income instruments. Performance against its peers is usually above average. However, in the year to June 30/01, when the average fund in its group lost 2.6%, this fund lost 6.1%. That result appears to have been an aberration, as five- and ten-year results are above average, with a five-year average return of 9.7% annually. Add a good safety record and you have a pretty decent fund.

## Canadian Bond Funds

### SCOTIA CANADIAN INCOME FUND $$$ → FI NO RSP CB

Manager: Romas Budd

MER: 1.16%     Fundata: C     Style: Yield Curve/Credit Analysis

Suitability: Moderate-risk income investors

In terms of bond funds, this is a strong entry offered by Scotia. It's conservatively managed but at the same time it produces above-average returns, aided by a low MER. Interest rate anticipation (a style in which the manager projects rate movements and adjusts the holdings accordingly) directs its strategy. The fund invests primarily in Government of Canada bonds, with provincial and corporate bonds rounding out the remainder. All bonds must be rated A or higher by a major Canadian rating agency and as a result, there's little default risk here. Interest rate risk is minimized through a conservative holding of long bonds.

The fund has lowered its average term to maturity since the end of 1998, thereby reducing its exposure to rising interest rates. A one-year return of 5.8% to June 30/01 beat the average bond fund by more than a percentage point. The five-year average annual gain of 7.4% was well above the average. All in all, a good representative bond fund.

## Mortgage Funds

### SCOTIA MORTGAGE INCOME FUND                    $$$ ↓ FI NO RSP M

Managers: Nicholas Van Sluytman and Bruce Grantier

MER: 1.56%      Fundata: D      Style: Credit Analysis

Suitability: Conservative investors

This fund was formed from the merger of the National Trust Mortgage Fund and the Scotia Excelsior Mortgage Fund. It invests primarily in residential first mortgages, with all the mortgages in the portfolio being guaranteed by the bank. Prior to the merger, the returns were about average for both funds, so it's not surprising to see continued average returns for the new fund. All in all, this is a low-risk choice for fixed-income investors.

## Foreign Bond Funds

### SCOTIA CANAM U.S.$ INCOME FUND                  $$$ → FI NO RSP FB

Manager: Bill Girard

MER: 1.89%      Fundata: B      Style: Yield Curve/Credit Analysis

Suitability: Moderate-risk investors seeking U.S. currency exposure

You may be investing in so-called "Yankee Bonds" and not even be aware of it. Quite simply, these are just foreign companies or governments (Canadian in our case) that issue debt denominated in U.S. dollars and sell in the U.S. Consequently, this Yankee bond fund offers investors full U.S. dollar exposure while being fully eligible for registered plans. The fund is a bet on the direction of the U.S. versus the Canadian dollar. When the Canadian dollar weakens the fund gains and vice versa. The risk comes from holding U.S. denominated securities. The fund invests mainly in federal and corporate bonds and has minimal interest rate risk. Performance over its life has been solid, with above-average returns over one to five years. The fund gained 12.8% for the year to June 30/01, while averaging 7.6% annually over the past five years. Those are healthy returns, particularly in light of an average risk rating. Investors who want more U.S. dollar exposure in their retirement plan without having to sacrifice foreign content room may want to look at this fund.

## SCOTIA CANAM U.S.$ MONEY MARKET FUND   $$$ → FI NO RSP FMM

Managers: Cecilia Chan and Amanda Ford

MER: 1.00%    Fundata: D

Suitability: Conservative investors seeking U.S. currency exposure

The average annual return for this RRSP-eligible U.S. money fund for the three years ending June 30/01 was 5.8%, way above the average for the group. The portfolio is split fairly equally between Canadian corporate and provincial issues, denominated in U.S. funds. This is an excellent U.S. dollar money market fund. The fund earns a rating increase to $$$.

## Also Recommended

## Canadian Bond Funds

## SCOTIA CANADIAN SHORT-TERM INCOME FUND   $$ ↓ FI NO RSP STB

Managers: Bill Girard and Nicholas van Sluytman

MER: 1.32%    Fundata: D    Style: Credit Analysis

Suitability: Conservative investors

As far as the risk and return spectrum goes, this fund lies between the companion Money Market Fund on the low end and the Canadian Income Fund higher up. This fund invests primarily in high-quality corporate bonds, followed by government bonds. It has a longer time horizon than a money market fund but a shorter one than most bond funds, reducing its volatility during times of sharp interest rate movements. During a period of declining interest rates, a fund like this will underperform most conventional bond funds. But when rates are rising, it will do much better. Five-year average annual gain of 4.8% was just above the 4.6% median for short-term bond funds. Recommended as a haven for your bond content when rates rise or if you're a cautious investor. But don't expect anything exciting in the way of returns.

## Canadian Money Market Funds

## SCOTIA MONEY MARKET FUND   $$ → C NO RSP CMM

Managers: Cecilia Chan and Amanda Ford

MER: 1.00%    Fundata: B

Suitability: Conservative investors

This fund was formed from the merger of the Scotia Excelsior Money Market Fund into the National Trust Money Market Fund. At mid-2001, the portfolio was invested mainly in federal bonds, followed by T-bills and a small sprinkling of provincial debt. Return for the year to June 30/01 was 4.6%, which was slightly above the average. Longer-term results are right on the median for the Money Market category.

## Promising Newcomers

None.

# SPECTRUM INVESTMENTS

## THE COMPANY

Spectrum Investments is part of the Sun Life organization and draws on several related companies for managerial expertise for its mutual funds. These companies include McLean Budden, one of the top institutional money management firms in Canada, and MFS Institutional Advisors of Boston, a leading U.S. firm. As well, Spectrum employs the services of several outside firms both in Canada and abroad.

This is a company that is often overlooked by investors because, despite a lot of marketing, it does not have much of a profile. But there are some very good funds in its line-up and they're worth closer attention.

## THE DETAILS

| | |
|---|---|
| Number of funds: | 46 |
| Assets under management: | $7.4 billion |
| Load charge: | Front: max. 6%; Back: max. 6% |
| Switching charge: | 2% maximum |
| Where sold: | Across Canada |
| How sold: | Through brokers, planners, and insurance representatives |
| Phone number: | 1-877-732-8786 |
| Web site address: | www.spectrum.com |
| E-mail address: | specinfo@spectrum.com |
| Minimum initial investment: | $500 |

## INVESTING TIPS

Spectrum offers several funds of the same broad type, but each is different in its style and the type of investor for whom it is best suited. For example, there are three large-cap Canadian equity funds in the company line-up, each of which has a distinctive risk profile and potential return. There are also three Canadian bond funds, again with different risk and return levels. Be sure that you understand the investment mandate of the fund you are considering before making a final decision.

Spectrum offers several "funds of funds." These are portfolios comprising a mix of their other funds, specially designed to meet specific investor needs. Although these portfolios are not bad in themselves, we note in most cases that the Spectrum Diversified Fund has a superior three-year record. You may wish to place your money in that fund rather than in one of the portfolios.

We note with dismay that the MERs on most of the funds in this group are up from last year, which will slightly depress returns.

# FUND SUMMARY

Top Choices: Canadian Equity, Canadian Investment, Diversified, Dividend, Mid-Term Bond, Short-Term Bond

Also Recommended: American Equity, Asian Dynasty, Canadian Growth, Canadian Money Market, Canadian Resources, Canadian Stock, European Growth, Global Bond, Global Diversified, Global Equity, Global Growth, Long-Term Bond, Optimax USA, U.S.$ Money Market

Promising Newcomers: Tactonics

The Rest: American Growth, Asset Allocation, Canadian Small Mid-Cap, Emerging Markets, Global Financial Services, Global Health Sciences, Global Telecommunications, RRSP International Bond, RRSP World Equity, World Growth Managers

# FUND RATINGS

## Top Choices

### Canadian Equity Funds

### SPECTRUM CANADIAN EQUITY FUND          $$$ → G #/* RSP CLC

Managers: Brian Dawson and Susan Shuter (McLean Budden), since May 1999

MER: 2.57%      Fundata: B      Style: Value/Growth

Suitability: Middle-of-the-road investors

When well-known manager Kiki Delaney resigned as manager of this fund in 1999, it was a blow to Spectrum. They had spent a lot of advertising dollars promoting her image as one of Canada's top money managers, so to see her decamp and move to competitor Trimark (now part of AIM) must have been a shock. However, replacements Brian Dawson and Susan Shuter of the highly respected money management firm of McLean Budden (which, like Spectrum, is part of the Sun Life empire) have proven more than adequate in the job. The fund has been an above-average performer since they took charge, recording a nice gain of 13.4% in 2000. It was in the red in the first half of 2001 by 6.8%, but that was a better performance than the majority of Canadian stock funds and the TSE. The managers use a "best ideas" approach from McLean Budden's growth and value teams, so there is no "pure" style here. Focus is on large-cap stocks (90% of the Canadian equities are drawn from the TSE 100), and there is a higher foreign content quotient than there was under Delaney's stewardship (almost a quarter of the assets were in U.S. and international equities in the first half of 2001). The goal here is steady, consistent performance with average volatility. We expect this fund to deliver just that, given McLean Budden's excellent reputation. It appears that Spectrum has survived the Kiki leave-taking quite well, thank you very much. Formerly called the United Canadian Equity Fund.

## SPECTRUM CANADIAN INVESTMENT FUND     $$$$ → G #/* RSP CLC

Managers: Kim Shannon and Gaelen Morphet (Mercury), since June 1999

MER: 2.53%     Fundata: A     Style: Value

Suitability: Conservative investors

This is the oldest continuously operated fund in Canada, running under the name Canadian Investment Fund since 1932. It had become almost moribund until Kim Shannon, then of AMI Partners, grabbed hold of it in 1996 and turned it around. She then surprised Spectrum by leaving AMI—and this fund—early in 1999. After searching for a new manager, they hired Shannon—again! This time, however, she wears the hat of chief investment officer for Mercury Asset Management in Canada, part of the Merrill Lynch organization. Her co-manager, Gaelen Morphet, also worked on this fund at AMI and moved to Mercury as well. So much for the revolving door—we're back where we began. The investment style here is a conservative buy-and-hold value approach, with a focus on blue-chip stocks within the TSE 100 Index. This fund is designed to have low volatility and will tend to lag behind when markets are strong, but will outperform when times get rough. We've recently seen dramatic evidence of that; the fund gained 13.8% over the year to June 30/01, placing it in the top 10 performers over that period. This fund is a good choice for a conservative investor who prefers a low-risk approach and it is especially well suited for an RRSP or RRIF.

## Dividend Income Funds

## SPECTRUM DIVIDEND FUND                 $$$$ ↓ FI #/* RSP DIV

Managers: Peter Kotsopoulos, Cort Conover, and Tony Magri (McLean Budden), since January 1995, January 1996, and February 2001, respectively

MER: 1.79%     Fundata: C     Style: Blend

Suitability: Conservative income-oriented investors

This is a genuine dividend fund, not a large-cap fund with "dividend" as part of the name. The focus is on high-quality preferred shares (over 60% of the assets in the first half of 2001). Only the top-ranking preferreds (P-1 and P-2 ratings) are used. For common stocks (about 9% of assets), the managers avoid the more cyclical sectors of the market and concentrate on stable businesses like pipelines, utilities, and banks. Total returns tend to be below average for the Dividend

Income category because of the defensive nature of the portfolio. Cash flow is very good, which is what really counts in a fund of this type. Distributions are paid monthly, currently at a rate of 4¢ per unit. During calendar year 2000, unitholders received distributions amounting to 4.2% of the fund's value on the first of that year, all of which was tax-advantaged. This fund is a good choice for income-oriented investors seeking to make use of the dividend tax credit. The safety record is one of the best for its category.

## Canadian Balanced and Asset Allocation Funds

### SPECTRUM DIVERSIFIED FUND $$$↓ FI/G #/* RSP CBAL

Managers: Brian Dawson, Susan Shuter, and Peter Kotsopoulos (McLean Budden), since November 1997

MER: 2.32%     Fundata: B     Style: Blend

Suitability: Conservative investors

This is a conservatively managed fund that invests mainly in blue-chip stocks and government bonds. It is run by McLean Budden, a top-notch money management company that is partly owned by Sun Life, which is also the parent of Spectrum. This fund is a good choice for risk-averse investors who want some growth potential but don't like big asset class bets. That makes it a sound choice for RRSPs. In the first half of 2001, the portfolio was slightly weighted toward stocks (55%), with bonds accounting for just under 40% of the mix. Foreign content was almost 25%, a big jump from last year. The fund produced a decent gain of 10.1% in 2000 and managed to keep its loss at just 3.6% in the terrible markets in the first half of 2001. This is a good core fund and is recommended over Spectrum's various portfolio funds.

## Canadian Bond Funds

### SPECTRUM MID-TERM BOND FUND $$$ → FI #/* RSP CB

Managers: Peter Kotsopoulos, Curt Conover, and Tony Magri (McLean Budden), since January 1995, January 1996, and February 2001, respectively

MER: 1.78%     Fundata: E     Style: Duration

Suitability: Middle-of-the-road bond investors

This fund focuses on mid-term bond issues, or bonds maturing in five to ten years. This mandate places it squarely in the middle of the three funds in the Spectrum bond fund grouping, both in terms of risk and potential return. It's for investors who want some fixed-income exposure without undue risk, making it most suitable to those about to retire, or for use in an RRIF. Lately it has been performing quite well, with a one-year gain to June 30/01 of 5.7%. Formerly known as the Spectrum Interest Fund.

## SPECTRUM SHORT-TERM BOND FUND　　　$$$ ↓ FI #/* RSP STB

Managers: Peter Kotsopoulos, Curt Conover, and Tony Magri (McLean Budden), since January 1995, January 1996, and February 2001, respectively

MER: 1.58%　　　Fundata: E　　　Style: Duration

Suitability: Conservative investors

This is the most defensive of the three Spectrum Canadian bond offerings, and therefore the fund that combines the lowest risk with the lowest potential returns. It was previously the United Canadian Mortgage Fund. The mandate was amended in August 1996 to allow investment in bonds and other debt securities that mature in five years or less, as well as in conventional first mortgages. It's only one step removed from a money market fund, but recent returns have been quite good with a one-year gain of 6.6% to June 30/01.


## Also Recommended

### Canadian Equity Funds

## SPECTRUM CANADIAN STOCK FUND　　　$$ ↑ G #/* RSP CE

Manager: David Antonelli (MFS), since June 1999

MER: 2.53%　　　Fundata: C　　　Style: Growth

Suitability: Aggressive investors

This fund is run out of the U.S. by one of Spectrum's associated companies in the Sun Life empire, MFS Institutional Investors of Boston. MFS has a long history (it claims to have introduced the first mutual fund in the U.S.) and is a growth-oriented company that uses a bottom-up selection, buy-and-hold approach, and brings a large-cap bias to this portfolio. Foreign content is supposed to be maximized, but in the first half of 2001 it was running at around 15%—much less than that of the companion Canadian Equity Fund. This fund is more aggressive than either the Canadian Equity or the Canadian Investment funds, so investors should expect a higher degree of volatility with potentially higher returns in strong markets. That's exactly what happened in the year to June 30/00 when this fund returned a very impressive 47.8%. However, when markets went south, this fund recorded a loss of 15.4% in the 12 months to June 30/01. Such a pattern is absolutely consistent with how the fund is positioned, so keep that in mind if you're considering an investment here.

## Canadian Small-to-Mid-Cap Funds

### SPECTRUM CANADIAN GROWTH FUND $$ → G #/* RSP CSC

Managers: Richard Howson and Robert Tattersall (Howson Tattersall), John Mulvihill and Alan Leach (Mulvihill Capital), and Lawrence Kymisis (Mercury), since May 1999

MER: 2.58%     Fundata: C     Style: Value/Growth

Suitability: Aggressive investors

Is this a case of too many cooks? After Kiki Delaney's company resigned the account, Spectrum turned to a multi-manager approach for this fund, drawing on the talents of three well-respected organizations. Howson Tattersall, which runs the Saxon funds, divides Canadian equity responsibilities with Mulvihill Capital Management. Mercury Asset Management looks after the foreign content. The style here is a blend of value and growth. The net result so far has not been impressive, however. In their first full year on the job, the team piloted the fund to a gain of 16.5% (to June 30/00). That result was much better than the previous year, but it was below average for the category. In the most recent 12-month period, to June 30/01, the fund lost 5.3% at a time when many Canadian small-cap entries were making gains. We think these folks can do better, which is why we're still recommending this one. But there are better small-cap performers out there right now (including Howson Tattersall's own Saxon Small Cap Fund), so this is not a top choice in the category. Previously known as the United Venture Retirement Fund and the United Canadian Growth Fund.

## Sector Funds

### SPECTRUM CANADIAN RESOURCES FUND $$ ↑ G #/* RSP NR

Manager: Gaelen Morphet (Mercury), since December 1999

MER: 2.66%     Fundata: E     Style: Value

Suitability: Aggressive investors

Most of the latter part of the 1990s was bad news for resource fund investors. But this fund in particular fared badly, losing an average of 22.7% annually over the three years to June 30/00. That's pretty shocking, especially if you had money in it; you would have lost two-thirds of your investment in three years! No wonder Spectrum decided to make a managerial change in late 1999, handing portfolio responsibility to Gaelen Morphet of Mercury Asset Management. She has done a credible—although not sensational—job with it so far, producing a gain of 8.2% in 2000 and managing to come in a bit over break-even in the first half of 2001. Not a great natural resources fund, but okay.

### SPECTRUM AMERICAN EQUITY FUND                    $$ → G #/* £ USE

Manager: John Laupheimer, since February 1999 and Michael Lawless (MFS), since April 2001

MER: 2.59%      Fundata: E      Style: Growth

Suitability: Aggressive investors

This fund offers a highly diversified portfolio of small-, medium-, and large-cap stocks, so you're getting the entire U.S. spectrum here. The investment style focuses on growth, and growth funds have not fared well recently with the high-tech collapse. As a result, it should come as no surprise that this fund lost over 21% in the year to June 30/01. The managers use a bottom-up, fundamental stock selection approach. That simply means they choose companies on the basis of their strength and prospects as opposed to which sector of the economy they happen to operate in. MFS has been running this fund since December 1995, although there was a change in the lead manager in early 1999. That change seems to have affected the fund's fortunes—not for the better—although it must be said that the investment approach here is out of sync with current market conditions. We'll retain this fund on our Recommended List for now, but we're not enthusiastic about it at the present time. Formerly known as the United American Equity Fund and before that as the United Accumulative Fund.

### SPECTRUM OPTIMAX USA FUND                    $$↓ G #/* £ USE

Manager: Fred Herrmann (Weiss, Peck & Greer), since April 1997

MER: 2.62%      Fundata: B      Style: Quantitative Model

Suitability: Conservative investors

This fund uses a computer programme to select stocks from the S&P 500 Index, using the principles of portfolio theory developed by Nobel Prize-winning economist Dr. Harry Markowitz. Sounds impressive, but the returns had been nowhere close to matching the Index and, in fact, were well below average for the U.S. Equity category. There was a managerial change in April 1997 and things have looked better since. This is not a shoot-out-the-lights type of fund, but it is a decent plodder with limited risk. Recently it has been a first quartile-performer in a weak market, limiting investor loss to just 3.7% in the first half of 2001. An okay fund if it fits your specific needs.

## Global and International Equity Funds

### SPECTRUM ASIAN DYNASTY FUND          $$ ↑ G #/* £ PRE

Managers: Chris Burn and Barry Dargan (MFS), since September 1998

MER: 3.13%     Fundata: A     Style: Growth

Suitability: Aggressive investors

Here's a fund that lost 25% in the year to June 30/01. So why are we recommending it? Because ever since the managerial team of Chris Burn and Barry Dargan took over in late 1998, this fund has been among the top performers in its category. They have managed to pilot it to a three-year average annual compound rate of return of 16%, placing it among the top five performers in the Asia/Pacific Rim category over that period. The fund invests throughout the Far East, including Japan. The focus is on mid- to large-sized companies, although some small-cap Japanese stocks may be included. We regard all Far East funds as essentially high risk, but if you must have one in your portfolio, this is one of the better choices. Originally the Bullock Asian Dynasty Fund.

### SPECTRUM EUROPEAN GROWTH FUND          $$ ↑ G #/* £ EE

Manager: Edoardo Mercadante (Mercury), since June 1997

MER: 2.93%     Fundata: C     Style: Growth

Suitability: Aggressive investors

This is a European small-cap fund, one of the few around. As such, it has a higher-risk profile than the more traditional European funds, but also offers greater return potential as well. The focus is on the bigger western European markets, but the manager may also invest up to 15% of the portfolio in emerging eastern European countries (only 10% in small caps, however). Major holdings in the first half of 2001 were in France (23% of the portfolio), Britain (16%), and the Netherlands (11.5%). This is a fund that offers investors a feast or a famine. It produced a one-year gain of 43% to June 30/00, but gave back a large chunk of that with a loss of 20.1% in the 12 months to June 30/01. In other words, there's a lot of volatility here—be warned. Formerly known as the Bullock European Enterprise Fund.

### SPECTRUM GLOBAL EQUITY FUND          $$ → G #/* £ GE

Manager: David Mannheim (MFS), since September 1998

MER: 2.72%     Fundata: C     Style: Growth

Suitability: Middle-of-the-road investors

This fund can invest around the world, but the main emphasis was on the U.S. (35%) and Europe (37%) in the first half of 2001, which has been the pattern since David Mannheim took over the reins in 1998. Performance during that time has been so-so. The three-year average annual compound rate of return of

3.3% is slightly below average for the category, although that result isn't terrible by any means in light of market conditions. Returns were depressed by a loss of 14% for the 12 months to June 30/01. The portfolio emphasis is on large-cap corporations with strong earnings growth. Stocks are chosen mainly on the basis of corporate fundamentals (bottom-up). We said last year that this fund was on the bubble of a downgrade. Performance has not been good, so we are dropping the rating to $$, although it remains on our Recommended List. This fund was originally formed from a merger of the Spectrum International Equity and United Global Equity.

## SPECTRUM GLOBAL GROWTH FUND $$ ↑ G #/* £ GE

Manager: James Skinner and Lawrence Kymisis (Mercury), since June 1997

MER: 2.70%     Fundata: B     Style: Growth

Suitability: Aggressive investors

This is the small-to-mid-cap global entry in the Spectrum line-up. Stocks are selected on the basis of corporate fundamentals and growth potential, and the portfolio was weighted toward the U.S. (55%) in the first half of 2001. As you might expect from a small-cap growth fund, recent results have been poor. The fund lost 28.2% in the year to June 30/01. However, it did so well in the late 1990s before the tech slump, that its three-year average annual compound rate of return was still a healthy 16.4%. Note that this fund will be higher risk by nature than the companion Global Equity Fund because of the focus on small-cap stocks. There is an RRSP-eligible clone available, although this seems to us like a rather volatile fund to be holding in a registered plan and we don't recommend it for that purpose. Previously known as the United Venture Fund.

## Global Balanced and Asset Allocation Funds

## SPECTRUM GLOBAL DIVERSIFIED FUND $$ ↓ FI/G #/* £ GBAL

Managers: Charles Prideaux and Gareth Fielding (Mercury), since April 2000

MER: 2.57%     Fundata: C     Style: Blend

Suitability: Middle-of-the-road investors

This is a global balanced fund that invests in stocks and bonds from around the world. Direction is by Mercury Asset Management of London, which uses an active asset allocation approach. Equities accounted for 60% of the portfolio in the first half of 2001, down slightly from the previous year. U.S. equities accounted for about half that total. The fund has had its problems recently, losing 10.6% in 2000 and another 6.2% in the first half of 2001. Consequently, it is hanging in on our Recommended List by a hair. If we don't see better results soon, it will be gone. We suggest that you check the most recent performance numbers before you put your money here. Formerly the United Global Portfolio of Funds.

## Canadian Bond Funds

### SPECTRUM LONG-TERM BOND FUND $$ ↑ FI #/* RSP CB

Managers: Peter Kotsopoulos, Curt Conover, and Tony Magri (McLean Budden), since January 1995, January 1996, and February 2001, respectively

MER: 1.93%     Fundata: E     Style: Duration

Suitability: Aggressive fixed-income investors

The fortunes of this fund will coincide with interest rate movements. When long-term rates decline, this fund will outperform. When they rise, it will underperform. As a result, it can go from first quartile in the Canadian Bond category to the fourth quartile within a few months. This kind of fluctuation is exactly what we have seen recently, with the fund diving to fourth quartile in the first half of 2001 as long-term rates moved up. The reason for this volatility is the term to maturity of the portfolio. Spectrum offers three Canadian bond funds and this is the most volatile of the bunch, as long-term bonds are more sensitive to interest rate movements, up or down. Over the long term, returns from this fund should be higher than from its short- and mid-term companions. But expect more unit value fluctuation along the way than you'd see in a more diversified bond fund. During the three years to June 30/01, this was the weakest of the three funds. But over five and ten years, it has turned in the best results. Therefore, this fund is best suited to patient investors with a long time horizon, or to high rollers who want to take advantage of rising bond prices when interest rates are on a downslope and then switch out when directions change. The trick with a switch, of course, is to get it right! Assess the situation carefully before you invest. The United Canadian Bond Fund and the Spectrum Government Bond Fund were folded together to create this entry.

## Foreign Bond Funds

### SPECTRUM GLOBAL BOND FUND $$ → FI #/* £ FB

Manager: Gareth Fielding (Mercury), since April 2000

MER: 2.22%     Fundata: C

Suitability: Investors seeking foreign currency exposure

This fund invests in bonds from around the world, mainly government bonds rated AA or AAA for quality. Currencies are actively hedged to protect the asset base. Returns are usually better than average, but keep in mind that this has been a very weak category. To be used only for currency diversification. Formerly the Bullock Global Bond Fund.

## Canadian Money Market Funds

### SPECTRUM CANADIAN MONEY MARKET FUND    $$ → C NO RSP CMM

Manager: Cort Conover (McLean Budden), since January 1996

MER: 1.05%    Fundata: B

Suitability: Conservative investors

This is a standard money market fund, investing in a mix of government T-bills, corporate short-term notes, and bankers' acceptances. Performance is average to slightly above. Note that although there is no sales charge for buying units in this fund, you will be subject to normal commissions if you transfer into another fund later. Formerly the Spectrum United Canadian T-Bill Fund.

## Foreign Money Market Funds

### SPECTRUM U.S.$ MONEY MARKET FUND    $$ → C NO £ FMM

Manager: Cort Conover (McLean Budden), since January 1996

MER: 1.27%    Fundata: D

Suitability: Conservative investors seeking U.S. currency exposure

This fund invests in U.S. dollar–denominated short-term securities, which is a great place to be when the loonie is tumbling. Results have generally been slightly above average, but remember that the numbers you see in the paper don't reflect your currency exchange profits or losses. Use this fund as a hedge if you're worried about a further decline in the value of the Canadian dollar. Formerly the United U.S.$ Money Market Fund.

## Promising Newcomers

### SPECTRUM TACTONICS FUND    NR → G #/* £ GE

Manager: Karen Bleasby, since inception (April 2001)

MER: N/A    Fundata: N/A    Style: Quantitative

Suitability: Middle-of-the-road investors

This is the only fund of its kind in Canada. It invests in exchange traded funds (ETFs) that are listed on North American stock exchanges, using a momentum/risk minimization strategy developed by Spectrum's vice-president of investments, Karen Bleasby. Some academic studies have indicated that stocks and industry sectors that performed well over a given six-month period are likely to continue to perform well in the next six months. This trend is called "winner persistence." However, the danger of relying solely on "winner persistence" to select securities was clearly demonstrated by the high-tech meltdown.

The technology market looked great—right up until the time it crashed. Mutual funds that relied solely on momentum to build their portfolios were slaughtered. To offset this danger, Bleasby has developed a technique called "risk metrics," which triggers a warning signal when the return on any market sector exceeds certain standards. If this signal sounds, the ETF replicating the sector, index, or country in danger will be dropped from the portfolio and the proceeds invested in cash until the next monthly review. In fact, the fund may hold significant amounts of cash at any time if the indicators are weak. The maximum cash percentage according to the back-tested models was 40% in August 1997, just prior to the October crash that marked the onset of the Asian flu that would go on to depress stocks worldwide. The net result of this combination of momentum and risk management is expected to be a fund that will match the MSCI World Index in strong markets and outperform it in weak ones. This action gives the fund a defensive characteristic that will appeal to investors who are concerned about risk. It is still too early to assess how this approach will translate into performance, but the initial results look promising.

# STANDARD LIFE MUTUAL FUNDS

## THE COMPANY

The Standard Life organization offers two distinct types of funds. The family described here is a regular mutual funds group. All funds are directed by Standard Life Investments Inc., a subsidiary company of Standard Life. See the segregated funds section for information on this firm's seg fund line, the Ideal Funds.

No individual lead portfolio manager names are made available. The company's rationale for this practice is that a committee approach "ensures that all clients benefit from the expertise of the total investment management group. We operate with a committee structure to ensure a centralized approach to decision making, not a guru driven one." The members of the company's investment strategy committee are Peter Hill (the president), Bill MacDonald, Tony Maturo, Norman Raschkowan, Charles Jenkins, Neil Matheson, and Dinka Kucic. We always prefer to know the name of the specific lead manager of every fund, and we think that is an important piece of knowledge for investors to have. That being said, this team has proven itself to be a very strong one and the funds offered by the company have been excellent performers over the years.

## THE DETAILS

|  |  |
|---|---|
| Number of funds: | 16 |
| Assets under management: | $423 million |
| Load Charge: | Front: max. 5%; Back: max. 6% |
| Switching charge: | 2% maximum |
| Where sold: | Across Canada |
| How sold: | Through brokers, dealers, and financial advisors |
| Phone number: | 1-888-841-6633 |
| Web site address: | www.standardlife.ca |
| E-mail address: | mutualfunds@standardlife.ca |
| Minimum initial investment: | $1,000 (except $5,000 for RRIF accounts) |

## INVESTING TIPS

These funds used to be available only through Standard Life representatives. In 1999, however, the company opened up its distribution network to allow stock-brokers, financial planners, and dealers to sell their mutual funds, making access to this family much easier.

If you're the type of investor who likes to do a lot of switching, note that Standard Life imposes what it calls a "short-term trading fee" of up to 2% if you indulge in what they consider "excessive trading." Their definition includes selling or switching units with 90 days of purchase, repurchasing units within 90 days of selling, or any activity that "disrupts the efficient and cost-effective management of the funds."

For wealthy investors, the company recently launched its Legend Series Investment Pools, 10 funds that carry much lower management expense ratios (MERs). You need a minimum of $250,000 to open an account, with at least $25,000 in each pool selected. These new pools have not been in existence long enough to determine if they will significantly outperform the regular mutual funds.

## FUND SUMMARY

|  |  |
|---|---|
| Top Choices: | Bond, Canadian Dividend, Equity, Growth Equity, International Bond, Money Market |
| Also Recommended: | Balanced, Natural Resource, U.S. Equity |
| Promising Newcomers: | Corporate High-Yield Bond |
| The Rest: | Active Global Diversified Index RSP, Active Global Index RSP, Active U.S. Index RSP, Canadian Healthcare & Technology, International Equity, S&P 500 Index RSP |

## FUND RATINGS

### Top Choices

**Canadian Equity Funds**

#### STANDARD LIFE EQUITY FUND                          $$$$ ↓ G #/* RSP CE

Manager: Standard Life Investments Inc.

MER: 2.19%      Fundata: B       Style: Bottom-up Value

Suitability: Conservative investors

This fund offers a large portfolio that includes a mix of small, medium, and large companies. It has produced some very good returns for its investors in both good and bad markets. Over the past year (to June 30/01), while markets were being hammered, the conservative style of the management team managed to limit the fund's loss to 4.6%, a much better performance than the average fund in the category or the TSE. Three- and five-year average annual returns are well above average, making this fund a top-quartile performer over those time frames. The safety record is one of the best in its category and the fund has a very low beta, a measure of volatility, of 0.69 (the TSE 300 is 1.00). This often-overlooked fund is a first-rate choice for investors and should be given serious consideration. We are maintaining our rating at $$$$.

## STANDARD LIFE GROWTH EQUITY FUND $$$$ ↑ G #/* RSP CSC

Manager: Standard Life Investments Inc.

MER: 2.17%    Fundata: B    Style: Bottom-up Growth

Suitability: Aggressive investors

This is Standard Life's small-cap entry, and it's a very good one. The portfolio focuses on Canadian stocks but there is enough U.S. representation within the foreign content limit to keep things interesting (8.5% in the first half of 2001). In addition, the fund may hold up to 20% of its assets in larger-cap stocks, to limit risk. In 2001, the fund was tilted toward the oil and gas sector, but the percentage of assets there has been trimmed back to 25% from 40% the previous year, due to some profit taking. Other large holdings included Industrial-Alliance Life Insurance, Finning International, and Torstar Corp. The fund managed a small gain of 0.6% in the year to June 30/01, compared with an average loss of almost 8% for the category. Three-year average annual compound rate of return was 9.8%. Risk is slightly higher than average for the Canadian Small-Cap category. Like many other fine funds in this group, this one is often lost in the shuffle. We are maintaining our $$$$ rating. More aggressive investors who can accept the added risk of a small-cap fund should investigate this one.

## Dividend Income Funds

## STANDARD LIFE CANADIAN DIVIDEND FUND $$$$ → G #/* RSP DIV

Manager: Standard Life Investments Inc.

MER: 1.60%    Fundata: B    Style: Bottom-up Value

Suitability: Conservative investors

This is really more of a blue-chip stock fund than a dividend income fund. The portfolio is invested almost exclusively in common shares, with no preferreds, royalty trusts, or the like. As a result, returns will tend to be more volatile than you'd find in a more conventional dividend fund holding a lot of preferred shares. That said, this fund has been a standout performer in its category in terms of total return. Over the year to June 30/01, with stock markets tumbling, this entry turned in a strong gain of 19.3%. Looking back five years, it was the number two performer in the category with an average annual compound rate of return of 21.5%. The main weakness in the past has been cash flow—this fund is not a great choice if steady income is your main need. Distributions are paid only quarterly and they have tended to be meagre. The exception was in 2000 when the fund paid out a total of $2.05. But the bulk of that amount ($1.79) was in the form of a year-end capital gains distribution, which is not likely to be repeated on a regular basis. However, if you want a conservative stock fund for your portfolio and cash flow is not a concern, this is a first-rate choice. On that strength, its $$$$ rating continues to be well earned.

## Canadian Bond Funds

### STANDARD LIFE BOND FUND                    $$$ → FI #/* RSP CB

Manager: Standard Life Investments Inc.

MER: 1.61%     Fundata: D     Style: Interest Rate Anticipation

Suitability: Conservative investors

This is another fine entry from this underrated group. This fund invests almost entirely in government issues. The bulk of the portfolio is in federal government bonds, but there are also some top-rated provincial securities (Alberta and Ontario) and a few corporates, so the quality of the assets is excellent. Returns have been above average for the Canadian bond category, with an average annual compound rate of return of 6.3% for the five years to June 30/01. The risk level is about average for a bond fund.

## Foreign Bond Funds

### STANDARD LIFE INTERNATIONAL BOND FUND    $$$ ↑ FI #/* RSP FB

Manager: Standard Life Investments Inc.

MER: 2.14%     Fundata: D     Style: Interest Rate Anticipation/Currency Trading

Suitability: Aggressive investors who want currency diversification

This fully RRSP-eligible fund offers international diversification by investing in bonds issued by the federal and provincial governments denominated in foreign currencies. Some bonds issued by international agencies like the World Bank are also held. Although this type of fund has not traditionally been a strong performer, this particular entry is one of the better bets in the category. It gained 7.4% over the year to June 30/01 and has a five-year average annual return of 5.1%, one of the best in the Foreign Bond category. Most of the portfolio was in U.S. dollar issues in the first half of 2001, which made the fund a good hedge against a further devaluation of the loonie. But be warned: the volatility rating of this fund is quite high in comparison with others of its type.

## Canadian Money Market Funds

### STANDARD LIFE MONEY MARKET FUND    $$$ → C #/* RSP CMM

Manager: Standard Life Investments Inc.

MER: 0.95%     Fundata: E     Style: Income

Suitability: Conservative investors

This is a useful entry that invests primarily in corporate notes, with some Canada and Province of Quebec T-bills tossed in. Returns have been above average. Don't pay a sales commission to acquire it, however.

# Also Recommended

## Sector Equity Funds

### STANDARD LIFE NATURAL RESOURCE FUND     $$ ↑ G #/* RSP NR

Manager: Standard Life Investments Inc.

MER: 2.15%     Fundata: C     Style: Bottom-up Growth

Suitability: Aggressive investors

As the name implies, this fund invests in the resource sector with a heavy emphasis on oil and gas in 2001 (55% of assets). With that sector performing well in the first part of the year (it slumped later), the fund chalked up a handsome gain of more than 20% in the 12 months to June 30/01. That was good enough to pull all longer-term results to above average. However, we are not convinced this fund isn't a one-shot wonder, as it has not been an impressive performer in the past. Moreover, its volatility record is higher than normal for this notoriously volatile category. We are raising the rating to $$ on the strength of the recent results, but investors should dip their toe into this one with caution.

## U.S. Equity Funds

### STANDARD LIFE U.S. EQUITY FUND     $$ → G #/* £ USE

Manager: Standard Life Investments Inc.

MER: 2.18%     Fundata: C     Style: Bottom-up Value

Suitability: Middle-of-the-road investors

This fund can invest across the entire spectrum of U.S. stocks, although the small portfolio tends to focus more on medium- to large-sized companies. It has a spotty performance record, unlike many other funds in this family that have shown good consistency. Over the year to June 30/01, it dropped 11.5%, but that was a better performance than the average for the U.S. Equity category. Results over three and five years are slightly below average. In the first half of 2001, the fund still had a heavy technology weighting (24%) despite the weakness in that sector. Names like Microsoft, Intel, and IBM were on the top-10 list as of mid-year. This is one of those funds that isn't terrible, but it isn't great either. The $$ rating fits it perfectly.

## Canadian Balanced and Asset Allocation Funds

### STANDARD LIFE BALANCED FUND      $$ → FI/G #/* RSP CBAL

Manager: Standard Life Investments Inc.

MER: 2.19%      Fundata: B      Style: Balanced

Suitability: Conservative investors

This fund offers a diversified portfolio that includes a large holding in federal and provincial bonds, a good representation of Canadian stocks, and some U.S. equities. In the first half of 2001, the balance between stocks and bonds was 56%–43%, with a small cash position. The fund lost 6.9% over the year to June 30/01, which was more than twice the loss of the average fund in the category. Longer-term results are still above average, however. Volatility is a little higher than normal for a fund of this type.

### Promising Newcomers

### STANDARD LIFE CORPORATE HIGH-YIELD      NR → FI #/* RSP HYB
### BOND FUND

Manager: Standard Life Investments Inc.

MER: 2.12%      Fundata: N/A      Style: Interest Rate Anticipation/Credit Analysis

Suitability: Aggressive investors

Funds of this type normally invest in what are commonly known as "junk bonds." However, this one is slightly different: the bulk of the portfolio is in high-yield corporate issues, but the mandate requires that the average credit rating of all the holdings be at least BBB. The end result is that this fund is less risky than others of the same type, at least in theory. Some of the top holdings in mid-2001 included issues from solid names like Sears Canada, Hudson's Bay Company, Shaw Communications, and Alberta Government Telecom. Initial results have been good; this fund gained 4.9% in the year to June 30/01, well above average for the category.

# STONE & CO.

## THE COMPANY

Richard Stone is a young entrepreneur who, after cutting his teeth on senior marketing assignments for other fund companies, decided to go it on his own. His fledgling company ran into some rough going in the first couple of years, with problems that ranged from finding good managers to persuading brokers and planners that there really was room for another option on their shelves. But Stone developed a unique investing approach that helps to differentiate his funds from the pack; his style is called "pure growth." Stone's portfolios contain growth stocks with, as he puts it, "no rocks, no trees, and no golds." So apart from energy stocks you won't find any resource issues (the so-called deep cyclicals) in his funds, which works pretty well more often than not.

To run the show he hired McLean Budden, one of Canada's best-respected money management firms. McLean Budden has altered its own style somewhat for these funds, but not a lot (they have always been primarily a growth manager, although they now have a value component to their operation). The Stone funds buy companies with strong earnings potential and growth rates that lead their peer group and the market as a whole. The managers stick with large, established companies and lean towards a buy-and-hold philosophy. In addition to the standard management fees, McLean Budden receives a performance bonus if it can beat an established benchmark.

The most recent addition to the Stone family is the Flagship Global Growth Fund, which focuses on stock picking outside of Canada. To date, it has been an average performer.

## THE DETAILS

|  |  |
|---|---|
| Number of funds: | 4 |
| Assets under management: | $225 million |
| Load Charge: | Front: max. 5%; Back: max. 6% |
| Switching Charge: | 2% maximum |
| Where sold: | Across Canada |
| How sold: | Through brokers, dealers, and financial planners |
| Phone number: | 1-800-336-9528 |
| Web site address: | www.stoneco.com |
| E-mail address: | info@stoneco.com |
| Minimum initial investment: | $500 |

## INVESTING TIPS

Until 2000, the Flagship Canadian Stock Fund was one of the most tax-efficient funds in Canada (although "tax-efficient" is really just another way of saying "tax-deferred"), due to the managers' buy-and-hold philosophy. In 1999, for example, this fund paid out taxable distributions of just 11¢ a unit. However, 2000 was a difficult year for stock markets and the fund managers did a lot more trading than usual. The capital gains that they realized in the portfolio as a result generated a year-end distribution of 97¢ a unit. That amount was equivalent to about 11% of the fund's year-end valuation and was taxable in non-registered accounts.

If you are considering this fund for a non-registered account, ask about the expected distribution for the current year. These distributions are usually paid in December, but the managers should have a general idea of how much they'll be by mid-autumn. If the payment is likely to be substantial, defer your purchase until after the distribution date and buy the units at the lower price that will result (the value of a distribution is deducted from net asset value per share). This action sidesteps what will amount to taxation on your capital.

## FUND SUMMARY

|  |  |
|---|---|
| Top Choices: | Stock |
| Also Recommended: | Growth & Income, Money Market |
| Promising Newcomers: | Global Growth |
| The Rest: | None |

## FUND RATINGS

### Top Choices

**Canadian Equity Funds**

### STONE & CO. FLAGSHIP STOCK FUND $$$ → G #/* RSP CE

Manager: McLean Budden, since 1996

MER: 3.16%    Fundata: C    Style: Large-Cap Growth

Suitability: Long-term investors looking for growth with reasonable risk

This is one of those funds that will probably never draw a lot of attention because it is not subject to wild swings, up or down. It's just a modest, steady performer that will add a nice growth component to a portfolio without causing anyone a lot of either elation or distress. Generally it's a second-quartile (above-average) performer, although it occasionally dips to the third quartile as it did in 2000. It will do well during periods when growth stocks are in favour (it had a nice run in 1999–2000), and will lag behind when they're not. It's lagged recently as growth has been out of favour and value in vogue. In the first half of 2001, the fund lost 8% in value. Significantly, however, that was somewhat better than average for the Canadian Large-Cap category. The portfolio is well diversified and the fund maintains a foreign content ratio of about 25% through a position in the companion Flagship Global Growth Fund. McLean Budden has a proven long-term record as a growth manager, so we expect this fund to continue to be one of the better choices of its type, despite the recent slump.

## Also Recommended

### Canadian Balanced Funds

### STONE & CO. FLAGSHIP GROWTH & INCOME FUND                    $$ → FI/G #/* RSP CBAL

Manager: McLean Budden, since inception (1996)

MER: 3.14%     Fundata: D     Style: Large-Cap Growth (Equities)

Suitability: Balanced investors

The investing style on the equities side is the same for this balanced fund as you'll find in the companion Stock Fund. Most of the holdings mirror the companion fund as well. That fact is hardly a surprise considering that McLean Budden handles the managerial chores in both cases. The fixed-income component was a mix of government and corporate bonds—mostly of short- to mid-term maturity—in the first half of 2001. The fund tends to be an average performer for its type, always in the second or third quartile. It showed a modest loss of 4.3% in the first half of 2001, but over three years it has been profitable. There's a large foreign component (19% in the first half of 2001), which is attained by investing in the companion Global Growth Fund. No one is likely to get very excited about this one, but it will do a decent job for you over time. You'll find blue-chip companies like Bombardier, the banks, CN Rail, and BCE in the mix. One negative: the MER is more than half a point above the average, which deflates returns.

### Money Market Funds

### STONE & CO. FLAGSHIP MONEY MARKET FUND   $$ → C #/* RSP CMM

Manager: McLean Budden, since inception (1996)

MER:   1.12% Fundata: E

Suitability: Conservative investors

This fund seems to hover around the average for its class, never much above or below the median. The portfolio is heavily weighted toward corporate short-term notes, which generate a somewhat higher return than T-bills. The MER is a bit on the high side, but not by a lot. Not a great fund of its type, but okay.

## Promising Newcomers

### Global Equity Funds

### STONE & CO. GLOBAL GROWTH FUND                    NR → G #/* £ GE

Manager: McLean Budden, since inception (December 1998)

MER: 3.20%     Fundata: C        Style: Large-Cap Growth

Suitability: Long-term investors looking for growth with reasonable risk

This fund takes owner Richard Stone's "pure growth" concept to the international level, using the managerial team from McLean Budden, an organization with plenty of expertise in this area. The fund scored a nice return of 18.9% in 1999, its first full year, but lost a little ground in 2000 with a return of –3.4%. The first half of 2001 was also weak, with a loss of about 8%. The portfolio is slightly weighted toward the U.S., with European stocks (including the U.K.) accounting for about a third of the holdings. Stocks are of the blue-chip variety, with names like Procter & Gamble, 3M, J.P. Morgan Chase, Microsoft, and Nippon T&T on the list. The portfolio is very well diversified. Over time, we expect this to be a sound, middle-of-the-road performer.

# STRATEGICNOVA MUTUAL FUNDS

## THE COMPANY

This firm appeared in last year's edition under the name of Nova Bancorp. The corporate title changed after Nova Bancorp acquired the Strategic Value funds (SVC O'Donnell) in 2000. And that was just the latest takeover by this aggressive company; previously it had purchased the Navigator and Centrepost funds. These acquisitions have moved the Montreal-based company (which has close ties to Quebec's powerful Caisse de Depot) into the 24th spot on the Investment Funds Institute of Canada (IFIC) list of member companies, with $2.8 billion under management. However, most Canadians are unaware of the firm's existence.

Now that StrategicNova has digested its various purchases, the company is launching new funds that target high net worth individuals and their financial advisors. One of these funds is the unique SAMI Fund, which invests in Canadian companies consistent with the principles of Koranic law. The firms are screened against criteria established by the Shari'ah Supervisory Board that relate to such matters as unacceptable levels of debt, impure interest income, and various ethical tests. The fund is designed to appeal primarily to devout Muslims and all investments will be eligible for inclusion in the Dow Jones Islamic Market Indexes. To our knowledge, this is the first fund of this type to be offered in Canada.

## THE DETAILS

|  |  |
|---|---|
| Number of funds: | 43 |
| Assets under management: | $2.8 billion |
| Load Charge: | Front: max. 5%; Back: max. 7% |
| Switching Charge: | 2% maximum |
| Where Sold: | All provinces |
| How Sold: | Through registered representatives |
| Phone Number: | 1-800-408-2311 |
| Web Site: | www.strategicnova.com |
| Email: | Through Web site |
| Minimum initial investment: | $500 |

## INVESTING TIPS

StrategicNova is one of the few fund companies that provides a negotiable back-end load structure. This means that if you buy units on a deferred sales charge basis, the commission you will be charged if you sell before six years will vary. The range here is very wide. The best deal is a maximum back-end load of 2%, which falls to zero after a two-year hold. The worst is a 7% deferred sales charge if you sell in the first year; you are off the hook only after a six-year holding period. The actual structure also varies depending on the specific fund purchased, so this process can get quite complicated. Consult the prospectus for full details.

The determining factor in the structure that applies in each case is the amount of commission the company pays to your sales representative. This amount can range from 1% to 6% on the total value of your purchase. The higher the sales rep's commission, the greater the fee you may be assessed if you cash out early. That's why it is important to discuss this deferred sales charge structure thoroughly with your advisor before you make a purchase. If you're a big client, with a lot of money invested, aim for the lowest rate structure possible. At worst, you shouldn't end up with a top deferred sales charge of more than 4% to 5%. If the advisor wants more, take your business elsewhere.

A word of warning about using RRSP clones from this company: Some are showing great divergences in performance from the parent fund. Be cautious and go with the parent if possible.

## FUND SUMMARY

| | |
|---:|:---|
| Top Choices: | Asia-Pacific, Canadian Balanced, Canadian Dividend |
| Also Recommended: | Canadian Asset Allocation, Canadian Large-Cap Growth, Canadian Large-Cap Value, Government Bond, Income, Money Market, U.S. Large-Cap Growth, U.S. Large-Cap Value, U.S. Mid-Cap Value, World Strategic Asset Allocation |
| Promising Newcomers: | Canadian Dominion Resource, Canadian Natural Resources |
| The Rest: | Canadian Aggressive Balanced Fund, Canadian High-Yield Bond, Canadian Mid-Cap Growth, Canadian Mid-Cap Value, Canadian Small-Cap, Canadian Technology, Commonwealth World Balanced, Emerging Markets, Europe, Euro-Tech, Japan, Latin America, Managed Futures, SAMI, TopGuns, U.S. High-Yield Bond, U.S. Mid-Cap Growth, U.S. Small-Cap, U.S.Tech, World Bond, World Convertible Debentures, World Equity, World Large-Cap, World Precious Metals, World Tech |

# FUND RATINGS

## Top Choices

### Dividend Income Funds

### STRATEGICNOVA CANADIAN DIVIDEND FUND    $$$ → G/FI #/* RSP DIV

Manager: Canadian Stock Markets Team (CDP Global Asset Management), since September 2000

MER: 2.76%     Fundata: B     Style: Value

Suitability: Conservative investors

This fund was previously the Strategic Value Dividend Fund under the direction of Mark Bonham, who was president of SVC O'Donnell before the Nova Bancorp acquisition. Bonham is now gone from the scene, however, and a new managerial team is in place. Under Bonham's direction, the twin objectives of this fund were capital growth and dividend income, and he made a concerted effort to enhance the cash yield with a goal to produce a fixed payout of between 4% and 5% annually. Distributions were on a monthly basis, set at 5¢ a unit (60¢ a year), and the fund paid out at that rate in calendar year 2000. However, the new managers have changed the composition of the portfolio somewhat. Previously, the typical portfolio mix was 40% preferred shares, 40% high-yielding common stocks, 15% bonds, and 5% cash, which gave the fund a more defensive tone in rough markets. As of the first half of 2001, however, the preferred share portion of the fund was down to 22.5%. Canadian common stocks accounted for just over 65%, and U.S. shares for about 5%, so this fund is now coming more into line with other funds in its category in terms of asset composition. Of course, this asset mix increases the risk factor, but the fund has done well so far under the new management team, recording a gain of 12.7% for the year to June 30/01. We'll maintain the $$$ rating on the strength of that performance. This is a good choice for an income-oriented investor seeking tax-advantaged cash flow.

### Global and International Equity Funds

### STRATEGICNOVA ASIA-PACIFIC FUND                  $$$ ↑ G #/* £ AXJ

Manager: Ian Beattie (WorldInvest Ltd.), since October 2000

MER: 2.64%     Fundata: A     Style: Value

Suitability: Aggressive investors

Not many Far East funds are making money these days, this one being the exception. Manager Ian Beattie, who is based in London, has been at the helm only since October 2000, so we can't give him full credit for this fund's remarkable gain of almost 29% in the year to June 30/01. But he can certainly take the lion's share of the kudos. His emphasis on stocks that trade at a deep discount to their intrinsic value has certainly paid off so far. This fund may invest throughout Asia, with the exception of Japan. The portfolio was heavily concentrated in Hong Kong (52% of assets) in the first half of 2001, with a 14% stake in South Korea, and the rest scattered around Asia. Most of the top names in the portfolio—with the exception of Samsung—will be unfamiliar to most investors, but if Beattie can keep producing results like this, who cares? We aren't currently enthusiastic about Asian funds, but if you want one for your portfolio this is the first place to look. Formerly the Navigator Asia-Pacific Fund.

## Canadian Balanced and Asset Allocation Funds

### STRATEGICNOVA CANADIAN BALANCED FUND
$$$ → FI/G #/* RSP CBAL

Manager: StrategicNova Asset Allocation Team, since August 2000

MER: 2.58%    Fundata: A    Style: Value

Suitability: Conservative investors

This fund differs from the companion Canadian Asset Allocation Fund in that the management team here uses a value approach to stock selection; the Asset Allocation Fund approach is growth oriented. The value style makes this fund more suitable for conservative investors. The focus is on medium- to large-sized companies that are undervalued. Recently, some of the top names in the portfolio included Manulife Financial, Brascan, Alcan, and Canadian Natural Resources. The fund has been a first quartile-performer since 1999 according to Globefund, and notched a small gain of just over 1% in the first half of 2001. This is a good choice for a core RRSP fund. Formerly known as the Centrepost Balanced Fund and renamed Nova Balanced Fund. The Strategic Value Canadian Balanced Fund was absorbed into the Nova Balanced Fund and the new name emerged.

## Also Recommended

## Canadian Equity Funds

### STRATEGICNOVA CANADIAN LARGE-CAP GROWTH FUND
$$ → G #/* RSP CLC

Manager: Steven Wippersteg, since October 1999

MER: 2.91%    Fundata: B    Style: Growth

Suitability: Middle-of-the-road investors

As you can deduce from the name, the mandate of this fund is to invest in domestic growth stocks of large corporations. The top 10 list in the first half of

2001 included firms like Bombardier, BCE, Canadian Pacific, TD Bank, etc. What's interesting is that four of the top-10 listings also show up in the major holdings of the companion Canadian Large-Cap Value Fund. We're not sure how a stock can qualify on both counts, but there you have it. Considering this is a growth-oriented fund, recent results have been quite good. The fund came close to breaking even over the year to June 30/01 and recorded a strong gain in the second quarter. We'd just like to see a little more separation between this and the Value Fund.

### STRATEGICNOVA CANADIAN LARGE-CAP VALUE FUND $$ → G #/* RSP CLC

Manager: Andrew Cook, since August 2000

MER: 2.34%     Fundata: B     Style: Value

Suitability: Conservative investors

Try to follow along here: The old Strategic Value Canadian Equity Fund and the Strategic Value Canadian Equity Value Fund were merged into the old Nova Canadian Equity Fund. The resulting fund was given the new name shown here, but this fund will carry the historic record of the Nova fund. All clear? Oh, yes—the mandate has also changed. The fund will now focus on large-cap stocks (previously it was an all-cap fund). And, of course, there is a new manager at the top. So in actual fact, you really can't give much credence to historic returns (which were extremely good, incidentally). Andrew Cook is still cutting his teeth on this one, so we won't judge him too harshly yet. But we are disappointed with a loss of 7.1% in the first half of 2001 at a time when many value funds were producing good returns. Top holdings recently included a lot of banks, Petro-Canada, Canadian Pacific, BCE, and, somewhat surprisingly for a value fund, Nortel. We're keeping this one on the Recommended List for now, but we expect better things from Cook over the next 12 months. This was formerly known as the Centrepost Canadian Equity Fund and became part of the StrategicNova Group in 1999.

### U.S. Equity Funds

### STRATEGICNOVA U.S. LARGE-CAP GROWTH FUND $$ → G #/* NO USE

Manager: Steven Wippersteg, since October 2000

MER:     2.92% Fundata: B     Style: Growth

Suitability: Middle-of-the-road investors

This fund was formerly the Strategic Value American Equity Fund. It's been given a name change and the mandate has been revised slightly (it used to invest in mid-to-large-cap companies; now the focus is on big firms only). You'll recognize a lot of the names in the portfolio immediately: General Electric, AOL

Time Warner, Citigroup, Exxon, etc. This investing concept should work just fine over time, but there are two short-term factors to consider. One is that growth investing is not in favour at present. The second is that we have not encountered new manager Steven Wippersteg before, and therefore are in no position to judge his performance. We can report that the fund lost just over 7% in the first half of 2001, which was not a bad performance considering general market conditions and the fund's mandate. But we're curious to see what Wippersteg can do in good market conditions. In the meantime, the rating moves up a notch to $$. Previously known as the Laurentian American Equity Fund and prior to that as the Viking Growth Fund.

## STRATEGICNOVA U.S. LARGE-CAP VALUE FUND   $$ → G  #/* RSP USE

Manager: Barbara Marcin (GAMCO Investors), since December 2000

MER: 3.08%     Fundata: D     Style: Value

Suitability: Middle-of-the-road investors

You may wonder how we can include a value fund on our Recommended List when it lost more than 20% in the year to June 30/01. It is a stretch, we admit. However, new manager Barbara Marcin can't be blamed for the poor showing. She took over only at the end of 2000 and the fund finished just below break-even in the first half of 2001, not at all bad given the market conditions. As the name suggests, the fund concentrates on big companies like Phillip Morris, Compaq, and Mattel. Historic results really aren't significant here, but the investment approach appears sound so we'll keep the fund on our Recommended List, with a $$ rating. The provenance here is the O'Donnell American Sector Growth Fund merged into the Navigator American Value Investment Fund, which was then renamed the StrategicNova U.S. Large-Cap Value Fund.

## U.S. Small-to-Mid-Cap Funds

## STRATEGICNOVA U.S. MID-CAP VALUE FUND     $$ → G  #/* NO USSC

Manager: Marc J. Gabelli (Gemini Capital), since inception (December 1995)

MER    3.19%  Fundata: C     Style: Bottom-up Value

Suitability: Aggressive investors

This is one of the few StrategicNova funds with management consistency. Marc Gabelli of the New York-based Gemini Capital Corp. was the founding manager when this fund was originally launched as the O'Donnell U.S. Mid-Cap Fund, and his services have been retained by StrategicNova. The fund has a somewhat spotty record but it has looked good recently with a gain of 6.4% in the first half of 2001. Gabelli searches out undervalued companies with a market cap between U.S.$1.5 billion and U.S.$6 billion. The top 10 holdings recently have included names like Tupperware, Blockbuster, and Ralston-Purina, and were heavily weighted toward consumer products. This is a decent fund, but not a great one, on the evidence to date. Note: there's an RRSP clone of this fund but it seems to be way out of whack in terms of tracking. While the parent fund showed a one-year loss of 5.2% to June 30/01, the clone dropped 15.8%! Until StrategicNova gets that problem squared away, avoid the clone.

## Canadian Balanced and Asset Allocation Funds

### STRATEGICNOVA CANADIAN ASSET ALLOCATION FUND
$$ → FI/G #/* RSP CTAA

Manager: StrategicNova Asset Allocation Team, since August 2000

MER: 2.65%    Fundata: C    Style: Growth

Suitability: Middle-of-the-road investors

This was previously the O'Donnell Balanced Fund and had been under the direction of Mark Bonham. Both name and manager are gone from the scene and the mandate has changed as well. The equities side of the portfolio now focuses on large-cap stocks (it was previously an all-cap fund) and the limit on the percentage of assets that can be held in any one category (e.g., equities, bonds) has been removed. Hopefully these changes will bring better results, as returns put the predecessor fund near the bottom of the heap. Initial signs are good; the fund was a first-quartile performer through the first half of 2001, despite recording a small loss. The portfolio was recently weighted toward stocks (65%), with companies like Bombardier and BCE holding prominent positions. Annual distributions have been running around 30¢, representing a very good yield for a fund with a net asset value in the $4 to $4.50 range. Rating moves up one notch.

## Global Balanced and Asset Allocation Funds

### STRATEGICNOVA WORLD STRATEGIC ASSET ALLOCATION FUND
$$ → FI/G #/* RSP GBAL

Manager: StrategicNova Asset Allocation Team, since December 2000

MER:    2.90%  Fundata: B    Style: Growth

Suitability: Middle-of-the-road investors

Two Strategic Value funds were combined to create this one: World Balanced and World Balanced RSP. The fund invests in a portfolio of international companies of all sizes and high-quality foreign currency bonds. It had been a chronic under-performer in recent years, but has looked somewhat better recently, although it just sneaks on to our Recommended List. Beware of the RRSP-eligible clone, which isn't coming anywhere close to tracking the return of the parent fund.

Formerly the Laurentian Global Balanced Fund and before that the Endurance Global Equity Fund.

## Canadian Bond Funds

### STRATEGICNOVA GOVERNMENT BOND FUND          $$ ↓ FI #/* RSP STB

Manager: Michael Labanowich, since June 1997

MER: 2.33%      Fundata: E      Style: Mix

Suitability: Conservative investors

This fund invests primarily in short-to-medium-term securities (not exceeding five years) issued or guaranteed by various levels of government. This strategy makes the portfolio less vulnerable to losses when interest rates rise, but returns in good bond years will tend to be lower. As a result, the fund is best suited to very conservative investors. Gain for the 12 months to June 30/01 was 5.3%. Main negative: the MER is too high for a fund of this type. Formerly the Strategic Value Government Bond Fund and prior to that, the Laurentian Government Bond Fund and the Endurance Government Bond Fund.

### STRATEGICNOVA INCOME FUND          $$ → FI #/* RSP CB

Manager: Michael Labanowich, since June 1997

MER: 2.29%      Fundata: E      Style: Interest Rate Anticipation

Suitability: Conservative investors

This fund invests mainly in corporate bonds of all durations, although there are some government issues in the mix as well. It hasn't been a strong performer in the past, but it has looked better recently with a first-quartile performance in the first half of 2001. Gain for the year to June 30/01 was 4.3%—you could have earned more in an average money market fund with less risk. This fund would look much better with a reduced MER; as things stand it's about 25 basis points above the average for its category. Those numbers mean the manager has to be a quarter point better than everyone else just to stay even. In a category where the difference between top or bottom quartile may be only 1.5%, that's a significant task. So this is not a top bond fund by any means, but it's an okay choice if you want to invest with the company. Previously known as the Strategic Value Income Fund, the Laurentian Income Fund and, going way back, as the Viking Income Fund.

## Canadian Money Market Funds

### STRATEGICNOVA MONEY MARKET FUND  $$ → C  #/* RSP CMM

Manager: Michael Labanowich, since June 2000

MER: 1.12%    Fundata: A    Style: Interest Rate Anticipation

Suitability: Conservative investors

There's been a significant increase in the MER here, which will cut into the returns of this decent money fund. StrategicNova pushed up the cost by 32 basis points, which is a lot. We do not approve of this move, believing it to be contrary to investors' interests, and we are lowering the fund's rating to $$ as a result. We don't think it's a coincidence that this fund's returns were below average in the first half of 2001 for the first time since it was launched. This fund brings together the Strategic Value Money Market Fund, the O'Donnell Money Market Fund, and the Nova Short Term Fund, which is the continuing fund for historic purposes.

## Promising Newcomers

## Sector Funds

### STRATEGICNOVA CANADIAN DOMINION RESOURCE FUND  NR ↑ G #/* RSP NR

Manager: Normand Lamarche (Tuscarora Capital), since inception (November 2000)

MER: 2.25%    Fundata: N/A    Style: Mix

Suitability: Aggressive investors

This natural resource entry got out of the starting gate like a flash. The fund registered a gain of 26.4% in the first half of 2001, making it one of the top performers in its category. Manager Norm Lamarche is a proven veteran who worked with Altamira for several years. Although his mandate covers all types of resource stocks, the emphasis is on the energy sector, which accounted for almost 80% of the fund's assets in the first half of 2001. This is high-risk/high-return stuff—not for the faint of heart—but if you're in a speculative mood, you might want to toss a few dollars at this one.

### STRATEGICNOVA CANADIAN NATURAL RESOURCES FUND  NR ↑ G #/* RSP NR

Manager: Normand Lamarche (Tuscarora Capital), since inception (November 2000)

MER: 2.25%    Fundata: N/A    Style: Value

Suitability: Aggressive investors

This fund differs from the companion Dominion Resource Fund in a couple of ways, even though they share the same manager. First, this fund has better diversification (Dominion Resource focuses mainly on energy). And while oil and gas is a big item here too, it's not as dominant. Second, Lamarche uses a value style for choosing stocks for this fund, seeking underpriced companies. Most of the stocks are small-to-mid-cap, so there's a lot of risk here. But initial returns have been very good, with a 34.2% gain in the first half of 2001. No one expects Lamarche to keep up that pace, but it's an encouraging sign.

# SYNERGY ASSET MANAGEMENT

## THE COMPANY

Synergy was established at the beginning of 1998 by Joe Canavan, a high-profile fund marketer and administrator who began his career with Fidelity, founded the GT Global family in Canada (since merged into AIM Funds), and then left that company as president in mid-1997.

The Synergy philosophy is to build a mutual fund family that offers investors the ability to diversify by four clearly defined styles: value, growth, momentum, and small-cap. The ability to differentiate in this way has paid off: Synergy has been one of the fastest-growing mutual fund companies in Canada in recent years.

The company's range of fund offerings has steadily expanded, and they now offer 17 basic funds plus another 7 RRSP clones. Synergy employs an "umbrella" approach for most of its funds, which allows investors with non-registered accounts to switch between "classes" without triggering capital gains tax liability. The original umbrella fund is Synergy Canadian Fund Inc. It offers six investment options, all of which are domestic. Synergy Global Fund Inc. replicates this structure with international funds.

The company also offers two "Extreme" funds. The first, created in April 2000, is the Synergy Extreme Canadian Equity Fund. This is a multi-manager fund that takes the best five ideas from each of its style-pure managers and then lead manager Andrew McCreath complements those picks with what Synergy calls "10 additional hyper-growth opportunity stocks." This process, according to the company, allows the fund to offer a highly concentrated portfolio of companies the managers believe have the potential to deliver significantly higher returns to investors, albeit with greater risk.

The same approach is taken with the Synergy Extreme Global Equity Fund, which was created in early 2001. So far, the jury is out on how well the concept is working, although the Extreme Global Equity Fund got off to a strong start.

The company also offers some quantitatively driven funds, including the Global Style Management Class Fund and the Tactical Asset Allocation Fund. In these funds, the security selection is based on Synergy's in-house style models. In fact, the Tactical Asset Allocation Fund is the first balanced fund in Canada that provides style diversification for its equity selections. David Picton is the lead manager.

Although not a balanced fund, the Global Style Management Class invests in equities, incorporating all investment styles of value, growth, momentum, and small-cap into one, and it does not discriminate with respect to country or industry. In this case, the company uses an in-house model that screens over 5,000 global stocks classified by investment style, geographic region, country, and industry. Next, it selects the best 100 global value, growth, momentum, and small-cap stocks. Managing the fund is Michael Mahoney, who is also the developer of the model.

## THE DETAILS

|  |  |
| --- | --- |
| Number of core funds: | 17 |
| Assets under management: | $1.3 billion |
| Load charge: | Front: max. 5%; Back: max. 5% |
| Switching charge: | 2% maximum |
| Where sold: | Across Canada |
| How sold: | Through financial advisors |
| Phone number: | 1-888-664-4784 (English) |
|  | or 1-888-664-4785 (French) |
| Web site address: | www.synergyfunds.com |
| E-mail address: | info@synergyfunds.com |
| Minimum initial investment: | $500 |

## INVESTING TIPS

The umbrella structure that Synergy employs for most of its funds makes this company a good choice for active investors with non-registered accounts. It allows them to move money around without having to worry about the tax consequences of every switch.

It works like this: Synergy offers two "master" funds, Synergy Canadian Fund Inc. and Synergy Global Fund Inc. Within each fund, there are several different "classes"—in effect, funds within the fund. For example, within the Synergy Canadian Fund Inc., you'll find Growth Class, Momentum Class, Small-Cap Class, Value Class, Management Class, and Short-Term Income Class. You can move your assets among any of these classes without triggering tax liability or a deferred sales charge. However, a financial advisor is allowed to charge up to 2% for each switch. If you plan to do a lot of trading, you should negotiate a zero switch fee before making your initial purchase.

## FUND SUMMARY

|  |  |
| --- | --- |
| Top Choices: | Canadian Growth, Canadian Momentum, Canadian Style Management |
| Also Recommended: | Canadian Small-Cap, Canadian Value |
| Promising Newcomers: | Extreme Global Equity |
| The Rest: | American Growth, Canadian Income, Canadian Short-Term Income, European Momentum, Extreme Canadian Equity, Global Growth, Global Momentum, Global Short-Term Income, Global Style Management, Global Value, Tactical Asset Allocation |

# FUND RATINGS

## Top Choices

### Canadian Equity Funds

### SYNERGY CANADIAN GROWTH CLASS $$$ → G #/* RSP CE

Manager: Andrew McCreath, since inception (December 1997)

MER: 2.91%     Fundata: E     Style: Growth

Suitability: Aggressive investors

This is Synergy's Canadian growth entry. It's an all-cap fund with stock selection based on expected strong profitability and sustained earnings growth. Top holdings in the first half of 2001 included companies ranging from the little-knowns like Baytex Energy and Gilden Activewear to giants like Bombardier, Petro-Canada, and Royal Bank. Note that almost a quarter of the fund's assets were invested in the Synergy Global Growth Class, to take advantage of the foreign content allowance. Unfortunately, Global Growth hasn't done well recently, so this position has been a drag on returns. One-year performance to June 30/01 showed a loss of 13.5%. However, the three-year average annual gain of 9.2% is well above average for the Canadian Equity category and better than many long-term growth fund leaders such as McLean Budden Equity Growth Fund. That result makes this fund worthy of a $$$ debut rating.

### SYNERGY CANADIAN MOMENTUM CLASS $$$ ↑ G #/* RSP CE

Manager: David Picton, since inception (December 1997)

MER: 2.68%     Fundata: D     Style: Momentum

Suitability: Aggressive investors

Manager David Picton seeks out fast-growing companies that meet his specific criteria, which includes accelerating earnings or revenues, positive earnings surprises, and strong relative price strength. As soon as a stock fails to meet his tests it is dropped, so this is not a buy-and-hold fund. Top 10 holdings in the first half of 2001 included several of the major banks, BCE, Bombardier, Canadian Natural Resources, and Hudson's Bay Co. Like most momentum funds, this one did very well in the late 1990s, scoring impressive gains. Those numbers account for its excellent three-year average annual compound rate of return of 12% to June 30/01. Also like most momentum funds, it has been in a slump recently (one-year loss of 15.4%), which explains its low Fundata rating. On a positive note, however, it held up much better than most momentum funds during the big tech market dive. This is a fund that will do well in a market recovery, which is why we are giving it a $$$ rating despite the recent setback. Average quartile ranking (AQR) over this fund's first three and a half years is a middle-of-the-road 2.00, but that result is heavily weighted by a fourth-quartile performance in the first half of 2001. A good choice for aggressive investors, but watch out for the volatility.

## SYNERGY CANADIAN STYLE MANAGEMENT CLASS $$$ → G #/* RSP CE

Manager: David Picton, since inception (December 1997)

MER: 2.69%     Fundata: D     Style: Mix

Suitability: Balanced investors

This fund gives you a bit of everything: value, growth, momentum, and small-cap. The manager uses a style allocation process, adjusting the weightings of the four components periodically to reflect market conditions. Mix in the first part of 2001 was 33% momentum, 32% value, 25% growth, and 10% small-cap. This style blend makes the fund less risky than the company's Canadian Momentum Class or Canadian Growth Class, so it represents a middle ground for investors. One-year loss to June 30/01 was 7.4%, but the fund's three-year average annual compound rate of return of 7.5% was well above average. This is the Synergy fund to choose if you can't decide what style you prefer. AQR for three-and-a-half years is 2.00.

## Also Recommended

## SYNERGY CANADIAN SMALL-CAP CLASS     $$ ↑ G #/* RSP CSC

Manager: Peter Hodson, since inception (December 1997)

MER: 2.76%     Fundata: E     Style: Growth

Suitability: Aggressive investors

Synergy takes the view that "small-cap" is actually a style of management, which is the rationale behind this fund. We don't see it that way, however. To us, this is a growth-oriented fund that focuses on small-cap stocks. Whatever your interpretation, the fact remains that this is a mid-range fund for its type. It's not great, but it's not terrible either. This fund would not be among our top five small-cap fund picks, if that helps to put things in perspective. But if you're a Synergy client and you'd like some exposure in this area, it will do the job. The fund showed a one-year loss of 21.6% for the 12 months to June 30/01, but had a three-year average annual compound rate of return of 5.6%, which was above average for the category. Main sector weighting in the first half of 2001 was oil and gas, holding 28.8% of the portfolio. We'll give it a rating of $$, but recommend you shop the small-cap market before putting your money here.

## SYNERGY CANADIAN VALUE CLASS                    $$ → G #/* RSP CE

Manager: Suzann Pennington, since inception (December 1997)

MER: 2.76%      Fundata: C      Style: Value

Suitability: Conservative investors

This is a pure value fund. Manager Suzann Pennington buys only quality stocks trading at discount prices, with special attention to downside risk. So this is a fund for investors who want to reduce volatility and keep their risk exposure to a minimum. This goal may mean giving up some profit potential during periods of strong market growth, however. The fund showed a one-year gain to June 30/01 of 8.1%, well above average for the period. That result was better than well-known competitor Ivy Canadian, but well behind the performance of the Spectrum Canadian Investment Fund and C.I. Harbour Fund, both of which use a value style as well. The three-year average annual compound rate of return of 4.9% reflects the fund's weak performance during the period when tech stocks were running wild (you won't find many of those here). It also comes in behind some of the other value fund rivals. While we like this fund's prospects in the current investment climate, there are better value funds available, which is why this one receives only a $$ rating.

## Promising Newcomers

## SYNERGY EXTREME GLOBAL EQUITY FUND        NR ↑ G #/* £ GE

Manager: Michael Mahoney, since inception (April 2000)

MER: 2.94%      Fundata: N/A      Style: Mix

Suitability: Aggressive investors

This is one of the increasingly popular breed of multi-manager funds that draws on ideas from several managers. In this case, the stock pickers all run other Synergy funds. They include lead manager Michael Mahoney and Andrew McCreath from the Synergy organization, Tom Marsico from Marsico Capital Management (Denver, Colorado), and Robert Treich from Pictet International Management (London, England). Each manager contributes stocks to the portfolio and may use aggressive investment techniques to capitalize on changing market and economic conditions worldwide. The company warns that risk here may be above average, which is the trade-off for potentially higher returns. It's still early, but the fund has been strong out of the gate with a three-month return of 18.2% for the period ending June 30/01. During that same period, the average global equity fund lost money, which highlights the impressiveness of this fund's result. Time will tell if the managers can sustain the pace, but this is certainly a fund to keep an eye on.

# TALVEST FUND MANAGEMENT

## THE COMPANY

Talvest Fund Management is the mutual fund arm of TAL Global Asset Management, a Montreal-based company with over $48 billion in assets (including their institutional business and the CIBC family of funds) under management. It is owned by CIBC but maintains independent management.

The mutual fund operation was established in 1985 and has since evolved into a healthy line of products that numbered 50 mutual funds at last count. In addition to its regular family of mutual funds, Talvest also distributes two labour-sponsored funds along with a group of segregated funds under the "Synchrony" brand name in conjunction with Maritime Life.

The past year has seen several additions to the Talvest family, including the Canadian Multi-Management Fund, the Global Multi-Management Fund, the International Equity Fund (including an RRSP version), and the Value Line U.S. RSP Fund.

Talvest is one of the world's pre-eminent currency managers and views currencies as a separate asset class. Rather than simply hedging currency risk, which is the approach taken by many other fund companies, Talvest attempts to "add value" through its currency management arm. This work is all done in-house, and the growth of the division has placed TAL among the top 10 currency management companies in the world.

The last two years have not been great for Talvest, as a number of its mainstream funds have suffered through some poor performance periods. On the other hand, the company has a few of the top-performing technology-based funds in the country.

Disclosure: Talvest has three funds known as the Talvest FPX Index funds. The funds include the FPX Income, FPX Balanced, and FPX Growth, designed to mirror the performance of the three FPX Portfolio Indexes, which represent a globally diversified portfolio. The FPX Indexes are listed daily in the *National Post*. Richard Croft and Eric Kirzner (the latter being one of the co-authors of this book) originally designed them at the request of the *Financial Post* in 1997. The three indexes are intended to be portfolio benchmarks that investors can use to judge how well their own portfolio is doing against a passive alternative. Richard Croft, Eric Kirzner, and the *National Post* earn royalties based on the assets under management within the FPX funds.

# THE DETAILS

Number of funds: 50
Assets under management: $4.7 billion
Load charge: Front: max. 1%; Back: max. 5%
Switching charge: 2% maximum
Where sold: Across Canada
How sold: Through brokers, dealers, and financial planners
Phone number: 1-800-268-0081
Web site address: www.talvest.com
E-mail address: marketing@talvest.com
Minimum initial investment: $500

## INVESTING TIPS

The Talvest Global Health Care Fund has been one of the top-performing sector funds in Canada in recent years. While most funds in the Science & Technology category posted huge losses, this one produced an amazing gain of almost 36% in the year to June 30/01. If you don't look at any other fund in this group, pay some attention to this one.

Talvest also offers one of the few China-focused mutual funds in Canada, the Talvest China Plus Fund. If you are interested in this emerging market, it is one of the best funds around.

## FUND SUMMARY

Top Choices: Global Health Care, Millennium High Income, Millennium Next Generation, Small-Cap Canadian Equity, China Plus, Global Small-Cap, Money Market
Also Recommended: Canadian Asset Allocation, Global Science & Technology, Income, Value Line U.S. Equity
Promising Newcomers: None
The Rest: Asian, Bond, Canadian Equity Growth, Canadian Equity Value, Canadian Medical Discoveries, Canadian Multi-Management, Canadian Resource, Canadian Science & Technology, Dividend, European, FPX Balanced, FPX Growth, FPX Income, Global Asset Allocation RSP, Global Bond RSP, Global Equity, Global Multi-Management, Global RSP, High-Yield Bond International Equity, International Equity RSP, Value Line U.S. RSP

# FUND RATINGS

## Canadian Small-to-Mid-Cap Funds

### TALVEST MILLENNIUM NEXT GENERATION FUND
$$$ → G # /* RSP CSC

Manager: Leslie Williams (Morrison Williams Investment Management), since 1993

MER: 2.50%    Fundata: B    Style: Bottom-up/Momentum

Suitability: Aggressive investors

This fund was formed when the Talvest Canadian Leading Industries Fund was merged into the Millennium Next Generation Fund (which had been acquired by Talvest) and renamed. Going further back, the Talvest Canadian Leading Industries Fund was previously the Talvest New Economy Fund, which was originally based on economist Nuala Beck's philosophy. That fund focused on companies involved in the "New Economy." But poor returns were the primary reason behind its closure. K. Leslie Williams, the original manager of the Millennium Next Generation Fund, is the manager here. The mandate of the merged fund is to look for small-to-mid-cap Canadian issues. At mid-2001, the fund held an assortment of such companies, including many found on the TSE 300. Many of its largest positions are small-cap, growth-oriented stocks, and the manager is doing a good job in this tough area. One-year returns to June 30/01 are superior to the peer group and comparable to the benchmark index (Nesbitt Burns Small-Cap Index), whereas three- and five year returns are more than double the average for the peer group and well above the benchmark index. Given the strong recent performance, we are upgrading to a $$$ rating.

### TALVEST SMALL-CAP CANADIAN EQUITY FUND    $$$ ↑ G #/* RSP CSC

Manager: J. Sebastian Van Berkom (Van Berkom and Associates), since inception (1993)

MER: 2.70%    Fundata: A    Style: Value/Growth

Suitability: Aggressive investors

Manager J. Sebastian van Berkom and his Small-Cap Equity Fund continue to impress. One-year numbers to June 30/01 (4.2%) were well above the average for its peer group (a 6.1% loss) and its benchmark, the Nesbitt Burns Small-Cap Index. The three- and five-year numbers are well above average as well. Add a below-average risk profile and you have an explanation for the high Fundata score. The fund's mandate is to scout out above-average growth prospects or under-valued situations, which suits Van Berkom fine since his boutique is highly regarded as a small-cap specialist. Formerly known as the Talvest/Hyperion Small-Cap Canadian Equity Fund. Rating raised to $$$.

## Global and International Equity Funds

### TALVEST CHINA PLUS FUND            $$$ ↑ G #/* £ CSE

Manager: Peter Chau, since 1998

MER: 3.00%      Fundata: N/A      Style: Bottom-up/Growth

Suitability: Aggressive investors

This fund invests primarily in companies located in China, Hong Kong, and Taiwan. Manager Peter Chau has the fund off to a good start. Although the fund suffered a 10.4% loss in the year ending June 30/01, the three-year return is a spectacular 46.1% per annum. The high returns were achieved with high volatility, however; the fund's standard deviation at 42.6 is at the upper end of risk profiles for all mutual funds. Nevertheless, if you are looking for a China investment, this is one of the best. We are starting this fund at a $$$ rating.

### TALVEST GLOBAL SMALL-CAP FUND            $$$ ↑ G #/* £ GE

Manager: Catherine Somhegyi, since 1998

MER: 2.90%      Fundata: C      Style: Bottom-up/Momentum

Suitability: Aggressive investors

This fund is off to a very unusual start. Fund manager Catherine Somhegyi racked up returns of 30% and 136% respectively in her first two years and then suffered a 31.2% loss in the year ending June 30/01. The fund invests in smaller companies and Somhegyi's bottom-up approach has the portfolio allocated across a wide range of nations, although the focus is Europe. The fund has a very high risk profile and is capable of wide swings. If you can stomach the volatility, this is a strong small-cap global entry. The fund debuts with a $$$ rating.

## Sector Equity Funds

### TALVEST GLOBAL HEALTH CARE FUND            $$$$ ↓ G #/* £ ST

Manager: Edward Owens (Wellington Management Co.), since 1996

MER: 2.90%      Fundata: A      Style: Bottom-up/Growth

Suitability: Aggressive investors

This is one of the top-performing funds in the country at the present time! It's diversified across several health care sectors, including major pharmaceuticals, medical devices, health care services, and biotechnology. Management shifts assets freely among these areas to capture the greatest value. The fund tries to benefit from three emerging trends: an aging baby boom population (25% of the population is projected to be over 65 in 2020), rising health care expenditures, and advances in technology. Manager Ed Owens is a veteran and one of the most highly respected professionals in his field in the U.S., where he runs the Vanguard Health Care Fund. The fund has produced some stellar returns of late; especially notable is the one-year 71.1% return to June 30/00 and the 35.8% return to June 30/01. The latter return compares with a 37.9% average loss for the peer group, although such comparisons are a little unfair because health care funds are lumped in with science and technology funds when, in fact, they have very different mandates. A closer examination tells a very compelling story: the average annual return for the three years ending June 30/01 was 47%. No other dedicated health care fund comes close to that longer-term number. Even more impressive, this fund held up remarkably well during the market tumble that began in April 2000. If you are interested in a health-oriented fund for your portfolio with some biotech action thrown in, you won't do better than this one. Roughly three-quarters of assets are invested in the U.S., although there are not a lot of recognizable names in the portfolio. The risk rating is excellent. We are giving this fund a well-deserved $$$$ rating. There is an RRSP-eligible clone available, but it is not tracking the parent fund as closely as we would like.

## Canadian Balanced and Asset Allocation Funds

### TALVEST MILLENNIUM HIGH INCOME FUND        $$$ ↑ C #/* RSP CHIB

Manager: Barry Morrison (Morrison Williams Investment Management), since 1997

MER: 2.50%     Fundata: C      Style: Bottom-up

Suitability: Aggressive income investors

The mandate allows this fund to invest in virtually anything: bonds, royalty trusts, convertible debentures, and common and preferred shares. So expect above-average volatility, although the fund has been consistently profitable in recent years. Monthly distributions are $0.06 a unit, some of which is tax deferred.

## Canadian Money Market Funds

### TALVEST MONEY MARKET FUND              $$$ ↓ C #/* RSP CMM

Manager: Steven Dubrovsky, since 1994

MER: 1.00%     Fundata: B      Style: Index

Suitability: Conservative income investors

The fund's low-risk portfolio consists mainly of corporate notes and government securities. Both the short- and long-term records are good, with the fund beating the averages virtually every year over the past 10. A good choice. If you make a purchase, try to negotiate for no load charges.

# Also Recommended

## U.S. Equity Funds

### TALVEST VALUE LINE U.S. EQUITY FUND $$ ↑ G #/* £ USE

Manager: Alan N. Hoffman (Value Line Inc.), since 1998

MER: 3.00%    Fundata: E    Style: Bottom-up/Momentum

Suitability: Aggressive investors

Fund manager Alan Hoffman has a Ph.D. from Yale and has been with Value Line since 1988. The investment strategy employs the Value Line system, where stocks are chosen based on a high timeliness ranking. Put another way, this is a growth fund that follows a momentum style of management. The Value Line methodology takes into account a number of measures, including earnings, price, and momentum. The fund will buy across all capitalization classes but it recently had a bias toward large-cap market leaders and growth stocks in its four core areas: technology, merchandising, financial services, and consumer products. To date, the results have been mixed. One-year return to June 30/01 was a loss of 18.9%, well behind the peer group (an average 13.8% loss). Three- and five-year returns were slightly below the peer group as well. We are downgrading to a $$ rating

## Sector Equity Funds

### TALVEST GLOBAL SCIENCE & TECHNOLOGY FUND $$ ↑ G #/* £ ST

Manager: Stephen Kahn, since 1996

MER: 2.53%    Fundata: D    Style: Bottom-up/Momentum

Suitability: Aggressive investors

This is your typical high-risk/high-return technology-oriented fund. When the market declines, this fund is more vulnerable because it is tied to a specific sector. A very volatile sector, we might add. When buying these types of funds, you should think long and hard about dollar-cost averaging your way into them. Buy a little now and a little more on dips. This advice is especially true when it comes to this fund, as manager Stephen Kahn tends to be more aggressive than his peer group. Case in point: Mr. Kahn's one-year return to June 30/00 was 160.7%, or more than twice the average for the peer group and almost four times the average for the benchmark index (the Nasdaq Composite Index). However, in the year ending June 30/01, the fund lost 61.2%. Put the two years together and through the magic of compounding the resulting number is a mere 1.15% per annum! Not surprisingly, this fund remains heavily weighted in U.S. tech stocks, although some of the biggest holdings in the fund are not household names. Companies like Agera Corp., Intersil Holding Corp., and Brocade Communication head the list. This fund is great if you are looking for some sizzle in your portfolio, but it's extremely volatile and we are downgrading to a $$ rating.

## Canadian Balanced and Asset Allocation Funds

### TALVEST CANADIAN ASSET ALLOCATION FUND $$ → G/FI #/* RSP CTAA

Manager: Jean-Guy Desjardins, since inception (1986)

MER: 2.44%     Fundata: C     Style: Top-down/Momentum

Suitability: Long-term balanced investors

The fund will actively shift between stocks of all capitalization classes, bonds, derivatives, and cash. The fund can invest as much as 75% of its assets in stocks at any point in time. It can also go as high as 60% in bonds and 55% in cash. As of mid-2001, the fund had about 56% of its assets in equities and 32% in bonds. The remainder was invested in cash. Clearly manager Jean-Guy Desjardins believes that he has a better chance to add value to his bond component with currency trades than with interest rate fluctuations. Loss in the year ending June 30/01 was 8.4%, below average for the peer group and the benchmark index. Over the long term, Mr. Desjardins has proven himself an above-average manager. However, on the basis of recent results, we are downgrading to a $$ rating.

## Canadian Bond Funds

### TALVEST INCOME FUND                          $$ ↓ FI #/* RSP STB

Manager: Jeff Waldman, since November 1998

MER: 1.69%     Fundata: C     Style: Top-down/Index

Suitability: Long-term income investors

After having managed this fund since its inception in 1974, John Braive was replaced by Jeff Waldman, who joined TAL in mid-1998 after stints at Confederation Life and ING Investment Management. That switch caused us some concern, as Braive generated some good numbers during his more than two decades with the fund. However, Waldman has done a decent job and has shown that he too can add value. The fund is geared toward conservative investors who want high monthly income and capital preservation. The bond portfolio is conservatively managed with minimal interest rate risk and is composed mainly of corporate bonds, followed by mortgage-backed securities and federal bonds. Returns tend to be higher than a money market fund but lower than a regular bond fund because of the short duration of the portfolio. A good choice if reducing risk is an objective—in an RRIF, for example—but you will sacrifice some return when bond markets are strong. Also, beware of the high management expense ratio (MER).

### Promising Newcomers

None.

# TORONTO DOMINION BANK

## THE COMPANY

The major development in the past year was the takeover of Canada Trust on February 1, 2000. The result was Canada Trust's mutual funds being merged into Toronto Dominion Bank's, effective October 1, 2000. The resulting funds are all named with the prefix TD, so the famous Green Line and Canada Trust names have disappeared.

We certainly applaud this attempt at clarity and transparency. While some other fund families are becomingly increasingly complex in structure, the result here is a neatly identifiable family of funds. Our only criticism—and this is generally industry wide—is that the management expense ratio (MER) of virtually every fund increased.

The TD family offers an extensive product mix that includes a strong presence in Canadian and foreign index funds, as well as a sprinkling of sector-oriented funds that concentrate on growth areas like science and technology and health care. The bank also offers a broad line of global funds, including RSP funds that are foreign in content but 100% eligible for registered plans. These 100% foreign RRSP-eligible funds have become increasingly popular in the marketplace.

Like some other mainstream fund companies, the Toronto Dominion Bank has expanded its product mix by offering its own line of segregated funds. Each seg fund mirrors the performance of an underlying TD mutual fund.

## THE DETAILS

|  |  |
|---|---|
| Number of funds: | 78 |
| Assets under management: | $30.2 billion |
| Load charge: | None |
| Switching charge: | None |
| Where sold: | Across Canada |
| How sold: | Through TD bank branches or through brokers, dealers, and financial planners |
| Phone number: | 1-800-268-8166 or (416) 982-6432 |
| Web site address: | www.tdcanadatrust.com/mutualfunds |
| E-mail address: | funderman@tdbank.ca |
| Minimum initial investment: | Non-registered: $500 to $2,000 (generally); Registered: $100 (generally) |

# INVESTING TIPS

TD was one of the first institutions to introduce index funds and its offerings have expanded in recent years. If you are interested in an index fund, this is a good place to start. Many of the foreign index funds are available in fully eligible RRSP form as well, with most of the portfolio invested in Government of Canada T-bills (to meet the Canadian content requirement), and with the balance in futures contracts on the underlying foreign market index.

Of special interest to online investors is the new series of funds offering "e" units. These units are available only for Internet purchase and have the advantage of a much lower MER. For example, A units of the TD Canadian Bond Fund carry an MER of 1.25%. However, the "e" units have an MER of 0.47%. The difference goes straight to the bottom line, enhancing your returns accordingly. Several index funds are now available with the "e" option.

Those who like working with TD funds can make use of the Managed Assets Program (MAP). Launched in late 1998, it is similar in format to the Bank of Montreal's MatchMaker programme. Depending on your investment objectives, MAP will help you select a different mix of TD funds for your account. Once a targeted asset mix is determined, the service will then automatically track and rebalance your portfolio in line with your asset mix. To participate, you must contribute a minimum of $5,000 into a non-registered plan and/or $2,000 into a registered plan.

# FUND SUMMARY

|  |  |
|---|---|
| Top Choices: | AmeriGrowth RSP, Balanced Growth, Balanced Income, Canadian Bond, Canadian Equity, Canadian Government Bond Index, Canadian Money Market, Canadian T-Bill, Dividend Growth, Dividend Income, Dow Jones Average Index, Health Sciences, Latin American Growth, Monthly Income, Real Return Bond, U.S. Index, U.S. Mid-Cap Growth, U.S. Money Market |
| Also Recommended: | Canadian Blue-Chip Equity, Energy |
| Promising Newcomers: | U.S. Small-Cap Equity |
| The Rest: | Asian Growth, Balanced, Canadian Index, Canadian Small-Cap Equity, Canadian Stock, Canadian Value, Dow Jones Industrial Average Index, Emerging Markets, Entertainment & Communications, European Index Fund, EuroGrowth RSP, European Growth, Global Government Bond, Global Growth RSP, Global RSP Bond, International Equity, International Growth, International RSP Index, Japanese |

Growth, Japanese Index, Money Market Plus
(closed), Mortgage, North American Equity,
Precious Metals, Premium Money Market,
Resource, Science & Technology, Short-Term
Bond, Short-Term Income, Special Equity, U.S.
Blue-Chip Equity, U.S. Equity, U.S. RSP Index,
U.S. Small-Cap Equity

# FUND RATINGS

## Top Choices

### Canadian Equity Funds

### TD CANADIAN EQUITY FUND                    $$$ → G NO RSP CE

Manager: John Weatherall, since 1997

MER: 2:27%      Fundata: C      Style: Primarily Growth

Suitability: Growth investors

Unlike the companion Blue-Chip Equity Fund, this fund is more growth-oriented
and invests across all capitalization classes. The end result is a much better fund that
has beaten both the average fund and the TSE 300 in recent years. This fund
employs a bottom-up approach, looking for a blend of both value and growth and
is directed by John Weatherall, the ex-chairman of TD Asset Management Inc.
While officially retired, Weatherall continues to provide advice to this fund. The
portfolio itself is well diversified, and with an emphasis on financial services and oil
and gas. For added diversification, the fund holds stocks from around the world,
with a bias toward the U.S. market as of mid-2001. Returns have been healthy.
Despite a 6% loss in the latest year, in the three years ending June 30/01 the fund
gained 9.2% per annum, well above the 4.8% average for the peer group. Its five-
year average annual return was a strong 14.5%. Recommended as a core Canadian
equity fund for a portfolio.

### Dividend Income Funds

### TD DIVIDEND GROWTH FUND                    $$$ → G NO RSP DIV

Managers: Doug Warwick, since 1993 and Paul Harris, since 1996

MER: 2.17%      Fundata: C      Style: Blend

Suitability: Growth-oriented investors

The word "growth" was added to this fund's name in 2000—it was previously the
Green Line Dividend Fund. The goal is to provide investors with superior after-
tax income and steady growth. It invests primarily in large-cap, high-yielding
common stocks and, to a lesser degree, in bonds, trust units, and preferred shares.

The portfolio holds a small core group of around 35 to 40 stocks, mainly in the traditional dividend-paying sectors of financial services, utilities, and pipelines. In terms of risk, this fund is a tad more aggressive than the average Canadian dividend fund because of its significant bias toward common stocks and lower holdings in bonds and preferred shares. In the 12 months to June 30/01, the fund gained an excellent 15% versus an 11.7% average return for its peer group. Longer-term numbers remain well above the average over two to ten years. Overall, this is an above-average fund for capital appreciation, but tax-advantaged cash flow is not its strong suit. The fund is therefore not recommended for those who need regular income.

## TD DIVIDEND INCOME FUND                    $$$ → FI/G NO RSP DIV

Manager: TD Asset Management Team, since 2000

MER: 2.00 %     Fundata: A     Style: Generally Value

Suitability: Conservative income investors

This fund was the Canada Trust Dividend Income-Inv Fund prior to the TD and Canada Trust merger. This fund is geared for investors seeking preferential after-tax monthly income and the opportunity for moderate capital gains. Since inception, the fund has generally been an above-average performer compared with its peer group. In the 12 months to June 30/01, the fund gained 15.8%, nicely above the average dividend fund. The fund's long-term returns were above average, as well. At mid-2001, the relatively diversified and value-oriented equities side of the portfolio accounted for 90% of assets, with two-thirds of the stocks in dividend-paying sectors like financial services, utilities, and pipelines. This gives the fund good tax-advantaged income, but also makes it more sensitive to rising interest rates. The bond side consists of government and corporate bonds and is very low risk. The safety rating is better than average for a fund of this type. The overall defensiveness of the fund makes it a good vehicle for long-term conservative investors. We are upgrading to a $$$ rating.

## U.S. Equity Funds

## TD AMERIGROWTH RSP FUND                    $$$ → G NO RSP USE

Manager: Kevin LeBlanc, since 2000

MER: 1.45%     Fundata: D     Style: Index

Suitability: Index investors

TD offers several international funds that are fully RRSP-eligible, and this is one of them. Most of the portfolio is invested in Government of Canada T-bills to meet the Canadian content requirement. The balance is in S&P 500 index futures. This fund was opened in 1993, so the S&P has been on the rise for most of its existence, explaining the excellent returns to date: average annual gain of 11.1% for the five years to June 30/01. But how did it contend with a bear market? It lost 14.2% in the year ending June 30/01, 1.6 points worse than the S&P 500 (just about equal to the MER). This fund should be purchased only with a long-term view and is a good choice for an RRSP where you'd like to add more U.S. content. This was previously the Canada Trust AmeriGrowth Fund.

## TD DOW JONES AVERAGE INDEX FUND          $$$ → G NO £ USE

Manager: Tim Thompson (TD Asset Management Team), since 2000

MER: 0.87%     Fundata: A     Style: Index

Suitability: Index investors

This fund is designed to match the performance of the Dow Jones Industrial Average. So far it's doing that and more, as the tracking error is on the positive side (which should even out in the future). If you are a passive investor looking to match the Dow, this is the fund for you. The fund managed a one-year gain of 4.3% over the year to June 30/01 (the "e" units did even better, at 4.9%). But remember, when the Dow drops—as it did in 2001—this fund will follow suit.

## TD U.S. INDEX FUND          $$$ → G NO £ USE

Managers: Tim Thompson, since 1996 and Enrique Cuyegkeng, since 1992

MER: 0.66%     Fundata: C     Style: Index

Suitability: Index investors

This is the original index fund launched by TD, which now has such funds covering all the major regions of the world. This fund tracks the S&P 500 Index—a broad measure of U.S. corporate performance. In the strong market we experienced in the 1990s, this passively managed fund was clearly ahead of most actively managed funds. But in weaker markets, index funds normally don't do as well. This fund's 15.4% loss for the year to June 30/01 exceeded that of the average U.S. stock fund. Longer-term results are above average, however. Over the past five years, this fund recorded an average return of 13.5%, about 1.7% annually above the average U.S. equity fund. If you want a U.S. index fund, consider this one. Just remember the risk in down markets. Formerly the Green Line U.S. Index Fund.

## TD U.S. MID-CAP GROWTH FUND          $$$ → G NO £ USSC

Manager: Brian W.H. Berghuis (T. Rowe Price), since 1993

MER: 2.45%     Fundata: C     Style: Growth

Suitability: Growth-oriented investors

As the name implies, the focus of this fund is on medium-sized U.S. companies. Behind the fund, you have a highly respected money manager in T. Rowe Price.

Since inception, Brian Berghuis has beaten the average U.S. mid-cap equity fund the majority of the time by using a bottom-up approach. The gain for the year to June 30/01 was only 1.8%. On the other hand, the average for the U.S. Small-to-Mid-Cap category was an 11.3% loss! Five-year numbers averaged 16.3% annually. Add this fund to a portfolio for more diversity in the mid-cap area.

## Global and International Equity Funds

### TD LATIN AMERICAN GROWTH FUND                $$$ ↑ G NO £ LAE

Managers: Michael Perl and Robert Meyer (Morgan Stanley), since 2001

MER: 2.81%      Fundata: A      Style: Primarily Growth

Suitability: Aggressive investors

This is a strong fund in a recovering region. In the three years to June 30/01, the fund's 4.2% per annum return exceeded the Latin America average by over five percentage points per annum. In the latest year to June 30/01, the fund recorded a 10.2% loss compared with a 13.7% loss for the average Latin American fund. The portfolio has a substantial allocation to Mexico, Brazil, and Argentina. The long-term performance is well above average and we consider this to be one of the better choices for investing in Latin America. We are keeping the fund's rating at $$$, but with the warning that Latin America funds are high risk by nature. Not recommended for registered plans.

## Sector Equity Funds

### TD HEALTH SCIENCES FUND                $$$ → G NO £ ST

Manager: Kris Jenner (T. Rowe Price), since inception (1996)

MER: 2.74%      Fundata: A      Style: Sector

Suitability: Aggressive investors

This fund has a strong record. Average annual compound rate of return for the three years to June 30/01 was 16.5%. The fund managed to break even in the 12 months ending June 30/01 when most funds were on the losing side. Volatility is among the lowest in the Science & Technology category, but this is still a sector fund, so expect greater ups and downs than you'd find in a more broadly diversified entry. It's a good choice if you want a health sciences component in your portfolio. Upgraded to a $$$ rating

## Canadian Balanced and Asset Allocation Funds

### TD BALANCED GROWTH FUND                $$$ → G/FI NO RSP CBAL

Manager: Mary Hallward (McLean Budden), since 1993

MER: 2.12%     Fundata: B       Style: Value/Growth

Suitability: Balanced investors

For those seeking more growth from their balanced funds, this one may suit your needs. Its equity side is well diversified with a value bias, including numerous blue-chip stocks and some mid-cap stocks for growth. The fund also takes advantage of the foreign content rule by holding the maximum limit in U.S. and foreign stocks, which adds further diversity. As of mid-2001, equities accounted for about 55% of its assets, with 34% in bonds. The bond side is conservatively managed, consisting mainly of federal and high-quality corporate bonds. Although the fund had a small loss in the year ending June 30/01, returns out to five years have been above average, coming in at 10.4% annually. A good choice, and one that would do very nicely in a younger person's RRSP. Formerly the Green Line Balanced Growth Fund.

### TD BALANCED INCOME FUND                $$$ → FI/G NO RSP CBAL

Manager: Margot Ritchie (Jarislowky Fraser), since 1988

MER: 2.12%     Fundata: A       Style: Blend

Suitability: Conservative income investors

This fund is the survivor of the merger between the Green Line Balanced Income Fund and the Canada Trust Retirement Balanced Fund. The mandate here is to generate income through a combination of high-quality fixed-income securities, money market instruments, and stocks. The fund had 56.8% in combined Canadian and foreign equities at mid-2001. In terms of portfolio risk, both the equities and fixed-income side are conservatively managed. The equity side is well diversified and maximizes its foreign content. Over time, this fund tends to trail the companion Balanced Growth Fund in terms of return, but it is more conservatively managed. Its five-year average annual gain to June 30/01 was 9.4% versus 10.4% for the Canadian Balanced category average.

## Canadian Bond Funds

### TD CANADIAN BOND FUND                $$$ → FI NO RSP CB

Manager: Satish Rai, since inception (1988)

MER: 1.00%     Fundata: C       Style: Credit and Term Structure Analysis

Suitability: Conservative investors

This fund is the product of the merger between the Green Line Canadian Bond Fund and the Canada Trust Bond Fund. This is a very steady bond fund and since 1994 it has beaten both the average of its peer group and the Scotia Capital Markets Universe Bond Index the majority of the time. To achieve this result, the fund manager has overweighted the portfolio toward high-quality corporate bonds, with the remainder in various government bonds. The fund is conservatively managed as far as interest rate risk goes. Gain for the year to June 30/01 was 6%, which was nicely above the 4.5% average for the bond fund category. This fund is a solid performer.

### TD CANADIAN GOVERNMENT BOND INDEX FUND   $$$ → FI NO RSP CB

Managers: Lori MacKay, since 1996 and Kevin LeBlanc, since 1993

MER: 0.86%     Fundata: D     Style: Index

Suitability: Conservative investors

This fund is structured to track the Canadian government bond portion of the Scotia Capital Markets Universe Bond Index and was the first such bond index fund marketed in Canada. Unlike the companion Canadian Bond Fund, this fund is predominately composed of federal bonds, followed by a mix of provincial and municipal bonds. As a result of this more conservative approach, results in the fund tend to have lower average returns than the Canadian Bond Fund. But having said that, this index fund has beaten the return of the average Canadian bond fund out to five years. Gain for the year to June 30/01 was 4.9% ("e" units came in at 5.1%); average annual compound rate of return for five years was 6.8%. This fund is the better choice for more conservative investors.

### TD MONTHLY INCOME FUND                          $$$ ↓ FI NO RSP STB

Manager: Doug Warwick (TD Asset Management Team), since 1998

MER: 1.27%     Fundata: N/A     Style: Credit Analysis

Suitability: Conservative income investors

This fund's objective is to earn consistent monthly income and it does so with a relatively low risk portfolio of short-term bonds and high-grade income trusts like Superior Propane. Its record is strong for its type. In the three years to June 30/01, it earned a return of 5.5% per annum. Over the most recent 12 months, it was way above average, at 8.9%. A good choice for an RRIF. This fund is off to a great start and well worth its debut rating of $$$.

### TD REAL RETURN BOND FUND                        $$$ ↓ FI NO RSP CB

Manager: Satish Rai, since 1994

MER: 1.64%     Fundata: D     Style: Duration Matching

Suitability: Indexed income investors

With inflation nowhere to be seen through most of the 1990s, it's not surprising that this inflation-hedged bond fund wasn't very popular. But recently, with inflation starting to pick up a bit, it has looked much more attractive. The fund's mandate is to generate yields based on the "real interest rate," which is the nominal rate plus inflation. Default risk is minimal due to the fund's 100% investment in Government of Canada guaranteed real return bonds (RRBs). Interest payments on these bonds are adjusted according to movements in the consumer price index. As well, the value of the bond at maturity is adjusted to protect investors from a loss of buying power due to inflation. These provisions make RRBs one of the best ways to invest in fixed-income securities when interest rates are on the rise. We're starting to see the impact here. The gain for the year to June 30/01 of 9.7% was among the best in the Canadian Bond category. Quarterly cash distributions improve the appeal of this fund in cases where income is important, such as in an RRIF. We are maintaining the rating at a well-deserved $$$ level to reflect the usefulness of this fund in the current environment.

## Canadian Money Market Funds

### TD CANADIAN MONEY MARKET FUND          $$$ ↓ C NO RSP CMM

Manager: Satish Rai, since inception (1988)

MER: 0.91%     Fundata: B

Suitability: Conservative income investors

This fund is the result of the merger between the Green Line Canadian Money Market Fund and the Canada Trust Money Market Fund. It has shown continued excellent performance since its launch in 1988, with consistently above-average returns. The portfolio invests primarily in commercial paper and short-term (less than one year) government notes.

### TD CANADIAN T-BILL FUND          $$$ ↓ C NO RSP CMM

Manager: Satish Rai, since inception (1991)

MER: 0.93%     Fundata: B

Suitability: Conservative income investors

An alternative money market fund from TD, this one invests exclusively in Government of Canada Treasury bills, giving a slightly higher level of safety. Returns tend to be lower than the Canadian Money Market Fund, but better than the average for the Money Market category.

## Foreign Money Market Funds

### TD U.S. MONEY MARKET FUND $$$ ↓ C NO RSP FMM

Manager: Satish Rai, since inception (1988)

MER: 1.19%     Fundata: D

Suitability: Conservative income investors

This fund invests in short-term securities denominated in U.S. dollars issued by Canadian governments and corporations, which makes it fully RRSP/RRIF-eligible. Over the past four years, straight returns have been higher than its Canadian counterpart. Factor in the strength of the U.S. dollar, and you're well ahead. This fund is recommended for investors who have a constant need for U.S. dollars and don't want the hassle of having to regularly convert from Canadian dollars. It is also a good choice for those who want to reduce Canadian currency risk in a registered plan.

## Also Recommended

## Canadian Equity Funds

### TD CANADIAN BLUE-CHIP EQUITY FUND $$ → G NO RSP CLC

Manager: Jarislowsky Fraser, since November 1999

MER: 2.45%     Fundata: C     Style: Primarily Value

Suitability: Conservative investors

As the name implies, this is your basic Canadian blue-chip, value-oriented fund, with a sprinkling of smaller technology companies thrown in for added growth, or risk, depending on your point of view. The fund is well diversified from the standpoint of industries and companies, with a good mix of foreign exposure from around the world. Historically, despite the large-cap bias of the late 1990s bull market, this fund has been inconsistent. However, it gained 8.6% for the year to June 30/01, which was way above the average Canadian large-cap equity fund. Longer-term numbers over two to ten years are now ahead of the peer group. The fund has had a good turnaround and we are upgrading to a $$ rating.

## Sector Equity Funds

### TD ENERGY FUND                               $$ ↑ G NO RSP NR

Manager: Margot Naudie, since 1999

MER: 2.28%        Fundata: D        Style: Sector

Suitability: Aggressive investors

Margot Naudie took this fund over in 1999 and has done a great job so far. Her focus on mid- and large-cap Canadian oil companies paid off with an 18.1% return for the year ending June 30/01. That was one of the better performances among pure energy funds over that time frame. This is a good choice if you want a no-load energy fund for your portfolio, but be aware that volatility is high. We are maintaining this fund at a $$ rating.

## Promising Newcomers

### TD U.S. SMALL-CAP EQUITY FUND            NR → G NO £ USSC

Manager: Gregory McCrickard (T. Rowe Price), since 1997

MER: 2.49%        Fundata: B        Style: Blend

Suitability: Aggressive investors

This fund specializes in small- to medium-sized companies, mainly the former. Many of the names in the portfolio are obscure, attesting to its small-cap focus. In the year ending June 30/01, the fund recorded a 7.6% return compared with the 11.3% loss for its peers. Definitely worth a look.

# UNIVERSITY AVENUE FUNDS

## THE COMPANY

There have been significant changes at this small, Toronto-based public company recently, and there are more on the way. In 2000, University Avenue purchased the @rgentum Funds of Montreal. The two groups were still operating independently as of late summer 2001, but plans were in the works to integrate them and to change the name of the parent company. So if you're considering investing, check out the situation before you act.

## THE DETAILS

| | |
|---|---|
| Number of funds: | 18 |
| Assets under management: | $41.6 million |
| Load charge: | University Avenue Funds: Front: max. 3%; Back: max. 5.75% @rgentum Funds: Front: max. 5%; Back: max. 5.75% |
| Switching charge: | 2% maximum |
| Where sold: | Across Canada |
| How sold: | Through brokers, dealers, and financial planners |
| Phone number: | 1-800-465-1812 |
| Web site address: | www.universityavenue.com |
| E-mail address: | info@universityavenue.com |
| Minimum initial investment: | $500 |

## INVESTING TIPS

The two fund groups have each taken a different approach to portfolio management. The University Avenue funds are run more or less in a traditional way. The @rgentum funds, however, combine traditional fundamental values with advanced technology to create high-performance investment portfolios through computer selection. The @rgentum funds have generally been the stronger performers, so you may wish to look there first if you are planning to invest with this group.

Again, we caution that there are company changes in the works that may result in mergers and/or managerial changes, so get the latest information before you invest.

# FUND SUMMARY

## University Avenue Funds

|                       |                                         |
|----------------------:|-----------------------------------------|
| Top Choices:          | Money                                   |
| Also Recommended:     | Balanced, U.S. Growth                   |
| Promising Newcomers:  | None                                    |
| The Rest:             | Canadian, Canadian Small-Cap, U.S. Small-Cap, World |

## @rgentum Funds

|                       |                                         |
|----------------------:|-----------------------------------------|
| Top Choices:          | None                                    |
| Also Recommended:     | Canadian Performance Portfolio, Short-Term Asset Portfolio |
| Promising Newcomers:  | Canadian L/S Equity Portfolio, Discovery Portfolio |
| The Rest:             | Canadian Equity Portfolio, Income Portfolio, International Master Portfolio, Market Neutral Portfolio, Quebec Balanced Portfolio, U.S. Market Neutral Portfolio, U.S. Master Portfolio |

# FUND RATINGS

## Top Choices/University Avenue Funds

### Canadian Money Market Funds

**UNIVERSITY AVENUE MONEY FUND**  $$$ → C  #/* RSP CMM

Manager: Robert Boaz, since February 1999

MER: 0.35%    Fundata: D

Suitability: Conservative investors

This fund offers a mix of T-bills and corporate notes that have a term of one year or less. It's been an above-average performer since inception (May 1996), a result aided by its very low MER. Average annual compound rate of return for the three years to June 30/01 was 4.8%.

# Also Recommended/University Avenue Funds

## U.S. Equity Funds

### UNIVERSITY AVENUE U.S. GROWTH FUND $$ → G #/* £ USE

Manager: Larry Jeddeloh (TIS Group), since May 2000

MER: 2.40%     Fundata: D     Style: Value/Growth

Suitability: Middle-of-the-road investors

Larry Jeddeloh, founder of the Minneapolis-based TIS Group, took over management responsibility for this fund in the spring of 2000, at just about the time when stock markets started to head down. He managed to hold the losses to a minimum here, however, recording a decline of just 6.5% over the year to June 30/01. The focus is on large-cap stocks, such as AT&T, Merck, and Abbott Laboratories. This fund historically has a high-risk rating, but that situation has improved recently. We want to see what this manager can do in a rising market (if he is still around after the impending changes) before adjusting the rating, however.

## Canadian Balanced and Asset Allocation Funds

### UNIVERSITY AVENUE BALANCED FUND $$ ↑ FI/G #/* RSP CBAL

Manager: Robert Boaz, since 1998

MER: 2.25%     Fundata: E     Style: Value/Growth

Suitability: Balanced investors

This fund displays more volatility than we like in a balanced fund, which is why it receives a higher risk rating. However, it's worth having in a portfolio when it's doing well. In calendar year 2000, for example, the fund recorded a very fine gain of 28.4%. However, it gave back 8.6% in the first half of 2001 despite a portfolio that was quite evenly balanced between stocks and bonds. We'll keep the rating at $$ for now while we await new developments at the company. Formerly the University Avenue Bond Fund.

## Promising Newcomers/University Avenue Funds

None.

## Top Choices/@rgentum Funds

None.

## Also Recommended/@rgentum Funds

### Canadian Equity Funds

### @RGENTUM CANADIAN PERFORMANCE PORTFOLIO  $$ → G #/* RSP CE

Manager: Chabot Page Investment Counsel Inc.

MER: 3.29%     Fundata: C      Style: Blend

Suitability: Middle-of-the-road investors

This fund uses the manager's proprietary computer screening techniques to iden-tify companies with above-average growth potential. At the beginning of 2001, oil and gas stocks represented the largest sector in the portfolio, at just over 30%. Top names included Methanex, Canadian Natural Resources, Chieftain International, and Talisman. The fund has a good three-year track record, with an average annual compound rate of return of 10.4% to June 30/01. Recent results have been weak, however, so hold off putting new money into this fund until there is a clear indication it's back on track.

### Canadian Money Market Funds

### @RGENTUM SHORT-TERM ASSET PORTFOLIO       $$ → C #/* RSP CMM

Manager: Chabot Page Investment Counsel Inc.

MER: 0.90%     Fundata: B

Suitability: Conservative investors

There's nothing particularly unusual about this fund, but it offers a low MER and has generated a decent return for its category, with an average annual gain of 4.6% over the three years to June 30/01.

## Promising Newcomers/@rgentum Funds

### Canadian Equity Funds

### @RGENTUM CANADIAN L/S EQUITY PORTFOLIO       NR ↓ G #/* RSP CE

Manager: Chabot Page Investment Counsel Inc.

MER: 2.95%     Fundata: N/A     Style: Hedge

Suitability: Conservative investors

This is a type of hedge fund, but without the high cost of admission normally associated with such funds. The managers attempt to minimize stock market risk by taking both long and short positions. The objective is to maintain a short portfolio of approximately 38% and a long portfolio of approximately 62% (so approximately 37.5% of the portfolio is exposed to the market). The fund invests mainly in large- and mid-sized companies, with a median market float of $250 million. This fund hasn't been around long enough for us to judge how it will perform over time. However, initial results are very encouraging: the fund gained 7.8% over the year to June 30/01. That was a very respectable performance and appears to validate the management thesis.

## Canadian Small-to-Mid-Cap Funds

### @RGENTUM DISCOVERY PORTFOLIO                    NR ↑ G #/* RSP CSC

Manager: Chabot Page Investment Counsel Inc.

MER: 2.85%     Fundata: A     Style: Blend

Suitability: Aggressive investors

This small-cap entry was launched in September 1998, so we don't have much of a track record to work with. But we like what we've seen so far. The fund gained a little over 12% in its first full year (1999), added 3% in 2000, and was ahead 8.2% in the first half of 2001. Those are good numbers under difficult market conditions, certainly are worthy of attention, though it should be noted that the fund did not match the pace of the Nesbitt Burns Small-Cap Index over that same time frame. Entering 2001, oil and gas stocks accounted for more than a third of the assets here, which contributed to the strong recent returns. This looks like a promising choice for small-cap investors.

# YMG FUNDS (MAVRIX FUNDS)

## THE COMPANY

In May 2001, it was announced that the YMG funds were being sold to a management group headed by Malvin Spooner, one of the key fund managers, for a price of approximately $4 million. The new fund group is to be known as Mavrix, and the names of the funds are being changed accordingly. Although this represents a change in the corporate structure, the funds themselves will be headed by the same people as before.

## THE DETAILS

|  |  |
|---|---|
| Number of funds: | 11 |
| Assets under management: | $61 million |
| Load charge: | Front: max. 5%; Back: max 5% (except Money Market at 2% and Emerging Companies at 4% for front and back) |
| Switching charge: | 2% maximum |
| Where sold: | Across Canada (except Emerging Companies; see "Investing Tips" for details) |
| How sold: | Through brokers, dealers, and financial planners |
| Phone number: | (416) 362-3077 |
| Web site address: | www.mavrixfunds.com |
| E-mail address: | sfernandes@mavrixfunds.com |
| Minimum initial investment: | $500 (except Emerging Companies, which has an initial minimum of $25,000 to $150,000) |

## INVESTING TIPS

These funds tend to be aggressively managed, which means investors in the equity portfolios can expect large swings, up or down, depending on market conditions. As a result, the family is recommended only for people who can accept this type of volatility.

Note that the Emerging Companies Fund is offered only on a private placement basis, and requires a minimum investment of $25,000 to $150,000 depending on your province of residence. It is available only in Ontario and the four western provinces. It is coming off a bad year (loss of 52.4% in the 12 months to April 30/01) and is not currently on our selection list.

# FUND SUMMARY

|  |  |
|---|---|
| Top Choices: | Income |
| Also Recommended: | Money Market |
| Promising Newcomers: | None |
| The Rest: | American Growth, Balanced, Bond, Canadian Value, Emerging Companies, Enterprise, Growth, Strategic Fixed Income, Sustainable Development |

# FUND RATINGS

## Top Choices

### Canadian High-Income Balanced Funds

**MAVRIX INCOME FUND**                    **$$$ ↑ G/FI #/* RSP CHIB**

Manager: William Shaw, since 1998

MER: 2.14%      Fundata: C       Style: Bottom-up Blend

Suitability: Aggressive investors seeking tax-advantaged income

This used to be a conventional, middle-of-the-road bond fund. No more! A couple of years ago, YMG reshaped it into a high-income balanced fund that can invest in a wide range of securities, including bonds, preferreds, high-yield common stocks, bond futures contracts, real estate income trusts (REITs), and royalty income trusts (RITs). Manager William Shaw may also use a covered call option writing strategy to further enhance returns. These elements add up to a very unusual portfolio mix that has produced good tax-advantaged cash flow, but also incorporates more risk than is usually associated with a fund of this type. (Note that the company officially classifies Income as a dividend fund even though it is a far cry from the usual conservative portfolios typically found in that category.) In the first half of 2001, RITs accounted for more than half the asset base, with the majority of those in REITs and energy trusts. The fund paid out 72¢ a unit in distributions in 2000, the same as the year before, so cash flow is good and consistent. Total return is another matter, however, with results bouncing all over the place. For example, the fund gained just over 1% in 1999. However, it enjoyed a terrific year in 2000, adding more than 30% as energy trusts came back, and was up 7% in the first six months of 2001. This pattern is typical of what you might expect from a high-income balanced fund, but it may be too volatile for more traditional income investors. This fund is worth a look if you want above-average tax-advantaged income and are prepared to accept above-average risk to achieve that goal. Formerly the HRL Bond Fund and before that as the Waltaine Bond Fund.

## Also Recommended

### Canadian Money Market Funds

**MAVRIX MONEY MARKET FUND**                    $$$ → C # RSP CMM

Manager: Jane-Marie Rocca, since 1996

MER: 0.80%        Fundata: C

Suitability: Short-term investors

This money fund invests in a mixed portfolio of T-bills, bankers' acceptances, and commercial notes. Results since the 1996 management change continue to be above average. Available only on a front-end load basis, with a maximum commission of 2%. Formerly known as the HRL Instant $$ Fund and before that as the Waltaine Instant $$ Fund.

### Promising Newcomers

None.

# The Top 10 Segregated Fund Families

*The entire field of segregated funds has been going through a major upheaval as a result of changes made by regulators to the reserve requirements for these insurance company products. In effect, companies are now required to put aside more money for contingency purposes in the event that they have to make good on the guarantee of principal, which is one of the most popular features of these funds.*

The result has been something approaching controlled chaos. Several seg funds have closed their doors to new business because it was no longer economical to operate under the new rules. Other funds have raised their management fees. In most cases, however, the reaction of insurance companies has been to withdraw their existing line of seg funds from sale, replacing it with a new series that carries lower (and therefore less costly) guarantees.

Predictably, this has taken a lot of the sheen off of what had been a booming market. During the late 1990s, we witnessed a virtual explosion of new seg funds in this country. We believe that in the coming years, we will see the market contract as investors and insurance companies adjust to the new reality. Don't be surprised if there are many mergers and closings in the future.

All this turmoil suggests investors should be very careful about putting their money into these funds. Make sure you understand exactly the terms stipulated. This isn't always easy, as we note with dismay that the information folders supplied by companies offering segregated funds are often very dense and difficult to understand. The mutual fund industry has made great strides in recent years to improve the quality of its prospectuses and better assist investors to understand the nature of each fund under consideration. The insurance industry would be wise to emulate this trend. If it doesn't do so voluntarily, regulators should force it to comply. As things stand now, we don't feel investors are receiving the required information in a way that can be easily comprehended and used for comparison with alternatives.

One other important point to note: In the past, U.S. and international segregated funds did not come under the foreign content rules because of a legal loophole. This is scheduled to change as of January 1, 2002, barring a last-minute reprieve by the Finance Department. So you must apply the 30 percent rule to your registered segregated fund portfolios, just as you do with regular mutual funds.

In this year's edition of the *Guide*, we've focused our coverage of segregated funds on the main players in this segment of the industry. The pages that follow contain information on the companies we regard as the top 10 seg fund leaders, with reviews and ratings of their best offerings.

# CANADA LIFE ASSURANCE CO.

## THE COMPANY

Canada Life is one of the country's oldest life insurance companies, with a history dating back to 1847. It has made aggressive inroads in the expansion of its family of segregated funds. In late 1998, the company launched 47 new segregated funds under the Generations and Generations Continuum brand names. The Generations Funds are a new family within Canada Life, while the Generation Continuum Funds are based on a strategic asset allocation programme that offers investors nine different investment modules ranging from conservative to growth-oriented, and are designed for both registered and non-registered plans. The company's original line of nine segregated funds is known as the Flex Funds.

With the new entries, Canada Life has increased its product line substantially, giving investors more choices and perhaps better-performing funds than they had had up to this point. Prior to the new additions, for example, there was only one Canadian equity fund. Now there are nine choices, each with a different outside manager. We think the choice element might be a bit overdone.

The management of the Flex Funds underwent some significant changes in 1999. After the merger of INDAGO Capital Management (the original managers) and Laketon Investment Management, the new firm assumed full control of the Flex Funds under the Laketon banner.

As for the new Generations line, the majority of the funds use external managers, including AGF, AIC, Bissett, C.I., Fidelity, Scudder, Templeton, Trimark, and TDQC (Toronto Dominion Quantitative Capital).

## THE DETAILS

| | |
|---|---|
| Number of funds: | 69 |
| Assets under management: | $4.36 billion |
| Load charge: | Back: max. 4.5% |
| Switching charge: | 8 free switches per year |
| Where sold: | Across Canada |
| How sold: | Through licensed insurance representatives |
| Phone number: | 1-888-CLA-1847 or (416) 597-6981 |
| Web site address: | www.canadalife.com/canadian/en/invest/individ/index.html |
| E-mail address: | canindserv@canadalife.com |
| Minimum initial investment: | $1,000 |

# INVESTING TIPS

Segregated funds can be quite complicated and the purchase terms for many of them have changed recently. In this case, redemption fees on all funds are payable if you cash in within seven years of purchase. You'll get a return of at least 75% of your contributions at maturity if you hold your units for 10 years. If you die, your estate will receive no less than the full value of your contributions. Any gains since purchase will be reflected in the payout. Check with a Canada Life representative for complete details.

# FUND SUMMARY

## Flex Funds

|                         |                                                                                                |
|------------------------:|------------------------------------------------------------------------------------------------|
|            Top Choices: | Enhanced Dividend                                                                              |
|       Also Recommended: | None                                                                                          |
|    Promising Newcomers: | None                                                                                          |
|               The Rest: | Asia Pacific, Canadian Equity, European Equity, Fixed Income International Bond, Managed, Money Market |

## Generations Funds

|                         |                                                                                                |
|------------------------:|------------------------------------------------------------------------------------------------|
|            Top Choices: | None                                                                                          |
|       Also Recommended: | None                                                                                          |
|    Promising Newcomers: | Balanced (Trimark), Canadian Equity (Templeton), Canadian Equity (Trimark), Enhanced Dividend (Laketon), Global Equity (Trimark), Harbour Canadian (C.I.) |
|               The Rest: | Balanced (Bisset), Balanced (Ethical), Canadian Bond (AGF), Canadian Asset Allocation (Fidelity), Canadian Equity (AGF), Canadian Equity (AIC), Canadian Equity (Bissett), Canadian Equity (Laketon), Canadian Equity (Scudder), Canadian Short-Term Bond (Scudder), Dividend (AGF), European Equity (Laketon), Fixed-Income (Bissett), Fixed-Income (Laketon), Global Boomernomics (C.I.), Global Equity (Laketon), Global Equity (Scudder), Global Equity RSP (C.I.), Global Equity RSP (Trimark), Greater Euro (Scudder), Growth (Ethical), Growth America (Fidelity), Harbour Growth & Income (C.I.), Income (Ethical), Index Canadian Equity (TD), Index U.S. Equity (TD), Indexed Balanced (TD), |

Indexed Canadian Bond (TD), Indexed International Equity (TD), International (Fidelity), International Bond (Laketon), International Equity (Templeton), International Portfolio RSP (Fidelity), Managed (Laketon), Money Market (Laketon), North American Equity (Ethical), Small-Cap Equity (Bissett), True North (Fidelity), U.S. Equity (Scudder), U.S. Value (AIC), U.S. Value RSP (AIC), World Equity (AIC), World Equity RSP (AIC)

## Continuum Modules

| | |
|---|---|
| Top Choices: | None |
| Also Recommended: | None |
| Promising Newcomers: | None |
| The Rest: | Conservative, Growth, Maximum Growth, Moderate, NR Aggressive Growth, NR Conservative, NR Growth, NR Maximum Growth, NR Moderate |

## FUND RATINGS

## Top Choices/Flex Funds

### Dividend Income Funds

### CANADA LIFE ENHANCED DIVIDEND FUND (S-39)  $$$ → G * RSP S DIV

Manager: Philip Wootten (Laketon), since 1997

MER: 2.00%    Fundata: A    Style: Bottom-up Value

Suitability: Income-oriented equity investors

This fund is off to a strong start. Fund manager Philip Wootten focuses on high-yield common and preferred shares as well as income trusts in managing this portfolio. In the three years to June 30/01, the fund returned an above-average 6.4% thanks largely to its 26.4% performance in the latest year. These numbers were sufficiently impressive to warrant a Fundata A rating. In fact, this fund placed first in the Fundata rankings for dividend funds in mid-2001 and also received a top rating from *Globefund*. We won't give it a $$$$ rating as yet, since we look for consistent superior results over a longer period. But we are prepared to give the fund a debut $$$ rating, and recommend that you add it to your portfolio if you are a Canada Life client.

## Also Recommended/Flex Funds

None.

## Promising Newcomers/Flex Funds

None.

## Top Choices/Generations Funds

None.

## Also Recommended/Generations Funds

None.

## Promising Newcomers/Generations Funds

### Canadian Equity Funds

#### GENERATIONS CANADIAN EQUITY FUND (TEMPLETON)

NR → G * RSP S CE

Manager: George Morgan (Franklin Templeton)

MER: 3.15%    Fundata: A    Style: Value

Suitability: Conservative investors

We think Canada Life is guilty of overkill with all the Canadian equity options they are offering in their Generations line (seven in total!). That said, we like the look of this one, at least in the current investment climate. The Templeton value style does particularly well when markets are going through a rough phase and we saw that kind of result here with a one-year gain to June 30/01 of just under 11%. The portfolio focuses on blue-chip issues, with names like TransCanada PipeLines, Bank of Montreal, and Shaw Industries topping the list. Value funds won't be top performers in booming markets, but if a conservative approach suits your needs, look at this one.

#### GENERATIONS CANADIAN EQUITY FUND (TRIMARK)

NR → G * RSP S CE

Managers: Ian Hardacre and Carmen Veloso (AIM)

MER: 2.90%    Fundata: A    Style: Value

Suitability: Conservative investors

The comments relating to the companion fund managed by Templeton pretty much apply here as well. The managers here form the same team that runs the

Trimark Canadian Fund, which has been performing well recently. So the portfolios of the two funds will be very similar. One-year gain to June 30/01 was a shade under 10%.

### GENERATIONS HARBOUR CANADIAN FUND (C.I.)    NR → G * RSP S CE

Manager: Gerald Coleman (C.I.)

MER: 2.90%    Fundata: A    Style: Value

Suitability: Conservative investors

As you would guess from the name of the fund and the manager, this is Canada Life's version of C.I.'s Harbour Fund. Returns will track the original fund very closely.

## Dividend Income Funds

### GENERATIONS ENHANCED DIVIDEND     NR → G/FI * RSP S DIV
### FUND (LAKETON)

Manager: Philip Wootten (Laketon)

MER: 2.05%    Fundata: A    Style: Blend

Suitability: Conservative investors

This is the Generations version of Canada Life's original Enhanced Dividend Fund. The manager and results are the same.

## Global and International Equity Funds

### GENERATIONS GLOBAL EQUITY FUND (TRIMARK)    NR → G * £ S GE

Managers: Angela Eaton, Darren McKiernan, and Judith Adams (AIM)

MER: 3.15%    Fundata: A    Style: Value

Suitability: Conservative investors

At the present time, it's the value-oriented Generation Funds that are producing the best results. This is another one of them that's run by the Trimark people (part of AIM Funds). It invests around the world and we expect its returns to be similar to those of the Trimark Fund. One-year gain to June 30/01 was 9.5%.

## Canadian Balanced and Asset Allocation Funds

### GENERATIONS BALANCED FUND (TRIMARK)    NR → FI/G * RSP S CBAL

Manager: Patrick Farmer (AIM)

MER: 3.00%    Fundata: A    Style: Value

Suitability: Conservative investors

Trimark's value-oriented style has been working very well recently and this fund is one of the beneficiaries. One-year gain to June 30/01 was a very strong

16.5%, which made this fund of the top 10 performers in the Canadian Balanced category over that time. In mid-2001 the portfolio was split about 60–40 in favour of stocks over bonds. There is significant foreign content here, which provides geographic diversification. This is a promising choice in the new Canada Life series.

## Top Choices/Continuum Modules

None.

## Also Recommended/Continuum Modules

None.

## Also Recommended/Continuum Modules

None.

# EMPIRE FINANCIAL GROUP

## THE COMPANY

This group is the marketing arm of the Kingston, Ontario-based Empire Life Insurance Company, which was established in 1923 and is one of the top 15 life insurance companies in this country. It is one of the most strongly capitalized firms in the insurance business today, so you don't need to worry about the safety of your investments. It owns Concordia Life Insurance and manages their five funds.

As with all segregated funds, the Empire entries offer death and maturity guarantees. Check with an Empire Life representative for details.

## THE DETAILS

|  |  |
|---|---|
| Number of funds: | 11 |
| Assets under management: | $1.59 billion |
| Load charge: | Premier Equity: Front: max. 5%; All others: Back: max. 5% |
| Switching charge: | 4 free transfers per year and $50 thereafter |
| Where sold: | Across Canada |
| How sold: | Through Empire Life agents and licensed brokers |
| Phone number: | (613) 548-1881 |
| Web site address: | www.empire.ca |
| E-mail address: | buildingempires@empire.ca |
| Minimum initial investment: | $500 |

## INVESTING TIPS

The Empire income-oriented and indexed funds have not performed well as a group, in part because of relatively high management expense ratios (MERs). For example, consider the high 2.39% MER associated with its U.S. Equity Index Fund (formerly the S&P 500 Index Fund). That number is well above the average for most index funds, and reflects the costs related to the guarantee. If your investment time horizon is longer term and you like index funds, we recommend going with a cheaper comparative fund (unless you like the guarantee and are willing to pay that kind of a price for it). On the other hand, its equity funds have done quite well. A number of them received an A rating from Fundata at mid-2001, which is not all that easy to achieve.

## FUND SUMMARY

|  |  |
|---|---|
| Top Choices: | Dividend Growth, Elite Equity, Premier Equity |
| Also Recommended: | Asset Allocation, Small-Cap Equity |

Promising Newcomers: None
The Rest: Balanced, Bond, Foreign Currency Bond, International, Money Market, U.S. Equity Index

# FUND RATINGS

## Top Choices

### Canadian Equity Funds

### EMPIRE ELITE EQUITY FUND                    $$$ ↓ G * RSP S CE

Manager: Vince Zambrano, since 1998

MER: 2.41%     Fundata: A     Style: Bottom-up Value

Suitability: Conservative investors

This fund has gone through a series of managers since the departure of Catharina Van Berkel in 1996. Vince Zambrano replaced Jill Pepall and has been at the helm since October 1998, which has added some stability to the fund. In the 12 months to June 30/01, the fund lost 1.8% compared with the 6.5% loss for the peer group. Longer-term results are strong: five-year returns of 12.6% were about 260 basis points above average. A major stumbling block is the fund's 2.41% MER, which is much higher than the Premier Fund's MER of 1.45%. As of mid-2001, this well-diversified fund had 90.6% of its assets in equities, including a wide mix of foreign issues. Smaller stocks are added for more growth potential, but the overall portfolio has a large-cap value bias. The very good safety record is a plus. Note: There is a difference in the purchase option and management fee between this and the Premier Fund; the Elite fund is back-end load, while the Premier has a front-end load but a much lower MER. So to benefit from the better performance with the Premier Fund, you'll have to hold it for several years. For long-term investors, it may be the better choice. Worthy of an upgrade to $$$.

### EMPIRE PREMIER EQUITY FUND                    $$$ ↓ G # RSP S CE

Manager: Vince Zambrano, since 1998

MER: 1.45%     Fundata: A     Style: Bottom-up Value

Suitability: Conservative investors

This fund is similar in every aspect to the companion Elite Equity Fund, but returns are slightly better here. The reason for the better performance is this fund's low MER, which more than offsets its front-end fee over time. If you hold for the long term, you should enjoy superior returns. As with the Elite Fund, Vince Zambrano replaced Jill Pepall as manager in late 1998. With the lower MER, returns are above average for this fund, with a three-year annual return of 10.9% to June 30/01. If you're purchasing an Empire Canadian equity fund, buy this one for the long haul and save on the MER.

## Dividend Income Funds

### EMPIRE DIVIDEND GROWTH FUND $$$ ↓ G * RSP S DIV

Manager: Vince Zambrano, since 1998

MER: 2.39%    Fundata: A    Style: Bottom-up Value

Suitability: Income-oriented equity investors

There are a number of strong equity entries in the Empire stable. This fund concentrates on high-dividend, large-cap Canadian common and preferred shares. In the 12 months to June 2001, the fund recorded an 18.9% return, some 8 percentage points above the average in this strong category. Over its first three years, the fund's 9.7% per annum return beat the peer group average by 2.5 points per year. If you are looking for a decent dividend fund, this is a good place to start. Debuts with a $$$ rating.

## Also Recommended

## Canadian Equity Funds

### EMPIRE SMALL-CAP EQUITY FUND $$ ↓ G # RSP S CSC

Manager: Vince Zambrano, since 1998

MER: 2.48%    Fundata: B    Style: Bottom-up Value

Suitability: Middle-of-the-road investors

This small-cap fund is run by the same team that manages the other Canadian equity funds. After a weak start, the small-cap orientation has created some fine results for this fund. Average annual return for the three years to mid-2001 was 7.1%; for the latest year it was a well-above-average 11.5%. Volatility is below average, an important consideration in a small-cap fund. The fund debuts with a $$ rating, but if the performance stays strong it will be in line for an upgrade.

## Canadian Balanced and Asset Allocation Funds

### EMPIRE ASSET ALLOCATION FUND $$ → G/FI * RSP S CTAA

Manager: Vince Zambrano, since 1998

MER: 2.41%    Fundata: A    Style: Top-down/Interest Rate Anticipation

Suitability: Balanced investors with an equity orientation

The difference between this and the companion Empire Balanced Fund (not on our Recommended List this year) is that this one is more aggressive in its approach. The portfolio could be entirely in one asset class (stocks, bonds, or cash) at any given time, depending on the circumstances. As of mid-2001, this actively managed fund had a fairly aggressive stance with 14.8% of its assets in bonds (low by historical standards), 72.2% in stocks, and the remainder in cash. Its equities are large-cap and diversified both by industry and geographic region. The bond portion is conservatively managed, consisting mainly of federal issues, followed by corporate bonds. Results have been average. It lost 3.3% for the year ending June 30/01, about 1.8 points less than the average for the peer group. Longer term, however, the five-year numbers are about 30 basis points below the average for the peer group. Worthy of a $$ rating.

## Promising Newcomers

None.

# GREAT-WEST LIFE ASSURANCE

## THE COMPANY

Established in 1891, Winnipeg-based Great-West Life is a behemoth among Canadian insurance companies. It is 99.5% owned by its parent, Great-West Lifeco, which in turn is 82.1% owned by Power Financial. The group also owns a 100% stake in London Life Insurance Company, whose funds remain independent. Segregated funds marketed under the "GWL" brand are quite extensive, making its product offering the largest of any insurance company.

Outside managers are used extensively for its funds, including AGF, Beutel Goodman, Mackenzie, Putnam, Sceptre, and Scudder Kemper. As a result, there is a large and somewhat intimidating universe of possible funds presented to investors. The problem is figuring out which funds to buy, since there are numerous choices within each category. Each type of fund, whether equity, fixed-income, or balanced, is offered through different fund managers, each with their own management style. With such overwhelming choice in mind, Great-West has tried to remove some of the confusion for investors through the creation of Windows-based asset allocation software called Discovery, designed to help people determine which funds are most appropriate, given their needs. If you're interested in this company's funds, you should ask a representative to lead you through it.

For reference, if you want to know which outside manager is running a given fund, check the initial in brackets after the name. "G" indicates the fund is managed in-house.

$$A = AGF$$
$$B = Beutel\ Goodman$$
$$M = Mackenzie\ Financial$$
$$P = Putnam$$
$$S = Sceptre$$
$$SC = Scudder\ Kemper$$

It should be noted that MAXXUM also provided management services for Great-West and some funds in the group are accordingly designated MX. As of October 2001, however, the responsibility for all MAXXUM funds was taken over by Mackenzie Financial managers.

Great-West Life does not provide the names of the lead managers for individual funds. In the past, they have indicated to us that this exclusion happens for several reasons:

1. GWL believes the underlying funds are all managed through a team approach, with people specializing in different areas. Consequently, GWL

has said the lead manager's job is really one of co-ordinating the fund rather than making all decisions. GWL thinks that investors are misguided if they believe a single manager of a team makes investment decisions. And on that point we can find some common ground.

2. GWL points out that the outside managers also thought it was inappropriate to list an individual as lead manager, fearing it would misinform clients.

We beg to differ on this point. We believe that the lead manager is ultimately responsible for the performance of the fund, much like the coach of a hockey team is seen as the one responsible for the team's performance. As a result, the manager should be listed, if for no other reason than to provide investors with some background on the investment philosophy that is guiding the decisions of the team. And in the real world, when a fund performs poorly, it's the manager who is replaced—not the team. Unfortunately, this issue will remain a sticking point for some companies.

We noted in our research that GWL did not provide manager's names to *Globefund* either. However, surprise! We found some of the names on *The Fund Library* Web site. We have included those names here, since GWL obviously felt that they should appear somewhere. We don't think it should be necessary to make people search so hard to find this valuable information.

The RS designation on funds in the GWL group indicates that they are available only under registered policies.

## THE DETAILS

| | |
|---|---|
| Number of funds: | 42 |
| Assets under management: | $3.94 billion |
| Load charge: | Back: max. 4.5% |
| Switching charge: | None |
| Where sold: | Across Canada |
| How sold: | Through insurance representatives |
| Phone number: | 1-800-665-5758 |
| Web site address: | www.gwl.ca |
| E-mail address: | Through Web site |
| Minimum initial investment: | $500 |

## INVESTING TIPS

Since guarantees are very important to seg fund investors, you need to fully understand the Great-West Life policies. Investors under age 70 can choose between two options:

1. A base guarantee of 75% of your investments, payable on either death or maturity (10 years).

2. A base guarantee with what the company calls "an enhanced guarantee rider." This rider increases your protection to 100% of your total investments at death or maturity. However, the death guarantee increases only in increments of five percentage points annually, so it will be five years before you reach the 100% mark. The cost of the enhanced guarantee is a higher annual management expense ratio (MER), which will reduce your return by a corresponding amount. This additional fee can range from as low as 0.1% annually for the most conservative funds/portfolios to as high as 0.8% for the most risky offerings, such as the Asian Growth (A) Fund.

There are two purchase options for all GWL funds. For A units, you can choose to pay a no-load charge up-front and be assessed a higher annual management fee. The back-end (DSC) funds have a maximum 4.5% load that declines to zero after seven years and are known as B units. With these funds, you pay a slightly lower management charge. The difference between the two is small—about a quarter of a percent a year. But if you're going to invest in a segregated fund it should be for the long haul, so you may as well realize some savings and choose the back-end load. In our reviews, the performance numbers quoted are for the DSC versions, as are the MERs.

GWL offers eight portfolio funds. Five are designed to match the risk tolerance level of the client (e.g., conservative, aggressive). The other three focus on specific asset classes (e.g., Canadian equity, global equity, fixed-income). We have adopted a policy of not reviewing portfolios of this type, which are really funds of funds. However, we note that the Great-West Life Balanced Fund (M), managed by Mackenzie Financial, has outperformed all the portfolios over the past three years, in some cases by a very wide margin.

## FUND SUMMARY

|  |  |
|---|---|
| Top Choices: | Balanced Fund (M), Dividend/Growth (M), Equity (M), Growth & Income (M), Income (G), Income (M), International Equity (P), Larger Company (M), North American Equity (B), Real Estate (G) |
| Also Recommended: | Balanced (B), Global Income (A), Government Bond (G), Smaller Company (M) |
| Promising Newcomers: | None |
| The Rest: | Advanced Portfolio (G), Aggressive Portfolio (G), American Growth (A), Asian Growth (A), Balanced Fund (S), Balanced Portfolio (G), Bond (B), Bond (S), Canadian Bond (G), Canadian Equity (G), Canadian Opportunity (M), Canadian Resources (A), Conservative Portfolio (G), Diversified Fund (G), Dividend (G), Equity (S), Equity Bond (G), Equity Index (G), |

European Equity (S), Growth & Income (A),
Growth Equity (A), International Bond (P),
International Opportunity (P), Mid-Cap Canada
(G), Moderate Portfolio (G), Money Market (G),
Mortgage (G), U.S. Equity (G)

# FUND RATINGS

## Top Choices

### Canadian Equity Funds

### GREAT-WEST LIFE DIVIDEND/ GROWTH FUND (M)      $$$ → G/FI */NO RSP S CLC

Manager: Mackenzie Financial Industrial Team

MER: 2.48%    Fundata: A    Style: Bottom-up Value

Suitability: Conservative investors

The emphasis here leans to the growth side rather than to income, which is why this fund is officially classified as a Canadian Large-Cap. As long as that classification isn't a problem for you, this fund is worthy of inclusion in any Great-West portfolio. Mackenzie's Industrial team is in charge, which means the fine hand of Bill Procter is operating unseen in the background. He has done very well with his Mackenzie funds, and this one certainly has benefited from his involvement. The one-year gain of 19.3% to June 30/01 made this the top performer in its category over that time. The three-year average annual return of 5.9% is less impressive, but better than average. As long as you aren't misled by the name into thinking this is a real dividend fund, it's a good choice. Debuts at $$$.

### GREAT-WEST LIFE EQUITY FUND (M)      $$$ ↓ G */NO RSP S CE

Manager: Mackenzie Financial Ivy Team

MER: 2.55%    Fundata: A    Style: Bottom-up Value

Suitability: Conservative investors

This fund's conservative approach resulted in an off year (relatively speaking) in 1999–2000. But the value style showed its merit when markets tanked in 2000–01. While the majority of Canadian stock funds were posting losses, this one came through with a decent 4.9% gain. Its five-year average annual rate of return at 10.3% is comfortably above the category average. The fund is run by Mackenzie's Ivy group and that shows in the portfolio composition (mainly blue chip), the large cash position (about 16% in mid-2001), and the fund's performance history. The historic risk level of this fund is very low, which adds to its appeal in turbulent markets. Rating is raised to $$$.

## GREAT-WEST LIFE LARGER COMPANY FUND (M)

$$ → G */NO RSP S CLC

Manager: Mackenzie Financial Industrial Team

MER: 2.65%     Fundata: A     Style: Bottom-up Value

Suitability: Conservative investors

This fund's long-term record is undistinguished, but it is coming off a very strong year with a 12-month gain of 15.3% (to June 30/01). That is an especially remarkable performance when you consider that the average Canadian equity fund lost ground during that time. The approach is similar to the companion Equity Fund (M), with a lot of blue-chip stocks in the portfolio. In this case, however, management is by the company's Industrial team, which has shown significant improvement in the past few years. The cash position in mid-2001 was quite small. Risk in both funds is better than average, but Equity (M) has the edge in that regard. This fund is looking better these days and we are raising the rating to $$. Another good year and we will add another $.

## GREAT-WEST LIFE NORTH AMERICAN EQUITY FUND (B)

$$ → G */NO RSP S CE

Managers: Tor Williams and Jim Lampare (Beutel Goodman)

MER: 2.49%     Fundata: B     Style: Bottom-up Value

Suitability: Conservative investors

This fund's mandate is to seek long-term capital appreciation through investing mainly in medium to large Canadian and U.S. companies that may be undervalued and/or show superior growth potential. It may also hold up to 25% of its assets in small-cap issues for additional growth potential and diversity. Although this is called a "North American" fund, its foreign content is restricted to the prevailing limit to retain full RRSP eligibility. As a result, we classify this as a Canadian equity fund. Like many value funds, this one struggled through the late 1990s and into 2000. But also like many value funds, it recovered in the latest 12 months to gain 12.7% for the year to June 30/01. Five-year numbers are slightly below average for the category, although another good year should change that. We are moving the rating up a notch to $$ on the strength of the most recent numbers.

## Global and International Equity Funds

### GREAT-WEST LIFE                                    $$$ → G */NO RSP S IE
### INTERNATIONAL EQUITY FUND (P)

Manager: Putnam Advisory Company

MER: 2.63%     Fundata: B     Style: Top-down Momentum

Suitability: Middle-of-the-road investors

Putnam Advisory is based in Boston and is one of the oldest and largest money management firms in the U.S. This fund doesn't invest in North America, settling instead for places such as the Pacific Rim, Europe, and South and Central America. This fund normally holds between 90 and 120 positions and is invested in at least 10 different countries at any given time. For added diversification, it will never hold more than 15% in one industry. Consequently, it is a very diversified fund. And despite the absence of U.S. stocks, the fund did very well until the latest year when it fell 21.7% (to June 30/01). As of mid-2001 the dominant regions were the U.K., Japan, and France. Top holdings emphasize energy and financial services, including such names as Total Fina and ING. Despite the recent slump, this fund remains an excellent performer over the long haul, with a five-year average annual compound rate of return of 11.1%. We expect Putnam will have it back on the rails before too long.

## Sector Equity Funds

### GREAT-WEST LIFE REAL ESTATE FUND (G)     $$$ ↓ G */NO RSP S RE

Manager: Paul Finkbeiner, GWL Investment Management

MER: 2.70%     Fundata: A     Style: Bottom-up Value

Suitability: Income investors

Over the past five years, this has been one of the best-performing real estate funds in Canada, with an average annual gain of 8.1% (to June 30/01). The fund invests in commercial and industrial real estate in Canada, including prime quality office, retail, industrial, and multi-family residential properties. These holdings make it more like a real estate investment trust (REIT) than most of the other open-end real estate funds, which tend to invest in stocks rather than bricks and mortar. This fund would be especially useful in a non-registered portfolio because it pays steady distributions that benefit from the tax advantages accorded to rental income. The risk level is very low, as long as the real estate industry doesn't go into a crisis like the one it experienced in the early 1990s. If there is any hint of that kind of situation, exit quickly.

## Canadian Balanced and Asset Allocation Funds

### GREAT-WEST LIFE BALANCED FUND (M)     $$ ↑ G/FI */NO RSP S CBAL

Manager: Mackenzie Financial Industrial Team

MER: 2.61%     Fundata: C

Suitability: Growth-oriented balanced investors

The risk level here is on the high side for balanced funds as a group, but the latest results have been very strong. At a time when stock markets were foundering, this fund turned in a handsome gain of 10.5% for the year to June 30/01. That result was enough to pull what had been some rather mediocre longer-term results to well above average. The fund aims for between 25% and 75% of assets in each of bonds and stocks, which means the fund is at the aggressive end of its mandate. At least 75% of the securities in the bond portfolio must have a credit rating of A or better, so default risk is low. In mid-2001, oil and gas was management's favourite sector, with 17.6% of total assets. Rating moves up to $$$.

### GREAT-WEST LIFE GROWTH & INCOME FUND (M)     $$$ ↓ FI/G */NO RSP S CBAL

Manager: Mackenzie Financial Ivy Team

MER: 2.37%     Fundata: A     Style: Value/Growth

Suitability: Conservative investors

This fund is operated along the same lines as the Mackenzie Ivy Growth & Income Fund, which has the same management team. However, the mandate here is more aggressive, as it doesn't limit the amount that can be held in stocks or bonds. So you could have 100% of the fund in a specific category, which makes it similar to a tactical asset allocation fund. As of mid-2001, equities accounted for only 61% of assets, including some U.S. exposure. Bonds were about 37% of the mix. Despite the ability to make large bets, historically this is one of the lower risk alternatives within GWL's stable of balanced funds. Of course, lower risk usually comes with a price. In this case, the price was lower-than-average returns through the late 1990s. However, that trend has now changed and the fund notched a solid gain of 5.5% in the year ending June 30/01, pulling up the five-year numbers to above average at 10.2%. Overall, this is a conservative balanced choice for growth and income. We are increasing our rating to $$$.

## GREAT-WEST LIFE INCOME FUND (G)   $$$ ↓ FI/G */NO RSP S CBAL

Managers: Terry Parsonage and Patricia Nesbitt (GWL Investment Management)

MER: 1.94%   Fundata: A   Style: Blend, with a Fixed-Income Bias

Suitability: Conservative investors

Of Great-West's balanced funds, this one is the most conservatively managed in terms of both its equity and bond sides. The fund is geared for those seeking more interest and dividend income with minimal risk. In fact, this fund is more like a bond fund than a balanced fund. The majority of the holdings are in government-guaranteed fixed-income securities with a minimum credit rating of A, while up to 20% can be invested in large dividend-paying companies. As of mid-2001, Canadian bonds and mortgage-backed securities dominated the asset mix (78.5%). Given the low risk, returns will generally lie between those of a bond fund and a balanced fund. Due to the recent stock market weakness, however, this fund has been outperforming most of its peers in the Canadian Balanced category, gaining 7.4% in the year to June 30/01. The five-year average annual compound rate of return was 8%, slightly better than average. A conservative fund looks pretty attractive these days, so we'll take the rating up to $$$.

## GREAT-WEST LIFE INCOME FUND (M)   $$$ ↓ FI/G */NO RSP S CBAL

Manager: Mackenzie Financial Industrial Team

MER: 2.10%   Fundata: C   Style: Top-down/Interest Rate Anticipation

Suitability: Balanced investors

This fund is designed for investors seeking a regular income stream along with capital appreciation. The mandate allows up to 40% of the assets to be held in stocks, making this entry relatively conservative as balanced funds go. The majority of its bonds are in federal or federal-guaranteed issues. Corporate debt is restricted to a maximum of 30% of assets. Moreover, at least 75% of assets will have a credit rating of A or higher. Performance-wise, five-year returns are about average compared with the peer group, but the latest one-year result to June 30/01 shows an excellent advance of 9.2%. This is a good fund for more conservative investors. We will increase our rating to $$$.

# Also Recommended

## Canadian Small-to-Mid-Cap Funds

### GREAT-WEST LIFE SMALLER COMPANY FUND (M)
$$ → G */NO RSP S CSC

Manager: Mackenzie Financial Ivy Team

MER: 2.61%     Fundata: A     Style: Value/Growth

Suitability: Aggressive investors

While the mandate of this fund is to focus on both small- and mid-cap stocks, it tends to have a bias toward smaller issues. It hasn't been a particularly strong performer over time, with a below-average compound annual rate of return of 4.4% for the five years to June 30/01. On the plus side, however, the risk here is less than you would normally find in a small-cap fund. That should come as no surprise, since Mackenzie's Ivy team runs this show. The conservative nature of the portfolio helped the fund post a 6.1% gain for the latest 12-month period, much better than the norm for its peer group. The fund is relatively well diversified, with no one dominant sector in mid-2001. This isn't a small-cap fund that really excites us, but the recent results warrant a move up to a $$ rating.

## Canadian Balanced and Asset Allocation Funds

### GREAT-WEST LIFE BALANCED FUND (B)
$$ → FI/G */NO RSP S CBAL

Manager: Denis Marsh (Beutel Goodman)

MER: 2.48%     Fundata: B     Style: Value

Suitability: Conservative investors

This fund aims to buy Canadian and U.S. stocks along with Canadian bonds and other short-term investments. Fixed-income securities may account for as much as 60% of the portfolio and require at least an A credit rating. On the equities side, the fund will hold between 20 and 40 Canadian stocks, with the same for the U.S. portion. The fund targets a 60% weight for its equities. Returns have been inconsistent. Five-year returns averaged 7.3% annually to June 30/01, which was below average for the peer group. However, the value style of Beutel Goodman showed its worth in the latest 12-month period, and the fund posted a very good gain of 8.1%. We are boosting the rating to $$ as a result.

## Canadian Bond Funds

### GREAT-WEST LIFE GOVERNMENT BOND FUND (G)

$$ ↓ FI */NO RSP S STB

Manager: Terry Parsonage (GWL Investment Management)

MER: 1.79%     Fundata: A     Style: Interest Rate Anticipation

Suitability: Conservative investors

This fund is geared toward very conservative investors who want returns that are generally between those of a money market fund and a regular bond fund. Default and interest rate risk is minimal, as the portfolio invests primarily in federal bonds followed by mortgage-backed securities. The average term of the portfolio will range from two to five years, so this is a short-term bond fund that will underperform in strong markets but protect your money when bond prices fall. Returns to date have been slightly below average for all measuring periods, but that's not bad considering the high MER. Our problem: Why pay for a guarantee on a low-risk fund like this? Rating remains at $$.

## Foreign Bond Funds

### GREAT-WEST LIFE GLOBAL INCOME FUND (A)     $$ → FI */NO RSP S FB

Managers: Clive Coombs and Scott Colborne (AGF)

MER: 2.00%     Fundata: C     Style: Interest Rate Anticipation

Suitability: RRSP/RRIF investors seeking foreign currency exposure

This entry is the counterpart to the companion International Bond (P) Fund (which is not recommended), with full RRSP eligibility. The fund invests mainly in foreign currency–denominated bonds that are issued or guaranteed by the Government of Canada, provincial governments, or corporations. The key risk here is foreign currencies and their movements against the Canadian dollar. At least half of the issues in the fund will have a credit rating of AA or higher. Recent returns have been good for the Foreign Bond category, with a one-year gain to June 30/01 of 4.6%. Five-year results are slightly above par. You won't get rich here, but if you want to hold some foreign currency in your registered plan, it's an acceptable choice.

## Promising Newcomers

None.

# INDUSTRIAL-ALLIANCE LIFE INSURANCE

## THE COMPANY

Established in 1892, Quebec-based Industrial-Alliance Life Insurance is a mutual life and health insurance company that offers its services and products across Canada and in the western United States. The company is ranked in the top 10 as far as life and health insurance companies go in Canada. The company recently acquired Vancouver-based Seaboard Life Insurance Company, the marketer of the Apex family of funds. The Apex line is sold through its sister company, North West Life Assurance Company of Canada, based in Vancouver.

Within Industrial's own group of funds, only the Ecoflex line is available for individual investors. All other funds are sold through pension plans and group RRSPs. The Ecoflex Funds are also sold through the North West Life Assurance Company of Canada. The funds, managers, and terms are identical between the two companies.

Industrial-Alliance's family of Ecoflex funds has grown to 28 in four main categories, based on investment objectives: income, moderate growth, growth, and superior growth. The full range is extensive and includes funds managed both in-house and externally. The external offerings are from the likes of AGF, Talvest, and Templeton.

## THE DETAILS

|  |  |
|---|---|
| Number of funds: | 8 |
| Assets under management: | $2.52 billion |
| Load charge: | Back: max. 5%, or no-load on a selective basis |
| Switching charge: | None |
| Where sold: | Across Canada |
| How sold: | Through life insurance agents |
| Phone number: | 1-800-463-6236 or (418) 684-5000 |
| Web site address: | www.inalco.com |
| E-mail address: | clientele@que.inalco.com |
| Minimum initial investment: | $500 |

## INVESTING TIPS

These funds are available either by back-end load purchase or through a no-load option. The no-load choice is not publicized or promoted, and is used only in "exceptional" cases at the request of a sales rep. But it is available, so if you're considering doing business with either Industrial-Alliance or North West Life, you should ask about it.

# FUND SUMMARY

Top Choices: Ecoflex T (Select Canadian), Ecoflex V (Dividend)
Also Recommended: Ecoflex D (Balanced),
Promising Newcomers: None
The Rest: Ecoflex A (Stocks), Ecoflex ABS (Canadian Equity), Ecoflex AFI (Canadian Stocks), Ecoflex AM (Multi), Ecoflex ANL (Stocks), Ecoflex B (Bond), Ecoflex BBS (Bonds), Ecoflex BNL (Bond), Ecoflex DFI (Asset Allocation), Ecoflex DMA (Balanced), Ecoflex DMO (Balanced), Ecoflex DNL (Diversified), Ecoflex DO (Balanced), Ecoflex DS (Balanced), Ecoflex E (Emerging Markets), Ecoflex G (Global Bonds), Ecoflex H (Mortgage), Ecoflex I (International Stock), Ecoflex ISS (International Stock), Ecoflex KAA (Euro), Ecoflex KFI (European Stocks), Ecoflex LAA (Global Growth), Ecoflex LFS (Global Equity), Ecoflex M (Money Market), Ecoflex N (Canadian Advantage), Ecoflex NFI (Canadian Stocks Best Choice), Ecoflex PFS (Asia Pacific), Ecoflex R (Short-term Bond), Ecoflex S (American Stocks), Ecoflex U (U.S. Advantage), Ecoflex USS (U.S. Stocks)

# FUND RATINGS

## Top Choices

### Canadian Equity Funds

### INDUSTRIAL-ALLIANCE ECOFLEX SELECT CANADIAN "T" FUND

$$$ → G */NO RSP S CLC

Manager: Luc Fournier, since 1998

MER: 2.56%      Fundata: B      Style: Bottom-up Value

Suitability: Moderate-risk investors

The fund's benchmark portfolio is 90% in Toronto 35 Index large-cap stocks and 10% in T-bills. However, at mid-2001, fund manager Luc Fournier had only a 75% allocation to stocks, which reduced the risk inherent in the weak markets. The fund invests primarily in large-cap stocks and is quite well diversified across both industries and companies. As of mid-2001, the largest allocations were to financial services (22%), oil and gas (9%), and industrial products (8.3%). In the year to June 30/01, the fund lost 6.8% relative to the peer group's average loss of

9.5%. Over the last three years, this fund has returned 8.4% annually, well above the group average. Volatility is below average. The fund debuts with a $$$ rating.

## Dividend Income Funds

### INDUSTRIAL-ALLIANCE ECOFLEX "V" DIVIDEND FUND $$$ → FI */NO RSP S DIV

Manager: Luc Fournier, since 1998

MER: 1.86%     Fundata: D     Style: Bottom-up Value

Suitability: Aggressive dividend-oriented investors

This diversified equity portfolio includes mainly high-yield large-cap Canadian stocks. Recently the dividend yield was about three times higher than the average dividend yield on the TSE 300 Composite Index. The fund's three-year return to mid-2001 was 11.1% compared with 7.1% for the peer group. Risk is above average, however, reflecting the common share orientation. If you want a more aggressive dividend fund, this is good choice. Debuts with a $$$ rating

## Also Recommended

## Canadian Balanced and Asset Allocation Funds

### INDUSTRIAL-ALLIANCE ECOFLEX "D" DIVERSIFIED FUND $$ → FI/G */NO RSP S CBAL

Managers: Luc Fournier, since 1993 and François Lalande, since 1998

MER: 2.48%     Fundata: B     Style: Bottom-up Value/Interest Rate Anticipation

Suitability: Moderate-risk investors

On average, this balanced fund is more aggressive than its peer group. The fund's mandate allows it to invest up to a maximum of 50% in Canadian stocks, 20% in foreign issues, and up to 60% in bonds. As of mid-2001, the fund had become more defensive, holding 48.6% of its assets in equities. Equities are well diversified across industries and companies, while the fixed-income side, composed mainly of federal and corporate bonds, has slightly above-average interest rate risk. At mid-2001, 42.7% of the portfolio was invested in Canadian bonds. The overweighted position in Canadian equity (i.e., overweighted relative to its peer group) helped the fund's performance in the year ending June 30/01 with a modest return of 2.3% compared with the 2.2% loss for the peer group. Longer-term, the three-year numbers are above average, although the five-year ones are below. Worthy of a $$ rating.

## Promising Newcomers

None.

# LONDON LIFE FUNDS

## THE COMPANY

The structure of the segregated line offered by London Life resembles that of its parent, Winnipeg-based Great-West Life, which acquired this company in 1997. The funds have remained independent, however. Like its parent, the London Life family of segregated funds makes extensive use of outside managers. In July 1998, London Life launched 33 new Freedom funds, which included new funds managed by London Life Investment Management. Its offering is very broad, which can make things confusing for investors in terms of choice. Some of these funds have performed quite well in the early stages.

The company chose a team of eight investment advisors for its Freedom funds, with a goal of providing clients with effective diversification. In theory, each Freedom fund has a specialized investment objective and management style. The eight managers are as follows: AGF Funds, Beutel Goodman, GWL Investment Management, Janus Capital Corporation, London Life Investment Management, Mackenzie Financial, Sceptre Investment Counsel, and Scudder MAXXUM. Note that the funds managed by MAXXUM were taken over by Mackenzie in October 2001.

In the list below, all funds managed by London Life have no identifier attached. Those managed by outside companies are marked as follows:

A = AGF

B = Beutel Goodman

GWL = Great-West Life

M = Mackenzie

Max = MAXXUM

S = Sceptre

In September 1999 the company announced a new fund line called the LFC Group of Funds. This addition to their stable further broadens the choices available. In October 1999 the company launched five new funds in the Freedom family, called the Profile Funds. Essentially, these are asset allocation funds, or funds of funds, that make asset mix calls through the purchase of other funds in the Freedom family.

## THE DETAILS

|  |  |
|---|---|
| Number of funds: | 45 |
| Assets under management: | $10.64 billion |
| Load charge: | Back: max. 5% |
| Switching charge: | None |

| | |
|---|---|
| Where sold: | Across Canada |
| How sold: | Through London Life agents |
| Phone number: | 1-800-LON-LIFE or 1-800-566-5433 |
| Web site address: | www.londonlife.com |
| E-mail address: | Through Web site |
| Minimum initial investment: | $300; $25 PAC (pre-authorized chequing) |

## INVESTING TIPS

Remember that a basic principle of investing in segregated funds is the guarantee. Back-end fees for most of the London Life funds (or withdrawal fees as London Life calls them) drop from 5% in year one to zero by year seven. Accordingly, you should always view seg fund investing as long term; otherwise, look elsewhere.

## FUND SUMMARY

| | |
|---|---|
| Top Choices: | Asian Growth (A), Balanced (B), Canadian Equity, Dividend |
| Also Recommended: | Income (M), Larger Company (M), North American Equity (B) |
| Promising Newcomers: | None |
| The Rest: | American Equity (J), American Growth (A), International Equity, Money Market, Mortgage, U.S. Equity, Balanced (S), Balanced Growth, Bond, Canadian Balanced (Max), Canadian Equity (GWL), Canadian Equity Growth (Max), Canadian Opportunity (M), Dividend, Dividend (Max), Equity (M), Equity (S), Equity/Bond (GWL), European Equity (S), Global Equity, Global Equity (Max), Government Bond (GWL), Growth Equity, Growth Equity (A), Growth & Income (A), Growth & Income (M), Income, Income (Max), International Equity, Mid-Cap Canada (GWL), Money Market, Mortgage, Natural Resource (Max), N.A. Balanced, Precious Metals (Max), Real Estate (GWL), U.S. Equity, Advanced Profile, Aggressive Profile, Balanced Profile, Conservative Profile, Moderate Profile |

# FUND RATINGS

## Top Choices

### Canadian Equity Funds

### LONDON LIFE CANADIAN EQUITY FUND $$$ ↑ G * RSP S CLC

Manager: London Life Investment Management

MER: 2.35%     Fundata: C     Style: Bottom-up Value

Suitability: Middle-of-the-road investors

Since taking over from long-time manager Rohit Sehgal, who left for Dundee Capital, the in-house managers have done a decent job with this fund despite the volatility in the markets. The goal is to scout for opportunities within the mid-to-large-cap market, represented by the TSE 300 Index. As of mid-2001, this well-diversified portfolio had a value orientation. With less than 60 stocks in this $1.9 billion fund, there is plenty of blue-chip exposure with solid representation from technology, financial services, oil and gas, and utility stocks. Returns have been above average in almost all measuring periods. In the three years to June 30/01, the fund realized a return of 7.3% per annum compared with a 5.7% return for the peer group. Five- and ten-year average annual returns are well above average. This fund deserves to maintain its $$$ grade.

### Dividend Income Funds

### LONDON LIFE DIVIDEND FUND $$$ ↑ G/FI * RSP S DIV

Manager: London Life Investment

MER: 2.25%     Fundata: B     Style: Value

Suitability: Conservative investors

This fund concentrates on earning above-average dividend income through high-quality common and preferred shares. The top holdings as of mid-2001 consisted of well-known large-cap Canadian companies, including BCE, Bank of Nova Scotia, and Canadian Pacific. The heaviest allocation was to financial services (25.8%) and utilities (11.9%). The fund is off to a solid start. Return for the three years to June 30/01 was 13.9%, well above the 7.2% average for the dividend category. Debuts with a $$$ rating.

## Global and International Equity Funds

### LONDON LIFE ASIAN GROWTH FUND $$$ → G * RSP S PRE

Manager: AGF Funds

MER: 2.60%    Fundata: B    Style: Value

Suitability: Aggressive investors

This fund, managed by the giant AGF group, concentrates on Asian companies with high growth prospects. In the three years to mid-2001, the fund recorded an 11% average annual return, which is quite respectable given the 4% per annum average for the peer group. The major country allocations, which compose over 80% of the portfolio, are China, Hong Kong, Korea, and Singapore. This is a highly unpredictable and volatile region but if you are looking for a fund in the area, this is a good one. Debuts with a $$$ rating.

## Canadian Balanced and Asset Allocation Funds

### LONDON LIFE BALANCED FUND $$$ → C * RSP S CBAL

Manager: Beutel Goodman

MER: 2.45%    Fundata: A    Style: Tactical Asset Allocation

Suitability: Moderate-risk investors

The Beutel Goodman folks use tactical asset allocation to manage this fund. This means they will adjust the asset category weights with their view of changing conditions and outlook. As of mid-2001, the allocation was 53% equity and 47% fixed income. The fund earned a Fundata A rating in the mid-2001 reporting period because of its high return (9.3% in latest 12 months compared with a 5.1% loss for the category) and moderate risk. The fund's beta (a measure of volatility) is a relatively low 0.53. Debuts with a $$$ rating.

## Also Recommended

## Canadian Equity Funds

### LONDON LIFE NORTH AMERICAN EQUITY FUND $$ ↓ G * RSP S CE

Manager: Beutel Goodman

MER: 2.45%    Fundata: A    Style: Bottom-up Value

Suitability: Conservative investors

The value specialists at Beutel Goodman manage this fund. Although the mandate is North America, the fund allocation so far has been primarily to Canadian large-cap companies. Sector weights as of mid-2001 were toward industrial products (21.1%), financial services (19.7%), and consumer products

(99%). The average annual return for the three years to June 30/01 was 6.4%, slightly above the norm for the category. Volatility was considerably less than the norm. Debuts with a $$ rating.

## LONDON LIFE LARGE COMPANY FUND $$ → G * RSP S CLC

Manager: Mackenzie Financial

MER: 2.50%      Fundata: A      Style: Value

Suitability: Conservative investors

This large-cap fund managed by the Mackenzie Financial management team concentrates on blue-chip Canadian companies. The top holdings as of mid-2001 included Royal Bank of Canada, Brascan, and CIBC. The heaviest allocation was to financial services (29.8%), industrial products (19.6%), and oil and gas (10%). After a very shaky start, the fund has recovered in the latest year with a return to June 30/01 of 14.9%, compared with a 9.5% average loss for the peer group. Return for the three years to mid-2001 is still below average, however. The fund's relatively low standard deviation and beta put it in the low-risk bracket for its category. Debuts with a $$ rating.

## Canadian Bond Funds

## LONDON LIFE INCOME FUND $$ ↑ FI * RSP S CB

Manager: London Life Investment Management

MER: 1.90%      Fundata: D      Style: Interest Rate Anticipation

Suitability: Higher-risk income investors

This entry is officially classified as a bond fund although it also holds common shares (24% at mid-2001), making it more of a balanced fund in our view, which means that the risk level is higher by definition than you'd expect in a bond fund. The portfolio holds mainly federal bonds, followed by some high-quality corporate issues. Interest rate risk is average. Returns have been above average since inception. In the three years to June 30/01, the fund's 6.4% annual return far outpaced the 3.9% average for the bond category. The outperformance is partially explained by the common share component, which was also a contributing factor to the fund's above-average volatility. The fund debuts with a $$ rating. If you're considering an investment here, be sure you understand exactly what you are buying.

## Promising Newcomers

None.

# MANULIFE FINANCIAL

## THE COMPANY

Waterloo, Ontario–based Manulife is one of Canada's leading insurance companies and boasts one of the largest stables of segregated funds. One of the great innovators, Manulife was the first to create a new type of fund when it made deals to put a seg fund wrapper on well-known mutual funds and sell them under the GIF (guaranteed investment funds) label. The Manulife GIFs are wrapper clones of well-known mutual funds.

In fact, Manulife was almost single-handedly responsible for the surge of investor interest in segregated funds in the late 1990s. Billions of dollars were poured into a rash of new seg fund offerings, many of them very aggressive. The trend caused concern for regulators, who subsequently raised the reserve requirements for seg funds in order to ensure money would be available if guarantees had to be paid. The new rules led to some major changes in the industry, including the demise of some funds and the creation of new lines with reduced guarantees (the latter is the course that Manulife has taken, as we explain below).

The majority of Manulife's GIF funds are run by outside managers, such as AGF, AIM/Trimark, Atlas, C.I., Dynamic, Elliott & Page, Fidelity, Merrill Lynch, StrategicValue, Sceptre, and Talvest. The GIF funds are investments in the underlying funds, but returns will differ from the underlying fund due to the higher management expense ratios (MERs) attached to the segregated funds and the timing of purchases. Choosing to go with the regular underlying fund or its segregated equivalent depends on the investor's risk preference. Buying segregated funds creates a bottom line for losses in a down market, but will also eat away at returns in a rising market due to higher management fees.

In 1999, Manulife launched its GIF Encore line of 50 seg funds, which emulates each of the existing funds except that the GIF Encore offers an escalating death benefit. This benefit is quite interesting and puts a different twist on the guaranteed concept. GIF Encore has removed the ability to reset at your discretion, meaning you can't periodically reset your guarantee as you can with many other segregated funds. This is one of the drawbacks of GIF Encore funds. On the positive side, Manulife provides an automatic reset on the death benefit. In a worst-case scenario, the automatic reset for a GIF Encore fund guarantees that the death benefit will increase by at least 4% per year (simple interest). This means that your death benefit is always guaranteed to be higher than your original investment. The reset occurs once a year on the anniversary date.

It works this way: Suppose you invest $10,000 today and one year later the portfolio is worth $9,000. The death benefit in GIF Encore will automatically be reset to $10,400. That's 4% higher than the previous year's value because the 4% escalation is higher than the current value of the underlying portfolio.

Manulife will also reset the death benefit to the market value of the fund if that is higher than the 4% escalation. For example, say you invest $10,000 and the portfolio is worth $11,000 on the anniversary date. The death benefit is reset to $11,000 because the market value is greater than the 4% minimum escalation. Finally, should the previous reset be higher than either the 4% escalation or the market value of the underlying portfolio, it will be your death benefit guarantee for the next year.

Here's another example: You invest $10,000 and in one year the portfolio is worth $9,000. The death benefit is automatically reset to $10,400 (4% above the initial deposit). In the second year, the portfolio value rises to $12,000 and the death benefit is reset to $12,000. In year three, the portfolio value declines to $11,000; the death benefit remains set at $12,000 because the previous death benefit is higher than both the current portfolio valuation and the minimum 4% simple interest calculation. As you can see, things can get complicated. The important point is that the death benefit will rise by at least 4% annually.

In January 2001, GIF Series 2 and GIF Encore Series 2 funds were launched. These funds are the same products as Series 1 except the maturity guarantee on Series 2 funds is 75% after 10 years instead of 100%. GIF and GIF Encore contracts purchased after January 2001 have only the Series 2 funds available. Since the guarantees on these funds are less valuable, the MERs are less than for Series 1.

## THE DETAILS

|  |  |
|---|---|
| Number of funds: | 69 |
| Assets under management: | $1.7 billion |
| Load charge: | Front: max. 3%; Back: max.5.5% (reduced charges for money market and bond funds) |
| Switching charge: | 5 free transfers per year and a 2% fee thereafter |
| Where sold: | Across Canada |
| How sold: | Through licensed life insurance agents and brokers |
| Phone number: | 1-888-MANULIFE or 1-888-626-8543 |
| Web site address: | www.manulife.com |
| E-mail address: | Through Web site |
| Minimum initial investment: | $500 |

## INVESTING TIPS

Here's one way to look at the GIF product: you are buying both the underlying mutual fund and a put option to sell the fund at the guaranteed value. Think of the extra MER you are paying as the cost of the insurance. The fairness of this insurance cost can be measured using a sophisticated option-pricing model. We wonder how many investors actually know if the price they are paying is indeed a representative one…

Don't get carried away by the "no-risk" aspect of seg funds. The chance of a properly run bond or balanced fund actually losing money over a five or ten-year period is very small; check out the long-term performance numbers of mutual funds and you will find this fact confirmed. We don't believe maturity guarantees are needed at all, and we certainly cannot recommend paying high fees to insure a bond or balanced fund. For older people or those in uncertain health, however, the death guarantee on high-risk funds provides some certainty in estate planning.

## FUND SUMMARY

All the Manulife GIF funds are segregated versions of existing mutual funds, most of which have well-established track records. The Manulife version of these funds is designed to allow investors to obtain the benefits of creditor protection, loss guarantees, and estate planning not available by investing in the underlying funds themselves. For these added benefits, you'll be assessed an extra management fee, over and above the one applied to the underlying fund. For information on our ratings of the underlying funds, see the appropriate entry in the mutual funds section.

# MARITIME LIFE

## THE COMPANY

Maritime Life began its operations in Halifax in 1922. Initially the company pro-vided services only to the Atlantic provinces, but in the early 1970s it expanded its business across Canada. In 1969 the firm was acquired by Boston-based John Hancock Mutual Life Insurance Company, although it maintained its original name and identity. In 1995, the firm took over the individual life and health business and the segregated funds of the bankrupt Confederation Life.

In October 1999, Maritime launched a whopping 33 new funds. These segre-gated funds are offered through three fund companies: AGF, Fidelity, and Talvest. The units are sold through each fund company in A, B, and C versions. The B units carry a deferred sales charge, while the A and C units are no-load. All these funds are restricted in that they may be purchased only for inclusion in Maritime Life's variable whole life insurance policies. Be careful about the differences between the sales charge identifiers, as they are different from Maritime Life's own funds.

Maritime also offers segregated versions of other company funds. The fund partners are AGF, Fidelity, and TAL (i.e., Talvest mutual funds). Funds under this classification include AGF American Growth Fund, AGF International Stock Fund, AGF RSP American Growth Fund, Fidelity European Growth Fund, Fidelity International Portfolio Fund, Fidelity Overseas Fund, Fidelity True North Fund, TAL Canadian Asset Allocation Fund, TAL Canadian Equity Growth Fund, TAL Global RSP Fund, TAL Global Bond Fund, and TAL Small-Cap Canadian Fund. For information on any of these funds, consult the regular mutual fund section under the appropriate fund family.

The Synchrony portfolios offered by the firm contain a mix of Maritime Life segregated funds and Talvest funds.

## THE DETAILS

|  |  |
|---|---|
| Number of funds: | 74 |
| Assets under management: | $3.9 billion |
| Load charge: | Three purchase options: Series A, No-load; Series B, Back: max. 6%; Series C, Back: max. 10% |
| Switching charge: | None |
| Where sold: | Across Canada |
| How sold: | Through insurance agents, brokers, dealers, and financial planners |
| Phone number: | (902) 453-4300 |
| Web site address: | www.maritimelife.ca |
| E-mail address: | cpa@maritimelife.ca |
| Minimum initial investment: | $500 |

# INVESTING TIPS

For the Maritime family of segregated funds, there are three purchase options. The Series A and Series B units are essentially the same, except that the B units are sold on a deferred sales charge basis. Choose A units if it comes down to a decision between the two. The C units are also sold on a deferred sales charge basis, declining to nil after 10 years, but they offer a bonus payment if they are held for 15 years or more. Ask a Maritime Life representative for details. If you know you're definitely going to be in for the long haul, the C units may be your best choice.

# FUND SUMMARY

|  |  |
|---|---|
| Top Choices: | American Growth and Income |
| Also Recommended: | Aggressive Equity, Dividend Income, Growth |
| Promising Newcomers: | None |
| The Rest: | Balanced, Bond, Canadian Equity, Discovery, Diversified Equity, Eurasia, Europe, Euro Growth, Global Equities, Pacific Basin Equity, S&P 500 Fund, Money Market, Synchrony Conservative, Synchrony Income & Growth, Synchrony Performance |

# FUND RATINGS

## Top Choices

### U.S. Equity Funds

### MARITIME LIFE AMERICAN GROWTH & INCOME FUND $$$ ↓ G */NO RSP S USE

Manager: John F. Snyder III (Sovereign Asset Management), since inception (1994)

MER: 2.55%     Fundata: B     Style: Stable Growth/Dividend

Suitability: Conservative investors

This conservative fund invests in companies that have had rising dividends, based on the theory that dividends increase as a result of higher earnings. In other words, you are investing in a fund that buys companies displaying steady growth. The focus is on large firms but the mandate does allow for some smaller-cap companies. Diversification is achieved by restricting any one sector to a maximum of 25% of the assets. Companies include a number of blue-chip value names like Chevron, Johnson & Johnson, and Citigroup. The fund was an underachiever in the late 1990s when this type of fundamental stock selection approach was pushed to the back burner during high-tech mania. Over the year to June 30/00, the fund actually recorded a loss of –6.1%, versus a

7.1% return for the average U.S. large-cap equity fund. However, the value bias worked well for the fund over the latest 12 months. The fund posted a gain of 6.2% while the average fund in the U.S. equity category was producing a double-digit loss. The plus with this fund is its conservative nature and great safety record to date. This is the type of fund that is working well in the present investment climate and we are accordingly upgrading it to $$$.

## Also Recommended

### Canadian Equity Funds

### MARITIME LIFE AGGRESSIVE EQUITY FUND    $$$ ↑ G */NO RSP S CE

Managers: Shauna Sexsmith (Altamira), since 1998 and Bernice Behar (John Hancock), since 1996

MER: 2.55%    Fundata: E    Style: Altamira: Top-down/Sector Rotation; John Hancock: Bottom-up Growth

Suitability: Aggressive investors

Results for this seg fund have trended from good to better to bad! The average annual return for the three years ending June 30/01 was 8.4%, above the 6.3% average for the peer group. In the year ending June 30/00 the fund returned 50.4%, which was almost double the peer group and better than the benchmark TSE 300 Composite Index—that's no small feat. But for the year ending June 30/01, the fund lost 21.3% compared with a 6.5% loss for the category. The managers invest in Canadian and U.S. equities, in industries they expect will outperform the market or that offer potential for superior growth. The Canadian portion of the portfolio invests in stocks that will benefit from expected changes in the economy, while the U.S. portion is invested in small-cap stocks that promise consistent or accelerating earnings growth. Having managers on both sides of the border has helped with results. Don't ignore the word "aggressive" in the fund name: volatility for this fund was high over its first four years. We are downgrading to a $$$ rating. This fund is suitable only for investors who can accept some additional risk, albeit with a guarantee that if things go sour, capital is protected.

### MARITIME LIFE GROWTH FUND    $$$ → G */NO RSP S CE

Managers: Ted Macklin (Montrusco Bolton), since 1997; David Knight (Knight, Bain, Seath & Holbrook), since 1989; and John Dunstan (Genus Capital Management), since 1992

MER: 2.55%    Fundata: D    Style: Multiple

Suitability: Aggressive investors

This fund is more diversified than the companion Canadian Equity Fund (not on our Recommended List) and will invest in all capitalization classes. It employs a multi-manager system, with the fund divided into three separate focuses: small-cap value, mid/large-cap growth, and large-cap value. The portfolio generally holds between 130 and 140 stocks, spread across a broad range of industries with a bias toward financial services, industrial products, and oil and gas. Top holdings are blue-chip stocks, but the fund will hold smaller stocks for added growth potential. Like its companion Canadian funds, the fund has no foreign content. As of mid-2001, the fund was holding 3.6% in cash, a very low amount by industry standards. Over the year to June 30/01, the fund lost 16.6% on the heels of its remarkable 43.8% performance last year. Returns over the longer-term remain solid and we will maintain the $$$ rating for now.

## Dividend Income Funds

### MARITIME LIFE DIVIDEND INCOME FUND     $$ → G */NO RSP S DIV

Managers: Alfred Samson and Peter Stuart, since January 2001

MER: 2.10%     Fundata: E     Style: Value

Suitability: Conservative investors

Let's make one thing clear at the outset: This is not a great dividend fund, as the Fundata rating shows. Don't choose the company just to get this one. But if you have an account with the company, then you may want to consider adding this fund to your mix. The fund offers investors a portfolio of large-cap, high-yielding, and value-oriented blue-chip stocks. In addition, it will hold preferred shares and fixed-income securities for added diversification and income. The portfolio is heavily weighted toward interest-sensitive financial services and utilities stocks. Returns are below the average for the peer group over all measuring periods. However, the fund did post a gain of 11% during the year to June 30/01, which was a better return than any of the company's regular equity funds managed to generate. If financial service companies rise, this fund will do relatively well and it holds its own in a down market, as we have seen. Also, there is a new managerial team in place, so the future may be brighter.

## Promising Newcomers

None.

# ROYAL & SUNALLIANCE INVESTMENT FUNDS

## THE COMPANY

At the time of writing, Maritime Life was expected to close a deal to purchase Royal & SunAlliance Financial on October 1, 2001. We were advised there would be no changes to the Royal & SunAlliance segregated fund family and its investment managers through to the 2002 RRSP season. Maritime Life plans to review the Royal & Sun segregated fund line-up after that time, so there could be some changes to this family in the future.

The company has run most of its funds with an in-house management team. However, they have also brought in some outside managers and introduced four new funds that are segregated versions of similar funds in the Trimark family. These funds are Advantage Bond Fund, Canadian Resource Fund, Discovery Fund, and Europlus Fund. For details on these funds, please see the regular mutual fund listings under AIM Funds, which now owns Trimark.

The company also offers several Simplicity Plus Portfolios, which invest in other funds within the group using an asset allocation approach.

## THE DETAILS

| | |
|---|---|
| Number of funds: | 19 |
| Assets under management: | $1 billion |
| Load charge: | No-load or back-end load options: max. 5% |
| Switching charge: | 4 free transfers per year and $50 thereafter |
| Where sold: | Across Canada except Yukon and Nunavut |
| How sold: | Through regional offices, managing general agencies, and independent brokers |
| Phone number: | 1-800-263-1747 (new clients); Fax (905) 842-6294 |
| Web site address: | www.royalsunalliance.ca |
| E-mail address: | Through Web site |
| Minimum initial investment: | $500; $50 PAC (pre-authorized chequing) |

## INVESTING TIPS

Like many other insurance companies, Royal & SunAlliance changed the guarantee structure on many of their segregated funds over the past year. For new investors, the maturity guarantee has dropped to 75% (from 100%). The death guarantee remains at 100% to age 80, after which it drops to 75%.

With this change, the company closed its original line of seg funds to new investors and launched new versions, known as Series II. They are the same as the original funds in all respects except for the guarantees they carry. Investors who had bought units in the original funds retain re-investment privileges.

## FUND SUMMARY

|  |  |
|---|---|
| Top Choices: | Balanced, Dividend, Money Market |
| Also Recommended: | Canadian Growth, Equity, Income |
| Promising Newcomers: | None |
| The Rest: | Canada 60 Index, Europe 50 Index, European Equity, Global Emerging Markets, International Equity, Pacific Rim Equity, U.S. 500 Index, U.S Equity, U.S. Opportunities 100 Index |

## FUND RATINGS

### Top Choices

#### Dividend Income Funds

**ROYAL & SUNALLIANCE DIVIDEND FUND**   $$$ → G/FI NO/* RSP S DIV

Manager: Brad Cann, since January 2000

MER: 2.20%      Fundata: B      Style: Value

Suitability: Conservative investors

This is a very impressive dividend fund that has been successful in its short existence, generating both decent income and capital gains. Manager Brad Cann invests mainly in common stocks, with an emphasis on financial services companies. However, the portfolio also holds a small number of preferred shares. After getting off to a slow start (a loss of 8.2% in 1999), performance has picked up. Recent returns have been very good; the fund gained almost 23% in the year to June 30/01. This is shaping up to be a very respectable entry.

#### Canadian Balanced and Asset Allocation Funds

**ROYAL & SUNALLIANCE BALANCED FUND**  $$ → FI/G NO/* RSP S CBAL

Managers: Rob Rublee, since 1990 and Brad Cann, since January 2000

MER: 2.40%      Fundata: B      Style: Value/Interest Rate Anticipation

Suitability: Conservative investors

The mandate here puts a cap of 75% on the proportion of the fund that can be in stocks or bonds at any given time, but usually the ratios are kept in closer balance. Equities with a large-cap value bias represented 49% of assets as of mid-2001, and were well diversified across industries. On the fixed-income side, default risk is low as the majority of assets are held in federal bonds and high-quality corporate debt. However, interest rate risk is above average; the fund uses an "interest rate anticipation approach." Overall portfolio risk is average. Results have been generally good, although the fund lost 4.1% in the year to June 30/01, slightly worse than average for the category. Longer-term results are average to slightly above. This is one of those funds that manages to produce profits most of the time with a modest level of risk.

## Canadian Money Market Funds

### ROYAL & SUNALLIANCE MONEY MARKET FUND                              $$$ → C NO/* RSP S CMM

Manager: Steve Locke, since 1999

MER: 1.20%     Fundata: B

Suitability: Conservative investors

This is a money market fund with above-average one- to five-year returns. To achieve this result, the fund invests predominately in higher-yielding corporate debt. The absence of government securities adds slightly to the risk level, although we don't see this as a major concern.


## Also Recommended

## Canadian Equity Funds

### ROYAL & SUNALLIANCE EQUITY FUND          $$ → G NO/* RSP S CLC

Manager: Brad Cann, since January 2000

MER: 2.45%     Fundata: B     Style: Value/Growth

Suitability: Conservative investors

While this fund seeks both value and growth, its overall bias is toward blue-chip issues, with the option to add smaller growth stocks. The bottom-up approach of this diversified fund has been generally effective in the past. However, Brad Cann replaced John Smolinski as head of this fund in January 2000 and the most recent returns have been slightly below par, with a one-year loss of 9.5% to June 30/01. We are reducing our rating to $$ for now. Nevertheless, we still view this as a steady fund for long-term investors.

## Canadian Small-to-Mid-Cap Equity Funds

### ROYAL & SUNALLIANCE CANADIAN GROWTH FUND $$ → G NO/ * RSP S CSC

Manager: Teresa Lee, since 1998

MER: 2.55%     Fundata: C     Style: Growth

Suitability: Aggressive investors

This is Royal's entry into the increasingly popular area of small-cap investing. The fund leans toward growth-oriented, low-dividend-paying industrial products companies, which trade at attractive valuations. The fund will primarily buy companies with a market cap of between $15 million on the low end to $200 million on the high end. This fund was an indifferent performer for some time but it's done better recently, with a gain of 8.8% for the year to June 30/01, much better than the average for its category. Five-year results are still sub-par, but the trend pattern is positive. Rating moves up to $$.

## Canadian Bond Funds

### ROYAL & SUNALLIANCE INCOME FUND $$ → FI NO/* RSP S CB

Manager: Rob Rublee, since 1992

MER: 1.90%     Fundata: D     Style: Index/Interest Rate Anticipation

Suitability: Conservative investors

Manager Rob Rublee uses a two-pronged investment approach here. Two-thirds of the portfolio is structured to mirror the SCM Universe Bond Index; the remaining third uses an "interest rate anticipation" approach, which simply means the manager trades actively in an attempt to benefit from changes in the bond/interest rate market. Interest rate risk is average while default risk is low, with the portfolio holding mainly government and high-grade corporate bonds. This is an average fund, with an average style, with average risk, and with results that are…well, about average.

## Promising Newcomers

None.

# STANDARD LIFE IDEAL FUNDS

## THE COMPANY

This is the Canadian arm of the Standard Life Group of Edinburgh, Scotland, established in 1825. The Canadian unit offers both a segregated line under the "Ideal" brand name and a non-segregated line. The segregated line has been expanded to 15 funds and includes several good performers. All funds are managed in-house. Please see the Standard Life entry in the mutual funds section for details on the non-segregated line.

## THE DETAILS

|                              |                                                   |
| ---------------------------: | ------------------------------------------------- |
| Number of funds:             | 15                                                |
| Assets under management:     | $1.43 billion                                     |
| Load charge:                 | Back: max. 6%; A no-load option is also offered   |
| Switching charge:            | None                                              |
| Where sold:                  | Across Canada                                      |
| How sold:                    | Through licensed agents and brokers               |
| Phone number:                | 1-888-841-6633                                    |
| Web site address:            | www.standardlife.ca                               |
| E-mail address:              | N/A                                               |
| Minimum initial investment:  | $1,000 ($10,000 for RRIFs)                         |

## INVESTING TIPS

You can buy these funds on either a no-load basis or with a deferred sales charge (back-end load) option. The latter carries a fee of 6% if you cash in within the first year, declining to zero after five years. If you choose the no-load option, you'll be assessed a slightly higher annual management fee (0.15%). Normally this would not be enough of a differential to dissuade us from recommending the no-load route. However, these are segregated funds. Presumably you are buying them for the long term to take advantage, among other things, of their guarantees. Therefore, it is less likely that you will want to pull out after a short period of time. As a result, the back-end load with its lower management expense ratio (MER) is the best choice in most situations. We use the back-end MER in the individual reviews.

Note that whichever option you select, the MER of these funds will be higher than that of the corresponding mutual funds, although not by a lot.

Investors should be aware that several of the funds in this group are not stand-alone portfolios. Rather, they invest exclusively in units of the corresponding mutual fund of the same name.

# FUND SUMMARY

| | |
|---|---|
| Top Choices: | Equity, Money Market |
| Also Recommended: | Balanced, Bond |
| Promising Newcomers: | Canadian Dividend, Corporate High-Yield Bond, Growth Equity, Income Balanced, International Bond Fund |
| The Rest: | Active Global Diversified Index RSP, Active Global Index RSP, Active U.S. Index RSP, International Equity, S&P 500 Index RSP, U.S. Equity |

# FUND RATINGS

## Top Choices

### Canadian Equity Funds

### STANDARD LIFE IDEAL EQUITY FUND           $$$ ↓ G */NO RSP S CE

Manager: Standard Life Investments Inc.

MER: 2.40%      Fundata: C      Style: Bottom-up Value

Suitability: Conservative investors

This fund differs somewhat from the companion Standard Life Equity Mutual Fund. It holds a core portfolio of the top companies on the TSE for stability and liquidity, with a large percentage of the assets (6.7% at mid-2001) in i60 units that track the S&P/TSE 60 Index. As well, there are some non-core holdings of smaller and less liquid growth stocks for added returns. A large holding of U.S. stocks provides further diversification. Financial services stocks, such as banks, represented about a quarter of the portfolio in mid-2001. Returns have been above average for many years, although they have slipped to the third quartile in the past 18 months. The fund lost 12.6% in the year to June 30/01, a much worse result than its mutual fund counterpart. That's somewhat surprising since both funds are run by the same team and have the same general mandate. Longer-term results are still well above average, although they too have fallen behind those of the mutual fund. This is still a good choice for those looking for a conservatively managed Canadian equity segregated fund. However, we are dropping the rating to $$$ in light of the latest performance numbers.

## Canadian Money Market Funds

### STANDARD LIFE IDEAL MONEY MARKET FUND

$$$ → C */NO RSP S CMM

Manager: Standard Life Investments Inc.

MER: 1.00%    Fundata: E    Style:    Income

Suitability: Conservative investors

With over three-quarters of the assets invested in higher-yielding corporate debt, returns here have been consistently above average over one to five years. The remainder of the fund is in T-bills and provincial bonds. It's a good haven for idle cash. This is one of the few cases where the seg fund version is outperforming the mutual fund.

## Also Recommended

## Canadian Balanced and Asset Allocation Funds

### STANDARD LIFE IDEAL BALANCED FUND    $$ → FI/G */NO RSP S CBAL

Manager: Standard Life Investments Inc.

MER: 2.40%    Fundata: D    Style: Value/Interest Rate Anticipation

Suitability: Conservative investors

The goal here is to focus on quality and liquidity, hence both the equity and bond sides consist of top companies and high-grade debt. Equities are diversified, including a good portion in U.S. stocks for foreign exposure. The portfolio is fairly standard and includes the traditional core areas of industrial products, oil and gas, and interest-sensitive stocks. The equity style leans toward mid-to-large-cap value, but with more stocks than the companion Ideal Equity Fund. To control risk, the fund cannot invest more than 60% in stocks at any time. The fixed-income side is conservatively managed with average interest rate risk and the majority of the assets in government bonds, with a dash of corporate bonds for added yield. As of mid-2001, the mix was 50% stocks, 44% bonds, and the rest in cash. Returns have fallen off to below average over the past 18 months. The fund dropped 8.8% in the year ending June 30/01 and its returns over all time frames out to five years now lag behind those of the companion mutual fund. The mutual fund looks like the better choice unless you're determined to invest in a seg fund.

## Canadian Bond Funds

### STANDARD LIFE IDEAL BOND FUND    $$ → FI */NO RSP S CB

Manager: Standard Life Investments Inc.

MER: 1.70%    Fundata: D    Style: Interest Rate Anticipation

Suitability: Conservative investors

This is a conservatively managed bond fund that invests almost exclusively in government issues, with a sprinkling of corporate debt for added yield. Recent returns have improved, although long-term numbers are still below average. The mutual fund counterpart generates slightly better profits.

## Promising Newcomers

## Canadian Small-to-Mid-Cap Funds

### STANDARD LIFE IDEAL GROWTH EQUITY FUND    NR ↑ G */NO RSP S CSC

Manager: Standard Life Investments Inc.

MER: 2.35%    Fundata: N/A    Style: Bottom-up Growth

Suitability: Aggressive investors

This fund invests exclusively in units of the very good Standard Life Growth Equity Fund. See the entry on Standard Life in the mutual funds section for more details.

## Dividend Income Funds

### STANDARD LIFE IDEAL CANADIAN DIVIDEND FUND    NR → G */NO RSP S DIV

Manager: Standard Life Investments Inc.

MER: 2.40%    Fundata: B    Style: Bottom-up Value

Suitability: Conservative investors

This entry is the segregated equivalent of the highly rated Standard Life Canadian Dividend Fund and its entire portfolio is in fact made up of units of that mutual fund. So the results will be almost the same, except for the variation in MERs.

## Canadian Balanced and Asset Allocation Funds

### STANDARD LIFE IDEAL INCOME BALANCED FUND

NR ↓ FI/G */NO RSP S CBAL

Manager: Standard Life Investments Inc.

MER: 2.40%     Fundata: A     Style: Bottom-up Value

Suitability: Conservative income investors

This fund has been especially designed to meet the needs of investors who require steady income along with modest growth potential and relatively low risk. In other words, it would be very well suited for an RRIF. In mid-2001, the portfolio was 46% in stocks, mostly of the blue-chip, dividend-paying variety. There was a large cash position of 16%, with the rest in bonds. Initial returns have been very good and the fund is a first-quartile performer. This looks like an excellent choice for low-risk investors.

## Canadian Bond Funds

### STANDARD LIFE IDEAL CORPORATE HIGH-YIELD BOND FUND

NR → FI */NO RSP S HYB

Manager: Standard Life Investments Inc.

MER: 2.10%     Fundata: N/A     Style: Interest Rate Anticipation/Credit Analysis

Suitability: Aggressive investors

Here again we have a seg fund that invests entirely in units of the underlying mutual fund of the same name. See the review in the mutual funds section for details.

## Foreign Bond Funds

### STANDARD LIFE IDEAL INTERNATIONAL BOND FUND

NR ↑ FI */NO RSP S FB

Manager: Standard Life Investments Inc.

MER: 2.20%     Fundata: N/A     Style: Interest Rate Anticipation/Currency Trading

Suitability: Aggressive investors

Invests entirely in units of the Standard Life International Bond Fund. See the review in the mutual funds section for details.

# TRANSAMERICA LIFE

## THE COMPANY

The GROWsafe family of segregated funds is offered through Transamerica Life Insurance Company of Canada, the Canadian subsidiary of U.S.-based Transamerica Occidental Life Insurance Company, which in turn is part of the Transamerica Corporation, a financial services company with more than $63 billion in assets. GROWsafe Funds are GIFs (guaranteed investments funds), now in their third version. GROWsafe 1 and 2 GIFs are now closed; new purchases are in the GROWsafe 3 version. The mutual fund lines available are essentially the same in all three versions; only the guarantee and reset terms differ. Check with an agent for complete details.

A major change during the past couple of years was the decision to replace several of the fund managers with the in-house staff at Transamerica. As a result, several of the funds have taken on a new look, following an index-driven mandate.

In general, many of Transamerica funds had a great year in 1999–2000 (to mid-year) and an awful one in 2000–01 (also to mid-year). Managers placed big bets on technology, which is reflected in the results and volatility.

Most recently, Transamerica purchased the ING family of funds, formerly the NN Financial family. Funds with the NN designation were renamed and they are now called the Transamerica Investment Management Series (IMS). They are not available for sale at this time (although existing investors can purchase additional units), so they will not be reviewed here.

## THE DETAILS

| | |
|---|---|
| Number of funds: | 22 |
| Assets under management: | $6.0 billion |
| Load charge: | Back: max. 6% |
| Switching charge: | Four free transfers per year; after that a 2% charge may be levied, or a minimum $250 per switch. |
| Where sold: | Across Canada |
| How sold: | Through Transamerica and independent financial advisors |
| Phone number: | 1-800-268-8814 |
| Web site address: | www.transamerica.ca |
| E-mail address: | webmaster.canada@transamerica.com |
| Minimum initial investment: | $1,000, with a $500 per fund minimum |

# INVESTING TIPS

We believe the guaranteed investment option is of limited value given the unlikelihood of negative returns over an extended period. However, one area to consider is some of Transamerica's more volatile funds. For example, The GROWsafe Canadian Equity Fund run by Glen Paradis scored a 96.9% return for the year ending June 30/00, followed by a 47.2% loss in the next year. Locking in the big gain with a reset option after the run-up would have looked like a very good move to have made in retrospect.

Our general advice, therefore, is to avoid paying higher management expense ratios (MERs) for guarantees on low-risk funds like bond funds, balanced funds, and conservatively managed equity funds. If you are going to pay more for what amounts to an insurance policy, do so with funds that have above-average risk.

# FUND SUMMARY

| | |
|---:|:---|
| Top Choices: | Canadian Balanced, Canadian Equity |
| Also Recommended: | None |
| Promising Newcomers: | None |
| The Rest: | Aggressive Asset Allocation, Bond, Canadian Dividend & Income, Canadian Money Market, Canadian 60 Index, Conservative Asset Allocation, European 100, Growth Asset Allocation, U.S. Balanced, U.S. Bond, U.S. Equity, U.S. 21st Century |

# FUND RATINGS

## Top Choices

### Canadian Equity Funds

### TRANSAMERICA GROWSAFE CANADIAN EQUITY FUND                    $$$ ↑ G */NO RSP S CE

Manager: Glenn Paradis, since 1998

MER: 2.69%    Fundata: E    Style: Top-down Momentum

Suitability: Aggressive investors

This fund now has three years under the stewardship of Glenn Paradis, and so far the results can only be described as dramatic. How about 96.9% return for the year ending June 2000, which was more than twice the return of the benchmark index (TSE 300 Composite Index) and almost four times the return of the peer group? This result was followed by a 47.2% loss in the latest year to mid-2001. Overweighting telecommunications and other technologies explains both the run-up and cascade in the fund's value. Overall, Paradis has a small number of high-growth stocks—less than 30—in the portfolio. The investment strategy makes the fund more aggressive, resulting in some stellar year-over-year numbers. But such a strategy also contributes to volatility and the latest terrible results explain why the fund got an E rating from Fundata and the lowest rating possible from *Globefund*. However, volatility is more tolerable when there is a guarantee on the fund's value, as is the case with seg funds. Overall, this is a high-risk fund and we are downgrading to a $$$ rating. The fund won the "Best Canadian Segregated Equity Fund" Analysts' Choice Award at the sixth annual Canadian Mutual Funds Award event in December 2000. It won't win this year.

## Canadian Balanced and Asset Allocation Funds

### TRANSAMERICA GROWSAFE CANADIAN BALANCED FUND    $$$ ↑ G/FI */NO RSP S CBAL

Manager: Mark Jackson, since 1998

MER: 2.37%     Fundata: D     Style: Top-down Momentum

Suitability: Aggressive investors

Mark Jackson took over this fund when Transamerica cleaned house in 1998. This fund has a strong growth bias. As of mid-2001, equities accounted for 55.9% of assets. The holdings are similar to those of the companion Canadian Equity Fund, with lots of technology issues and a small core group of less than 30 stocks. This mix generates higher risk than one would expect in a balanced fund. At mid-2001, bonds accounted for 43.5% of total assets and the investment mix was divided between federal and corporate issues. The bond component is more aggressive than the average balanced fund, but why not? You are paying for a guarantee—use it. Recent results have been reflective of this family—highly volatile. The fund had a 63.5% gain for the year ending June 30/00, well above the average for the peer group (13.4%) and the benchmark index (27.5%). The latest year spelled disaster, with a loss of 25.8% compared with 2.2% for the peer group. Three- to five-year returns are well above average. We are downgrading to a $$$ rating and warn potential investors that, in its current state, this is a very aggressive balanced fund. The fund won the "Best Canadian Segregated Balanced Fund" Analysts' Choice Award at the sixth annual Canadian Mutual Funds Award event in December 2000. It will not be a repeat winner.

## Also Recommended

None.

## Promising Newcomers

None.

# Labour-Sponsored
# Funds

*It's been an up-and-down few years for Canada's labour-sponsored venture capital funds. Just when they seemed to be headed into oblivion, Finance Minister Paul Martin breathed new life into them in the fall of 1998 with some improved tax incentives.*

Then the summer of 1999 brought a number of blockbuster deals that enriched unitholders in several of these funds, making them much more attractive as investment vehicles. Returns soared and by the time the 2000 RRSP season rolled around, investors could hardly wait to get in on the action.

The high-tech collapse of 2000–01 hit many of these funds hard, however. Losses were widespread, even among previous high flyers. The slump led to a cooling of investor interest as the heady gains of the late 1990s gave way to depressing negative returns of 25 percent and more in some cases. It's fortunate that these funds are a long-term hold (if you cash in before eight years you forfeit the tax credits), as most investors will ride out this setback. But it's painful nonetheless.

From the outset, the main attraction of these funds was the tax credits that came with them. At federal level, these credits amount to 15 percent of the value of your investment (up to $5,000 a year). So the maximum annual federal credit is $750. Some provinces, including Ontario, offer the same credit, while others, including Saskatchewan and Nova Scotia, limit the annual investment to $3,500, for a maximum provincial credit of $525. As a result, while the federal credit is consistent across Canada, we now have four levels of provincial tax credits for these funds, as follows:

1. 15% of $5,000, to a maximum of $750 a year (e.g., Ontario, New Brunswick)

2. 15% of $3,500, to a maximum of $525 a year (e.g., Nova Scotia, Saskatchewan)

3. 15% of $13,333 to a maximum of $2,000 a year (B.C. only)

4. No provincial credits (e.g., Alberta, Newfoundland, P.E.I.)

As if the tax credits for labour-sponsored venture capital funds weren't already attractive enough, the Ontario government added an extra sweetener that took effect for the 2000 tax year. The province created a special category of labour funds, known as research-oriented investment funds (ROIFs). To qualify, the fund has to invest a portion of its assets directly into projects being carried out by a university, college, research institute, or hospital. Investors in qualifying funds receive an extra 5 percent provincial credit, which is not to exceed $250 in any year (based on a maximum investment of $5,000). For qualifying funds, that brings the total tax credit in Ontario to 35 percent (20 percent provincial, 15 percent federal).

Only two funds met the ROIF criteria for the 2001 RRSP period: the New Generation Biotech Equity Fund from Triax and the Canadian Medical Discoveries Fund. However, eligibility is determined on a yearly basis, so if you live in Ontario, check which funds get this bonus before making your investment decision for the 2002 RRSP season.

There are several other wrinkles to labour fund investing that can be useful. One is the recent elimination of the three-year "cooling off" period. This was a rule that prevented anyone who redeemed shares in a labour fund from making a new purchase and claiming a tax credit within three years. The change is important, because people who bought units at a time when the holding period was five years (it is now eight) are now able to cash them in. Without a rule change, some funds were looking at potentially large redemptions. The prospect of a new tax credit may be enough to persuade a significant number of people ready to redeem to reinvest their money, either into the original fund they purchased or another one.

Another wrinkle is the foreign content bonus. The federal government allows shares in labour-sponsored funds that are held in RRSPs to be classified as qualifying small business assets for purposes of calculating allowable foreign content. This allowance means you can increase the foreign content in your RRSP to above the allowable limit if you hold any labour fund units; the additional allowable foreign content is three times the value of the labour fund assets. However, your total foreign content may not exceed 50 percent of your plan. For example, suppose you buy $5,000 worth of labour fund units for your RRSP. That purchase entitles you to an additional $15,000 in foreign content, over and above the limit. For investors who have large RRSPs and have been buying labour funds for some years, this could open up many thousands of dollars of foreign content room.

When this rule change was originally introduced, there was a three-month phasing-in period before it fully applied. That phase-in has now been eliminated and you can take advantage of the foreign content bonus immediately. To illustrate, a $350,000 (book value) RRSP would normally be limited to $105,000 in foreign content under the 30 percent rule. But if you've bought $22,000 worth of labour funds over the past five years, you will be able to add another $66,000, bringing your total foreign content maximum to $171,000, or 48.9 percent of your plan.

Two notes here. First, labour funds are not confined to RRSPs, but most people have been purchasing them that way. Second, you cannot purchase labour fund units directly for a registered retirement income fund (RRIF). However, if you hold units in your RRSP at the time it is converted to a RRIF, you may retain them.

## Tax Savings

The main attraction of labour-sponsored funds until recently was the tax credits. If you invest the maximum amount eligible for a tax credit into an RRSP, here's how the numbers will look for you, presuming a 50 percent marginal tax rate in a province where a provincial credit is available on the full amount:

| | |
|---|---|
| Amount invested: | $5,000 |
| Federal tax credit: | $750 |
| Provincial tax credit: | $750 |
| Cost before RRSP deduction: | $3,500 |
| RRSP deduction @ 50%: | $2,500 |
| Net cost: | $1,000 |

If you reside in a province that allows a 15 percent credit on only $3,500, here are your numbers, again using a 50 percent marginal rate:

| | |
|---|---|
| Amount invested: | $5,000 |
| Federal tax credit: | $750 |
| Provincial tax credit: | $525 |
| Cost before RRSP deduction: | $3,725 |
| RRSP deduction @ 50%: | $2,500 |
| Net cost: | $1,250 |

Of course, your tax bracket will be a major factor when you're deciding if labour-sponsored funds are a sensible investment choice. If you're in a 27 percent bracket, for example, the net cost of a $5,000 investment in a province where a combined $1,500 credit is available increases to $2,150 because the tax saving generated by the RRSP contribution is less for low-bracket taxpayers. If this is your situation, you should ask yourself if there are better investment choices available.

In cases where the labour-sponsored investment is made into a spousal RRSP, tax credits may now be claimed either by the contributor to the plan, or by the spouse (the plan's annuitant).

## Investment Performance

Until the late 1990s, the performance of labour-sponsored funds left much to be desired. The tax breaks were attractive, but the rates of return had been generally unimpressive. Entrepreneurial investments of this type often take several years to come to fruition, however. During the summer and fall of 1999, several megadeals were announced, resulting in big profits for a number of these funds. B.C.'s Working Opportunity Fund had to temporarily close its doors to new investors in the summer of 1999 when one of the companies in which it was a major share-holder announced a merger deal worth $440 million with a California-based firm. The windfall profit to the fund's unitholders was estimated at $100 million—this for a fund that previously had total assets of $235 million.

Covington I Fund also had to suspend sales in mid-1999 for the same rea-son: one of its holdings was involved in an Internet merger that was going to produce a big gain for unitholders when the deal closed. By mid-2000, some of the numbers posted by funds in this category were looking quite attractive. Some examples (all for the year to June 30, 2000) are as follows:

| Capital Alliance Ventures | +103.4% |
|---|---|
| Working Opportunity Balanced | + 79.1% |
| B.E.S.T. Discoveries | + 65.7% |
| Centerfire Growth | + 60.9% |
| VenGrowth I | + 55.8% |

The average one-year gain for all funds in the category came in at 34.5 percent.

But the collapse of the high-tech market brought a sudden end to much of the lucrative deal-making and the subsequent 12 months were pretty dismal ones for labour-sponsored funds. The average fund dropped 8.9 percent over the year to June 30, 2001. The top performer only gained 5.6 percent over that time. What a contrast! Neither of these years shows typical returns, however. The long-term prognosis for any fund lies somewhere in between the two extremes, although we can expect the occasional bonanza going forward.

Of course, being in a top-performing labour fund is something akin to winning the lottery: there is no way of predicting in advance where lightning is going to strike. As always, diversification is a good idea here. By spreading your money among the most promising funds, you improve your chances of being in on a big score.

The key point, however, is that labour-sponsored funds are now starting to demonstrate that they do have the capability to provide decent investment returns (in addition to tax credits) under the right conditions. This potential makes the selection process even more important. We want to find those managers with the best nose for picking the future winners. As we see more performance numbers, that process becomes a little easier.

## Labour Fund MERs

One thing you may notice when you look closely at labour funds is what appears to be very high management expense ratios (MERs). An MER includes the fees and costs assessed against a fund's assets, which come right out of the unitholder's pocket. Labour fund MERs have always been on the high side, but this situation has been exacerbated by a change in the way they're calculated. Some labour funds allow for manager performance bonuses if certain benchmarks are surpassed. In some cases, such as with the Capital Alliance Ventures Fund, these bonus fees are paid only once gains are realized within the portfolio, and then only when any losses have been subtracted. (To date the fund has paid no performance fees.)

The Ontario Securities Commission has ruled that any performance fees accrued must be reflected in the fund's MER, even though those fees may never be paid. As a result, the MERs of high-performance funds with these bonus provisions have shot up and will continue to increase as long as results remain strong. Conversely, if the fund suffers losses, the amount of money held in reserve for performance fees will decline and so will the MER.

This reporting rule creates an unusual situation where a fund's low MER may actually be telling a negative story, rather than a positive one. So don't allow a high MER to influence your choice of a labour-sponsored fund—it may actually mean that the fund is doing extremely well.

## What to Look For

If you are considering an investment in labour-sponsored funds, here are some of the issues to look at:

SEE WHAT TAX CREDITS THE FUND QUALIFIES FOR All funds get the federal tax credit, but they all won't necessarily get a provincial tax credit. Some provinces offer no provincial tax credits at all; others (like Quebec, Manitoba, and B.C.) restrict them to just one or two provincially sponsored funds. Ask before you invest.

ASK IF THE FUND IS ELIGIBLE FOR DIRECT RRSP PURCHASE. Some investors have adopted a strategy of buying labour-sponsored funds inside an RRSP, using "old" money to generate a tax credit outside the plan. This can be done with no problem in provinces like Ontario, but the rules are different across the country. If you're interested in this approach, ask a sales rep if it is allowed where you live.

REMEMBER THAT THE CREDITS CAN REDUCE YOUR TAX ONLY TO ZERO. The tax credits generated by labour-sponsored funds aren't refundable. So if you don't owe enough tax to make full use of them, you won't get the maximum benefit from this strategy.

**RECOGNIZE THAT THE UNITS CARRY ABOVE-AVERAGE RISK.** The mandate of all these funds is to invest in small-to-medium-sized companies that are usually not publicly traded. Such companies may have above-average growth potential, but they also incur a higher risk than more established firms. Also, as a result of previous deals, some funds may find themselves with a significant portion of their portfolio in publicly traded shares. This kind of scenario can materialize when a previously private company in which the fund has invested goes public. Often under the terms of such an arrangement, the fund is required to retain part or all of its position for a certain amount of time, ensuring that a large block of shares isn't dumped into the market, depressing the price of the fledgling company. Another source of public shares is the takeover of a private company in the portfolio by a firm that is already public in a share-swap deal. Triax Growth is an example of a fund with a large percentage of publicly traded stock. As a result, it was especially vulnerable to the collapse in the high-tech market and lost 38.5 percent in the year to June 30, 2001.

**DON'T FORGET THAT YOU CAN'T GET YOUR MONEY OUT.** All labour-sponsored funds have a minimum holding period of eight years. If you take your money out early, you'll have to repay your tax credits, up to 30 percent of the value of your total investment! There are no exceptions to this eight-year rule. Consequently, these funds are not suitable for people who are likely to need access to their cash within eight years.

**LOOK AT THE TRACK RECORD.** These funds have now been around long enough to establish an investment history, some of which are much more impressive than others. Big scores are always great, but you'll do better to focus on those funds that have shown the ability to produce above-average gains consistently, with minimal risk. Diversification is a good strategy if you live in a province where several funds are available. Ontario residents are especially blessed in this regard, as they have the widest range of funds available to them. There's no way of knowing which funds will perform best over the long term, so instead of putting all your money into just one, spread it around among three or four.

By the way, in case you're wondering why these funds are denoted "labour-sponsored," it's because each one has to be sponsored by a trade union. Sponsorship is basically political window-dressing, and in most cases it doesn't have any impact on how the money is invested.

Here is a rundown of the labour-sponsored funds now available. Only those with a three-year record have a rating. "NR" in the legend means the fund doesn't yet qualify for a rating. As a group, these funds have a higher-than-average risk factor because of their venture capital approach. The risk rating for each fund ($\downarrow$ for low, $\rightarrow$ for medium, and $\uparrow$ for high) is relative to other funds of this type, not to the total fund universe.

# FUND RATINGS

## B.E.S.T. DISCOVERIES FUND $$$ ↑ G #/* RSP LAB

Managers: John M.A. Richardson and Alan Huycke, since inception (1996)

MER: 7.16%      Fundata: C      Style: Growth

B.E.S.T. stands for Business, Engineering, Science, and Technology. Those categories give you the focus of this fund in a nutshell. The managers use a number of criteria to evaluate companies, including competitiveness, growth potential, past performance, and senior staff. The portfolio includes companies in various stages of development, with an emphasis on technology. The fund got off to a slow start but did very well in 1999 and 2000, with gains of 34.7% and 18.6%, respectively. The first half of 2001 was a tough period, however; the high-tech market crumbled and the fund gave back 12.6%. Still, its three-year average annual compound rate of return of 11.5% to June 30/01 is very good. Because of its high-tech emphasis, this fund may be more volatile than some of the other entries in the labour category. Keep that detail in mind if you're considering this fund. Minimum investment is $1,000. Sold in Ontario only, through brokerage firms and financial planners. Call 1-800-795-2378 or (416) 214-4616 for information. You can also visit the Web site: **www.bestcapital.ca**.

## CANADIAN MEDICAL DISCOVERIES FUND $$ → G #/* RSP LAB

Manager: Dr. Calvin Stiller, since 1995

MER: 4.80%      Fundata: D      Style: Bottom-up Growth

When this fund was first launched, many investors thought it would be one of the best prospects in the labour-sponsored universe. It operates in an area of rapid growth (medical technology) and the principals are extremely well connected in the medical world (the chairman and CEO, Dr. Calvin Stiller, is a renowned physician and scientist, one of Canada's leaders in the field of organ transplants, and the co-founder of Diversicare). The fund also has the advantage of being associated with MDS, the leading medical services company in Canada. So far, however, the fund has not lived up to its potential. Its five-year average annual compound rate of return to June 30/01 was a tiny 1.4%. We're still waiting for this fund to make a major breakthrough, which could happen at any time considering one of the main areas of investment is the hot field of biotechnology. The good news is that the downside risk here is somewhat less than in other funds of this type. The portfolio is well diversified, with all kinds of potentially promising medical ventures ranging from cancer therapies to diagnostic procedures for detecting Alzheimer's disease. This is one of the few labour-sponsored funds that is available across the country. Residents of Ontario, Saskatchewan, Nova Scotia, and New Brunswick who buy these units qualify for a provincial tax credit as well as a federal one. In all other provinces, only a federal credit is available. As well, the fund qualified for the bonus 5% Ontario research credit in 2001. The fund is distributed by Talvest and is available through brokers and financial planners. Call 1-800-268-8258 for more information, or consult a broker or planner. You can find out more at the Web site: **www.cmdf.com**.

## CANADIAN SCIENCE & TECHNOLOGY GROWTH FUND $$$ → G * RSP LAB

Managers: Peter Day, Paul Johnson, and Glen Smeltze (Technology Investments Management Corporation)

MER: 5.50%    Fundata: A    Style: Growth

Here the managers seek investment opportunities in the technology sector, working in partnership with the National Research Council, the Natural Sciences and Engineering Research Council of Canada, and the Canadian Space Agency. The fund also benefits from a blue ribbon advisory board that includes some of the top names in Canada's research community. The fund managers stated in the 2000 annual report that they had not yet achieved an exit from any of their positions. This revelation may be a key reason behind the fund's turning in the best record in the category over the year to June 30/01, with a gain of 5.6%. Also contributing to this success was the strong performance of one of the few publicly traded companies in the portfolio, Xplore Technologies. The fund invested about $1 million in the company, which produces computerized products for use in the field (e.g., police forces). Over the past three years, the average annual compound rate of return is a very good 12.8%. Even more impressive is the fact that we have not seen any big losses here so far. Available nationally. Minimum initial investment is $1,000. A provincial tax credit is available to investors in Ontario, Saskatchewan, New Brunswick, and Nova Scotia. The units are distributed by Talvest and are sold through brokers and financial planners. Call 1-800-268-0081 for more information. The fund also has its own Web site: **www.cstgf.com**.

## CAPITAL ALLIANCE VENTURES INC. $$$ → G * RSP LAB

Manager: Richard Charlebois, since inception (1994)

MER: 4.80%    Fundata: B    Style: Growth

This is another fund that specializes in technology issues, with special emphasis on companies in the Ottawa area, where it is based and where most of the shareholders live. The fund's original goal was to reach $75 million in assets and then close the doors to new money. But as of mid-2001, it was well past that target with some $84 million in assets and no one was saying anything about closing up shop. You can understand why when you look at the returns. Despite its focus on the volatile high-tech area, the fund has performed very well. Investors enjoyed a gain of 23.4% in 1999, followed by a big 41.7% advance in 2000.

The fund managed to hold its own in the first half of 2001, a notable accomplishment in the face of the high-tech collapse. The founders obviously knew that Ottawa would be a high-tech hotbed long before the rest of Canada did, and they've cleaned up for their investors as a result. The fund is available through brokers and financial planners in Ontario, with a minimum initial investment of $500. Call 1-800-304-2330 for additional details. There is also information on the Web site: **www.cavi.com**.

## CENTERFIRE GROWTH FUND                    $$ ↑ G * RSP LAB

Managers: Normand Lamarche and Gary Selke (Tuscarora Capital), since inception (1996)

MER: 7.00%     Fundata: E     Style: Growth

This fund invests in a broad range of industries (no sector focus here) with strong growth potential and with what is known in the venture capital business as a clear "exit strategy." This term refers to the manager's ability to foresee a way of cashing in on an investment and taking profits within a reasonable period of time. This result can be achieved by taking the company public or selling the fund's interest to a third party. Norm Lamarche is a former Altamira fund manager, so he has experience running this type of operation. The plan is to cap this fund when it reaches $50 million, which is a long way off (it was at only $12.7 million in mid-2001). By limiting the number of investments, the managers feel they can concentrate more effectively on improving performance. Initial results were so-so, but that's what you'd expect from a start-up venture fund. But then things started to jell and the fund scored a big advance of 60.9% over the 12 months to June 30/00, thanks to handsome gains in positions in Indian Motorcycle Co. and World Heart Corporation. Unfortunately, the fall of the high-tech sector took its toll here and the fund dropped 13.9% in the subsequent 12 months to June 30/01. Still, the average annual compound rate of return of 11% over three years is quite respectable. We're maintaining this fund's $$ rating (it has had only one good year, after all) while we see if any clear-cut pattern develops. Available only in Ontario. StrategicNova acts as distributor. Call 1-888-777-2949 or (416) 777-0707 for information. There is also information offered on the Web site: **www.centerfirecapital.com**.

## COVINGTON FUND I                    $$ → G * RSP LAB

Managers: Grant Brown and Chip Vallis, since inception (1999)

MER: 4.72%     Fundata: E     Style: Disciplined Diversification

This labour-sponsored venture capital fund is now closed to new investors. However, you can purchase units in Covington II, which has replaced it. This fund did very well a year ago, but suffered a huge setback in the year to June 30/01, dropping slightly more than 30% as some of its key technology holdings were battered. As a result, the three-year average annual return fell to a weak 2.6%. However, we expect to see this fund pull out of its nosedive. Co-manager Grant Brown has a sound reputation in the venture capital business and Chip Vallis brings a wealth of experience. If you have units in this fund that have exceeded the mandatory holding period, you may wish to remain invested, although the risk is higher here than with Covington II, which has a larger cash position at this time. Conversely, the reward potential here is greater if markets rebound. It's a judgment call, with your risk tolerance as the determining factor.

## COVINGTON FUND II                               NR → G * RSP LAB

Managers: Grant Brown and Chip Vallis, since inception (2000)

MER: 4.65%     Fundata: N/A     Style: Disciplined Diversification

This is the fund that replaced Covington I when it was capped. Due to the time it takes for venture capital investments to mature, we expect it will be a couple of years before investors start to see much in the way of returns with this fund. Its newness worked to investors' advantage when the high-tech market took a dive; a large percentage of this fund's assets were in cash, cushioning it from the fall. In fact, the fund actually managed to record a small gain of 1.1% in the 12 months to June 30/01. We expect that, over time, it will show similar characteristics to Covington I. The fund is available in Ontario only. For more information call 1-888-746-4751 or visit the Web site: **www.covington.ca**.

## CROCUS INVESTMENT FUND                         $$ ↓ G NO RSP LAB

Manager: James Umlah, since 1995

MER: 3.54%     Fundata: E     Style: Balanced, with a Growth Bias

This fund was created to promote industrial development in Manitoba and is open only to residents of that province. It does not limit itself to any specific sector of the economy. The fund has been quite successful in raising money from its limited base ($172 million to date). Performance had been among the best in the labour category until some other funds scored huge coups, pushing their numbers to the sky. Over the most recent 12 months to June 30/01, the fund posted a loss of 9.7%, slightly worse than average for the category. The main contributor to the drop was the bankruptcy of one of its holdings, Isobord Enterprises, which represented an investment of more than $7 million. The decline pulled longer-term results down below par as well. The fund invests in a wide range of Manitoba-based businesses, from clothing stores to auto body shops to video production firms. These holdings give the fund a kind of mom-and-pop feel that no other labour-sponsored fund can offer. Units can be purchased through brokers, some mutual fund dealers, credit unions, and directly from Crocus Capital. Minimum initial investment is just $250. Call 1-800-361-7777 or (204) 925-7777 for more details. You can also visit the Web site: **www.crocusfund.com**.

## CROWN VENTURES FUND INC. NR → G * RSP LAB

Manager: Crown Capital Management Inc., since inception (2001)

MER: 6.00%     Fundata: N/A     Style: Growth

This brand-new fund is available only to residents of Saskatchewan. It was just launched in March 2001, so we have no track record to go by so far. To the end of July 2001, it had attracted about $6.5 million in investments. The management company is a joint venture between Prairie Financial Management and a subsidiary of Crown Life. Minimum initial investment is $500. For information call (306) 791-4833.

## DGC ENTERTAINMENT VENTURES CORP. $ → G * RSP LAB

Manager: EVC Management Inc., since inception (1993)

MER: 5.60%     Fundata: A     Style: Growth

This fund invests in the exciting world of movies, television, the Internet, pop music, and just about any other entertainment venture you can think of. Performance is weak; the five-year average annual compound rate of return of 2.9% to June 30/01 is well below average for the category. The fund is closed to new investors.

## DYNAMIC VENTURE OPPORTUNITIES FUND $$$ ↑ G * RSP LAB

Manager: Ray Benzinger (Dundee Investment Management), since 1996

MER: 5.22%     Fundata: B     Style: Growth

This fund began life as the Integrated Growth Fund but was a sad performer in that guise, recording big losses for investors. But the fund has looked much better since Ray Benzinger of Dundee Investment Management took it over in 1996. Since that time, it has had one of the best records in the category. Although it was on the losing side in the first half of 2001, the performance was still above average as several of its competitors suffered double-digit declines. The portfolio is quite well diversified, with positions ranging from biotech firms like Dimethaid Research, which is developing treatments to reduce drug side effects, to PetHealth, which is in the pet insurance business. Over the 18 months to June 30/00, investors more than doubled their money here. They've given a little back since, but we doubt they're complaining. This has become a more attractive labour fund today than it was a few years ago. Available only in Ontario through brokers and financial planners. Minimum investment is $500. Call 1-888-527-4811 for information.

## ENSIS GROWTH FUND  $ \rightarrow$ G * RSP LAB

Managers: O. Kenneth Bicknell, William E. Watchorn, Jenifer A. Bartman, and Steven W. Stang (ENSIS Management Ltd.)

MER: 4.68%     Fundata: D     Style: Growth

This is Manitoba's second venture capital fund, competing with the province's original Crocus Fund. The fund invests in small-to-medium-sized businesses based in the province and favours companies with high-value-added products or services. No specific area is targeted; the managers will look at companies in all sectors of the economy. The company that oversees the money, ENSIS Management, was once named as one of Canada's 50 best privately managed companies by the *Financial Post*. Results so far have not been very exciting, with a three-year average annual compound rate of return of –1.1% to June 30/01. About the best that can be said about the fund is that it hasn't had any big losses. For information call 1-800-937-5146.

## FIRST ONTARIO FUND  $ \downarrow$ G * RSP LAB

Managers: Venture Portfolio: First Ontario Management and Crosbie Capital Management, since 1995; Liquid Portfolio: Co-operators Investment Counselling, since 1995

MER: 6.52% (Traditional Shares)  Fundata: C     Style: Value
    7.19% (Growth Shares)

This fund has expanded through mergers; it absorbed the Trillium Fund and the FESA Enterprise Fund in 1999. As a result, total assets under management have increased to $65.3 million, which is a lot for a fund that hasn't come up with the same big scores as many of its competitors. Neither was it a heavy loser in the first half of 2001, however, when many funds in this category were pulled down by their high-tech holdings. What sets this fund apart from other labour-sponsored choices is its commitment to socially responsible investing. That mandate makes First Ontario the labour fund of choice for Ontario residents who want to put their money into companies that are committed to environmental protection, good labour relations, and community support. It would be nice if those noble objectives were accompanied by great returns, but that has not been the case. The best one-year gain was a mere 5.6% in 1998. There are two types of units available. Class A shares (Traditional Shares) invest 75% of the assets in venture capital businesses and 25% in liquid reserves (bonds and cash), reducing risk. The newer Class B shares (Growth Shares) invest that extra 25% in index-linked securities that track the TSE. So when the Canadian stock market is strong, you'll get an extra boost. When it drops, however, the Class B shares will suffer, which is exactly what happened in the first half of 2001 when the Growth Shares dropped almost twice as much as the Traditional Shares. It's a matter of trading off higher potential returns for greater risk—the classic investment dilemma. Sold in Ontario only. Call 1-800-777-7506 or (416) 487-5444 for details. You can also visit the Web site: **www.firstontariofund.com**.

## GOLDEN OPPORTUNITIES FUND    NR → G * RSP LAB

Manager: Doug W. Banzet, Grant J. Kook, and Trevor S. Giles (Westcap Mgt. Ltd.), since inception (1998)

MER: 5.46%    Fundata: C    Style: Growth

This is Saskatchewan's original indigenous labour-sponsored fund and if you're a resident of the province you might take a look at it, if for no other reason than it qualifies for an extra tax break. Most labour-sponsored funds get only a 15% provincial tax credit on a $3,500 investment in Saskatchewan. But this one qualifies for a 20% credit on an investment up to $5,000. On top of the federal 15% credit, that works out to a 35% tax write-off—very attractive! This small ($15 million) fund got off to a good start, with a gain of 12.1% in 2000. And it managed to hold its own in the first half of 2001, when many labour funds were being clobbered. The portfolio holds positions in companies dealing in everything from real estate to grain elevators, although most of the assets (73%) were in cash in the summer of 2001. For more information, call (306) 652-5557.

## QUEBEC SOLIDARITY FUND    $$ ↓ G/FI * RSP LAB

Manager: Raymond Bachand, since April 1997

MER: 2.00%    Fundata: N/A    Style: Growth

This is the oldest and biggest of the labour-sponsored venture capital funds, with assets of more than $2.7 billion in mid-1999 (we were not able to secure any more recent information about this fund). Unlike most funds in this category, Quebec Solidarity is a balanced fund with a significant portion of the assets in bonds. Unfortunately, details about this fund are hard to obtain since they don't report to any of the tracking companies as far as we can determine. Open only to residents of Quebec. Investments can be politically motivated at times. The risk factor here is lessened by the size of the fund, which allows for greater diversification.

## RETROCOMM GROWTH FUND    $ ↓ FI/G * RSP LAB

Manager: J. Roger Keane, since 2001

MER: 4.17%    Fundata: A    Style: Growth through Convertible Debt

The focus of this fund is the construction industry, but it also will invest in firms involved with energy conservation and the environment. Investments are mainly in the private sector, with very few publicly traded companies held. You'll find a lot of real estate in this portfolio, like industrial parks and shopping malls. The fund is conservatively managed to keep risk low. Investments are generally made by way of convertible debentures (debt that can be converted to equity). This fund has never had a big year; its largest 12-month gain was 5.2% in 1997. Conversely, it doesn't get clobbered in falling markets. While many of its competitors suffered double-digit losses when stock markets were weak in the first half of 2001, this fund just about broke even. Still, that performance doesn't add up to very impressive long-term numbers. If safety is your priority, then this is one of the few labour-sponsored funds that fit the bill. But if you're looking for above-average returns, don't expect to find them here. The fund is steady and low-risk, sure, but it's not very exciting. In mid-2000, the assets of Sportfund were merged into this fund. Retrocomm Growth is now available in Ontario, Nova Scotia, and New Brunswick, with registration pending in Saskatchewan. Check with a broker or financial planner in your area or call 1-888-743-5627 for more information. You can also visit the Web site: **www.rgfjobs.com**.

## TRIAX GROWTH FUND                                $ ↑ G * RSP LAB

Managers: Alex Sasso and Stephen Masson (Altamira), since 1999

MER: 4.97%      Fundata: E       Style: Growth

This fund was an immediate hit with investors when it was launched just in time for the 1996 RRSP season. The dual attraction was the reputation of original manager Susan Coleman and the fund's stated intention to focus on companies that already had a public listing or would soon be in a position to come out with an IPO. The result was an astonishing inflow of $135 million within six weeks of the fund's launch. But that flood of money was reduced to a trickle for a time; the fund's assets stood at $200 million in mid-1999. The slowdown reversed when performance picked up. The fund gained 42.8% in the year to June 30/00 and, not surprisingly, assets soared to just under $360 million. But now the hard times are back. The fund lost 38.5% in the 12 months to June 30/01, and assets tumbled to $234 million as a result. So this fund has turned out to be either a feast or a famine for investors. If you were in at the start, the net result is just about break-even over five years (not counting the tax credits, of course). The collapse of the high-tech sector hit this fund especially hard because a large percentage of its holdings are publicly traded. In fact, one of the top 10 holdings entering 2001 was Nortel Networks, which represented 3% of the portfolio. The Nortel shares were acquired when that company purchased Architel, an original fund investment. The deal produced a good profit at the time, but Nortel shares subsequently tumbled, contributing to the fund's recent losses. Such are the hazards of labour fund investing! One advantage this fund does offer is wide distribution; it is now available in all parts of the country except Saskatchewan, but only residents of Ontario, Nova Scotia, and New Brunswick can claim a provincial tax credit in addition to the federal credit. For more information call 1-800-407-0287 or visit the Triax Web site: **www.triaxcapital.com**.

## TRIAX NEW GENERATION BIOTECH FUND    NR ↑ G * RSP LAB

Managers: Kelly Holman and Damian Lamb, since inception (2000)

MER: 4.25%    Fundata: N/A    Style: Growth

If you want to put some of your labour-sponsored fund money into the cutting-edge biotech sector, this is the fund for you. It's a newcomer, launched by Triax for the 2001 RRSP season, so we don't have much of a track record for judging it at this stage. There are actually two classes of shares within the fund. The Balanced Shares take a more conservative approach, investing about 65% of the assets in stripped bonds to protect investors' principal. The rest is invested in Community Small Business Investment Funds, which in turn invest in companies with assets of $1 million or less. The Equity Shares invest at least 70% of their capital directly into companies that meet the fund's mandate and comply with the guidelines of Ontario's new Research Oriented Investment Funds programme. That action makes these shares higher in risk, but also qualifies them for a bonus 5% tax credit if you're an Ontario resident. If you're considering investing in this fund, study the two classes of shares carefully. They are quite different and will likely produce very different returns over the long haul. Conservative investors should choose the Balanced Shares, while those willing to accept more risk for greater potential return may opt for the Equity Shares.

## TRIAX NEW MILLENNIUM VENTURES FUND    NR ↑ G * RSP LAB

Manager: Rod Baker (New Millennium Venture Partners), since January 2000

MER: 5.98%    Fundata: N/A    Style: Growth

This fund must have seemed like a great idea when it was launched in November 1999. The high-tech craze was in full flight and Internet stocks were booming. How times have changed! These days, attracting new money into an Internet-based fund must be a very tough slog for the folks at Triax. Actually, performance has been a lot better than you might expect under the circumstances. The fund managed to almost break even over the year to June 30/01, a pretty decent accomplishment in light of the high-tech meltdown. The manager delayed making the bulk of his investments until late 2000, by which time there were some very good values available in Internet and e-commerce companies. It may take a while for these investments to pay off, but so far at least, investors haven't had to face big losses. There were originally two types of shares offered, but the Balanced Series was discontinued after February 29, 2000. Only the higher-risk Venture Shares are now available. The risk element here is clearly very high, but younger, more aggressive investors may be attracted by the potential for above-average long-term growth. The fund is currently available in Ontario only. Minimum initial investment is $500. For more information call 1-800-407-0287 or visit the Triax Capital Web site: **www.triaxcapital.com**.

## VENGROWTH I INVESTMENT FUND $$ → G * RSP LAB

Managers: Earl Storie, David Ferguson, Allen Lupyrypa, and Michael Cohen, since inception (1999)

MER: 4.50%     Fundata: D     Style: Growth

For several years we singled out this fund as being one of the better bets in the crowded labour-sponsored funds marketplace. Hopefully you got in on it because now it is too late. The fund was closed to new investors in December 1999, and was replaced by a new fund, VenGrowth II. If you did invest and still hold your units, you may be feeling a bit unhappy right now; after five consecutive profitable years, this fund took a big hit in the first part of 2001, dropping 24% by mid-August. However, let's keep matters in perspective: despite that setback, the fund showed an average annual compound rate of return of 10.1% for the five years to June 30/01. Combined with the tax credits, it's been a pretty good long-term investment. The portfolio is quite large, with a heavy emphasis on technology and communications, which explains the recent poor results. We expect better things from this fund as the stock markets improve and recommend holding on to your units.

## VENGROWTH II INVESTMENT FUND NR ↓ G * RSP LAB

Managers: Earl Storie, David Ferguson, Allen Lupyrypa, and Michael Cohen, since inception (1999)

MER: 2.00%     Fundata: N/A     Style: Growth

This is the new fund currently on offer from VenGrowth. The management team is well experienced in the venture capital field (they've been in the business since 1982) and they bring a highly disciplined approach to the difficult task of analyzing the profit potential of small operations. They have also proven that they know how to successfully manage funds of this type. Like the first fund, this one focuses on privately held small- and medium-sized leading edge businesses in growth or expansion stages. The managers like companies that are already up and running, with annual sales of at least $3 million. That preference reduces the investment risk to some extent and increases the possibility of an early, profitable exit from their positions. As of mid-2001, a large percentage of the assets were still in cash, which greatly reduced the fund's exposure to falling stock markets. The units are distributed through brokers and financial planners in Ontario only. Call 1-800-387-0614 for more information or visit the Web site: **www.vengrowth.com**.

## VENTURELINK FUND                                    NR → G NO RSP LAB

Managers: Leon Rudanycz and Susan Coleman, since inception (March 2001)

MER: 3.50%     Fundata: N/A     Style: Growth

This new fund features the return to active management of Sue Coleman, previously with Altamira and the original manager of the Triax Growth Fund. The fund invests primarily in technology companies. It is too new to have any meaningful track record. Available in Ontario only. Minimum initial investment is $500. Call 1-877-711-2440 for more information.

## WORKING OPPORTUNITY FUND                          $$$ → G NO RSP LAB

Manager: GrowthWorks Capital Ltd.

MER: 2.40%     Fundata: N/A     Style: Growth

This is a labour-sponsored venture capital fund that's available exclusively to British Columbia residents. The investment focus is on B.C.-based industries in the biotechnology, manufacturing, high-tech, tourism, and knowledge-based sectors. To be eligible, a firm must have less than $50 million in assets and be 80% located in B.C., with at least half the salaries and wages paid to B.C. employees. The fund had a slow start and returns in the early years were low because most of the assets were held in short-term notes while investment opportunities were reviewed. The fund lost 3.9% over the 12 months to June 30/99, but then blew out the lights with a huge 79.1% advance in the subsequent 12 months. That growth pulled all the longer-term results to above average. The main reason for the big gain: one of the fund's holdings, HotHaus Technologies of Vancouver, merged with Broadcom Corporation of Irvine, California in a deal valued at $414 million. Working Opportunity was a major shareholder of HotHaus, and realized a profit of more than $100 million for the fund and its unitholders. This is the kind of elephant deal that all venture funds look for, which can drive up the returns dramatically overnight. Working Opportunity was temporarily closed to new investors in mid-1999 so that people couldn't jump in while the price was still cheap and benefit from the huge windfall. The fund is now open again. Due to a recent development, investors now have the choice between two types of shares. The Balanced Shares invest in a portfolio that includes a percentage of fixed-income assets to reduce risk. The Growth Shares hold a portfolio of venture investments, Canadian public equities, and regular and index-linked debt securities. The Growth Shares thus offer greater profit potential, but with more risk, as was demonstrated over the year to June 30/01, when they declined by 8.6% while the Balanced Shares finished with a fractional profit. In another recent move, the outgoing NDP B.C. government raised the limit on the amount of shares the fund can sell each year to $100 million. It had been raised from $60 million to $80 million the previous year, but continues to sell out annually. Sold by brokers and planners throughout B.C. Call 1-800-563-3863 or (604) 688-9631 for details, or visit the Web site: **www.wofund.com**.

## WORKING VENTURES CANADIAN FUND $ ↑ G * RSP LAB

Managers: Ron Begg and Jim Hall, since inception (1989) and Don Morrison and Jim Whitaker, since 1995.

MER: 4.90%     Fundata: E     Style: Growth

This was the first labour-sponsored fund to be offered outside a single province, and money came flooding in faster than anyone could have imagined. However, assets have declined considerably in recent years and now stand at about $420 million. The fund invests in a wide range of businesses across Canada, from golf courses to packaging companies. Unfortunately, it has never been a particularly strong performer and was socked particularly hard in the year to June 30/01 when it plunged more than 33%. That weak performance pulled down its 10-year average annual return to barely above break-even, at just 0.3%—not good. Thank goodness for the tax breaks! This is one of the few funds available throughout Canada. However, provincial tax credits are available only in Ontario, New Brunswick, Nova Scotia, and Saskatchewan. Call (416) 922-5479 for information or visit the Web site: **www.workingventures.ca**. Distribution duties have moved to AGF.

## WORKING VENTURES II TECHNOLOGY FUND NR → G * RSP LAB

Managers: Ron Begg, Jim Hall, Don Morrison, and Jim Whitaker, since inception (2001)

MER: N/A     Fundata: N/A     Style: Growth

This fund is a new addition to the Working Ventures family, and was launched in January 2001. It focuses on start-up technology companies, particularly in areas like e-commerce, the Internet, semi-conductors, communications, software, and services. It has the advantage of starting up at a time when such companies are cheap as a result of the tech meltdown, which could lead to a "buy low, sell high" situation. At least that's what the managers and investors hope for. We'll see. This management team has not done particularly well with the original Working Ventures Canadian Fund, which has barely broken even over the past decade. Unlike Working Ventures, this one is sold only in Ontario. It's also distributed by AGF.

# The Top Small Funds

*In this year's Guide, we have focused primarily on the larger fund companies. However, there are a number of small funds that deserve a mention—and your attention— because of their long-term performance, special nature, safety record, or other factors. Only funds with at least a three-year track record are included.*

Here are the ones we recommend:

## Canadian Equity Funds

### CHOU RRSP FUND $$$$ ↓ G # RSP CE

Manager: Francis Chou, since inception (1986)

MER: 2.12%      Fundata: A      Style: Value

Suitability: Conservative investors

Manager Francis Chou holds a senior position with Fairfax Financial and runs this and the companion Chou Associates Fund more or less in his spare time. The funds grew out of an investment club and are very small (this one has assets of just $5 million). They're available only in Ontario. But those few people who own units are very glad that they do. Chou is a dedicated value manager who absolutely refuses to overpay for a stock. This mandate means he did not participate in the tech boom and consequently, he avoided the tech bust. One comment he made to unitholders sums up his views: "Paying 500 times for hot air is not an investment, it's pure speculation." This fund focuses on companies with sound fundamentals, many of which will be unfamiliar to most investors. No matter—it's results that count and this fund delivers. One-year return to June 30/01 was 24.3%. Long-term results are equally impressive; over the past decade the fund has averaged 13.6% annually, putting it in the top 10 performers in the big Canadian Equity category. One other thing you should know about the manager: he is a unique person. When the fund was underperforming in 1994 and 1995, he waived the management fees, refusing to accept any payment for what he regarded as poor results. It was a matter of "fairness and honour," he told unitholders. He also reduced his fee in 1999 due to the weak performance. That's the kind of management approach this industry needs to see more of. We are moving the rating up to $$$$ in recognition of this fund's very fine long-term performance. It's too bad Chou RRSP is not more widely available. Call (416) 299-6749 for more information. Minimum initial investment is $25,000.

## CO-OPERATORS CANADIAN CONSERVATIVE FOCUSED EQUITY FUND     $$$ ↓ G #/* RSP CE

Manager: George L. Frazer (Leon Frazer, Black and Associates Ltd.), since April 1976

MER: 2.56% Fundata: B  Style: Top-down/Blend

Suitability: Conservative investors

Here we have a new name for an old fund. Mutual fund buffs will remember it as the Associate Investors Fund, and it has a history of more than half a century under the management of the same house: Leon Frazer, Black and Associates. It has always been a solid, low-risk performer and it is especially well suited to the current investment climate. It is coming off a very strong year, with a gain of almost 32% in 2000, placing it at the top of the list in its category. The first half of 2001 was pretty well a break-even situation, a good showing in a down market. The portfolio is very blue-chip oriented, with an emphasis on Old Economy stocks in mid-2001. In a letter to investors, the management team said they were targeting companies with good earnings, book values, and steady dividends. There were several banks in the top 10 holdings along with companies like BCE, Enbridge, Canadian Utilities, and TransCanada PipeLines. There is no foreign content. Not many people know about this fund, but it's a worthwhile entry for conservative investors. Safety record is very good. This used to be a no-load fund but it is now sold on an optional front- or back-end load basis through investment advisors. For more information call 1-866-866-2635 or visit the Co-operators Mutual Funds Web site: **www.cmfl.ca**.

## THE GOODWOOD FUND     $$$ → G * CE

Manager: Peter Puccetti, since inception (1996)

MER: 1.97%     Fundata: A     Style: Bottom-up Value

Suitability: Experienced long-term investors

This is a fund for "sophisticated" investors, hence the high entry fee (as much as $150,000 depending on your province of residence). Manager Peter Puccetti will take short positions in the portfolio as well as going long on stocks, to reduce market risk. In mid-2001, 74% of the portfolio was long, 12% was short, and the rest was in cash. Performance has been spectacular. The fund shows a three-year average annual compound rate of return of 34.4% to June 30/01. The relatively few investors who went in at the start must be delighted with their good fortune! Puccetti's stated goal is to achieve an average annual return of 20%, so he's way ahead of target so far. He takes concentrated positions in just a few stocks, so performance very much depends on his selection ability. So far, he's pulled the right strings. Few people know about this fund, but if you have the spare change lying around, take a look at it. Otherwise, check out the new Goodwood Capital Fund, which only requires an initial minimum of $5,000. It has performed very well but has not been in existence long enough to qualify for a rating. For more information call (416) 203-2022 or visit the Web site: **www.goodwoodfunds.com**.

## MCELVAINE INVESTMENT TRUST $$$$ → G NO RSP CE

Manager: Tim McElvaine, since inception (October 1996)

MER: 1.60%     Fundata: A     Style: Value

Suitability: Long-term conservative investors, willing to accept some risk

The manager of this fund wears several hats. Tim McElvaine is also chief investment officer of the Mackenzie Cundill funds and is one of the managers responsible for the Mackenzie Cundill Value Fund. In effect, he runs this fund on the side and does a heck of a job with it. As you might expect from a manager associated with Peter Cundill, his style is value-oriented. He puts a lot of emphasis on finding a "margin of safety" when making investment decisions. In other words, he seeks to limit risk wherever possible. The numbers tell you how well he has done: this fund has generated double-digit profits in every year of its existence. It even managed a double-digit gain in the first half of 2001, when markets everywhere were sliding. The three-year average annual compound rate of return to June 30/01 was 21.9%, placing it in the top spot in the Canadian Equity category. Low risk and high return—it doesn't get any better than that! However, investors should be aware that McElvaine will take big bets on individual companies, a practice that has the potential to backfire if he makes a bad pick. For example, in the first half of 2001, Mattel Inc. shares accounted for 16.2% of the portfolio, while Fairfax Financial was 11% and Rainmaker Entertainment 10.1%. So far this approach has not hurt results, but we have to rate the fund as medium risk because of it. That said, you can't quarrel with the returns. The only problem is that the Trust is available only by offering memorandum, which means you need a hefty $150,000 to get in. For more information, call (604) 685-4275.

## TWENTY-FIRST CENTURY CANADIAN EQUITY FUND

**$$$ → G NO RSP CE**

Manager: Joel Raby (Magna Vista Capital), since inception (July 1997)

MER: 1.40%    Fundata: N/A    Style: Value

Suitability: Conservative investors

This large-cap Canadian stock fund is available only by offering memorandum, which means you'll need $150,000 to get in. What you'll get is a conservatively run portfolio with lots of bank stocks plus names like BCE, Power Corp., Alcan, and Thomson. Results have been good; the fund returned just over 22% in both 1999 and 2000, and hovered around break-even in the first half of 2001. For information call 1-888-299-2121.

## Canadian Small-to-Mid-Cap Equity Funds

## MULTIPLE OPPORTUNITIES FUND

**$$$ ↑ G # RSP CSC**

Manager: Normand Lamarche and Gary Selke, since 1999

MER: 2.89%    Fundata: B    Style: Growth

Suitability: Aggressive investors

This small microcap fund used to specialize in junior mining companies traded on the Vancouver Stock Exchange. It was available only to residents of B.C. and had a record of extreme volatility. However, things changed in 1999 when the team of Norm Lamarche and Gary Selke acquired the fund for their firm, Tuscarora Capital, and assumed management responsibility. It was transformed into a more conventional microcap fund and was made available through financial advisors across the country. Performance has been very good under the direction of Lamarche and Selke. The fund scored a nice gain of 35% in 2000 and managed to post a small profit in the first half of 2001, despite the weak markets. The fund has kept a pretty low profile, but expect to hear more about it as RRSP season approaches. The reason? Tuscarora recently completed a merger with a firm run by former Altamira Equity manager Frank Mersch. Lamarche and Mersch will split up the management responsibilities for this fund and the companion Special Opportunities Fund, but we didn't know at the time of writing who would take which fund. However it works out, the intention is to more actively promote the two funds once they have been repositioned. If you are interested in investing in either fund, check with your financial advisor for the latest details.

## RESOLUTE GROWTH FUND $$$ ↑ G #/* RSP CSC

Manager: Tom Stanley, since inception (1993)

MER: 2.00%    Fundata: B    Style: Growth/Value

Suitability: Aggressive investors

It isn't often that you come across a fund that is so far ahead of the rest of its category that no one else is within 10 percentage points. It's even more unusual when that fund holds the top spot over one-, three-, and five-year periods. That's the kind of rarefied atmosphere being enjoyed by the Resolute Growth Fund, a small entry out of Toronto that few people have ever heard of. It's run by Tom Stanley, a broker with the firm of Thomson Kernaghan & Co., and the fund is very much his personal baby. In fact, if anything should happen to him it would probably be wound up ("I'm in good health and I look both ways before crossing the street," he jokes). How does he manage a one-year return of 36.6% (to June 30/01) and a five-year average annual compound rate of return of 18.9%? By ignoring the crowd and picking stocks that are below everyone else's radar scopes. Often this approach means buying microcaps—ultra-small companies with a market cap of $20 million or even less. He doesn't worry if the stock is thinly traded, since he buys for the long haul and believes investors pay too high a premium for liquidity. "Nortel is highly liquid," he observes. "Look what happened." His style is a blend of value and growth: "If the market is paying too much for growth, I focus on value." Stanley's willingness to buy thinly traded stocks and the small number of positions he has held have made this a highly volatile fund in the past. However, he has recently broadened his base and currently holds about 20 names in the portfolio. He likes companies that are in a sound cash position, have good management, and enjoy a sustainable, competitive advantage. If his strong numbers make you itchy to jump on board, Stanley probably doesn't want you as a client. He's not interested in hot money: "We don't want to be one of those funds that blows up." In order to discourage short-term investors, he's seeking regulatory approval to raise the minimum initial investment to $25,000 (it's currently $10,000) and to introduce a 90-day holding period for front-end load purchases. If you cash in before that time, you'd be hit with a 5% penalty. If he obtains approval, the changes are expected to be in effect by the time you read this *Guide*. The fund is for very aggressive investors only. It's eligible for registered plans, but we do not recommend it for that purpose because of the volatility. For more information visit the Web site: **www.thomsonkernaghan.com**. You can also call 1-800-216-4398 or (416) 350-3232. The fund is available for sale in Ontario, B.C., and Alberta.

## SPROTT CANADIAN EQUITY FUND $$$ ↑ G NO RSP CSC

Manager: Eric Sprott, since inception (September 1997)

MER: 2.50%     Fundata: B     Style: Value

Suitability: Aggressive investors

Sprott Securities is a Canadian brokerage house that specializes in small-cap companies. This fund was created in 1997 and, without any fanfare, has evolved into one of the top performers in its category in recent years. Its debut was not auspicious; it posted a loss of 16.6% in 1998, its first full year. But since then investors have been reaping rewards with gains of 53.4% in 1999, 44% in 2000, and 34.7% in the first half of 2001. What is even more remarkable is that the recent strong performance was achieved with a large cash position of 24%, into which the manager had moved for defensive purposes. Clearly Eric Sprott and his team know how to pick winning small-cap stocks! In the mid-year 2001 report to investors, the manager was highly pessimistic about the economic outlook for the immediate future and said that the portfolio would continue to remain defensive. We're very impressed with the results to date and recommend that you take a look at this fund if you're in the market for a small-cap position. The minimum investment is $10,000 and there are no load charges. For more information call 1-800-461-2275.

## U.S. Equity Funds

## CHOU ASSOCIATES FUND $$$$ → G # £ USE

Manager: Francis Chou, since inception (1986)

MER: 2.00%     Fundata: A     Style: Value

Suitability: Conservative investors

This is the companion to the Chou RRSP Fund (see page 583). It concentrates on locating U.S. stocks trading at a deep discount to their underlying value. Manager Francis Chou professes to ignore exotic selection techniques, preferring the KISS (keep it simple, stupid) approach to choosing securities. His strategy is buy-and-hold. Results slipped in the late 1990s because of the manager's refusal to invest in high-priced tech stocks, which were the driving force of the U.S. market. But his decision was vindicated by the subsequent collapse in technology shares. This fund avoiding the clobbering that most U.S. stock funds were subjected to in 2000–01, actually gaining 15.6% over the 12 months to June 30/01. The 10-year average annual compound rate of return of 16.3% was third best in the U.S. Equity category. Entering 2001, there were only 15 securities in the small portfolio, ranging from giants like Citigroup and Reebok to several small companies few people have even heard of. One point to note: this is not a pure U.S. fund; there are also some Canadian assets in the mix like Westshore Terminals. This fund was originally conceived in 1981 at an investment club; it gained fund status in 1986. Unfortunately, the Chou funds are available only in Ontario. See the Chou RRSP entry for purchase information. Minimum initial investment is $50,000.

## SPECIAL OPPORTUNITIES FUND $$$ ↑ G # £ GE

Manager: Normand Lamarche and Gary Selke (Tuscarora Capital), since 1999

MER: 2.42%     Fundata: B     Style: Growth

Suitability: Aggressive investors

Originally intended as the international stablemate of the companion Multiple Opportunities Fund, this fund still retains foreign status for registered plans. But there is some overlap between the two funds and, like Multiple Opportunities, the emphasis here was on the energy sector in 2001. The fund invests in ultra-small companies, or microcaps, as they are known in the fund industry. Like Multiple Opportunities, performance has been extremely volatile, ranging from a loss of 30% in 1998 (the year prior to the Lamarche/Selke takeover) to a gain of about 49% in 1999 and 17% in 2000. The first six months of 2001 saw a small gain despite falling stock markets. There are some important changes in the works here, however. See the Multiple Opportunities Fund entry for details.

## Sector Equity Funds

## DOMINION EQUITY RESOURCE FUND $$$ ↑ G NO RSP NR

Manager: Crescent Capital Corp., since 1998

MER: 2.30%     Fundata: B     Style: Growth

Suitability: Aggressive investors

This Calgary-based resource fund specializes (as you might expect) in oil and gas stocks. It has a spotty record, reflecting the ebb and flow of prosperity in the oil patch. Lately it's been looking very good, thanks to a strong performance in the energy sector. One-year return to June 30/01 was 44.8%, the best in the Natural Resources category by a wide margin. Returns for all longer time periods are also well above average. In fact, this is the top performer in the category over the past decade with an average annual compound rate of return of 16.7%. Just remember that this fund can be very volatile—it produced double-digit annual losses on several occasions during the 1990s. So this is not a buy-and-hold fund. Get in when the energy sector is hot, make your money, and then exit and await the next opportunity. Note that the minimum initial investment is $20,000. The fund is available only in Alberta, B.C., and Ontario. For information call (403) 531-2657. It's a no-load fund.

## SENTRY SELECT CANADIAN ENERGY GROWTH FUND $$$ ↑ G # RSP NR

Manager: Glenn MacNeill, since September 2000

MER: 2.41%     Fundata: A     Style: Value

Suitability: Aggressive investors

As the name suggests, this fund concentrates on the energy sector, which has been strong in recent years. There are a lot of large-cap stocks in the top holdings, including Petro-Canada, Alberta Energy, Talisman, and Shell Canada. The fund has been a solid performer, with a 13.5% average annual compound rate of return over the three years to June 30/01. However, the tight focus on energy means there will be nowhere to hide when oil and gas stocks tank, and they are notoriously cyclical. Keep that fact in mind when you're contemplating an investment decision. Minimum initial investment is $500. For more information call 1-888-246-6656.

## Canadian Balanced and Asset Allocation Funds

## COMMON SENSE ASSET BUILDER FUND I, II, III, IV, V          $$ ↓ FI/G * RSP S CBAL

Manager: Martin Hubbes, since August 2000

MER: 2.10%     Fundata: A     Style: Growth

Suitability: Conservative investors

Primerica Life offers this Common Sense line and the funds are segregated. These funds offer an innovative approach to retirement investing, with each one designed for a specific age level and time frame. Each Asset Builder fund is differentiated by portfolio composition and maturity date. However, all are classified as balanced funds. All funds aim for a high level of long-term growth and capital preservation through investment in a specific mix of equities and fixed-income securities depending on the maturity date. For example, as you move from Asset Builder I to Asset Builder V, the fund will become more aggressive, holding a larger portion in stocks. The range is about 40% equities for Asset Builder I, which is designed for older people, to 75% for the Asset Builder V. The closer you are to retirement, the more conservative the portfolio and the higher the percentage of fixed-income securities. For example, Asset Builder I is designed for people who will need their money in 2010 and 2011, so it will normally have the lowest percentage of stocks in its portfolio (the maturity date must be at least 10 years after the issue date of the contract). At the other extreme, Asset Builder V is for young people who won't retire until 2041 to 2050, so the percentage of stock holdings will be much higher. All of these funds were originally managed by Jerry Javasky of Mackenzie Financial's Ivy family, who did a fine job with them using a value approach. However in August 2000, managerial responsibility shifted to Martin Hubbes of AGF.

Hubbes is more of a growth-oriented manager, so we are somewhat concerned about the implications of this managerial switch. Despite our reservation, however, all the funds held their ground quite well in the first half of 2001, recording only small losses in rough markets, so we're prepared to bide our time and see how Hubbes fares. Focusing on Asset Builder I, this fund is designed for people who will retire in about 10 years. The stocks are the same here as in all the other Common Sense funds, the only difference being the percentage of total equities in the overall portfolio. As of mid-2001, the split was 49.5% stocks, 43.8% bonds. The equity side is conservatively invested and generally includes between 30 and 40 well-established stocks across many sectors. Recently, major holdings included Berkshire Hathaway, George Weston, and Royal Bank of Canada. A few small growth companies are added for enhanced profit potential. All five funds make good use of geographical diversification, holding a portion of their assets in foreign issues, mainly consisting of U.S. companies. Returns for all five funds have generally been above average. The funds with the lowest stock content, as is the case here, do better when the markets are soft. In the 12 months to June 30/01, Asset Builder I gained 2.4%, compared with a loss of 5.9% for the peer group. Five-year average annual compound rate of return was 9.4%, well above the average of the peer group. The other Common Sense funds have higher five-year returns because their increased equity component enabled them to profit more when stock markets were strong. This family is suited for long-term investors looking for strong-performing segregated funds, and represents a sound strategy for investing for retirement.

# Top Choice Funds at a Glance

The following list summarizes all the funds we've ranked as Top Choices for 2002. We suggest you use this list as a starting point when making your mutual, segregated, and labour-sponsored fund investment decisions. It is always a good idea to consult with a financial advisor for up-to-date information before proceeding.

## Canadian Equity Funds

ABC Fundamental-Value Fund
AGF Canada Class
AGF Canadian Dividend Fund
AGF Canadian Stock Fund
AIC Advantage Fund
AIC Diversified Canada Fund
AIM Canadian First Class
Altamira North American Recovery Fund
Bissett Canadian Equity Fund
BMO Equity Fund
Chou RRSP Fund
Clarica Summit Canadian Equity Fund
Clarington Canadian Equity Fund
Co-operators Canadian Conservative Focused Equity Fund
Empire Elite Equity Fund
Empire Premier Equity Fund
Fidelity True North Fund
The Goodwood Fund
Great-West Life Dividend/Growth Fund (M)
Great-West Life Equity Fund (M)
Great-West Life Larger Company Fund (M)
Great-West Life North American Equity Fund (B)

Harbour Fund
Industrial-Alliance Ecoflex Select Canadian "T" Fund
Investors Summa Fund
Leith Wheeler Canadian Equity Fund
London Life Canadian Equity Fund
Mackenzie Cundill Canadian Security Fund
Mackenzie Industrial Horizon Fund
Mackenzie Ivy Canadian Fund
Mackenzie Universal Canadian Growth Fund
Mawer Canadian Equity Fund
McElvaine Investment Trust
McLean Budden Canadian Equity Growth Fund
Merrill Lynch Canadian Core Value Fund
Northwest Growth Fund
O'Shaughnessy Canadian Equity Fund
Optima Strategy Canadian Equity Value Pool
Phillips, Hager & North Canadian Equity Fund
Phillips, Hager & North Canadian Growth Fund
Royal Canadian Value Fund
Saxon Stock Fund
Scotia Canadian Mid-Large Cap Fund
Signature Select Canadian Fund
Spectrum Canadian Equity Fund
Spectrum Canadian Investment Fund
Standard Life Equity Fund
Standard Life Ideal Equity Fund
Stone & Co. Flagship Stock Fund
Synergy Canadian Growth Class
Synergy Canadian Momentum Class
Synergy Canadian Style Management Class
TD Canadian Equity Fund
Transamerica GROWsafe Canadian Equity Fund
Trimark Canadian Fund
Trimark Canadian Endeavour Fund
Trimark Select Canadian Growth Fund
Twenty-First Century Canadian Equity Fund

## Canadian Small-to-Mid-Cap Funds

Beutel Goodman Small Cap Fund
Bissett Microcap Fund
Bissett Small-Cap Fund

CIBC Canadian Emerging Companies Fund
Clarington Canadian Microcap Fund
Clarington Canadian Small Cap Fund
Ethical Special Equity Fund
Fidelity Canadian Growth Company Fund
GBC Canadian Growth Fund
GGOF Guardian Enterprise Fund
Mackenzie Ivy Enterprise Fund
Mawer New Canada Fund
Merrill Lynch Canadian Small Cap Fund
Multiple Opportunities Fund
National Bank Small Capitalization Fund
Resolute Growth Fund
Royal Canadian Growth Fund
Saxon Small Cap Fund
Scotia Canadian Small Cap Fund
Sprott Canadian Equity Fund
Standard Life Growth Equity Fund
Talvest Millennium Next Generation Fund
Talvest Small Cap Canadian Equity Fund
Trimark Canadian Small Companies Fund

## Dividend Income Funds

BMO Dividend Fund
Canada Life Enhanced Dividend Fund (S-39)
Clarica Summit Dividend Growth Fund
Empire Dividend Growth Fund
GGOF Guardian Monthly Dividend Fund
HSBC Dividend Income Fund
Industrial-Alliance Ecoflex "V" Dividend Fund
London Life Dividend Fund
Mackenzie Industrial Dividend Growth Fund
MAXXUM Dividend Fund
National Bank Dividend Fund
Phillips, Hager & North Dividend Income Fund
Royal & SunAlliance Dividend Fund
Royal Dividend Fund
Scotia Canadian Dividend Fund
Signature Dividend Fund
Signature Dividend Income Fund
Spectrum Dividend Fund

Standard Life Canadian Dividend Fund
StrategicNova Canadian Dividend Fund
TD Dividend Growth Fund
TD Dividend Income Fund

## U.S. Equity Funds

AIC Value Fund
BPI American Equity Fund
Chou Associates Fund
Desjardins American Market Fund
GGOF Centurion American Value Fund
HSBC U.S. Equity Fund
Investors U.S. Large Cap Value Fund
McLean Budden American Equity Fund
Mutual Beacon Fund
Optima Strategy U.S. Equity Value Pool
Merrill Lynch U.S. Basic Value Fund
O'Shaughnessy U.S. Growth Fund
O'Shaughnessy U.S. Value Fund
Special Opportunities Fund
TD AmeriGrowth RSP Fund
TD Dow Jones Average Index Fund
TD U.S. Index Fund
TD U.S. Mid-Cap Growth Fund

## U.S. Small-to-Mid-Cap Funds

BMO U.S. Special Equity Fund
CIBC U.S. Small Companies Fund
Fidelity Small-Cap America Fund

## Global and International Equity Funds

AGF European Growth Class
AGF International Stock Class
AGF International Value Fund
Altamira Asia Pacific Fund
Altamira Japanese Opportunity Fund
Bissett Multinational Growth Fund
BMO NAFTA Advantage Fund
CI Global Fund

Clarica Summit Foreign Equity Fund
Great-West Life International Equity Fund (P)
HSBC European Fund
Investors North American Growth Fund
London Life Asian Growth Fund
Mackenzie Cundill Value Fund
Mackenzie Ivy Foreign Equity Fund
Merrill Lynch Select Global Value Fund
StrategicNova Asia-Pacific Fund
Talvest China Plus Fund
Talvest Global Small Cap Fund
TD Latin American Growth Fund
Templeton Growth Fund
Trimark Fund
Trimark Select Growth Fund (Class)

## Sector Funds

BMO Precious Metal Fund
CI Global Consumer Products Sector Shares
CI Global Energy Sector Shares
CI Global Financial Services Sector Shares
CIBC Financial Companies Fund
Dominion Equity Resource Fund
Dynamic Focus Plus Wealth Management Fund
Great-West Life Real Estate Fund (G)
Investors Canadian Natural Resources Fund
Investors Real Property Fund
Mackenzie Universal Canadian Resource Fund
Optima Strategy Real Estate Investment Pool
Royal Energy Fund
Sentry Select Canadian Energy Growth Fund
Signature Canadian Resource Fund
Talvest Global Heath Care Fund
TD Health Sciences Fund
Trimark Canadian Resources Fund

## Specialty Funds

Quebec Growth Fund

## Labour-Sponsored Venture Capital Funds

B.E.S.T. Discoveries Fund
Canadian Science & Technology Growth Fund
Capital Alliance Ventures Inc.
Dynamic Venture Opportunities Fund
Working Opportunity Fund

## Canadian Balanced and Asset Allocation Funds

ABC Fully-Managed Fund
AGF Canadian High Income Fund
BMO Asset Allocation Fund
Clarica Summit Growth & Income Fund
Clarington Canadian Balanced Fund
Clarington Canadian Income Fund
Common Sense Asset Builder Fund I, II, III, IV, V
Desjardins Quebec Fund
Fidelity Canadian Asset Allocation Fund
Great-West Life Balanced Fund (M)
Great-West Life Growth & Income Fund (M)
Great-West Life Income Fund (G)
Great-West Life Income Fund (M)
ICM Balanced Fund
Investors Mutual of Canada
Leith Wheeler Balanced Fund
London Life Balanced Fund
Mackenzie Industrial Balanced Fund
Mackenzie Industrial Income Fund
Mackenzie Industrial Pension Fund
Mackenzie Ivy Growth & Income Fund
Mavrix Income Fund
Mawer Canadian Balanced Retirement Savings Fund
Mawer Canadian Diversified Investment Fund
McLean Budden Balanced Growth Fund
Merrill Lynch Select Canadian Balanced Fund
Northwest Balanced Fund
Perigee Accufund
Phillips, Hager & North Balanced Fund
Royal & SunAlliance Balanced Fund
Royal Monthly Income Fund
Scotia Canadian Balanced Fund

Spectrum Diversified Fund
StrategicNova Canadian Balanced Fund
TD Balanced Growth Fund
TD Balanced Income Fund
Templeton Balanced Fund
Templeton Canadian Asset Allocation Fund
Transamerica GROWsafe Canadian Balanced Fund
Trimark Income Growth Fund
Canadian High Income Balanced Funds
Bissett Income Fund
Elliott & Page Monthly Income Fund
GGOF Guardian Monthly High Income Fund
Merrill Lynch Canadian Income Trust Fund
Saxon High Income Fund
Signature High Income Fund

## Global Balanced and Tactical Asset Allocation Funds

AGF American Tactical Asset Allocation Fund
Altamira Global Diversified Fund
CI International Balanced Fund

## Canadian Bond Funds

Altamira Bond Fund
Beutel Goodman Income Fund
Bissett Bond Fund
CI Canadian Bond Fund
CIBC Canadian Short-Term Bond Index Fund
Fidelity Canadian Short-Term Bond Fund
HSBC Canadian Bond Fund
ICM Bond Fund
Jones Heward Bond Fund
Leith Wheeler Fixed-Income Fund
Lotus Bond Fund
Mawer Canadian Bond Fund
Mawer Canadian Income Fund
McLean Budden Fixed Income Fund
Montrusco Select Bond Index+ Fund
Optima Strategy Canadian Fixed Income Pool
Optima Strategy Short-Term Income Pool
Perigee Active Bond Fund

Perigee Index Plus Bond Fund
Phillips, Hager & North Bond Fund
Phillips, Hager & North Short-Term Bond & Mortgage Fund
Sceptre Bond Fund
Scudder Canadian Bond Fund
Spectrum Mid-Term Bond Fund
Spectrum Short-Term Bond Fund
Standard Life Bond Fund
TD Canadian Bond Fund
TD Canadian Government Bond Index Fund
TD Monthly Income Fund
TD Real Return Bond Fund
Trimark Canadian Bond Fund
Trimark Government Income Fund

## Foreign Bond Funds

Scotia CanAm U.S.$ Income Fund
Standard Life International Bond Fund

## Mortgage Funds

National Bank Mortgage Fund
Scotia Mortgage Income Fund

## Canadian Money Market Funds

Altamira Short-Term Canadian Income Fund
Altamira T-Bill Fund
Beutel Goodman Money Market Fund
Bissett Money Market Fund
CI Money Market Fund
HSBC Canadian Money Market Fund
Jones Heward Money Market Fund
Leith Wheeler Money Market Fund
Lotus Income Fund
Mackenzie Cash Management Fund
Mawer Canadian Money Market Fund
McLean Budden Money Market Fund
Montrusco Bolton T-Max Fund
National Bank Corporate Cash Management Fund
National Bank Treasury Bill Plus Fund

Perigee T-Plus Fund
Phillips, Hager & North Canadian Money Market Fund
Royal & SunAlliance Money Market Fund
Royal Canadian Money Market Fund
Sceptre Money Market Fund
Standard Life Money Market Fund
Standard Life Ideal Money Market Fund
Talvest Money Market Fund
TD Canadian Money Market Fund
TD Canadian T-Bill Fund
Trimark Interest Fund
University Avenue Money Fund

## Foreign Money Market Funds

AGF U.S.$ Money Market Account
CI U.S.$ Money Market Fund
Fidelity U.S. Money Market Fund
HSBC U.S.$ Money Market Fund
National Bank U.S. Money Market Fund
Phillips, Hager & North U.S.$ Money Market Fund
Royal U.S.$ Money Market Fund
Scotia CanAm U.S.$ Money Market Fund
TD U.S. Money Market Fund

# The Fund Lists

## Ten Funds That Are Doing Well

ABC FUNDAMENTAL-VALUE FUND. Some investors thought manager Irwin had lost his touch when this fund went into a slump in the late 1990s. Not at all. He was simply waiting for deep value investing to come back into style. Now that it has, this fund is back near the top of the performance lists again, with a one-year gain of 22.9% to June 30/01.

AGF INTERNATIONAL VALUE FUND. Charles Brandes wrote the book on value investing (well, one of them anyway) and his San Diego–based team certainly know how to translate theory into results. This fund held up remarkably well while international markets were heading south in 2000–01. One-year gain to June 30/01 was a remarkable 23.4%. Over the past decade, no global equity fund has been better.

FIDELITY SMALL-CAP AMERICA FUND. Small-cap funds were all over the lot during the market slide of 2000–01. Some plunged, while others did remarkably well. This was the best of the bunch by far, gaining 43% over the year to June 30/01. That result came as a bit of a surprise, as the fund had been lukewarm in recent years. But right now, it's hot again.

MACKENZIE CUNDILL VALUE FUND. Peter Cundill's investment philosophy has always been to try to buy a dollar for half price. It works better during some times—like right now—than others. The fund was a top performer in the lousy markets of 2000–01, with a 12-month gain of 22.6%.

MUTUAL BEACON FUND. This Franklin Templeton entry didn't get much attention when it was launched in Canada in the late 1990s, as its deep value style ran completely counter to the high-tech mania of the day. But now it has come into its own, following in the footsteps of its parent fund in the U.S., a top performer for more than 15 years. One-year gain to June 30/01 was 24.1%.

**O'SHAUGHNESSY U.S. VALUE FUND.** The Royal Bank did a deal a few years back with U.S. money manager Jim O'Shaughnessy to offer three funds bearing his name. His investing theories are quite original, so no one knew what to expect. Turns out that his funds have been among the few stars in Royal's line-up lately, especially this one, which chalked up a return of almost 30% in the year to June 30/01.

**PHILLIPS, HAGER & NORTH DIVIDEND INCOME FUND.** There are several good funds in the PH&N stable and this is a top entry. How good is it? Well, over the past ten years, it was the number one performer in the Canadian Dividend category. Ditto for five years. And three years. Unfortunately, over the latest one-year period (to June 30/01) it slipped to the number nine position. But it still managed to gain more than 20%. No one is complaining.

**SAXON SMALL CAP FUND.** This is one of the perennial top performers in the small-cap category, but it is doing especially well these days because of its conservative value approach to stock selection. One-year gain to June 30/01 was a very fine 14.1%. Plus it's no-load. You won't find a much better fund.

**TALVEST GLOBAL HEATH CARE FUND.** With the Science & Technology category in tatters, this fund stands out like a lone beacon at midnight. It invests across the health care sector, including some biotech issues, and manager Ed Owens has done a phenomenal job with it. One-year gain to June 30/01 was an amazing 35.8%.

**TRIMARK FUND.** This long top-rated fund is back on track under the direction of Bill Kanko after a brief slip into mediocrity. Good one-year return of 11.5% to June 30/01. But avoid the DSC units with their high management expense ratio (MER).

## EIGHT FUNDS FOR LOW-RISK INVESTORS

**AGF EUROPEAN EQUITY CLASS.** It's hard to believe there could be a European stock fund that has never lost money over a calendar year, but here's the evidence. It had a close call in 1999, just squeaking into the black with a 0.9% gain, but in every other year since its 1994 launch, it has produced a double-digit advance. It was even able to make a profit in the first half of 2001, when European markets were diving. Amazing!

**CLARINGTON CANADIAN EQUITY FUND.** Peter Marshall and his team at Seamark Asset Management run several funds for Clarington, all of which impress us. This is a consistent first-quartile performer that has never recorded a losing calendar year since its 1996 launch.

**HARBOUR FUND.** It took Gerry Coleman a while to find his feet after his much-publicized move to C.I. a few years back, but his flagship Harbour Fund is now delivering a very attractive cargo for investors.

**ICM BALANCED FUND.** You get two different investing styles in one package with this little-known fund: top-down growth and bottom-up value. The net result is decent returns and a very good safety record. The last time this fund had a calendar-year loss was way back in 1994, and then it was only a fraction of a percent.

**MACKENZIE IVY CANADIAN FUND.** Nothing very flashy here, just decent returns year after year and a very low level of risk, which makes a lot of people comfortable.

**PHILLIPS, HAGER & NORTH SHORT-TERM BOND & MORTGAGE FUND.** Here's the ultimate in low risk: a fund that confines itself to bonds with a maturity of less than five years and conventional mortgages. You won't get rich, but your capital will be safe. A very good choice for an RRIF.

**SPECTRUM CANADIAN INVESTMENT FUND.** With value investing back in the saddle, Kim Shannon and Gaelen Morphet are playing starring roles again. They actually work for a subsidiary of Merrill Lynch and run this fund for Spectrum on contract, but it's doing better than their own ML Canadian Core Value Fund, with a one-year gain of almost 14%. All equity funds carry some risk, but this one has less than most.

**STANDARD LIFE CANADIAN DIVIDEND FUND.** Although it's officially classified as a dividend fund, in reality this is simply a blue-chip stock fund, and a very good one. One-year gain to June 30/01 was more than 19% in a very tough market. Over the past five years, it has averaged 21.5%. Those are great numbers for a conservatively run fund.

## TEN IMPRESSIVE CANADIAN STOCK FUNDS

**AIC DIVERSIFIED CANADA FUND.** The Warren Buffett school of investing is back and this fund is profiting as a result, under the direction of Jonathan Wellum. We like this entry better than the companion AIC Advantage Funds because of the broader diversification it offers.

**BEUTEL GOODMAN SMALL CAP FUND.** Small-cap funds are usually higher risk, but this fund manages to keep the volatility in check with a conservative, value-based approach to stock selection. Returns are running way above average for the peer group.

**BISSETT CANADIAN EQUITY FUND.** It's now part of the Franklin Templeton organization, but this fund is almost as good as ever. We say "almost" because most investors will now have to pay a sales commission to buy it, and the MER of the A units is higher, which will cut into returns. But the manager is the same and the results are still impressive.

**MACKENZIE CUNDILL CANADIAN SECURITY FUND.** This fund was a fine performer when it was a small-cap entry. Now that it's expanded its horizons to include the entire Canadian market, it continues to pour out good results. One-year gain to June 30/01 was a very fine 20.5%, which puts it among the top performers in the category.

**MAWER CANADIAN EQUITY FUND.** A steady performer year after year. This fund, from the Calgary-based company, has a very low profile in eastern Canada. Montrealers and Torontonians should look west more often. One-year gain of 11% in a tough market is impressive.

**MCLEAN BUDDEN CANADIAN EQUITY GROWTH FUND.** A first- or second-quartile performer every year since 1995, this fund has a great record of consistency. Although it uses a growth style, it's conservatively managed so risk is contained. Ideal for long-term investors, but don't go in if all you're looking for is a one-time big score.

**MERRILL LYNCH CANADIAN CORE VALUE FUND.** The tandem of Kim Shannon and Gaelen Morphet has combined to bring a new level of respectability to the Merrill Lynch (formerly Atlas) line-up. This value fund is one key addition, and it is working very well.

**O'SHAUGHNESSY CANADIAN EQUITY FUND.** James O'Shaughnessy has his own unique method of picking stocks, and it works. In fact, it worked so well that this fund chalked up a gain of almost 13% in the year to June 30/01, at a time when most equity funds were taking losses. It's part of the Royal Bank family.

**SIGNATURE SELECT CANADIAN FUND.** Under the direction of Eric Bushell, this entry has emerged as one of the top Canadian stock funds in recent years. Unfortunately, only a few people have noticed.

**TRIMARK CANADIAN ENDEAVOUR FUND.** You may have once owned this entry's units under the old name of Trimark RSP Equity Fund, but you probably bailed out when performance lagged. If you held on, good on you—the fund is doing very well these days. One-year gain to June 30/01 was 18.8%. That's amazing, given the market conditions.

# THREE U.S. EQUITY FUNDS TO NOTE

**INVESTORS U.S. LARGE CAP VALUE FUND.** It took a while, but Terry Wong now seems to have found the success formula for this one after a rocky start when he took over from his mentor, Larry Sarbit. This fund was one of the top U.S. equity performers in the year to June 30/01, gaining a fat 23%.

**MERRILL LYNCH U.S. BASIC VALUE FUND.** U.S. stock markets were in disarray in 2000–01, but this fund bucked the slide. Employing traditional value screening techniques, the managers found a bunch of large-cap winners and guided the fund to a gain of almost 14% over the year to June 30.

**MUTUAL BEACON FUND.** No one cared about deep value investing when this Canadian version of a U.S. stalwart was launched in 1997. But the economic downturn brought this style of stock picking to the forefront and the fund gained an impressive 24% in the year to June 30/01. It's not right for all times, but it's right for these times.

# TEN GOOD SMALL FUNDS YOU'VE PROBABLY NEVER HEARD OF

**@RGENTUM DISCOVERY PORTFOLIO.** This small-cap entry has been around only since 1998, but so far the results have been impressive. One-year gain to June 30/01 was a fine 14% under difficult market conditions. The @rgentum funds joined forces with University Avenue recently, so there may be a name change coming here.

**CHOU RRSP FUND.** Francis Chou's full-time job is senior manager at the highly respected Fairfax Financial firm. He runs this and the companion Chou Associates Fund more or less in his spare time. It's enough to produce great returns for his few investors—24.3% in the year to June 30/01.

**CO-OPERATORS CANADIAN CONSERVATIVE FOCUSED EQUITY FUND.** This entry's been around for more than 50 years, most of the time under the name Associate Investors Fund. Now it's owned by Co-operators Mutual Funds, but the same management team headed by veteran George Frazer is still at the helm. What has it done for investors lately? It won the award for top-performing Canadian equity fund in calendar 2000.

**DOMINION EQUITY RESOURCE FUND.** This is an energy-focused fund that is managed out of Calgary. It's been the number one natural resource fund in Canada over the decade to June 30/01, averaging 16.7% a year. That's a heck of a run, especially when you consider that the number two finisher, Royal Energy, was almost four percentage points behind.

**LEITH WHEELER CANADIAN EQUITY FUND.** This company isn't well known, even in its home city of Vancouver. But the conservative investment style it offers works very nicely for low-risk investors. Nothing flashy here, just decent returns at minimal risk.

**NORTHWEST GROWTH FUND.** This fund is based in Toronto, despite the name. Northwest refers to the quadrant on an investing chart that represents high-return/low-risk. This little entry fills the bill very nicely, using a little-known style called economic value added (EVA). One-year gain to June 30/01 was a very good 12.5%.

**RESOLUTE GROWTH FUND.** Tom Stanley of the Toronto brokerage firm of Thomson Kernaghan runs this high-performance small-cap entry and his results show that he knows a thing or two about stock picking. Over the past five years, investors have profited to the tune of 19% annually. Just be careful of the risk.

**SAXON STOCK FUND.** This is one of the best Canadian equity funds you'll find, and it's a no-load fund to boot if you buy it direct from the manager (Ontario residents only). It deserves a lot more attention than it gets. You owe it to yourself to check it out.

**SENTRY SELECT CANADIAN ENERGY GROWTH FUND.** Here's another energy fund that has been quietly posting some very nice gains. In the past three years, it's returned 13.5% annually.

**SPROTT CANADIAN EQUITY FUND.** This is another small-cap fund that's run out of a brokerage firm, in this case Sprott Securities. Its profile has been so low that hardly anyone has heard of it, but those who have are overjoyed. It gained almost 35% in the first half of 2001. That's right—35% in just six months, while the markets were plunging! Wow!

## TEN FUNDS FOR YOUR RRSP

**CLARINGTON CANADIAN BALANCED FUND.** The Clarington fund line is still a mystery to many investors, but there are some excellent choices available. This fund fits perfectly into an RRSP because it offers a combination of above-average returns, below-average risk and a conservative value style. Hard to go wrong with that.

**FIDELITY CANADIAN ASSET ALLOCATION FUND.** This conservatively managed entry offers a combination of large-cap, dividend-paying stocks and carefully selected government and corporate bonds. Over the five years to June 30/01, it was the number one performer in the Canadian Tactical Asset Allocation category. Moreover, it has never lost money in a calendar year and is almost always in the first or second quartile of its peer group. You won't find credentials much better than that.

**MACKENZIE INDUSTRIAL HORIZON FUND.** For several years this fund suffered in the doldrums. But Bill Procter has returned it to respectability and the fund scored a gain of more than 15% in the latest year, while most Canadian stock funds were in the red.

**MAWER CANADIAN BALANCED RETIREMENT SAVINGS FUND.** Above-average performance, good safety record, broad diversification, and no load charges. A first-rate choice from this Calgary-based company.

**MERRILL LYNCH SELECT CANADIAN BALANCED FUND.** When Merrill Lynch overhauled the old Atlas Funds line-up, they were smart enough not to throw out the baby with the bathwater. Veteran manager Len Racioppo, president of Jarislowsky Fraser, was kept on at the head of this fund and, as usual, he turned in a winning performance. The fund has consistently outperformed the averages in recent years, and its low risk is a bonus.

**NORTHWEST BALANCED FUND.** Steady performer, good safety record; this is a first-quartile performer that should do your RRSP proud.

**PHILLIPS, HAGER & NORTH BOND FUND.** If you have the $25,000 to open a PH&N RRSP, this fund is a must for inclusion. It has consistently been among the top-performing Canadian bond funds over the past decade, and the safety record is first-rate.

**ROYAL DIVIDEND FUND.** A superb blue-chip stock fund that offers just the right combination of growth and income for an RRSP or an RRIF. Manager John Kellett delivers the goods with this one year after year.

**SIGNATURE DIVIDEND INCOME FUND.** If you're looking for a true dividend fund without a lot of gimmicks, here it is. But act quickly. C.I. has warned it plans to close Dividend Income at some point.

**TRIMARK INCOME GROWTH FUND.** The whole Trimark family is looking much better these days. It's not because they've moved under the AIM umbrella, but because value investing is back in style and that's these folks' forte. This is a good core RRSP fund with nice balance and results that are improving.

# TEN GREAT MONEY MARKET FUNDS

**ALTAMIRA SHORT-TERM CANADIAN INCOME FUND.** Excellent performance, low risk, low MER, no load. What a combo for your cash!

**BEUTEL GOODMAN MONEY MARKET FUND.** It has beaten the averages every year since 1991. That's a decade of first-rate performances. We love that kind of consistency. Top marks.

**CI U.S. MONEY MARKET FUND.** Many investors are looking to hedge their currency bets by adding U.S. dollar money funds to their portfolios. This is one of the better ones around.

**JONES HEWARD MONEY MARKET FUND.** In 1998, the company cut this fund's MER from 1% to 0.5%. That was all it needed to move into the top ranks of its category. Since then, the annualized return has been almost half a percentage point more than the average Canadian money fund.

**MACKENZIE CASH MANAGEMENT FUND.** This entry's been one of our top money market choices for years, and remains on the shortlist. If you have some money with Mackenzie that you want to park for a while, this is the spot.

**MCLEAN BUDDEN MONEY MARKET FUND.** The numbers tell the story: this fund has been a top-quartile performer ever since 1995. The low MER of 0.6% really helps to boost returns.

**PERIGEE T-PLUS FUND.** The low MER of 0.48% helps to boost returns to above average. The conservative portfolio—mainly T-bills—provides the ultimate in safety. That's an unbeatable one-two punch.

**PHILLIPS, HAGER & NORTH CANADIAN MONEY MARKET FUND.** One of the lowest management fees in the industry contributes to the consistently above-average results.

**PHILLIPS, HAGER & NORTH U.S.$ MONEY MARKET FUND.** The top-performing foreign money market fund in Canada over the past five and ten years. The low MER really helps returns here.

**SCEPTRE MONEY MARKET FUND.** This fund has been in the top half of the money market category for as long as we can remember. The safety rating is among the best.

# FIVE BIG DISAPPOINTMENTS

**AGF AGGRESSIVE GROWTH FUND.** From penthouse to cellar in just one year. That's the story here. Last year it was our Fund of the Year, with a gain of 121%. This year it finished dead last in its category, with a loss of 52%. Manager Richard Driehaus has a big turnaround challenge here.

**CAMBRIDGE BALANCED FUND.** Balanced funds are supposed to be low risk. This one has managed to lose an average of 9.4% a year over the past decade. Something is terribly out of line here. If you wondered why the Sagit Funds are not included in this year's *Guide*, this fund is part of the answer.

**EXCEL INDIA FUND.** Everyone expects India to emerge as one of Asia's investment powerhouses, but it never seems to manage. This is one of two funds that specialize in India and it beat out the rival from AGF for worst performance of the year with a loss of almost 55%.

**TRIAX GROWTH FUND.** An instant hit among labour fund investors when it first came out, this fund looked like it was going to become one of the leaders of its type. But the past year was a disaster. The fund lost 38.5% in the 12 months to June 30/01. Main reason: it held a lot of shares in crashing high-tech companies like Nortel, Research in Motion, and Descartes Systems.

**VENGROWTH I INVESTMENT FUND.** For years, this fund ran up above-average gains in the labour fund category, thanks to the acumen of its veteran managers. It did so well that it finally closed its doors to new money, and a second fund, VenGrowth II, was started. Meanwhile, original investors here sat back and waited to reap profits. Or so they expected. The high-tech plunge took its toll here and the fund dropped 24% in the latest 12 months.

# THREE BIG COMEBACKS

**INVESTORS RETIREMENT MUTUAL FUND.** For years this fund did nothing. Its long-term record is among the worst in the Canadian Equity category. Suddenly, it's acting like the manager found the Midas Touch. While stock markets were diving, this one gained almost 22% in the year to June 30/01. Now we'll see if it can keep it up.

**MACKENZIE INDUSTRIAL GROWTH FUND.** We've been panning this one for years, so it's only fair for us to recognize that it is finally performing well again. Manager Alex Christ has been patiently awaiting a turnaround in the resource sector, and he finally got it. The fund gained 24% in the first eight months of 2001. Unfortunately, many investors lost patience long before Mr. Christ did and bailed out, so they weren't around to pick up the rewards.

**OPTIMA STRATEGY U.S. EQUITY VALUE POOL.** Here's a fund that had never recorded a calendar year loss since it was launched, earning a $$$$ rating as a result. It immediately responding by losing almost 23% over the year to June 30/00. The loss was all the more astonishing because stock markets were strong and this is a conservatively managed fund. But now it has righted itself and is back where it belongs, with a 31% gain in the subsequent 12 months. Great, but conservative investors shouldn't be subjected to such shocks.

## FOUR FUNDS THAT SHOULD BE DOING BETTER BUT AREN'T

**AGF MANAGED FUTURES VALUE FUND.** The idea here is to avoid the ups and downs of the stock market by diversifying into commodity futures. Of course when you do that, you expose yourself to the ups and downs of the commodities markets. Result: a loss of 20.3% annually over the past five years.

**ETHICAL GROWTH FUND.** For years, this was one of our favourite entries: a fund that combined decent returns, low risk, and a large dose of social responsibility. The social responsibility remains, but all else has vanished. Three-year numbers are now in negative territory, which is even more surprising in light of the value investing style that has generally served managers well recently. We're rooting for an early comeback here.

**TEMPLETON GROWTH FUND.** For years, this was the fund that set the industry standard. But recently, it's been labouring. Perhaps that's why it just got its third manager in two years, George Morgan. He happens to be a Canadian, the first in the fund's history. Since this was the fund that gave the Templeton organization its start, it seems fitting somehow that a Canadian should be given the task of restoring it to glory.

**WORKING VENTURES CANADIAN FUND.** This is the oldest nationally distributed labour fund. It has had plenty of time for its initial investments to mature and produce profits. So what do investors have to show for their years of patience? An average annual return of 0.3% over the past decade. That's just not good enough!

## THREE FUNDS FOR HIGH ROLLERS

**CIBC GLOBAL TECHNOLOGY FUND.** You don't normally think of bank funds as highly speculative, but this one fits the profile. When things were going well for high-tech, it outperformed almost every other fund. When the sector tanked, it did the same trick on the downside. If you think tech will roar again, go ahead and roll the dice. It may not come as a big surprise that the fund is run by Stephen Kahn, whose comparable Talvest fund also makes this list.

**MONTRUSCO TSE 100 MOMENTUM FUND.** For starters, you need $150,000 as an entry fee for this fund. Then you need a very strong stomach, because there are a lot of ups and downs with this momentum-driven fund. Take a look at the five-year record from 1997 to mid-2001 and you'll see what we mean: +34.4%, +4.9%, +70.3%, +17.3%, −21.8%. Those are big swings!

**TALVEST GLOBAL SCIENCE & TECHNOLOGY FUND.** From top to bottom in one easy step. This fund gained 160% last year. This year it lost 61%. Next year, it may be up over 100% again. That's the way the manager operates. If you like to throw those kinds of dice, here's your fund.

# THE RICH PERSONS' CLUB

**ABC FULLY-MANAGED FUND.** Value investing went into a slump in the late 1990s, but this entry is now back as one of top-performing balanced funds in Canada with a one-year gain of 22.1% to June 30/01. But you need $150,000 to get in and even then manager Irwin Michael may not take your money if it represents too high a percentage of your net worth.

**CIBC PREMIUM CANADIAN T-BILL FUND.** A low MER plus the safety of T-bills combine to create a great place for your cash reserves—if they add up to $100,000 or more, that is.

**GBC CANADIAN GROWTH FUND.** One of the best entries if you're looking for a small-to-mid-cap fund and have $100,000 available. Only two other funds in the category have beaten its 10-year average annual return of 15.9%.

**THE GOODWOOD FUND.** How does an average annual return of better than 34% over the past three years sound to you? Pretty good? Sure it does. And all you need is $25,000 to $150,000 for a ticket to ride, depending on where you live.

**MCELVAINE INVESTMENT TRUST.** Tim McElvaine is another of those money experts who holds down a full-time job elsewhere and runs a fund of his own on the side. His major role is chief investment officer of the Mackenzie Cundill funds, but he set up this small fund for friends and associates a few years ago and it has done very, very well, with a three-year average annual compound rate of return of just under 22% to June 30/01. You can climb on board too—if you have $150,000 to invest.

**OPTIMA STRATEGY CANADIAN EQUITY VALUE POOL.** When you compare this fund with others on this list, it looks like a bargain. You need only $25,000 to get in (only!). But that's just the price of admission. This is one of those fund groups that keeps encouraging you to up the ante by offering bigger discounts on their management fees if you put in more cash. Get your total up to $100,000 and save a quarter point on most fees. Get up to $250,000 and save another quarter point. Work your way up to the $750,000 level and they almost pay you. Well, not quite, but you get the idea. Still, it's a pretty good fund.

**SCOTIA PREMIUM T-BILL FUNDS.** What's that they say about the rich get richer? It's true here. The more money you have, the more you'll make. Ordinary folk have to invest in the regular Scotia T-Bill Fund, which carries an MER of 1%. But if you have $100,000 to invest, you can get into the Premium T-Bill Fund, in which case your MER drops to 0.52%. That means you end up with almost half a percentage point a year in your pocket. If you've got really big bread, say a million or so, they'll give you a fund with an MER down around your socks, at 0.3%. See what we mean?

## FOUR FUNDS THAT ARE NOT WHAT THEY SEEM

**AGF CANADA CLASS.** This equity fund invests exclusively in Canadian stocks. Yet it is classified as foreign content for RRSP purposes. Why? Because it is a sub-section of the company's International Group, an umbrella fund that allows investors to move money around among various "classes" without exposure to capital gains tax. AGF International Group is officially foreign content, so everything within it is too.

**AGF DIVIDEND FUND.** Don't expect any dividends from this "dividend" fund, which the company admits isn't one at all. It's a very good Canadian large-cap equity fund, but it isn't even slotted in that category where it would have been a top-quartile performer over the past year. Instead, AGF insists on maintaining the fiction that it is a dividend income fund. The result? It finished near the bottom of its category in the year to June 30/01, giving a completely misleading impression to investors.

**CLARICA ALPINE GROWTH EQUITY FUND.** It's supposed to be a small-to-mid-cap fund. So why do we find names like Nortel Networks and Petro-Canada among the top 10 holdings?

**GREAT-WEST LIFE DIVIDEND/GROWTH FUND (M).** The unseen hand of Bill Procter and Mackenzie's Industrial team drives this entry, which has been churning out very good returns recently. But don't let the name mislead you. It's officially classified as a Canadian Large-Cap fund, not a Dividend Income entry.

# SEVEN GOOD SEGREGATED FUNDS

**CANADA LIFE ENHANCED DIVIDEND FUND.** Few people have heard of this one, but it was the top performer in the Dividend Income category over the year to June 30/01, with a return of 26.4%. Manager Philip Wootten of Laketon has this fund off to a strong start.

**GREAT-WEST LIFE LARGER COMPANY FUND (M).** While many Canadian stock funds were plunging, this one chalked up a return of better than 15% in the year to June 30/01. Give credit to Mackenzie's Industrial team of Bill Procter and friends, who pulled the strings behind the scenes.

**GREAT-WEST LIFE REAL ESTATE FUND (G).** If you want a real estate fund that puts its money into bricks and mortar instead of stocks, this is it. There's good tax-advantaged cash flow if you keep it in a non-registered account.

**LONDON LIFE BALANCED FUND.** This relative newcomer has been churning out decent returns for investors in tough markets. It also has a better-than-average safety profile. A good bet for an RRSP.

**PRIMERICA COMMON SENSE FUNDS.** There are five of these funds, all structured according to the number of years you have left before retirement. The longer you have to go, the more equities you have in your portfolio. It all makes a lot of, well, common sense. Our only concern is a recent managerial change, with Martin Hubbes of AGF taking over from Mackenzie's Jerry Javasky, who had pulled the strings here for several years.

**ROYAL & SUNALLIANCE DIVIDEND FUND.** Any fund manager who can produce a return of almost 23% in the lousy market conditions that prevailed in the 12 months to mid-2001 deserves a pat on the back. Kudos to Brad Cann.

**STANDARD LIFE IDEAL INCOME BALANCED FUND.** This segregated fund has been especially designed to generate good cash flow while keeping risk to an absolute minimum. It's a relative newcomer, but performance so far has been first-rate. RRIF investors with $10,000 available should take a close look at it.

# TWELVE FUND COMPANIES WE THINK ARE PRETTY GOOD

**ABC FUNDS.** Few companies work as hard at educating investors as this small firm does. Plus, president Irwin Michael sticks to his value style in good times and bad, and these days things are working pretty well for him.

**AGF FUNDS.** For a while, this was a pretty dull company. But all that has changed. They now have some terrific funds in their line-up and the Global Strategy acquisition has strengthened their international connections.

**AIM FUNDS MANAGEMENT.** The Trimark takeover has turned out even better than anticipated, giving the company a top-performing value line just when it was most needed as an alternative to the sagging fortunes of the growth-oriented AIM family.

**FIDELITY INVESTMENTS.** This company has finally come to grips with their biggest weakness, domestic Canadian funds. Now the line-up is imposing right across the board.

**FRANKLIN TEMPLETON.** The acquisition of the Bissett funds brought an entirely new dimension to this company. The rise of Mutual Beacon and the launch of several new Franklin funds served only to enhance the image of a revitalized organization.

**HSBC ASSET MANAGEMENT.** Unless you're a client of Hongkong Bank of Canada, you may not know about this neat little operation. Too bad. Some fine fund selections here.

**MACKENZIE FINANCIAL CORPORATION.** Mackenzie's Cundill, Industrial, and Ivy lines are all doing very well in these difficult market conditions. Just avoid most of the funds with Universal in the name.

**PHILLIPS, HAGER & NORTH.** Sound, solid, ready, reliable, conservative, and low cost. All those good adjectives apply here. Invest your money and forget about it.

**SAXON FUNDS.** Most investors overlook this small company. Perhaps that's because Saxon doesn't have the marketing budget necessary to trumpet their terrific long-term record. Do yourself a favour and take a look.

**SPECTRUM INVESTMENTS.** Too often overlooked by investors, this company has done a first-rate job of restructuring its line-up. Some of the funds are turning in top results.

**STANDARD LIFE.** Most people don't realize that Standard Life offers a line of non-segregated funds, and very good ones at that. You could build a nice portfolio from Standard Life funds alone.

**TD ASSET MANAGEMENT.** The merger of Green Line with the Canada Trust funds has produced a unified product group that is a lot stronger than the two individual parts. The useful range of bond funds is very impressive and the line-up of index funds is first-rate.

## SEVEN GOOD IDEAS

**@RGENTUM CANADIAN L/S EQUITY PORTFOLIO.** Here's something that looks like a hedge fund without the exorbitant entry fees most of that breed command. A combination of long and short positions is intended to reduce risk and enhance returns. So far it seems to be working; the fund gained almost 8% in the year to June 30/01 in a rough market.

**FIDELITY DISCIPLINED EQUITY FUND.** This entry is a cross between an index fund and an actively managed fund. The sector weightings are exactly the same as those of the TSE 300. The difference is that manager Robert Haber then picks stocks he considers the best in each sector. So far, the formula looks promising.

**INVESTORS MERGERS & ACQUISITIONS FUND.** How about a fund devoted to pin-pointing companies that are candidates to be taken out at a premium price? Strange no one has thought of it before. But now Investors Group has seized on the idea and the result is a new entry that gained 32% in the year to June 30/01.

**MACKENZIE CUNDILL RECOVERY FUND.** You've heard of junk bond funds? This entry might be described as a junk stock fund. Its mandate is to invest in companies that are underperforming, are in turnaround situations, or have low credit ratings— or any combination thereof. It is certainly off to a fine start. One-year gain to June 30/01 was an excellent 19.5%.

**NATIONAL BANK CANADIAN OPPORTUNITIES FUND.** There aren't many sector rotation funds in Canada, and none that excite us very much. But National Bank decided to stick its toe into the water with this one and so far it has come up with a winner. Gain for the year to June 30/01 was a very fine 16.6% in a weak market. What can we expect when markets are strong? We will watch with interest.

**OPTIMA STRATEGY CANADIAN EQUITY DIVERSIFIED POOL.** You can't get the combined talents of three of Trimark's top managers in any one fund offered under their own banner. But you can get Heather Hunter, Ian Hardacre, and Kiki Delaney to pick stocks for you with this new entry. They're off to a pretty good start, too.

**SPECTRUM TACTONICS FUND.** Exchange-traded funds (ETFs) are threatening to cut into the traditional mutual funds market. Well, if you can't beat 'em, join 'em. This new fund uses a formula developed by Spectrum chief investment officer Karen Bleasby to zero in on the top ETFs of the day and bring them together into a winning portfolio. The concept sounds great. We'll watch to see how well it works.

## FOUR SURPRISING FUNDS

AGF CHINA FOCUS FUND. The Far East has been a disaster zone for fund investors, right? For the most part, yes. But here's an exception. In the face of all the gloom, this little-known entry pulled off a gain of almost 40% in the 12 months to June 30/01. That's even more astonishing when you realize that most Asian funds recorded double-digit losses. Kudos to manager Raymond Tse of Nomura Capital Management, who took over a weak performer in June 2000 and pulled off this mini-miracle.

MACKENZIE UNIVERSAL PRECIOUS METALS FUND. It's not often these days that we single out a precious metals fund for special mention, but this one merits a look. Most of the funds in the category have looked better recently, but this one turned in an amazing gain of 38% over the past year. It's also number one in its category over three years, with an average annual compound rate of return of almost 11%. When you consider the average precious metals fund lost 4.2% over that time, it makes the performance even more astounding.

NATIONAL BANK SMALL CAPITALIZATION FUND. Few people have ever heard of this fund, but it has been one of the top performers in the Canadian Small-to-Mid-Cap category for many years. In the year to June 30/01, it posted an amazing gain of 18.7%, which was so dramatically above the 6.1% average loss for the category that it is hard to believe it is operating in the same universe. If you live in Quebec, Ontario, or New Brunswick, it's worth a trip to your National Bank branch to check it out.

STRATEGICNOVA ASIA–PACIFIC FUND. This was the other Far East fund that emerged from the pack to score a big gain while almost everyone else was going down the tubes. Manager Ian Beattie managed to score a 29% profit for investors in the year to June 30/01 by concentrating on stocks trading at a deep discount to their intrinsic value. Maybe everyone else should switch to his style!

## FIVE TOP BALANCED FUNDS

ABC FULLY-MANAGED FUND. Manager Irwin Michael is one of Canada's top exponents of value investing. This fund underperformed in the late 1990s when technology dominated, but it's back on course again. Over the past decade, it's the number one balanced fund in the nation with an average annual gain of 14.4%.

**GREAT-WEST LIFE BALANCED FUND (M).** Not many balanced funds managed a double-digit return in the past year. This one did. If you want to know why, check out the entry on the Mackenzie Industrial Pension Fund. Same team.

**MACKENZIE INDUSTRIAL PENSION FUND.** Bill Procter has done great things with the Industrial Horizon Fund, but he hasn't been ignoring this neat balanced fund. Returns have been very good in these tough markets, with a gain of almost 16% in the latest 12 months.

**MACKENZIE IVY GROWTH & INCOME FUND.** The Ivy line-up offers a blend of decent returns and relatively low risk. This fund is typical of that approach and did well in the down markets of 2000–01 with a one-year gain of 6.6%. Not impressed? The average fund in the group lost 3.1%, so this one was almost 10 percentage points better.

**PHILLIPS, HAGER & NORTH BALANCED FUND.** This fund was launched in 1991 and up to the end of 2000, it never had a losing calendar year. Performance is steady, but not spectacular. This is one of those low-profile entries that just keeps doing the job.

## FIVE GOOD-LOOKING NEWCOMERS

**AIC AMERICAN FOCUSED FUND.** When Larry Sarbit left Investors Group after many years, it created a stir in the mutual fund community. He's now running funds for AIC and this entry is one of his. The style is the same as it was when he piloted Investors U.S. Large Cap Value Fund to great results—careful and conservative. Looks like the results will be similar, too. This fund gained 28% in the year to June 30/01.

**FIDELITY AMERICAN OPPORTUNITIES FUND.** We like the look of this new Fidelity entry. Manager John Muresianu uses a growth-at-a-reasonable-price (GARP) style to pick his stocks, with an emphasis on the Old Economy. His goal is to outperform the S&P 500. We think there's a good chance he'll do it.

**ICM U.S. SMALL-CAP EQUITY FUND.** The term "small cap" gets stretched a bit here. The fund can invest in companies with a market cap up to U.S.$2.5 billion, which brings in some big names like Bell & Howell and Barnes & Noble. But let's not quibble. The managers seem to know their stuff and this fund was a top-quartile performer over the past year and a half. One-year gain was a very good 28.5%.

**IRIS SMALL-CAP CANADIAN EQUITY FUND.** Laurentian Bank has been working hard to build a credible fund line-up. This newcomer, managed by Elliott & Page, represents a big step in that direction. Good no-load small-cap funds with reasonable entry fees are hard to find. This one qualifies nicely and the managers have shown they can turn good profits even in weak markets.

**MCLEAN BUDDEN CANADIAN EQUITY VALUE FUND.** A company that built its reputation on growth investing shows it can handle the value side of the equation, too. This fund chalked up a nice gain over the first several months of 2001, at a time when the TSE was plunging.

## TWELVE FUNDS FOR INCOME INVESTORS

**AGF CANADIAN HIGH INCOME FUND.** There's a little bit of this and a little bit of that in this mix, but the net result is a low-risk fund that offers decent cash flow, with an annualized yield of 5.75% in the first half of 2001. Good for an RRIF.

**BISSETT INCOME FUND.** The cash flow is excellent, and much of it comes with tax advantages as a bonus. The management team is also first-rate. But you have to accept above-average risk if you decide to invest here. If safety of capital is a priority, check elsewhere.

**CLARINGTON CANADIAN INCOME FUND.** You receive distributions of 8¢ per unit each month and good overall returns, with very little risk. Do you need anything more?

**GGOF GUARDIAN MONTHLY DIVIDEND FUND.** Good news for income investors. This fund, which was closed for over five years, is back in business. If cash flow is your goal, this is the fund for you. It invests mainly in preferred shares, which means steady income and the advantage of the dividend tax credit. Just don't expect big capital gains. They don't come with the territory.

**GGOF GUARDIAN MONTHLY HIGH INCOME FUND.** This companion fund also offers good cash flow, but with more capital gains potential. It also carries a lot more risk. That's because it invests primarily in volatile royalty income trusts (RITs). But when it gets hot, it can blow the income competition out of the water. One-year gain to June 30 was a scintillating 24%.

**MAVRIX INCOME FUND.** Avoid this one if you want your income to come with a high degree of safety. But if you're looking for good capital gains potential as well as cash flow, plus a lot of tax advantages, this may be your home. It could be a wild ride, though, because the portfolio concentrates on high-risk royalty trusts. So be sure you have the stomach for it.

**MERRILL LYNCH CANADIAN INCOME TRUST FUND.** There's a fair amount of volatility in this fund, which invests mainly in real estate investment trusts (REITs) and RITs. But the cash flow is excellent, and comes with some tax breaks as well.

**NATIONAL BANK DIVIDEND FUND.** Nothing fancy here. Just a plain, old-fashioned dividend fund that invests mainly in preferred shares and does its job of producing tax-advantaged cash flow very well, with minimum risk.

**ROYAL MONTHLY INCOME FUND.** You get good cash flow and some growth potential out of this one. Plus, the risk level is relatively low for a fund of this type. Works well in an RRIF.

**SAXON HIGH INCOME FUND.** The Saxon folks have shown over the years that they know how to pick stocks. Now they're demonstrating that they can deliver cash flow as well, and with relatively low risk for a fund of this type. It's no-load as a bonus.

**SPECTRUM DIVIDEND FUND.** This is a true dividend fund, one that invests mainly in preferred shares to produce tax-advantaged cash flow. Monthly distributions ensure there is always a cheque in the mail. Excellent safety record.

**TD MONTHLY INCOME FUND.** Here's a fund that offers a decent revenue stream with very low risk. Many people, especially retirees, are looking for that combination exactly.

# The Year's Best Investor Questions

*Every year we receive hundreds of questions relating to mutual funds. We can't answer each one individually, but we post as many responses as possible on the Building Wealth on the 'Net Web site (**www.gordonpape.com**) and in the "Money" section of the Fifty-Plus Web site (**www.50plus.com**). If you have a mutual fund question you would like to submit, you can visit either Web site or send it along directly to **gpape@istar.ca**.*

What follows is a selection of some of the more interesting questions we have received in the past year.

## Should I Sell My StrategicNova Fund?

**Q** Around 1995 I had invested some money into the then new and much heralded O'Donnell Canadian Emerging Growth Fund, managed by Wayne Deans. It has now been named the StrategicNova Canadian Small-Cap Fund and currently has a sub-par track record. My questions are as follows:

1. Do you predict that this fund and Canadian small-caps will recover generally, or should I consider another fund within this company?

2. Bearing in mind the fund is in my RRSP, could you suggest a more appropriate conservative fund for a 58-year-old closing in on retirement?—M.E.S.

**A** We're not impressed by the fund you mention and it does not make the StrategicNova Recommended List in this book. However, many other small-cap funds have been doing well recently so if that's what you're looking for, check around. Among the better performers in the category are Beutal Goodman

Small Cap, Clarington Canadian Small Cap, CIBC Emerging Company, Ethical Special Equity, Northwest Specialty Equity, Resolute Growth, Saxon Small Cap, Sprott Canadian Equity, and Trimark Canadian Small Companies, so there is a lot of choice.

More to the point is whether you should really have a small-cap fund in your RRSP at this point. It depends on the rest of your asset mix, of course, but you may want to take a look at the current allocation in your plan. Value funds are doing well right now and there are lots of conservatively managed ones around including Spectrum Canadian Investment, CI Harbour, Mackenzie Ivy Canadian, and more. Within the StrategicNova group, we are giving good ratings to the Canadian Dividend Fund and the Canadian Balanced Fund.

## Mother-in-Law in a Pickle

**Q** My father-in-law passed away two years ago, leaving his wife in a very comfortable financial position. Taking advice from her eldest son, my 67-year-old mother-in-law consulted with a financial advisor employed by one of the big-name banks. The financial advisor suggested she put half her savings ($100,000) into GICs and the other half into mutual funds. The mutual fund asset allocation mix is very aggressive in my opinion, with approximately 40 percent in equity funds, including tech funds.

And now, you guessed it: the funds have performed terribly over the past two years—and my mother-in-law has lost approximately $15,000 on paper. She now wants to sell, cut her losses, and transfer everything into GICs. Her financial advisor has told her to wait and give her funds time to rebound. I think he's an idiot for getting an elderly woman into this mess. What do you think she should do? —B.K.

**A** Actually, the asset mix itself isn't that aggressive. The way we read your numbers, only 20 percent of a total $200,000 went into equity funds. That percentage certainly seems to be on target for an older person. The question is more about the nature of the funds chosen. Technology funds certainly do not seem appropriate, and in hindsight they weren't. Dividend income funds and conservatively managed, broadly based equity funds would be a more logical mix for someone of her age and in her situation.

We suggest you have a meeting with the advisor to determine how the selection was made. Ask to see the investment profile that should have been prepared at the time. If your mother-in-law was classified as a conservative or very conservative investor, you may have a case for trying to claim restitution (this has happened). If she wasn't, find out why not. Did it come down to how she answered the questions? If you aren't satisfied with the responses you receive, arrange a meeting with the local branch manager and make your case.

As for whether she should put the remaining money in GICs, we can't answer that question. It depends on many considerations, including her willingness to accept risk, her tax situation, her income needs, etc.

## Commodity Funds

**Q** Do you know of any mutual funds that invest in commodities other than the usual natural resources and precious metals funds? —Y.B.

**A** No, but there are two funds that specialize in commodity futures. One is the AGF Managed Futures Value Fund. We doubt you'd be interested in it, however. Its five-year average annual rate of return is −20.3 percent (to June 30, 2001). The other is the Friedberg Futures Fund. It has a losing three-year record, but gained 22 percent in the past year. Of course, such funds will be very high risk by nature.

## Mixing Value and Growth

**Q** A significant portion of my RRSP is in value funds (AGF International and Cundill Value "C"). You suggest investors have growth-oriented funds in addition to value funds in a portfolio. I already have a few labour-sponsored funds. Can I count labour-sponsored funds as a growth component? —K.M.

**A** Labour-sponsored funds can certainly be considered growth funds in a portfolio.

## AIC Distributions

**Q** Having heard about the great performance of the AIC Advantage Fund, I contacted my financial advisor. He cautioned me, saying that while the fund has been tax efficient for a long time, one of these days there could be huge capital gains distributions. Also, I am wondering if I did decide to invest in this fund, would it be suitable for the systematic withdrawal plan in one or two years? —A.A.

**A** There would be a large cash distribution from the AIC fund only if the manager were to sell several of the positions at a big profit. Under the laws governing mutual fund trusts, net realized capital gains within a portfolio must be distributed to unitholders each year. This is always possible, but the fund's investment mandate is buy and hold, which makes such large sales unlikely. Such a move would run contrary to the company's stated policy. Of course, if you should sell your units there could be a large capital gain realized that would be taxable, but this decision is within your control.

Usually we recommend choosing an equity fund for a systematic withdrawal plan that has fairly consistent distributions. Otherwise, units have to be constantly cashed in to generate the cash flow needed for the withdrawals.

One other point to remember is that AIC Advantage focuses on the financial services sector (banks, mutual fund companies, etc.). It is therefore not considered a "core" fund position. For that, you would look for a fund that is more broadly diversified.

### Wants Out of Fidelity Fund

**Q** I own Fidelity Canadian Asset Allocation Fund in three portfolios and I noticed that the mutual fund was heavily weighted in Nortel and has been a poor performer in the last year. I want a conservative balanced fund that is performing reasonably well. Would you recommend selling, and if so, what would be a good replacement? —F.R.

**A** Obviously, any mutual fund that had a significant holding in Nortel has been badly chewed up. However, the worst is over. If Nortel hasn't hit bottom, it's very close to it and a few years from now the current price of the stock may look like a bargain. So there doesn't appear to be much downside risk in the Fidelity fund at this point, at least as far as Nortel is concerned.

That said, we are not sure why you are unhappy with Fidelity Canadian Asset Allocation. You say that it has been a poor performer, yet its returns over all time periods are well above average for its category and it was the top-performing Canadian Asset Allocation fund over the five-year period to June 30/01. Fidelity is known as a top-flight company, with a conservative style. If you want an even more conservative approach, however, take a look at Templeton Canadian Asset Allocation Fund. Its one-year record is better, although its long-term results don't come close to the Fidelity entry.

### Should I Sell AGF American TAA Fund?

**Q** I bought AGF American Tactical Asset Allocation Fund as a defensive, pre-retirement play years ago. Could you comment on how well it has weathered the storm and whether I should now sell it?

**A** This fund has a stellar long-term record, but it had difficulty keeping its head above water in the tough markets of 2001. The fund has never suffered a calendar-year loss but over the year to July 31, 2001, it declined just over six percent due to weakness in both the bond and stock markets. No one likes to lose money, but given market conditions that's a reasonable performance. You invested in this as a defensive fund, and that's exactly what you're getting. You say you have been in for several years. The five-year average annual compound rate of return to that date is 12.6 percent while the 10-year number is 13.1 percent—both excellent results for a balanced fund. Whether you should sell now depends on your current priorities. If a U.S. balanced fund still has a place in your portfolio, we can see no reason to dump this one.

## A Question from Egypt

**Q** What is a third-party sponsored mutual fund? —S.N., Egyptian Capital Market Authority

**A** Very nice to hear from someone in Egypt, a country Gordon Pape has visited on two occasions and greatly enjoyed.

A third-party fund is a fund sold by a financial institution that is not one of their own products. In Canada, all the major banks have their own lines of mutual funds. Using the Royal Bank as an example, their funds are called the Royal Funds. But the banks have found that there is a demand for one-stop shopping, so they now also offer access to mutual funds from other companies, such as Fidelity and AIM. These additional offerings are called third-party funds.

## Foreign Stocks or Funds?

**Q** Is there an advantage to holding foreign (U.S.) stocks over holding a mutual fund that invests in foreign companies outside the RRSP for long-term appreciation? —B.K.

**A** There is no tax advantage in holding foreign stocks individually as opposed to a mutual fund, if that is what you are referring to. But from a cost perspective, you won't have to pay any annual management fee for the stocks, so if you feel comfortable picking your own and can diversify properly, that might be your best choice. However, if you are planning to invest beyond the U.S., choosing and buying foreign stocks can be more difficult, unless they trade in the U.S. as an American Depository Receipt (ADR). So for foreign stocks, mutual funds are generally recommended.

## Labour Funds Outside an RRSP

**Q** I am following the strategy of putting the maximum amount into my RRSP. This year I filled my unused contribution room. Now I am considering borrowing a modest amount to invest outside my RRSP. Should I include a labour-sponsored fund outside my RRSP? —T.C.

**A** There is nothing to prevent you from making this kind of investment. You will still qualify for the tax credits, which can be claimed next year when you file your return. However, give careful consideration to the eight-year hold requirement.

Inside an RRSP, this rule isn't a serious deterrent for most people because they don't expect to make use of the money in the plan until retirement. But in a non-registered plan, holding labour-sponsored funds will reduce your flexibility to react to changes in the market.

## Avoiding Deferred Sales Charges

**Q** Is it true that mutual fund investors are able to withdraw up to a maximum of 10 percent of their investment annually without incurring deferred service charges? —K.W.

**A** Yes, this is correct in most cases. But check the prospectus to be sure it applies to your funds.

## What is "Return of Capital"?

**Q** My year-end mutual fund statement shows, along with the usual items (i.e., capital gains, dividends, interest, etc.) an item called "return of capital," with an amount showing. This amount, however, does not appear on my T5 slip. Can you explain exactly what this item might represent in addition to its accounting and tax explanations? —S.R.

**A** Return of capital is the term used to identify income that you received on a tax-deferred basis. Often this income originates from royalty income trusts (RITs) that have certain tax advantages and from real estate investment trusts (REITs). The amount does not appear on your T5 because it is not taxable in the year received. However, you must subtract such tax-deferred income from the cost base of your units, producing what is called an "adjusted cost base" for tax purposes. This is the figure used to calculate your taxable capital gain when you sell. For example, suppose you paid $10 a unit and received a $1 per unit return of capital last year. Your adjusted cost base is $9 ($10 − $1 = $9).

## Labour Fund Performance Bonuses

**Q** I've been looking into investing in labour-sponsored funds because of the tax savings, but most of them seem to pay extravagant performance bonuses to the fund manager even though they all have approximately the same MER. Would it be better for me to invest in a fund that gives all of the returns to its shareholders? Why don't fund managers include performance bonuses in the cost of managing the fund? —B.J.S.

**A** Not only do many labour funds have performance bonuses for managers, but this policy is increasingly being applied to regular mutual funds as well.

Typically these bonuses come into play when a fund's performance exceeds that of a particular benchmark (like the TSE 300 Index) by a specified amount.

You have to read the fine print to see just how onerous the bonus might be. For example, some funds do not pay any bonus if the portfolio has recently underperformed. There is a formula whereby the fund must, in effect, catch up before future bonuses will be paid. Additionally, you need to see if there is a cap on the bonus, or if it is open-ended. The worst situation is a bonus formula that does not take past results into account and has no cap. In this situation, the manager could reap huge rewards at investors' expense for just one strong year.

Of course, the bonus is designed as an incentive to maximize returns. However, all fund managers should be seeking to do that anyway, as part of their fiduciary responsibility to investors. For this reason, we are not big fans of the bonus provision. In the end, however, what matters is how well the fund does. If you end up with a 30-percent gain while all the other funds in the category are returning 10 percent, you certainly won't complain because you had to pay the manager a bonus.

Our advice is to be aware of any bonus provisions, but not to make them the main criterion for an investment selection.

## Wants Information about MD Funds

**Q** I've been an avid buyer of your mutual fund and RRSP books for the last eight years, but it always disappoints me to notice the absence of the MD Management Funds in these guides each year. Since I do respect your opinion and would like to see what you have to say about them, I'm just wondering if there's a chance of them appearing in your guides in the future, or if you have some kind of religious conviction against those exclusive doctors' organizations. —D.S.

**A** No religious conviction and only the greatest respect for doctors—and for the MD Funds, for that matter. But if you read the section "How to Use the Mutual Fund Ratings," you will see that every year we repeat the same thing: We do not include coverage of any fund groups that are not offered to the general public. The reason for this exclusion is that there are too many of them: funds exclusively for doctors, dentists, pilots, teachers, public servants, etc. We have to draw a line somewhere. So, sorry, you won't see MD Funds reviewed in our guides—not now, not in the future.

We can say this, however: Most of the MD funds have proven decent performers—not sensational, but quite respectable. You could do far worse.

## Do Mutual Funds Have Ticker Symbols?

**Q** Do mutual funds have ticker symbols like stocks? I'm using a finance software package that allows updates of mutual fund prices if I input the ticker symbol. I can't seem to find the symbols for Canadian mutual funds. —C.H.

**A** No, they do not have ticker symbols but each fund has its own code, which is used to identify it for the purpose of sales, tracking, etc. Also, every version of a fund has its own separate code. For example, a fund that offers Canadian dollar, U.S. dollar, segregated, and clone versions will be treated as four separate funds, each with its own code.

This coding is the reason why you often see discrepancies in the numbers of Canadian mutual funds that are mentioned in the media. It depends on how you count; is the example we just referred to really four separate funds, or just one fund in four different forms? We believe the latter is actually the case, but if you're updating the fund in your software programme you must have the correct code for the version you actually own. The fund company can supply that code for you, or it may appear on your brokerage statement.

## Is a Managed Money Account a Good Idea?

**Q** The large brokerage company I deal with has been pushing its managed money programme. While entry is a reasonable $50,000 minimum, do the track records of these programmes generally outweigh the extra costs involved? Would it be wiser to put that money into two "good" mutual funds with modest MERs? —C.J.

**A** There is no way to generalize if "wrap accounts" of this type are good value for your money or not. The performance figures are not published anywhere, so we have no way to measure them. Complicating the matter is the fact that your personal allocation among the different pools within the programme will be somewhat different from another person's, depending on your investment strategy.

We suggest you ask the brokerage firm for a performance history of each of the separate pools within the plan (Canadian Equity, U.S. Equity, etc.). Also ask for clarification on how the firm determines these numbers —do they include management fees, for example. If they don't, then you have to discount the returns if you want to compare the results against an average mutual fund of the same type. For instance, suppose you are told that the Canadian Equity pool gained 12.5 percent in the past 12 months, not including a management fee. Your management fee, paid separately, is 1.5 percent. This fee has the effect of reducing the net return to 11 percent. Now you have something you can use to compare against a benchmark of your choice—the TSE 300 Index, the average Canadian equity fund, or whatever seems right. When you apply this test to all the possible pools into which you might invest, you can get an idea as to whether the programme as a whole is outperforming, underperforming, or about even with the relative benchmarks.

## Has Fund Company Complaint

**Q** Please! Can you provide me with a contact I can speak with regarding lodging a complaint against a mutual funds company? —T.G.P.

**A** It depends on the nature of the problem. You may be able to get satisfaction simply by writing to a senior executive of the company. A letter sent to the president will usually find its way to the desk of the appropriate person, assuming the complaint is legitimate and serious.

The Investment Funds Institute of Canada (IFIC), which has its headquarters in Toronto, is a voluntary association of mutual fund companies. While it does not act as a police officer for the industry, it does set regulations for its members so if you have a situation that appears to violate one of their regulations you could address a complaint there. The Web site address is as follows: **www.ific.ca**.

Finally, if the matter is very serious and appears to involve some kind of unethical or even illegal activity, you should complain to your provincial securities commission. Each province has its own commission. Contact them directly for information about how to file a complaint.

## Wants to Invest in Biotech

**Q** Is there an equivalent to a Nasdaq 100 for Biotech companies? I would like to buy some Biotech stock and reduce my risk by investing in some of the top companies. —L.R.

**A** Yes, there is a security you can buy that represents a basket of biotech companies. It's called Biotech HOLDRS (Holding Company Depository Receipts) and it trades on the American Stock Exchange under the symbol BBH. The portfolio consists of 20 biotech stocks. As you might expect, the price has been extremely volatile, so if you plan to invest any money here, be aware of the risk. Biotech is an exciting and potentially high-growth field, but you may need to have nerves of steel if you want to play it in this way.

## Does the Amount You Have to Invest Change the Asset Mix?

**Q** Do you recommend the same asset mix regardless of how small or large an amount of money a person has to invest? For example, would you use the exact same formula whether a person had $10,000 to invest or $1,000,000? —D.C.

**A** The amount of money involved would not normally be a significant factor on asset mix appropriation, which should be based on such considerations as age, risk tolerance, economic climate, tax status (for non-registered portfolios), etc. The total available to invest might influence the mix only to the extent that someone with a large amount of assets and a long time horizon might decide he or she can assume more risk and therefore increase their growth percentage.

What would be more significant in asset mix determination would be whether the portfolio is registered or non-registered. In the latter case, tax considerations would figure in, and the weighting might be more heavily skewed to tax-advantaged securities that generate dividends and capital gains.

### Not Happy with Advice

**Q** Can you advise us on whether we are risking too much by allowing our bank representative to manage our portfolio? We just received our quarterly report today and again we lost nearly $9,000. In fact, we have been losing for the past two quarters since signing up with them. We are getting scared! My husband just turned 62, and he wants to work two more years. We were also advised at the outset that we can expect downturns in the markets. Do you think we are too old to be risking our life savings? The bank is responsible for investing approximately $400,000 of our money. Thanking you advance for any advice you can give us. —L.W. & M.W.

**A** This is a tough question to answer. Your rep may be doing a fine job based on the instructions you have given him or her—after all, stock markets have been taking a beating recently. Did you make it clear at the outset that you did not want to take on a lot of risk? Did you discuss the way in which your assets would be allocated between lower-risk fixed-income securities and higher-risk growth securities? If you didn't, you should have.

We suggest you sit down with the representative, discuss your dissatisfaction, and jointly decide on an investment strategy that would be more appropriate for you.

If you are investing in the bank's mutual funds, check the write-up on the company in this book to see which ones we currently recommend.

### Sell Funds Like Stocks?

**Q** When purchasing a mutual fund should I pay attention to the present price relative to its price history? Should I buy low and sell high like a stock? —R.F.

**A** No. Mutual funds don't operate like stocks and past price history means nothing, although the performance record does. The price (meaning the current net asset value, or NAV) can be deceiving because distributions will reduce the

NAV. For example, if a fund was priced at $10 and made a distribution of $1 on December 31, the NAV on January 2 would appear as $9. It looks like the fund has lost value, but of course it hasn't. It has just passed some of the value on to unitholders.

That said, buy low and sell high is a good strategy for any investment. So when fund prices are low, say because of a stock market drop, it's a good time to average down.

## Should I Switch Companies?

**Q** I have a question regarding an investment decision, and was wondering if you could tell me what you think. I have $50,000 with TD funds (both RRSP and non-registered) and I have $50,000 with Investors Group (again, both RRSP and non-registered). I'm concerned about being overdiversified, so one option I was thinking about was putting all my money with Phillips, Hagar & North. I know they're a good company, but would that be putting all my eggs in one basket? —N.M.

**A** For starters, we cannot give you personal investing advice. For a decision involving sums of this magnitude, you should consult a professional advisor in your area.

We can say, however, that Phillips, Hager & North rates very highly as a money manager and was named the top fund company of the 1990s in the 2000 edition of this *Guide*. However, their strength is in fixed-income and North American funds. Their international funds continue to be weak, although they are making determined efforts to improve that situation.

Our general view is that it's not a good idea to tie up all one's assets in a single company, regardless of how good that firm may be; every company has some weaknesses. Splitting your assets between two or more companies allows you take advantage of the strengths of each, presuming you have researched those strengths in advance.

## What's a Good Source for Socially Conscious Funds?

**Q** I'm interested in investments that support environmentally and socially conscious companies and I'm not sure where to find this information. I'm aware of the Ethical Funds Group and a couple of other organizations such as Investors Summa, but I'm hoping there is a Web site or other source that has a consolidated list of ethical funds and/or individual companies. I'm also interested in investing in companies that are attempting to improve the environment, such as those in the area of wind or solar power, for example. Is there a way to find out about these types of companies? I haven't been very successful in receiving this information from a broker and would really appreciate any advice you can give me. —S.S.

**A** We suggest you visit the Web site of the Social Investment Organization, which is based in Toronto: **www.socialinvestment.ca**. You'll find information about all the mutual funds that meet their criteria. The site also contains several other articles and features of interest to socially conscious investors.

## Lost Funds

**Q** You have recommended BPI American Equity Fund in the past, but where is it? I tried finding it on BPI.com—no go. I've tried to find it through the financial pages—another no go.

Also missing in action is Jim O'Donnell and his group of funds. I'm sure many of your readers would appreciate an update on these disappearing funds. I certainly would. —J.F.

**A** The BPI funds were purchased by the C.I. organization a couple of years ago. Several of them have been merged into other C.I. funds or had their names changed, but a few are still sold under the BPI brand, including BPI American Equity. You'll find information on this fund in the C.I. section of this book or by going to the C.I. Web site.

The O'Donnell funds were sold to Strategic Value and Jim O'Donnell left the organization shortly thereafter. The whole family was later sold to Nova Bancorp and has been renamed StrategicNova. The O'Donnell name has disappeared. See the StrategicNova section for more information.

## Clones and Currencies

**Q** You have recommended at least 25 percent of one's assets should be held in U.S. dollars. This advice raised a question in my mind with respect to the RRSP-eligible foreign ("clone") mutual funds: Even though these funds are essentially futures contracts held in Canadian dollars, are they in fact U.S. dollar assets in real terms? —A.P.P.

**A** No they're not. In fact, one of the reasons why the RRSP clones of the TD and Royal U.S. index funds have done so much worse than the parent funds is that they did not benefit from the appreciation of the U.S. dollar against our currency. The clones may be designed to replicate the performance of the parent funds, but the futures contracts underlying them are in Canadian currency, at least in these cases. Investors in the non-registered funds had their S&P Index losses reduced by their currency gains. The clone fund investors didn't get that break.

## Needs Independent Advice

**Q** I am 78, widowed, and have the bulk of my portfolio with a financial advisor who is a mutual fund salesperson. Every time a GIC comes due, this advisor recommends a mutual fund. I don't have a lot of money and depend on my investments for additional income.

I am concerned about this situation. My daughter has suggested that I have an independent financial advisor (fee-for-service) assess the situation and suggest an appropriate portfolio. I don't know if you can have this type of analysis done on a one-time basis and I don't know where to look for this type of service. Do you have any advice?—Initials withheld by request

**A** Certainly we think an independent financial review of your assets is in order if for nothing more than your own peace of mind. The mutual funds being recommended by the advisor may be just fine, but if they are heavily oriented toward equities, they may be inappropriate for your situation.

There are indeed fee-for-service financial planners who will perform such an analysis on a one-time basis for an hourly rate. One way to locate someone in your area is through the Canadian Association of Financial Planners. Their Web site (**www.cafp.org**) has a search programme with a filter that enables you to identify qualified planners in your city operating on a fee-for-service basis.

## Fund Switching in an RRSP

**Q** My question is about buying and trading mutual funds inside an RRSP. All of my funds are with CIBC, which does not charge switching fees. Is it a good idea to switch between funds to enhance returns? I believe that natural resource or energy funds are not really long-term funds to hold on to, so switching between these and other funds when market conditions permit is a good idea. I don't believe in switching all the time, but there are occasions when a fund is down so I shift some money into it and in turn lower my average cost per unit. Any comments on this strategy? —P.O'T

**A** We call such funds "opportunity funds" and yes, we believe switching in and out of them at appropriate times is good strategy, as long as you are comfortable with what you are doing. Natural resource funds have not proven themselves to be good buy-and-hold candidates; in fact, the average fund in this category has returned about the same per annum over the past decade as the average mortgage fund, with much more risk. Don't overdo the switching, but it certainly is a viable way to potentially boost returns.

## Is AGF International Value Really a Value Fund?

**Q** Is the AGF International Value Fund truly a "value" fund? Would it be suitable for inclusion at a rate of about 30 percent in the RRSP portfolio of a 57-year-old? —K.W.

**A** Yes indeed, it is a genuine value fund. In this case, the "value" part of the name is not misleading. (What is misleading is the word "international," technically implying that the fund does not invest in North America, which it most assuredly does.) The fund is managed by the Charles Brandes organization of San Diego, California. Brandes is a disciple of the legendary Dr. Benjamin Graham, credited as being the father of value investing. Brandes himself has written a well-known book on the subject, *Value Investing Today.*

The fund has been a star performer in an otherwise dismal market, with a one-year gain of 17.9 percent to July 31, 2001. It has slipped a bit recently, but is still holding up much better than most of its competitors. All of that said, we can't recommend committing 30 percent of your portfolio to this or any other fund. Every fund experiences ups and downs over time and we have seen high performers go into prolonged slumps in the past. Certainly include this fund in your foreign equity section, but provide some diversification by adding at least one quality global growth fund so that you will benefit when the markets turn around. Diversification is the key to keeping risk to a minimum while maintaining a good potential for above-average returns.

# General Index

Gerber, Martin, 168, 265
Giasson, Erik, 405
Gibbs, Carolyn, 191, 192
Gifts, 93
Giles, Trevor S., 577
Girard, Bill, 449, 450
Gleeson, Tim, 370, 371, 380
Global equity fund, 51
Global fund, 113
Gluck, Richard, 377
Good performers, 601, 602
Goodman, David, 276
Goodman, Jonathan, 280
Goodman, Ned, 274, 277
*Gordon Pape's 2002 Buyer's*
  *Guide to RRSPs*, 60
Graham, Benjamin, 76, 149
Graham, G. Keith, 194, 196
Graham, Trevor, 422
Grammer, Mark, 205, 206
Grantier, Bruce, 449
Great-West Life Assurance,
  527–536
Gregoris, David, 226
Grestoni, Dom, 342
Griffiths, Stephanie, 372
Growth funds, 18–20
Growth managers, 50, 77
Growth potential, 67
Guardian Group of Funds
  (GGOF), 314–321
Guthrie, Chris, 322

**H**

Haber, Robert, 291, 297
Habermann, Dick, 289,
  293, 296
Hall, Jim, 385, 582
Hallward, Mary, 502
Hardacre, Ian, 193, 199,
  216, 520
Harmon, James, 289
Harris, Paul, 498
Harrison, Dale, 422
Harrop, Bruce, 199, 201
Heal, David, 422
Herold, Jeffrey, 234
Herrmann, Fred, 458
High-income balanced funds,
  18, 95, 108
High rollers, 610, 611
High-yield bond funds, 17, 107
Hill, Peter, 464

Hirsch, Veronika, 44, 322,
  323, 324
Ho, Ed, 277
Hochachka, Gene, 422
Hock, John, 232, 233
Hodson, Peter, 487
Hoffman, Alan N., 493
Holland, Paul, 242
Holman, Kelly, 579
Holzer, Jason, 188, 191
Howson, Richard, 437, 436,
  439, 440, 457
HSBC Investment Funds,
  328–332
Hu, Christine, 422
Hubbes, Martin, 167, 168,
  590, 591
Hughes, Christine, 175
Hunt, Vince, 196–202
Hunter, Heather, 194, 216
Huycke, Alan, 571

**I**

i60 units, 119
IFIC, 629
Ihnatowycz, Ian, 163
Income funds, 30, 108
Income investors, 618, 619
Income taxes. *See* Taxes
Index funds, 114, 119–122
Index investing, 78
Industrial-Alliance Life
  Insurance, 537–539
Insurance companies,
  517–564. *See also*
  Segregated funds
Insurance sales people, 83
Integra Mutual Funds,
  328–332
*Intelligent Investor, The*
  (Graham), 76
Interest rates, 108
International fund, 113
Investment Funds Institute of
  Canada (IFIC), 629
Investment personality, 27–29
Investment strategies, 52–58
  asset mix, 55, 56
  buy and hold, 52, 53
  closed-end funds, 134, 135
  dollar-cost averaging, 53, 54
  equity funds, 114–116
  fixed-income fund strategies,
    109, 110

leveraging, 56, 57
  questions, 630, 631
  switching, 54, 55
Investor questions, 621–634
  asset mix, 629, 630
  bank representative
    management, 630
  biotech companies, 629
  capital gains, 623
  clones, 632
  commodity funds, 623
  complaints, 629
  deferred sales charges, 626
  distributions, 623
  foreign stocks or funds, 625
  fund switching in RRSP, 633
  independent advice, 633
  investment strategies,
    630, 631
  labour funds outside
    RRSP, 625
  managed money account,
    628
  MD Funds, 627
  performance bonuses,
    626, 627
  return of capital, 626
  single company, all assets
    in, 631
  small-cap funds, 621, 622
  socially conscious funds,
    631, 632
  systematic withdrawal plan,
    623, 624
  third party funds, 625
  ticker symbols, 628
  value/growth mix, 623
  widowed mother-in-law, 622
Investors Group, 333–343
iPerformance Fund Corp.,
  344–346
iShares, 119
i60 units, 119
iUnits, 117

**J**

Jackson, Mark, 563
Jacobs, Alan, 443
Javasky, Jerry, 44, 152, 372, 373
Jeddeloh, Larry, 509
Jenkins, Neil, 464
Jenkins, Richard, 198, 201
Jenner, Kris, 501
John, Juliette, 309

# Fund Index